Entrepreneurship

To our families

Olga, Max, and Rosa

and

Doreen, Erinn, Jacquelyn, and Brenna

An Innovator's
Guide to
Startups and
Corporate Ventures

DISCARDED

Entrepreneurship

Marc H. Meyer
Frederick G. Crane
Northeastern University

$SAGE

Los Angeles | London | New Delhi
Singapore | Washington DC

For information:

 SAGE Publications, Inc.
2455 Teller Road
Thousand Oaks, California 91320
E-mail: order@sagepub.com

SAGE Publications Ltd.
1 Oliver's Yard
55 City Road
London EC1Y 1SP
United Kingdom

SAGE Publications India Pvt. Ltd.
B 1/I 1 Mohan Cooperative Industrial Area
Mathura Road, New Delhi 110 044
India

SAGE Publications Asia-Pacific Pte. Ltd.
33 Pekin Street #02-01
Far East Square
Singapore 048763

Printed in the United States of America

Library of Congress Cataloging-in-Publication Data

Meyer, Marc H.
Entrepreneurship : an innovator's guide to startups and corporate ventures / Marc H. Meyer, Frederick G. Crane.
        p. cm.
Includes bibliographical references and index.
ISBN 978-1-4129-5560-7 (cloth : acid-free paper)
ISBN 978-1-4129-9265-7 (pbk. : acid-free paper)
    1. Entrepreneurship. 2. New business enterprises. 3. Venture capital. 4. Success in business.
5. Business planning. I. Crane, Frederick G. II. Title.

HB615.M49 2011
658.1'1—dc22   2010028213

This book is printed on acid-free paper.

10   11   12   13   14   10   9 8 7 6 5 4 3 2 1

Acquiring Editor:	Lisa Cuevas Shaw
Editorial Assistant:	MaryAnn Vail
Production Editor:	Brittany Bauhaus
Permissions Editor:	Karen Ehrmann
Copy Editor:	Terri Lee Paulsen
Typesetter:	C&M Digitals (P) Ltd.
Proofreader:	Eleni-Maria Georgiou
Indexer:	Sheila Bodell
Cover Designer:	Candice Harman
Marketing Manager:	Helen Salmon

Brief Contents

Detailed Contents

Chapter 2: Developing the Venture Concept   36

Chapter 3: Getting Into the Hearts and Minds of the Target Customers   55

Chapter 4: Defining the Business Model for a Venture   78

Chapter 5: Transforming a Product or Service Idea Into a Product Line and Service Strategy   108

PART II: WRITING THE BUSINESS PLAN AND MAKING THE PITCH   179

Chapter 8: Sources of Finance for Startups and Corporate Ventures   183

Chapter 9: Projecting the Financial Performance and Requirements for the Venture   219

Chapter 10: Organizing the Venture Team   257

Chapter 11: Writing the Business Plan!   276

Chapter 12: Making the Pitch 324

Acknowledgments

This book is the product of many helping hands.

The examples and teaching cases used throughout the book would not have been possible without the contributions of our friends who are entrepreneurs, investors, and corporate innovators. Our deepest thanks go to Tom and Darr Aley, Brian Chaney, Russ and Jeff Curran, Aaron Gowell, Alvin Graylin, John Helferich, Harry Keegan, Tom Kelly, Al Lehnerd, Mel Litvin, Jeff McCarthy, Dan Michael, Jeff Noce, Scott Pollister, John Ready, Rob Seliger, Jacques Torres, Neil Willcocks, and Margot Woodworth. Your dedication to sharing insights with the next generation of innovators and entrepreneurs is inspirational and goes well beyond this book.

We also extend our thanks to Professors Matthew Allen, Gordon Adomzda, Tucker Marion, and Cheryl Mitteness—and our other colleagues in the Entrepreneurship and Innovation Group at Northeastern University–who helped test and refine the methods in this book. We are also indebted to Professors Jeffrey Sohl and Richard Sudek for their contributions to our section on angel financing.

The SAGE Publications team has been tremendous. In particular, we would like to thank our sponsoring editor, Lisa Cuevas Shaw. We also wish to thank our copy editor, Terri Lee Paulsen, and production editor, Brittany Bauhaus. The assistance of Richard Luecke was also invaluable.

In addition, this book would not have been possible without the support and encouragement of Robert Shillman. Thank you, Dr. Bob!

Perhaps most all, we will remain forever grateful for the patience of our wives, Olga Smulders-Meyer and Doreen Crane.

The authors and SAGE also gratefully acknowledge the contributions of the following reviewers:

Jeffrey R. Alves, *Wilkes University*

Wasim Azhar, *University of California, Berkeley*

Shawn M. Carraher, *Minot State University*

Todd Finkle, *The University of Akron*

Dmitri Kuksov, *Washington University in St. Louis*

Phil Laplante, *Penn State*

Wally Meyer, *University of Kansas*

John E. Mulford, *Regent University*

Stephanie Newell, *Eastern Michigan University*

Gerald Smith, *Boston College*

Introduction

Welcome! This is a book for venturesome students who want to build great companies. *It is likely that you are that very type of person.* Why else would you be taking a course on entrepreneurship? There is a big difference, however, between being a venturesome individual and being a successful builder of a new enterprise. As a venturesome person, we are sure that you are not reluctant to try something new, challenge yourself to accomplish things that others might not, and take calculated risks in achieving goals. You are probably also someone who relishes the thought of greater independence and control over your work and the desire for the rewards of successful entrepreneurship—true and unshakable financial independence. These personal characteristics are important and good. However, building a successful new enterprise requires other qualities of mind and spirit—from the creation of winning new product and service concepts, to business modeling and pragmatic financial planning, to building a great team and deploying it to all the various things that a company needs to launch and then prosper. Each is a skill that can be learned and *will be learned* in the pages of this book.

Our goal in writing this book is to help you be the builder of a successful new enterprise: to conceive, plan, and execute on a new venture idea. The chapters that follow are designed to create a bridge between your venturesome nature and a future in which you are the founder, major shareholder, and leader of a growing enterprise. And while the methods apply generally to all types of entrepreneurship, our focus is not on the "lifestyle" business, such as a small specialty retail store or monthly industry newsletter, but rather, on ventures that can grow substantially in market reach and equity value. The material that follows is based on the findings of business scholars, our own experiences as entrepreneurs, and our work with dozens of young entrepreneurial companies.

Innovation is at the core of our design for this book. That is why we think of this book as an *innovator's guide to entrepreneurship.* We define innovation as the embodiment of new ideas or insights in the form of products, services, processes, or business models that have value for people or society. Business innovators create solutions to problems and satisfy customers in new ways.

There are plenty of books on innovation and many more on entrepreneurship. However, in the world of startups and corporate ventures, these are hardly separate disciplines. That is why we wrote this book. Innovative, high-growth ventures, ones based on dynamic marketing, new technology, and robust business models, reveal that innovation is, indeed, inextricably linked with entrepreneurship. The great companies, small and large, have applied new technology to address the compelling needs and challenges in industry and society in areas such as health, energy, environment, communications, security, transportation, education, food and water that cut across all geographies and industries.

For example, some of you might be customers of Zipcar, a Boston-based startup that is now growing across the United States. Zipcar's founders created an innovative solution to the transportation problem faced by millions of modern urban dwellers: the high cost and inconvenience of owning and finding parking for an automobile that is used only occasionally. Zipcar's solution: make vehicles conveniently available on a membership and rent by the hour basis as opposed to by the day. When a Zipcar member needs a car for a Saturday trip from the city to the seashore, the individual goes online, reserves a vehicle, and picks it up from a nearby lot. The member's magnetic card opens the door and logs in the time of beginning usage. Upon returning the vehicle to its parking spot that evening, the member swipes the card once more, registering the total time and mileage used, which will be reflected on a monthly bill. And then the member walks away, leaving all the headaches associated with car ownership in the city behind. Problem solved. From a business perspective, Zipcar is a wonderful example of a *market innovation,* because it has reached out to an untapped market of primarily young urban consumers who shun traditional rent-by-the-day car rental companies.

Another way to bring innovation to new ventures is to simply target an untapped market. For example, one of the book's case studies is about corporate venturing in Mars, Inc., the world's largest chocolate manufacturer. The company ventured into custom-printed candies. These are candies where the consumer can have the product delivered with specific messages or jpeg images of friends and loved ones directly on the blank side of the M&M's Candies. This transformed the traditional business from just commodity candy to the emerging market for customized food products. Suddenly, the target application expands from traditional snacking to a broad range of gifting occasions such as birthday parties, graduations, weddings, retirements, and so forth. This also led the company to a new business model: printed candies that could be sold for a handsome premium (up to ten times) price per pound of traditional M&M's. It is an entirely new way of making money for Mars, Inc.—a classic case of business model innovation.

Or, a venture can be innovative by virtue of breakthrough technologies or services—pure technological innovation. For example, emerging from the research labs at the authors' own university is an ingenious innovation that is a novel Petri dish that can grow cultures from an amazing range of organic materials (dirt and slime!). This new technology has opened the doors for discovery of new types of antibiotics and cancer drugs derived "from nature." The technology has showed so much potential for new drug discovery that alumni and professors of our university seed-funded the venture as "angel" investors. All these examples show just how broad the connection between innovation and entrepreneurship can truly be. A venture can flourish with a technological innovation, a market innovation, or a business model innovation—or a combination of all these innovations. This is what makes entrepreneurship based on innovation so cutting edge and exciting.

A Market- and Customer-Driven Process

Successful business innovators do not simply think of ways to profitably serve customers. First, they watch, meet, and talk with customers to generate concepts and then press on to test their concepts with potential customers, prototype new products or services, and re-test these prototypes to improve the designs and the business models surrounding the designs with each iteration. Only then does the successful entrepreneur write a business plan and use it to raise funds. And when the entrepreneur completes his or her product or service and launches it in the market, the learning never stops. Instead, customer reactions are closely observed and used to improve those commercial offerings and revise the business plan. The innovative type of entrepreneurship we focus on here rests profoundly on the ability to learn from customers, to understand their current solutions and problems, and to translate this learning into a new set of value-rich solutions that are the basis of any great company.

Figure I.1 provides an overview of the market- and customer-driven venture process offered by this book. The front end of that process is substantially different than the one traditionally offered to most students. Most books put an "idea" at the very beginning of the process. In this traditional process, the entrepreneur has an "Aha!" moment. He or she gets a great idea or recognizes a promising business opportunity. All else flows from that flash of inspiration: designing the product or service, writing a business plan, obtaining financing, and launching the business.

Many entrepreneurs follow this idea-driven approach. A few succeed, but most, regrettably, do not. Indeed, according to the U.S. Small Business Administration, 78% of new businesses fail. The reasons for failure are many: inadequate financing, poor management skills, and so on. In our experience, however, most failures are the consequence of the founder's inadequate attention to the marketplace of customers and competitors. What entrepreneur does not fall in love with his or her own idea? Energized by what appears to be a great, internally generated idea, the eager entrepreneur pushes forward (prematurely) to a business plan, and then tries to infect potential financiers with his or her misplaced enthusiasm. Sadly, most idea-driven ventures fizzle upon contact with the real world of customers and competitors.

The antidote to the deadly odds faced by entrepreneurs is what we call *market- and customer-driven* venturing—a process in which the new business is built on a compelling idea that emerges from a clear and methodical understanding of a particular industry, its various segments, and the customers and competitors who populate them. In this process, the idea, or venture concept, and the entrepreneur's business model are tested at every stage of development against market realities and real user needs and preferences. The voice of the market, and not the entrepreneur's inner voice, calls the shots. The result: The likelihood of financing and operational success is vastly greater.

Our approach in this book is to have you first develop problem-solving concepts and to then test them directly with target users. Then, you can turn your ideas into pragmatic yet exciting new products, services, and branding strategies. Only then, we believe, are you ready to write a business plan, to raise your startup capital, do a quick launch, and learn what it really takes to grow a scalable, dynamic company.

What's Ahead in This Book? _____

A market-tested concept, a solid product or service strategy, and a powerful business model are three of the things that today's investors look for in an entrepreneurial venture. Part I of this book—**Defining the Venture Concept**—teaches you how to:

- Determine the focus of your venture by defining the industry, its major segments, a target segment for your venture, and the type of business that makes sense for that target segment. We call this defining the *venture scope*.
- Define your target market and users in that market, the types of products or services you will provide to them, and the initial positioning of these offerings relative to competitors (e.g., premium, parity, lower priced). These choices produce your venture concept.
- Specify the business model the venture will adopt to make money.
- Create a product/service strategy that offers choice and variety to target customers.
- Determine competitive positioning and customer positioning of the venture.
- Conduct a market-based reality check on both the venture concept and the business model, not only with prospective customers but also against direct competitors.

Part II—**Writing the Plan and Making the Pitch**—will guide you to create a concise but powerful business plan, realistic financial projections, and an accompanying PowerPoint presentation. Doing this *after* the work of Part I is complete will make the task easier and produce a far better result. Traditional textbooks encourage plan writing from the early stage of idea development. Our experience has shown the error of this approach. Entrepreneurs learn so much in the course of developing their strategies, prototyping their products and services, and testing them with potential users that the initial business plan must be scrapped and created anew, wasting time and energy. In this part of the book, we will also look at essential issues that include:

- Building your startup team so that it has a balanced set of skills and experience and not just people like yourself!
- Selecting external advisors—those folks with a few gray hairs that have "seen it" and "done it" before—who can help you with key decisions and perhaps even provide access to seed capital.
- The different forms of startup capital, which might work best for your type of venture, and how to approach those all-important equity sharing decisions.

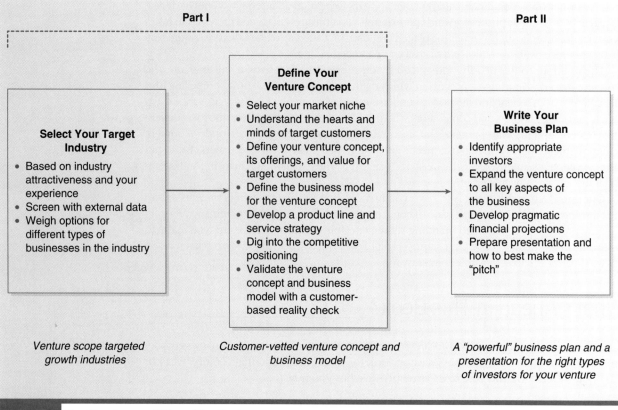

Part I

Part II

Select Your Target Industry

- Based on industry attractiveness and your experience
- Screen with external data
- Weigh options for different types of businesses in the industry

Define Your Venture Concept

- Select your market niche
- Understand the hearts and minds of target customers
- Define your venture concept, its offerings, and value for target customers
- Define the business model for the venture concept
- Develop a product line and service strategy
- Dig into the competitive positioning
- Validate the venture concept and business model with a customer-based reality check

Write Your Business Plan

- Identify appropriate investors
- Expand the venture concept to all key aspects of the business
- Develop pragmatic financial projections
- Prepare presentation and how to best make the "pitch"

Venture scope targeted growth industries

Customer-vetted venture concept and business model

A "powerful" business plan and a presentation for the right types of investors for your venture

Figure I.1 The Structure and Flow of the Book

With respect to investors, most textbooks spend a great deal of time on venture capital (VC) firms. Not this one. Only a tiny percentage of new ventures are ever funded by institutional venture capital. One in a thousand is perhaps generous! Most entrepreneurs find other sources of funding. Consequently, this book gives much greater attention to obtaining capital from "angels" and corporate investors. It also covers self-funding ventures and how to anticipate future funding requirements, given your business model and the type of products and services offered. For the financial projections, our focus will be on the first three years of the business, with a specific eye on detailed revenue and expense projections. From these we will look at annual projections for the fourth and fifth years of the venture. As any experienced entrepreneur will tell you, any numbers projected beyond the third year are more speculation than anything else. Still, those outlying years provide an indication to prospective investors on the upside potential of your venture based on industry standard multiples of revenue and profit. All this will be covered in Part II of the book.

In this book, we have two ways to bring these ideas to life for students—and as students in MBA or undergraduate business courses, you know both well. The first way is to provide you with a series of interesting venture cases, many of which profile our former students who have launched successful ventures! In these cases, we also try to cover the gamut of products, systems (such as software or hardware systems), and pure services—for each is an important aspect of our entrepreneurial economy.

The second way to help you learn the concepts of this book is to have you apply frameworks to your venture ideas. We call these "Reader Exercises" at the end of a chapter. Each chapter will feature one or two key frameworks that are presented as templates, visual representations of an approach for thinking about and solving a task or problem. An example might be a template for framing the target market, users, and positioning of your venture. Or another might be a template for presenting the business model for your venture. A reader exercise will simply ask you to apply this visual template using the research and integrative thinking that you have done on your project, hopefully with some teammates. Working in a team in a project-focused course not only fosters the shared learning that comes with discussion, but it also makes the work a lot more fun. Moreover, successful companies may have a visionary entrepreneur, but successful ventures invariably are created by strong, diverse teams that learn together and can trust each other's commitment and skill sets.

Pathways to Success

For many readers, graduation will be the launching pad to an exciting new venture. As business professors, we've observed scores of enterprising students develop and test venture concepts in parallel with their classroom studies. Quite a few of these students hit the ground running after graduation. Funded by family and friends, or by "angel" investors, many have succeeded. And we have taught a number of students who cannot wait for graduation. They, like one of your authors, actually start companies while still in school and still, importantly, managed to complete their academic programs. If you are young and have a burning passion to start a company, *do not drop out of school to start a company*. Do both and be the master of your own destiny.

Most entrepreneurs, however, do not make the leap until they have gained three to five years of work experience upon graduation, learned how to manage people and projects, and saved enough money to self-fund the first stage of a venture. If that's your plan, here is our advice: Work first for a top-flight company—a market leader in your target industry, meet highly qualified and effective individuals who have different skill sets, and do everything you can to get to know customers, what they wish to buy, and how to best sell to them. Never stop thinking about various ventures that you might launch into the market to serve those customers. When the timing is right—and don't wait too long!—form your team with the people you have met either at work or at school, apply the methods that are in this book, and launch that venture with all the passion and fortitude that you can muster.

There is yet another venue in which the entrepreneurial spirit expresses itself: inside large corporations. At least a third of our own entrepreneurial experiences have taken place within large, mature corporations. Corporate venturing—or "intrapreneurship"—has its own challenges and intrigues. Corporate venturers, for example, must deal with the power of the status quo, which uses its weight to push innovators aside when they ask for commitment and resources. Corporate venturers must also compete for the attention of senior management, which is usually more focused on the business of today than the opportunities of tomorrow. Innovating within the shell of a mature corporation, however, can be incredibly exciting. It's always a good way to cut through many layers of management and interface directly with top executives. For some, it's a fast path to the C-suite. We will do our best throughout this book to share our insights into corporate venturing with you.

But now, here's a little bit about your authors—you probably want to know about us before spending the coming semester reading our book. First and foremost, we are guided by four passions. The first is a passion for user-centered innovation—that is, designing products and services that make target consumers or corporate users *smile*. If they smile, the innovator can usually charge more than can competitors who offer the standard, boring stuff that populates most consumer, industrial, technology, health care, and energy categories.

Passion No. 2 is helping innovators think about how to make money from interesting ideas. Many worthy ideas fail in the marketplace when their advocates fail to offer them in ways that benefit *both* the customer and the innovator. This is a passion for *business model innovation*.

Our third passion is how to design and build innovative, fully-featured product lines and services that utilize underlying product or service platforms. In our experience, it is rare that a company can succeed with just a "onesie," yet many entrepreneurs fail to think beyond their first product or service. To achieve rapid growth, you need to offer choice and variety to customers and be prepared to do so soon within the first year of your new business.

Our fourth passion is branding—that is, creating exciting, dynamic marketing images for innovative products and services. Effective branding commands attention in a chosen market and builds the kind of excitement that propels venture growth. Every entrepreneur wants to create a "hot" company, but doing so rarely happens by chance. Branding and market development takes just as much work as creating products or services. We have done our best to bake these four personal passions into our book; we hope they will generate the same enthusiasm within you.

The best way to use this book is to read each chapter and then get a reality check on your ideas and approaches. We provide templates for doing this at each step of the venturing process. Examples of different types of products, systems, and service ventures are used to illustrate these templates. It is up to you and your teammates to go into the real world and apply them. Once you've obtained this feedback from your target market, learn, adjust, and retest your ideas. *Create, test, refine* is the mantra of this book. It should guide your work in building an innovative and successful venture.

part 1
Defining the Venture Concept

Defining and Testing Your Venture (Before Writing the Business Plan!)

The process for creating a new venture is just that—creation. It involves ideation, refinement, testing, and more refinement. Unlike a piece of art, however, creating a new business requires that you ideate not only what you will do as a business, but how you will make money doing what you do—for example, manufacturing and selling products, or producing and selling services.

Within the creation of a new business, there is a balance between discovery of new technologies and the application of proven technologies to solve people's problems. It is easy to get confused by the difference between "invention" and "innovation." As an entrepreneur, you must understand these differences because your path toward success will likely be very different if you are focused on one or the other.

Invention is the discovery of new science and technology. For example, one of our former students led the team that developed a new flexible solar film that can be layered on top of radios, backpacks, vehicles, and so forth. A spin-off out of a state university research lab, no matter how promising the long-term prospects for flexible solar films, he knew he was in for a long haul because the team had to first make the underlying technology work—including an entirely new, capital-intensive manufacturing process for making the flexible solar films—before ever launching a single product application to market. And a long haul it was! (Readers can go to http://www.konarka.com to see what has become of this amazing technology). "Invention" takes a long time and is typically best left to a funded university or corporate research lab.

In most cases, however, neither the startup or corporate entrepreneur have the time to wait for what often turns out to be a decade or more to see if a disruptive technology actually works and can be scaled into commercial form. For the entrepreneur involved in an invention business that takes many years to fulfill, hopefully, there's enough money left over at the end of the discovery process to get on with the business of actually making money with the technology.

Biotechnology startups are the classic "invention" venture. Most need to raise $10 million just to get started and another $50 million to get to animal trials—even before testing a single drug on humans! Not many people can raise that sort of money. Nonetheless, the rewards can be immense, with hundreds of millions of dollars, and sometimes billions, garnered by successful therapies.

Innovation, on the other hand, is the application of science and technology to solve problems for consumers, companies, governments, or society at large. Entrepreneurs, in particular, tend to apply their innovative thinking to find and address *new market applications* (e.g., new sets of emerging problems, new challenges, and new opportunities). For example, we see myriad mobile software development startups creating new applications—for mobile advertising, mobile health monitoring, or smartphone-based financial transactions—based on existing communication standards or protocols and published software development toolkits from Research in Motion, Google (Android), or Apple. Or it might be the application of known nutritional science to create a new product line of healthy, great-tasting snacks for people—or their pets! Or, it might be applying known materials to create new energy-efficient or sustainable household goods.

Regardless, using an existing set of hardware, software tools, chemicals, or any type of elemental ingredients does more than just reduce an important element of risk for the entrepreneur. An innovation focus is a market-driven focus. The drive becomes to understand what customers need and to design products or services to satisfy that need. It also allows the entrepreneur to focus heavily on the go-to-market aspects of being a successful business—the branding, the distribution or selling, and the additional follow-on services that can be provided to customers.

This holds equally true for corporate entrepreneurs reading this book. You want to be in the position of taking and deploying existing—or if it's new, well-proven—technology out of your company's research labs to new market applications to create new streams of revenue for your corporation within a year, or perhaps two, and the very most, three. Try to select technologies that are ready to hit the ground running.

Successful entrepreneurs and investors alike working on innovation want to know three basic things about a new venture:

- Is the target market—the *addressable market*—significant and growing in terms of the annual revenue of products and services flowing into that market?
- Is there a clear target customer, and does that customer need and want to buy what the venture intends to sell, be it a product, a service, or both?
- Does the venture have a clear way of making money—a business model that is both pragmatic and exciting?

This leads to a series of questions that guide the first section of this book. These questions need to make sense to you, because then the work that you have to do to answer these questions will seem logical and reasonable.

We would like you to read these questions slowly, and carefully think about them. You cannot rush blindly into a startup process; it is done step by step, solving one set of issues first and then moving onto the next, in a disciplined, orderly way.

1. *In what industry and sector in that industry are we going to focus our entrepreneurial efforts?* Does your target industry sector have robust growth? Apart from whatever passions you or your team's members might have for a technology or a business or social activity, do these find a home in a larger industry that has the customer demand—the market power—that will reward all of your hard work? In other words, is the industry a good place to start a new venture over the coming decade? And within this industry, where is a good place to make money? Is it primarily as a manufacturer of products? Or, a developer of software and systems? Or, is it as a service company, specialized in some certain way to differentiate against other existing services in that industry segment? Just as industries are so very different, each of these three types of business has a completely different business model—a different way of making money. The process for selecting a target industry and a target business type in that industry is the first step along your entrepreneurial journey. It results in what we refer to as **a venture scope**—which, at a very high level, defines who the target market and type of business the venture will be. The best way to show a strong target market is to gather *data*—lots of it. It can come from government sources, industry trade associations, trade shows, or articles in publications. Today, much of this information is available with diligent searches on the Web.

2. With the venture scope in hand, *who, specifically, will be our target customers?* This defines the addressable market for the venture. If you are seeking investment from professional investors, that addressable market needs to be clear, fairly substantial, and hopefully growing. And as the company itself grows, how might that target customer group expand? This might be starting in one city and expanding regionally, selling to one part of an industry and expanding to closely related or adjacent parts, or selling to Baby Boomers and then expanding to the elderly. Typically, there are several or more fundamentally different types of customers in any market, and you need to pick those that you think will be the best customers for what you wish to sell. The clever entrepreneur also thinks about *reference customers,* for example, those first customers whose very use of your products or services will help convince other customers to try them as well. Furthermore, the entrepreneur needs to be crystal clear about whether there is a difference between *who buys* and *who uses* the product or service (as in any business-to-business [B2B] venture—an IT manager buying software for the rest of us to use, or in a business-to-consumer [B2C] business—just think about diapers!). Answering these questions is the first part of developing **the venture concept**—it defines the all-important "who" in the venture equation. Answering this set of questions typically involves *field research,* getting to know different types of customers in their places of work or leisure or care.

3. Now that the venture has a defined a target customer, *what are the primary uses or applications that we wish to solve or address, and what do we wish to sell to them?* The key to success here is to understand how customers themselves define their problems and, as an innovator, how to best meet their needs in terms of features, performance, and price. For example, is the customer a football player for whom you have developed a new type of helmet to greatly reduce the probability of concussions? Or, is your target customer a building owner for whom you wish to develop an energy management system to automatically power equipment on and off to save money? Or, is it the medical director of a hospital who needs to gather data from all sorts of systems, analyze it, and point the way to improve the quality of care in the hospital? All three of these are clear customers with compelling needs. *That is what you want for your venture.* Field research with customers is the only way to get to the root of customers' needs and new, compelling solutions. With these insights, and some clever performance-price positioning relative to existing competitors serving the same market, you will then have all the information you need to create a **complete venture concept.** In addition to the *who,* it defines the *what, why,* and *where* for the basic aspects of the venture. A completed venture concept is the soul of a new business.

4. Once the venture concept is defined, entrepreneurs need to answer the all-important question of *how is the business going to make money?* We call this defining **the business model** for the venture. A robust business model is one that defines an approach for making money in a venture—hopefully, a lot of money! Business models for a venture can be just as much a point of competitive advantage as the venture concept itself; the former is the idea, and the business model is the execution of that idea—and it is the execution of a venture concept that separates the true winners from the wannabes. It also results in projections of revenue, expenses, and operating profit—where you use a spreadsheet to help envision how your venture concept can produce a money-making business.

5. *What will be the full range of our products or services?* The answer to this question builds directly on the venture concept and business model. No enterprise makes money on a "onesie," that is, a single product or even a single service. Rather, growth ventures require a fully featured product line or services that can be tailored to specific types of customers. The strategy for defining that range of products or services is called creating **a new product strategy** that matches targets customers. We think of new product strategy more simply as defining "good, better, best" in a way that offers different levels of features and price within a given target. More variety, within reason, typically produces more revenue. It is the essence of being a growth venture as opposed to a "Mom & Pop" operation. The "good, better, best" approach also helps the entrepreneur to decide where to start and where to grow. So often, an innovator will want to focus first and foremost on the very, very "best," which only serves to extend market launch and consume vast amounts of venture capital, whereas a "good" or "better" suits the majority of target customers just fine and can be introduced to them far more rapidly. The *innovative entrepreneur* wants to develop and launch distinctive new products and services to market as rapidly as possible, for it is only then that true market learning begins.

6. *What will be our* **competitive positioning**? *How will we differentiate from other companies already serving our target customers?* The answer to this question also builds upon your venture concept and its business model. Most young entrepreneurs are so optimistic about their venture concepts and business models that they fail to adequately consider current competition and probable competitive responses to the venture's own launch into the marketplace. A lack of competitive due diligence leaves you subject to nasty surprises, even after a lot of hard work getting to launch. Further, in the fundraising process, you might find potential investors pounding you for a lack of insight into competitors who they are likely to know all too well. We don't like nasty surprises, and neither should you! It is amazing just how much information can be surmised about competitors by examining their own Websites. And your field research with customers reveals the reality of features, performance, and price behind those Websites.

7. *How will we know that the venture concept, the business model, the product and service strategy, and the competitive positioning not only make sense but will also excite our target customers and put competitors on notice?!* These all need to be vetted with prospective customers and against current and emerging competitors. **A reality check** on the venture concept, its business model, its product/service strategy, and its competitive positioning are all essential—particularly for younger entrepreneurs. This reality check must be performed as a field-based exercise with target end-users and buyers. Any seasoned investor is going to ask after hearing your pitch, "Those new products and services sound great, but how do we know that any of this is really going to fly with target customers?" or "Your business model sounds unique and potentially a source of sustained competitive advantage, but has anyone else ever succeeded making money this way? Is it really feasible?" Being able to anticipate these questions and answer them with some degree of certainty—which means data—is where you need to be to launch your venture.

We will help you explore these questions and develop answers in the next seven chapters of this book. Each of the seven basic questions above has its own chapter. We want you to read these chapters and apply the exercises to your own projects before writing the formal business plan. In other words, we want you to perform all the in-market learning and thinking first before writing a single page. There are no shortcuts. Sure, you might get lucky and write a quick plan, raise a little money, and launch some products or services in a month or two. However, unless you are extraordinarily brilliant or have tried a similar type of business before and failed but are going at it again with the benefit of your prior mistakes, the chances are that you will have to scrap most of what was in your short and quick business plan and reinvent your business on the fly.

In contrast, going through the first section of this book successfully will make the second part—writing the actual plan—relatively straightforward. It will also greatly increase the chances of success in terms of raising money and executing with that money. You will bring all the research, insight, and integration of ideas from Part I into your business plan writing and money-raising efforts. In short, the time spent in the first section pays handsome dividends later on.

Now, *we hope you are ready not only to work but also to have fun in doing that work*. Think of this as not just working for a grade but working for yourself, for your own future. Creating something from scratch—seeing a business launch and grow from simply an idea in your head—is one of the most rewarding, exciting, and energizing things that anyone can do in their lives. It doesn't always work, but when a venture succeeds, *there is nothing else quite like it* for the mind and spirit.

## chapter 1

Identifying Your Industry, the Target Sector in the Industry, and Type of Business

The Purpose of the Chapter

The biggest mistake a would-be entrepreneur can make is to follow blindly his or her passion about a particular invention or technology without regard or knowledge about the industry and applications to which that invention or technology will be applied. To be successful as an entrepreneur, you must select an industry and market that can reward your hard work with customers who need what you have to sell and will pay you for it. Select a strong industry—one that is growing and hungry for innovation, new products, and services—and with proper execution, your innovative idea can be the basis of a wonderful company. This is a market-driven approach to entrepreneurship as opposed to one where you simply create technology and pray that it finds a good market and application to serve. Also, if you are going to raise money from professional investors, you are going to have to defend the attractiveness of your target market with data—with facts that prove size and growth.

This chapter describes the first step in the market-driven venture process:

1. Identifying the industry you wish to enter based on your experience, education, family connections, and personal interests

2. Selecting the sector of that industry where opportunity beckons

3. Determining the type of business (product, system, or service) with the greatest potential

At a deeper level, the purpose of this chapter is to get you into the mindset of working diligently to understand markets, customers, and business opportunities. Successful entrepreneurship rarely happens by accident. Sure, timing is extremely important, but being in the position to take advantage of fortuitous circumstances is what entrepreneurship is all about. Though "hunches" or intuition may open your eyes to real commercial possibilities, they may also lead you into a trap, where even a great idea is pulled down the drain by the overwhelming forces of a declining industry. Why bother to seek opportunity in such an industry when others offer more possibilities and a brighter future?

This chapter also discusses the dynamic between your own personal experiences and interests, and the market realities needed to support a prosperous business. Entrepreneurs have passion for their new venture concepts. However, often we find a tension between an entrepreneur's own personal internal influences—such as work experience, education, and family background—and external market factors that help set the stage for a promising new venture. Just because you are wildly enthusiastic about a particular hobby or sport or industry does not mean that starting a company based just on that personal interest will be worth the effort. This chapter will help you think about these two sides of the entrepreneurial coin and, we hope, strike a balance.

Moreover, successful entrepreneurship requires that you be brutally honest and pragmatic about the facts on the ground. You must do your utmost to gather the best information available around any particular decision, and then take the information you gather seriously. You cannot pretend that a "bad" market will suddenly turn around and become a fertile ground for a new venture. And, if you come up empty, you can then check other parts of an industry for better hunting. Entrepreneurship requires market knowledge as well as innovative thinking, plus a determination to keep working through what might at first seem to be difficult barriers.

Learning Objectives

This chapter offers practical methods for:

- Gathering information on the attractiveness of a particular industry
- Identifying industry sectors and determining which are most appealing, including a method called "industry ecosystem mapping."
- Using industry analysis to define the scope and purpose of your venture

Selecting a Target Industry

Most people who aim to start a business get their initial ideas from one or more of the following "internal" sources:

• **Work experience:** We watched as Cheryl moved up the ranks as a successful salesperson for selling medical instrumentation for a market leader in eye surgery, including cosmetic surgeries. She was determined to start her own business. Fashionable, engaging, and market-focused, Cheryl saw the combination of increasing skin cancer rates and the spending of disposable income on cosmetic products and minor procedures (such as dermal abrasion and Botox injections) as creating an opportunity to start a chain of skin health centers focused on upscale professional women in urban areas.

- **Educational background:** Matt, a business school student at our university, took various entrepreneurship courses and believed that there must be a better way to design customized business models and create financial statements than using his professor's spreadsheet templates or buying off-the-shelf packaged software sold for creating business plans. He formed a team to create a Web-based software package for business models and financial planning for new ventures—seeking to provide this as a service to business school educators. Matt convinced his business professors and their students to be the test users!

- **Family background and business experience:** Walter was an old friend from high school. It turns out that Walter's father created a company that provides de-icing services to major airlines at many airports across the United States and Europe. Walter worked in the business and became the CEO after his father retired. Walter developed great connections through the industry, and one of his customers was Federal Express (having a large fleet of its own airplanes). Walter wanted to make his own mark on the industry. He envisioned raising additional capital to start a small, feeder airline to transport FedEx packages to small, local airports in the southeastern United States. And that is precisely what Walter did.

Among student entrepreneurs, the fad seems to be to propose yet another social networking idea, following in the footsteps of Twitter or Facebook. The vast majority of these fail to become viable businesses because even though the idea is "cool," there is no clear recipe for monetizing the innovation, particularly if the Website is geared toward fellow students who are well trained not to pay for anything on the Web. This is not to say that the social networking trend is a passing fad or that you can't make money creating a social networking service. One of the teaching cases in this book (Generate) is about one of our students who developed a "LinkedIn on steroids" combined with Hoover's-style business information to empower business-to-business (B2B) salespersons. This fellow, Tom, ended up selling his company for more than $50 million within just four years of start up!

But we also encourage you to buck the trend of thinking about popular fads for new ventures. Consider mature markets that are in desperate need of innovation. Many mature industries are in the process of business and consumer transformation. Just look at the energy utility sector, once the most "boring" and today, one of the most exciting areas for new devices, software, and systems.

Moreover, often the most successful entrepreneurs avoid highly competitive spaces where lots of other entrepreneurs are trying to win. For example, we have a friend Jim who introduced a new approach to the tired, old workers' compensation industry—preventing injuries from occurring in the first place and sharing that benefit back with customers through reduced premium rates. Within ten years, Jim had built himself a $200 million a year industry. And now he is doing it again for outsourcing employee counseling services for major corporations. The same type of innovation in mature segments can be found in health care, energy, and transportation. And the advantage is that cash is already flowing in these industries—money that could be yours for the taking.

None of these factors—work, education, family experience, or the current trend—function in isolation toward new venture creation. In fact, in many cases, these factors combine in a type of synergy that makes entrepreneurship its own special life form. Take the case of Alvin, another former student. Alvin was born in China and immigrated to the United States at a young age. Over the years, he earned an undergraduate degree in electrical engineering, a master's degree in computer science, and an MBA. The family heritage was a strong pull for Alvin. He also knew opportunity for new products and services for the domestic Chinese market was virtually unlimited. On his journey to be an entrepreneur, Alvin first took a job with Intel and then got himself an assignment in the Shanghai office to explore mobile consumer applications and services for China. A few years later, he left Intel to start what is now one of the leading mobile search and pull-based advertising companies in China. His new company was named the official mobile search provider to the 2008 Summer Olympics in Beijing. Alvin was on his way!

These are all wonderful stories, and they can happen for you as well. Each one of these individuals was a "smart" but regular person—the type of individual with whom you would enjoy having lunch or grabbing a beer: a good listener and a careful thinker, and highly attuned to how to merge his or her own personal portfolio of skills and contacts with robust market opportunities.

Figure 1.1 is designed to help you weigh how your own personal internal factors might direct you toward a particular industry as well as the target sector or niche within that industry. Take a look at it now and begin to think about filling in the boxes on the left side of that figure and how the combination of your own work experience, education, family background, and personal business goals point to an industry focus where your history and interests provide insight and understanding needed for the road ahead.

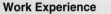

Work Experience
- (Position, type, and depth of experience gained)
- Etc. . . .

Education Experience
- (University, skills gained)
- (Other education, skills gained)

Family Experience
- (Family business, experience gained, source of finance, access to channels and suppliers)

Personal Business Goals
- Long-standing personal goals as an innovator and entrepreneur

Characteristics of the Target Industry
And the sector or niche within the industry

Potential Venture Ideas
- a product venture opportunity
- a systems venture
- a service venture opportunity
- combination/hybrid

Do this individually for the members of your venture team, then compare notes, and share your ideas about the different business types of opportunities that might exist in the target industry.

Figure 1.1   Balancing Internal and External Factors to Shape New Ventures

However, it is critically important to note that following any of these internal factors blindly down the path to a venture concept may just as easily lead you into a lot of hard work with little return. Internal factors are seldom sufficient in and of themselves for success. To capitalize on the value they do contain, the entrepreneur must integrate them with favorable "external" factors such as rising market demand, positive industry trends, unsatisfied customer needs, and so forth. The best approach to do this is to find an industry or industry sector with those positive characteristics and then build an enterprise that capitalizes on them and the entrepreneur's internal factors.

The importance of finding the "right" industry cannot be overemphasized. Being in the right industry is like bicycling with the wind at your back, making your journey easier. The key is to identify a source of powerful market demand and let that demand drive the design of your venture as well as the team that you build around the venture. And that market demand is itself an unfolding story. In doing your research, you might go after a particular market niche and find that an adjacent area actually offers even higher growth and the potential for higher profits. Consider the experience of your authors.

As an undergrad at Harvard, one of your authors worked four nights each week as a chef at a high-end restaurant just off the campus. Despite his expertise and passion for the culinary arts, however, he never seriously considered starting a restaurant business as an entrepreneur. There were already dozens of high-quality restaurants in the area, and many of these seemed to have a shelf-life of only four or five years. The likelihood of earning a decent financial return on invested capital and 12-hour work days six days each week was slim.

Instead, technology—and in particular software—was the "hot thing" in the Cambridge area during that time. To pay for graduate school at MIT, your author took another three-day-a-week job working for a large commercial bank running a software-based project management system for major back-office information technology implementation. While he considered starting his own project management software company, there were already very large software players in that market space. He kept looking, thinking, and networking with individuals like himself who were hungry to start a software company.

Over the coming months, your author was determined to either start or join a fledgling software venture. It seemed a good idea to take an entrepreneurship course. From this course, he banded with a team of MIT graduate students with a vision of putting Unix on a PC and applying a "real-time" operating system kernel that they had developed for science experiments to commercial applications. This venture was to be a classic university spin-off. The team developed software products that became market leaders in real-time process control and then expanded into fast, memory-resident database software. One of our favorite applications was for factories for brewing beer! Customer visits were a "must!" Medical equipment, robotics, and telecommunications all came next. It was an excellent business that grew rapidly, forming partnerships with companies such as Digital Equipment Corporation and Microsoft, and eventually, it was acquired by Citrix as part of that company's virtualization software play.

The important lesson is that your author saved his passion for cooking to please his future wife as opposed to trying to make it his life's work. And his expertise in project management software was used to gain a general comfort with software technology but was not the focus of a venture due to existing competition. That was a very good thing because Microsoft Project came into existence a few years later and has "crushed" the market. Instead, your author looked for an emerging niche and team of skilled peers who wanted to gang-tackle the opportunity.

If you want a business that will provide you with a modest income and the benefits of self-employment—a lifestyle business—follow your passion and forget about external market and industry factors. However, don't be surprised if you fail to achieve financial independence and the sense of accomplishment and freedom that comes with it. And you may spoil your passion by turning it into a job. Could you imagine running a commercial kitchen, day in and day out? Or, if your passion is fishing (such as is the case with both of your authors), being a fishing guide, rain or shine? Or, being within a family that owns a business that you are expected to take over after getting your education, and you simply know that the family business lacks growth potential and is barely making a profit? This, in fact, was the expectation of your second author.

> The Crane family had been in the retail and wholesale food distribution business for many years. As a family member with plenty of work experience in the enterprise, your author could have stepped into this business in a leadership capacity. But he chose to look elsewhere for an occupation. Why? His education and experience told him that family-owned food businesses faced tough sledding in the years ahead. Huge national food distributors were sweeping across North America, rolling over "Mom and Pop" businesses like his as they went. The idea of running a small food business was appealing, and the idea of following in his parents' and grandparents' footsteps was compelling, but Fred's business education and industry experience told him that going head to head with well-financed competitors with enormous buying power would be nothing but a series of exhausting and disheartening rear-guard actions. The profit margins of his family business were already slim and would be under continuous downward pressure as those larger competitors exercised their greater market power.
>
> So, your author struck out in a different direction. He entered a field where his grasp of market information, branding, and customer behavior was in high demand, and where he would charge a premium price for his consulting services. By integrating external information with his internal capabilities, Fred stepped away from the troubled food distribution industry and caught the rising wave of market consulting.

Many others entrepreneurs, including many former students, have successfully adopted this same winning formula: Find an industry or industry sector with favorable supply/demand and competitive characteristics, *and* where one's internal strengths can be profitably applied. This is how we want you to approach your own venture.

The other important context-setting decision is whether you wish to start a new company from scratch or create a venture within an established corporation. Our examples and teaching cases in this book deliberately cover both types of situations, because each is a venture in its own right that can bring you satisfaction as well as considerable personal wealth. We have already provided you with lots of startup examples, so let's take a quick look at a classic corporate venture.

Steve, a gifted electrical engineer and MBA student in one our weekend classes for working professionals, was considering how to create a product line that would leverage his company's technology to an *adjacent* market application. The company made highly specialized chips that were used to process 3D images in medical equipment—CT (computed tomography) and MRI (magnetic resonance imaging) in particular. Steve searched and searched for other medical applications but came up with nothing. Working with the professor, both came to the conclusion: Think outside the medical field.

Several weeks later, while returning from a business trip, Steve noted the poor quality of the luggage scanning system deployed at the airport. He realized that the government would demand far better solutions—if there were any. Steve now had a venture target. He developed a plan for the course, which he took to the company's head of R&D. With the support of this executive, Steve received funding to lead a project to deliver improved scanning for airport security. September 11 had not yet happened, but it would soon rear its ugly head. Steve's project could not have been better timed. In the years since, his company has become a major supplier of imaging subsystems technology to manufacturers of explosive detections systems.

For the entrepreneur, startup or corporate, having a market mandated by a federal government agency is perhaps as good as it gets.

Situations like Steve's are not usual. Ventures often emerge from the frustrations that people encounter. Thanks to their work experience and technical educations, midlevel corporate personnel like Steve often see problems or opportunities that their companies overlook, find too small to pursue, or might view as a new growth opportunity if only a well-considered plan is brought to management's attention. You can do the same by looking at the problems and frustrations you experience as potential opportunities.

Taking Stock: Your Internal Factors

What is your relevant business experience? What are the facets of your educational background that might come into play in a venture? What connections do you have amongst your family and friends that might be brought to bear in a venture? And at a deeper level, what are your personal interests for business? In your heart of hearts, where might you want to commit yourself for a 24/7 effort for the next five years?! What motivates you to commit a big chunk of your life to building a business?

Take some time to think about these internal factors as they apply to you personally, using Figure 1.1. Like other frameworks in this book, Figure 1.1 is intended to stimulate your thinking, searching for facts and planning of your own venture.

Work, education, and family experience are factual in nature—what have you done or what exists in these three areas and the level of accomplishment in that area? Your skills and experiences might well "suggest" a fit toward a particular industry. Moreover, there will typically be multiple sectors within an industry. We want you to note all of these. We will show you how to do research on them in just a moment to identify which specific parts of an industry look best from a business creation perspective. But before we do, consider the following two examples.

Starting From Ground Zero

Unlike the characters in our two previous examples, some people lack the industry or work experience that would help them recognize and pursue an entrepreneurial opportunity. Many graduating students fit this description. How about you? Are you at a point in life where you have no real work experience? And you don't come from an enterprise-owning family that discusses business around the dinner table every night. But the idea of working for someone else leaves you cold. Don't despair. You are starting at ground zero, but your passion and a bit of good old-fashioned luck might open the door to something special.

We once had several students who, frankly, were not stellar students. School, books, and classrooms were not their thing. However, they had other admirable qualities of mind and spirit. As graduation drew near and their need to find employment became more tangible, they approached their professor.

"Professor, can you help us find a job at a bank or something?"

"I don't think you fellows are cut out for banking," the professor said.

"Then what about consulting? That pays well, doesn't it?"

"Yes, it pays well, but consulting firms only hire graduates with 4.0s," he responded.

"Then, what should we do?"

"Well, you'll soon have business degrees from a fine university, and you seem to have plenty of energy and guts. Maybe you should start your own company. That way, you can control your own destiny."

"Great," they said, "what should we do?"

"Do something you really love, because you're going to have to work harder than you have ever worked in your life—and definitely harder than you've worked in my class!"

One of the young men laughed, "Well, we sure love beer. Maybe we should open a bar!"

"Have you ever worked in a bar?" the professor cautioned. "Do you have any idea how hard it is to run a bar? You never have a night off and the employee problems are rampant."

They looked puzzled. "My guess is that you guys are going out to a bar tonight, am I right?" (Nods all around.) "Well, instead of being customers as usual, keep your eyes on the bar owner. Watch everything he does. And think about what it would be like being him six nights a week. *Really* think about it. Then come back and talk to me."

The students were back the next day, this time with long faces. "Professor, we love beer, and we like hanging out in bars, but after watching that owner for hours, we would hate his job."

"In that case, how about *making* beer to sell to bars? I had some microbrewery beer the other day and it was great. Was expensive, too. I bet there is room for another specialty beer label, as long as it's premium quality and has a good story crafted behind the product. Think about it and come back to me next week," the professor said.

Well, one of those students thought about it, and after graduation he created a plan: to enter the premium segment of beer industry, with a great Boston "story" behind the brand. This student, the professor discovered later, did not simply love to drink beer—he loved the craft and culture of brewing and had gone to great lengths to learn about how great beers are made and about the ingredients that go into them. Following his muse, he learned the lore of a unique industry. Ten months after graduation, he and a partner started a specialty beer company that a few years later won the "Best of Boston" award in its category. A dozen years later, the two partners sold that company for millions to a large national specialty brewer. Those two guys made a lot of money!

Yes, passion and energy can take you a long way in your search for the right opportunity.

Investigating the External Dimension: The Potential of the Target Industry

Up to this point, the notion of selecting a target industry may seem to be largely a "gut" call, using one's work background, education, and family experience—plus personal passion—to decide where to direct the entrepreneurial effort. But there is a difference between blind insight and informed insight, between guessing and *calculated risk-taking*. From the gut, we must now move to the head—to detailed research on the fundamental characteristics of the industries that interest you.

Industries and Their Sectors

An *industry* is a group of firms that produce products or services that are close substitutes for each other and which serve the same general set of customers. Industries are defined by the markets served by their competing participants.

Most industries can be subdivided into specific *sectors,* which, in turn, include a set of competitors that address particular customer groups. For example, the financial services industry includes many sectors: investment banking, commercial and retail banking, insurance, money management, and so forth. Each of these sectors includes its own set (often overlapping) of competing firms, customer groups, products, and services. Some sectors may have low growth, low profitability, and little innovation; others may exhibit dynamic growth and an abundance of opportunities to make money. As entrepreneur, you probably cannot take on an entire industry, at least in the beginning. The path to success is to develop a venture within a particular niche or area within a larger industry, to grow to a leading if not dominant position within that niche, and expand from there. This lends focus to the new enterprise, and focus is all important for any new venture. And the key to success is to focus on a particular sector (or subsector) of an industry that is most promising for you in terms of a range of critical factors such as growth rate and clear channels to customers. Thus, you need to understand the industry in broad strokes and understand its sectors in detail.

As you study a particular industry and sectors of interest, look for positive indicators in the following areas:

- The size, growth rates, and profitability of the customer markets served by the industry
- The concentration and intensity of competition
- The industry, or sector's, life cycle stage
- Barriers to entry

Be as thorough as possible investigating these areas. The result should point the way to a robust market opportunity, one that can support and reward all of the hard work that you will have to do when actually launching a company based on a vision and a plan to act on that vision.

Size, Growth Rates, and Profitability

Starting a new venture in a flat or declining sector is usually a waste of time, so look for areas where robust growth is anticipated for years to come. For example, if you were looking into the imaging industry, you'd be wary of any sector that involved film-based imaging, which has been in decline ever since digital imaging gained a market foothold. Further, rarely does an entrepreneur take on an entire industry—at least in the beginning. Rather, he or she focuses on a particular sector of that industry. Markets tend to be comprised of multiple sectors. Each sector contains different types of customers and different uses for products and services. Some of these sectors might have low growth and low profitability; others have dynamic growth and lots of opportunities to make money. The entrepreneur therefore needs to know the size, growth, and profitability of key sectors in a given market. "A rising tide," as the saying goes, "lifts all boats."

Likewise, determine the profitability of the companies battling for market share in sectors of interest. If the firms that already have a foothold in a growing market cannot make a profit, what's the chance that you, a newcomer, will? If there is a publicly traded company participating in your target industry, even if not the same exact sector of that industry that you wish to target, the financial performance of that company might be indicative of what you can achieve should your venture scale into a major business. A quick trip to Yahoo! Finance or Hoover's can reveal the margins enjoyed by successful players.

Concentration and Intensity of Competition

Some industries have one or two large leaders and half a dozen second-tier competitors, all jockeying for incremental gains in market share by introducing a new product or service and, just as often, lowering prices. It's very tough for a startup to compete in such an environment. A new corporate venture, on the other hand, stands a chance because it can often leverage the corporation's brands, distribution channels, manufacturing, and credibility to break into the market with a new solution.

Most entrepreneurs should avoid areas of concentration and intense competition and seek out *fragmented markets* in which there are many small competitors and no dominant leaders. In fragmented markets, anyone with an attractive value proposition, a strong work ethic, adequate capital, and imagination has a fair shot at success. A123 Systems of Watertown, Massachusetts, for example, entered an industry with large, established battery manufacturers. In the high-performance sector of this mature industry, however, only a handful of other small startups were competing to create the rechargeable lithium-ion batteries needed to power large equipment and vehicles. A123 raised more than $50 million of venture capital and received a U.S. government grant for $259 million to build manufacturing capacity. A month later, it raised another $400 million through an initial public offering. Those had to be some pretty special high-performance rechargeable batteries!

Life Cycle Stage

In the strategy literature, technological and product/service innovation are important components of what is referred to as the industry life cycle. This life cycle has several stages: *emergent, growth, maturation, and decline.* This cycle is sometimes expressed as an S-curve[1] similar to that shown in Figure 1.2.

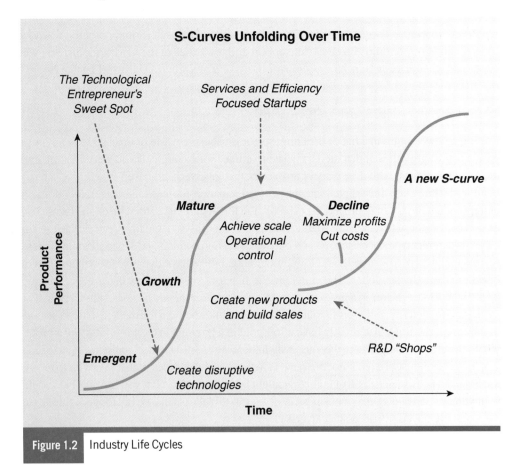

Figure 1.2   Industry Life Cycles

The emergent stage is an initial period of slow revenue growth and few if any direct competitors. Many entrepreneurs in this stage are still working out their product/service concepts. A credible market may not yet exist. Nanotechnology (which is new material science working on

---

[1] For a fuller explanation of S-curves, see Richard Foster, *The Attacker's Advantage* (New York: Summit Books, 1986), and James M. Utterback, *Mastering the Dynamics of Innovation* (Boston: Harvard Business School Press, 1994).

the scale of a billionth of a meter!) is in this emergent stage—although we already see it taking hold in certain mainstream applications such as apparel, house paint, and drug delivery.

The next stage is characterized by rapid growth. This is when the product or service concept really clicks with customers. The cell phone sector of the telecom industry entered this stage several years ago. Cell phone companies and service providers had finally worked out the technical kinks, and more and more areas of the country were offering service to roaming users. Suddenly, everyone wanted one of these handy devices. Today, the companies that are developing new types of batteries and energy management systems are clearly in the growth stage. As growth hurtles forward over time, more and more competitors and more capital are attracted to the sector.

Eventually, growing markets become saturated, the rocketing growth curve tapers off, and competitors find themselves in the maturity stage of the cycle. The many companies now in the field resort to price discounts and other mechanisms to generate revenues and poach customers from their competitors. They enhance their products and services in an attempt to make them stand out from the crowd. Gradually, the weaker firms exit the field, and a handful of firms are left standing. The office productivity sector of the software industry is in the mature stage of its cycle, with just a few players holding the majority of market share.

As you can see in Figure 1.2, the *S-curve* of an industry sector or product category (and companies) may eventually enter a stage of *decline*. In most cases, industry decline occurs when a discontinuous technology enters the market. The market for manual and electric typewriters, for example, tumbled when computers with word processing software came along. The same happened to the photographic film industry when digital camera technology became price competitive. Likewise, the incandescent lighting industry that Thomas Edison pioneered at the end of the nineteenth century is now moving from maturity to decline as energy-conscious users move to fluorescent and LED substitutes.

To fully appreciate the S-curve concept, look again at Figure 1.2. Notice the new S-curve on the far right. Even as one industry sector or product category is in decline, a rival, usually armed with a new and better technology, is increasing its product performance and entering a period of buoyant growth—typically at the other's expense.

TIP: OPPORTUNITY ALERT!

Many new business opportunities can be found in the turmoil created by disruptive innovations. For example, the U.S. global positioning system (GPS) changed the way ships, aircraft, and field armies navigate on the earth's surface. Those were the obvious and intended applications. Once the technology was made available for civilian use, corporate and individual ventures quickly found new applications and markets for that technology: smart bombs, handheld GPS devices for hikers, dashboard-installed auto GPS devices, downloadable maps for national parks, and "kid-track" units to name just a few.

So, when you see a new technology driving a mature industry into decline, think of the opportunities that technology may create elsewhere.

Life Cycle Implications for New Ventures

The life cycle has important implications for ventures seeking to produce new products. At the front of the life cycle, a nanotechnology entrepreneur simply has to find an application that will show his or her technology not only working but also producing value for customers. At the back side of the life cycle, a brilliant engineer seeking to develop software, systems, or services for oil or gas producers is going to surely face several cost and pricing pressures, as will the entrepreneur targeting automotive industry (original equipment manufacturers—OEMs). Costs are counted down to the pennies in mature industries. Experience shows that technology-based ventures enjoy the greatest success when they enter the field *near the beginning* of the growth stage. This is the entrepreneur's sweet spot, shown in Figure 1.2. A123 Systems, the battery company, was in this spot, using its proprietary technology (actually, nanotechnology) to create a high-energy discharging lithium-ion battery for mainstream applications—such as cars or power tools. Apple was in the same spot with iTunes. The early to midpoint of a growth stage of a broader market is where an entrepreneur should ideally enter with a specialized application or solution. Anything much earlier—technology that is nowhere close to prime time—can mean a long and painful journey for the entrepreneur. Because no markets currently exist for these pioneering concepts, the entrepreneur starves for cash before paying customers appear. Instead, such technologies best belong in corporate R&D or in university laboratories until the technology matures to the point where it can be effectively commercialized.

On the other hand, entering the industry or sector late in its cycle—in the mature or declining stages—is a hopeless errand for the entrepreneur unless he or she has a powerful concept for reinvigorating the product or service and thereby regenerating solid growth. Lacking that, he or she will fight against entrenched competitors for a dwindling number of customers.

Exceptions to the Rule

For startups that offer new systems or services (as opposed to products), opportunities can be found at *all* stages of the life cycle, particularly for B2B plays. In these cases, industry participants are the venture's customers. For instance, makers of home refrigerators in the U.S. market are in a mature stage characterized by many competitors and modest profit margins. Demand is growing very slowly. The predicament in which these manufacturers find themselves creates healthy demand for entrepreneurs who can provide:

- Cost-saving production methods
- Operating efficiencies
- Imaginative marketing concepts
- Customer-pleasing product innovations

Thus, in B2B situations, identify areas in which companies are feeling pain and desperately seeking solutions. If you can relieve their pain or solve their problems, you will have customers, no matter what stage of the life cycle your B2B customers are in. For example, a new information system or data mining application that can substantially help a company such as Staples improve customer knowledge and supply chain efficiencies is going to get a good look, and if Staples decides to buy, it is world-class reference accounts with which to sell other retailers. Or, large, mature utility companies are actively investing in new "smarter planet" technologies in the form of software and sensors to more efficiently manage electrical grids and consumption. Even the most mature and static of industries can become hotbeds for innovation. And when that happens, the entrepreneur often becomes pivotal in business and industry transformation.

Barriers to Entry

A thorough investigation of a target industry must also consider (1) the presence of barriers to entry, and (2) what, if anything, can be done to surmount them. A barrier to entry is any requirement—capital, technical know-how, and so on—that makes industry or market entry difficult or impossible. Of the many barriers faced by industry outsiders, three are particularly important for new venture entrepreneurs: capital and time, manufacturing, and marketing.

Capital and Time

Entry to some industries/sectors requires huge amounts of capital—amounts that few entrepreneurs can raise. In other industries/sectors, years of R&D are needed to develop marketable products. As you can imagine, these two barriers usually go hand in hand. Consider, for example, the pharmaceutical industry where more than ten years and close to a billion dollars are typically needed from start to launch for a single new drug! On the other hand, Web-based social networking presents minimal time and capital barrier. Launching a new Web-based business can be fast and inexpensive.

Manufacturing

Certain manufacturing industries require particular types of machines to produce a given category of products. For building products, complex wood cutting, forming, and assembly machines are needed; for certain plastics and food products, specially built extrusion machines are required. And the list goes on. These machines can cost millions of dollars. An entrepreneur who insists on entering a capital-intensive industry needs to consider external manufacturing options—often called contract or comanufacturers—to source his or her products. An increasing variety of these options exists both here and abroad.

On the other hand, we have seen students create new data mining and analytical "production" for the institutional investment industry with nothing more than several affordable servers.

Marketing

Marketing is the third major barrier to entry that an entrepreneur needs to consider. Gaining access to customers may be difficult and costly. Consider these examples:

- A new food venture with a natural fruit snack for kids faces a serious financial obstacle: paying "slotting fees" to get its products on the shelves of major grocery and convenience store retailers. Slotting fees can reach to several million dollars or more.
- A software company's products need to be sold by knowledgeable sales people. It faces a $300,000 annual price tag (compensation, benefits, and training) for each highly qualified salesperson. Half a dozen salespeople are typically needed in the second year of business by companies in this field.

Situations such as these make entry challenging. But don't give up too easily. An imaginative entrepreneur can sometimes circumvent typical barriers by finding new and unconventional challenges to customers. This is how Dell Computer made its mark. Instead of selling through expensive retail stores like everyone else, it marketed PCs directly to customers. eBay founder Pierre Omidyar operated his new company from his rented apartment using a PC, a small server, and a second-hand table until such time as he could easily afford more space, personnel, and equipment.

Additional Environmental Scanning Can Also Uncover Rich Entrepreneurial Opportunities

Environmental scanning can uncover new venture opportunities, or at least help identify the types of users you want to get to know. Successful entrepreneurs regularly scan their market, technology, and competitive landscapes to look for opportunities, threats, and partners—to understand the ecosystems in their dynamic marketplaces.[2] As you scan the environment:

- Pay attention to trends and market changes, and how users are reacting to them; for example: a consumer trend toward purchasing locally grown food.

---

[2] Crane, F. G., & Sohl, J. (2004). Imperatives for venture success: Entrepreneurs speak. *The International Journal of Entrepreneurship and Innovation, 5*(2), 99–106.

- Closely look for structural changes in society and determine how those changes will affect the needs of consumers; for example: an aging population of homeowners seeks smaller, low-maintenance housing.
- Study the *trajectory* of new product introductions by leading competitors in your chosen industry; for example: Manufacturer X launches a new product generation every four years, each with more electronic systems, and each with analog features replaced by digital features.
- Keep up to date on government actions that could affect your venture; for example: the U.S. Environmental Protection Agency taking public testimony in advance of new regulations on disposable medical products.

What you learn from scanning will greatly inform your venture concept. And you may uncover an opportunity that is even better than your initial concept. It is also important to keep track of what you learn from environmental scanning and then see how it affects your choice of target customers, products, and/or services.

Figure 1.3 shows a simple environmental scan in terms of key facts, constraints, and emerging trends driving the North American landscape. Each one can shape your venture concept. While Figure 1.3 shows some over-arching trends that are affecting businesses on an aggregate level, you will have to prepare an environmental scan specific to "your industry" and "your venture." Revisit it from time to time to see if and how the external environment is changing.

Environmental scanning can hugely affect the design of a business. Here are some examples from different industries:

Trends	Over-Arching Examples	Venture Opportunities
Social	- Growing ethnic diversity - Aging - Time poverty - Value-consciousness - Eco-consciousness	- Ethnic foods - Adult diapers, nursing homes - Personal services - Dollar Stores - Green-based businesses
Economic	- Growth in electronic commerce - Shift toward experience economy	- Online businesses - Businesses that "market" experiences like ecotourism
Technological	- Diffusion of digital and mobile technologies - Growth in biotechnology and nanotechnology - Advances in medicine and medical treatments	- Social media companies - Miniature medical devices - Personalized medicine based on DNA
Competitive	- Increase in global competition - Emergence of and as competitors - Mergers and acquisitions	- Access to foreign markets; encroachment by foreign competitors here - Opportunities to partner with Chinese and Indian firms - Opportunities to merge with a partner or acquire a partner
Regulatory	- Increased protection for intellectual property - Increased emphasis on free trade - Deregulation	- Leverage IP as competitive advantage - Opening up of foreign markets for venture expansion - Reduction of entry barriers to allow new startups

Figure 1.3   Environmental Scanning Matrix

- Security: September 11 created a whole new market for startups and corporate ventures in the industry sector of Homeland Security. Many of these businesses deploy various types of sensors, databases, and workflow software to monitor, alert, and respond to terrorist threats.[3] The choice of target customer went to new buying agencies in federal, state, and local governments, as well as corporations needing protection from terrorist threats (such as utilities).

- Health: The aging of the population, as well as new government regulations, is creating new growth opportunities in home health care. We will have a dedicated case on this in a later chapter; but for the time being, imagine various noninvasive sensors deployed in someone's house that can monitor physiological conditions and well-being, and send alerts in the case of medical emergencies.

- Energy: The cost of oil is driving the creation of a new generation of electric car manufacturers; by some estimates, there are dozens of startups and corporate ventures focused on this opportunity. Energy costs are also creating opportunities not only for alternative energy sources (solar and wind, for example) but also for widely distributed energy management systems that track and balance energy consumption.

- Government regulations for specific industries: Government regulation can also be a powerful external factor that can make or break a new venture. For example, in financial services, fraudulent company accounting led to Sarbanes-Oxley legislation and a host of new software and service ventures to help companies become compliant. Publicly traded companies spend millions of dollars each and every year on software and services for accurate financial reporting and consolidation across divisions and countries. *There is no choice.*

Three Steps to Industry Analysis

If you've applied your thinking to Figure 1.1, you will have some notion of where in the universe of industries your internal factors (experience and passion) should direct you. You might then say with some assurance that your future lies, for example, in the load management sector of the energy industry or social networking sector of Web commerce. It is now time to dig deeper with three straightforward and relatively simple steps for analyzing a target industry or sector. To illustrate these steps, put yourself in the shoes of a would-be entrepreneur, Jake, who is attracted to the organic foods sector of the agriculture industry. Here is the situation:

> Jake has some personal experience with the agriculture sector. He spent several summer vacations working on his uncle and aunt's family farm, and selling their organic produce to city people each Saturday morning at an outdoor farmers market. Jake has also read widely on agri-environmental issues and the subject of sustainability. He is passionate in his belief that the nation, environment, and individuals would all be healthier, and small farmers would be more prosperous, if consumers would shift more of their food spending to locally grown organic produce. Thinking broadly, he has sketched out a rough idea for automated hydroponic greenhouses capable of providing 10 to 20 times the yield of the field-grown operations. He has gone so far as to test out a miniversion of this concept using grow lamps and other equipment in one of his university's science labs. The results are encouraging. Jake wonders if he could create a viable business by marketing certified organic food to upscale food stores and expensive restaurants.

[3] Meyer, M. H., & Poza, H. (2009, May). Venturing adjacent to the core: From defense to homeland security. *Research Technology Management,* 31–48.

With Jake's situation in mind, let's move on to the steps an entrepreneur can use to analyze a target industry. (Note: Jake and his business are based on an actual case. One of your authors helped that business obtain angel financing, which it used to construct two dozen greenhouses. The business became a supplier to upscale retail food companies and restaurants, generated substantial cash, and within six years sold out to a large food grower.)

Step 1: Correctly Identify the Industry

The first job is to *name* and accurately *describe* the industry in which you intend to operate. The North American Industry Classification System (NAICS) and accompanying U.S. Census Bureau data linked to it is a good place to begin (http://www.census.gov/eos/www/naics). NAICS provides common industry definitions for the United States, Canada, and Mexico, and groups the economic activities of specific companies into specific industries and industry subsectors. This information can help you to evaluate industry size, customer demand, competitive market share, and so on for many industries and their subsectors. Similar classification systems exist in Europe, Japan, and the BRIC countries (Brazil, Russia, India, and China).

Let's now revisit Jake's organic greenhouse concept in terms of Step 1, putting you in his shoes as entrepreneur.

Where would you start in defining this industry in a broad sense? Using NAICS, you will find an "industry" defined as Sector 11 under NAICS—called Agricultural, Forestry, Fishing, and Hunting. You will find "aggregate information" on the industry including value of production for most recent years. That is your starting point. But, given that you want to play in the "agricultural space" you do not want to analyze forestry, fishing, and hunting. Thus, you can drill down to Crop Production—Subsector 111. In doing so, you have refined your industry space to a specific sector. You can now start examining what is happening in this specific industry sector (see Step 2).

Step 2: Determine Market Size, Growth, and Profitability in a Sector

Using Subsector 111—Crop Production—you can examine market size, growth, and profitability across a range of crops. But, given that you intend to operate in the "greenhouse" space, you should define and identify your sector more narrowly, in this case by focusing on Subsector 1114—Greenhouse, Nursery, and Floriculture Production. Doing this will provide some more specific insight into your industry niche. But wait! It is even possible to drill further to Subsector 11141—Food Crops Grown Under Cover (exactly what you will be doing). It is possible to drill down to another level—Subsector 111419—and examine data on specific crops grown under cover. Using this data, you discover that organic tomatoes are in greater demand and selling at significantly higher margins than mushrooms! This industry data will help you to properly plan your product offerings.

Remember, you can gather growth rate and related data through NAICS and its direct links to U.S. Census Bureau data (or visit the Census Bureau site directly at http://census.gov/econ/census07). If the U.S. Census Bureau doesn't have the information you need, there are other sources of industry-level data. For example, *Fortune* magazine reports profits and profit growth for single and for 5-year periods for a variety of industries (see Figure 1.4 for 2008 and 2003–2008 data).[4] This single table serves as a useful benchmark for assessing the relative attractiveness of your target industry. Notice that only five of the ten industries listed for 2003–2008 are on the list for 2008. Yesterday's profitable industries are not necessarily the best ones for you to start a business today or in the future. That is what makes this type of research so important to do. Never take the health of any particular industry for granted.

If you cannot find an aggregated report—or report supplement—the sales, profitability, and balance sheet strength of publicly traded industry leaders can be readily obtained. Growth rates

---

[4] Industry Profit Potential, *Fortune* Survey, 2008, May 4, 2009.

Growth in Profits (2003–2008)		Growth in Profits (2008)	
1. Metals	57.9%	1. Food Service	43.1%
2. Internet Services	58.5	2. Engineering, Construction	38.0
3. Oil and Gas Equipment	48.9	3. Health Care, Pharmacy	36.9
4. Wholesalers	36.9	4. Internet Services	35.5
5. Engineering, Construction	29.5	5. Pharmaceuticals	24.5
6. Construction/Farm Equip.	26.5	6. Info Technology Services	24.2
7. Network Comm. Equip.	24.2	7. Oil and Gas Equipment	18.5
8. Railroads	23.6	8. Pipelines	18.0
9. Aerospace/Defense	23.2	9. Railroads	16.4
10. Pipelines	22.6	10. Medical Product Equip.	15.4
Some of the worst performers			
Motor Vehicles/Parts	−11.8	Chemicals	−22.5
Insurance	−18.3	Hotels/Casinos/Resorts	−101.0
Entertainment	−35.1	Airlines	−564.0

Figure 1.4   Industry Profit Potential, *Fortune* magazine Survey, 2008 Survey

Source: Fortune magazine, May 4, 2009.

can be calculated directly from those data. Go to Yahoo!Finance, type in the name of an industry leader, and look at the "competitors" section. If the company has a lengthy history, you'll find a wealth of information. For example, if you know of publicly traded companies in the agricultural sector engaging in greenhouse farming, you can check them out at Yahoo!Finance.

Step 3: Assess Industry Dynamics

The final step in our process is to understand and assess the dynamics of the industry—the many forces at work in the industry and that impinge on its fortunes. The purpose of this assessment is to shed light on developments that make yours a favorable or unfavorable industry in which to start a new enterprise. Objectivity in this assessment is essential; without it, personal enthusiasm can cloud your judgment. People have a bad habit of seeking out data that confirms what they already believe to be true while avoiding or discounting data that contradicts those preconceptions. Objective assessment is the antidote to that human foible, which is why we offer you the following "screening factors."

1. Market growth. Determine the rate of growth for the industry or sector you have identified above. If you can't find that information for the industry, try to find the growth rate of the industry's leaders and "hot companies."

2. Industry profit potential. Again, use either an aggregate figure from a source such as *Fortune* or research on publicly traded industry leaders and "hot companies." Yahoo!Finance and Hoover's are sources for this information.

3. The industry's rate of technological change and innovation. Opportunities are often found in the turbulence created by technological change and innovation. Deregulation can create a similar effect. News stories on company events, product announcements, and customer applications can give you a sense of change and innovation. Look also to specialized industry publications such as *ComputerWorld* (for hardware and software innovations) or *New Scientist* (for chemistry and hard science breakthroughs). For environmental innovation, see Hot Topics on http://www.EarthPortal.com and online publications of the National Council for Science and the Environment. Or, once again, go to Yahoo! Finance and read the news stories on industry leaders. And, of course, a carefully constructed Google search may turn up incredibly valuable information on industry dynamics.

4. *The volume of venture financing to startups in the target industry or sector.* The venture capital (VC) industry employs thousands of highly trained professional analysts to do exactly what you, an amateur, are trying to accomplish: Identify areas of commercial growth and opportunity. When they find those areas, venturing financing quickly follows. So let these professionals be your reconnaissance scouts and follow their money trail. Pricewaterhouse Coopers' *MoneyTree Report* (http://www.pwcmoneytree.com) tabulates recent quarter venture capital investments by technology industry. While most startups do *not* attract VC funding, VC behavior is a good indicator of where growth is anticipated and where other venture financiers, such as angel investors, are placing their bets. At the time of this writing, biotechnology, software (generally), and medical devices are the top three destinations for venture capital, accounting for nearly 60% of all such investments in the second quarter of 2009. *MoneyTree Report* will give you the most recent information and also indicate the regional breakdown for investments by industry. Within these larger categories, certain niches will be hot. For example, in mid-2009 the $60 billion storage management industry, the niche of virtualization through software and/or hardware, was receiving much attention. Similarly, certain natural resource plays were strong in the industry and energy category (wind energy, solar energy, and biomass energy conversion), while others (oil and natural gas) were not.

5. *Strong, clear channels to markets that are receptive to new product or service innovations.* The third-party software business development programs of Microsoft, IBM, or any computer technology company are a path to their installed base. These and other technology giants generally require that your technology uses or integrates with their own tools and products, and often, undergoes some type of certification process for which you might have to pay a fee. In return, your company and its offerings are listed in catalogs and Websites, and sometimes, actually sold by their own sales forces as part of a larger enterprise solution. Or, if you are doing a consumer products venture, understanding the willingness of premium specialty retailers to try new products such as yours is an essential consideration. Examples of highly receptive retailers that are always on the search for distinctive, premium-priced innovations include Whole Foods Market, PETCO, and Trader Joe's. If you are doing a life sciences venture, today large pharmaceutical companies are desperate to fill their depleting pipelines with new potential drugs. Each one of these represents channel as well as development partners. New, small firms can prosper by aligning themselves with giants. It can provide corporate investment, credibility with customers who do not want to take a risk with a new startup, as well as broader access to markets.

6. *The concentration and intensity of competition.* An oligopolistic industry, with half a dozen major players, could create a lock on channels and suppliers. Every venture will have competitors; however, you strongly prefer that these competitors not be market leaders who spend a lot of R&D money on your exact area of innovation and show prowess in bringing it to market. Who wants to compete directly with an Apple or a Microsoft or a Dell or an IBM? Some startups succeed, but typically it is far better to focus on a complementary product or service. As part of this, you must also try to understand if there are offshore players that are strongly affecting price and, therefore, profitability. Samsung, Lenovo, and Acer are all highly effective cost competitors that are even giving Dell a run for its money.

7. *Poor access to key supplies and suppliers.* If you are thinking of manufacturing solar energy panels, you should check the availability of key inputs, such as silicon. On the same note, how eager to deal with small firms like yours are suppliers of key materials? You may

find, for example, that a major competitor has "locked up" those suppliers, thereby creating a barrier to entry. You have to be proactive and actually ask whether or not suppliers are open to cooperate with you. Suppliers will be honest if you ask. But, it is your responsibility to determine this situation.

8. Concentrated customer power. Who has the power in your sector, customers or producers? If your plan is to make and sell things through small, independent retailers (which are fast disappearing these days), the power to set prices and dictate terms of trade may be well balanced. If your customer is Walmart, Target, or Best Buy, you will be a price taker and an acceptor of terms. Customers like these have the power to protect their margins and drive yours down. How would a power imbalance like that affect your intended business? Big firms (e.g., Walmart) can dictate terms and conditions. But, those conditions will not be self-evident until negotiations begin. This is when you, as an entrepreneur, must hold the line and decide whether or not you will accept terms and conditions that are likely to be detrimental to the long-term success of your business.

Take a look at Figure 1.5. It shows how we can use these aspects of industry analysis to assess a target industry, breaking them down into more specific dimensions. The sample shown in that figure is for Jake's business.

	Facts / Data About Your Target Industry	Industry Score
Market growth	Double-digit growth, above 15%	7
Profit potential for the sector (or) Operating margin of sector leaders	Excellent margins by taking out the manual labor	10
High rate of technological change and new products	Agronomics is steadily advancing the knowledge on optimizing nutrients, seeds, and greenhouse technology	7
Flow of venture financing	Bootstrap or angel financing, with some government financing	4
Presence of clear channels to customers	Whole Foods Market was a perfect channel to target users	10
A lack of concentrated competition	Highly fragmented. Mid-sized Israeli, Dutch, and Mexican suppliers. No ConAgra.	10
A lack of offshore entrants driving down prices	For standard grocery, yes. For organics, no downward price pressure.	10
A lack of barriers to gain access to channels	Premium speciality retailers highly receptive to greater supply of organics.	10
A lack of barriers to gain access to suppliers	No problem. Seed and nutrient suppliers available. The automation technology readily available.	10
A lack of concentrated customer buying power	Walmart was just getting into the organic food business. (Today it is the No.1 seller of organic foods!)	6
	Total Score	84

Figure 1.5 Understanding the Dynamics of Jake's Target Industry

Scoring Key: 1 to 10, where:
1 is "a tough barrier for a new venture," 3 is "a challenge," 5 is "neither a barrier nor supporting success,"
7 is "conducive to a new venture," and 10 is "an ideal setup for venture success."

Each area of the assessment can be scored along a 1 to 10 scale using the key at the bottom of the figure. If you feel that a particular factor is not relevant to your venture, it can be deleted from the table. However, we strongly urge you to consider each and every item before dismissing anything. Any one of these areas can turn around and bite you in the back later on. When these are totaled, you will have an overall score that can be used to either (1) assess industry/sector attractiveness, or (2) compare alternative target industries or sectors. (Note: The last five screening factors in the template are placed in the reverse—for example, using the words "A lack of . . ." in front of *barrier to entry*.)

For the first two screening factors, market growth and potential profitability, we consider data showing growth over 30% as outstanding, 20% to 30% as very good, 10% to 19% as tolerable, and 3% to 9% as poor. Anything below 3% is unacceptable. Profit potential can be considered between 5 and 10 percentage points lower than growth percentages. This is based on our own personal experience in ventures. You need to see sufficient growth in an industry because this shows that there are enough customers predisposed and having the cash to buy the products and services you wish to create in your new venture.

Jake is actually doing pretty well in his industry assessment. The only two dark spots on the horizon are (a) that hydroponics is not a "hot" area for traditional venture capital and (b) that Walmart is becoming a major player in organic foods, which means severe downward price pressure. The way Jake ended up dealing with these negatives was to raise capital from angel investors and to work a good deal with Whole Foods Market and other premium specialty retailers. That is how most entrepreneurs deal with difficult venture finance and route-to-market issues.

Perhaps as important as anything else is that Jake modeled the benefit of his new automated system in terms of productivity in growing organic vegetables. In fact, that is how we came to know about Jake. One of your authors helped him develop productivity calculations based on a single prototype greenhouse that Jake had used his own money to build. They compared its growing rates to traditional commercial greenhouses. They realized that a hydroponic, automated greenhouse could provide 10 to 20 times the yield of field-grown methods and five times the yield of greenhouses that are not hydroponic or fully automated. This became a key part of Jake's ability to raise startup capital—he had designed a *better mousetrap*.

An industry scoring over 75 in this template is very much worth consideration as a venue for a venture. Any industry scoring below 25 should probably be avoided. If your industry scores in the midrange on the scale, say 50, then you must think about how you will overcome industry problems and obstacles. We'll return to this template in the Student Exercises section of the chapter.

Mapping Out the Key Players in an Industry Sector

With industry data and your assessments of the industry on hand, it is then important to focus on a venture's specific role in an industry. To do this in a powerful, simple way, we like to use a technique called *industry ecosystem mapping*.

An industry ecosystem includes all the players within a given industry, from raw material suppliers, to value-added suppliers, to assemblers and integrators, on through the distribution and support channels and their respective players. Mapping the industry ecosystem as a network of interconnected players can help you to understand the industry at a deeper level and suggest where your enterprise might fit in. Figure 1.6 is the industry ecosystem map for our friend Jake, the automated, organic gardener!

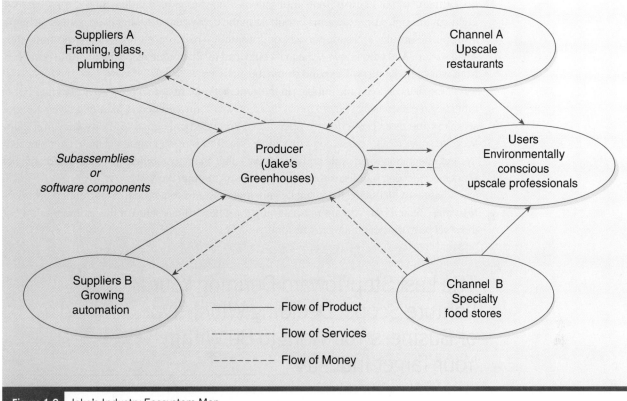

Figure 1.6 Jake's Industry Ecosystem Map

You can see that we have placed the typical startup venture squarely in the middle in the figure. Pay particular attention to the colored lines, which represent the flows of product (or components or raw material), services, money, and information and referrals. We want you to think about creating this type of diagram for your own target industry. Also note the four different types of lines connecting the actors in the chart:

- The flow of product (from raw materials to assembled products to shelf, or software development tools to completed software applications to OEM or value-added reseller to the customer or user)

- The flow of services (which may include consulting to integration to training to maintenance or repairs)

- The flow of money (often, but not always, a different colored arrow going the opposite direction as product or services)

- The flow of information (one aspect of which may be marketing referrals)

The combination of the circles filled in with company or customer group names and the lines connecting the various circles tells the story of the industry in which you wish to play.

In some cases, a major, dominant player—an IBM, Microsoft, Goldman Sachs, or Walmart—sits squarely in the middle of the industry ecosystem. These are analogous to the sun in our solar ecosystem. They are at the center and, like the planets, all other industry participants orbit around them. It would be foolish to compete directly with these behemoths because of their financial, marketing, and technological power.

It is then that you can use this mapping to identify niche opportunities within an industry. For example, if you were to draw out the ecosystem for Apple iTunes, there is clearly the opportunity to build new iPhone applications. Entrepreneurs building these "apps" and sell-ing them through Apple are a major bubble in the ecosystem diagram. Even a small niche—as a supplier, consultant, testing service, or distributor—may represent a good opportunity for a small startup. And who knows what that could lead to? That same niche might be the beachhead from which the startup will expand within the industry.

The spaces *between* the bubbles in the generic figure may also present outstanding oppor-tunities. An enterprising venture might find a way to connect different industry players for more seamless and more cost-effective operations. You need only go to IBM's own Smarter Planet Website pages to find case studies that show how IBM is using instrumentation, interconnectiv-ity, and integration to link one end of a global value chain to another. Or you might be the next iTunes, connecting music creators with music users through the Web.

Whatever you decide to do, make sure that your ecosystem map is current and *forward-thinking*. Remember, you are not planning for where things stand at the moment but where they will be in the near future and beyond.

The Last Step Toward Defining Your Venture Scope: Deciding Which Type of Business You Want to Be Within Your Target Industry

Figure 1.7 shows the first two steps of the venture scoping process: understanding the internal strengths and experiences of the entrepreneur, and understanding the characteristics (we hope positive) of the target industry for which personal strengths seem to fit and serve as the basis for a successful enterprise. Think of this as balancing and blending personal and industry analysis. We have also learned that since industries are enormous entities that the key to success is to develop a venture within a particular niche or area within a larger industry. Every successful company used to illustrate a point in this chapter is an example of this focus in one form or another—the authors' ventures included!

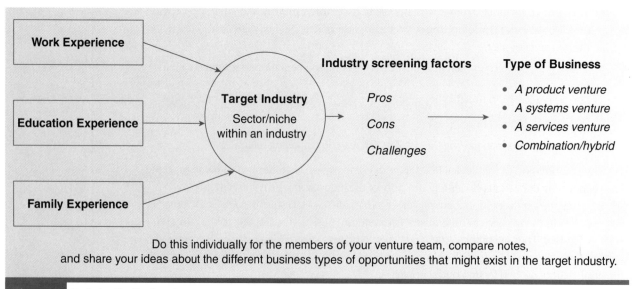

Figure 1.7   Defining the Venture Scope

Figure 1.7 also shows the third and last step of defining the scope of a venture: deciding what type of business to be in terms of creating and providing products, systems, services, or a hybrid combination thereof. There are usually many ways to "make a buck" in a given industry or sector. In general, these fall within these three categories—or a hybrid of the three. It is also important to appreciate the differences between these types of businesses in terms of how they generate revenues. It is to the last step of venturing scoping that we now turn our attention.

Different Types of Business Possibilities for the Same Target Industry Sector

It is not unusual to find customers in the same market being served by different companies focused totally on products, focused totally on systems, or focused just on providing different types of services. Suppose, for example, that we wanted to start a venture in the supply chain management industry, with a focus on mass market retailers. Those retailers, led by Walmart, want to track every product they sell from suppliers' factories to their store shelves. Now, let's consider how different business "types" created by entrepreneurs could serve the needs of Walmart and others in the supply chain management industry:

Products: Create radio-frequency identification (RFID) sensors and readers capable of tracking products in transit by item and by pallet. The venture will obtain patents on its sensor technology and find third-party manufacturers to produce its sensors and readers.

Systems: Create software-based systems to acquire sensor information in real time, communicate those data to central servers armed with sophisticated workflow management software, and use software applications to inform customers of the status of products in production, in transit, and in stock. Customers will use these data to optimize inventory planning and distribution center operations.

Services: Create any one of many service-based businesses; for example, provide Walmart employees with access to tracking data through a simple, secure Web browser. Alternatively, the venture will create a portal to facilitate competitive bidding by shippers to manufacturers and mass market retailers such as Walmart, Target, Tesco, or Carrefour.

Making Money Is Different Based on the Type of Business

The three business types not only differ in how they create value for customers, but they have, in most cases, very different revenue, cost, and margin profiles. Consider first a product-type business. For every $100 in product sales revenues, $30 to $40 is spent on manufacturing; another $25 to $40 is spent on selling, marketing, R&D, and administration, leaving a net operating profit margin in the range of $15 to $25. The point of leverage in this business is to design a great set of products and manufacture thousands if not millions of them at a low cost per unit. Such businesses often require huge capital outlays for production capacity. Using our example of A123 Systems again, this venture raised about half a billion dollars in 2009 to develop manufacturing capacity, about ten times the amount raised for its research and development of the batteries.

Now consider the typical systems company. For every $100 of revenue, $20 to $30 might be spent on R&D; another $10 to $20 is spent on sales, marketing, and administration, leaving a net operating profit of $50 or more. At least, that is the goal! The point of leverage for a systems company is to hire the smartest programmers, have them create fantastic software, and then ship it electronically with virtually no cost of goods. The high profit margin enjoyed by this type of business explains why software continues to draw heavy venture capital investments.

Services companies aim to be product and systems *agnostic*. They are consulting firms, equipment service firms, transportation services providers, home health care providers, energy production and management firms, and so forth. Most are labor intensive. Thus, for every $100 of revenues, a typical services firm spends a third on labor; a third on technology, marketing, and administration; and tries to walk away with $33 or more in operating profit. Its point of leverage is the design of the service, the people who deliver the service, and the technology that helps them deliver the service efficiently and effectively. Think of the UPS drivers in your area and their handheld devices. UPS's combination of people, trucks, and information technology is its secret for profitably delivering more than 18 million packages a day!

In short, the three basic types of businesses—product-focused, systems-focused, and services-focused—are completely different in terms of what they do and how they make money. Their points of leverage are also entirely different. You can learn about the revenues, costs, and margin profiles of companies operating in your target industry or sector through Yahoo! Finance and similar sources. Look up the industry leaders and examine their income statements.

Making the Choice of the Business Type for Your Venture

And so, having selected an industry and screened various possible target sectors in that industry, you must now decide, "What type of business do I want to have?" Apple's decision in the mid-2000s to shift some of its energy to a service business—iTunes—demonstrates the power of type choice on earnings and company value.

Most entrepreneurs make the "type" decision by considering internal factors and the analysis they used in screening industries:

- For which type of business do I have the experience and education needed to succeed?
- What am I really good at? This is not only in terms of creating a product or system or service but also in terms of *selling* the innovation.
- Do I want to create a new product or simply integrate different products together within a system or service? Am I most comfortable with the idea of providing a service?
- Which type of business in my chosen industry sector is in greatest demand by customers?
- For which type of business is there the least direct competition?

Time is another issue to consider in making the choice of business type. The longer it takes to generate revenues, the more difficult it will be to obtain financing—and the greater the risk for the entrepreneur.

As a general rule, product companies seem to take the longest time to move from business idea to first paying customer. A unique and appealing product must be designed, prototyped, customer tested, and manufactured. Even a simple product can take 18 months or longer to move to market. Medical products can take much, much longer! Systems companies tend to face a one- to two-year run-up to workable product: lots of software development and iterative testing, a beta site with a few lead users, and then it's off to the races. Service companies, on the other hand, can start providing services right away if the team is right and be making money soon thereafter. Time to market is not the only consideration, of course; make a great product and there is far more leverage on time and effort and capital than all but the best of services businesses. Software can be even better.

*** *** ***

In this chapter, you learned the importance of gathering information on the attractiveness of industries and the sectors within those industries. Successful entrepreneurs use information to drive their venture decisions. It is critical that you use objective information to determine if the innovative concept you have in mind also has the makings of being a good business, the foundation of which is to compete in a growing, attractive market space. Do not let your passion for an idea get in the way of applying common business sense to find those areas where your experience and industry dynamics combine to make for a promising journey.

Reader Exercises

Now it is your turn to apply the venturing scoping ideas of this chapter to help shape your own entrepreneurial vision. The following exercises should be done sequentially.

Also, a few words about student project teams. This type of work is often performed in teams to emulate the venture team startup process. If you do recruit team members for a project, have a separate discussion off-line in terms of roles and responsibilities. Do this early in the project so that everyone understands the amount of "skin in the game" that each team member is willing to contribute. Then, have a process for reviewing each other's work.

This commitment to getting the work on time is so important. You don't want to have people join your team just because they think your idea is "cool." They must be willing to work because it is only through that work that your venture idea will continue to improve. As a fledgling entrepreneur, you do not have the time nor should you have the patience to carry noncontributors on your back.

Now on to the assignments for this chapter. It is time to define your venture scope!

Step 1: Each Team Member Needs to Complete Figure 1.8

Put down your specific work and educational experience as well as family history events. After each team member does this for themselves, you then need to assemble a composite list for all team members. Just as important as what is on that list, note in a different color (such as red) those items in terms of skills and work experience that appear to be missing for a successful venture. If you have gaps, don't let these stop you. However, these will also help direct you in terms of what new team members you need or which other professors or advisors you might seek out in the weeks and months ahead.

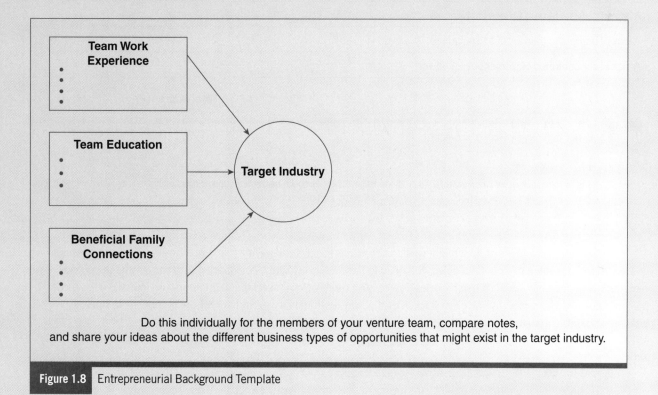

Do this individually for the members of your venture team, compare notes, and share your ideas about the different business types of opportunities that might exist in the target industry.

Figure 1.8 Entrepreneurial Background Template

Step 2: Conduct a Target Industry Analysis

This is a very important exercise. You need to search the Web and other data sources for information regarding your target industry. This includes hard numbers of the profitability of current market leaders and some intensive research on technology changes, channel changes, and competitors entering your target industry sector. You also need to search sources such as *MoneyTree Report* (http://www.pwcmoneytree.com) to see the current flow of angel and venture financing into that sector. Examples of industry sectors might be biotechnology, software, medical devices, energy, media and entertainment, networking and equipment, or health care services.

Then, once you have gathered these data, we want you to score the attractiveness of each dimension in Figure 1.9 for your industry sector. Then, make an honest assessment of this data-driven analysis. Is the sector a good place to start a venture? Does it have favorable industry dynamics or not?

	Facts / Data About Your Target Industry (Bullet-point facts)	Industry Score (1–10)
Market growth		
Profit potential for the sector (or) Operating margin of sector leaders		
High rate of technological change and new products		
Flow of venture financing		
Presence of clear channels to customers		
A lack of concentrated competition		
A lack of offshore entrants driving down prices		
A lack of barriers to gain access to channels		
A lack of barriers to gain access to suppliers		
A lack of concentrated customer buying power		
	Total Score	

Figure 1.9   The Industry Dynamics Scorecard

Scoring Key: 1 to 10, where:

      1 is "a tough barrier for a new venture," 3 is "a challenge," 5 is "neither a barrier nor supporting success,"
      7 is "conducive to a new venture," and 10 is "an ideal setup for venture success."

If the assessment score is low, you might wish to consider strongly looking at a different industry or a different sector of the industry that interests you. Otherwise, you need to have a serious discussion about how to overcome the negative dynamics you have uncovered. When it comes time to raise money from professional investors, assume that they know the potholes just as well as anyone else. What seasoned professionals try to find are "show stoppers," defined as an industry dynamic that makes even a well-managed venture hard to grow.

Step 3: Conduct an Environmental Scan for Your Target Industry

Figure 1.10 presents an environmental scanning to further enrich your target industry sector analysis. Pay particular attention to the five key dimensions of environmental scanning: changes and trends in the social, economic, technological, competitive, and regulatory conditions surrounding your venture concept. Record these with references to supporting data sources directly on the template. Then, try to identify venture opportunities that take advantage of or respond to these trends. Remember, trends can be either positive or negative from the end-user's point of view. A venture can be positioned within a larger trend—and from that "ride a wave" toward success. Ventures targeting the aging population, environmental regulations on energy production and consumption, or obesity are examples of "matching venture opportunities."

Trends	Over-Arching Examples	Venture Opportunities
Social	• Look for aging, health, ethnic, and other socio-demographic trends	• Make a list of matching venture opportunities
Economic	• Look for macro-economic trends such as globalization and economic cycle	• Make a list of matching venture opportunities
Technological	• New, disruptive technologies • Current and emerging "standards"	• Make a list of matching venture opportunities
Competitive	• Offshore competitors • "Plays" by large corporations through acquisitions	• Make a list of matching venture opportunities
Regulatory	• Regulation/deregulation • "Green" regulations • IP protection in emerging markets	• Make a list of matching venture opportunities

Figure 1.10 The Environmental Scanning Template

This template will be useful when you get to the point of discussing the venture with your professor or advisors. It will demonstrate that you have done your homework and that you recognize both opportunities and dangers on the horizon. Revisit your venture concept statement with the environmental scanning template in hand. Does it still make sense? Which if any of that statement's four elements should be revised or otherwise improved?

Step 4: Draw the Ecosystem Map for Your Target Industry

Identify all key players within the ecosystem. If there is financial information on the Web about these key players, gather it and look at their revenues, their revenue growth rates, their operating margins, and the even the number of employees. Begin to get smart about your competitors and potential partners such as OEMs, distributors, and complementary innovators or service providers. As you are doing this, look at their Websites and see if there are management team members who are alums of your university.

Step 5: Have Breakfast or Lunch With an Experienced Entrepreneur, Investor, or Executive in Your Target Industry Sector

A term project is a great excuse to reach out to business people. Students are always amazed at how executives are willing to help young aspiring entrepreneurs. Go to the Websites of local companies that are either members of your target industry sector or investors in new companies in that sector. See if any are alums of your university. Usually there is contact information for high-level managers. Try to use your professor for an introduction. Your assignment is simple: have breakfast or lunch with just one of these individuals. Armed with your industry research, you should bounce ideas off your guest and then *listen*. This will provide a world of information about your target industry sector.

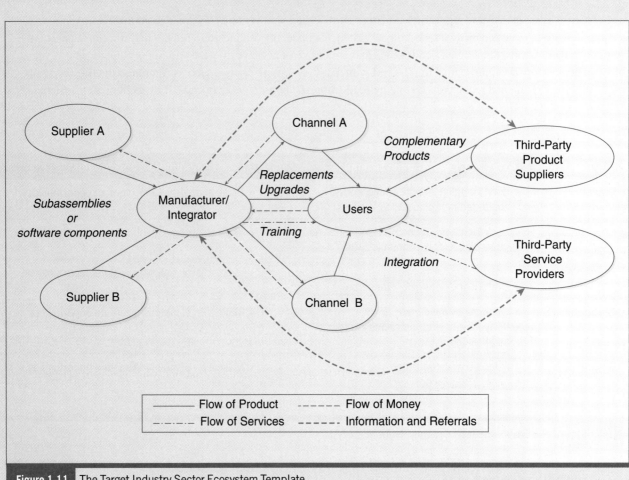

Figure 1.11   The Target Industry Sector Ecosystem Template

Knowledge is power; your job is to get as smart as you can about an industry as quickly as you can. Time is your enemy. Friendly alums can be powerful allies and, more often than not, are willing to help.

Don't worry about how to design and produce these offerings yet; specific planning for that will come later in this book. You don't really know what users truly need at this point, so keep your type of business at a very high or general level.

Step 6: Bring All of This Learning Together: Create Your Venture Scope

Figure 1.12 integrates all of the prior work into a set of venture opportunities. Based on your personal work/education/ family network background, your target industry sector analysis, and your environmental scanning, you should now be able to identify several or more venture ideas. At this point, you don't need to get too specific about the products or services in these venture ideas. Instead, focus on what they will do—or the value they will bring—to users in the industry sector.

With these venture ideas placed in the template, we then want you to circle that idea which is your favorite one. Be prepared to explain why it is the favorite based on your industry analysis. The following chapters in this book will help you refine and test that venture idea.

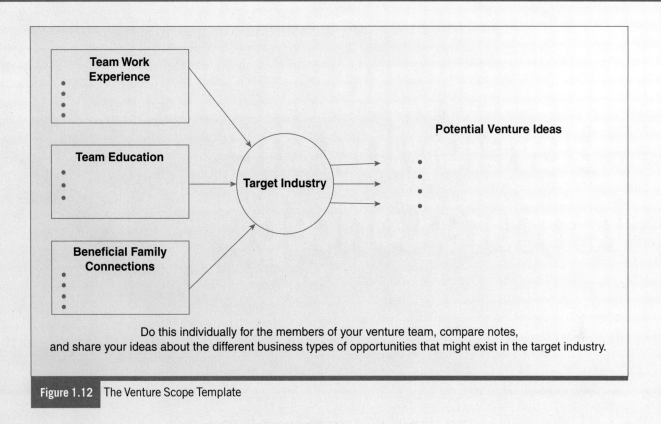

Figure 1.12 The Venture Scope Template

Great work! You have now created your "venture scope"—the definition and boundaries of the venture that you want to create. Now it's time to get feedback on your templates. Your professor will organize an in-class presentation session where you can share your ideas with the rest of your classmates and benefit from their experiences and insights. Be prepared for some people wanting to join your team or you wanting them to join.

chapter 2
Developing the Venture Concept

2

The previous chapter helped you determine the *scope* of your venture: the industry and sector of that industry in which you wish to start a company, and the "type" of business you will launch. Scope defines the boundaries of your intentions. That is an essential first step. But within those boundaries, who precisely should you serve? How much of the larger market do these target customers represent as an addressable market? And exactly how do you propose to create value for these customers?

This chapter will help you start to answer that question by creating a customer focus. From this focus, in the next chapter you will then develop a *specific business idea*—what we call the *venture concept*. The process for creating a robust venture concept is equally applicable to corporate as well as startup ventures.

A fully developed business idea has two key dimensions: (1) the *venture concept* and (2) the *business model associated with the venture concept*. We will deal with the venture concept over the next two chapters and save the business model for Chapter 5.

The venture concept includes the following elements:

- The market niche with your target industry sector (i.e., the addressable market)
- The target customers and, when the "users" are not the "buyers," customer insight into both
- The primary problems or activities of the customers that the venture seeks to solve, improve, or otherwise address

- The venture's basic commercial offerings, its products, systems, services, or some combination thereof
- The competitive positioning of the venture and its commercial offerings

Each of these elements must make sense individually *and* together! In this chapter, we will target the first two bullet points: the target market niche and customers in that market niche. And in the next chapter, we will then learn how to mine customer needs, create winning product and service ideas, and position them against competitors.

All of these elements are important for success. Great companies are characterized by alignment between their choices of market segment or niche, intended customers, commercial offerings, and the positioning of those offerings in terms of price and performance relative to existing competitors. An entrepreneur's choices for these strategic elements must make them mutually reinforcing. For example, conceiving richly featured products and services and positioning them as having a premium value makes little sense if the target niche and its customers have little money or appreciation for premium offerings. On the other hand, a strongly growing market niche with appreciative customers will support the same premium product set. The key ingredients of the venture concept recipe must fit and blend to make a powerful result.

As in our prior chapter, we will first explain target markets and customers through a series of simple templates and examples. And then we will want you to apply these templates to your own venture ideas—within the scope that you established in Chapter 1.

Learning Objectives

- Segmenting your target markets
- Developing a crisp definition of the customers and their uses or applications that the venture will address.
- Using these market and customer definitions as a launching pad for further customer research to more fully understand user pain points and needs.

Building Upon the Prior Chapter: Determining Your Market Niche Within a Target Industry

You should now have a good notion about your initial target industry and the sector of that industry that will be the object of your entrepreneurial efforts. You have also considered the type of business you wish to create in that industry sector, for example, a product, systems, or services type of company, or some combination thereof. We called this the venture scope.

Now, we need to advance this forward to the next level of focus. The goal of this chapter is to develop a specific venture concept within the venture scope you defined in Chapter 1.

First, let's make an important conceptual bridge. In Chapter 1, we used the word "industry," and then "industry sector" to reflect a part of a larger industry in which you wish to create a business. Once you make that decision, that "industry sector" becomes your "target market." It has customers who have problems that you wish to solve, customers to whom you wish to sell, and customers from whom you wish to collect money.

We need to get even more specific. Successful entrepreneurs start their companies by targeting a specific "niche" within a target market (e.g., industry sector). There are many ways to get to a target market niche, but the best, most systematic way to arrive at that conclusion for a new venture is to:

1. Segment or divide the broader target market by clear, "physical" properties to identify major groups of customers. For business-to-business (B2B) ventures, this might be size of the customer's own industry orientation (often called a vertical market), its size (small, medium, or large), and geographic location. For business-to-consumer (B2C) ventures, these physical properties might be as simple as age and gender. From this, we get major buckets of customers who have similar characteristics. This is called *market segmentation.*

2. The next step is to focus in on a particular segment of the broader market and identify subsets of the larger customer group in that segment. These subsets are defined by collections of customers who share core needs. This is traditionally called *customer segmentation.* The needs of each group are "homogeneous" with each group and different than other groups—all within the same market segment. If there are "no differences" in customer needs, then you have "a mass market"—no segmentation or customer groupings are necessary. Typically, however, most markets consist of customers with different needs; the entrepreneur's job is to determine the needs of different customers and to determine which customers have needs that are currently being met and those that are going unmet. *Those unmet needs* become your opportunity!

3. Our bridge from selected industry sector to target market niche is almost complete. The last step is a refinement of *customer grouping* with a market segment to include uses or activities by customers. From this we can define the term "market niche" in a way that works best for the entrepreneur. A market niche is also part of a particular market segment. However, it is more than just a specific group of customers. Rather, it is a combination of that group of customers and *what* they are using–a particular set of products or services to get done or otherwise achieve. College students use computers to do homework, socialize, and shop; adults use computers to work professionally, shop, and sometimes, to socialize. The market niche is that intersection between "the customer" and the "uses" of the product or service by the customer. Specific market niches therefore equal "customers and uses." Once again, the entrepreneur must find the "met" and "unmet" needs within the selected customer group and for the various uses or activities of customers in that group. From this you can define products, services, and market strategies that are specific, distinctive, and which aim directly at the heart and minds of your target customers.

This three-step process and the terminology that goes with it are very important. It helps you focus on a specific market niche and, in doing so, learn everything you can about the customers and their uses in that niche. This knowledge becomes the entrepreneur's greatest competitive weapon. It drives the design and pricing of the venture's products and services, its selling strategy, and its branding. Focus creates a powerful alignment in everything that the venture does. And this, if well executed, generates revenue.

These Three Steps in Action

Let's take a specific example of a company that one of your authors helped get started—a spin-out of technology from what used to be the medical division of Hewlett-Packard. The startup was a software venture for clinical information systems. The industry was health care. The sector in that industry was hospitals. The goal of the venture team was to introduce a new type of security software for doctors and nurses accessing clinical information systems running on the computer networks of hospitals. (There is a case written on this successful spin-out in the back of this book. It is called Sentillion.)

From hospitals as a broad market, the team first segmented the market by its clear physical dimensions: the size and location of the hospital. To do this, the team gathered data on the size of the hospitals (small, medium, and large, based on the number of beds in the hospital) and geography (United States, Canada, Europe, and so forth). These data were readily available from government and other freely available sources. The amount of money being spent in this market for clinical information technology at the time pointed us to large hospitals, and since we were just a startup, to those customers just in North America. Our initial market segment was therefore large hospitals in North America—a specific intersection point between these two key dimensions.

Next, the team started grouping customers by actually visiting a number of local, large hospitals. They distinguished between the traditional keepers of computer technology—the IT staffs of hospitals—and the end-users, such as doctors, nurses, and other care providers. In the specific area of information security, the team found that practicing physicians and nurses were having lots of trouble remembering passwords and IDs to sign into the dozen or more clinical information systems that they had to use over the course of a day—*and often forgot to sign out!* There was really no sure way to tell who had actually entered a drug order or medical observation or a recommendation for a procedure into a particular computer system. This chaos was unacceptable to the managers running hospitals and no longer tolerated by the federal government. The doctors and nurses wanted one simple way to sign on to the myriad applications that they had to use throughout the course of the day. Their driving need was convenience. Remembering all sorts of various passwords was a hassle, and remembering to sign out was problematic given the pace of action during the day and night in large medical centers.

The data processing staff, on the other hand, wanted to know the *who, what, when, and where* for all doctors and nurses accessing clinical information across a very large and often multifacility operation. The federal government was actually requiring them to assure this accountability as part of Medicare and Medicaid reimbursement compliance.

This field work by the venture team led to two specific uses within hospitals: a simple, single way to log into all systems permissible for any given doctor or nurse and a powerful underlying set of tracking databases to store all access information so that it could be audited later on. The venture then quickly developed single sign-on solutions for care providers and detailed tracking databases for the IT managers. *The focus on specific customers, their uses, and their driving needs* were the key factors for success for this company. It grew to be the market leader in single sign-on for health care and was later acquired by Microsoft for a handsome sum.

Creating a Picture of Your Market Segmentation

Figure 2.1 shows the market segmentation grids for a B2C venture within the snack foods industry sector. We have seen similar grids both in a number of new ventures and within the internal venturing groups of large consumer products companies. This particular approach was used by an internal venture group of a large corporation to innovate beyond its core brands and products.

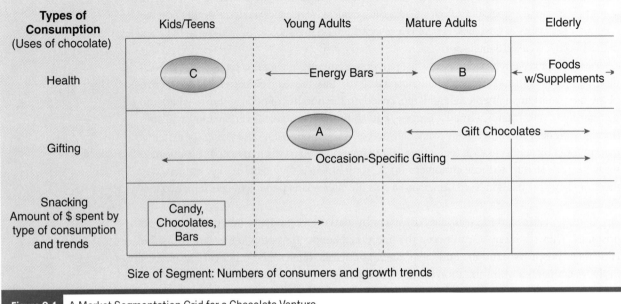

Figure 2.1 A Market Segmentation Grid for a Chocolate Venture

The horizontal access is straightforward and meaningful: It has different types of customers as measured by age groups. The vertical axis is based on three major types of snack food consumption, each of which already has current products yet still offers a lot of "white space" for the development of innovative concepts. The bottom row is the region of the market segmentation grid that is most difficult to innovate—a new mass market candy for kids and teens, such as another M&M'S Candies, Hershey's bar, or Snickers. Trying to venture into this space runs into the teeth of well-entrenched competitors who own powerful brands as well as shelf space. Seeing this competitive landscape on one part of the gird, the entrepreneur looks elsewhere. There are many ventures, for example—either within established manufacturers or as entirely new startups—that are seeking to provide healthy snacks in the form of bars, cookies, and dried vegetables for different types of consumers in the top row. The health snacks and treats section of grocery stores expands year by year, filled with new product innovations. Other ventures—such as online beverage sellers or apparel companies like Vermont Teddy Bear—are bringing occasion-specific gifting ideas to market. The market segmentation grid for an industry sector shows the entrepreneur where it is best to focus his or her attention. We have drawn circles on the gird to indicate possible areas for venture development:

- Circle A: Develop a venture around healthy energy bar products that are flavorable and less fattening for mature adults. (Most energy bars have high caloric density—and don't taste all that great.)
- Circle B: Develop a venture around a more contemporary type of gifting chocolate that would be "cool" for young adults still in college or just out of it (e.g., a much more contemporary type of Godiva).
- Circle C: Develop a venture on the notion of disrupting the established confectionary business by making healthy snacks that are not only good for kids but that they also love to eat! An example might be "fun fruit"—a whole serving of fruits in different fun flavors in a shelf-stable, kids-designed package.

The corporate venture team decided to go for Circle B and located the business in Manhattan with a combination retail and online business. Arguably one of the best chocolate chefs in the country was a key team member, and he had both the product knowledge and a strong empathy with that particular target market segment. Besides, all the data showed that gifting was a strong and growing category with well-established routes to market—including the Web.

As another example, Figure 2.2 shows a market segmentation grid for a computer consulting venture. This was a team of MBA students who were already midlevel IT managers in companies near our university. They were very strong at designing and implementing service-oriented architectures (SOA) to link up different types of applications in a much simpler way within large enterprises. Another way of thinking about SOA is simply as a "Web services model" where users can access and use any and all software through a Web browser. Two of the team members worked in financial services and another in e-commerce for a major retailer. Like many of you, they had taken the entrepreneurship course with a goal of starting their own business! Chapter 1 told them to focus on what they knew and enjoyed: enterprise computer technology. Within that sector, however, there were myriad possibilities. Rather than make a simple checklist that would run on page after page, the team created the framework in the figure to guide its research and decision making. On the horizontal axis are key vertical markets; on the vertical axis are the sizes of the client company. Each axis could be clearly identified or measured (the prospective client's industry affiliation and its size in terms of the number of employees or approximate level of sales). Moreover, the team was able to gather specific information on the size of IT spending within each vertical market, the growth rates of that spending, as well as the number of prospective client companies within the categories of small, medium, and large corporations.

During the year in which these data were gathered (during the post-9/11 time period), it became clear to the venture team that information technology "spend" in financial services was taking a huge hit given economic conditions. However, the team saw tremendous growth continuing in Web-based retailing. Their data also indicated that large sums of money were projected to be spent on modernizing and connecting health care information systems. In terms of client size, they knew that the large consulting outfits—such as Accenture, IBM, and Hewlett-Packard—would be hard to beat in the large retailer-company market. They further suspected that small companies did not have much cash to spend on external consultancies. They therefore targeted the midmarket and aimed at

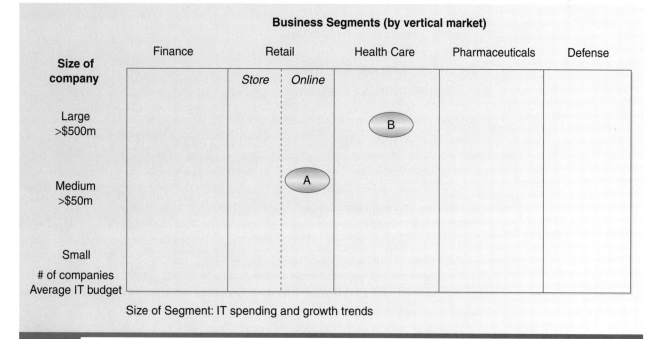

Figure 2.2   A Market Segmentation Grid for an IT Consulting Venture

a vertical market other than their own traditional niche of financial services. Helping midsized online retailers became the venture's target market segment (the circle labeled A in the figure). The team also decided to allocate some of its time and energy to get smart in the health care arena as a potential second target down the road. (This is represented by the circle labeled B in the figure.) The lesson in both of these stories: segment your target market into its logical pieces and let the market data in terms of growth and customer need direct you to the most fertile ground.

Keep Your Market Segmentation Simple Yet Powerful

These two examples also show that it is important to keep market segmentation within your industry section simple, easy to explain to others, and yet powerful in terms of providing clear differentiation between different possible types of customers. This will make your strategy easier to explain to investors, employees, vendors and channel partners. It will also be easier to explain to your professor! For this reason, we limit our market segmentation framework to just *two, and at most three, dimensions*. It is fairly easy to explain phenomenon that have two major dimensions. Once we get into three, it becomes a lot harder!

And as these two cases show, the entrepreneur tries to find the "white space" on his or her own market segmentation grid for an industry sector. Each cell on the grid represents a specific market segment. The entrepreneur selects one or two segments to investigate deeply and then gathers all sorts of information about the current level of revenues for products or services sold into the segment, growth rates, and competitors. This information provides the entrepreneur with a picture of the attractiveness of any particular market segment—and tells the entrepreneur where to aim first.

Market segmentation should help you to focus your business and all the various aspects within the business, such as the design of the products and services you create or how to bring these to market. In general, you will know that you have a powerful market segmentation framework when its segments are:

- Measurable (such as decennial age groups or industry groups)
- Meaningful (the behaviors and emotions of people or businesses in these segments are truly different)
- Actionable (we know what is needed to make and market Toyota Camry for commuting adults, versus a Scion for Gen-Yers)

Established Market Niches Versus Emerging Niches

As we have discussed above, entrepreneurs like to hit a particular niche of a larger market—a specific combination of a group of customers with shared needs for specific uses or activities—rather than attack the market more generally. For example, in the single sign-on software corporate spinoff described earlier, large hospitals in North America was the market segment, and the user authentication and tracking became the market niche within that segment. There are two types of niches for the entrepreneur: established niches and emerging niches.

An *established niche* that is suitable for a startup is one that is rather obvious to the observer but *too small* to merit the attention of large, established competitors. "It doesn't move our meter if it's less than a $50 million annual revenue opportunity," they will say. Well, $49 million in annual sales revenue is a big number for almost anyone launching a new company (particularly when that same established company will probably want to buy you for two to three times sales should you achieve even $30 million).

An *emerging niche* is a small but growing slice of a large market characterized by customers and uses that no company quite understands or knows how to fully serve at the moment; it is therefore seen as either too small or too risky by most large, established competitors serving the larger market. For example, as we write this book now, it is obvious that the application of medical monitoring devices for home health care is a niche that is on the cusp of explosive growth. Such a solution can save society lots of money by reducing expensive hospital admissions, all for the cost of a few medical sensors, some wireless connectivity in the home, and a connection to some monitoring server software—just like ADT for home security. In contrast to this opportunity, monitoring devices in hospitals is the larger, established market, and it is already served by many major medical device manufacturers.

Similarly, mobile advertising on your cell phone is an emerging niche that many major players such as Nokia and Microsoft are trying to understand and exploit with new services. The core print and media advertising represents the large, well-established market.

Entrepreneurs try to find market niches that are riding the wave of a rapidly expanding larger market. This is the story behind the hopes of so many social networking startups, seeking to leverage the beachhead established by Facebook for the mass market or LinkedIn for professionals. The same is occurring in energy and in health care. The bottom line is that successful entrepreneurs target niches within robust markets and *so should you.*

Some entrepreneurs even try to create a niche—as was the case with eBay, which created online auctions within the burgeoning e-commerce market. When we hear that an entrepreneur has "created an industry," what they have really done is to create a tiny new niche in an established industry that over time grows large. Fred Smith of Federal Express started with a couple of airplanes delivering mail overnight. Now expedited delivery is a global industry. People who have the vision and courage to create new niches within an industry are nothing short of business geniuses, be it Bill Gates and Steve Ballmer with a PC independent operating system or Bob Metcalfe with a communications technology to link computers, for example, Ethernet.

If the entrepreneur can successfully launch a product or service into an emerging niche, then learn and grow, he or she might have the opportunity to eventually dominate that niche. At that point, the firm becomes an acquisition target for the larger, traditional companies in the main market, or as in the case of Microsoft and others, goes public and uses the capital to build or buy expansion into the broader market.

The Importance of Identifying Segments With Innovative Customers

Selling the innovative products of innovation companies often means finding customers who have innovative attitudes and behaviors, who desire innovation, and who appreciate the benefits of innovation for improving their lives and businesses. To create a "hot" innovative company, find those segments known to have customers who want a taste of your hot sauce—even though it is not yet well proven. These are customers who want to try the new—or at least to test the new.

This might be a segment with retail consumers who enjoy trying new things in a store or online. Or it might be certain types of buildings in certain locations where owners are proving themselves to be highly receptive to installing solar cells on rooftops. Or it could be the CIOs of large tertiary care hospitals who are just dying (sorry for the pun!) to use Web 2.0 technology to keep patients on proper rehabilitation after leaving the hospital.

The reason why the entrepreneur tries to find segments with innovative customers is that it makes selling so much easier for innovative new products or services.[1] The sales cycle for bringing new revenue in the door is one of the most painful realities of venturing. Shorten your sales cycle—particularly for a technology-intensive product—and you are well on your way to a successful business—assuming, of course, that your product or service *works!* When you are selling to an innovative customer, there can be many benefits. That type of customer is seeking to build a partnership with you, one based on trust and respect that goes both ways. You will supply great products and

---

[1] Moore, G. A. (1999). *Crossing the Chasm: Marketing and Selling High-Tech Products to Mainstream Customers.* New York: Harper Business Essentials.

services at a price that is fairly commensurate with value; he or she will not beat down price and will also turn first for new solutions. In fact, that person will help you build your next-generation solutions.

If you are starting an innovative business, target segments with innovative customers first. It's that simple. Figure out who they are, what they need, how much they will spend, and what other products or services they want to use with the ones you wish to create. Think "partnership," regardless of whether your target innovative segment is initially a dozen large enterprises or 10 million Gen-Yers/Millennials.[2] Provide and market *real value* to a specific customer group within a target market niche and you will typically be able to maintain some form of premium pricing for your products or services relative to competition. From these operating profits on initial sales, you can then fine-tune your products or services and reach out to more risk-adverse segments and the customers within them.

The bottom line is that successful startups typically target a specific market segment.[3] Choose wisely, which means making yourself informed of the size, growth rates, and appetite for innovation across different potential segments in your industry sector. And remember, once you establish a foothold in a particular market segment, you can begin to consider expansion to adjacent segments. Getting there, however, will take a lot of work.

Now take a few minutes to sketch out what you think is the market segmentation within your industry sector. Use the examples above to try several different combinations, and pick the one you think makes the most sense. Then write where you think you can obtain higher-level, aggregated data for the rows and columns of your framework.

With that done, let's move on to the next step of the process: understanding the needs and wants of customers within a market segment.

Digging Deeper: Defining Major Customer Groups Within Your Target Market Segment

The next step is to segment even deeper within your target market. We can also think of this as grouping customers by common core needs and behaviors. Our objective is to understand the template shown in Figure 2.3.

Customer Group	Description of Typical Customer Needs and Behaviors (Use bullet points)	Segment Size/Share (Use words or actual numbers)	Priority in Terms of Startup Focus

Figure 2.3 Identifying Different Types of Customers in a Market Segment

Customer Segmentation Based on Common Core Behaviors and Needs

Reference in Reader Exercises

---

[2] Gen Y generally refers to individuals born between 1985 and 2000 and are the children of the Baby Boomers. The Millennial term refers to these individuals who came of age and entered college around the turn of the millennium.

[3] Derrick Abell, author of *Defining the Business* (Prentice-Hall, Englewood Cliffs, NJ, 1980), was a master at deploying this simple user and uses framework to develop strategies for business growth.

You do not need to find a large number of different customer groups within a given target market. In most cases, you will find two or three distinct types of customers. And, if the buyers are not the end-users, you should create a second version of Figure 2.3 that focuses just on the different types of buyers within your market segment.

Let's quickly consider the two examples above to put these ideas to work. The first example of contemporary gift chocolates for young adults has specific types of (a) end-users and (b) buyers. Let's get personal. On Valentine's Day, we trust that you will buy chocolates for your *amore:* You are the buyer, and your boyfriend, girlfriend, or spouse is the end-user. If we were starting a venture here, we would want to understand the different types of customers first, for example, the different types of attitudes and behaviors of gift receivers within our target market segment of "young adults." We might find gift receivers that relish receiving expensive brand-name gifts of just about any sort, others who prefer discrete personal gifts, and those who value the thought of the gift more than the gift itself. For buyers, we might find consumers who think a lot about their purchases and carefully select amongst different options versus those who are impulse buyers (largely you men!). In fact, given what we learned we might want to create a premium, fashionably packaged product (e.g., expensive) for young men who are impulse buyers (e.g., not price sensitive for that special moment) who want to impress (or say they are sorry to!) their significant others. We would create two templates from Figure 2.3, with three rows for the customers and two rows for the buyers. This simple example is actually more complex than meets the eye, because there is the additional set of retailers who are the actual buyers of our products and within these there are specialty stores, mass merchants and purely online retailers. As entrepreneurs, we need to appreciate the differences in types across all three participants, and then connect the dots to create the right types of products, the right messaging, and the right channel to market.

For a B2B example—our students' IT consulting firm venture—the customers are the buyers. From our earlier discussion, we would visit customers in two potential market segments being the midsized online retailers and hospitals needing help with implementing a services-oriented architecture in their IT operations. We would look with a keen eye to understand core needs and behaviors that distinguish between different types of customers in each segment. In either segment, we might differentiate between really smart customers who prefer highly customized services and understand that such services must come at a moderately high cost, versus those that simply want "quick and cheap" solutions. Or, we might also find meaningful customer grouping based on users that lean heavily to well-known brands of proprietary hardware and software versus those that wish to explore the new generation of powerful "open systems" software. In fact, the combination of these two behaviors might lead us to four distinct types of customers within each market segment: smart-proprietary, smart-open, quick-and-cheap-proprietary, and quick-and-cheap-open. We would then try to populate each type of category through the "reality check" in Chapter 7 and see who is the most receptive type of customer and also needs our help. Our students ended up focusing on "smart-open" for online retailers for this very reason.

Figure 2.4 provides a general template for B2C and B2B businesses to describe important information for each major customer group within a market segment. In that figure, you create a name for the specific customer group, and further identify it by noting end-user or buyer, demographic or industry information, decision-making level, and most important, key attitudes and behaviors. We want you to be able to provide this type of information for the major customer groups in your target market segment.

Once we have a handle on the major types of customers by virtue of their core needs and behaviors, we can then say with greater confidence and specificity *who* we wish to serve first and then drive everything in our business concept to serving that type of customer.

As with our IT consulting team, there should be a good reason for that selection. For example, let's say your chosen customer group appreciates high-quality products and services and

	Business to Consumer	Business to Business
Customer Group Name		
User Type	• Buying for self • Buying for others • Using what others have bought for me	• Buying for self • Buying for others • Using what others have bought for me
Demographics	• Age, income, gender, marital status • Health condition (for some categories) • Geography/Culture (for some categories)	• Industry—vertical market/segment • Size of organization • Status—profit/nonprofit
Decision-Making Level	• Head of household • Influencer • None of the above	• Business unit/department • Rank and authority • Role in buying decision
Needs & Behaviors	• Physical activities around product/service use • Used alone or with others • Attitudes and emotions, positive and negative • Only buys at certain occasions during the year	• Focused on revenue growth • Focused on reducing operating expenses • Risk-taking versus conservative • Only buys at certain times in the budget cycle

Figure 2.4   Factors to Consider When Describing Target Customers

therefore is less likely to price-discount you. Or a particular customer group is particularly stuck with a problem and is desperate for help. Either situation can make for a great business with loyal repeat customers.

Alan McKim, an alumnus of our university, started what has become the largest environmental hazardous waste removal company in North America. He started his company by driving his own truck to oil and other waste spills that local and state agencies needed help removing. He and his first three employees personally provided this service with a high level of quality. They then grew from there. Today, Alan is the CEO of a multibillion-dollar-a-year concern and is amongst the top 15 fleet owners in the United States with over 5,000 trucks and has incineration sites across the continent. His company played a major part in dealing with aftereffects of 9/11 in lower Manhattan as well as Hurricane Katrina in New Orleans and now, oil spills large and small. (See http://www.cleanharbors.com.) This all resulted from Alan's razor-sharp attention to the needs of government agencies who were in great need of help, fast.

Application of Customer Segmentation to Farming of the Future

These frameworks apply equally well to corporate ventures. Let's populate the customer segmentation template from one such case. A few years ago, we came across a corporate venture team seeking to create software services for farm management. This was in the farm belt of the United States. The company had forever been in the "product business," and this team wanted to move into "services." Companies like John Deere had aggressively pursued this strategic path, and this venture team thought their company needed to get started down this path.

The industry was agriculture and the specific sector was "grains." Within this sector, the team segmented the market according to the type of grain (corn, wheat, soy, and specialty crops) and the size of the farm based on the number of acres. Given that the vision was to create computerized services to improve farm efficiency, they thought it best to focus on the large farm segment—those with more than 10,000 acres of land under management. The initial product idea was to create a software tool that would allow the farm owner to specify all grain farm inputs (seed types and quality, pesticides, herbicides, planting and harvesting machines, etc.) and agricultural outputs, and monitor profit and productivity to better plan the next growing season. This tool would be provided as a "hosted" service to farmers because the customer wasn't expected to have fancy computer systems.

Over the coming month, team members visited a dozen farming operations in their state. Those visits revealed four distinct types of grain farmers that are shown in Figure 2.5. There were farmers who followed traditional methods who were called "Steady Eddies." Then, there were "performance optimizers," younger farmers who were comfortable with computers and truly ran their farms as growing businesses. The team also visited weekend farmers as well as dairy farmers whose only interest was to grow corn to feed their livestock. The team took photographs of these customers and developed "personas" for each type of farmer type. A persona is a fancy way of referring to a set of bullet points that describe the attitudes, behaviors, needs, and preferences of a particular type of end-user or buyer. The team then went to the Web and found federal government sources that provided data on size, growth rates, and trends in each customer group. Information from industry sources, such as trade associations and from government agencies, is increasingly available on the Web. All this is shown on Figure 2.5. The team decided with good reason to target the innovative farmer—the performance maximizer—who already owned a significant percentage of grain production acreage and was buying up the land of the Steady Eddies.

Customer Group Label	Description/Persona	Segment Size/Share	Priority/Status
Steady Eddie	Wants to stay the same if possible, stay profitable, sell the farm in 5–10 years and move to someplace warm in the winter. Thinks intuitively. If he doesn't use a computer to run the business now, he is never likely to.	About 35% of U.S. acres for grain growing, and 160,000 farms Declining share	May be large in market share but not a good target
Up & Comer	Thinker, Planner, Tester. A Performance Maximizer. Trained to use computers to manage business. Likely attended an agriculture college and may have an MBA. Trades commodities. Tracks inputs/outputs acre by acre.	20% of U.S. acres, about 70,000 farms Growing share fast	No. 1 Top Target Customer
Sun Downer	Part-time farmers. Running the farm as a lifestyle choice, not to make money. May use computers in the city, but the farm is an escape from technology. Price focused in buying seed and equipment.	About 10% of U.S. acres, About 35,000 farms Growing slowly	Not a target
Livestock Farmer	Looks for quality, but growing grains is not the top priority. Might be interested in a service to take the problem off his hands, but using his land. Includes dairy, poultry, and pork farmers.	14% of U.S. acres, 89,000 35% Stable	No. 2 Priority Find third parties who grow grains on their land.

Figure 2.5 Farmer Customer Segmentation—The Major Groups in Grains Production, data circa 2006

Take a good look at the figure because this is what we believe you need to create for your venture!

TIP: FIND THE "RIGHT" CUSTOMERS _____

This book is not about starting a Mom & Pop pizza shop or other "lifestyle" business. It is about building a dynamic, high-growth, and innovative venture that creates and sells technology or services that employ advanced technology. We trust that this matches your goal.

With that said, innovative companies must find customers with innovative attitudes and behaviors—who will invest in innovative products and services, and who appreciate the benefits of innovation for improving their lives and businesses. They are much different than customers who take a wait-and-see approach to anything that is new and different. So, as you conduct your customer groupings, look for people on the leading edge of the wave—who enjoy your "secret sauce." Avoid the laggards.

Innovative customers are less cautious about adopting new approaches and technologies. The laggards, in contrast, want to wait and see. They drag out the sales decision process for longer than a startup company can afford to wait to hear the cash register ring. You can get to them later, after you've built credibility and leadership in your niche.

The bottom line of this discussion on customer segmentation (or grouping if that is an easier term for you to use) is that it is insufficient for the entrepreneur to say that all customers within a given market are the same. There are likely to be distinctly different types of customers who want different things, act in different ways, and have preferences for buying products or services that are very different.

With Segment and Target Customers in Hand, Now Look at Their Different Uses_____

Defining Your Market Niche as a Function of Customers and Their Uses

This is one step beyond simple customer segmentation or grouping. Now we begin the process of truly learning what makes customers *tick in what they do*.

In general, the innovator—either as entrepreneur or corporate entrepreneur—wants to create a powerful brand backed by equally powerful products or services that dramatically *improve the customer's experience*. That might be in finding the best way to avoid a traffic jam when driving a car, securing all of your company's data across all types of computer systems, or simply enjoying a new type of beverage. *Improving the customer experience* is in part substance—actually delivering the goods—and style, marketing the promise of that enjoyment or improvement, and then reinforcing those benefits with additional marketing to induce repeat purchases—be it for your product, your software, or your services.

Before we can get to the wonderful moment of defining a product, system, or service idea to dramatically improve the customer's experience, we've got some homework to do with the target customer. But this homework is going to be a lot more fun than going to the library or searching around on the Web. This is a hands-on, face-to-face type of homework.

We now proceed to an important template for gathering customer insights. We call it the Customer and Their Uses Grid Template. It is shown in Figure 2.6. On the horizontal axis are distinct groups of customers as we have defined them above—specific types of customers that share core needs and behaviors. We also indicated that in certain types of ventures, the customer is not the end-user. In enterprise software, an IT (information technology) manager might buy the software for all employees, just as a mom buys diapers for her new child. It is also important to estimate the relative size and value of each customer group within a target market. Let's say that we have a venture making a new consumer product in the area of healthy eating. We have a wide range of potential customers, from the young to the old. You can quickly search statistical databases maintained by government agencies to find out the percentage share of these various demographic customer groups. We find out from that work that Generation Yers and Baby Boomers are two large groups in terms of relative share of consumers. Then, in terms of "value," further research shows that the while Boomers spend more money on food consumption generally, it is the younger populations that are more focused on healthy eating— our target application.

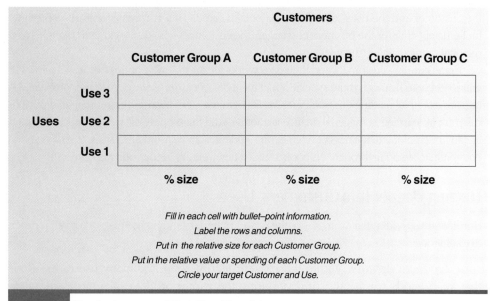

Figure 2.6 The Customers and Their Uses Template

On the vertical axis is a second term: *uses*. A customer use is a key activity in their daily work, leisure, or learning. Uses in the food example above might include main meals, snacking, and "fast food." The intersection of the customer and their specific-use occasion forms the target market niche for the entrepreneur. Thus, our venture might target healthy "fast food" for Gen Y customers. Venture capitalists would call this our "addressable market," that is, who we are going to sell to and for what purpose they are going to use or apply our products or services. As someone planning a venture, you need to continue the research from Chapter 1 to determine specific sizes for the various customer groups on the Customers and Their Uses Template. Industry trade journals, research reports, magazines, and government statistical databases provide a rich set of information to help you define the size and spending value of your addressable market.

Entrepreneurs create businesses and make money by solving the problems of individuals, companies, and governments. The two sides of the equation of a target market niche—the customer and the use—exist because the entrepreneur improves the work, function, or enjoyment of specific groups of consumers, companies, or government organizations. It is that simple. Without understanding both sides of the equation—and in particular, digging into what we call *specific use cases*—you cannot form that product, system, or service idea that will have a transformational impact on the customer's experience.

Use cases are categorizations of activities. In an earlier book, we described how Honda thinks about use cases in designing its new cars.[4] Driving to work is a use case. Driving off-road is a different use case. Using your vehicle to move furniture—or to party with your friends—is yet another use case. These also mean different things for different types of car drivers/customers. Partying for your 50-plus-year-old authors is a completely different matter than when you, our readers, go out to party. Honda even distinguished between older guys like your authors who don't act their age and those who do. Each one of these use cases and customer behaviors affects what a car manufacturer might build into its vehicles. This might include flexibility in the seating to accommodate the move-in, move-out use case scenario or a high-volume bass in the sound system for the young party scenario. The amount of seating in the car, the type of tire and chassis built into the car, and the styling of the exterior for the "youthful" or "young at heart" customer are all types of design decisions that can accommodate particular use case scenarios for different types of customers. The whole idea is to find opportunities to improve the customers' experience. For a venture, Honda finds its market niche in the combination of the customer and the uses served. HondaJet is the result of a corporate venture to provide a fuel-efficient craft for the business passenger (the customer) who desires a "taxi" flight between regional municipalities (the use).

Understanding customers and their uses works great for new ventures because it allows the entrepreneur to be much more specific about the *who, what, and how* for customer problem solving. For example, reading this book presents its own use case. Learning entrepreneurship is a use case, just as learning managerial finance is another. And these apply differently depending if you are an undergraduate business or engineering student, a 25-year-old MBA student, or a corporate entrepreneur working through this book to start a new venture inside your corporation.

Digging Deeper Into Customers' Uses

Consider these additional examples of the power of understanding use cases to develop distinctive solutions:

- *Products: Apparel.* Within the glove category, there are many use cases: gloves that keep hands warm (and/or dry) during the winter or gloves for more specialized applications. 3M is a wonderfully innovative and intrapraneuerial company. It has created special gloves (called Greptile) for playing golf, baseball, softball, and race-car driving. Military, construction, and health care will be future market applications. In each case, gloves use the same materials technology but vary in style, fit, and tactile feel that serve each customer's specific purpose. These gloves function equally well in wet or dry environments and provide the performance and safety needed by these various applications. Here, the Greptile material is *a platform* from which various stylings and designs are created to fit particular use case situations. 3M's target market niches for this corporate venture are high-performance gripping (the use) by a set of specific customers (golfers, soldiers, carpenters, etc.).

---

[4] Meyer, M. H. (2007). *The Fast Path to Corporate Growth: Leveraging Knowledge and Technologies to New Market Applications.* New York: Oxford University Press. See Chapter 6, which focuses on the concept development of the Honda Element SUV.

- *Software:* You are a guy and only buy presents for your wife or girlfriend at the last second before a major holiday or event. You never get the advantage of special sales because you never read the advertising sections of the newspaper to learn about them. Well, cell phone manufacturers such as Nokia and software companies such as Microsoft are investing heavily into location-based mobile services. Let's consider one use case: You are walking down a fancy shopping street with your cell phone GPS-enabled. By looking at your location, the service provider knows which stores are nearby. Also, by looking at your cell phone registration and monthly billing, the company has a rough idea of your disposable income and a very clear idea of your gender. Now, let's say that you receive a mobile alert that says that if you stop by a particular store located right down the street in the next hour, you can purchase that nice leather handbag for your better half at a 15% discount. Further, you can redeem the discount at the point of sale by showing them a coupon code contained in the advertising message. Simple, targeted, and value-added (if not a little bit intrusive!). By the way, this already works in certain foreign countries and was pioneered by a hot, venture-backed startup (Enpocket) located right on Newbury Street in Boston (a fancy shopping street!) that was bought for a hefty some by Nokia. The firm's target market niche was location-based mobile advertising to accelerate shopping (the use) by young, affluent adults (the customers).

- *Services:* You are elderly and your greatest single fear is falling down in your home alone, breaking your hip, and dying without anyone knowing about it. That's a compelling need. A brilliant medical device engineer from Johns Hopkins develops an ultrasensitive sensor cone that can be programmed to detect the vibrations of a person falling (as opposed to a book or lampshade). Further, he builds in wireless connectivity. A hungry entrepreneur teams up with the engineer to create a new home monitoring capability and invests the money needed to build backend server software to alert families and emergency medical services should falls occur. "You will never die alone" becomes a powerful selling message for the elderly customer, as does relief from fear and guilt as the message for the families. The venture's target market niche becomes home medical monitoring for the elderly (the customer) to detect falls (the use).

As you can see, the entrepreneur as innovator needs to put him or herself into the shoes of the customer and feel what the customer feels. And the best way to learn about the major uses within a customer group is through direct contact and observation. You can do Web searches until your eyes glaze over, but the only way to truly understand different types of customers and their uses in a particular segment is to leave your desk, put yourself in a place where you can observe, and talk to potential customers in market segments of interest.

For example, we had an undergraduate student team that developed a social networking Website for new types of Xtreme sports. The team went to these sporting events to talk with prospective customers. They then got to know the business people behind the sport (e.g., the league owners and product manufacturing sales representatives who often hang out at these competitions). They found a wealth of information existed around the actual sporting activity.

Or, another MBA team created a firm to bust into the paid obituary market—perhaps the only real money-maker left for newspapers. This team wanted to provide obituaries online and let them last for weeks if not months for loved ones to read. As you might expect, asking families of the elderly what they wanted for an obituary before the parent died was awkward. Instead, they visited several large funeral home corporate chains and found a great need to help sell a new high-value obituary service to consumers—multimedia, in fact, with videos as well as text. One of the funeral home chain managers suggested going into revenue sharing model with funeral home owners. Through that one conversation, the startup had found an amazing channel to the consumer.

Here are some additional ideas on how to best define distinct customer groups and uses for the purpose of venture concept creation:

- If you are developing a consumer product, such as a new type of healthy prepared meal or snack: Go to different types of grocery and specialty stores and discretely observe who is shopping in the aisle where your products would logically appear. For smaller retail outlets, store personnel are quite approachable and will give you a wealth of information. Customer groups can be differentiated by *what* they like to buy, *where* they buy, and *how much* they are willing to spend.

- If your venture concept is a piece of enterprise software—for example, a customer analytics package for financial services firms: Visit professionals working in the marketing and customer service departments of local financial services firms, with an eye on large companies versus the small, independent ones. Different types of enterprise customers come in the form of industry or vertical markets, market, size, and sometimes, geographical location.

- If your venture is a new type of travel or tourism business: Visit travel agents as well as the locale to which you wish to target your business. Identify the different types of travelers—business travelers, families, young couples, or individuals seeking new adventures. Each of these customers has its own behaviors, needs, and buying preferences.

"Needs," "attitudes," "behaviors," and "demographics" are very important words with specific meanings. We define each of these terms as follows:

- Core needs are the customer's specific desires and frustrations as these relate to a specific "use case." These needs drive the features, performance, and price of a product or service. Uncovering core customer needs lies at the heart of entrepreneurial innovation. We like to think of these core needs as, in part, being derived from the attitudes and behaviors defined next.

- Attitudes are cognitive value or belief systems of end-users and buyers for those use cases. An example might be a young male's attitude toward driving versus Mom driving the kids to school versus professional commuters. In a corporate setting, "you can never get fired by selecting IBM" might be the attitude of mature IT managers, whereas younger ones prefer to go with "open systems" and use smaller, independent service suppliers to get the job done.

- Behaviors represent the physical activities surrounding the use case—including preferred places and frequency of purchase. Once again, using the car example, a young male wants to move lots of "stuff" and "party" with his buddies in his transportation; Moms and commuters display other behaviors, be it driving around with lots of kids or requiring an "office in the car" through communications technology. Purchasing behaviors are important here as well. Customer behavior at the place of purchase provides essential insights for consumer-focused entrepreneurs. For example, it is well known that males generally do not like to shop down the aisles of a grocery store. Rather, they prefer to shop the periphery, which includes the produce, deli, and chilled sections of the store. An entrepreneur trying to make tasty, convenient meals geared for husbands (who may have to cook for their family one or two nights a week) needs to know this. The entrepreneur had better be thinking about new meal formats for the chilled section of the store rather than stuck in the frozen aisle. Otherwise, most male shoppers will never see those products, regardless of need.

- Demographics are age, gender, and ethnicity based for B2C ventures, or industry sector, geography, and size of a company for B2B ventures.

You need to understand not only the present realities but also the evolving dynamics for each of these four areas for the target customers and buyers of your proposed venture. *There is no other path to success*—other than perhaps pure luck or years of trial and error through which you learn these things "the hard way."

In fact, often the very things that tie a set of individuals or business customers together into a "group" are common demographics, attitudes, and behaviors. That commonality induces a generally similar set of attitudes and belief systems. You can often learn all of these factors by simply observing different customers in their places of work, leisure, and in their homes. This applies to both business and consumer products and services. Collectively, these produce a set of core needs that become the target for your rifle-shot strategy in a venture.

Further, within any given customer group, there are often "tensions" in key attitudes, behaviors, and core needs. Understanding this tension—and relieving it with an innovative product or service—can be the genie in your venture bottle.

For example, we all experience tension when buying food. We want our food to be healthy, but we also want good taste. More and more people are experiencing an analogous tension in their car-buying decisions. They want excellent fuel economy, but they also want enough power to accelerate out of dangerous traffic situations. Ventures that successfully eliminate buyers' tensions are one step closer to commercial success.

*** *** ***

In this chapter, we have shown you how to identify different types of customers within a target industry sector, and then how to think about their different types of uses for various products, systems, or services. By finding the intersection between customers and target uses, you come to a very specific definition of your target market niche. We also referred to this as your "addressable market." These are the customers and their problems that your venture will address. The next chapter examines how to understand how these target customers think, feel, and act, which is the foundation of designing distinctive commercial offerings and figuring out how best to sell them.

Reader Exercises

Apply the Methods to a Sports Venture

a. Develop a market segmentation grid for your favorite sport. First, list all the potential segmentation criteria, then experiment with different combinations of two- or three-dimensional grids. For customers, consider age as well as gender as a potentially "hard," measurable, and actionable criteria upon which to construct the axis of the grid. Then give attention to customers' uses which are a reflection of their various attitudes toward physical activity, including sports (e.g., learning, recreational play, and competitive/professional play). Draw the market segmentation grid that you think is best.

b. For one of your segments, such as recreational play for young adults, identify three distinctly different types of customers, employing your common sense. You can even give them names, such as the "weekend warrior," "the marathon man," or "outdoor Susan" to reflect the *personas* that emerge from your segmentation chart. These customers should have different attitudes, behaviors, and motivations in playing the sport. That is the definition of a clear customer group. Then ask a friend or two who play the sport to tell you what they think of your customer groupings.

c. Then, as a prospective entrepreneur, consider all the different products that are possible for your grid, such as balls, racquets, and clothes. Next, consider all the different services possible for your grid: camps, clubs or leagues, facilities, learning CDs, archived multimedia, and even online communities. Find a product that applies to multiple market niches and determine how that product would have to vary, if at all, to serve those different niches. Then do the same thing for a service—how would it have to vary to serve different market niches? Use your market segmentation grid to show the application of that product and its variation; then do the same for the service.

Draw each framework on a separate page and write a sentence or two that explains your reasoning.

Apply the Methods to Define the Addressable Market for Your Venture Idea

Next, we want you create the Customers and Their Uses Template for your own venture idea.

a) Label the columns and rows for the Customers and Their Uses Template (Figure 2.6) for your venture. That means identifying the specific customer groups and their primary uses for products or services, such as the ones you might create.

b) Next, hit the Web and find data to support the relative size and "value" or spending for each customer group. You might get lucky and find data for the size and spending for each "use" as well. For example, your authors enjoy fishing. We are both older, experienced fisherman (and we spend a lot of money on the sport). Another customer group is the younger sport fishermen who don't fish as often and prefer not to purchase $500 rods. For the customers' uses, we have freshwater fishing and saltwater fishing and within these, fishing for specific types of fish. A quick search of "recreational fishing demographics" brings us to all the data we require. An entrepreneur could then target products or services for young beginners versus older, experienced customers, and focus on particular types of fishing (e.g., fishing for trout versus fishing for striped bass).

c) After constructing your grid, now circle what you believe to be your primary customer and customer use for your venture's offerings. Be prepared to defend your choices.

## chapter 3

Getting Into the Hearts and Minds of the Target Customers

The Purpose of the Chapter

The previous chapter helped you segment your markets and groups into different types of customers within those markets—all with the intent of developing an increasing focus on that person or business that is going to be your No. 1 primary target for product or service development and marketing. In this chapter, we go about the business of understanding what these customers need. From this, you can then create your product and service concepts and develop a positioning for them against competitors in the target market. This whole package tied together into a cohesive strategy will be your *venture concept*. Having you develop your own venture concept is the goal of this chapter.

As in the prior chapters, we will explain each of these elements and help you apply them through a series of templates. A final template will help you combine all of them into a clear and powerful one-page description of your venture concept. That document can serve as a basis of discussion with mentors, colleagues, and potential backers. We will end the chapter with *environmental scanning,* a method you can use to test your concept against market forces, technology trends, and government regulations that you may have overlooked.

Taken together, a clear venture concept, a workable venture business model, and a method for testing them with target customers and competitors form the vital foundation on which every successful enterprise is built. Having them will put you far ahead of other would-be entrepreneurs once you get to the point of writing a business plan and launching your enterprise.

Learning Objectives

- Refine your definition of the customers and their uses that the venture will address
- Define your product or service idea based on customers' needs
- Position these offerings, and your company as a whole, against current competitors within your chosen market space
- Put your market segmentation, customer grouping, product or service concepts, and positioning all together into a single, powerful venture concept

Getting Ready to Jump Into the Hearts and Minds of the Customers in Your Target Segment

If you are not representative of the customer in your target market niche—and this entire process of talking to customers feels at first a little threatening—no worries. You simply need to go observe and talk to actual customers in that niche. We guarantee that you will find fears, frustrations, and concerns. It is then up to you to create the venture concept that serves this need. When the origins of the idea are of this negative type and you solve the problem, your solution can often be a "must-buy" as opposed to a "nice-to-buy" product or service.

Also, it is often advisable to consider several potential market niches before deciding on the one best suited for your venture project. Think about the different major types of customers and for which purpose they are using products or services.

- Products: Is it for moms to diaper their babies, or men and women diapering themselves? This contrasts the traditional baby care market with the adult incontinence market, the latter in a growth phase given the aging of the population.
- Systems: Is it a medical device to measure breathing capacity for asthma patients for use by trained physicians in a hospital or clinic or by individual consumers in their homes? This contrasts the medical market between traditional inpatient services and the booming market of home health care.
- Services: Is it energy consumption analysis for facilities managers in large corporate office buildings, or energy analysis and management by homeowners for the devices in their homes? Once again, we contrast the difference between two parts of the energy consumption market: corporate users versus the home. There are implications not only for the design of the solution for these customers, but also in how to sell to them and provide ongoing service.

Once you have identified several adjacent parts (often called *niches*) within your target market, select several that seem the most promising based on user need and industry dynamics. The reason for examining more than just one market niche is to hedge your bets. If one initial target niche pans out, you might have another close by that is in great need of the innovation provided by your venture.

Arm Yourself With a Few Innovative Ideas

Entrepreneurs typically approach their field observation and conversations with target customers with a new product, service, or distribution innovation idea in mind. But you must be willing and open to being told that the idea is wrong or misguided; and, in that process, invariably you might learn *what* might indeed be a better concept. So where do these initial business ideas come from?

You Are a Representative Customer and Have Been Frustrated for Years

A lot of great companies get started in this manner. As a user of a particular product or service, you may recognize critical flaws. You are frustrated with what you have and envision the design and performance of a much better solution. Many products and companies, in fact, emerge from the frustrations of innovative users.

For example, Procter & Gamble's successful development of a commercially viable disposable diaper, the LUVS, has been traced to an employee's experience running a pin from the old-style cloth diapers through his thumb while changing his grandchildren's diapers. Getting rid of the pins was his design inspiration! His frustration, followed by his insight, created a multibillion-dollar global industry! Or, as another example, consider the Dustbuster portable vacuum cleaner. One of our closest friends, Al Lehnerd, was a manager at Black & Decker. Al had six kids. His wife left for a church meeting, leaving poor Al alone with all the kids for the weekend. After two days of bending up and down to plug in the vacuum cleaner, Al went to work with a pain in his back on Monday morning and in just a day designed and prototyped a portable vacuum cleaner that didn't have to be plugged in![1]

We remember an MBA student who was already a gifted orthopedic surgeon. Based on his surgical experience and frustration in spinal cord surgery, Scott helped form a company around a new medical device he designed as a user. That device served as a spacer of sorts for compressed vertebrae. Necessity is not only the mother of invention, but often of new companies. Ingenuity often starts with a frustration. The use case problem *becomes* the problem to solve and hence, the business opportunity.

Even with this personal insight, remember that you still need to validate your idea with other customers in your target market niche. Either the core or the nuances of the idea might change—don't let your own insight blind you to the needs of the larger user community.

A Customer in Your Target Market Has Already Created the Innovation!

Wouldn't that be great! A lot of the hard thinking will have already been done by someone else who has no intention of creating a separate business from his or her invention.

In fact, history has shown that the early forms of successful commercial innovations can sometimes be found right in the hands of customers in a market niche. With careful observation and good discussion, you might well find origination in the frustration or dissatisfaction of *lead users*. These are potential customers for a venture whose technical and problem-solving abilities

---

[1] Meyer, M. H., & Lehnerd, A. P. (1997). *The Power of Product Platforms*. New York: The Free Press.

are a step or two above most other market participants. They face a problem; but rather than sit on their hands waiting for a solution, lead users create their own solutions.[2] These lead users tend not to be interested in patenting and commercializing their ideas. A clever, resourceful entrepreneur will recognize these as prototypes of what might become the products for a new venture.

There is no better example than Harry, a remarkably successful alumnus of our own university. Harry has his own privately held pharmaceutical company that has what is approaching ten new drug discoveries, a large number by any measure and extraordinary for a firm self-funded by the entrepreneur with a little help from angel investors. Harry tells the story of starting his company by providing medical research tools involving mice experiments to various medical schools. In that process, he became acquainted with various medical researchers. One of these was a brilliant physician whose daughters suffered from kidney disease and required frequent dialysis. Dialysis is a terrible thing to put anyone through, particularly the young. The process would rob the patient of his or her good blood chemistries and eventually lead to death. This physician was in a race against time to save the lives of his daughters. He invented a "prep" that would retain the electrolytes in the blood even through dialysis, but he needed help producing it. Harry recognized the genius of this solution. The two formed a partnership to create a company to get the job done. From this first drug, other applications emerged, all focused on the biochemistry of the human gut and colon! (Harry is now a market leader in the laxative and "lavage" market.)

The Ideas Exist as Technology in Companies and Universities Waiting to Be Applied

Other ventures form in the wake of scientific and technological breakthroughs that occur within large corporations. We see this most clearly in today's bio-tech and new-energy companies, but it has been occurring for decades in electronics, communication systems, and software-only products. These breakthroughs sometimes occur in large corporate research labs. For example, Xerox's California research lab (which was called Xerox Park) is credited for being the spawning ground of bit-mapped screens and user interfaces, Ethernet for communications, and the first personal computer, known as the Alto.[3] Many of the pioneering companies in Silicon Valley are said to have been spun out of Xerox Park by technical staff that saw their old company doing nothing with their hard-won innovations.

Many ventures are started by employees of larger companies who find opportunity in niches that their corporate bosses deem too small to matter, or which they dismiss because they don't understand them. "This is a distraction for us. Perhaps you can make something of it. Good luck." The enterprising employee leaves and raises the capital needed to exploit the orphaned niche. In our MBA classes for working professionals, we always encounter enterprising midlevel marketing or engineering managers who shortly leave his or her company to do a venture based on technology licensed or not thought important by their former employers.

Or technology breakthroughs are spawned in university research labs and spun out by graduate students and their professors. Akamai (Cambridge, Massachusetts) accelerates the delivery of Web pages for industry, and A123 Systems is a leader in high-performance rechargeable lithium-ion batteries. Both were MIT spinouts that have market capitalizations of about $4 billion and $1 billion, respectively, at the time of this writing.

---

[2] Von Hippel, E. (1988). *The Sources of Innovation.* New York: Oxford University Press; Thomke, S., & Von Hippel, E. (2002). Customers as innovators: A new way to create value. *Harvard Business Review,* 80(4), pp. 74–81.

[3] Smith, D., & Alexander, R. (1988). *Fumbling The Future: How Xerox Invented, then Ignored, the First Personal Computer.* New York: William Morrow and Company.

Take an Idea That Works in
One Geography and Adapt It to Another

Some ventures originate in an entrepreneur's recognition of an opportunity to transfer a product, service, or technology from one regional context to another. Company folklore in Mars, Inc. has one of the Mars family members in Spain on vacation during the time of the Spanish Civil War. He observed peddlers selling beans coated in a hard shell of sugar. Villagers told him that the coating preserved the inside material. From this he got his "Aha!"—a chocolate core coated in a sugar shell that would melt in your mouth, not in your hands (M&M'S).[4]

In services entrepreneurship, Zipcar is a membership club for car rentals by the hour and mile. This business idea was originally conceived and executed in European cities. An American team adopted the model and applied it first in Boston. With this successful test in hand, the team took the company public and used the proceeds to expand to additional North American cities. Or, as another example, Howard Schultz's idea for Starbucks emerged from a vacation he took in Italy, where he enjoyed and was impressed by that country's coffee bistros. Schultz wondered if he could recreate a similar service and ambiance in America. This proved to be a winning venture concept.

Doing the Field Research: Learning About the Attitudes, Behaviors, and Core Needs of Target Customers

Armed with some initial ideas for innovative solutions to customer needs, your key to success from this point forward is to identify and spend time with several or more target customers.

That experience tells the entrepreneur more about the intended customers' needs and wants and their willingness to pay rather than rely on opinions of any industry guru or consultant. Furthermore, this insight cannot be gained remotely. Communication over the telephone or through e-mail removes the intimacy of observation and nonverbal expression that lies at the heart of identifying and understanding a customer's pain and frustrations. You are going to have to roll up your sleeves or otherwise get into the attire of your target customers and go "exist" with them for short but concentrated periods of time to get your true "Aha!" and march forward.

Understanding the customers' frustrations with current products or services in your chosen market niche is an essential element of a new business opportunity. Finding these frustrations, paying particular attention to knowledgeable, thoughtful customers, pays rich dividends.

If your field work does not unearth any clear customer frustrations, do not despair. Continue to look at the edges around your initial focus. Rarely are there no problems to solve.

Therefore, a mandatory requirement for successfully creating a new venture is to spend time with customers in a selected market niche. This is one of the most important parts of your team work in using this book. At the very least, time spent with customers helps you think more deeply about the business you could create and the products and services it may offer. More often, it will provide you with a direct indication of desirable products, services, pricing, and strategies for beating current competitors. Moreover, investors will know in a second if you are smart about your target customers.

Do not expect doing this customer research to be easy or something that you can save for two days before your next class meeting when presentations are due. It takes time to plan your attack, to conduct the meetings, and to synthesize the results. Reaching out to customers

---

[4] Meyer, M. H. (2007). *The Fast Path to Corporate Growth*. New York: Oxford University Press.

does not come naturally to some entrepreneurs, especially to those with strong technical backgrounds. Get over it. You and your team need to be deeply grounded in the world of your target customers—for products, services, and business model development.

Moreover, many users of consumer or business products or services will tell you that they are "somewhat pleased" or "very pleased" with the products and services they currently buy from existing businesses. This is because the fierce competitive nature of our economy has already driven most inferior products and services from the field. As if following some Darwinian law, the truly bad choices have probably been purged from the market and your venture will have to supplant products and services that have some good points. Thus, your venture must be distinctive in some clear way. For many ventures, this distinctive edge comes in the design and functionality of the products or services. For others, the edge comes in the go-to-market aspect of the business—such as the best sales force or the coolest Website. And yet for a few others, the competitive advantage comes in the approach to pricing. An example might be creating a powerful software application that saves customers demonstrable time and money. Instead of charging them a hefty licensing fee, the ventures request a percentage of the time and money saved.

Spotlight on Innovation: Working With Customers Can Bring Innovation Even to Life Insurance!

Let's say that we are a software startup hoping to develop a next-generation portal for insurance brokers to enroll customers in the field and get their initial premium payments. The larger industry is insurance. For industry sectors, we have life insurance, property and casualty insurance for homeowners and businesses, health insurance, and long-term care insurance. Each one of these sectors is a potential "target market" for a venture.

One of our team members has a dad who ran a very successful independent life insurance brokerage. Even though he is retired, this dad still knows everyone in the business throughout New England. We make him an honorary board member and decide to create a new agent's portal for life insurance. We are not making systems for consumers nor are we making a system for the home office administration of policies and claims in life insurance companies. No, our focus is on the traveling life insurance agent, and even more specifically, on agents who work for independent insurance brokerages throughout the country. We proceed to follow a small group of life insurance salespeople in their work to deeply understand their needs and wants, their use of technology, and how we can make something far better than what they use today. We also learn what it takes to communicate with the computer systems of the life insurance companies. From all of this we design a mobile application that runs on an iPod, a brokerage Web portal with a database behind it, and interfaces to the major new life insurance policy systems in the life insurance industry.

Some technologists believe that they can *think their way* to breakthrough business concepts from the comfort of their labs or offices. They are uneasy with the prospect of meeting with strangers and listening to people who have much less technical knowledge. However, technologists cannot assume that they know what is best for customers. Personal brilliance works occasionally, but most of the time it channels entrepreneurs into a disastrous "build it and they will come" mentality. Accordingly, your mindset must be that origins of winning venture concepts lie first and foremost with the customers in your target market niche.

Further Appreciating the Differences Between Target End-Users and Buyers

As we described earlier, the buyer and the end-user are not always the same, and this has implications for the business you wish to create. The buyer places the order and pays the bill; the user consumes or interacts with that purchase. Each is a "customer," and both must be listened to.

Consider the case of pet foods. For pet food makers, the buyers are pet owners; the end-users are dogs and cats. Buyers include both women and men; their attitudes are different and must be understood. Most women enjoy preparing meals for their pets, mixing kibble with sauce or leftovers; for them, pets are akin to children. Most men, according to trade experts, are convenience oriented. On the user side, dogs and cats have different nutritional requirements, and many have taste preferences. Pet food developers must appreciate both human buyer attitudes and pet requirements and tastes.

Similar examples can be found in systems and services ventures. Workers in companies use software every day that has been purchased by decision-makers somewhere else in the company. Or in the emerging field of residential energy management systems, the buyers of the new technology are often utility companies that provision new electronic sensor and management technologies into user households or workplaces. Selling to and through the utility company brings with it many additional requirements—and some would say burdens. In the case of services, simply consider this book. Your professors have decided that *this* is the book you should use to guide your journey toward starting an innovative company.

To reiterate, *the target customer can be a target end-user and/or a target buyer.* It is essential that you determine and keep track of the precise meaning of "customer" as you advance your venture concept from idea, to plan, to reality.

Structuring Your Field Research

First, forget any preconceived notions of having a highly structured questionnaire that you learned how to create in a marketing class and might be expected to apply to hundreds of customers to get precise answers to well-known product or service features. It is far too early in your venture concept development *for that*. Instead, we are directing you to conduct exploratory field research to ferret out a new business idea in a series of in-depth conversations with a much smaller panel of target customers. The approach of this research is called *ethnography:* direct observation and depth interviewing in the customer's place or context of use.[5] Later on, in Chapter 6, when we learn how to do a "reality check" on your venture concept, we will create a small, structured discussion guide or questionnaire—but that is later. For now, we want you to work directly with customers to get your "Aha!" from the perspective of their needs and frustrations.

From this point of view, there are a series of basic questions. First, how can you identify target end-users and buyers? Who are they, *precisely?*

The answer regarding who to speak to comes from your Customers and Their Uses Templates explained in Chapter 2 (Figure 2.6). Remember that your choice of industry sector drives your market segmentation, which in turn drives your customer grouping, which then drives your understanding of the major use cases or activities for each customer group. Each step takes us into a deeper understanding and knowledge. That knowledge is the foundation for designing distinctive products, systems, and services. Those use cases will have problems to solve. Those problems become your business opportunity.

What Is the Correct Number of Interviews for This Stage of the Process?

Students always worry about the number of customers to observe and converse with to get "reliable" results. Conventional marketing science tells us that a sample of a hundred or more is essential to do any serious statistics. Here, however, we are more concerned with deep insight

---

[5] Leonard-Barton, D., & Rayport, J. F. (1997). Spark innovation through empathic design. *Harvard Business Review;* Schrage, M. (2000). *How the World's Best Companies Simulate to Innovate.* Cambridge, MA: Harvard Business School Press; Norman, D. (2002). *The Design of Everyday Things.* New York: Doubleday; Atkinson, P., & Hammersley, M. (2007). *Ethnography Principles and Practice,* 3rd ed. New York: Routledge.

than statistics. Deep insights rarely come from a one- or two-page survey. Instead, customer insights come from deep and thoughtful observation and conversation.

A recently completed study of a large number of design firms—companies that innovate for large corporations and are commonly accepted as experts in product and service innovation—showed that nearly 80% of those firms surveyed preferred depth interviewing with fewer than ten people for a specific design. The reason is two-fold: First, after a while, you don't learn anything new. In fact, that is the best measure for saying "enough" rather than any hard and fast number. Second, time and money are short. Learn what you need to learn and get on with the process of building a company. Once you launch a business and its products or services to living, breathing customers, you will learn so much more and will have to adjust accordingly.[6]

We have given some indication in the examples above that no more than a dozen or so in-depth conversations with customers is the scope of this activity. That's a pretty good rule to follow, particularly for business-to-consumer (B2C) ventures. The actual number of people you should talk to depends on your venture concept, available time, and your access to potential customers. In general, B2C target customers are more easily identified and accessed than business-to-business (B2B) target customers. In B2B ventures, identifying and gaining access to those potential customers requires greater persistence and connections. In fact, six really good, in-depth interviews with target customers are worth their weight in gold at this point in the ball game.

Most Important: Work With Target Customers in Their Places of Use

Once you've identified target customers—end-users and buyers—how will you approach them for information and insights? We suggest the following: Do not ask them to visit you or meet in a neutral space. Instead, go to their place of activity—be it a place of leisure, of family activities, or of work, depending on your venture idea. Half of the insights you gain will probably come from observing customers in the appropriate settings.

For example, the widely used WD-40 household lubricant was originally just an industrial degreasing and rust-preventing spray used, for example, in aerospace applications. The company, Rocket Chemical Company, had an early industrial customer named Convair, where engineers used WD-40 to spray the outside of its military missiles. Norm Larsen, WD-40's inventor, learned that engineers were taking the lubricant home. His own in-depth interviewing with these engineers revealed a wide range of interesting household applications. So Norm developed a new aerosol can for household use!

Today, the WD-40 company is about a $250 million a year company based on his field research with these lead users. More recently, WD-40 reinvented its cans by creating the straw directly into the can top—solving the frustration that all of us have by losing that little but essential straw!

The Mindset and Approach for an Effective Conversation With Target Customers

If at all possible, we want you to observe first and talk second. Simply observing the customer's activities for an hour or so may reveal a wealth of opportunities. Your authors never cease to be amazed at what inconvenience, poor quality, or simple nonperformance users across a rich

---

[6] Meyer, M. H., & Marion, T. (2010, May). Innovating for effectiveness: Lessons from design firms. *Research Technology Management*.

array of industries and industry sectors put up with time and time again. Seeing that, with your own eyes, will be the source of your greatest opportunity.

Then, after you are done observing and begin a conversation, please try to listen more than you talk. You are not selling anything yet. In fact, you want the user to sell you on the importance of his or her needs and concerns. And when a user tells you that something is important or a problem, *ask why that is so.* Trust us: This makes standard interviewing become "in-depth interviewing," a standard conversation much deeper, more meaningful, and useful for you as the entrepreneur.

Also—and even if you have some initial business ideas from your prior work experiences—*leave your personal views and preferences on the shelf.* Enter their world unencumbered by personal preferences and preconceived notions of customer needs. Never assume that what excites you will excite others or that your problem is a problem for the target customer. Be objective. Think about the customer's own experience and how to best improve it. Your mission is to discover what *they* like, what *they* need, and what frustrates *them.*

Also, come prepared. You should have an idea of the type of information that you want—information will help you focus your venture concept.

Figure 3.1 expands upon these questions. Please read through them now. The italicized sentences in parentheses after each question are the results you should pursue in these conversations. We also want you to make these questions your own questions by tailoring the words to suit your venture idea.

1. How do you define the activity or problem? *(Teach me how I should think about the activity or problem area. It is probably bigger than how I define it now.)*

2. What do you use now in terms of products or services in this activity? *(Teach me the current competitive set.)*

3. Where or from whom do you buy products or services? What is good about that channel? What is not so good? *(Teach me the realities of the channels or the preferred routes to market.)*

4. How satisfied are you with your current products or services that you use in this activity? What is your greatest source of dissatisfaction or frustration with using these? *(Please tell me who you think is the best and the worse!)* What are your workarounds? *(I would love to see them!)*

5. Who is responsible for the buying decision? Is it you or someone else? *(Can you help me speak with them also?)* How is the buying decision made? Who and what are the key influencers? *(You should be writing down notes because this is where most entrepreneurs slip up!)*

6. What are the criteria used when evaluating alternatives? Is there a clear set of metrics as part of those criteria? *(Can you teach me how you currently evaluate current products and services?)*

7. How much do you spend each month of the year on products or services within this activity? *(Tell me if you think you are getting your money's worth, either by your facial expression or in words.)*

8. What would be the ideal solution for you? How would you measure its value to you? *(Let me know what you think will be better than anything on the market today, and how customers would make their buying decisions.)*

9. What fears would you have in trying this solution? *(Would you ever buy something from a startup? Do you need to see a well-established brand name? Do I have to partner with a market leader in order to get you to try my wares?)*

10. Who would be the ideal supplier? What would be their approach, not just in terms of products, but in other things around the products? *(Teach me how to partner with you as opposed to just being a vendor.)*

Figure 3.1   A Discussion Guide for Conversations With Target Customers

Also note the following:

- This is *a conversation,* not an interview. The customer is the teacher, and you are the student. This means detaching yourself from the solution for the moment—even if you are the smartest person in the room and think you know five times more than the person with whom you are speaking.

- Use *open-ended* questions—that is, questions that cannot be answered with *yes* or *no.*

- As noted above, when the customer gives you a decided opinion or thought, ask *why that is important or a priority for them.* And if they give you a great answer, try to ask why that is important! This is a technique called *laddering* as a series of "why is that important to you?" This reveals underlying motivations.

- Don't ask about the customer's ideal solution right away. Establish the use case context and competitive solution set first. The use case context simply means the activity set associated with the product or service category: Making a meal, engaging in a sport, or doing a business task are examples. Don't first ask about products; ask about the larger activity set. Only then, dig into what the customer has now for solutions, and then his or her frustrations with any aspect surrounding those solutions.

- Always offer genuine thanks, both before and at the end of the conversation. If you have a meeting with ten target customers, three or four of those individuals may participate in subsequent prototype design and testing. If you treat these people as partners, they may help you again during those later stages. Treat them with utmost respect; let them know that you value their insights.

Within Core Needs, Look for Latent Needs and Clear Customer Frustrations

We had a friend who was interested in the pet industry, realizing that pet owners were increasingly treating their pets as family members. This was a "veiled" trend, emerging but not yet mainstream. Pet owners increasingly wanted to care for their pets as if the pets were children but were frustrated that there were no credible health insurance programs to help cover the cost of premium care. He thought to himself, "Valued family members have health insurance—what about pets?" From this insight, he test marketed the service among affluent consumers and then proceeded to create a new, exciting business. Today, pet insurance is becoming mainstream. What our entrepreneur friend discovered was a *latent need* within a growing trend (pet as family member) within a target customer base (affluent pet owners) of an established market (pet owners).

A latent need is a fear or frustration that the customer doesn't know how to solve. The need may be expressed with a quick phrase, a swear word, or some type of physical expression such as a sigh or clenched fist. Part of that frustration is that the customer knows the problem but does not know the answer or solution.[7]

Then later on, when you present that customer with a solution to his or her problem, they say, "Great! That's perfect!" Most hypersuccessful ventures have had entrepreneurs who worked hard to find and validate some type of latent need amongst customers in a growing market niche and then delivered solutions to solve those user frustrations with a form, function, and price that screamed "value" to the marketplace. This should be your recipe for success as well.

Latent needs stand in contrast to *perceived needs*. A perceived need is one that customers already recognize and, in many cases, have a fair idea of how it can be addressed. "I need it to drive faster!" "I need it to last longer!" "I need it to cost less!" Performance, quality, and price tend to be the "big three" perceived needs. All competitors in a target market can understand these with just a little customer research. As an entrepreneur, you must understand perceived needs

---

[7] Meyer, M. H., & Lehnerd, A. (1997). *The Power of Product Platforms.* New York: The Free Press.

as well as any competitor. But to truly differentiate yourself and your offerings, you must discover customers' latent need and build toward them. If you can find one or two latent needs and address them with attractive products and services, you will be on the path to success.

Latent needs are often found in the following areas:

- *Safety.* This latent need is driving entire industries, including border and facility security systems. Many of these ventures are spin-offs from large defense contractors. At the consumer level, the Spot Satellite Messenger (http://www.findmespot.com) is designed for outdoor adventurers, allowing them to send emergency locator beacons from any place in the world directly to emergency response teams and loved ones.

- *Reuse.* Reuse is a growing concern and source of frustration in industries. In software, it has become a major play of market leaders such as IBM (with its Services Oriented Architecture and associated software tools). In consumer products, it is transforming manufacturers' approaches to packaging volume and materials.

- *Sustainability.* Once they have finished using a product, customers are frequently frustrated in disposing of it. In many U.S. cities and towns, for example, one must pay a $20 fee to dispose of an old refrigerator, air conditioner, TV set, or computer monitor. Some ventures have flourished by recycling used equipment or replenishing equipment (e.g., inkjet and laser printer cartridge refills).

- *Personalization.* In a world of mass-produced products and services, many customers appreciate—and will pay extra for—items tailored to their specific needs. Few suppliers know how to address this need. Those that do can differentiate themselves. Dell rose from obscurity, in part, thanks to its ability to use flexible manufacturing to customize and quickly deliver PCs.

Here are some interesting facts about *latent needs:*

- *Expression.* Users tend to express their latent needs as a partial, poorly articulated sentence—or an unpublishable word! Sometimes body language is used. To get them talking, ask about their greatest fears and frustrations within the activity set on which your venture is focused. For example, imagine that you were the entrepreneur who created the first automatic radio-frequency identification (RFID) systems for car identification at drive-through toll booths. You have received permission to observe car drivers waiting in long lines and searching for correct change. You capture this on film to show your investors. Will those car drivers use complete sentences to express their frustrations with coin and cash toll booths during rush hour? Where are the toll-booth lines and the disgruntled customers for your venture?

- *Premium pricing.* Products and innovations that effectively address latent needs are seldom subject to price discounting—at least during the early stages of market penetration. Apple iPod/iTunes addresses a common frustration: having to purchase an entire CD to get the one or two tracks one really wants. The price per song stayed at $1.29 for a number of years, and then lowered to $.99 a song. In fact, all of Apple's products seem to command a price premium over competitors by striking a chord with customers in terms of elegant, fashionable design and ease of use.

- *Effort.* Mature companies tend to be lazy when it comes to spending the time and resources in the field, observing customers, and uncovering latent needs to drive their next-generation products and services. The market research departments in these companies are more likely to focus on incremental improvements to existing product lines and services than on true innovation. They send out surveys, hire consultants, and go to trade shows. The best of the large companies, however, companies like Cisco, IBM, and Honda, precisely understand the fears and frustrations of target customers in different markets, and those insights drive many of their innovations.

We have found, as will you, that translating a frustration into a solution is one of the most exciting and rewarding of business activities. Make this one of your primary goals—a litmus test—in developing your own venture concept.

Examples of statements that might be found for perceived and latent needs in a product, system, and software are provided in Figure 3.2.

	Perceived Needs	Latent Needs
For a product	• I want my truck to get better fuel economy.	• *Darn, I had no idea that my tire was about to blow a flat! I almost got killed!*
For a system	• I want my engineering CAD software package to work as software as a service so that I don't have to worry about upgrading individual engineers' computers.	• *This is unacceptable. All my engineers make individual CAD drawings on their computers, but nothing allows them to make sure that they use the same common components. There isn't any reuse across our product lines!*
For a service	• I want my MBA because I want to fill in gaps in my knowledge and skills so I can advance my career.	• *I want my MBA because my peers in my company are pigeon-holing me just as a technology person with no clue about the business. I am much more than that.*
	• I want to get my MBA online because I don't have the time to sit in class.	• *I took an online class, and I never got to know my professor or any of my fellow students. I could have just read the books. I didn't learn anything from my classmates.*

Figure 3.2   Perceived and Latent Needs: Examples of Customer Statements

Positive and negative customer motivations go hand in hand with latent needs. One of the examples that might work for you is getting an MBA. Here, the perceived need is to learn new things, but the latent need is the fear of being boxed into a particular career path. Does the young male drink beer because it is so refreshing? Or does he drink beer to bring down his own social inhibitions so as to more comfortably engage with members of the fairer sex? Does the technology manager in a large corporation "go with Oracle" because that company's software is faster and more fairly priced than other software on the market? Or does he or she select Oracle because "no one ever gets fired for picking Oracle," but just might if a mission-critical application is built on some open-source database like MySQL (which independent tests show is just as fast and certainly less expensive than Oracle's competitive offering). Call all of these the "sunny side" and the "dark side" of customer motivation.

Finding a latent need can be all so powerful for entrepreneurs. We warmly think of twin brothers Tom and Darr, now in their 40s, who held impressive corporate jobs, one at ZDNet (of Ziff Davis Publishing) and the other at Amazon. In calling on key accounts for their employers, they felt frustrated that it took so much time to prepare for each sales call. They would read dozens of industry-specific magazines, *The Wall Street Journal,* local business journals, and do searches on the Web for news stories about the companies and executives they were about to visit—and then have to boil all that information down into a call sheet. What if they could automate the entire process and filter down the most important tidbits of current information based on a salesperson's account's preferences and interests? So that became their venture concept, positioned as a premium information service to high-ticket sales forces in major companies. With funding, the twins created a team to harness the online information of the world into personalized information packages for sales professionals. This enabled more efficient selling. Dow Jones acquired this startup just three years after its formation for a healthy sum. (There is a case in the back of this book, Generate, Inc., that describes Tom's and Darr's startup adventure.)

Now, before proceeding forward, take a moment to read the customer statements in Figure 3.2. Jot down some notes on what you might expect to find for some of the customers and uses in your target market niche.

TIP: "TAKE ONE!"

Whenever your authors study a use case, we always take along a digital camera or digital camcorder to grab images of people in action. This helps us remember the insights we gained on the visit. It also helps us communicate our ideas to others—team members or investors—who were not there to see what we saw. Of course, you may not be allowed to take pictures in a manufacturing plant or an R&D lab. In that case, take good notes!

Look at the Before, the During, and the After of Each Use Case

Use cases involve the element of time. A use activity almost always has a before, during, and after time dimension. And though "during" is the main event, each may contain a perceived or latent need that the astute entrepreneur can profitably serve.

For example, an amateur astronomer takes his equipment to a backyard viewing location, aligns the telescope's mounting with the celestial pole, and sets out his star charts, red flashlight, and other accessories. He may also have to drag out a long electrical extension cord. This may take 10 minutes, and it occurs *before* any stargazing activity can begin. The *during* phase involves finding the desired celestial objects in the sky, which may involve some calculations and searching, examining them under different magnifications and with different light filters, and perhaps some photography. The *after* part of this astronomer's use case involves bringing in and storing his equipment, logging his observations in a notebook, and possibly working with a number of digital images.

It's so easy to be fixated on the *during* part of a use case activity that people overlook what happens before and after—though each is important for the customer and each may hold perceived or latent needs. Using our backyard astronomer's experience as an example, equipment makers have been highly innovative in making the *during* activity easy and enjoyable. A new generation of computer-guided telescopes will point directly to a deep sky object selected by the user from a handheld menu, eliminating the need to work with charts, make calculations, and fumble around in the dark. But customer needs in the *before* and *after* activities remain largely untapped, though one small company has introduced a fiberglass shed with a roll-off roof and electrical connection that makes telescope setup and breakdown unnecessary.

Take a look at Figure 3.3. This is the result of a team's field research with consumers of premium gift chocolate. This represents a template to guide your work in each time stage of the customer's use case, whether it involves products, services, or systems. It is a method that has helped innovators create more fully featured, robust solutions, and in some cases, shift their focuses toward a more promising venture concept. So, when you go into the field to understand target customers, keep your eyes and ears open. Look to the *before* and the *after*.

For the chocolate team, Figure 3.3 shows two use cases: one for the male buying for his female partner and the other of the female buying for herself and her friends. We find it useful to write down phrases that express the customer's perceived needs and latent

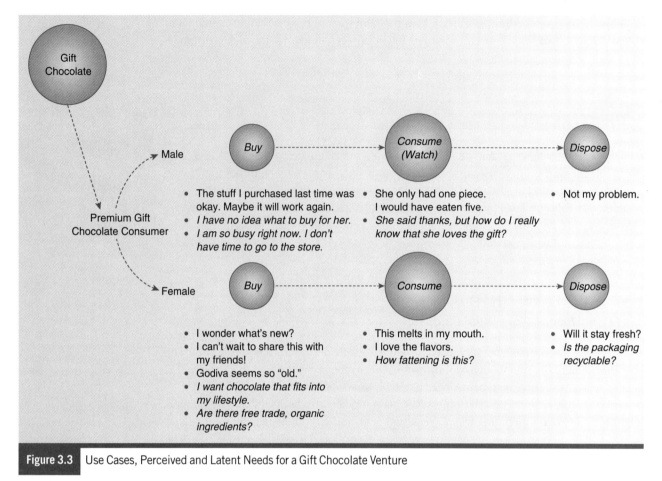

Figure 3.3   Use Cases, Perceived and Latent Needs for a Gift Chocolate Venture

Source: Product image Copyright © Jacques Torres Chocolate. Reproduced with permission.

needs, and we use italics to highlight the latter (e.g., the frustrations). The observations by the team revealed that indeed, men and women are completely different "animals" when it comes to chocolate, with different motivations and preferences in buying chocolate, eating it, and disposing of the packaging. The statements in the figure are not only humorous but highly revealing. And it is this type of insight that drives distinctive product or service development. The male consumers need help making purchase decisions, which lends itself to interesting marketing messages to induce "trial" and a successful consumption by the female to induce "repeat." That success in actual consumption means contemporary styling, "fair trade" organic ingredients, and small sizing or portion control—all suggested directly in the latent needs expressed by female customers.

Creating the Initial Product or Service Offering

With target customer insights in hand—the problems and needs of a specific set of customers for a specific use case—the next step is to translate your idea into an initial product or service idea, or a combination of the two.

This is the creative part of your entrepreneurial process. You have done a lot of thinking to get to this point. Remember, you want to be highly focused on a target customer and use. Also, when you create a product or service idea, you want it to be distinctive, not just a me-too idea like others already on the market. To make it distinctive at this point of the process, the best thing to do is to make your initial product or service idea directly address the latent needs you uncovered in your user research. Entrepreneurs score by leveraging latent needs into new solutions—be they products, systems, or services.

For now, all we want you to do is to come up with a general description of your product line or services. In Chapter 4, we will flesh out your product and service concepts into more fully featured offerings.

Now, let's turn to Figure 3.4 as an approach for presenting a product idea. Think of the figure as a dynamic triangle with three parts: the product or service idea itself; the value of that idea to your target customer for his, her, or its use; and the positioning of that idea relative to competitors. The case shown continues the example of contemporary chocolate gifts for adult men to purchase for their adult female partners, or for affluent women to buy for themselves and their friends.

Look at the diagram. It has a picture of the target customer (a woman as the end-user and her husband as the buyer) and a textual description of the specific use case, gifting for romance on Valentine's Day. Underneath is a picture of an actual product idea developed into a contemporary gift chocolate product by a small entrepreneurial firm that is part of a large company. The left side of the triangle has the customer value statement from both of the customers' perspectives; the right side, a competitive positioning statement. Note that this gift chocolate idea is not the most expensive type of chocolate on the market but rather, a discrete, personal expression of affection at a moderate price within the reach of young professionals.

Figure 3.5 presents a service idea, this time for the other case used at the beginning of this chapter, the IT consulting service focused on fast-growing, medium-sized companies seeking a

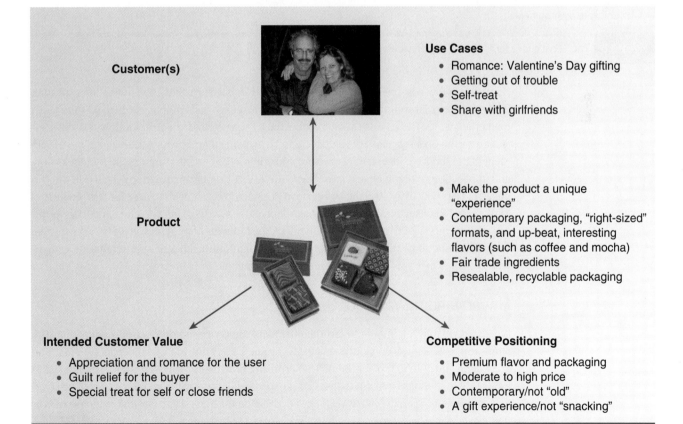

Customer(s)

Use Cases
- Romance: Valentine's Day gifting
- Getting out of trouble
- Self-treat
- Share with girlfriends

Product

- Make the product a unique "experience"
- Contemporary packaging, "right-sized" formats, and up-beat, interesting flavors (such as coffee and mocha)
- Fair trade ingredients
- Resealable, recyclable packaging

Intended Customer Value
- Appreciation and romance for the user
- Guilt relief for the buyer
- Special treat for self or close friends

Competitive Positioning
- Premium flavor and packaging
- Moderate to high price
- Contemporary/not "old"
- A gift experience/not "snacking"

Figure 3.4 The Product Idea for Contemporary Gift Chocolate

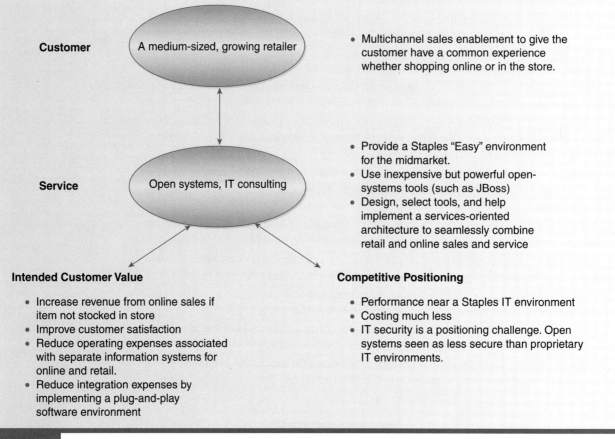

Customer   A medium-sized, growing retailer

- Multichannel sales enablement to give the customer have a common experience whether shopping online or in the store.

Service   Open systems, IT consulting

- Provide a Staples "Easy" environment for the midmarket.
- Use inexpensive but powerful open-systems tools (such as JBoss)
- Design, select tools, and help implement a services-oriented architecture to seamlessly combine retail and online sales and service

Intended Customer Value

- Increase revenue from online sales if item not stocked in store
- Improve customer satisfaction
- Reduce operating expenses associated with separate information systems for online and retail.
- Reduce integration expenses by implementing a plug-and-play software environment

Competitive Positioning

- Performance near a Staples IT environment
- Costing much less
- IT security is a positioning challenge. Open systems seen as less secure than proprietary IT environments.

Figure 3.5   The Service Idea for IT Consulting Services

powerful yet low-cost open-systems service-oriented architecture (SOA) computing infrastructure. It has a picture of the customer, an IT professional in a midsized company (which was the target market segment). There is also a statement of the use case, transforming a Windows-based architecture into an open-systems SOA architecture. Then, rather than a picture, the diagram has a statement of the service concept: infrastructure and applications architecture design, tools selection, and applications integration services. The value to a customer organization is stated in the language of IT productivity. And the competitive positioning is essentially "more for less" compared to the large IT consultancies that are not as adept at open-systems infrastructure and tools as this new consultancy aspires to be. If you remember, the founders of this firm were working in a large company hiring some of these large consultancies for infrastructure and applications integration-type projects. There was a basis for their hopeful aspirations.

Understanding Value for Users

We also need to think about the *customer value* of the proposed product or service idea. The litmus test for a venture concept is whether customers see value in its commercial offerings and are willing and able to pay for them. It is surprising how many would-be entrepreneurs fail to look at their offerings from the customer's perspective. It is not what *you* think about the offerings that matters but rather what your intended customers think. Here is a three-step process to understand value from the perspective of your intended customers:

1. *Create a mental picture of your customer.* Who is that person? Create a picture in your mind of the target customer—his or her face, behavior, and attitudes. What turns this person on, and—as important—what turns him or her off? (Don't worry if you haven't yet zeroed in on this customer;

exercises in this chapter and the next will help you to do that. For now, create a straw man image of the customer in your mind, and write down bullet points around that image.)

2. *Does the venture's offering represent significant value to the intended customer?* Try to express that value as a series of features—benefit bullet points surrounding the picture of your customer.

3. Is the value of your offer something that *target customers will pay for?* There's a huge difference between a customer saying "That's nice" or "Wow, that is really useful!" and the motivation to reach for their wallets.

Value is, of course, a function of the short- and longer-term benefits of a product or service exceeding the costs of purchasing and maintaining it. But value can take many forms: a more effective solution than what the competition is offering or faster or more reliable delivery.

Value can also be created by exceeding customer needs in ways that they truly appreciate. The innovations in noninvasive surgical devices and procedures over the past several decades are certainly things that both doctors and patients can fully appreciate! Hospital-based infection is still running rampant in the United States at the time of this writing. Getting "cut open" seems to have as many risks in the "after" element of the surgery use case scenario as the surgery itself!

And again, when the entrepreneur can make something possible which in the customer's eye is not yet possible, a venture is poised for hypersuccess. As an example of this, we want a next-generation Kindle book that will keep on reading to us when our eyes are tired! Or, for illustrations to have a third dimension to take users onto the Web to learn more about the subject or individual shown in the illustration. As the Kindle software is now broadly available on PCs (as opposed to just Kindle devices), the processing power and connectivity needed for that next generation of hybrid, three-dimension audio-book lies at the feet of innovators. With dynamic books might come more engaged, youthful readers!

The world of energy is ripe with latent needs. Consider Konarka, a company cofounded by one of our former students. It produces sheets of thin film solar cell technology that can be wrapped around cell phones, radios, and laptops, and so forth to provide power on the go. (Visit http://www.konarka.com for an example of a fascinating energy sector venture.) The "value" for active cell phone users will be immediate and compelling.

With these thoughts in mind, return to your prototype product or service idea and, if need be, modify your description of the value to the target customer.

Creating an Initial Positioning for the Venture

With these customer insights into "value" in hand, you can now position the venture against competitors in your target market niche.

Competitive positioning describes how your products or services stack up against those already available to and being used by customers. If you don't think you have competitors, look harder—even if that competitor is a manual or completely outdated process.

Competitive positioning is traditionally based on performance and price. In Chapter 6, we will learn a different type of positioning that often works well for highly innovative products and services. This is called *customer positioning* and is highly subjective, looking at emotional response as opposed to functions, features, and price.

Here, we focus on objective competitive positioning—the "hard" stuff. A new BMW 5 series car, for example, has measurably greater driving performance and a higher price than the venerable Honda Civic, which delivers reasonable driving performance at a much lower price. The data used for this positioning sometimes come directly from product or service sales sheets, which list features and prices.

Figure 3.6 provides a framework for competitive positioning for a venture. As the figure shows, in any given market niche there tends to be a high-performance, high-price leader

(Competitor A, think IBM or Oracle); a medium-performance, low-cost leader (Competitor B, think Dell or salesforce.com); and a low-cost, low-performance leader (Competitor C, such as Walmart or some other firm that competes largely on price). If you find a company that has low performance and high price, its days are probably numbered.

The entrepreneur needs to think about the venture's intended products and services and place them and those of competitors on the map shown in Figure 3.6. This determines much of your tactical strategies for developing and selling your products or services. How fully featured will they be? How will they be priced? How and where will you sell them?

Typically, entrepreneurs focus on one of two positioning strategies: provide demonstrably better performance than Competitor A in the figure, but charge the same or somewhat less to gain a foothold in the market, or have somewhat lesser performance than a Competitor A and charge a lot less (in the position around or near Competitor B). Trying to take a startup positioning against a Competitor C is so hard because within a given market there tends to be usually only one high-volume, low-cost leader—one or two dominant players such as Walmart, for example. Traditionally, startups begin with lower volumes and, therefore, must strongly consider highly featured offerings that go to market at a moderate to high price so that operating profits flow from sales.

First-time entrepreneurs are often tempted to create great products and give them away to win customers. However, why would you "give away" value? If you have something great, charge for it! Moreover, sometimes if you discount a great product or service, your target customers will think less of it. The price is part of the perception of value and quality. Resist the temptation. Position the offerings of your venture in a way that is commensurate with the value that you hope to provide—and all the work that will go in the creation of that value.

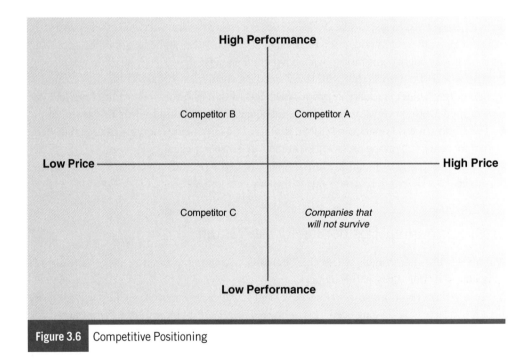

Figure 3.6   Competitive Positioning

Creating the Venture Concept Statement

We now come to this chapter's capstone: creating a statement of the *venture concept* in a single, powerful page. Think of this concept statement as the calculus of your venture—how all the different important pieces fit together to solve the equation of success.

The idea here is to assemble all the elements covered in this chapter into a powerful statement that captures the focus, purpose, commercial offerings, and positioning of your venture. This statement should be a synthesis of all the thinking, field research, and work that you have done up to this point. More than just an "idea," the venture concept statement reveals the meat on the bones; it has shape and specificity—enough so that an intelligent stranger, a mentor, or a backer can examine it and give you useful feedback on its merits and weaknesses.

Figure 3.7 shows a team's venture concept statement for the chocolate idea described earlier in this chapter. We have a picture of the target customers in the middle column, which includes a male buyer and a female user, who, as the field research revealed, is also purchasing chocolate for herself and to share with her friends. On the left side is the target market, with size, segment, and growth rates provided. You can see that this team is focused on the premium segment that is also the fastest-growing segment of the gift chocolate market. Also shown is a specific list of the target customers for the venture, different types of males and females.

The template's middle column contains customer insights presented in as straightforward and powerful a way as possible. What are your profound customer insights? This example shows various statements from males and females that express distinct use occasions: chocolate for love, chocolate for self-treating, chocolate for sharing with others, and chocolate to say "I'm sorry." These are need statements. This may be the most important part of your venture concept statement—for your professors and for potential investors—so think carefully. You can also include links to any observational videos taken in the field research. In this case, it might be a male shopping for chocolate for his wife showing his reactions to product appearance, sampling, packaging, and price.

In the right-hand column are the implications of the other two columns. The first of these are the customer solutions: specifically, how a venture addresses customers' needs. List any

---

Target Market

- Gift chocolate
- $18 billion (U.S.)
- Premium segment is fastest growth segment, 20% of total market

The Customer Insight

- For love
- For a treat

Solutions for Customers

- Boxed chocolate, with upscale contemporary packaging, solid in specialty or premium retail, and Web
- Permissable portioning to meet health concerns
- Organic chocolate SKUs

Target Customers and Uses

- Romance: Married guys buying for women; young men buying for women
- Self-treat: Women buying for themselves
- Share: Women buying to share with their friends

Need Statements by Different Users

- F: I love chocolate. I have a passion for really good chocolate.
- M: A nicely packaged box of truffles always does the trick with my wife.
- F: I love to treat myself with chocolate.
- F: When my girlfriends come over, chocolate is perfect with coffee and tea.
- M: I work too much. I need a special present to get out of the dog house.

Extra Credit

- This might be a video of a male shopping for chocolate for his wife.

Value for Customers

- An expression of love and tasteful self-indulgence

Competitive Positioning

- Great taste and ingredients
- Contemporary
- Medium-high price

Figure 3.7   A Chocolate Team's Venture Concept

combination of products, systems, and services. Then state the *value* of your solutions for customers. In the chocolate case, you can see that the team is focused on creating great-tasting chocolate in contemporary packaging sold through premium channels. For B2B ventures, on the other hand, customer value might be expressed in terms of operating cost savings or reduced inventory requirements. For a B2C venture, value might take the form of customer enjoyment, safety, or convenience. At this point, value is hypothesized. Later on, we will show you how to validate and specify that value in a "reality check." Then at the bottom of that column is the positioning of your commercial offerings. The chocolate team seeks a premium, contemporary positioning. Remember, every venture needs a crystal-clear positioning statement.

The power of summarizing the entirety of your insights and information on a single page cannot be underestimated. You can show a friend, mentor, or colleague your venture concept in a single, clear statement, and then talk about how the different pieces connect with and support one another. Some of our students take the poster board approach. Go to Staples. Buy a large, fold-down poster board, and assemble the different pieces of the venture concept on it. And do not forget the pictures of the customers! This brings your audience into the world of your customers. It will make your conversations and presentations all the more real and poignant by addressing the needs and concerns of real people and organizations.

Get Your Information Organized and Keep Track of the Unanswered Questions

As you start prioritizing the most promising niches, try to gather data that shows the growth rate of sales or demand in each niche and other indicators of future growth. We recommend that you create a separate folder on your computer to store spreadsheets and the like for these industry data. We recommend that you also create a folder to store financial and product information about competitors operating in your market niche. When it comes time to speak to investors for capital, they will expect intimate knowledge of competitors as the basis for a strategy for beating them! Folders should also be created for major distributors or channels supplying products or services for a niche, as well as suppliers of materials, manufacturing, or information needed to compete effectively in that niche. These are all common-sense buckets of information that will be worth their weight in gold as you fine-tune your venture concept and create a more fully featured strategy for it in the business plan.

Perhaps most important, create a simple spreadsheet containing all the questions that emerge for which you don't have an answer—yet. You might even want to assign a name to find out an answer to that question if you are working in a team. One of your author's oldest and dearest mentors—an executive with large firms and small—taught me to keep an "I Dunno" file or folder for each new project. Often we forget the questions we had earlier when we could not answer them at the time. When important questions disappear, they invariable come back to bite us. Keeping an "I Dunno" file of some sort that you revisit every week or so as the project rolls along prevents this from occurring.

Where We Go Next

In completing this chapter, you have come a long way on the road to creating a successful entrepreneurial venture. You now have much more than an "idea" for a business. Ideas are cheap and plentiful. What you have now is much more valuable: an idea that is supported with an understanding of the market and customers the business will serve, the products or services it will offer, and how those offerings will measure up to the competition and provide value for customers. That's your venture concept.

The next question is how to make money from this venture concept. That is the subject of the next chapter.

Reader Exercises

You have done a lot of industry analysis by this point in your project. You have also hopefully had that breakfast or lunch with a seasoned business person from your target industry sector. Now it is time to take your research to the next level. The only way to truly understand customer needs—and therefore the solutions you need to create and sell—is to enter in the realm of the target customer.

Step 1: Hit the Streets! Apply Figure 3.1

Accordingly, your field work for this part of the book is to go observe and talk to target customers. That might be just two or three users at this stage, or it might be six or seven. No need at this point to talk to a lot more. We want quality as opposed to quantity. That means spending serious time observing and talking to target users in their own *place of use*. We also want you to gain insight into their place of purchase. If it's dog food, that means in their kitchen and also the shopping trip to PetSmart. If it's premium chocolate, that means visiting one of those chocolate boutiques or coffee shops selling premium chocolate and forming a small focus group with your friends (where you should definitely split up the men from the women so that they can talk freely!). If it's software, that means going into the companies to spend time with the end-users of your type of software: a few doctors or nurses for medical equipment software, or a few architects, builders, and building supply dealers for energy systems software. Use Figure 3.1 as your discussion guide.

Spending time in the field with customers is what the most successful *innovators* do—their inspiration comes from users. Remember, this is a difference between *invention* and *innovation*. Invention is a brilliant engineer or scientist sitting alone in a lab creating new technology or basic science. Very few inventors create category-leading companies. Innovation, on the other hand, is the application of known technology or science to solve consumer, industrial, or societal problems. Innovators learn *what* to do from end-users and then work to figure out the *hows*. Successful entrepreneurs then take the matter one step further, transforming those users into paying customers.

The discussion guide goes well beyond product or service issues. The marketing and business model insights it seeks to gain from customers are the foundation of designing a powerful, dynamic venture strategy. We guarantee that if you follow the discussion guide in your conversations with prospective customers, you will come back to your team with new insights and inspiration. While this is "serious" work, it is also the most fun an innovative entrepreneur can have other than the joy of experiencing a multimillion dollar exit five or six years down the road.

Step 2: Develop Use Cases. Apply Figure 3.8

You should come back from your field interviews with notes, perhaps videos, and fresh memories. The next step is to develop the primary use cases that will be the focus of your venture. We saw how this worked for the premium chocolate team. Now it is your turn to create this for your venture idea. To do this, use the template shown in Figure 3.8. Don't forget to try to incorporate the before, during, and after for your primary use case(s). And then try to distinguish between perceived and latent needs, for example, needs that customers expect all competitors to solve, and other needs that are pure, maddening frustrations that they aren't sure anyone can solve!

Step 3: Develop the Product, System, or Service Idea

We saw this method applied to the gift chocolate idea—affluent couples or women buying for them and their female friends, small-portioned chocolates made with fair trade ingredients, contemporary packaging, and resealable and recyclable packaging. Now it is time to construct this framework for your venture using the template shown in Figure 3.9. Enough said. Go to work!

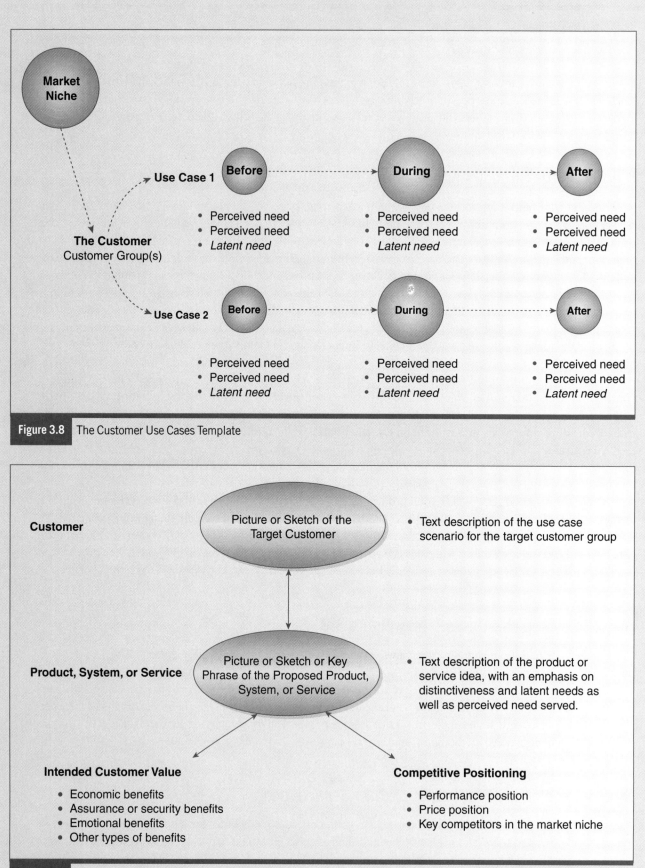

Figure 3.8   The Customer Use Cases Template

Figure 3.9   The Product, System, or Service Idea Template

Step 4: Bringing It All Together

This is where your venture concept should come together into a single, powerful, and hopefully compelling page. Once again, you can use the chocolate gifting case as an example. Create your own venture concept using the template provided in Figure 3.10.

Keep your phrases short and focused to prove the key points you want to make. The template is meant to be the basis of a conversation with your team members, your advisors, your professors, and potential investors. The key question is, Do all the elements in your own venture concept, as expressed in the template, hang together to form a powerful, forceful idea? If so, you should be excited. If not quite yet, keep working it. Don't give up. If you have selected an attractive industry sector, performed solid field research with customers, *something is there*. You just need to find it, work it, and express it.

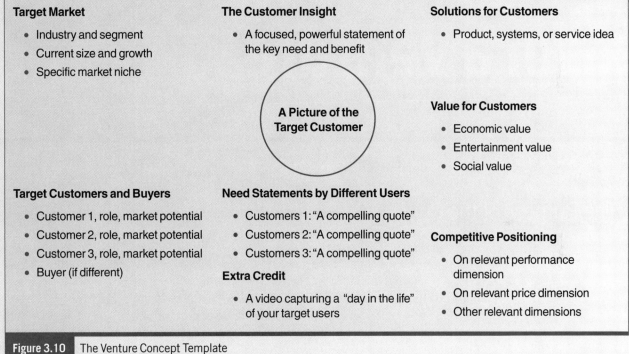

Target Market
- Industry and segment
- Current size and growth
- Specific market niche

The Customer Insight
- A focused, powerful statement of the key need and benefit

A Picture of the Target Customer

Solutions for Customers
- Product, systems, or service idea

Value for Customers
- Economic value
- Entertainment value
- Social value

Target Customers and Buyers
- Customer 1, role, market potential
- Customer 2, role, market potential
- Customer 3, role, market potential
- Buyer (if different)

Need Statements by Different Users
- Customers 1: "A compelling quote"
- Customers 2: "A compelling quote"
- Customers 3: "A compelling quote"

Extra Credit
- A video capturing a "day in the life" of your target users

Competitive Positioning
- On relevant performance dimension
- On relevant price dimension
- Other relevant dimensions

Figure 3.10 The Venture Concept Template

*** *** ***

This should be another major checkpoint with your professors and your classmates. Show them your venture concept; use your data to explain its key elements. Be confident about your work. At the same time, *listen and think*. And as you hear comments or criticisms, learn to place yourself once again *into the heart and mind of the target customer* as the filter for what you hear and how you respond.

chapter 4
Defining the Business Model for a Venture

The Purpose of the Chapter

The previous chapter described a market-driven process for identifying an idea with business potential and framing it within a broader venture concept. Here you will learn how to think about making money with that concept using the *business model*. You will see how a strong business model can turn a good venture concept—for a product, technology, or service—into a great and profitable new enterprise. Dell, Southwest Airlines, and iTunes, for example, have good products or services, but so do most of their competitors. What has set them apart and made them so spectacularly successful has been their innovative business models.

Dell bypassed traditional retailers to bring a new level of value to the PC industry; Southwest's lean, no-frills operating model made it a leader in terms of number of passengers carried by increasing the numbers of potential consumers who thought they could now afford to fly instead of drive. iTunes used the Web to provide single songs and other media to disrupt, and soon own, the mobile media distribution business. These are not only phenomenal business model innovations but also stunning and tenacious business model executions. For some of you, the term "business model" might suggest dry finance and accounting. As these three cases show, do not make that assumption. A business model is the architecture of a venture—soup to nuts—that leads to financial outcomes. In this chapter, we are going to learn about *business model innovation*. While one tends to think about innovation in terms of new technology for new products and services, innovating on a traditional business can be just, if not, more powerful in terms of making a tremendously successful venture.

Moreover, business model innovation around your venture concept might be a necessity to achieve a distinctive market position and a sustained competitive advantage. As Dell, Southwest, and iTunes show, a newer, better way to make money can be the way to disrupt and take position in a mature industry. Not only that, we have found designing business models to be fun as well as interesting. You might come to find it as satisfying a "head-game" as any you will encounter during your business career.

Learning Objectives

In the pages that follow, you will learn the following:

- A definition of what a business model *is* and *is not*
- Different types of business models and guidance for knowing which are well suited to particular ventures
- The different ways ventures monetize their innovations
- Levers for creating robust business models, such as premium pricing, recurring revenue, and sharing productivity gains or revenues with customers
- The importance of business model innovation for new ventures

The chapter concludes with exercises designed to advance your venture idea to the next level.

Defining a Business Model

There is a lot of confusion about the precise meaning of a business model, so let us take a moment to explain what it is, and what it is not. The relationship between the three elements is shown in Figure 4.1. Note the feedback loop in the figure. Financial outcomes can convince a venture team to either pour more capital into its current business strategy or change that strategy.

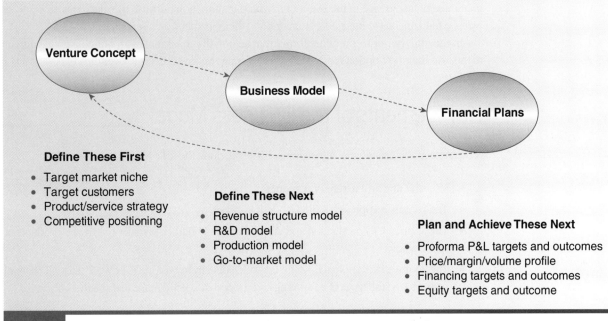

Define These First
- Target market niche
- Target customers
- Product/service strategy
- Competitive positioning

Define These Next
- Revenue structure model
- R&D model
- Production model
- Go-to-market model

Plan and Achieve These Next
- Proforma P&L targets and outcomes
- Price/margin/volume profile
- Financing targets and outcomes
- Equity targets and outcome

Figure 4.1   A Business Model Is the Link Between the Venture Concept and Financial Plans

Simply put, a *business model* describes how a company plans to make money.[1] It is not what you *do,* but how you will *make money* doing what you do. For entrepreneurs, it also explains how the venture will create value for themselves and their investors in terms of building a company that will one day be acquired or be taken public. This is not to be confused with business strategy, which describes *what you do:* your choice of target market, the types of customers within that market, your choice of products/services, and the positioning of those offerings with respect to price and performance—for example, the venture concept we covered in the previous chapter. While there are many other aspects to business strategy, these four are the most important. Once a team determines *what* the business will do in these four key areas, the manner and method of *how* the business will make money must be determined.

Consider the following example of how attention to the business model—and a dose of inventiveness—can spell the difference between success and failure. Your authors both share a passion for fishing. Well, we encountered a team of entrepreneurs who had developed a *self-sharpening* de-heading and fillet machine for use in commercial fish processing plants. (Yes, you read correctly: for cutting the heads off fish!) All de-heading machines at that time had to be taken off-line once each week so that their blades could be sharpened. Every time this occurred, the processing lines would be idle, costing the plant owners money. The new machine's self-sharpening mechanism allowed processing lines to continue working.

Plant owners loved the idea and bought the new machines as fast as the company could make them. However, because the machine's self-sharpening blades lasted for a very long time, every purchase closed the book on the customer relationship; there were no repeat purchases or recurring revenues for the entrepreneurs. Their business model had led them into a dead end.

The venture team thought about other approaches to making money. One member suggested an alternative model: Sell the machine at a premium price, and then sell an annual service maintenance package. Another person suggested that they rent the machines to customers for a reasonable fee and include service as part of the rental agreement. Both business models were vetted with prospective customers. For the entrepreneurs, the rental model was attractive because it would ensure a long-tailed, recurring stream of revenue. However, the customers interviewed had a different perspective on renting equipment. Because de-heading was such an integral part of the business, they almost unanimously favored owning their machines in case the supplier went out of business. They were receptive to a premium service agreement, however. Customers wanted the guarantee of fast service in the event of machine malfunction because the machines themselves were so fundamental to business operations and the customers' own revenue.

In the end, our entrepreneurs found that selling the machines with annual service agreements was their best option for capturing a recurring stream of revenue over the years.

Key Elements of the Business Model

A business model has several key elements. They include the following:

- The structure and nature of revenues
- The venture's approach to R&D—do it in-house or use third parties
- The approach to production and/or fulfillment—whether to make or buy the products or services sold
- The go-to-market approach—whether to sell directly to customers or work through channel partners, and the types of advertising and support needed to make that channel effective

---

[1] Hamermesh, R. G., & Marshall, P. W. (2001, January 22). *Note on Business Model Analysis for the Entrepreneur,* Note 9–802–048, 1. Boston: Harvard Business School Publishing.

Each of these four key elements involves one or more important decisions that you—the entrepreneur—will have to make in dealing with revenues, expenses, and capital—the primary components of every money-making venture. Look at Figure 4.2, which is an extension of the previous figure and shows key decisions regarding the venture concept, the business model for the concept, and the financial planning needed to get the venture up and running. We want to pay particular attention to the business model decisions listed in the figure's middle column.

Venture Concept	Business Model	Financial Plans
Target Market Niche	**Revenue Structure**	**Projected Income Statement**
Is it robust and growing?	The structure and nature of revenue?	Size and growth of revenues, gross margins, and operating profit
Is competition fragmented and/or vulnerable to innovation?	The number of distinct revenue streams?	Time to first sales dollar from startup
	Pricing relative to competition?	Time to operating profit from startup
	Recurring revenue?	
	Product /service mix?	
Target Customers	**R&D**	**Price/Margin/Volume Profile**
Target group?	Build technology or buy?	A premium-priced, high-margin, low-volume business or visa-versa?
What are their needs and frustrations?	Focus of "value-add" in product/service R&D?	
Is it a premium or "value" buyer?		
Behavior toward the innovation/new?		
Products & Services	**Production**	**Financing**
Are we selling products, services, or both?	Manufacturing—internal or outsourced?	Stages of financing
What is the value of these to the customers?	Gross margin targets on products & services.	Amounts for stages
Roadmap for "good, better, best"?	Capital required to create internal assets.	Sources for stages (self, angel, VC, strategic corporate investor)
Key partners around the product/service ?		
Positioning	**Go-To-Market**	**Equity**
How are products/services perceived by customers in terms of value?	Preferred channel?	Company valuation
How are your offerings positioned against current competitors?	Cost to build awareness?	Shareholder worth
	Startup approach versus ramp-up approach?	

Figure 4.2   Tying It All Together: The Venture Concept, the Business Model, and Financial Planning

The same venture concept can have two very different executions in terms of business model, as we saw in the case of the automated fish fillet machines above. If we enter the world of software, for example, Microsoft charges a hefty initial licensing fee ($400 at the time of this writing) for its standard Office suite, Hewlett-Packard (through its acquisition of Sun Microsystems) offers its own Star Office suite for less than $50, and Google Apps Premier Edition (with Office & Exchange type functionality) is $50 per customer per year instead of an upfront licensing fee. These cases represent three very different approaches to "the structure and nature of revenues" within the business model for like products of the same general category. Or, as another example, Red Hat offers its JBoss software development tools for $99 per year but charges thousands of dollars for its technical support service agreements. In contrast, IBM and Oracle charge tens of thousands of dollars for initial licensing fees for their own proprietary software development tools; they also have premium-priced support offerings. One might say that the venture strategy and business models are modular—two different pieces of the successful business equation. An effective venture, however, will make a tight, mutually reinforcing connection between the two.

Business Models and Financial Outcomes

Business models drive financial strategies and financial outcomes, which are contained in the third column of Figure 4.2. A financial strategy involves key decisions, which include how a company will finance its startup and growth. For most ventures, the most important financial outcomes are the following:

- The size and growth rate of revenues
- Gross margins
- Operating profits
- The time required to reach the *first dollar of sales* (as measured from the beginning of R&D)
- The time required to reach operating profitability (positive cash flow from operations)

Another outcome entrepreneurs must focus on is the valuation of the business as it grows. These are shown as the equity outcomes in Figure 4.2. Seasoned entrepreneurs have a keen nose for their "exit" outcome—for example, when their company is acquired or issues stock on the public market—meaning that their own holdings are liquid.

It is also important to note that Part II of this book will dig deeply into the last column of Figure 4.2—how to plan and project the financial outcomes that emerge from a venture concept and its business model. But in this chapter, we will look at a few examples of the financial strategies and outcomes that emerge for different business models. We want you to understand the difference between a business model and the financial outcomes of that model, just as we ask you to appreciate the differences and connection between a venture concept and its business model.

Cohesion Within the Business Model

In the prior chapter, we dug down from top to bottom on the four elements of the venture concept. Our goal was to assure that those elements fit well into a powerful, synergistic whole. Now, we will do the same for the four elements of the business model. For example, a venture's revenue strategy needs to be reinforced by its go-to-market strategy. A premium food product does not typically belong on the shelves of Walmart because shoppers in that environment are not looking for premium-priced products. Alternatively, a social networking product that relies on advertising as its primary way of making money needs a complementary Web deployment and traffic-generation strategy to attract and maintain the millions of "eyeballs" needed to make the advertising structure of revenues attractive for investors. All the various elements of a venture's business model need to sit comfortably together.

Revenues

Revenue is the source of operating profit and, ultimately, enterprise value. Creating a revenue stream and increasing it over time can make you and your fellow shareholders wealthy! If your technology or your products fascinate you, try to be just as fascinated with the revenue side of the venture. This mindset is essential for successful entrepreneurship. In this section, we will examine the structure and nature of revenues, premium pricing, recurring revenues, and the product–service mix.

Revenue Does Not Necessarily Mean Cash

First, a lesson that every new entrepreneur needs to learn: *Revenue is not necessarily cash*. Thus, the business model must consider how and *when* sales revenue can be *realized* by the company and when that revenue is translated into cash.

Here's an example. A close friend of one of your authors launched an exciting new business in 2009 that finds missing charges in the billing records of large physician groups and hospitals. Studies have shown that upwards of 3% of all medical charges for health care are actually missing—not charged to health insurers—due to human and computer error. There are surgery charges without associated anesthesia charges, or anesthesia charges without surgery charges, and so forth. Our friend developed data mining software to find these inconsistencies, and his business model is take a percentage of the new revenue that he finds for his customers—typically the revenue managers or CFOs of health care providers. His team has had little difficulty selling this service—it costs the customer nothing up front, adds precious revenue to their cash-strapped operations, and they only pay for the service when they get paid by their insurers. And each account, on average, is worth a half-million dollars or more in annual revenue for our friend's company.

However, our friend has learned the difference between revenue and cash. If he receives the billing records for analysis in Month 1 of a new engagement, produces a set of possible missing charges and validates these with the customer during Month 2, and submits new claims to the health insurers in Month 3, he must wait another 30 days for the hospital to get paid—so *he can get paid*. Add all of this up and the cash conversion cycle for our friend ranges from four to five months. Four to five months is a lifetime for a startup! And our friend can only book revenue on his own financial statements in Month 3 once the missing charges are validated and invoiced to the health insurers.

Many exciting new ventures are like this: great businesses in terms of the sales but tough in terms of hard cash—at least during the startup phase. Our friend had to raise several million dollars from angel investors for working capital to pay programmers and analysts needed to work with customers to generate the missing charges.

None of these problems are insurmountable: raise some money, sacrifice cherished equity, and do everything possible to get customers to move quickly and *pay*. However, the entrepreneur needs to clearly understands the cash conversion cycle of his or her venture—to know when revenue from customers can be legitimately recognized in the eyes of the law and then, when that revenue turns into hard cash.

The Structure and Nature of Revenues

As an entrepreneur entering an industry, you must take the time to search the Web and use data sources available at your university library to understand:

- How your target industry operates in terms of the flow of raw materials, assembly, the shipment of finished goods, the delivery of services, the handling of returns, and the process for upgrading current customers with newer, fresh products or services. The industry is going to be your sandbox; you must develop intimate knowledge of the entire ecosystem in which your business will exist.

- The key industry ratios and statistics for market leaders and on average for the industry as a whole. One simple way of doing this is to go to Yahoo!Finance, enter the name of a market leader in your target industry, go to its financial information, and then hit the "Competitors" button. In a matter of seconds, you will have the sizes, growth rates, gross margins, and profitability of the major players in the industry shown before you. Then read the news stories associated with the industry provided by Yahoo! to learn more about current industry dynamics. Through very simple, convenient means, you can get numbers for competitors in your industry and the story behind those numbers.

You can then go into any publically traded company's annual report to find a specific breakdown of the revenues associated with various lines of business. These are important because they show the business model of a market leader and the operating margins that entrepreneurs and investors alike can expect to see in a scaled-up version of your own venture. These are important benchmarks to consider for your own financial planning. To take one example, IBM reports revenue and gross margins on multiple lines of business: selling computer hardware, computer software, technology services (such as outsourcing), business services (such as business consulting), and financing equipment and other purchases for customers.

Print out these summaries to show to your teammates. Highlight the key facts that pertain to your business model development. Become fluent in the structure and nature of revenues and operating profits enjoyed on those revenues by current market leaders. It is a club that you aspire to join in one form or another.

Having done this homework, you will be better prepared to ask yourself questions that emerge from the venture concept statement created in the previous chapter:

- *Where is the money in the target market?* The answer to this question will help you to decide which market niche to focus on first (e.g., that specific choice of customers whose professional, leisure, or social activities your venture will seek to improve).

- *Who has the money?* With a target market niche, which customer group should you address first, second, and so forth? Not all customers are equally predisposed to spending money. Not all have the same amount of money to spend!

- *How can we best reach the customers who have the money to spend?* What is the best sales channel to reach them?

- *What must we provide in exchange for their money?* The answer to this question will inform your final choice of product/service offerings.

- *How can we get customers to give us their money faster?* The answer will help you design a customer proposition in which the customer's decision making (e.g., the selling cycle) is quick and easy and involves less risk.

- *How can we convert the customer's money into cash sooner rather than later?* As the story above shows, the sooner you can convert a sale to cash, the less working capital (or loans on your own personal property!) you will need to carry the business. Credit card purchases by customers, for example, put cash into the vendor's hands within a few days. For larger offerings—such as a major systems integration project—what percentage of the total sale can you state as an upfront payment before delivery of products or services?

- *What can we do to make repeat sales to the same customers?* A repeat customer is a gift that keeps on giving. This typically involves having follow-on products and services as well as marketing efforts such as customer loyalty programs, upgrade pricing, and special promotions.

- *How can we add additional streams of revenue over time?* This question speaks to the expansion of the product–service mix or expanding your business to new but related customer groups.

Try to answer these questions in terms of your venture. In doing so, you may see reasons to alter or expand your choice of target market, customers, product mix, and positioning.

Pricing/Volume

Business models generally fall into one or another category:

1. A high-price, high-margin, and low-volume business (businesses that fit this description tend to have selective retail distribution or direct selling)

2. A low-price, low- or moderate-margin, and high-volume business

As an example of the first category, consider a high-priced law firm. It may have perhaps 50 attorneys, some charging more than $500 per hour, and clients numbering in the hundreds or low thousands. The legal work done by this firm is customized for each client.

Now, consider Legal Zoom. It falls into the category of a venture with a business model based on low price but high volume. It also applies high levels of automation to try to boost its margins on sales. Legal Zoom provides services through the Web and has package prices for a wide range of legal services. It will charge, for example, 10% to 20% of the price of the face-to-face premium firm and uses software to automate legal document preparation. Legal assistants perform final reviews. Unlike a traditional law firm, Legal Zoom must draw tens of thousands of clients through its Web portal to generate substantial revenue.

Note: One of the case studies included in this book—My M&M'S—involves an internal corporate venture that successfully launched a high-price, high-margin, low-volume business *within* a mature company that had built its success on a low-price, low-margin, high-volume business model. The comparison point is standard M&M's. The retail price of M&M's comes in at about $3 a pound. For My M&M'S, it is close to ten times that price per pound!

Every venture must decide which type of business it aims to be—high price and low volume, or low price and high volume—because that decision will affect positioning, branding, choice of channels, and the design of products and services.

TIP: BE CAREFUL IF YOURS IS A WEB-BASED BUSINESS

The Web offers a way to get high volumes at very low prices or, in the case of Facebook, at no price at all for direct end-users! But remember, companies such as Amazon and Google have had to spend enormously to build and sustain consumer awareness. Most investors now shun Web portal business plans that rely solely on advertising to make money—just because so many saw their investments in Web businesses based on the premise of "eyeballs" fail.

Recurring Revenue

Recurring revenues should be a goal when developing a business model. Yes, it is fine to make the initial sale to a customer, but developing a stream of recurring revenue from that customer is finer. Consider these examples of recurring revenue for different types of business:

Manufactured products. Motorcycle maker Harley-Davidson's target customers, typically Boomer men with average incomes over $80,000, spend more than $20,000 on their "Hogs." But that is not the end. Replacement parts and accessories comprise about 15% of Harley-Davidson's net revenues. Apparel and other "soft" accessories contribute another 5%. The vast majority of this private-label merchandise is sourced from third parties, which means that Harley-Davidson makes no investment in manufacturing.

Electronics. Let us say that we are creating energy monitoring chips—using a wireless communications standard for household devices, such as what a company called Ember has done with the ZigBee communications protocol. We plan to sell our technology to companies that make refrigerators, washing machines, dryers, lighting systems, and other household appliances. Recurring revenue comes our way as every new appliance is built. This is an OEM (original equipment manufacturer) deal. Plus, if we develop software that reads electricity use signals from these chip-enabled household appliances and sends messages back to adjust energy consumption, the licensing of that software to software developers becomes another stream of recurring revenue. (Take a moment to look at http://www.ember.com and, in particular, its products page.)

Traditional services. As a simple example, the other day a man from our gutter cleaning service was up on the ladder cleaning the leaves. We made no call; rather, we had signed up for the service through a homeowners' repair and maintenance portal with links to homeowner reviews. The gutter cleaning was one of the automatic services offered by the portal. Homeowners move onto an annual plan of preferred maintenance services. This means recurring, repeat revenue for the gutter cleaner. The same approach works for the financial auditing firm that certifies the recordkeeping and information security needed to comply with government regulations such as Sarbanes-Oxley or HIPAA (Health Insurance Portability and Accountability Act).

Recurring revenue for the service firm means getting customers to rely on it time after time to do something that they are not qualified or have any desire to do. This may be easier said than done. An architect, for example, has little basis for recurring revenue. Unless he or she works for a major real estate developer, the architect's business sells and performs one project at a time. Many innovative, technical services have the same problem—they are "onesies." It's hard to make a lot of money from onesies!

Software products. For a software company, the typical approach for achieving recurring revenue is to sell the customer an initial customer license, and then charge a maintenance fee (typically 10% to 20%) for bug fixing and new releases. Alternatively, the vendor may charge another licensing fee for each new software release. Microsoft has done this successfully with its operating system and office applications software, with the sometimes not so subtle pressure of announcing that it will no longer provide support and updates to older versions of certain products! A different business model is to sell "plug-ins" of one form or another. Apple's iPod is the example that keeps on singing. For every $100 of iPod sales, Apple takes in another $30 or so in follow-on downloads. Lastly, there is selling software essentially as a service. Symantec's Norton AntiVirus pioneered the approach of following the initial software license with an annual service charge that enables the customer's computer to automatically check and download software and virus detection rules to respond to new threats. Service renewal is automatic for most customers.

The Product–Service Mix

Building a mix of products versus services is another critical area for business model design. This should be driven by what customers need. Consider SAP, one of the world's leading software companies. SAP develops and sells a suite of software products that include enterprise resource planning (ERP), product life cycle management, customer relationship management, supply chain management, and supplier relationship management. SAP's software is complex and expensive; consequently, its technical support for developers and customers is heavy. Further, neither the complexity nor the expensive price of this software can match the complexity and cost that large organizations incur in implementing it. Good implementation requires business process consulting as well as custom applications development. Then training must be provided to customers.

The table in Figure 4.3 shows the revenue outcomes of SAP's business model: the 2009 revenue reported in both euros and U.S. dollars. Actual software licenses—the traditional software business model for enterprise software—were only about one-third of total revenues for SAP! Traditional software support comprised another third, and high-value-added services such as process consulting and custom programming added roughly another third. Because customers need every item shown in SAP's revenue structure, we would call its product–service mix "well balanced."

	Euros (millions)	Dollar Value 12/31/09 1.44 exchange rate	Percentage of Total
Software revenue—ERP Product Suite	2,606	$3,753	24.4%
Support revenue	5,285	7,610	49.5%
Subscription and other software-related service revenue	306	441	2.9%
Consulting revenue—business process improvement	2074	2,987	19.4%
Training revenue	273	393	2.6%
Other service revenue	85	122	0.8%
Other revenue	42	60	0.4%
Total revenue	10,671	$15,366	100%

Figure 4.3 The Financial Outcomes of SAP's Business Model: 2009 Revenues

Source: SAP's 2009 Annual Report.

The product mix has important implications for operating margins:

- Manufactured products are usually 40% or greater.
- Software products are around 80%!
- Services are about 30%.

On the other hand, products tend to be more capital intensive than services and require greater amounts of startup capital. The product mix also influences the type of managerial experience the venture must recruit as it grows. Service operations managers have different skills than product R&D managers; both would probably be lost in a manufacturing plant.

For some entrepreneurs, how your company gets valued by professional investors can also drive the choice of business model. This valuation issue is not without controversy, but it can be an important consideration in how you structure your business model *if you intend to pursue institutional venture capital as a funding source.*

Your customers might require a full range of products and services and pay your firm handsomely for the delivery. We can see this in the success of SAP. However, for new ventures working with venture capital firms, the logic for customer success sometimes gets lost in the discussion of maximizing valuations for "exit" (e.g., achieving an initial public offering [IPO] or acquisition). Over the past decades, service company valuations have tended to be substantially less than those of product-based ventures because of the nature of operating leverage in these two types of businesses. As we saw earlier, the operating margins of a good service company are around 30%; for a software company, those margins can be in excess of 80%! When it comes to exit valuations among software product companies, depending on the type of software, valuations generally run between four and five times current revenue. Thus, a $25 million revenue software or systems company might be acquired for more than $100 million. A $25 million services company might fetch between one and a half and two times revenue, or only about $40 million to $50 million. A company with a balance of products and service might end up somewhere in the middle.

Thus, the drive to achieve successful exit valuations has led to what might appear to be somewhat odd or perverse discussions of having too much service in the mix even though customers are gladly willing to pay for such services! This is but one of the oddities of working with venture capitalists. As the next section of this book will discuss, however, only a tiny percentage of ventures receive VC funding, and most get their start with funds from family, friends, and angel investors, or directly from large corporate customers. The best thing to do is to follow the voice of the customer in designing your product–service mix and to fully appreciate what it takes as a business to deliver excellence in each, and then to market them.

Market trends and business needs often force companies to reconsider their mix of products and services. This provides opportunities for corporate entrepreneurs to create recurring revenue or to improve the profitability of existing products or services. The measure of profitability that managers often use for portfolio reconstruction is simply gross margin—the profitability of a product or service after its cost of goods (and before subtracting SG&A [selling, general and administrative expenses] to achieve net operating profit).

IBM provides one of the best examples of business model reinvention driven by major market forces. IBM transformed itself from being primarily a computer hardware manufacturer with dwindling operating profit to a company with hardware, software, and services offerings. IBM had about $40 billion in revenue at one point in the mid 1990s, yet managed to lose almost $8 billion! This near-death experience put the entire company on war-footing, and management has not let its foot off the gas pedal ever since. By 2009, IBM was approaching $100 billion in sales. Take a look at Figure 4.4. Note just how different the gross margins (sales minus cost of goods) differ across IBM's lines of business. Software is truly a star in this regard, a highly profitable $20 billion business in its own right and the focus of an aggressive acquisition strategy in recent years. The company's technology and infrastructure services—including outsourcing—has also been a juggernaut in terms of sales and also with attractive gross profit.

	Revenue (thousands)	% of Total Revenue	Gross Profit
Global Technology Services	$37,347	39%	35%
Global Business Services	17,653	18%	28%
Software	21,396	22%	86%
Systems and Technology	16,190	17%	38%
Global Financing	2,302	2%	48%
Other (Technology licensing, etc.)	869	1%	12%
Total	**$95,757**		

Figure 4.4   IBM's Revitalized Business Model: 2009 Revenue and Gross Profit

Source: IBM 2009 Annual Report.

The old IBM was primarily a hardware company with four major product lines (mainframe, midrange, workstation, and PC) and some proprietary software; today, over half of its revenues come from services. These services include computer systems integration services (often for global corporations—these can be huge projects worth hundreds of millions of dollars), outsourcing customer computer operations, as well as more general business and IT strategy consulting. Because most have recurring revenue structures, revenues flow into IBM year after year. IBM has also transformed itself into a software powerhouse, standing second in the world after Microsoft. The gross profit of 85% on software (2008) helps explain IBM's eagerness for this initiative! Recurring revenue and profitability have been two strong drivers in IBM's transformation. Breaking into emerging markets such as India and China with the entire portfolio has been another.

If you aim to be an *intrapreneur*—an innovator within a large company—consider which might be the better sales pitch to senior management:

A. "Boss, I have an exciting new technology that none of our competitors have put to good use."

B. "Boss, I have a vision for a new line of technology-enabled services that will produce a new stream of monthly revenues and twice the profitability of our current products. Even better, we can sell it to our current customers and use it to attract new customers."

If you found *B* the stronger pitch, you got it right.

The Venture's Approach to R&D: Where to Create the "Secret Sauce"

You would think that a technology-focused venture would conduct its research and development in-house, and in years past you would have been right! R&D was and largely remains an essential activity for technology-intensive ventures. However, R&D can be partitioned into activities that can be addressed either in-house or by third parties. The question is, which should be retained in the business and which can be outsourced?

To answer that question, ask yourself, "What are the things we want to do that will absolutely give us a competitive advantage and are essential in providing value to our customers?" Those activities are your "core competencies." Let us call them your company's "secret sauce"— the stuff that will make it special. In general, any part of the value-creating process that involves your "secret sauce"—whether it is R&D, production, or distribution—should be kept in-house.

Spotlight on Innovation: Coca-Cola's "Secret Sauce"

If you are familiar with the history of Coca-Cola Company, you know that its business model (which goes back to the 1880s) is built on a geographically extended network of franchised independent bottlers. In this arrangement, Coca-Cola provides a syrup, or concentrate, made from a highly guarded formula—its secret sauce. Franchisees combine the company's syrup with carbonated water, bottle it, and take responsibility for distribution within assigned territories.

Coca-Cola Company has never shared its formula, which is held in an Atlanta, Georgia bank vault, with any of its bottlers.

If an activity does not involve a core competency, then carefully consider options for developing trusted external partners to whom you can outsource that work. Think "lean." Every single person in your company should be "high-value-added," contributing to some aspect of competitive advantage of your company. Of course, anytime you outsource work, you need to develop an effective process for assessing the quality of what comes back. So, for example, if you are starting a Web company and you outsource the design and development of the Website to a third party, you still need to invest your time and those of key members of your team to review the work done by that outside firm. Your Website is the face of your company to the outside world!

Customer insight is the most important core competency for any venture. That means doing your homework in Chapter 2 to gain keen insights into customer needs, problems, and frustrations. That knowledge needs to be your defining wedge that drives everything else in your business. You and your team *must* become experts in the needs and wants of customers and their activities in your target market niche. You can farm some of the development work and production work to others, but the customer insights are the crown jewels of your business. Learn them, refresh them, and be careful about disclosing them freely to anyone who comes for a visit.

With those insights, you can then decide on potential development partners. Where should the venture focus its "value add" in terms of R&D? Software companies regularly hire outside "guns" for particular areas of technical expertise—a database expert, for example, or another highly proficient in designing graphical user interfaces. Over time, however, these same companies try to bring these talents in-house. If products and technology are the engines of growth for your company, you have to control the design and development of that engine!

For ventures creating complex systems with both hardware and software, it is not uncommon to see venture funds raised to pay for highly focused, external development of certain pieces of the overall system. We know of several well-funded new ventures that have forgone the traditional approach of doing all software R&D in-house and instead outsourced that work to other partner companies. The motivation for doing this is typically time to market. It takes at least six months to hire and integrate a first-rate software development team. The downside, of course, is that the crown jewels of the software company lie in a third-party developer, creating a dependency on that partner for ongoing improvements and bug fixes. It is more common these days to see a new venture keep its core software development in-house and, instead, farm out specific smaller developments, such as specialized reporting modules or hardware components to specialty R&D shops. Doing everything yourself in R&D for complex systems is no longer advisable or necessary given the depth and breadth of talent in the industry. However, working with others requires strong relationships with managers in your external partners and strong legal contracts.

Outsourcing R&D is regularly done in the field of biotechnology. For example, ventures frequently contract with external research organizations to help "productize" new science. These outsourced activities include conducting analytical chemistry to identify and synthesize new compounds, setting up and conducting animal tests, and doing the same for human trials. Charles River Laboratories—a market leader in such services—provides the full gamut of services needed to turn discovery into therapy. In fact, some of our former students have created contract research organizations in Russia staffed by PhDs who will work at far lower rates than their North American counterparts. We have asked them, "How do you give your clients here in the United States the assurance that their intellectual property is safe on the other side of the world, in a country not known for the rule of law?" The only way, they answered, was to start small with their biotech clients and earn their trust.

While we are not so sure that outsourcing the *R* in R&D is the right decision for the long term, an entrepreneur has many alternatives to the capital-consuming proposition of hiring the technical staff it needs to do everything in-house.

Hiring someone else to do your discovery, design, or other important links in the value chain does have risks, however. By sharing important information with today's value chain partner, the entrepreneur may be creating tomorrow's competitor. For product companies, some part of the venture's "secret sauce" is often found at the junction of product design and manufacturing. A contract firm with access to that special knowledge may, despite intellectual property protections, become a competitor—or a partner of a competitor. One would think that the legal agreement between the venture and its third-party contractor would eliminate this risk, and the best contractors live by the terms of their agreements. However, take care. A startup seldom has the cash to sue anyone. So, hire outside help if you require it—but at first, give that outside contractor a small piece of the work. See if they perform and are reliable. Only then, expand the relationship. Moreover, if you wish to create a business of lasting and substantial value, keep the "secret sauce"—the knowledge of customers' needs and wants and the design of your product or services—inside the company and in the hands of loyal employees.

Production: In-House or Outsourced?

The use of third-party manufacturers has become commonplace. For startup ventures, this approach saves significant capital, as the cost of purchasing, installing, operating, and servicing production equipment is avoided. For corporate ventures, the benefit is that the team does not have to beg for time on existing manufacturing assets that may be running 24/7.

The drawback to outsourcing production, again, is that a third-party contractor with access to the intellectual capital of the venture, or its unique production process, may exploit it for its own benefit, legal agreements notwithstanding. This danger is particularly acute when ventures use overseas contractors, who may be difficult to observe or control. A123 Systems, the new lithium-ion battery company, views its process for battery making as a form of intellectual property. Rather than send all of its production to Asia, A123 is building a new plant in Michigan to manufacture battery packs.

Software does not involve much manufacturing, other than printing CDs and documentation, which is easily outsourced. However, a number of software startups are turning to Amazon and other "on demand" computer services vendors to rent computer time for machine-intensive processing—such as mathematical modeling, software program compiling and "builds," and large-scale graphics processing. As they see it, why buy computers that will be obsolete in a few years when they can rent them at very low cost from Amazon? Systems companies, on the other hand, typically take software they have created or licensed and place it on a microprocessor, or printed circuit boards, or entire computers—themselves typically manufactured by a third party. However, systems companies do the final integration and testing of completed systems before shipping them to customers. These backend stages, however, are also available from large third-party manufacturers such as Solectron Corporation. Again, using contractors for assembly and testing saves time and capital for a new venture. The contract manufacturer needs to perform its tasks with a high level of quality. Timeliness of delivery of parts or of finished products is crucial. Many entrepreneurs have preferred to keep the final assembly of finished products in-house so that they can test everything with complete visibility.

Services firms, by their nature, do nearly all "production" in-house. The service operation *is* the production plant. It is also the all-important "touch point" with customers and, as such, is not a candidate for outsourcing. If we were to start an energy improvement business for private homes, our own technicians would "produce" the service and directly interface with customers under a strict regimen that we would measure and control. Financial services and information products ventures are also services organizations that do information "manufacturing" in-house.

Go-to-Market Approach

In our experience, entrepreneurs consistently undervalue the importance of their "go-to-market" approach. By go-to-market, we refer to a venture's plan to engage and deliver products and services to customers. Inexperienced entrepreneurs tend to focus instead on their technology, the products or services themselves, and the financial projections for the venture. Your company's approach to marketing its commercial offerings must be as powerful and as much a source of competitive advantage as what it sells. In addition, that go-to-market approach has a direct impact on financial planning and outcomes. In creating a business model, the key go-to-market decision is going to be channel.

A business's distribution channel is its pipeline to customers and is often a key element in a successful business model. Staples, for example, innovated the first office supply "superstore." Dell famously bypassed the traditional retail channel, selling directly to PC buyers—first by phone and then online. When Apple opened the doors of its iTunes Music Store, it did so via the Internet.

The basic channel choices are:

- Sell direct with your own sales force
- Sell through sales reps or distributors
- Sell through various types of retail stores
- Sell through the Web or mail order catalogues

From these, the venture can choose one or more. Using multiple channels, however, can lead to channel conflict. For example, if one channel partner starts discounting, another partner, who is selling the same product at the suggested list price will be upset. And customers may be confused. One must think carefully about how channels can support each other and create a more satisfying customer experience. The best example of this today is Staples, the No. 1 office supplies retailer, whose e-commerce site is second only to Amazon in sales generated on the Web. For Staples customers, shopping on the Web or in a retail store is an integrated experience. Promotions, shipping, and other types of services are personalized through internal systems across channels.

As an entrepreneur, your go-to-market questions are:

- Where do our target customers prefer to buy the type of products or services we aim to sell?
- How much information do they require to make the purchase? If it is a lot—as in buying enterprise software—then you will need a direct sales force that can speak to the advantages of your products.
- How important is convenience to these customers? If it is a major factor in their decisions, an e-commerce Website backed by UPS fulfillment might be the way to go.

Putting yourself in the shoes of targeted customers will help you answer these questions and build those answers into your business model. In Part II of this book, we will cover tactical decisions on structuring channels, incentivizing channel partners, and creating dynamic branding campaigns. For now, however, focus on your choice of channel. What makes the most sense for your intended customers, and what you are trying to sell to them? It has huge implications for everything you do in the business.

Warning! Going for the "Big Bang" right away might be your undoing. Trying to launch a consumer product through a mass market retail leader such as Walmart or Target could exhaust you and your bank account. A smaller, independent retailer such as Ace Hardware or a sports apparel chain might be more feasible and provide you with better margins.

Different Types of Business Models

In our first chapter, you were asked to decide which *type* of business you want to be: a product company, a systems company, or a services company. To really understand business models, we must consider what a business model looks like for each of these three businesses. Our examples are drawn from ventures launched by the authors' successful students; you can take inspiration from them! These examples are:

- A manufactured pet snack product
- A hardware/software system for home health monitoring
- A consulting service in the field of telecommunications and data network design and implementation

Let us get started with the first business model example.

A Manufactured Product Venture: HealthyWags

Your authors are avid pet owners and have worked extensively in the pet food industry. It is an industry that is surprisingly fun and high tech! A student venture team aimed to find a niche in the $30 billion North American pet food industry. Its venture concept and business model are shown in Figure 4.5.

Over recent decades, families have come to regard their pets more as four-footed children than as animals. This has resulted in greater spending on pet products such as food, accessories, pet grooming, and veterinary medicine. Pet specialty retailers, dominated by PetSmart and PETCO, have risen to meet this growing demand for products and services.

The pet *food* category contains markets for main meals and snacks. Demand for main meals has been addressed with increasingly nutritious, higher-protein foods. Snacks, on the other hand, generally fall into the "junk food" area—less than optimally nutritious. They are heavy on corn meal and meat flavorings, and are often shaped as cookies or bones. Snacks also include heavily processed raw hide "chews" and chicken strips—many of which are made in Asia in low-cost, poorly controlled facilities. Despite their lack of nutrition, pet snacks are highly profitable because a high price is charged for a small amount of food.

The venture team—which was two dog owners—became knowledgeable in pet nutrition. Its members decided to create a venture that would bring health and nutrition to the pet snack category. They approached a small, upscale pet snack bakery in the city where they had gone to school and offered the owners a partnership arrangement. The motivation was to partner with people who already understood how to bake dog snacks, handle food safety and quality issues, and package product in ways that appealed to upscale buyers. If things went well and they got along in terms of business and personality, the two parties would then merge into a single business entity in which the venture team would handle sales, branding, and finance, and the bakers would focus on product design and manufacturing.

The venture concept is shown at the top of Figure 4.5: Target Market Niche (pet snacks), Target Customers (affluent owners), Products (whole, nutritious cookies and bars), and Competitive Positioning (better for your pet, a premium positioning.)

The financial planning of the team was very straightforward. They would invest $60,000 in high-volume baking and packaging equipment to be installed in the bakery. For their part, the bakery owners would design tasty and nutritious cookies and health bar pet snacks made from natural ingredients and few preservatives. The venture team would create a new brand and bring the products to market. The team planned the initial roll-out to focus on independent pet specialty stores, and later to the large high-end pet store chains such as PetSmart and PETCO. Altogether, the team figured that they would need an additional $60,000 for an effective regional launch to the small retailers, plus another $5,000 or so in travel expenses to keep the team members on the road selling into the channel. When combined with the manufacturing investment, the total funds needed to start the business came to about $125,000. Between the founders' own assets and those of some close friends, that amount of capital was within reach.

In return for buying the baking/packaging equipment for the small pet bakery, the venture team planned to pay the bakers a royalty for new product designs and to also pay the bakery for finished, packaged goods. The sweetener for the bakery owners was that they would be free to use the new baking assets for their own production once orders from the new venture were satisfied.

You can see from the figure that the team's business model has a revenue structure based on multiple items sold at retail. The goal was to create a high operating margin business (charge a lot per unit and preserve a 50% margin over cost of goods sold). As sales grew by geographic expansion, the margins would improve through economies in purchasing raw materials. In addition, recurring revenue is built into that structure because most owners shop for snacks on a

Venture Concept for HealthyWags

Market Niche:	Pet owners, dog
Target Customer:	Affluent women, any dog; snacking
Products/Value:	All-natural, wholesome snacks; value is good nutrition means a long, healthy life
Positioning:	Premium, better-for-your-pet, healthy snacks

Business Model

Revenue Structure:	Standard retailer markup on pet products Multiple SKUs (cookies in a box, bars in flow wrap)
R&D Model:	Outsource; work with local boutique Pet Snack baker
Production Model:	Partner with local shop $50,000 commercial baking machine, $10,000 flow wrap machine
Go-to-Market Model:	Independent pet specialty first, then Specialty Chains (PetSmart, PETCO) $65,000 for marketing launch to regional independent stores

Figure 4.5   The Venture Concept and Business Model for a Healthy Pet Snacks Venture

biweekly if not weekly basis. The venture's production model is to collaborate with the local pet snack bakery. In terms of marketing, the independent pet store retail channel is the initial target to gain market exposure, followed by the large specialty chains.

Both the R&D and manufacturing approaches involved having the bakery develop the product recipes, formats, and packaging designs, as well as do all the manufacturing. This model aimed for a win-win situation. The bakery owners would get much better baking assets than they could afford to buy on their own. Moreover, they would have business partners who could help them succeed financially. As a husband and wife team, they had not taken a real vacation in five years! They were tired of going it alone and welcomed that help.

The go-to-market approach in this venture involved the team going out to independent pet store owners, one by one, and selling them on the attractiveness and wellness of the new snacks. Special in-store displays and checkout counter samples were also thought to be a good idea to gain traction. To get this done, the baker-partners would have to get to work developing a set of half a dozen new, healthy snacks as well as some preliminary packaging. Samples were essential for selling the independent storeowners.

Note that all four dimensions of the model "fit" well together for purposes of starting a venture at relatively low cost and in a short time. Recognize also that the venture team could have pursued an entirely different model for the same business strategy. For example, the venture team itself could have handled all production and product/package design in-house. However, that model would have required the hiring of at least three employees and entailed the risk of enlisting people with less experience in food design, safety, and packaging than the bakery owners.

The design of a business model also allows the entrepreneur to establish certain critical business goals for a new company.

- The launch strategy: Typically, a local or regional launch, or within a specific set of accounts within an industry sector for B2B plays. This limited launch then expands to national or some other form of larger scale.

- The time to first dollar: This period spans from the start of R&D to completing it, then getting manufacturing or whatever form of production makes sense for your venture, and finally, actually booking initial sales with paying customers. The time to first dollar is an incredibly important metric for both entrepreneurs and venture investors.

- Revenue for a scaled-up business: This is the annual sales level for a startup that has jumped the hurdle, had a successful launch, and has effectively penetrated a reasonable part of its target market. A scaled-up business is one that has gained a sufficiently large number of customers to support a stable and growing level of revenue and is generating operating profits from that revenue.

- Exit valuation: This is the valuation of the business at the time of "exit"—either through acquisition or an IPO (initial public offering). For planning purposes, entrepreneurs apply a multiple that is standard in their target industry against their scaled-up business revenue goal. In a manufacturing company, that might be two to three times revenue; in software, four to six times revenue; or in pure services, one to two times revenue.

Think of these as goalposts for the venture. In the next section of this book on venture financing and projecting financial performance, we see how these goal points emerge from *pro-forma* financial statements. In the case above, the answers were clear: a regional launch through independent retailers following by national expansion, a go-to-market in just three months that was also the time to first dollar, and a goal of $10 million to $15 million in sales after five years. In this industry, with profitability, that revenue level could be expected to garner a $20 million to $30 million acquisition.

A Software and Systems Venture: Health Monitoring Systems

Manufacturing is not the only type of enterprise that requires deep thinking about the business model. If your venture concept involves systems and software, this example warrants your attention.

Figure 4.6 shows the venture concept and its associated business model for a systems venture that targeted the burgeoning home health market. Its venture concept aimed to provide basic blood testing and physiological monitoring for seniors using computer and medical technology. This monitoring would be free of home health care worker intervention after initial setup.

The venture team in this case addressed a large opportunity. Forrester Research had described the remote personal health monitoring market as one of the most attractive technology markets and expected sales to reach $5 billion in 2010, exploding to $34 billion by 2015. This growth would be fueled by the aging of Baby Boomers and would accelerate over the next 20 years. Opportunity within the elder care technology market was validated by a GE and Intel announcement to invest more than $250 million over the next five years in the research and development of home-based health technologies for seniors. Earlier VC-funded ventures, as well as corporate ventures, had tried to penetrate this market but failed. The venture team would have to work smart to be successful.

We need not go into the same detail as we did for the pet food venture; the figure speaks for itself. The venture concept was to target the elderly at home, provide basic physiological and related health monitoring systems in a minimally obtrusive way, and send the alerts up to a centralized server to initiate responses by trained home health care workers. The positioning of the venture was one of low-cost, reliable, and easy-to-use. The goal was to provide "smart" 24/7

Venture Concept for Health Monitoring Systems

Market Niche:	Home health
Target Customer:	Seniors, Cognitive Okay
Products/Value:	Self blood testing and physiological monitoring; value is "staying alive!"
Positioning:	Low cost, reliable, easy to use

Business Model

Revenue Structure:	Basic testing unit with consumable test packs; Monthly access/monitoring fee to record data and send alerts. Accessories (weight scales, breath measurement)
R&D Model:	Design firm for basic kit; license blood test pack chemistries; develop software to report data and send alerts
Production Model:	Outsource manufacturing of basic kit and consumables; buy and resell accessories.
Go-to-Market Model:	Partner with local home health agencies, visiting nurse associations, etc.

Figure 4.6   The Venture Concept and Business Model for a Health Monitoring Venture

care at an affordable cost to reduce emergency room admissions as well as to provide a sense of comfort to both the elderly and their families living in different locations.

The team thought long and hard about its options in each of our four business model dimensions: the nature and structure of revenues and approaches for R&D, production, and sales. The venture's technology would employ different types of blood testers and sensors, and custom-developed workflow software for detecting patient problems and initiating alerts. The traditional approach would have been to charge customers for the "hardware" as well as a set-up fee. However, the team thought that the home security model was most attractive: to offer a reasonable, recurring monthly service fee and, if possible, to provide all the sensors and set-up at no additional charge. Given advances in technology, the team could obtain sensors very inexpensively. Software would be built on a Web services architecture using inexpensive but powerful open-source tools (JBoss Linux-type tools, for those of you who relish venturing in software). To penetrate households, the pricing had to be perceived as affordable for seniors and their loved ones—no more than the monthly fees charged for existing home security systems such as ADT. Since some of testing requires customers to take their own weights or, in the case of diabetics, draw a blood drop, the team thought that it should initially target seniors who were not cognitively impaired.

To avoid the huge costs associated with manufacturing sensors, blood kits, and accessories, the team planned to outsource that activity, or if items already existed, purchase them under volume discount agreements. A local design firm with expertise in medical devices would be engaged to make blood testing and monitoring sensors pleasing to seniors and very easy to use. The software was another matter, however. This would be its "secret sauce." One of the team members was a skilled software architect and programmer. They all agreed that he would need a team of at least five additional programmers to get the job done and then tasked him to get started right away—with his own "sweat equity"—to build a prototype that could be shown with the business plan to venture investors.

Perhaps the most important feature of this business model is its go-to-market strategy. The team determined that it had to partner with local home health care agencies. As one team member put it, "For a share of the monthly service fee, they would install our system, teach seniors how to use it, and replace sensors when necessary." Plus, there would be highly trained, experienced people behind the ongoing use and maintenance of the system. This included nurses who would continue to visit the elderly in their homes. The team thought these nurses could provide feedback on the design of the system as well as a wealth of new product development opportunities over time. As fortune would have it, one of the team members knew several executives in two large home health care agencies in two cities nearby who were seeking ways to automate their field operations as well as create a new stream of revenue. With the right incentives, a strong, lasting partnership could be in the works—to the point that one of the executives offered to visit a few venture capitalists that he knew with the venture team.

The goalposts for this venture emerged in a logical manner from the business model decisions above. If properly funded, the team thought that it could have a working system in its lead customer's hands within a year, and after running a hands-on trial with 50 elderly residents in their homes, begin booking actual revenue in 18 months. While we will delve into planning rounds of investment, companies of this sort usually get started with between $2 million to $4 million from venture capital firms to complete the technology and get the system up and running in the first one or two major customers. This is then followed by a second round of $6 million to $10 million for business expansion.

The team had dinner with the friendly home health care agency executive. They collectively thought that $50 a month as a home monitoring fee was reasonable, given the rates charged by security companies. The executive also thought that a served population of 50,000 customers within the geographic region was also achievable if the system worked as promised. A half dozen home health care agencies working with several large health insurers could deliver that number and he personally knew the key decision makers in each account. That usage would translate into $30 million in annual sales. Exit valuations for large-scale systems types of ventures were currently four to five times revenue. It sounded even more promising when the executive offered his own home health company as the lead customer for development and testing.

This is the type of forward-looking thinking that every venture team should do as it designs its business model. In many if not most ventures, the financial reward that you receive for all that hard work comes from your founder's equity, and not the salary or profits you take home from the business. Be assured that your investors will be thinking about this, too!

A Technical Services Venture: Telestructures

We expect that a number of you have created an innovative service concept in the previous chapter—one that primarily is not product or systems based but largely some form of technical, systems integration, or consulting service; if you did, you will find the case example in this section useful.

Figure 4.7 describes the business model for a venture started by some former students—people with strong technical backgrounds who were earning their MBAs through our weekend program. Their aim was to form a consulting firm specializing in telecommunications infrastructure design and implementation for commercial buildings and commercial campuses. Their vendor-independent consultancy would configure a set of voice and data switches, routers, and communications management software that would meet a client's requirements. They would also manage implementation and training as needed. The business would be positioned as a premium, "high-touch" technical service for building owners and facilities managers.

Venture Concept for Telestructures

Market Niche:	Commercial properties
Target Customer:	Building owners and facilities managers
Services/Value:	Design and implement telecommunications and data network infrastructure; value is to meet our occupants' needs without wasting money!
Positioning:	Customized, premium service, with "high touch" for clients relative to large telco service departments

Business Model

Revenue Structure:	a) Infrastructure design fees, package price b) Implementation (general contractor and testing) fees c) Network maintenance fees
R&D Model:	Telco network design software to be licensed and customized. Network testing software developed in-house with MSFT Software Development Kit
Production Model:	In-house—using our own highly trained engineers
Go-to-Market Model:	Proposal to property owners, first in New England, and then expand

Figure 4.7   The Venture Concept and Business Model for a Telecommunications Systems Design Firm

The second box in Figure 4.7 reveals the business model. Revenues could come from design fees, implementation fees, and ongoing maintenance fees. Each was a specific stream of revenue, each following the former. The entrepreneurs planned to recruit their engineering friends to provide services, and expand with new recruits. Selling would require identifying property owners with a value proposition along the lines that telecommunications infrastructure was an increasingly important dimension for building occupants and would provide building owners a nice selling point for their properties to prospective tenants. For example, shared teleconferencing facilities were increasingly viewed as a way for occupants to save travel costs and increase productivity for geographically dispersed development teams and customers. Current and prospective tenants would pay additional money to have access to such facilities if conveniently located within the building or building campus. Moreover, since the technology was changing all the time, a highly skilled, vendor-independent service company would be the best way for a property owner to stay current with technology that was the best "bang for the buck" for certain applications.

For the R&D approach, it was clear that the software used by field technicians to quickly assess a new building and make recommendations could become one of this venture's crown jewels. Accordingly, the software should probably be done in-house. The team had already developed some software that analyzed a building's requirements and infrastructure to recommend networking technology solutions. They figured that a full-time programmer could make that program suitable for use by trained field staff. Also, the database and rules engine in that software had to be expanded to include different types of buildings (such as greener infrastructures) and new types of networking and telecommunications technologies (such as new mobile networks). For example, in certain properties, building owners wanted to install radio-frequency identification (RFID) readers that would scan employee badges and provide selective access to secure areas. These new requirements and technologies could spell additional revenue for the venture.

The rest of the business model was straightforward. "Manufacturing" simply meant arranging delivery and managing installation of specific equipment by known and trusted vendors or systems integrators. And sales would by its nature be direct to the property owner. In some cases, this would be facilities managers working for large corporations who owned and managed their own commercial campuses; in other cases, it would be large commercial property owners who leased facilities to companies.

Based on interviews with other area computer services firms that were not direct competitors, the entrepreneurs estimated that success would create a profitable $10 million per annum business over the course of five years. Owners of these services firms tended to sell their businesses to employees or to large services firms, typically for one and a half times sales. That, if anything, was the likely "exit strategy" for this particular venture team. The two founders thought that $7 million each would be a nice sum for retirement. These became their long-term goals. Once again, this is a healthy exercise for any entrepreneurial team to think about as it designs its business model.

One of the property owners they visited liked their "spunk" and offered to be an advisor, introduce them to his lawyer and banker, and even provide them with a desk or two from which to work on the startup process. Further, since the students were already working full-time, there was no reason why they could not pool their savings and fund the first six months of software development themselves, with an actual services launch once all had earned their degrees. What had begun as a classroom exercise was ready to roll.

Comparing the Three Business Models

We have just examined three ventures, each with a different venture concept, business model, and the goals that emerge from that model. Now let us compare the different business models. Doing so may help you identify features that can invigorate your venture. Figure 4.8 does that for the three cases above.

	Type of Business	Profile of Revenues and Gross Margins	Goals
Healthy pet snacks	Product	Low volume, high price, healthy margins (>50%)	• Launch: Regional, then national • First dollar: No reason why it can't be 3 months • Grow to $10 million sales, • Sell to CPG company for 1–2X sales
Home health monitoring	System (hybrid of products, software, and services)	High volume, moderate price, strong margins on services (monthly fees >80%)	• Launch: Local w/a home health agency, then national • First dollar: At least a year for development, and another 6 months for trial. Probably 18–24 months until first revenue. • Grow to $30 million sales • Sell for 3X revenues, and be worth $100 million, or else seek to become the next ADT.
Telecom design services	Services	Low volume, high price, healthy margins (>35% on services)	• Launch: 1 site per month in first year, regional; growing to 5 sites per month • First dollar: Almost right away, at least within 2 months • Grow to $10 million • Maintain the business and sell to employees down the road

Figure 4.8 A Comparison of Key Business Model Goals for Three Different Types

One major result of a business model is what you hope to be the structure of revenues and gross profit from sales. In the figure, we call this the "profile of revenues and gross margins." Deciding between products, systems, and services is certainly a crucial decision for any entrepreneur and, as we have discussed, is intimately connected with the choice of target market niche and the needs and pain points of customers within that niche. With that decision made, the business model developed to pursue that market opportunity leads to a certain revenue and gross margin profile. Being able to explain that profile in a simple, clear way is essential in winning the confidence of investors.

Take a look at the second column in the figure. In the three cases above, we have three very different revenue-margin profiles. The pet snack venture is a relatively low-revenue, high gross margin business. The health care monitoring venture has two profiles given the nature of the business. On the product side, sensors are provided at no charge as part of the initial sale. Sensor replacements (due to normal wear and tear) are expected to be infrequent but when they do occur, reasonably priced but with a healthy margin. Services are a different matter. The monthly recurring fee is at a moderate price ($50 per month), but the margins on that service are expected to be high given that most of the work will be done through automation and intelligent server software. The telecom services business has its own particular profile: low volume but strong gross margin across all three lines of service—network and telecom applications design, implementation, and monitoring.

The third column then shows the various major goalposts that the entrepreneur wishes to achieve in his or her venture. This set of milestones is largely financial in nature. Launch target and the time to first dollar are the first two to consider.

Launch refers simply to the venture's strategy for bringing the first set of products or services to market. The pet snack folks are going to do a limited, regional launch to independent pet retailers and then expand to the national premium chains. The health monitoring entrepreneurs are going to team up with several local home health care agencies to get started and then, too, expand geographically. Working with a local customer is essential for this team given the need to test, refine, and test again. Proximity is important. The telecom service entrepreneurs are fortunate to be living in a region (the Northeast) with lots of potential customers. Their launch is local as well with an initial target of securing one new property per month.

Company founders count every day until the cash registers rings—that is, until the day they record their first sale. The first sale is a landmark moment. Many businesses frame that first dollar as a good luck talisman. Time to first dollar (or euro, yen, renminbi, or whatever coinage you use) refers to how long it will take to complete the development of your product or service and bring it to market. The pet snack business, for example, can get to market quickly—say in three months. As we noted earlier, the first dollar booked as a sale is usually not the first dollar of cash for the business—and for certain large industrial sales, the lag between sales and actual cash can be long and treacherous. The health monitoring business is going to take much longer to execute, because of not only the complex workflows and real-time data feeds that have to be designed and programmed, but also because of the anticipated six-month testing phase with live customers. This is simply the nature of the industry. Lives are at stake! In contrast, the telecom services venture can start booking sales tomorrow. The founders are the providers. They can start working the next day to sell design services. In fact, in their case, they should probably not even write a business plan if they cannot sell an initial account as the ultimate "reality check" for their venture concept. A services firm should be able to create revenue almost immediately and reach an operating profit shortly thereafter.

We then show the scale-up revenue and exit goals for each of the three ventures. Scaled-up revenue means the annual sales of a business once it has achieved that balance of a large number of customers, stable revenues, and most important, operating profits, that is, it is generating real cash from the business (after R&D, marketing, and general administrative expenses). That number for scaled-up revenue obviously differs for different types of companies, even in the same industry. Exit valuations, for planning purposes of the entrepreneur, can be estimated as a multiple of current sales based on acquisitions that are occurring in his or her industry sector. You might be able to get to an IPO, but that is indeed so very rare. Being acquired by an industry or segment leader is far more realistic as an exit strategy. For our three companies at hand, the entrepreneur's goals in these two dimensions are fairly clear and reasonable. For the pet food business, $10 million with an exit goal of $20 million at two times sales. For the health care team, the scale-up revenue target is $30 million, which should fetch more than $100 million based on current deals in the industry. And for the telecom services firm, the goal is to reach $10 million in sales leading to an employee buyout a decade or more down the road.

Note two very important things. First, as an entrepreneur, you do not have to exit unless, of course, you are one of those select few who actually bring in institutional venture capital to fund your startup. In that case, your venture capitalists will be working from Day 1 to get your company acquired or to reach an IPO, because *that is the only way they make money.* Second, operating profits should be achieved as soon as possible in any business. For example, the telecom design consultants should be profitable in the first month or two of their business—if they are careful about taking on administrative expenses. For ventures generally, if you can start generating small amounts of cash from your business within the first year of the business, a huge congratulations will be in order to you from your investors. Indeed, if you achieve this, your company would be a fine candidate for use as a case study in this book! Achieving operating profits as soon as possible should be your goal.

Now for the Advanced Class: Business Model Innovation _____

Many people mistakenly think that designing a distinctive product or service that shines uniquely in customers' eyes is the sole path to competitive differentiation and business success. There is also another path, sometimes as compelling as the new product or service itself. This is business model innovation—disrupting the way an entire traditional industry does business with its customers.

We define business model *innovation* as an important change to the traditional way of making money in a given industry. For example, before Dell came along, PCs were built-to-stock and sold through retail middlemen. One of Dell's business model innovations was to sell directly to customers. That made low-cost PC customization possible. It also eliminated the need to build and hold huge inventories of finished machines, whose value was eroded daily by the lightning fast pace of technology change. Customer-direct sales gave Dell an opportunity to collect payment immediately (through credit card transactions); unlike its competitors, it did not have to sit on a mountain of 30 to 60 days' receivables from retail vendors.

Examples of business model innovation lie within successful startups across a broad range of industries, even those that appear at first glance to be *highly noninnovative.*

A great example of business model innovation was introduced by Automated Data Processing (ADP), a software company that grew throughout the 1970s and 1980s to about $400 million in revenue. ADP rented "time sharing" accounting software to millions of small businesses. Management decided to try a new business model. In addition to software rentals, the company began to handle customer payments and deposits, including paying federal and state tax payments on payrolls processed through its software. This saved small-business owners the hassle of writing all those checks and going to the bank to make pay-roll tax deposits. ADP held the customer's payroll deposits for a few days, earning interest off "the float." An alumnus of our university, Bill, was a top executive at ADP and helped lead this transition to a new business model. We were not surprised to learn that Bill was a math major in college and as his career evolved, he made "the numbers" of ADP work for sustained competitive advantage. This is a skill as impressive as any technology feat. With it, ADP transformed itself from a software company into a financial services juggernaut, and quickly grew from $400 million revenue to $2 billion!

The take-away is clear: Entrepreneurs who can create, launch, and scale up new business models in mature industries can win big!

Repositioning Products as Services

Business model innovation can sometimes be achieved by repositioning products as services or, at least, making products part of an overall set of services. The benefit of services is that they typically have a recurring revenue structure. Products, on the other hand, are one-time pur-chases (unless you can offer plug-ins or add-ons like Apple or consumables like Gillette).

To see products as services in action, consider salesforce.com (http://www.salesforce.com), one of the first ventures to successfully deploy this business model innovation. The revenue structure of the traditional software business model has been to create "products" and license them to customers based on a fee for a particular sized "server" or a much larger enterprise-wide license for all of the customer's servers. Annual maintenance and support fees are added to the initial licensing fee.

Salesforce.com turned this traditional model on its head, providing companies with "lead" management and related customer relationship management (CRM) capabilities. Tens of thou-sands of companies use this software. Our own university, like many others, uses salesforce.com to track candidates to our various MBA programs through the inquiry, application, and enrollment process. Salesforce.com's innovation was to charge *per user* month, tiered into a good, better, best model based on the number of users and the range of capabilities—from basic sales management, to sales process workflow modeling, to customization. (Go to sales force.com to see their current pricing structure. At present, for example, $65 per user per month provides lead tracking, custom dashboards, sales forecasting, and much more.) Customers do not have to buy, maintain, or upgrade their own computers; everything is delivered through a secure Internet "cloud." Salesforce.com has been highly successful. Its current annual revenues have surpassed the $1 billion mark.

In the future, many software companies will find this the preferred option for their clients, and it will challenge the traditional server licensing approaches of traditional giants such as Microsoft and Oracle.

Designing a Win-Win Solution

Another approach to business model innovation is to bake a win-win solution with customers into the model. For example, we once worked with what we initially thought was an account-ing consultancy, the Mitchell Madison Group. We quickly learned, however, that it performed forensic accounting to help large corporations reduce operating expense by reducing costs in printing, temporary labor, purchasing PCs, and renting cars and hotel rooms. Instead of charging the usual consultant day rate, this company shared the risk with clients, taking 20% to 30% of the amount of money found and saved. Fueled by this business model, the partners scaled up their business to 900 professionals and eventual sold their practice for $500 million! All on a business model innovation.

Business model innovation can help the entrepreneur dramatically shorten the sales cycle. A benefit of a "win-win" business model is that it can lessen the up-front risk for prospective customers and therefore shorten the sales cycle. Mitchell Madison Group could approach a CFO of a major corporation without asking for any money up-front and, even better, payment only when the customer saved money. For "enterprise" selling, this can be so very important.

Many software ventures find themselves working 18 months to create a new product, only to find that it takes another nine months or more to actually book sales for enterprise customers. This is why software companies need to raise millions of dollars in early VC rounds to withstand that one- to two-year period of bleeding cash prior to booking revenue. Those days in VC funding are probably over for a while. Shortening the time to first dollar and sales cycle sometimes requires an entirely different approach with customers. Plus, the entrepreneur can keep more of his or her stock by reducing the amount of venture capital raised for startup.

Remember, the entrepreneurial process is fundamentally one of learning with target customers about their problems and how to best solve them, both for the customer and for the entrepreneur. How you charge is just as important as what you sell in the calculus of a venture.

Closing Thoughts on Business Model Innovation

Business model innovation may be the only way to break into entrenched markets and to grab share from existing competitors. Everyone rightly thinks of Dell as a multibillion dollar market leader in personal computing. However, at one point, it too was a startup venture based in a college student's dormitory room. Michael Dell assembled personal computers for fellow students by pulling together inexpensive components in his dorm room and selling them to customers at a lower price because the sale avoided the standard retailer markup. He then morphed this in the Web, challenging existing PC manufacturers whose business model was to manufacture and sell through distribution retail channels. By going direct to consumer through the Web, Dell was able to bring a substantial price discontinuity to the PC market: excellent computers, less expensive than those on the shelf, customized to individual consumer preference through a Website, and shipped direct to the customer.

If you are a corporate entrepreneur, business model innovation can be a key to success but also very hard to explain to your senior management. We wrote a case in the back of this book on an internal corporate venture that did just that— it created a new way of making money leveraging company assets. This is the story of My M&M'S and its custom-printed M&M's candies. The venture has figured out a way to charge ten times as much per pound for printed candies! (Go to http://www.MyMMs.com.) The key to success for the My M&M'S team was to develop a new business model for taking orders directly from consumers through the Web, developing specialized printing machines to print text and pictures on the candies, and forming a partnership with UPS to ship finished product directly to customers. This "make to order" business model, personalized for each customer, was profoundly different than the company's traditional approach of manufacturing tonnes of standard products, shipping these finished goods to large warehouses, and seeing that inventory end up in checkout counters and vending machines around the world.

Many mature companies find themselves desiring adjacent growth into new markets and new use occasions. Executives look toward corporate ventures as a means of developing and launching such ideas. The challenge, however, is that corporate entrepreneurs often have difficulty getting their more traditional corporate executives to fully understand the new business model required to build and scale such exciting new ventures! It takes careful thought, patience, and persistence to sell a senior executive on a business model that is different than the one ingrained in the current thinking of the corporation.

Please, don't give value away for free! Entrepreneurs often make the mistake of creating a next-generation product, system, or service that is a lot better than anything currently in the marketplace, and then charge less for it than those competitors offering inferior products. They think that this is the best way to ramp up sales. The problem is that a great product, system, or service is nothing if it does not also lead to a financially successful company. At some point, sooner rather than later, your venture will have to start generating cash from operations. If you train customers to get a lot and not pay a lot, it is very difficult to get them to switch into a pay-more mode. It is also very difficult to support a flood of new customers in any new venture. We believe it better to get a solid yet constrained initial set of customers and serve them well. Learn what it takes to be a successful enterprise. Then, raise the capital required to scale the business.

Consider EMC, started by the late Dick Egan and his partner, Roger Marino, two alumni of our university. They started selling office furniture to generate cash to fund R&D for the product they really wanted to sell: a large-scale storage system to take on existing systems from IBM. EMC deployed a new architecture—called RAID—that permitted customers to hot-swap added storage arrays to their system. This allowed their systems to be more powerful yet have a lower cost of goods by using more common PC disks than other high-end systems on the market that used rarer 15-inch disks. Egan and Marino could have charged less than IBM, since their cost of goods was less. Instead, they priced their products at a 25% premium over IBM because EMC's RAID systems were 25% faster and more scalable. More than two decades later, EMC remains the market leader in storage.

Resist the allure of mass numbers of customers possible through the Web if it relegates making operating profits from each new customer unlikely for a number of years. Sooner or later, the chickens will come home to roost, and your investors will want to see cash generated from each sale.[2] In fact, a worthy goal is that a business model should seek profitability on the very first sale. Even if you have difficulty achieving this right away, it will provide the mindset and discipline needed for long-term success. It doesn't necessarily have to be cheaper—just better.

---

[2] Facebook is the great counter example. We know that Facebook sounds so attractive to younger would-be entrepreneurs—a company that gives its primary services away and has hundreds of millions of customers. However, be mindful that Facebook's primary revenue stream is an advertising fee per impression, a fee that at the beginning of 2008 was about $7 per 1,000 unique visitors per month, but which today is hovering around $1 per 1,000 unique impressions. With such a seven-fold drop in revenue per unit, any firm faces a tough road. Nonetheless, Microsoft invested $240 million in Facebook for 1.6% of the stock, leading to a $15 billion valuation. More recently, *BusinessWeek* reported a valuation of between $3.75 billion and $4 billion ("Facebook Stock for Sale," August 7, 2008). Facebook announced that it had turned cash flow positive for the first time in September 2009, 5 1/2 years after launch. That, dear readers, combined with massive amounts of venture capital, makes for the ultimate high-wire act!

Reader Exercises

Your Turn—Create a Business Model for Your Venture

Let's go to the template shown in Figure 4.9. It asks you to specify approaches in each of the major dimensions of the business model described in this chapter. Using the template makes this easy. Just follow these steps:

Business Model Dimensions	The Approach for Your Venture	Rationale for That Approach
1 **Revenue Model** Products and services The structure and nature of revenue? The number of distinct revenue streams? Pricing relative to competition? Recurring revenue?		
2 **R&D Model** Build technology or buy? Focus of "value-add" in product/service R&D?		
Production Model Manufacturing—internal or outsourced? Gross margin targets on products and services.		
Go-To-Market Model Channel? Strategy for building awareness Startup approach versus ramp-up approach?		
3 **How do these Drive Financial Performance?** Revenues, gross margins, and net operating margins	**4** **Taken as a Whole, is this Business Model Distinctive Relative to Competitors in the Marketplace?**	

Figure 4.9 Define Your Business Model Template

Think back to the venture you developed in the previous chapter. It identified your (1) target market niche, (2) target customer(s) within which the niche and their primary activities or uses that you will be solving or improving, (3) your products and/or services offerings, and (4) the positioning of those offerings relative to competitors. These should have been summarized in your *venture concept statement*. Take out your completed version of that template and keep it handy for the next steps.

Step 1: Define the Revenue Model

Take out your Venture Concept Template completed for the prior chapter. Now, turn to Figure 4.9. Begin at the top row—the Revenue Model. Describe what you propose to be the structure and nature of your venture's revenues and the rationale for that approach. What is your product–service mix? How many streams of revenue are you shooting for? Will there be recurring revenue? (We hope so!) Can you achieve premium pricing? And, what is your product–service mix for which you will be charging money? As you answer these questions, think beyond the startup phase to a scaled-up version three to five years down the road. You want to design the structure and nature of revenues with that scaled-up business in mind. Map all of this out on a whiteboard, and then fill in the worksheet. For your choices, state your reasoning for that decision (in the second two columns with the arrow labeled as *1*). Show this to your friends or colleagues. See what they think. Are there analogies in the market that help show that your revenue model is in fact feasible? How is it the same, or different, than current players who operate in your chosen market niche?

Step 2: Define the Models for R&D, Production, and Sales

Do the same for your approach to R&D, manufacturing or production (fulfillment for services), and for branding and distribution. Once again, always ask yourself why your approach for each area makes sense and if there are analogies in the marketplace. What is the reasoning for these decisions? Also, we want you to anticipate the learning in Section II of this book by already thinking about the financial implications for the amount of startup capital needed to start your company and get to the moment of actual product or service launch. Be smart about this. If there are suppliers or channel partners with good reputations in your market niche, consider working with them. In the beginning of any venture, your goal should be to minimize fixed costs (Lease office space, do not buy the building!) and instead, make them variable expenses. The less you have to raise, the less stock you have to give up as a founding team. Then, of course, the goal is to provide enough value in your products or services so that you can charge a sufficient price to generate the operating profit needed to grow the business—and potentially, bring some of these external activities *back into* the business as part of a scaled-up business model.

Step 3: Integrate

Take a step back. Consider all of the above steps as a whole. How well do the four rows integrate? This first pass should be in a logical sense. Do the strategies form a cohesive whole? Following the arrow starting at No. 3 on the template, work vertically down the columns, reading your own words and reflect as you do so. Is there a tight fit, or does one piece seem out of alignment with the others? Re-examine your reasoning behind the different approaches and try to make a more cohesive, powerful business model.

Step 4: Financial Outcomes From the Business Model

Next, what do you expect to generate in terms of gross margins for each dollar of revenue, and net or operating margins (before taxes, depreciation, interest, and amortization—for example, any of the "funny business" in corporate accounting)? What do other companies in your same field of business generate in terms of gross and operating profit/EBITDA (earnings before interest, taxes, depreciation, and amortization)? How have the most successful startups in your industries "scaled" in terms of ramping up their revenues over the first five years of business? Beyond this, how do similar firms in your industry charge customers? What is their product–service mix? How and where do they do their R&D and manufacturing? Where can customers buy their products or services? Given the approaches in your current business model, is your venture competitive? How is it better or distinctive relative to competitors? A little digging on the Internet for news stories and product announcements, or a visit to points of sale or with current customers, will help you answer these questions. "I don't know" is not an acceptable answer if you are serious about starting a venture.

Step 5: Internal Corporate Venture Business Model Difference Template

Only for corporate entrepreneurs: If your project is to start a business within a business, then fill out the template in Figure 4.10. Use it to highlight the difference between your venture and the core business of the corporation. Then, highlight differences in the two respective business models, for example, the structure and nature of revenues, and the approaches to R&D, production, and channels. If you have not already done so, read the My M&M'S case in the back of this book.

	Core Business	New Venture
Business Strategy • *Target market* • *Target customers/uses* • *Products/services* • *Competitive positioning* **Business Model** • *Revenue structure and margins* • *R&D approach* • *Production/Supply approach* • *Go-to-market approach*		

Figure 4.10   The Differences Between Internal Corporate Ventures and Core Business Template

*** *** ***

Make no mistake: Steps 1 through 4 can be a lot of work. For you corporate entrepreneurs, Step 5 can be both fun to do and frustrating as you try to sell it to your senior management. You might as well start the process now because without their support, your venture is grounded. Your goal is to find that one or two executive champions who will provide the "air cover" you require and help sell the other senior staff.

As you work the business model template, have a computer handy because this will allow you to check on the Web for competitors and analogous business model situations. Also, this type of work is best done in teams. Working by yourself does not necessarily give you the objectivity and broader experiences required to think deeply and creatively about the business model for your venture. Running your ideas by a trusted outside party is certainly a good idea at this point.

And we also encourage you to organize a show and tell session for your business model with your professor and your classmates. Show your listeners your Venture Concept Template from the last chapter and the Business Model Template from this chapter. The two templates should represent a powerful synergy that is the essence of any new venture. *This is the time to be bold. Speak with conviction.*

## chapter 5

Transforming a Product or Service Idea Into a Product Line and Service Strategy

5

The Purpose of the Chapter

In this chapter, we take your single product, system, or service idea from your venture concept and strategize on how to create a more fully featured product line or family of services that offers choice and variety to the customers in your target market niche. The most important words in this chapter are "good, better, best." It is easy to see how this applies to a product line. It takes more careful thinking to apply the framework to software and services. Nonetheless, experience strongly suggests that offering choice and variety to the customer is necessary for sustained success.

Learning Objectives

- Understand the importance of creating product lines or a range of services with variations for "good, better, best"
- Creating an architecture underneath products, systems, and services as the basis for providing "good, better, best"
- The meaning and importance of modularity for innovation in products, systems, and services
- The role of product and service platforms in a product line or family of services
- The importance of complementary products and services and how to think of them as "plug-ins"

Principles for Success

A new product strategy is the plan for developing and launching specific products, systems, or services for specific uses or applications within a selected set of market segments. For the entrepreneur, this simply means which products, systems, or services will you provide to your target customers today and then tomorrow. As we learned in Chapter 2, understanding customer needs and building these into the core design of your commercial offerings is the foundation stone. Now, we build up this to product lines and families of services.

Our experience suggests eight important principles of defining a new product–service strategy that you must think about from the start:[1]

1. Bring a product *line,* not a single product, to the market. The same goes for customizing systems and services for individual customers.

2. Create an architecture of the product, system, or service that is modular—revealing major parts or subsystems and how these interconnect.

3. Provide variety and choice to customers through a "good, better, best" strategy that builds on the product, system, or service architecture.

4. Consider the platforms within the architecture that can make offerings within the product line or service all the more powerful as well as cost effective.

5. If you are a manufactured products company, strongly consider offering services *in addition to* products. These are also a possible form of recurring revenue from each customer.

6. If you offer software-based systems, figure out how to offer an array of "plug-in" modules that offer variety, choice, and customization for the customer and how to make these easily incorporate into your base system.

7. If you do offer services—financial services, health care, consulting services, systems integration services, and so forth—figure out how to "productize" these services to gain efficiencies in delivery. Also, learn what it takes to provide levels of "good, better, best" in those services.

8. Consider the products and services from other individuals or companies which, when combined with yours, provide a rich portfolio for the target customer. In particular, if you are creating a software venture, develop a strategy to get other third-party developers to create plug-in modules for your solution set, transforming your company into a channel for others.

Now, let's see how to put these principles to work.

---

[1] Meyer, M. H., & Lehnerd, A. P. (1997). *The Power of Product Platforms.* New York: The Free Press.

The Product Portfolio:
The Importance of Choice—
Single Versus Multiple Offerings

Creating robust product portfolios requires deep insight into the needs and behaviors of different customer groups in target markets. The goal is to have each element of the product portfolio bring delight to each specific target customer and his or her intended product or service use along a continuum of performance and price. Portfolio planning should also establish the clear streams of revenue derived from specific product offerings for target market applications. In other words, the product portfolio becomes a revenue map. Getting to a strong portfolio requires the development of *a new product or service strategy*.[2]

Many new entrepreneurs think in terms of a single product with a rich combination of features included in the product at an attractive price. "Let's give the customer a bang for the buck" is the common thought. Based on our work in Chapter 2, however, we know that not all customers in the given market niche are the same in terms of what they need and what they expect in a product or system or service. In other words, not every customer wants a fully featured product. Moreover, in many categories, customers want to be able to customize their product or service with elements of their choice and even of their own making. This makes the single monolithic product, system, or service idea limited. Yes, it was good for our initial planning in Chapter 2, but now we need to do something better and different. *The most successful ventures quickly learn to offer customers choices.*

We take inspiration for designing new product strategy for ventures from a select few large corporations, including Honda, one of our favorite large innovative companies. Employees within the company like to remark that the company tirelessly creates new products to drive its engines, and those engines—fuel efficient and reliable—are deployed as common platforms across different brands and product lines. The company also has a straightforward approach to "good, better, best." In its automotive business, Honda offers passenger sedans, SUVs, pickup trucks, and minivans. Within each category, it then offers different levels of performance, luxury, and price. Different feature bundles and price points usually work best, but keep decision making simple for customers. While it is important to offer variety and choice to customers, one can also over-apply the concept. For example, some car manufacturers have periodically forgotten this lesson, making every feature an additional charge and forcing customers to make a series of stressful price-feature decisions. During the 1990s, we know of one automaker that forced its customers to choose between over a dozen wheel covers and an equal number of steering wheel and floor carpeting choices!

An entrepreneur does not want to make potential customers labor over their purchase decision. Most buying, even for industrial products, has an important element of impulse—supported by good branding. Provide variety but keep it sensible and simple by putting yourself into the shoes of the target end-user and buyer. A great way to do this is by thinking about "good, better, best."

Whether it is a commercial bank, an insurance company, a health care provider, or a retailer, success relies on providing a portfolio of related services that are well positioned for the organization's target customers. For example, we worked with a life insurance company whose primary market niche was selling life insurance for physicians, another whose target was military personnel and their families, and yet another whose target, more generally, was families. Each one of these insurers succeeded by providing a suite of insurance products (term, whole life, variable life, and annuities) whose terms and pricing were finely tuned to the lifestyles and predicted mortality of their respective populations. Health care providers in urban areas provide a full suite of specialty

---

[2] Wheelwright, S., & Clark, K. (1992). *Revolutionizing New Product Development*. New York: The Free Press.

as well as general services and have the populations to support the entire portfolio; rural community hospitals, on the other hand, provide a narrower range of essential services.

Product Line or Service Architecture

The architecture of a product or service defines its key parts and how those parts are connected. It becomes a product line architecture when multiple variations of products adhere to that same design and are modified at certain points to suit market niche requirements. The same goes for services.

A strong, flexible product line architecture allows the engineering team in a venture to create a powerful base-level product, system, or service, and then quickly make variations to certain elements within or surrounding that base-level design for point-specific offerings for different types of customers. Once in production mode, the venture can "turn the crank" on the core elements and have other parts of the business add the variations needed to customize the final result to specific customer needs. This is a recipe for keeping customers happy while operating the business in a highly cost-effective manner.

Figure 5.1 provides a simple yet effective framework for specifying the design of a new product or system. It shows levels of technology, where each level has a specific purpose, and then specific modules within each level. Each of these modules has a predefined function.

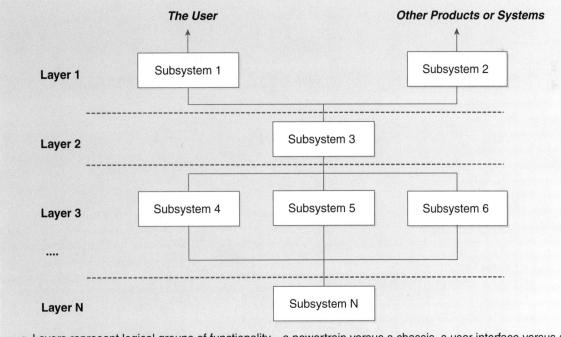

- Layers represent logical groups of functionality—a powertrain versus a chassis, a user interface versus a computation or database access.
- A subsystem can be an electrical component, a motor, a housing or packaging, a software module, and so forth.
- The lines shown connect different subsystems. Good architecture has a limited number of powerful, flexible interfaces between subsystems.

Figure 5.1 Designing a Product or Systems Architecture

Then, there are interfaces defined to link modules within the architecture. This type of approach allows your company to swap in newer, better modules without ruining all the rest. It also allows your company to create different types of products or systems that utilize much of the same core technology. That reuse, together with replacing older modules with newer ones, is a good working definition of modularity. And it applies even to products that on the surface seem "low tech." Packaged food companies, for example, are replacing certain core ingredients (such as preservatives) with healthier ones. Moreover, many of these same firms are eagerly searching for new packaging solutions that are made from recycled materials and are themselves recyclable—while still protecting the food and providing adequate shelf life. None of this is possible without modular product and package design.

Services are best modeled as workflows. Here the modules or subsystems are the major steps within a larger process. As shown in Figure 5.2, each step has a purpose. And with each step, there may easily be a series of substeps. Each step or substep has its inputs and outputs, which tend to be either information or activities. If you are planning to start a services venture, you had best apply that framework in fine detail to learn not only the steps along the way but also the types of information you will need to be effective in each and every step. There is an old saying about services businesses versus product businesses that still rings true. In a product company, you can lose a customer if a competitor beats you on price. However, in a service business, customers tend to be less aggressive shoppers. Once you have the customer trying your services, they typically become wedded to and dependent on them. The only way to lose the customer is through poor execution and failed delivery.

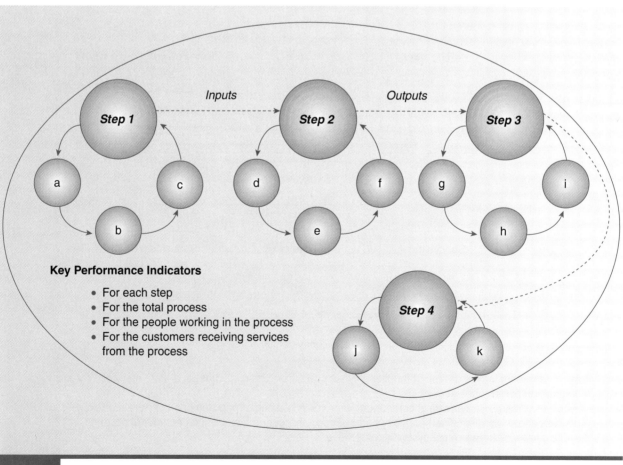

Figure 5.2   Designing a Services Architecture

The Importance of "Good, Better, Best" for a Product or Service Strategy

We recommend that venture teams consider different levels of functionality and price for their product or service portfolios. A modular architecture should be able to accommodate variations at incremental cost.

The terms "good, better, best" have a powerful meaning for customers.[3] If a customer thinks a particular offering is too expensive, he or she can get something less costly with less functionality. On the other hand, if the customer needs more, he or she can have it by paying more. By adding choice and variety, "good, better, best" can increase your sales.

What does "good, better, best" mean for different types of products, systems, or services? Consider these examples:

- *Physical products.* Go to Dell or Lenovo's Website and browse their computer offerings. Each model has basic step-up functions for performance. What is even better about the online channel is that these Websites allow customers to specify the step-up functions they prefer to create personalized products from common components. And only then does Dell or its competitors start the final assembly process and direct-to-consumer delivery. Imagine the inventory carrying costs if Dell had to manufacturer and ship every single possible version of its computers to retailers! Its business model was transformative, and it allowed Dell to bring a price discontinuity to the marketplace.

- *Software.* Many software firms offer "basic" and "premium" versions. Most small businesses in North America today use Intuit's QuickBooks for their bookkeeping. At the time of this writing, Intuit provides three tiers of price-performance: Simple Start for about $100, Pro for about $150, and Premium for about $300. Pro is a major step up over Simple Start, and Premium is a major step up in functionality over Pro. If you have a moment, go to the Intuit Website and see the variations in functionality between these three levels for yourself. The company is a master in its execution of "good, better, best" to provide simplicity and variety to the customer. Other category leaders in software, such as Symantec with its Norton AntiVirus package, have comparable tiers of price-performance, prominently displayed as part of the online purchase process.

- *Services.* Computer support companies offer the equivalent of Bronze, Silver, and Platinum services featuring different levels of support. Car rental companies offer "preferred" customer plans that provide certain guarantees and expedited service. American Express's Platinum and Gold cards are associated with different levels of benefits. The idea is to provide a basic service for most customers and premium offerings for customers who are willing to pay for greater richness in services. Levels of warranty are also commonly used to differentiate levels of service and are priced accordingly.

Defining "Good, Better, Best"

Figure 5.3 shows a method for the entrepreneur to define levels of incremental functionality or additional services to a base-level product or service. The end result is a "good, better, best" suite of commercial offerings that gives customers choice and variety. Take a look at the figure now and jot down some ideas for your own venture.

---

[3] Meyer, M. H., & Lehnerd, A. P. (1997). *The Power of Product Platforms.* New York: The Free Press.

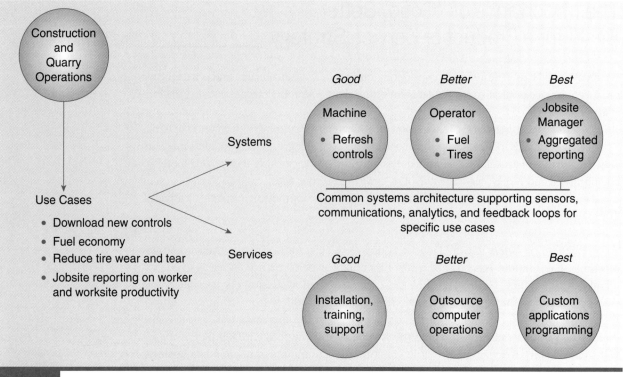

Figure 5.3   Defining "Good, Better, Best" for Monitoring Industrial Equipment

The figure shows the method applied to another monitoring venture. In this case, the venture was an internal initiative within a major corporation to monitor and manage industrial equipment on jobsites. These jobsites include highway and building construction and operating in quarries. The venture concept was GPS-enabled moving equipment such as tractors and trucks and then to monitor operations in a variety of ways. The information and analytics derived from this system could help equipment owners control operations and reward high-performing machine operators for their productivity. The business model was to sell these new features as a subscription service on a machine-by-machine basis—software as a service on computers with wheels!

This vision translates into a "good, better, best" product strategy. The "good" included using satellite communications to download new controller instructions for the machines themselves—automating a manual process. The "better" was to monitor fuel consumption and tire pressure. These data are used to inform the operator of driving habits and the need to inflate tires. You can imagine that large articulated trucks, tractors, and excavators do not get many miles to the gallon of diesel fuel. The "best" was to monitor the productivity of the operators on the jobsite. This would allow construction and quarry managers to pay for performance and retain their best workers. All of this would transform the jobsite in these major industrial worksites from a largely noncontrolled environment to one where all assets and operators were visible in real time.

For services, the team also defined three levels: basic installation, training, and support; outsourcing the running of this system for the customer (construction companies prefer running excavators to computers); and then, custom software programming to tune and tailor the dashboards and reports by industry and application for client companies. This approach allowed the team working on this internal corporate venture to present a rich array of offerings in a way that was simple both for customers and the team/company. The framework also made for an easier sell to the team's senior management.

In practice, companies test these options with customers to gain insight into the prioritization of what comprises "good, better, best" across different segments of customers. Entrepreneurs tend not to have the time or staff to conduct such experiments, but they must have a strategy and then follow carefully the results of market launches and adjust accordingly.

How Offshore Markets Affect Product Design Variety

One of realities and delights of today's venturing is the number of teams that target foreign markets from the very beginning. Twenty years ago, we professors rarely saw this in student business plans. It is now commonplace for both corporate ventures and startups.

Growing interest in offshore markets by intrapreneurs should not be surprising, given that many large companies anticipate that a majority of their sales growth will come from emerging markets. Experience indicates, however, that not all commercial offerings travel well—many companies work to understand and design in the preferences of foreign buyers into their core products and services. The product design and performance needs, price preferences, sales channels, and promotional campaigns that we find appealing in the United States or in Europe may be ill suited to markets such as India, China, Brazil, or South Africa. For example:

- Performance: In shaving, "The best blade a man can get" in North America will actually cause skin burn, in-grown hairs, and blemishes on the skin of the typical African male.

- Price: An Indian male living in a rural community on a dollar per day may stick with his old double-edge blade shaver rather than switch to the more costly cartridge system. His middle-class neighbors, on the other hand, may be attracted to Tata's Nano, an India-manufactured four-seat passenger car of Italian design that gets 52 miles per gallon and retails for about $2,500! Pricing for emerging markets can be an order of magnitude less than standard pricing for traditional mature markets.

- Packaging: Japanese consumers value product packaging far more than do Americans—it must be as stylish and appealing as the product itself. As you think about designing packaging for your own products as an entrepreneur, consider the five senses: the impression made when you first see a product, then when you potentially hear it, then when you touch it, smell it, and finally, if it is food, taste it. Designing for the five senses is an incredibly powerful discipline—for any market.

- Product adaptation: Gerber baby food comes in different varieties in different countries. Vegetable with rabbit is a favorite in Poland; freeze-dried sardines with rice is popular in Japan.

- Promotion adaptation: L'Oreal sells the same product in many countries but with different promotional messages. For example, its Golden Beauty brand of sun-care products is promoted to Northern Europeans as a dark tanning solution, to Latin Europeans as a skin protecting solution, and to Mediterranean Europeans as a beautiful skin solution.

As an entrepreneur, you must understand these differences in consumers and build that insight into your product or service portfolio. Even if your venture develops a so-called "global" product or service, it will have to vary it in terms of packaging and communication. For many years, Honda's best-selling Accord in Japan was the station wagon version; in the United States, it was the sedan. In fact, Honda discontinued its Accord station wagon in 1998 and replaced it with a sports utility vehicle (the CR-V).

Governmental regulations also vary from country to country, as do methods and structures for doing business. For example, U.S. and European companies have had to establish new joint ventures with Chinese affiliates in order to conduct business in China.

Intellectual property protection is another matter that entrepreneurs must contend with when crossing borders. A software venture that plans to do business in emerging markets must understand that a majority of all PC-type software used in countries such as China, Kenya, Russia, or Indonesia is stolen or "shared," depending on your point of view.[4] It seems that the only way for entrepreneurs to be paid for what they do in those regions is to provide their software as a Web-provisioned service, with a low-cost subscription model for end-users and companies.

Perhaps most important, the notion of the price-performance equation for "good, better, best" typically is downshifted when focused on emerging markets. Consumers and companies simply have less money—or if they have it are reluctant to spend it—for products and services. There are always exceptions to the rule. Many Asian countries have urban areas where real estate, retail shopping, information technology, and financial services are on a par in terms of price and performance with Boston, London, or Tokyo. However, the majority of buyers in emerging markets typically expect price levels that can be an order of magnitude less than the prices of products in the same category in developed markets.

Establishing a Beachhead Strategy for Venture Launch

A beachhead is where you get started penetrating the market.[5] This comprises the first one or two years of business. Then, from that success, you can consider expanding to other adjacent areas in the market. By areas, we mean specific market niches, which by our definition in earlier chapters is a specific combination of a customer group and an important use case for those customers. Therefore, to determine your beachhead strategy, you require:

- The target market segment within the industry sector of your choice
- The target customer group in that market segment
- The specific use case or activity set that you have chosen as focus of improvement and innovation, which together with the customer group forms your target market niche
- The specific products, systems, or services that you will deliver to that target market niche
- The definition of what "good, better, best" can mean for those products, systems, and services

The beachhead you select determines the focus for aspects of your business well beyond commercial offerings. It affects how much you can charge, your go-to-market strategies and therefore your marketing expenses, and for some firms, the structure and cost of logistics needed to convert customers' orders into cash. Beachheads are important!

A representation of the merging of your beachhead product strategy—and then your next stage of growth product strategy—is shown in Figure 5.4. In that figure, you can see a representative beachhead in a target market niche and then, an expansion strategy denoted as one every two or three years. This is common for high-growth ventures. Tackle a niche and become a leader; then leverage the technology and marketing channel to penetrate an adjacent niche. Win that and move on to the next adjacent niche. All the work that we did in Chapters 1, 2, and 3 determines the point of focus for your beachhead: the demand in that market niche, your ability

---

[4] International Data Corporation (2008, January). *The Economic Benefits of Reducing PC Software Piracy*. This report is available on the Web. The countries with the lowest piracy rates are the United States, Japan, New Zealand, and Luxembourg, all near 20%. The highest piracy rates are in Armenia, Bangladesh, Georgia, and Zimbabwe, with all more than 90%!

[5] Meyer, M. H., & Lehnerd, A. P. (2007). *The Power of Product Platforms*. New York: The Free Press. See Chapter 3.

to understand and serve the needs of customers, and the competitive intensity in the niche. When you have the ability to grow to another region on the market segmentation grid, you will have to apply the same logic all over again. Except then, it will be a lot easier. First, you should be able to leverage your products, services, and technologies in a much more expeditious way. The same might also apply for the investments you will have already made in branding. If the new niche is truly adjacent to your beachhead, the channels of distribution you have developed might also be leveragable. That is why when once-small companies get on the fast track, their growth accelerates. Many of the uncertainties involved in startup and launch are well behind the entrepreneur. Now, it is a matter of rapid planning and execution to hit adjacent applications and market segments, year by year.

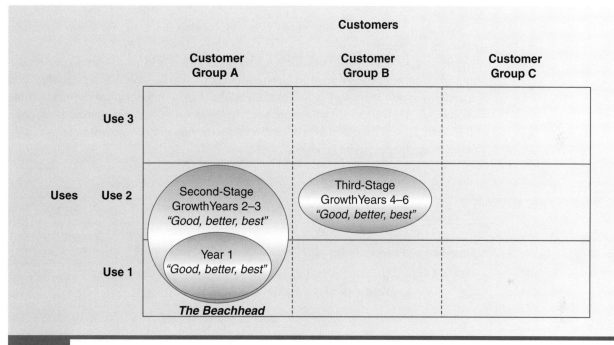

Figure 5.4 Defining Your Beachhead Strategy—and then Next-Stage Growth

A great example of this beachhead strategy applied to technology-intensive services is Kinko's (now part of FedEx). It was a student venture! Founded in 1970 by Paul Orfalea, and named after his own curly red hair, Kinko's got started next to the University of Southern California. (Orfalea was a finance undergraduate student.) With a $5,000 bank loan cosigned by his father, Orfalea set up a Xerox copier stand next to the university and made copies for fellow students and also sold class materials. He then opened up similar student-focused stores on other campuses, forming partnerships with other students. The idea spread across the country. In the 1980s and 1990s, Orfalea then leveraged his idea to the small-business market. He first added Apple computers to allow small-business owners to generate their publications right in the store in addition to copying. He urged small-business owners to use Kinko's as "your branch office" and loaded them up with desktop publishing systems, sophisticated color copiers, laser printers, fax machines, and video-conference technology (for $150 an hour). These small or home-based businesses grew to be a majority of his business. In fact, Orfalea was approaching 1,000 stores in 2004 when FedEx agreed to buy his company for $2.4 billion! Kinko's is truly a case where the entrepreneur was highly customer focused, grew into adjacent markets, and figured out how to scale the business along the way.

A Beachhead and Growth in Software

Here's a concrete example, even if it is in software! It is of a venture—we will call it Highground—that was acquired for over $400 million. One of your authors worked hard to help define the new product strategy. This was an open-systems storage management play—to create a repository to gather from information on storage files and specific data sets across an enterprise's dispersed computer networks. All storage disks were profiled in terms of how much data existed on them and the trends for the amount of data and the frequency of access. This was all highly granular information—perfect in the hands of the nerdy storage administrator who needed visibility across an organization's storage networks. It was also the first commercial software to seamlessly integrate information from across the proprietary storage devices of IBM, EMC, Hitachi, Hewlett-Packard, and Sun. That is why it was referred to as an "open systems" application.

So far, so good. But the company had heavy VC backing and these investors wanted 100% growth year in, year out.

Following the principles of this book, management took a field trip to learn more precisely about who was using the software and *who else* might want to use other outputs possible from the underlying data repository. It first segmented the market by key industry verticals. If you look at Figure 5.5, you can see what these were: financial services, pharmaceutical, health care, and so forth. Most of the business at this stage was in the financial services segment, as was the case for most storage systems vendors.

		Large End-User Customers				OEMs
		Finance	Pharmaceuticals	Health Care	Government	Storage Service Providers
Best	CIO	3	Financial applications such as "chargeback"			4
Better	Computing Managers	2	Storage assets: capacity, bottlenecks, and growth			4
Good	Department Technical Staff	1	Current "sweet spot" Storage/Data locator and administration			4

Figure 5.5   A Product Strategy for an Enterprise Software Company

Then, the team dove deeply into customers and use cases. The first step was to talk to the primary customer's boss—not the nerdy storage administrator but the data processing department chief. The team quickly learned about their latent needs, enough so that we could rapidly build a second product. Across a dozen or so customers, the message came back repeatedly: "Give me advanced warning of when I am going to run out of disk space at any place and on any vendor's system in my enterprise so that I can plan ahead and budget appropriately. Right now, my job is to put out fires and not outspend my IT budget. Help make me look smart!" If you look at the figure, you will see that this became our next target for growth—shown as the number *2* at the end of the bottom left arrow. Think of this as a set of graphs and reports showing trends in various types of storage capacity across the enterprise and projections of new data that would be placed on that capacity. What-ifs could then be performed to see the impact of spending more money on storage assets.

The team gained entry into the offices of CIOs. Very quickly, the discussion turned to a new form of value. The CIOs of these large corporations were under tremendous budget duress even though the end-user departments were requesting greater amounts of computer capacity. (This is still the case.) The CIO had no objective way to charge end-user departments for their storage utilization—a classic latent need. The software team created some algorithms that reported the storage across all devices used by a specific department, set a pro-rated price for that storage utilization based on the overall storage asset utilization, and then generated *a charge statement for the department*. The CIO could also "jigger" charge rates and other aspects of the system. The company called its new module *Chargeback*. Today, major storage software firms have this plug-in. In fact, today's "cloud computing" initiatives have the key benefit of allowing CIOs to chargeback for an increasing variety of shared infrastructure and application services. At the time, however, this module too was an important innovation. It also provided our sales force a good reason to visit CIOs in industry. "Selling up" an organization is always preferable than selling down into its bowels where price always seems to be the order of the day. We show this addition to the firm's growth strategy as the number *3* in Figure 5.5. The venture also started making a play to privately label its software to Managed Service Providers—storage farms—that outsourced companies' computer operations. That is shown as the number *4* in the figure. All the R&D team had to do was add an additional column to the various databases containing "client IDs" so that the data could be sorted and analyzed for each of these service providers' own customers. That database turned out to be a highly flexible, leveragable platform.

More on Modularity

First, what is modularity? Most people think of it strictly in these technical terms. As we discussed earlier, the architecture or design of a product, system, or service should be modular in nature. Within that design, there are different parts or subsystems that connect to one another through predefined interfaces that allow all the elements to work together. For the engineer, this means that he or she can optimize a product execution by selection from a basket of different components to get the best performance for the least cost. Modularity also means that he or she can create new products much more rapidly by making changes at certain levels of the design that appeal directly to the needs of different groups of customers, even within the same use case. Take driving. The Honda Element and the Honda CR-V both share power trains and chassis, yet their interiors and exteriors are richly and finely designed for active male customers on one hand, and adult women with families on the other.

Why is modularity important for the entrepreneur from a business perspective? *Modularity helps you create new streams of revenue.* The entrepreneur can conceive of all sorts of attachments, accessories, and other forms of complementary products to enrich the customer's experience. Be it the ability to download and play iTunes songs on your iPod or PC, or simply to switch between regular tires to snow tires to allow your car to achieve optimal performance in different driving conditions, modularity is good for both the customer and the supplier. The modularity of the iTunes software benefits the music listener as well as the music seller. The modularity of the chassis benefits both the car driver and the tire manufacturer. Alternatively, the entrepreneur can use modularity in the design of his or her products to create a powerful consumables business. That P&G Gillette can continue to feast on the profits generated by its blades is a testament to importance of modularity for any innovator seeking to make a great business out of his or her inventions. If these great companies can do it, *so can you*.

Modularity in Physical Products

One of my favorite examples of an entrepreneurial firm using modularity to create a highly differentiated, multi-element product line is from Korkers Products, LLC, a Portland, Oregon–based company. Both of your authors share a passion for fly-fishing. We have fished in calm streams; in slippery, fast-moving rivers; as well as in the ocean. We have both hiked over mountains to reach remote streams and sledged through the night down beaches in search of bass. Each is a different use case for the fly angler. And for reasons of safety and comfort, each has traditionally required a different type of wading shoe, be it to prevent slippage, to withstand salt water, or of late, to prevent the spread of water-borne parasites from one river to another.

Each of these use cases required at least a different sole: felt-soled for the calm water, metal-studded for the treacherous water, rubber-soled for salt-water beaches, and hiking boots for the treks to remote fishing spots. Moreover, these soles are integral to the shoe. When the felt sole wears out after two or three seasons, the angler must purchase new boots. And for some odd quirk of behavior, the avid angler never seems to throw worn-out boots into the garbage, leading to an ever-growing pile of worn-out useless boots in "man-caves" or mudrooms across the country.

Along comes Korkers, a small, innovative company on the West Coast. It designed a boot with interchangeable soles (See Figure 5.6). In that figure, you can see on the left three different assortments of fishing shoes: boots, sneakers, and sandals. Korkers actually has many more varieties of shoes than those shown here, and you are welcome to visit their Website to see current offerings and prices. We have used all three and find them well suited for different fishing occasions. Fishing boots are standard rugged fare; the sneakers are lighter, more contemporary, and having used them, a wonderful product; and the fishing sandals are great for surf-casting on the beach. In the middle of the figure are the various soles for these three types of shoes. These soles include two standard soles: felt and a rubber lug. In addition, you can see studded felt and studded rubber for slippery conditions. And to help solve the problem of anglers mistakenly

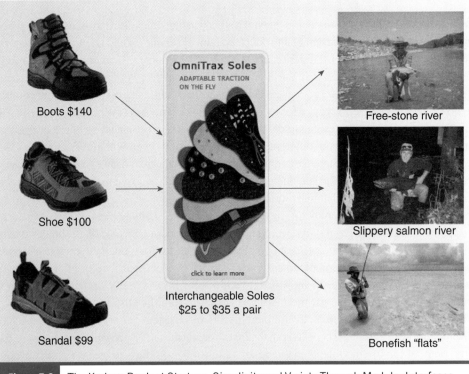

Figure 5.6 The Korkers Product Strategy: Simplicity and Variety Through Modular Interfaces

Source: Portions reproduced with permission of Korkers Products, LLC.

transporting fish-killing parasites from one infected stream to another, Korkers has followed the industry trend by providing its own new sticky rubber sole material called "Kling-On." The little critters do not stick to this material as they do to felt-based materials. Then, on the right side are the specific use case scenarios. (Yes, your authors will do anything to get their fishing pictures printed in a book!) The beauty of the design is that the soles are interchangeable across any of the footwear products, making those footwear products multipurpose for different use cases. This eliminates the need to buy a different set of shoes for fishing in different types of streams or in the ocean.

The key to the Korkers solution is the interface between the front of the sole and the front of the boot, as well as the attachment mechanism on the back of the sole. This interface architecture makes it easy for the customer to switch between different soles. The boots and sneakers are built on rugged shoe lasts making them comfortable on long, overland treks. An angler can walk on roads or trails wearing the rubber soles, and upon reaching the river determine if plain felt or studded felt is required. He or she can then substitute the rubber sole with whichever one is most suited to the conditions. Since the soles weigh very little, they can be carried in one's fishing vest or backpack.

The Korkers design translates into a robust product strategy that serves different niche applications for the angler. It also translates into a business model with recurring revenue and strong margins. The shoe products are durable and last for years. The soles, however, depending on the angler's passion for fishing, may last a season or two at which point they can be replaced for around $30. Moreover, when an angler buys a new pair of shoes, he or she will be tempted to buy and experiment with additional types of soles to match different fishing occasions. Just like Gillette, it is a business modeled where consumables—manufactured at low cost and sold at a high margin—become as important if not more important to operating profitability as the razor handle or fishing shoe itself. This generates extra spending by each customer sold, and it is based on providing value, be it in the form of new sharp blades or application-specific gripping soles for land, boat, or water. Nice stuff, and you should try to do the same.

More generally, the entrepreneur should be able to tell the story about how his or her product architecture translates into a new product strategy and then how that product strategy translates into a business model that generates recurring revenue at high margins.

Modularity in Software

These days, software tends to be highly modular. Not only are there numerous modules that can be connected to one another but these modules are organized into specific layers of technology that have different functions. For example, there are modules for logging and tracking usage in a security layer, other modules for communicating and sharing data over networks, other modules for storing and accessing data, and yet others for executing application-specific logic, and others for generating reports on the screen or on a piece of paper. These layers of functionality, the modules in these layers, and the predefined programming interfaces for connected modules and layers define the architecture of a software product. It is that simple and, at the same time, that complex.[6]

You know that your team has created a modular software design when the overall system can evolve in an organized and efficient manner over time because necessary changes made to any one module are transparent to the other modules that already exist in the architecture. If you don't have modularity, then the code eventually becomes a mess, with all sorts of crazy procedure calls between an ever-growing set of modules. We call this "spaghetti code" because it

---

[6] Want to read an entertaining and spot-on book on the peculiarities of software development for commercial endeavors? Read Arnold Cooper's *The Inmates Are Running the Asylum* (Indianapolis, IN: Sams Publishing, 2004).

looks just like a pile of spaghetti dumped on the kitchen counter, where nothing seems to connect with anything else.[7]

Just as in Korkers shoes, modularity also has clear strategic benefits for a software venture. It allows the entrepreneur to quickly create a family of point-specific solutions that leverage a stack of pre-existing code. That means broader market reach, happier customers, and yes, more revenue. And in software, one of the great things about modularity is that it allows a software venture to transform itself into a channel for other software companies who make their own point-specific application modules and sell them as "plug-ins" for your base-level software.

To see this approach in action, let us consider The MathWorks, a privately held firm that is the leader in the market for mathematical modeling software. The company was founded in 1984 based on the premise that desktop computers would provide a viable platform for numerical computation. Think of this software as a scripting language that allows engineers to create, store, and process vast arrays of numerical matrices and from this, produce all sorts of analyses and simulations. This vision was on target: today, desktop computers are the primary platforms for mathematical modeling in corporations and professional organizations. Core applications are quite nerdy: digital signal processing and the design of sensors and controls used in equipment—such as the antilock braking systems on your car.

Figure 5.7 provides an overview of The MathWorks' software product offerings. The company built its core software engines (MATLAB and Simulink, which are shown as the base products) and then created specific application modules for digital signal processing and the design of industrial controls. Software developers outside the company developed their own specific applications and toolkits on top of MATLAB and Simulink as well. The company then developed

	Digital Signal Processing	Control Design	Test & Measurement	Financial Product Design	Biotechnology
Third Party Plug-ins	• DirectDSP • FUSE Toolbox • GPS Receiver Toolbox • UTRA FDD Blockset **1**	• Code Composer Studio • dSpace Prototyper • Spacecraft Control Toolbox **1**	• Keithley Data Acquisition Boards • Pro/MECHANICA • TekVISA • Acoustic Ideas Toolboxes	• Quantitative Energy Models • RisKontroller • STABLE Toolbox	• Altia Design • Chemometrics Toolbox • GeneX • TrueAllele
MathWorks Plug-ins	• Real-Time Workshop • Digital Sig Proc Blockset • Stateflow Blockset • Stateflow Coder	• Real-Time Workshop • Control System Toolbox • Stateflow Coder	• Wavelet & Statistics Toolbox • Sig Proc Instrument Control Toolbox • Data Acquisition Toolbox	• Financial Derivatives Toolbox • Time Series Toolbox • Optimization Toolbox	• Systems Biology Toolbox
Beachhead Core Business		**2**	**3**	**4**	

Figure 5.7   The MathWorks Product Strategy and Growth

---

[7] Meyer, M. H., & Webb, P. (2005). Modular, layered architecture: The necessary foundation for effective mass customization in software. *International Journal of Mass Customization,* (1:1), 14–36.

a third-party marketing program where it offered to be the Pied Piper for these other programmers. Sure enough, The MathWorks portfolio expanded beyond what it could have developed by itself. This is shown by the number *1* next to the arrows in the figure.

Figure 5.7 also shows the rest of the company's growth strategy.[8] Over the years, we have had a series of brilliant students from The MathWorks. Using the approaches that form the principles of this book, they have taken the company into new market segments—and within each segment, focused on specific customers and uses cases, for example, market niches.

So, for example, one of our students helped lead the company into real-time data collection and analysis (through partnership with instrumentation manufacturers such as Tektronix.) His growth strategy is shown as the number *2* in the figure. One of his peers led the charge to develop models for new types of financial products (such as financial derivatives). This is the number *3* in the figure. The company also started a project to develop mathematical modeling toolkits for bioinformatics, focusing on systems biology. This is number *4* in the chart. And for each of these new segments, the third-party market program came into play. The MathWorks launched into these new markets with highly knowledgeable partners.[9]

Platforms for Products and Services _____

In addition to modularity, we need to consider "platforms" as a core part of any new venture strategy where technology is at play.

Platforms are the "under the hood" recipe for getting specific products out fast and achieving high levels of operating profitability. *A platform is a subsystem, module, or process that is used in more than one product, system, or service.* For example, a product platform might be an engine design used across many car models. In software, it might be a library of graphic interface objects shared across a word processor, a spreadsheet, a database, and a charting program. A platform might also be a common process, such as an underwriting process used across multiple lines of property and casualty insurance.

It takes a lot of careful thinking and effort to create platforms that can readily scale across different products, systems, or services. But the payoff can be substantial. Consider the classic case we described in a book—to no surprise—titled *The Power of Product Platforms.*

Black & Decker revolutionized the manufacturing of power tools by treating motors, armatures, power cords, and switches as product platforms. A picture tells it all. Take a look at Figure 5.8. It shows the single "universal" motor designed to serve the needs of *all* Black & Decker consumer power tools up to 650 watts in power. This motor had a plug-in interface to the rest of the motor assembly, and the entire assembly was designed for automated balancing. Prior to these innovations, the firm had more than 120 different motors for its various consumer power tools; these were attached manually to the motor assembly and balanced through operator-assisted machinery.

---

[8] Meyer, M. H., & Webb, P. (2005). Modular, layered architecture: The necessary foundation for effective mass customization in software. *International Journal of Mass Customization*, (1:1), 14–36.

[9] Beyond this product strategy, The MathWorks' go-to-market approach fascinates us. The CEO has always had a warm spot for universities. Universities and entrepreneurship were in the family blood; the CEO's dad was a famous professor at MIT and a successful software entrepreneur in his own right. The CEO created a go-to-market strategy where engineers and scientists would first learn how to use The MathWorks' software in school under highly favorable academic licensing arrangements. Then, when these same students graduated, they would want to use the same software in their new jobs, but this time, with premium pricing reflecting the superior functionality of the software. This strategy has worked well. Today, The MathWorks enjoys well over a million customers worldwide.

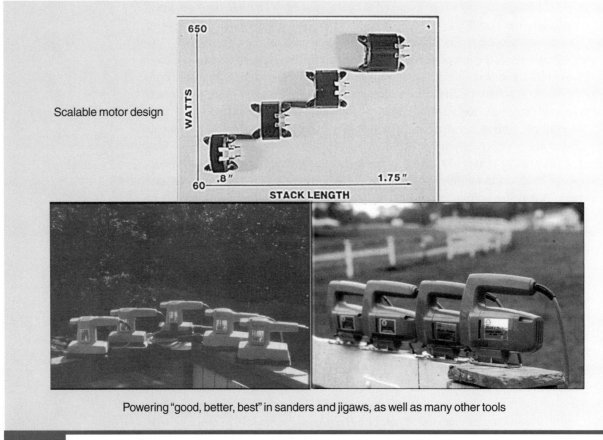

Powering "good, better, best" in sanders and jigaws, as well as many other tools

Figure 5.8   The Motor Platform in Power Tools: The Classic Brilliance of Black & Decker (now owned by Stanley Tools)

Source: Images used with permission of Alvin P. Lehnerd.

Black & Decker's scalable subsystem allowed the manufacture of a wide range of motors through a *single* production process, using the same materials, and the same quality control process. This process and its common, scalable motor assemblies were deployed across all major products: drills, sanders, circular saws, jigsaws, and so forth. And within each product line, Black & Decker cleverly designed "good, better, best" offerings. Moreover, Black & Decker carried the platforming into its high-end tools for builders and carpenters, which come under the DeWalt brand. Even though DeWalt tools are priced at four to five times the price of the consumer tools, "under the hood" much is shared. You can well imagine how that translates into operating profitability through the economies in volume purchases of raw materials and various components. Also, the utilization of capital soars when a company can operate expensive machines at high rates to produce common parts.

The bottom line for the entrepreneur is that platforming can be as important a part of a new product strategy as tackling new adjacent market segments or designing streams of recurring revenue.

Innovation and Platforming in Services

Throughout these first four chapters, we have presented examples of services innovation. Zipcar, iTunes, eBay, or Nokia's location-based advertising are all examples of the new services that reach directly out to consumers. Just like products, the drivers of these service innovations tend to be a fear or frustration in a well-defined customer group—a latent need waiting to be solved. Across different services ventures, we find common themes of providing higher levels of service quality, greater convenience, and in some cases, aggregate and personalized choices for purchase in broad categories of products and services. And of course, low cost has been a design driver for the fastest-growing sectors of the retail/e-tailer industry.

Services innovation also drives ventures providing technology to services industries. We have described a number of software ventures whose purpose is to enable new types of customer-facing services or new business processes within corporations. For example, CRM (customer relationship management) software has transformed the corporate selling processes around the world. Salesforce.com is a major winner that emerged as a venture only a decade ago, and now it has in excess of 60,000 business customers and more than a million end-users. Or, software powerhouses such as Parametric Technology Corporation have developed software that has transformed the product design, engineering, and manufacturing processes in the aerospace, automotive, and industrial sectors. Whenever you see a service innovation in a company or government organization, the chances are that underneath it lies a powerful, new information system that supports the service itself. And it is that information system—the engine under the hood—that can be the focus of a new, dynamic venture.

If you look at what is common across these services innovation opportunities, one clear factor is the design of better workflows. Entrepreneurs hoping to apply technology to improve business processes need to spend substantial amounts of time in the bowels of friendly organizations where they can identify the major steps in a workflow and the interfaces between those steps. Then the entrepreneur thinks about how to best eliminate certain steps that are antiquated or avoidable with automation and more intelligent decision making based on data analysis and situational awareness. The better workflow model that results from this activity becomes a next-generation service.[10]

For example, large drug distribution companies have remodeled processes to prevent fraudulent pharmacy orders for narcotics and other potentially harmful drugs. Or, tire manufacturers have provided retail dealers with Web-based applications to locate a particular tire across an entire supply chain so that it can be delivered quickly to meet a particular customer's need and, yes, generate cash. Entrepreneurial systems development firms are helping these large corporations get the job done.

A common factor within services innovation is the computer technology itself. And while this might appear technical, it is not that hard to understand once you dig into it a little. This is where software modularity comes into play. For services innovation, there is no doubt that the services-oriented architecture espoused by IBM has taken hold across all industries and across computing environments that go well beyond those of IBM itself. A services-oriented architecture simply means that any computer application can be delivered as a service, over the Internet and through a Web browser. In fact, the original program does not even have to sit on a company's own computers. It can be operated from another computer shop over a secure "cloud" network. Moreover, in this new architecture, all programs are modular and are much easier to connect together—or to add new programs and connect them to existing programs. All this spells flexibility and versatility, and the age of large-scale monolithic programs is over. Again, the services entrepreneur needs to invest his or her time to learn about these matters—and only at the level that is needed to create a vision and approach for creating new services or improve business processes for clients. Later on, you can hire the programmers you need to do the actual implementation.

In sum, there is increasing need to interconnect all the disparate elements of operations and activities in society at large corporations and households for the purposes of improved health, energy utilization, security, and asset utilization. This is clearly the future direction of technology to improve services and internal business processes. It will be a world filled with instrumentation, sending signals and data up into powerful servers, where highly intelligent analytics will monitor, adjust, and respond to conditions as needed. IBM calls this "Smarter Planet." We think this presents boundless opportunities to create new IT-enabled service opportunities for technology- and workflow-savvy entrepreneurs.

---

[10] An example of this is how a large health care network in Boston has used computers to reduce the transition of patients from hospitals to outpatient facilities from on average three days down to a single day or less. Imagine hotels.com meets electronic medical records. For your health care entrepreneurs, see: Meyer, M. H., Jekowsky, E., & Crane, F. (2007). Applying platform design to improve case management across the continuum of care. *Managing Service Quality, 17*(1), 23–40.

Reader Exercises

Now it is the time for you to build your own product or service strategy. We have created some simple templates from the examples shown in this chapter. As in prior chapters, use these templates to think about your venture. Take out your Venture Concept Template and your Business Model Template. Bring all your customer and competitor research to the table. Then begin.

Step 1: Define Your Beachhead and Growth Strategy

Figure 5.9 provides the template. Your beachhead is your launch focus in your target industry sector by customer and the customer's use or use case.

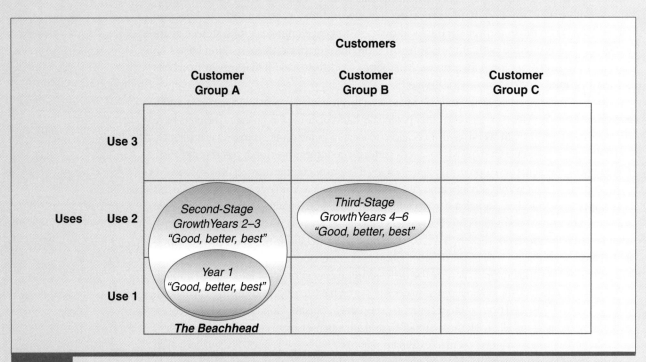

Figure 5.9   The Beachhead and Next-Stage Growth Template

Take the time to write down the clearly different customer groups that you encountered in your field research. We have used age, gender, size of company, type of pet, and other dimensions as customer grouping examples in this book. What are these for your venture? Also, what are the primary use cases? Think of the different types of fishing in our fishing boots example. Or for services, think about the industrial equipment example where downloading machine controls, monitoring tire pressure, and measuring worker productivity were three distinct use cases for large construction and mining companies. What is the analogy for your customers? For certain teams, going to a new offshore market is by itself a new customer group by virtue of the huge differences in customer preferences and buying behaviors in those new markets.

After structuring your template, circle the region on the template that will be your unswerving focus for at least the first two years of your venture. Then, where might you grow for the next stage of growth? What is your reasoning?

Step 2: Define "Good, Better, Best"

This next step is to use the template shown in Figure 5.10 to define your product line or suite of services. Again, all the customer and competitor research you have performed should guide your work. Think about the use cases you have studied. These, too, can drive different types of offerings from your company.

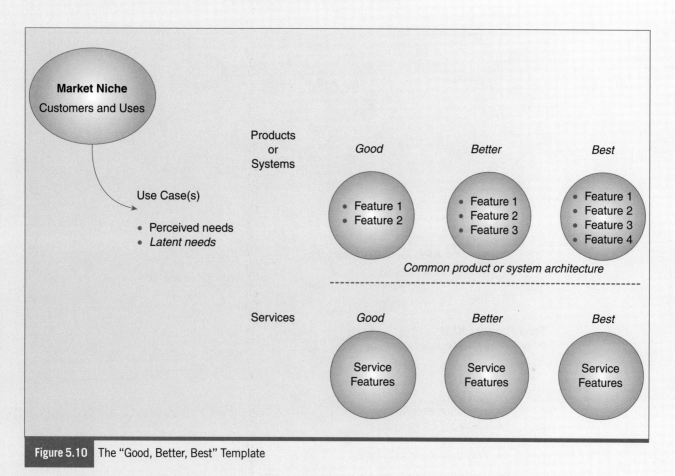

| Figure 5.10 | The "Good, Better, Best" Template |

Then, step back and look at the result. Does the combination of products and services make for a more powerful whole? Lastly, consider the pricing strategy that fits with your "good, better, best" portfolio design.

Step 3: Define an Improved Workflow for Your Customers (optional)

Figure 5.11 shows a template for modeling workflows and identifying needed and unneeded steps. It also shows the metrics or key performance indicators (KPIs) needed to measure efficiency and quality. If you plan to develop a product, system, or service that touches some type of workflow or process within an organization or between organizations, you need to apply this template to the use cases of your typical target customer.

Think of how this template might be applied to the industrial equipment monitoring case. Without the automation, field specialists have to manually insert "cards" into tractors, excavators, and trucks with new machine controls. With the new system, all that labor is completely eliminated: new machine controls download through a wireless connection.

Same goes for the process of checking tire pressure or trying to measure the productivity of workers. Turn on the switch, and these happen without human intervention. The technology makes the process *much simpler and more effective*. Measures (or KPIs) include machine downtime, fuel consumption, and operator productivity.

So if it fits, use this template. It may drive the design of your system or service and be the basis of a compelling sales pitch to your customers.

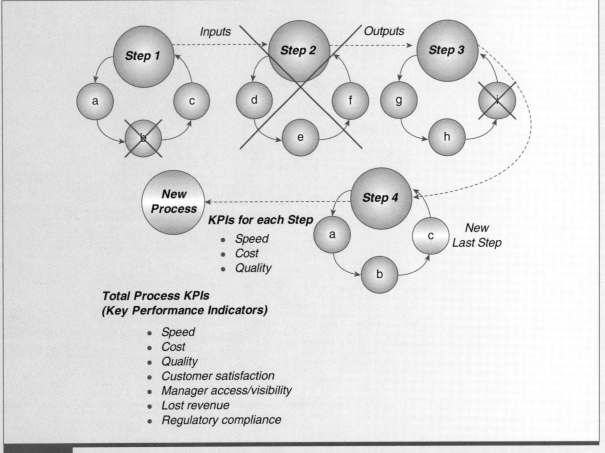

Figure 5.11 The Workflow Redesign and Measurement Template

As you complete the template for your customers, once again, be creative and be bold. Find areas in your customer that need substantial improvement. As always, listen to the user's greatest pain points. Design to those pain points. We have seen many entrepreneurs convince a specific customer to pay for the development of a custom software system to solve these problems. And afterwards, the custom application becomes a prototype that the entrepreneurs take to their venture capitalists for funding, supported with a strong customer testimonial. The system also becomes the basis for a more generalized commercial offering. Bottom line, this template can serve as a powerful tool for your venture. Please take the time to think things through mindful of the context and problems of your target customer.

*** *** ***

As in the prior chapters, it would be foolhardy (and perhaps a little lazy) to design these templates in a vacuum. Show your work to a trusted advisor and then to your professor and your classmates.

chapter 6
Positioning Your Venture
Thinking Deeply About Competitors and Customers

6

The Purpose of the Chapter

In reaching this point in the book, you have achieved a number of important milestones. You have:

- Developed a venture scope and a venture concept that defines your target market niche, target customers, intended products and services, and an initial positioning of your offerings against competitors

- Developed a business model that includes the structure and nature of your revenues, and your approaches for R&D, production, and go-to-market

- Refined your venture concept with an improved understanding of target customers through market segmentation and customer grouping, and developed a more robust product or service strategy based on that understanding—with some element of "good, better, best" to offer choice and variety

This is powerful stuff that must be done *before* writing a single word of a formal business plan. *It is the thinking behind the plan.* This chapter will help you with two final pieces of venture concept fine-tuning: competitive and customer positioning. It will be impossible to do a better job of meeting customer needs than the competition without a thorough understanding of your competitors. In short, you need to determine who your competitors are and how you intend to compete against them. This includes determining your competitive positioning—your ability to compete in your space. For example, how do you measure up on key metrics such as product or service quality and on your costs to deliver on your promised product or service quality? Is it possible for you to be in a winning position? Additionally, you have to think about positioning from the customers' perspective—how do they perceive you in terms of measuring up to the competition? And, does the position you intend to occupy "differentiate you," and is this differentiation valuable and meaningful to the customers you are seeking? In other words, positioning involves competitive positioning (ability to compete—can you win against competitors?) and positioning as perceived by your customers (will they perceive how you intend to compete as a valued and meaningful alternative to the competitors?).

While related, competitive and customer positioning are not the same. For example, competitive positioning often involves a straightforward and objective assessment of your venture's ability to compete on important features and functions that define the market space. It involves measuring the performance of your offerings against those of direct competitors. But, positioning for the customer may be much more subjective and certainly much more "emotional." For example, you might have a better product or service, but you may lack a trusted brand and have no track record. This may lead the customer to stay with a tried and true brand. In short, it is not enough to measure up or outperform competitors from an objective measurement of particular metrics (e.g., quality). The customers must believe you measure up and be willing to select you as their vendor of choice (e.g., perceived quality). Importantly, the customer has to believe that your positioning is relevant, believable, and valuable. In the end, both types of positioning (competitive and customer) are essential for the entrepreneur. This is the last part of the fine-tuning we need to do for your venture concepts before taking them out into the field for the "reality check" described in our next chapter.

Learning Objectives

By the end of this chapter you should be able to:

- Articulate your competitive positioning and your presumed basis for beating competitors
- Explain how target customers will perceive your offerings relative to all possible options for solving their problems or meeting their needs
- Complete templates for positioning your venture relative to both competitors and customers

The Importance of Positioning for New Ventures

If you have taken a formal marketing class, you may have encountered a method called STP, which stands for segmentation, targeting, and positioning. In many ways, we have mirrored this method in the previous chapter—segmenting even the most mature markets for growth, understanding different types of customers within target market niches, identifying the customers for whom our venture represents real value, and fine-tuning our original venture concepts with those insights. We now get to the *P* word—positioning. This, too, can help a venture team improve and sharpen its venture concept.

Let's look at some examples where the notion of how to best compete (position against the competitors) played a significant role in refining or redefining a venture.

A Product Example

A corporate venture team wanted to use new types of proprietary materials in making energy-efficient windows. As its members surveyed all high-efficiency windows on the market, however, they realized that the market included many strong players, all of whom claimed to have the most energy-efficient windows.

On going into the field and directly observing potential customers (home builders), team members realized that energy efficiency was not the only metric that mattered; "ease of installation" was another important consideration for customers. With more observations they learned that all windows on the market required installation *from the outside,* which meant that building crews often had to work from tall ladders or scaffolding—an inefficient and often dangerous situation when multistory dwellings are involved. The team returned to the shop and designed its windows to be easily and quickly installed from *inside* the new structure. For contractors and multifamily housing builders, that design would reduce installation time and labor costs, both important customer metrics. Note that the venture *scope* in this example remained the same; however, the venture concept, and even the business model, changed (selling windows to big-volume builders and renovators).

A Software Example

A student venture team with an interest in energy management created a software prototype that, when installed in a commercial building, could monitor the energy consumption of major appliances and utilities—HVAC units, data processing shops, lighting, and so forth. Their professors were enthusiastic. Market research revealed that several major companies, including Honeywell and Schneider Electric, were already offering server-based energy management software that promised to shut off lighting and adjust heating and cooling as needed, for example, at certain times of the day. Even with much better technology, the student venture would have trouble competing with these industry giants.

Rather than give up, the team adjusted its aim to pursue a market niche where competition would be less intense. Research forecasted that most new construction during the coming ten years would take place in emerging markets. Further, most buildings in China, India, South America, and Africa would be much smaller and have far less expensive heating and lighting systems than their North American counterparts. The team agreed that this different building context would create the need for a new, low-cost, small building energy management system. This positioning exercise completely changed the students' venture concept and business model.

A New Drug Example

A pharmaceutical research team was working on a cancer therapy that would target cancer cells much more accurately than existing drugs. The new drug would be at least as effective but, because of its targeting capabilities, would have fewer side effects, allowing patients to carry on their lives with fewer disruptions. Therapeutic effectiveness coupled with reduced side effects was seen as a powerful positioning statement. The team also believed that its cell targeting therapy would command a premium price.

As these examples indicate, positioning can have a profound impact on the venture concept and its associated business model. Being able to measure how your product or service will compete is essential to positioning. How does your venture concept measure up on key metrics such as quality, cost to the buyer, easy of use, or effectiveness? Are you positioned to win on the competitive battlefield?

Positioning Against Direct Competitors _____

Most markets can be described in terms of a *competition continuum* like the one shown in Figure 6.1. A new venture must position itself against direct competitors in this continuum.[1]

	Low/No Cost	Moderate Cost	High Cost
Product (Drinks)	Generic tap water	"Product" Bottled water Iced tea	"Branded" Veryfine V8 Energy drinks
Systems (Productivity Suites)	Google Apps	Star Office	Microsoft Office
Services	Do-it-yourself w/tax software	H&R Block	Accounting firms

Figure 6.1 | The Competition Continuum

Suppose, for example, that you intend to enter the beverage industry with an all-natural bottled blueberry drink. In the continuum of competition, you would encounter "generic" rivals; a customer might simply go to his or her household tap for a thirst-quenching drink of water. Next there would be "product competition." In the beverage category these would include bottled water, tea, or beer. Finally, your most direct form of competition would be "branded" rivals—products similar to yours, including V-8, branded bottled fruit juices, and a variety of new "energy drinks" of water mixed with natural ingredients. Your all-natural bottled blueberry drink would fit into this last category—and from here you can look at price, taste, and claims with respect to health benefits.

TIP: DON'T IGNORE COMPETING ALTERNATIVES _____

When we think about positioning, we naturally think about direct competitors and the concrete measures that customers could use to evaluate their products and services. However, direct competitors do not always represent the universe of possibilities available to customers. They may see alternative solutions outside that circle. For example, the hourly car rental service, Zipcar had to position itself against not only car rental companies but against personal car ownership and public transportation. Lower cost, convenience, and the concept of sharing came to bear as positioning statements.

What alternative solutions do targeted customers have to the offerings you propose in your venture concept statement?

[1] Crane, F. G. (2010). *Marketing for Entrepreneurs.* Thousand Oaks, CA: Sage.

Redefining a market with a new dimension of functionality creates open running space for the startup or corporate entrepreneur. The importance of creating a distinct positioning against current competitors cannot be overstated. For example, "cloud computing" is reshaping the software industry. Traditional software programs that have run directly from code residing on a computer are being transformed into "services" delivered through Web browsers on any device, delivered from central servers, and metered to enable new "chargeback" business models—just like water or electricity. Cloud is so transformative that some would rightly argue that it becomes a new axis on a competitive position map across the universe of software products and services. It will enable innovative entrepreneurs to make new fortunes and place traditional market leaders in certain categories of software obsolete.

The need for competitive positioning extends to traditional services as well. The service example in Figure 6.1 is tax preparation. Its competitive continuum extends from "do it yourself" to H&R Block, which charges about $100 for a 1040 return, to the typical accounting firm that charges more than $500 for anything but the simplest returns.

To position yourself effectively, you must identify and monitor all competitors who target your intended customer base. This includes determining the number, size, strengths, weaknesses, and behaviors of those competitors. It also includes how similar their products are to yours. However, because you do not have the time or resources to conduct detailed analysis of every single competitor, you must find a way to identify the most relevant rivals. You must also determine the optimal advantage upon which to compete, and then employ it to effectively position your venture.

Competitive Intelligence

Understanding the competition begins with intelligence work. Competitive intelligence is the process of legally and ethically collecting data on potential competitors, including their products, services, channels, pricing, branding, and market communications activities. There are plenty of quick and inexpensive ways to gather such information. Here are a few of your options:

1. **Competitors' Websites.** Most company Websites have substantial information about the management team, product or service offerings, and how these companies are funded. Look for recent press releases and announcements.

2. **Websites that contain financial information and news stories.** These include Yahoo!Finance (for publicly traded companies), Hoover's (http://www.hoovers.com), and Morningstar Document Research.

TIP: SMALL, PRIVATE COMPETITORS

Many of you will create ventures for which direct competitors are, or will include, small private companies. The fact that they are private will make gathering information about them more difficult—particularly financial information. In such cases, make an effort to understand the relative sizes of these firms (e.g., Firm A is two times the size of Firm B). Estimate the number of their employees and customers. Ask customers, "Which of these small companies is the market or niche leader?"

3. **Competitors' customers and suppliers.** Your competitors' customers can speak with authority about the strength and weaknesses of those competitors' products and services, the qualities of their sales forces, and the channels they use for distribution. Ask customers and suppliers what the competition does well and poorly.

4. **Go into the marketplace and see where and how your competitors' products are bought and sold.**

5. **Ask directly.** As crazy as it sounds, you can sometimes talk directly to your competitors. Tradeshows and conferences are two typical opportunities to "talk shop" with these rivals. If a tradeshow has an exhibit area, chances are that all major competitors and many customers will be there. Be bold—go into vendor booths, ask about what they do. Try to find out where you might fit in and the dimensions on which you will have to compete.

You must treat competitive intelligence gathering as a continuous process. And remain vigilant about competitive activities as you grow the venture.

Competitive Analysis

With competitive intelligence in hand, you must now begin the process of competitive analysis, which, like competitive intelligence gathering should be an ongoing process. This process should examine competitors' revenues, profits, market shares, marketing expenditures, product or service portfolios, and other market-related and operating performance statistics. Figure 6.2 contains a template in which a company has summarized its analysis of direct competitors.

Assessing Your Competitive Position

The outgrowth of your competitive analysis is an assessment of your competitive position—examining your potential venture's ability to occupy a competitive position compared to key competitors that will allow you to win business. This will require you to drill deeply and to assess several dimensions of competitiveness. The goal is to discover your competitive position

Operating Factors	Competitor A	Competitor B	Competitor C	Advantage
Revenue	$100 million	$75 million	$50 million	Competitor A
Return on Assets	13.0%	8.0%	10.0%	Competitor A
Sales Growth	10.0%	12.0%	15.0%	Competitor C
Operating Profit	15%	12.5%	18%	Competitor C
Marketing Factors				
Market Share	25%	18%	12%	Competitive A
Marketing Budget (% of Sales)	10%	8%	5%	Competitor C
Sales per Employee	$2.5 million	$1.7 million	$2.8 million	Competitor C

Figure 6.2 A Template With an Example of Performing Competitive Analysis

relative to your most direct and key competitors. The thorough approach to understanding competitive position is to compare your venture to two or three other competitors according to:

- Relative price
- Product/service performance
- Product/service quality
- Market coverage
- Sales force quality
- Marketing "spend"
- Manufacturing costs
- Operating costs

For your venture, these are all "planned" phenomenon—what you intend to do. For competitors, these are based on talking to prospective customers who use competitors' products and services, and for publicly traded companies, analysis of their financial statements.

With these key metrics you can make a determination of how your proposed product or service strategy, together with the business model, yield a competitive positioning. Don't expect it to be positive on every dimension. Planning to be the best at everything—quality, low price, and lowest operating costs—usually turns out to be very unrealistic. At the same time, you must be superior in one or more of these dimensions in order to thrive.

Competitive Advantage

The competitive advantage of a venture is a distinctive factor that gives it a clearly superior or favorable position relative to its competitors. Importantly, a competitive advantage must be valuable and meaningful to the target segment and not easily copied by competitors. In general, your venture can pursue a few broad choices when it comes to competitive advantage: cost advantage or noncost-differentiation advantage.

If you have a cost advantage it means you have significantly lower costs and can occupy the low-cost position compared to competitors. This means you have lower variable costs, lower marketing costs, or lower operating costs. With low variable costs, you are able to achieve the same or better unit margin at lower prices compared to your competitors. Those variable costs can include manufacturing costs, distribution costs, or transaction costs. To achieve lower variable costs, volume is a critical factor. On the other hand, you may be able to leverage lower marketing costs. If, for example, you have a family of products, your salespeople can reach customers with more products to sell to the same customers and achieve a marketing cost advantage. Finally, lower operating costs compared to competitors can provide a low-cost advantage.

While it is important to control costs, you may not be able to realize a cost advantage. Thus, you may have to turn to a noncost-differentiation advantage. This differentiation advantage can be in the form of a superior product, service, brand, channel, or sales force. For example, you might be able to leverage a superior product advantage such as reliability, durability, technical performance such as speed, or conformance to a customer's specifications. Or, you might be able to use service as a differentiation advantage. Differentiating on service requires that the differentiation be on a particular dimension of service deemed important to the customer such as responsive customer service. An increasingly important differential advantage for new ventures is branding. While players in a particular competitive arena may be able to "objectively" obtain parity with one another on product or service, the brand as perceived by the customer may create the differentiation. For example, many watchmakers believe they can match the product quality of a Rolex watch, but they cannot match Rolex's brand advantage.

It is also possible for your venture to achieve *a channel advantage*. Experienced entrepreneurs fully appreciate that excellence in channel is as important, *if not more important*, than excellence in product or service. And the mistake that young entrepreneurs often make is to leave the development of a robust channel strategy as an afterthought behind R&D and early, opportunistic sales.

Channel excellence can be achieved in many ways. For many entrepreneurs, it is to create a dynamic e-commerce portal that is engaging, easy to use, and supported by backend analytics to create a "single view" of customers needed for promotions and service. In more traditional channels, securing the high-quality distributors or dealers for your products is essential. For example, let's assume you will use channel members to distribute your product. If you can lock up high-performing channel members, it lends credibility and most often a better presentation of your product to customers. This leads to channel advantage. Or, another possible advantage is differentiation by having a superior direct sales force. In many B2B markets, a sales force is required in order to close business. Large companies achieve sales advantage by placing a large sales force in the field. But, for the entrepreneur who typically is resource constrained and cannot quickly build a large sales force, the only path forward is to be highly selective about each and every salesperson hired. They should have substantial industry experience, a track record of success, and the ability to attract other sales professionals to your company as it grows. And, perhaps most important, they need to be both fearless selling against industry giants and, at the same time, know how to ally with other industry leaders to gain a foothold in the market.

Most companies in this day and age employ multiple channels: one physical and the other, Web based. The driver of channel excellence here is to create a seamless integration and overall experience between the two for customers. Look no further than Staples for a great learning example. The "Easy" theme stretches across both its retail stores and its Website. The two channels share customer and product databases and there are Web kiosks in retail stores to provide access to the thousands of additional SKUs for which there is no room on the shelf in retail stores. The consumer can indicate home/office delivery—or store pickup—from either channel depending on preference. With this focus on channel excellence, Staples.com has grown to be the No. 2 e-Commerce site on the Web in terms of dollar value, second only to Amazon. Channel integration—and the avoidance of channel conflict—is essential for a superior go-to-market strategy.

Using a Perceptual Map to Examine Competitive Positioning

A *perceptual map* for competitive positioning helps to reveal a venture's points of differentiation. It can help you to determine (1) which rivals you will compete against in a particular market segment or niche and (2) your competitive position relative to other players in attracting customers in that segment or niche. A traditional perceptual map for competitive positioning has two dimensions: performance and price. These dimensions can be objectively measured using information found in specification sheets and price lists. Consider these examples.

A Manufactured Product

A venture team wanted to create a new convertible sports car. It used Edmunds.com (http://www.edmunds.com) to gather the retail price and acceleration performance information needed to position competing vehicles in the map shown at the top left quadrant of Figure 6.3. The best power train experts were then hired to design an engine with incredible performance.

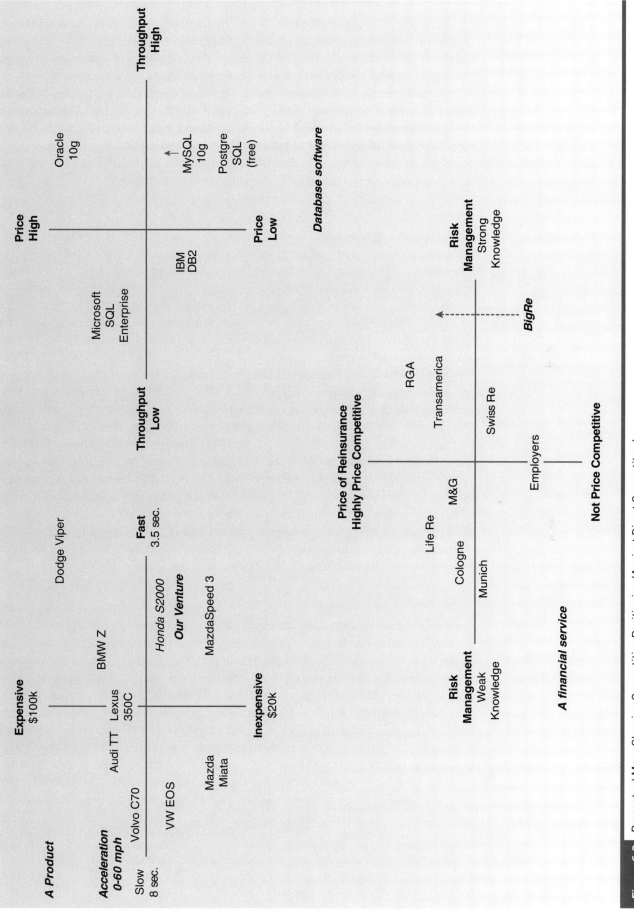

A Product

Expensive $100k

Acceleration 0-60 mph

Slow 8 sec.

Volvo C70 | Audi TT | Lexus 350C | BMW Z

Dodge Viper

VW EOS

Honda S2000
Our Venture

MazdaSpeed 3

Fast 3.5 sec.

Mazda Miata

Inexpensive $20k

Database software

Price High

Microsoft SQL Enterprise

IBM DB2

Oracle 10g

MySQL 10g

Postgre SQL (free)

Price Low

Throughput Low — Throughput High

A financial service

Price of Reinsurance
Highly Price Competitive

Risk Management
Weak Knowledge

Life Re

Cologne | M&G

Munich

RGA

Transamerica

Swiss Re

Employers

Risk Management
Strong Knowledge

BigRe

Not Price Competitive

Figure 6.3 Perceptual Maps Showing Competitive Positioning (Against Direct Competitors)

137

Learning that one outstanding vehicle—the Honda S2000—was being discontinued, team members wonder if its disappearance would open space in the market for a reasonably priced, fast sports car: a vehicle with the performance of a z4 at the price of a Miata. Sure enough, research showed that a gap existed, as shown in the lower left quadrant of Figure 6.3.

The same exercise could be performed for a hybrid car venture, using miles per gallon instead of acceleration as one of the key dimensions. In that case, our mapping would show that Toyota's Prius is a higher priced, higher mileage hybrid, relative to Honda's Insight, which is about $8,000 less but not quite as fuel efficient. We would also notice a third dimension: Toyota is pushing the interior features and comfort of its hybrid in addition to fuel economy, while Honda's hybrids are seeking to differentiate by delivering more "fun to drive."

Software

A team of skillful programmers aimed to create a new relational database management system that was as fast as any other database product then on the market, but which would reduce costs for end-users. Current competitors charged an annual server license fee of $10,000. The team's business model took a different approach, proposing a $10 per month per user subscription fee.

To create a perceptual positioning map, team members went to the Web for "benchmarks" on all four major competing systems. The relevant benchmarks measured the time required to access a single record in a large database file or to "join" two large tables on an indexed key. The licensing costs for customers of these products were also found. From these data, the team then worked to define its own open "white space" in the market. An example of such a direct competitor mapping is also provided in Figure 6.3. The map shows the number of read/write database transactions per second for a simulated e-commerce application (throughput) and the licensing price per CPU (central processing unit) with unlimited users. These two metrics formed the two dimensions of the positioning map found in the upper-right of Figure 6.3. Each of the current large competitors was fitted to the map, revealing many "white spaces" in which the venture might position itself. Note that one of them, MySQL, had traditional been not only "fast" but "free" as open-source software. But then Oracle purchased MySQL (through its purchase of Sun Microsystems) and many developers quickly came to suspect that the party was over since Oracle is the 800-pound gorilla in the market. PostgreSQL, a high-performance derivative of the Ingres database management system that originated out of the University of California at Berkeley, seems to have taken up the high-performance, open-source mantle.[2]

Services

Perceptual mapping can be applied with equal utility to service ventures. A corporate venture team in a large financial services firm set about creating a new "reinsurance" service for life insurance companies. (Note: *Reinsurance* is purchased by insurance companies to protect themselves against the risk of loss on policies they themselves issue—insurance for insurers.) Rather than charge a certain amount of money to reinsure each individual policy, the venture team decided to help insurance companies create profitable policies for less expensive "term" insurance. Because its parent company had deep risk management expertise, the team knew that it could design attractive yet profitable "cheap" term insurance policies. Rather than reinsure individual amounts, coverage would be provided for aggregated blocks of insurance policies, thus lowering the price per policy reinsured.

Figure 6.3 shows this venture's positioning (disguised here as "BigRe") relative to its direct competitors. The arrow indicates how the venture sought to move BigRe into the price competitive quadrant.[3]

---

[2] Sources: http://www.jonahharris.com/osdb/mysql/mysql-performance-whitepaper.pdf which compares IBM DB2, MySQL, Microsoft SQL Server, and Oracle 10g in terms of e-commerce read/write transactions per second for 1,000 simultaneous users; and Web searches for pricing at the time of this writing.

[3] Meyer, M. H., & DeTore, A. (2001). Creating platform-based approaches to new services development. *Journal of Product Innovation Management, 18,* 188–204.

These examples have been fairly simple. However, more complexity can be introduced. Sometimes, by considering a larger list of product/service capabilities and features, an aggregate score can be created. For the automobile example above, this might be accomplished through a broader definition of "driving performance," to include acceleration, braking, handling on curves, and so on. For the database example, a composite measure might include the size of databases handled, the number of indexes allowed, security provisions, as well as transaction speed.[4] For services, "total service" capability often includes timeliness and quality of customer service in addition to price.

Customer Positioning: Again, Find the White Space _____

Understanding the competitive positioning of a venture (your ability to compete) is a fundamental part of the entrepreneur's job. We have approached positioning thus far in terms of "hard," objective metrics such as price and performance relative to direct competitors. Let's now consider positioning in terms of "soft," more subjective, even emotional measures important to the customer when purchasing products or services. We call this customer positioning. A venture team must consider both "hard" and "soft" metrics when determining its positioning in the market.

Customer positioning aims to find out how a venture concept can be valuable and meaningful in the hearts and minds of target customers. To do this, you must abandon the notion that customers base their purchase decisions solely on *features, functions, and price*. Yes, having the right feature set, functionality, and price are important. These appeal to the rational side of buyer behavior. Too few of the right features and functionality will cause customers to pass over your offer; too high of a price will scare many away. But, customers must also "feel good" about the products and services they buy. "Feeling good" can take many forms: the socially conscious consumer's satisfaction in driving a 60 mpg hybrid car or the sense of security that an IT manager feels in buying from IBM instead of from a tiny startup ("No one around here ever got fired for choosing IBM!").

What does "feel good" mean for your venture concept and its intended customers? If you can do this well, you will have entered the realm of branding. A well-positioned and branded startup or corporate venture can literally take the market by storm.

Customer perceptions and emotions can play important roles in buying decisions—even for high tech products. Many successful software companies, for example, make specialized "turn-key" systems for particular industries—such as a point-of-sale system for retailers, or a real-time process control system for chemical and beverage manufacturers. The customer positioning associated with the most successful of these niche players is the perception that their software is developed by people "who know your industry" as opposed to a bunch of smart kids from a technical university who throw software together with no concept of business process and measurements, be it in retail or manufacturing.

This thinking can be generalized into another type of perceptual map, one that captures customer perceptions of direct competitors as well as other possible solutions to meet their needs. To construct such a perceptual map, the following information is needed:

1. The important attributes that customers consider when making a purchase decision

2. Customer judgments in terms of how well competing brands deliver on those important attributes

---

[4] See "Comparison of Relational Database Management Systems" at Wikipedia.com for a list of features and functions for a variety of database offerings. A composite score could be made for each major product from such a list.

3. Customer understanding of what would constitute an "ideal" offering.[5] As with perceptual maps used for competitive position, customer positioning maps typically have just two axes, each representing a key dimension for products and services of a general category as *perceived by customers*. Customer perceptions may be based on rational, objective decisions or evaluations, but in most cases, they are strongly influenced by emotion and brand association.

Typically, to construct a customer perceptual map you have to engage the customer and have them build this map, including determining which dimensions should be measured on the map: where they would locate the "ideal offering" on the map; where they would locate competitors on the map; and, importantly, where would they locate your venture and its offerings. In general, it is better to work with customers in a one-to-one situation. You will continue to sample your customers until a clear picture emerges that reveals a perceptual map that captures the customer reality of all the offerings in your specific space, including your proposed offering.

For example, for our blueberry drink example mentioned earlier, the dimensions could be high nutrition/low nutrition and all-natural/artificial (Figure 6.4).

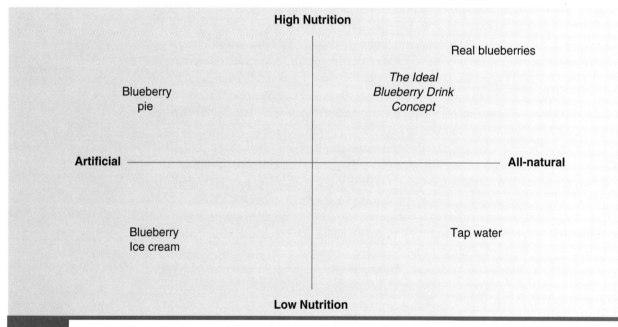

Figure 6.4　Perceptual Map—The Customer's Perspective for an All-Natural Blueberry Drink

Perhaps the best example of creative customer positioning that has led to a branding and product positioning strategy is the perceptual map of the My M&M'S®, the custom-printed candy business created by an internal venture team at Mars, Inc.[6] Figure 6.5 is the perceptual map for that business (http://www.mymms.com). Clever entrepreneurs sometimes add an axis to the perceptual map *that no one else has explicitly used before for competitive positioning*. In the case of the custom-printed candies, the corporate venture team developed two axes that were totally *different from those used* within the company with respect to developing strategy for gifting products and services. One of those axes represented volume: from "mass produced"

[5] Crane, F. G., Kerin, R., Hartley, S., & Rudelius, W. (2008). *Marketing* (7th Canadian edition). Toronto: McGraw-Hill Ryerson.

[6] See Chapter 10 in Marc H. Meyer's, *The Fast Path to Corporate Growth* (New York: Oxford University Press, 2007).

to "personalized." The second axis represented the emotional connection to the offering, along a spectrum of "serious" to "fun." By characterizing the market with these two dimensions, the My M&M'S team was able to create white space for itself, occupying the upper-right-hand quadrant—the intersection of personalized and fun. Note that Disney (in the lower right quadrant) is fun but clearly mass produced, just as traditional M&M candies at checkout counters around the world are both "fun" and "mass produced."

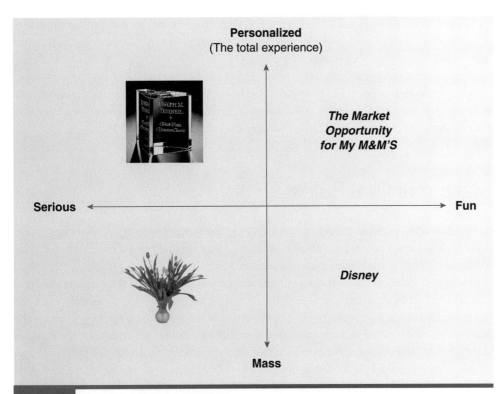

Figure 6.5 | Perceptual Map for My M&M'S

Gift products such as Stueben Glass can indeed be personalized but are also clearly "serious." 1-800-Flowers is mass produced and used for more serious gifting occasions. My M&M'S created a unique market space for itself by focusing its branding and product on fun, personalized gifting.

In the My M&M'S case, the perceptual map is a customer positioning because it is looking at products and services outside of directly competitive chocolate gifting. Note further that while most entrepreneurs use performance and price in their mapping, the My M&M'S team redefined performance as "serious" to "fun," and used "personalized" versus "mass produced" as surrogates for price. My M&M'S was going to sell for a lot more money per pound than traditional M&Ms because of the competitive differentiation of "fun" and "personalized." Soon, the personalized product was selling for a ten-times premium over the mass candy product.

A perceptual map crafted by your customers will also reveal how similar or dissimilar customers judge competitors to be. This is important since, for example, if two competitors are perceived to be very similar, customers might switch from one to the other. A perceptual map will also reveal how close a given competitor is to the "ideal" offering. Or, importantly, how closely your offering is to the ideal offering.

On the other hand, a perceptual map may reveal no available white space. In other words, it may show that competitors currently occupy all the valuable landscape. This should not necessarily deter the entrepreneur since a superior offering can dislodge an existing competitor and take over its space. This is referred to as "repositioning the competition." Here is a good example of repositioning in practice.

Gillette developed a long-lasting battery called Duracell. When Duracell developed its long-life alkaline battery, it created a lucrative new battery category or segment with margins three times greater than the regular battery category. Duracell held this valuable market space for over a decade. Its rival, Eveready, decided to compete head-to-head with Duracell with its new long-life battery called "Energizer." To dislodge Duracell and take over that valuable space, Eveready had to convince customers that its batteries lasted longer than Duracell's. It did so through a very effective marketing campaign featuring the famous "Energizer Bunny." Duracell lost its positioning to Energizer and has been unable to regain it.

Remember, perceptual mapping is a technique used to capture *customer perceptions* of competing products or services. What you hope to find is that customers perceive your offering as being as close as possible to the "ideal" offering. In addition, you want customers to perceive clear differences between your offering and those of competitors.

Make Your Own Rules

As the My M&M'S example indicates, changing how customers perceive a market can turn the rules of the game to your own advantage—by having your venture being the only game in town to fill a new "white space" defined within a market.

In the end, doing a better job of meeting customers' needs requires a deep understanding of competitors and their positioning. One of the two biggest mistakes made by aspiring entrepreneurs is underestimating the extent of competition he or she will face on entering a market and failing to plan for how the venture will compete successfully. The other mistake is failing to consider possible competitor responses to their own market entries, a matter we will get to shortly.

Smart entrepreneurs do not allow their rivals to define the competitive landscape and establish rules of the game. Consider the example of Farrington's Farm Shop, an independent United Kingdom retail store located between Bath and Wells. Farrington's competes against food giant Tesco, which has one of its supermarkets located just down the road. Both offer many of the same things: meat, milk, bananas, carrots, cheese, jam, bread, easy parking, loyalty cards, and a café. If you ask Farrington's how their prices compare to Tesco's, they do not know. Moreover, Farrington's does not send in mystery shoppers to find out and does not subscribe to retail data that would tell them. They do not know Tesco's prices at a granular level, because Tesco's is not seen as a direct competitor.

The founders of Farrington's have beaten all their revenue projections and won awards because they don't compete on price. They compete on delivering a unique shopping experience. From the baby barn where customers see and touch calves, lambs, guinea pigs, and rabbits to the milking parlor where children can see where milk comes from, Farrington's is not about price—it is all about the "shopping experience." And Tesco cannot compete on that unique dimension.

Farrington's knew that if it tried to compete with Tesco on price, it would be slaughtered. So, instead, it defined it own market—wrote its own rules—and pursued its game plan with passion and intelligence. Instead of playing the competitor's game, Farrington's chose its own rules to compete by offering something different to customers. An enterprise that does this can spend less time worrying about competitors and more time focusing on its customers! This type of thinking keeps quality businesses such as Farrington's alive and well![7] The secret, of course, is to understand what customers value and *are willing to pay for.*

---

[7] Heffernan, M. (2004, March). Country competition. *Real Business Magazine,* 18.

Be Prepared for a Competitive Response

In many cases, your competitors are not going to welcome you warmly into their arena. In fact, they may try to prevent your entry, and if that does not work they may try to crush you and put you out of business. In an attempt to keep you out of the market, a competitor may utilize a "barrier to entry" strategy. In essence, this competitive practice might make it difficult for you to enter the market. The higher the entry barrier, the less likely it is that you can successfully enter. For example, a competitor might offer customers lower prices, thus deterring customers from trying your product. The competitor may also spend substantial money on marketing, which might significantly increase the cost of your entry into the market. Or, competitors might use their power with channel members and block distribution access (e.g., they may threaten a distributor by telling it if they carry your product, they may withhold distributing their products through this channel member). Finally, even if you succeed in entering the market, you may still face additional competitive responses designed to push you out of the market including very bloody price cutting. For example, what would happen to your forecasted P&L if you were forced to cut your own prices by 20% to 25%? The key is to anticipate and plan for such eventualities—otherwise, the life of your venture may be truncated.

Key Takeaways for Competitor and Customer Positioning

- Recognize that you will encounter *some form of competition,* whether direct, indirect, or even the customer as a competitor.

- Assess the most direct competitors and determine if you are in a position to vanquish these competitors on the metrics that determine success in your competitive space. Use objective data in this positioning exercise. Determine "how you will compete"—that is, what differentiation will provide you with a sustainable competitive advantage?

- Prepare a competitive positioning map to analyze the rivals that you will compete with and your ability to compete with them.

- Assess customer perceptions of your offerings by preparing a perceptual map with your customers. The information used here tends to be "soft," incorporating customers' emotional responses to products or services in your category. Done correctly, the customer perceptual map will dimensionalize the important attributes customers use in evaluating competitive offerings, provide insights into how you and your competitors stack up against those attributes, reveal if customers perceive offerings as similar or dissimilar, and indicate which competitor, if any, is in close proximity to the customer's "ideal" offering.

- Decide whether your venture will accept and play by the current competitive rules of engagement, or play by its own rules. Accepting traditional rules of competing may weaken your position in some cases; being a "disruptor" and changing the rules may do the opposite.

- Business competition is dynamic, with each competitor responding to the moves of its rivals. So think ahead. Anticipate tactics your competitor may use to either keep you out of the market or, once you have arrived, drive you from the field. Anticipate how they will respond to your moves.

Reader Exercises

Now it is your turn to develop a competitive positioning for your venture and use that positioning to further refine your venture concept, your business model, and your product/service strategy. If you don't think you have competitors, think again. At the same time, the goal of competitive positioning is to create some space between your proposed venture and current competitors in a way that is meaningful and relevant to target customers—just as in the case of My M&M'S (see page 371).

Step 1: Do Your Homework on Competitor Strengths and Weaknesses

a. Identify your two to three most direct competitors. Identify the key metrics in your market space. The template shown in Figure 6.6 is a boilerplate that we want you to tune to suit your own venture. What does product or service quality or product/service performance mean for your target industry sector? Be specific. If there are key performance or quality metrics used in your target industry, apply these to competitors' offerings.

b. Then, examine your own venture concept, your business model, and your product/service strategy. Together, how do these essential documents translate into a competitive positioning for your venture against the metrics you create and apply for competitors?

c. On what dimensions of Figure 6.6 do you see a clear "win" relative to competitors? On what dimensions are you in a negative position compared to the competitors?

Dimensions of Competition	Your Venture Concept	Competitor 1	Competitor 2	Competitor 3	+ or – Position
Relative Price					
Product/Service Performance					
Product/Service Quality					
Market Coverage					
Sales Force Quality					
Marketing "Spend"					
Manufacturing Costs					
Operating Costs					

Figure 6.6   Competitive Position Research Template

Step 2: Prepare a Customer Perceptual Map

Talk to some customers and then construct a perceptual map. Refer to Figure 6.7.

a. Dimensionalize the map—that is, create the two axes from the customer's perspective. What are these dimensions?

b. Based on your customer research, how do you think target customers will locate the leading competitive offerings and then your offering on the map?

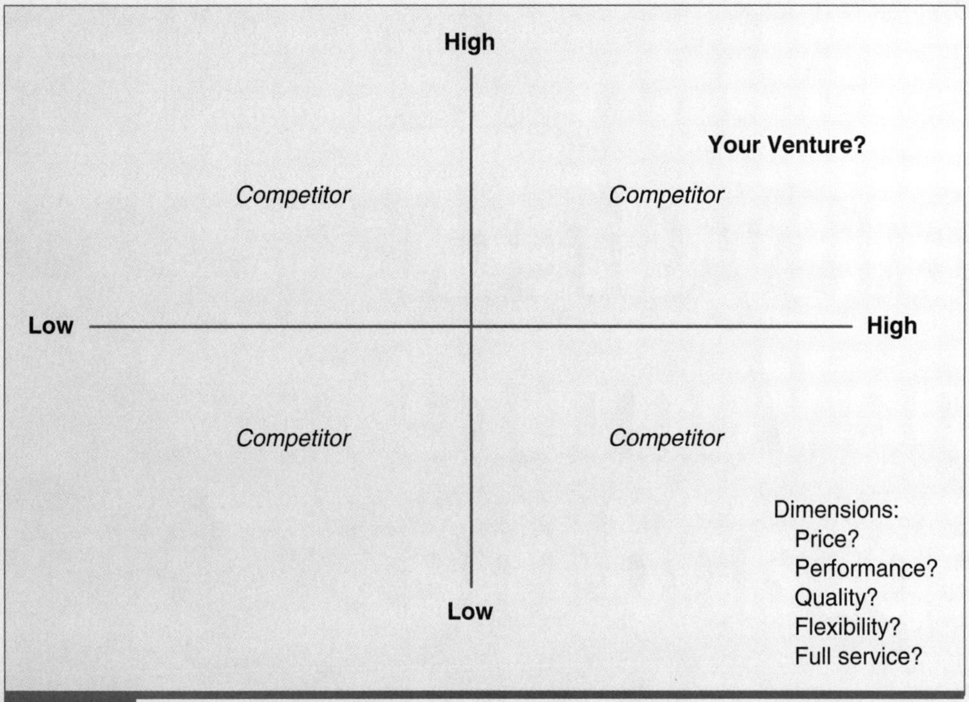

Figure 6.7 | Perceptual Map Template

c. Where would they position the "ideal" offering on the map? What is the distance between your planned venture and that ideal solution? If you were to ask customers what your venture must do to achieve the ideal positioning on the map, what would they tell you? (In the next chapter, you will get the chance to ask them!)

Step 3: Revisit Your Venture Concept Statement, the Business Model, and the Product/Service Strategy

a. With your venture concept statement in hand, does the "positioning" part of that statement still makes sense, given what you have learned in this chapter and your answers to the exercises above? If not, correct it now.

b. Split up your initial or revised positioning statement into competitor and customer positioning—now that we have learned the important difference between these two forms of positioning.

c. Based on your competitive and customer positioning, does the structure of revenue in your business model (and, in particular, the volume/price equilibrium you have chosen) still make sense? If not, make adjustments. Perhaps you can charge more! Or, perhaps you cannot charge as much.

d. Lastly, reexamine your product/service strategy. Does your competitive analysis suggest that the best way to differentiate is to offer greater variety than competitors—making that an axis of the perceptual map—and that the best way to achieve this is to design a whole bunch of specific plug-ins or third-party plug-ins for your products? Or, perhaps it is best to position your offerings as a service, rather than a product.

All four of these activities require that your sit down with your teammates, *reflect,* and then *decide.*

*** *** ***

The development of a competitive positioning lends itself well to another checkpoint with your trusted advisors, your professor, and your fellow classmates. Get that feedback!

chapter 7

A Reality Check on the Venture Concept and the Business Model

7

The Purpose of the Chapter

Every year, millions of individuals come up with a venture "concept" that they believe could be the beginning of a fundable startup venture. While many of these concepts may have merit at the 50,000-foot level, it is the process of transforming a venture concept into a valuable business proposition for both you and your target customers that makes all the difference.

To help accomplish this, we are going to learn how to do a field-based reality check for venture concepts that is fast and effective. This should be your second pass at interviewing target customers. In Chapter 2, we had you perform ethnography with a dozen or fewer target customers to get your basic "Aha!" by understanding their needs, wants, and frustrations. Now, it is time to go back out into the field once again to validate these ideas with a more structured questionnaire and interviewing method. This is in the spirit of developing a solid and exciting venture concept before writing a single page of the business plan for it. Your goal here is to become even more expert about your target customers and their core needs than anyone else, *even your professors!*

In our experience, too few budding entrepreneurs spend enough time to properly conceptualize their ventures. Done correctly, constructing and testing your venture concept can save you a lot of headache and possible heartache down the road.

*** *** ***

Let us summarize the path you have taken and what you need to test as the last step in this section of the book:

1. You have defined a venture scope, the target industry sector, as well as the type of business (product, system, service, or a combination) that you wish to start in that industry. Your industry research should have already validated that your chosen sector has the size and growth rate necessary to support your entrepreneurial efforts.

2. You have translated that industry sector into a target market for your venture by identifying different types of customers within it (the end-users and buyers). Then, you have selected a particular set of target customers upon which to focus your venture. You have observed and talked with these customers to understand different use cases or activities, and you have found needs and frustrations that customers have with current product and service solutions in those use cases. Those needs and frustrations become your problems that your venture will solve. This combination of target customers and problems to solve for those customers become your initial target market niche and, together with your new product or service idea, comprise your initial *venture concept*. These ideas are all contained in the template shown in Figure 7.1—for which you should have a good first draft to take into this reality check.

3. You have also developed *a business model* for your venture concept. The business model shows how you plan to make money by working with your target customers. That model includes the structure and nature of revenues as well as strategies for doing R&D, production, and selling. The basic aspects of the business are contained in the template shown in Figure 7.2—again, and need to be flushed out for your venture.

4. You have further fleshed out your product or service ideas into a more fully featured product or service strategy that provides a meaningful offering of "good, better, best" for your target customers. Again, Figure 7.3 contains a generic template for defining a new product or service strategy that you should have filled out for your venture.

5. Lastly, you have refined your initial positioning in your venture concept to create clear separation between you and existing competitors in terms of performance and price. You have also learned how to think about how customers might position you, which typically gets into behavioral and attitudinal factors beyond just performance and price. Figure 7.4 provides the template, and you should have your own version for it to take into this reality check.

Applying the first six chapters of the book to your venture idea is a lot accomplished, by any measure! The "whiteboard" in your office or notepad or computer should be filled with ideas from each one of these activities. If you have done the exercises at the end of the chapters, we bet that your new business idea has much more substance and perhaps an entirely different focus than what you imagined at the end of Chapter 1.

Now is the time to take the very important step of testing your concept in the field with target end-users and buyers. After this, you can start writing your business plan with confidence. And at that point, you should give yourself a big slap on the back for getting to this stage. You are already a winner.

Learning Objectives

- Planning the "reality check"
- Digging into the different elements of the reality check—the "stuff" you need to learn from this reality check
- Creating a Venture Concept Statement with specific questions underneath it to test levels of interest, buying preferences, competitive positioning, and more to show to customers
- Organizing customer panels—with an eye to getting this research done in one or two weeks
- Quickly conducting the field research itself—methods that work best for approaching end-users and buyers who you don't already know
- Analyzing the results of the field research to validate the venture concept and its business model
- Using the reality check to understand the size and structure of revenue for a scaled-up venture
- Integrating the results of the reality check to improve the venture concept and business model as the foundation for moving on to the next section of this book

Developing the Field Research Instrument for the Reality Check _____

While you might be able to show some customers your versions of the charts shown in Figures 7.1, 7.2, 7.3, and 7.4, you cannot count on getting them to say *yes* or *no* in order to perform a proper

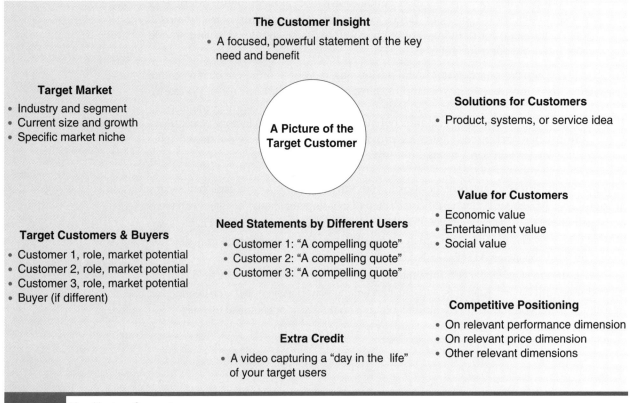

The Customer Insight
- A focused, powerful statement of the key need and benefit

Target Market
- Industry and segment
- Current size and growth
- Specific market niche

A Picture of the Target Customer

Solutions for Customers
- Product, systems, or service idea

Value for Customers
- Economic value
- Entertainment value
- Social value

Need Statements by Different Users
- Customer 1: "A compelling quote"
- Customer 2: "A compelling quote"
- Customer 3: "A compelling quote"

Target Customers & Buyers
- Customer 1, role, market potential
- Customer 2, role, market potential
- Customer 3, role, market potential
- Buyer (if different)

Competitive Positioning
- On relevant performance dimension
- On relevant price dimension
- Other relevant dimensions

Extra Credit
- A video capturing a "day in the life" of your target users

Figure 7.1 Your Venture Concept

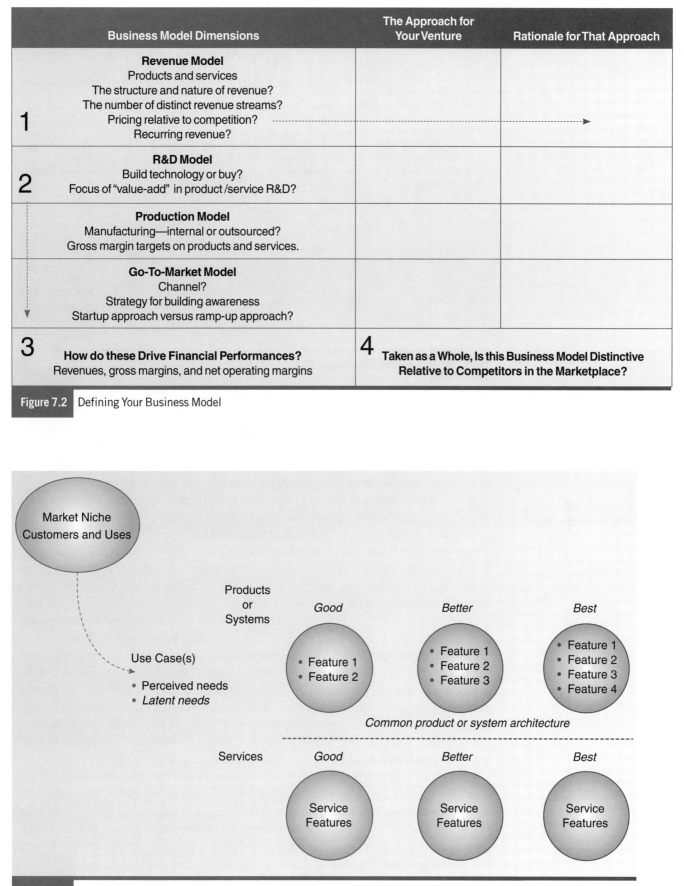

Business Model Dimensions	The Approach for Your Venture	Rationale for That Approach
1 **Revenue Model** Products and services The structure and nature of revenue? The number of distinct revenue streams? Pricing relative to competition? Recurring revenue?		
2 **R&D Model** Build technology or buy? Focus of "value-add" in product /service R&D?		
Production Model Manufacturing—internal or outsourced? Gross margin targets on products and services.		
Go-To-Market Model Channel? Strategy for building awareness Startup approach versus ramp-up approach?		
3 **How do these Drive Financial Performances?** Revenues, gross margins, and net operating margins	**4** **Taken as a Whole, Is this Business Model Distinctive Relative to Competitors in the Marketplace?**	

Figure 7.2 Defining Your Business Model

Figure 7.3 Your Definition of "Good, Better, Best" for Your Products, Systems, or Services

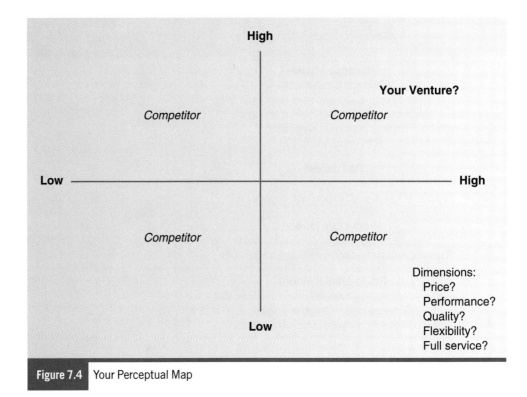

Figure 7.4 Your Perceptual Map

reality check. Your target customers are not ordinarily thinking about connecting the dots of a venture strategy as you must do. Rather, all they are thinking about is their own needs, problems, and opportunities.

A more typical scenario is to first create a simpler one-paragraph statement of your venture concept that you can show to customers more quickly and without much explanation. This statement is something you can say to customers in less than 30 seconds in a way that is clear and meaningful so that they can give you a response.

The goal of a venture concept statement is to give you ammunition for testing ideas with target customers in a systematic way to validate your venture concept. The types of things we want to know are the customers' reactions to your proposed solutions and how you plan to bring these to market. And, we want you to do this not just for your primary target customer group but also for one or two groups that are adjacent to it.

Figure 7.5 shows the basic insights that we want you to try to get from the field research. Each type of insight is critically important. For example, does the customer really want to buy a set of products and use them or integrate them on their own, or does the customer really prefer a service in which products are potentially included? Does the customer do his or her own buying, or is there another person in the household or organization that is making the purchase decision? What is the customer problem solved, the point of clear differentiation in your proposed products or services, the price positioning, the point of preferred purchase, as well as complementary products and services that you might include by one means or another with your own primary offerings? Figure 7.5 walks you through all of the key questions that we have explored in the prior chapters and boils them down into one simple page.

Plus, there is the very last question: Can we produce a strong stream of revenue in this venture? In Chapter 3, we learned how to define a business model for a venture and, as part of that, the structure of revenues for the venture. We learned about the importance of healthy gross margins (the selling price minus the cost of goods sold) and also the beauty of recurring revenues (by selling add-on products or services). Now, in this chapter, we simply need to combine that with an understanding of the "purchase intent" of customers for what we wish to

---

A venture team must answer these questions with clarity, focus, and purpose:

1. What is the business? (product, system, service)
2. Who is the target end-user? Who is the target buyer?
3. What problems does it solve for the customer?
4. How is it different from competitors in terms of what "it" does?
5. Would the customer pay more, the same, or less than what they use now if your product was available today?
6. Where does the customer want to buy offerings like yours?
7. How much and how often will the customer buy your offerings? Are there occasion-specific or budget cycle drivers?
8. Where do customers normally learn about offerings such as yours?
9. What else do they want to buy with offerings such as yours?
10. Can we produce a strong stream of revenue in this venture?

Do the answers to these questions add up to a cohesive, powerful venture concept and an attractive revenue model?

Figure 7.5 The Reality Check: Ten Essential Questions for the Entrepreneur

---

sell. If a significant percentage of target customers are strongly interested in your proposed solution and the structure of revenues is one that provides healthy margins and recurring revenues, the stream of revenues from the venture is going to look promising. (In the next section of this book, we will explore the financial modeling needed to understand if the venture can turn an operating profit.)

Our goal—and your goal—is to be able to express each question in a single sentence or set of bullet points. Concise, clear answers to each question will indicate that your venture strategy is solid and meaningful.

To answer these questions, we need to develop a research "instrument" that we can take to end-users and buyers to get their feedback for your venture ideas. At the very top of this instrument is a simple, clear statement about your venture concept for customers, followed by a series of specific questions. The goal is to be able to get through your instruments in less than ten minutes—and preferably five—with each specific customer that is interviewed.

The Venture Concept Summary for Customers

A venture concept summary has a specific structure. We recommend that you apply the following format to your own venture idea that focuses on the target customer, the problem to be solved, the difference from competitive offerings, and the benefits that customers will expect.

ABC is our business that (solves *what problem*) for (*who—which target customers*). It is different from the current competitors because of (*why customers buy*). The benefits that we expect to provide (name the major benefits) will make ABC stand out from all competitors.

Now, let's build some venture concept summaries to show to customers. To do this, we can use the three business model cases described before in Chapter 3. One of these was a new healthy pet snack venture; the second, a home health monitoring system; and the third, a telecom/networking infrastructure consulting service for corporate buildings.

For those of you wishing to create manufactured products business, let's look at the pet snack idea. The following might be a reasonable venture concept summary to show to prospective customers:

HealthyWags (disguised) is a startup that will bring health and nutrition to pet snacks for those of you who feel that your pet is a special member of your family. Our special variety of tasty snacks will use all-natural ingredients, be nutritionally complete, and have the meaty flavors that dogs relish. We will also carry nonmeat snacks for those of you who prefer only grains and vegetables. Our packaging is also made from 100% recycled materials. Our goal is to keep your pet healthy for a long, healthy life.

Next, for those of you building software or system-type ventures, let's build a venture concept summary for the home health monitoring company. Remember that this venture seeks to deploy a series of monitoring sensors in the homes of the elderly in partnership with home health agencies.

Health Monitoring Systems (disguised) keeps a 24/7 electronic monitoring for the elderly living at home or assisted-living centers. Rather than rely on your elderly loved ones to make the emergency call on their own or a visiting nurse to detect a problem, our system constantly monitors basic heart rate, movement, and other key factors and uses advanced software when problems arise and alerts our partner home health care agencies as well as family members. And we do this monitoring without having to make your loved ones wear any special equipment or bracelets or install video cameras that invade privacy. Our sensors are woven into bedding, seats, and other living spaces. In actual trials, our system significantly reduces stressful and costly hospital admissions, plus it gives loved ones that peace of mind that comes from 24/7 health monitoring.

Remember, the concept summary should state the what, how, and why in terms of customer value. In other words, it should clearly state the benefits of the venture concept from the perspective of the target customer. This actual venture team behind this concept did its reality check by talking to dozens of loved ones as well as assisted-living center administrators and, at the same time, built and ran a prototype installation in a limited number of residencies. It was rewarded in 2009 with a $7.5 million Series A or first-round financing!

Lastly, there are undoubtedly those of you reading this book that wish to start consulting or technical services ventures. The telecommunications infrastructure venture described in the business model chapter should be a useful example. This team wished to provide vendor-independent services to design suitable, cost-effective telecommunications and computer networking systems for corporate buildings. You will also recall that this venture did not need much in the way of startup funds and was off to the races with its very first client engagement:

Telestructures (disguised) is a consultancy to design, install, and service the communications and computer networking infrastructure needed by your company. We are vendor independent and have highly experienced engineers who select the technologies that most suit your business needs. We also deploy advanced software to remotely monitor, diagnose, and fix any problems that might arise in daily operations on a 24/7 basis. Instead of going to equipment vendors who will try to sell you complex solutions, we deliver simple yet powerful solutions using the most cost-effective technologies, and we get your new systems up and running fast.

Now take a moment to write down a few sentences that you might show to prospective customers. This should be based on your venture concept diagram from Chapter 2. Later on in the reader exercises, we will have you complete this task.

Questions Following the Venture Concept Summary

The next step is to develop specific questions that test different aspects of your venture concept, business model, product/service strategy, and positioning. The questions will also help you forecast the potential revenue for your venture.

Look at Figure 7.6. This figure contains questions to be asked to customers. You should provide your venture concept statement on a separate page that can be handed to customers so they can refer back to it as you work through the questions.

Please trust us that it takes a lot of careful thinking to write a powerful, clear concept summary in two or three sentences. The more abstract the venture—such as a software or information services business—the harder it is to be brief. Spend sufficient time with your team getting the ideas and words down correctly. A poorly worded statement destroys the efficacy of your reality check.

---

1. Can you tell us a little bit about yourself or your company? (Open ended but look for key demographic descriptors to align with your market segmentation and customer groups)

2. This is what our product or service generally does (provide a quick description or a picture/sketch on a separate page.) Do you view yourself as a potential customer of this offering? What would be the different ways that you would want to use the (product or service)?

3. How satisfied are you with the current products/services you use now?
    Very dissatisfied   Dissatisfied   Neither Dis/Sat.   Satisfied   Very satisfied

4. Do you see the proposed offering as distinctive from the competitors?
    Not different   Somewhat different   Highly distinctive

5. How much would you be willing to pay for this offering compared to the current products/services you use now?
    Less   Same   More

6. How often do you buy similar products or services? (Open ended)

7. How much do you spend each time you make a purchase? (Open ended but looking for a dollar amount. Also, try to validate the structure of revenue — e.g. , does the customer want to purchase, license, subscribe, try before buy, etc.?)

8. Where is the best place to buy products/services such as this? (Open ended but look for a specific preferred channel and ways in which they test or try products/services)

9. Where do you get your information about products/services such as this? (Open ended but look for preferred information sources.)

10. How likely is it that you would be willing to buy this offering?
    Very unlikely   Unlikely   Neither   Likely   Very likely

11. What additional features do you think are important in a (product or service) such as this? (Open ended)

Figure 7.6 The Field Research Instrument for the Reality Check

(To be applied with different potential target customers. Provide your Venture Concept Statement for Customers on a separate page. Also, provide a simple description of your product or service using a sketch or diagram if this helps customers understand your venture.)

The questions shown in Figure 7.6 help customers assess the attractiveness of your venture concept as well as important aspects of the business model. Each question gathers information about an important aspect for the venture:

- The end-users and buyers
- The major problems addressed by the venture's offerings and the value of solving those problems for the customer
- Since innovation rarely happens in a vacuum, the degree to which customers already like the solutions they already have now
- The competitive positioning and distinctiveness of the venture
- Purchase intent, as well as the frequency and amount of purchase

- The preferred point of purchase, be it a store, the Web, or face to face

- And the preferred venues for learning about offerings such as yours

- Complementary products and services that customers might want in addition to those proposed here.

Now, take a few minutes to work down the questions in Figure 7.6 with pencil in hand. You might wish to refine these questions to best suit your proposed venture (but not too much!). Don't leave any of the key points out, because you will need all of them not only to do a reality check but to create a foundation for building your business plan and financial models in the next section of this book.

Organizing Customer Panels _____

Structure Customers Into Distinct Potential Groups and Ask Members of Each Group for Their Thoughts on Your Venture Concept

In earlier chapters, we learned the importance of identifying specific groups of customers and the use cases or activities that you, as an entrepreneur, wish to target. Now, an essential part of the reality check is to make sure you have targeted the best customer group for your products or services and that these offerings are positioned appropriately for their tastes and preferences. The best way to do this is to directly apply your survey to several groups adjacent to your initial target. This has many benefits. First, it will help you appreciate how the different groups vary. And, you might actually find a better set of customers for launching your venture (such as those who have more money to spend or have greater need of your solutions). Or, you might learn what needs to be added to your product line or services to expand your business at the next stage of growth.

For example, if we were making a new type of tasty energy bar for young adults in their twenties, we would also want to find out reactions to that product concept by teenagers on one hand and adults in their 30s on the other. This information will help sharpen your focus. You might find that your tasty energy bar concept actually applies better to an older crowd, for example, or to a broader population that includes two or three distinct customer segments.

As a quick exercise, pretend that you are a pet owner and are answering the questions for the pet snack team. Pretend (or not!) that you are a young, professional woman, single or married, and have a dog (Spot) for whom you have a special, almost mother-child relationship. You tend to shop at Whole Foods Market, buy the all-natural pet food brands there, and spend whatever it takes at your veterinarian to keep Spot healthy. When it comes to snacks, you explicitly read labels and look for natural, healthy ingredients. Now, switch your customer group by virtue of demographics, attitudes, and behaviors. Pretend to be a pet owner that has a more distant relationship with the pet. You shop at Walmart for inexpensive pet food in bulk. You have never been to the vet. You also make the animal sleep in the mudroom. And, you feed your pet cheap cookies for snacks. Now, switch one more time again. Let's say that you are a single male (as many of you are), live in an urban area, and often eat "on the run." You go to PetSmart or PETCO to buy what seems like really healthy pet food—but you don't bother reading any labels. When it comes to snacks, you want Spot to have fun and will buy things that look like chews or are colorful, even to the point of being silly. Besides, if it is in a premium retailer, the snack can't be all that bad.

In each role, you will come up with very different answers with respect to demographics, attitudes, behaviors, and core needs for pet snacks in key areas such as ingredient type and quality, price, and preferred place of purchase. *As an entrepreneur, this is the type of information you need to know for targeting and execution.*

It is important to get feedback from members of each adjacent customer group on your venture concept. You might find, in fact, that your original idea appeals more strongly to a group of customers different from your original target. In the pet snack case, that might be the young urban male or female, as opposed to the grocery shopping Mom. Or, in the telecom infrastructure services case, the realization that medium-sized companies are truly the sweet spot for your venture because they are big enough to have cash, make decisions fast, and are not so large as to have their sufficient IT capabilities in-house to do all the thinking and work. You might also find ways to expand or refine your core offering to adjacent customers in the target market. For example, in the home health monitoring case, that might be special screens and reports for assisted-living center administrators beyond the basic monitoring and alerting software. Beyond simple validation, the reality check for a venture is all about refining your targeting and fleshing out your product or service strategy. *Listen* to the customers and *learn*.

Deciding the Number of Customers to Target for Reality Checking

There is no "magic" number of potential customers that you should communicate with. In fact, smaller samples of customers selected properly are perhaps a better way to go than selecting larger numbers of potential end-users/buyers that are not well qualified and screened as customers. As we learned in Chapter 2, many of the leading design firms in the world shoot for intensive conversation with a dozen or less highly representative target customers of a new product or service idea. That applies to testing a venture concept. Quality wins out over quantity. It is far more important to spend focused periods with the potential customers for your venture, engaging in real dialogue.

As a rule of thumb, we suggest talking to at least ten customers. And, if you have three specific types of target customers, you would talk to 30 people (ten in each grouping). However, another key rule of thumb is that you only "stop" talking with customers when no new information is being obtained that will help inform you about your venture concept. Thus, it is possible you may obtain a consensus opinion from your customers after only speaking to a small number of prospective target customers, say ten to 12 respondents—either positive or *negative*. If it is a negative consensus then, obviously, you and your team need to either re-work your proposed offerings toward something that customers really want, or look to adjacent customer groups where demand might be greater. If in this work an overall consensus has not yet emerged—either positive or negative—you must keep talking to customers until that consensus develops. If after your analysis of the data you are able to write those one or two sentences for each of the questions presented in the table in Figure 7.5, you have reached a consensus.

Conducting the Field Research _____

In Chapter 2, we had you observe and talk to target customers to gain the insights into your customers' needs required to define the solutions for your venture. Now, we are seeking more specific responses—data—for more specific things. You will be generating these data by asking people questions and recording their responses. You have several options for doing this: You can collect the data by:

- Personal interviews (face-to-face) following a structured discussion guide,
- Telephone interviews also following a structured discussion guide,
- Mailed surveys that respondents complete and mail back to you, or
- Online surveys, using one of the popular survey tools offered on the Web. There a number of such tools that you can use at no initial cost with a simple Google search.

In choosing between these alternatives, you will have to make important trade-offs, such as the cost of gathering the information against the expected quality of information obtained. Figure 7.7 provides some of the pros and cons of each particular method.

Personal interviews (face-to-face) have the major advantage of enabling you to ask probing questions or see reactions of the respondents. But personal interviews can be time consuming and expensive to conduct, particularly if the people you want to talk to live in a different city or region. Yet, just as we learned in Chapter 2, any face-to-face time with a target customer is worth its weight in gold to the entrepreneur. You simply cannot get enough of it—and this is our preferred method for testing venture concepts—particularly if you only often need a dozen or so respondents to get good directional input from the target market. As we also learned in Chapter 2, try to do this research in situ—in the customer's actual buying environment. If this is not possible, do so in an environment that is most comfortable for the respondent. In other words, on their home turf, not yours.

Basis of Comparison	Personal Interview	Telephone/Skype	Mail	Online
Cost of completed survey	Most expensive	Moderately expensive	Not very expensive	Very inexpensive
Ability to probe and ask complex questions	Much; this is a face-to-face conversation	Some; interviewer can probe and elaborate	Little to none	Depends; can go back and ask respondent to clarify responses; or make changes to the concept and retest.
Potential of interviewer bias on the results	Significant; voice, appearance, gender, and "know it all" attitude can easily bias the results	Also significant, although appearance is taken out of the picture	None	Little, if done correctly
Anonymity given to respondent	Little, because of face-to-face contact	Some, because of telephone contact	Complete, unless coded instrument is used	Some; e-mail/ customer name may be known
Response rate	Good	Fair; refusal rates are increasing	Poor or fair	Very good, if done correctly
Speed of data collection	Moderate depending on travel time to customers	Good	Poor	Very good

Figure 7.7   Comparing Field Research Methods of a Reality Check for a Venture Concept

As for the other possible methods, collecting data by mail can be slow and response rates low. Also, in mailed surveys, there may be bias in the data because those likely to respond will typically have either strong positive or negative reactions to your venture concept. Additionally, a mailed survey does not give you the flexibility to explain to the customer what you mean by a particular question or idea. Often, customers misunderstand what you mean or simply get lost and therefore fail to complete a research instrument. Mail seems to be something of the past.

Collecting data by telephone allows the flexibility to talk to customers and walk through a research instrument. For business-to-business (B2B) ventures, we have seen this method used to great effect, grabbing 15 minutes of a busy manager's time to run through a set of important questions. However, for business-to-consumer (B2C) ventures, the telephone method is becoming increasingly difficult because consumers are sick and tired of marketing calls. Also, with many unlisted telephone numbers, it is becoming increasingly more difficult to obtain a good sample of respondents.

Using the Web to collect data, on the other hand, is becoming increasingly popular. In our MBA classes, we find that student teams have no trouble finding 30, 40, and sometimes well over 100 people to complete their online "concept tests." One of the nice things about the online survey route is that you can make changes to various aspects of the product or service offering and "re-test" to get customer or buyer reactions.

Importantly, the key driver you must consider when determining a data collection method is whether or not you wish to present a "prototype" or visual of your core offering. If it is important for the potential customer to actually see the prototype or visual, then you must use the personal interview or the online method. Remember, an online survey can include a picture of the proposed product or a strong description of the proposed service. Visuals bring a concept to life for target customers. We strongly encourage you to use pictures, sketches, or actual prototypes whenever possible.

Analyzing Your Data and Interpreting the Results

The Goal: Validate Your Customer Insights and Business Model Vision

So, let's say that you have designed your key questions, identified target customers and buyers, and have reached them either face to face, through the phone, or through the Web. You have gathered data for these questions and are ready to start your analysis. The purpose now is to consolidate what you have learned about the demographics, attitudes, behaviors, and core needs of the potential target customer groups you have identified and to then validate your product/service strategy and its competitive positioning.

The next step is to consolidate all the data from your field research into a simple, single source of information. We recommend that you use the Field Research Discussion Guide as a template for doing this. Take a look at the series of Figures labeled as 7.8A through 7.8D. We have used the HealthyWags case as an illustration for what a consolidated data set might look like as a result of the reality check field research. We have chunked up a single consolidated data set into four pieces to make it easier for you to read—but on the team's computer this is a single document (supported by a number of supplemental files). In the pages to follow, we are going to show you how to analyze various parts of these data to validate and improve your venture concept.

Question 1: Can you tell us a little bit about yourself or your company? (Open ended but look for key demographic descriptors to align with your market segmentation and customer groups)

Results: (Combination of earlier ethnography and the reality check field research)

Mother Goose (Attitude: dog as family member, but still a pet) Customers are health conscious when purchasing at the grocery store, and many are going to Whole Foods Market. They expect quality ingredients, but they are not label readers. They are explicitly focused on taste but value is also important because dog snacks are part of the overall household food budget. They will accept fortification of ingredients, as opposed to all-natural recipes. They take supplements themselves! Key motivation for feeding snacks: "I feed my dogs just for love." Key target customer. **50% of market**

Dog Mommy (Attitude: dog as family member, dog as child—and may be a surrogate child for some) Customers are very health conscious. These customers want quality ingredients and not a lot of fat and calories. All-natural is another key driver. They want all-natural ingredients, good taste, and minimally processed products. They are deliberate shoppers including reading the ingredient list. Key motivation for feeding snacks: "I want my dog to be as healthy as I am." Key target customer. **40% of market**

Pet Buddy (Attitude: dog as pet friend) Predominantly male. They are focused on ingredients on a more scientific basis. All-natural is less of a concern. He does not mind using a dog snack as an indulgence. Milk Bones will do for this customer. Key motivation for feeding snacks: "If he is happy, I am happy." Looks at dog as exercise buddy. **10% of market**

Question 2: This is what our product or service generally does (provide a quick description or a picture/sketch on a separate page). Do you view yourself as a potential customer of this offering? What would be the different ways that you would want to use the (product or service)?

Mother Goose	100%	Snack pet	N = 12
Dog Mommy	100%	Snack pet	N = 12
Pet Buddy	50%	Snack pet	N = 6

Figure 7.8A   HealthyWags' Consolidated Field Research Data: Questions 1 and 2 (N = 30)

Question 3: How satisfied are you with the current products/services you use now?

Very dissatisfied	*Dissatisfied*	*Neither Dis./Sat.*	*Satisfied*	*Very satisfied*

Mother Goose: 30% Dissatisfied or Very dissatisfied
Dog Mommy: 40% Dissatisfied or Very dissatisfied
Pet Buddy: 5% Dissatisfied or Very dissatisfied

Question 4: Do you see the proposed offering as distinctive from the competitors?

Not different	*Somewhat different*	*Highly distinctive*

Mother Goose: 20% Highly distinctive
Dog Mommy: 30% Highly distinctive
Pet Buddy: 10% Highly distinctive

Question 5: How much would you be willing to pay for this offering compared to the current products/services you use now?

Less	*Same*	*More*

Mother Goose: 10% Would pay more
Dog Mommy: 20% Would pay more
Pet Buddy: 100% Would pay the same

Figure 7.8B   HealthyWags' Consolidated Field Research Data: Product/Service Strategy and Positioning Questions

Question 6: How often do you buy similar products or services? (Open ended)

Mother Goose:	Once a month
Dog Mommy:	Once a month
Pet Buddy:	Once every 2 months

Question 7: How much do you spend each time you make a purchase? (Open ended but look for a dollar amount)

Mother Goose:	$5
Dog Mommy:	$7
Pet Buddy:	$3

Question 8: Where is the best place to buy products/services such as this? (Open ended but look for a specific preferred channel and ways in which they test or try products/services)

Mother Goose:	Supermarket, pet specialty store
Dog Mommy:	Pet specialty store
Pet Buddy:	Supermarket

Question 9: Where do you get your information about products/services such as this? (Open ended. Look for preferred information sources.)

Mother Goose:	Print, television, friends
Dog Mommy:	Internet, friends
Pet Buddy:	In-store

Figure 7.8C HealthyWags' Consolidated Field Research Data: Go-to-Market Questions

Question 10: How likely is it that you would be willing to buy this offering?

Very unlikely   *Unlikely*   *Neither*   *Likely*   *Very likely*

Mother Goose:	25% Likely or Very likely
Dog Mommy:	50% Likely or Very likely
Pet Buddy:	10% Likely or Very likely

Question 11: What additional features would make you more likely to buy this (product or service)? (Open ended)

Mother Goose:	Bulk packaging to buy it for less money per pound
	Want smaller portion treats for training purposes
Dog Mommy:	A no-meat version because "I don't eat meat myself"
Pet Buddy:	"Can you make it look like a bone?"

Figure 7.8D HealthyWags' Consolidated Field Research Data: Purchase Intent Questions

Validating the Core Needs, Attitudes, Behaviors, and Demographics of Your Target Market

Successful entrepreneurs become experts in their target customers and their uses for a product or service. While many of the insights shown in a figure such as Figure 7.9 should emerge in the ethnography done earlier in Chapter 2, the reality check is the time to test these insights against a set of closely related customers.

Remember, in Chapter 2 we learned about identifying distinct customer groups—where "customers" might be customers and/or buyers. The venture concept template (repeated as Figure 7.1 at the beginning of this chapter) lists the specific end-users and buyers in a target market. It also includes a picture or sketch of your primary target customer together with simple needs statements based on your ethnography. Now, we want to validate and improve those insights, to create even crisper "personas" of the various target customers in your target market. This helps focus everything else in the venture: your commercial offerings, your positioning, your go-to-market strategy, and the structure and nature of revenues.

Also to refresh, customers are often their own buyers. But just as often, they are not. In the B2C space, for example, many readers may have just purchased their first new automobile—and hopefully a lot of careful thinking as well as brand emotion went into that decision. When you were much younger, however—say still in diapers—your mother made the Pampers, Huggies, or store-brand purchase decision for you. Similarly, in the B2B space, self-employed home office entrepreneurs make their own decisions about the office productivity and other forms of software to be used; but in any larger sort of corporation *someone else* makes that decision for us, and the process for that decision making is typically more complex based on volume discounts, support agreements, and so forth.

Let's stick with the pet snack case—it's a fun case and we bet that quite a few of you come from households that own a dog. Take a quick look at what might emerge from a reality check for HealthyWags. Our focus here is primarily on Questions 1 and 2 of the Field Research Discussion Guide. Look at the consolidated data set in Figure 7.8A:

Question 1: Can you tell us a little bit about yourself or your company? (Open-ended, but look for key demographic descriptors to align with your market segmentation and customer groups)

Question 2: This is what our product or service generally does (provide a quick description or a picture/sketch on a separate page). Do you view yourself as a potential customer of this offering? What would be the different ways that you would want to use the product (or service)?

Figure 7.8A shows the consolidated data set for these two questions for HealthyWags. The team applied its discussion guide to 30 dog owners in all, speaking with dog owners in their neighborhoods or in dog walking parks. There were three distinct customer groups that emerged from this research as distinguished by owners' attitudes and behaviors toward pets. Demographics also supported the customer grouping. In Figure 7.8A, you can see specific descriptions for each of these three groups: Mother Goose, Dog Mommy, and Pet Buddy. Those descriptions contain lots of useful information on attitudes and behaviors that drive needs for both products and services. You can also see that all the prospective customers in the first two groups saw themselves as potential customers for healthy dog snacks, while only half of the Pet Buddy customers saw themselves as customers (the other half were satisfied with their current relatively unhealthy snacks).

What is particularly interesting—and the type of insight you need to discover for your venture—is the how different target customers perceive themselves as customers for your proposed product or service. In the case of HealthyWags, here are the results:

Questions 2: This is what our product or service generally does (provide a quick description or a picture/sketch on a separate page). Do you view yourself as a potential customer of this offering? What would be the different ways that you would want to use the product (or service)?

Mother Goose	100%	n = 12
Dog Mommy	100%	n = 12
Pet Buddy	15%	n = 6

The female customers have a much stronger identification with healthy dog snacks than the male pet owners. For HealthyWags, the second part of the question is rather obvious: snacking the pet. However, the venture team found other use, occasions—snacks specifically for training (which might suggest a smaller portion size for each snack), and snacks for in the car (which might suggest resealable packages rather than boxes to avoid mess). In other types of business, the range of use cases coming from actual surprises can be a real eye-opener! For example, in our Home Monitoring Case, the very same system is not only to identify and initiate responses for health problems in the elderly but to also provide loved ones with the ability to stay in closer touch with their parents' health and well-being.

Now, we want you to make a simple chart—but one with a complex array of information. Do you remember the customer grouping of the farmers in Chapter 2—Figure 2.5—with the "Steady Eddie," the "Up & Comer," the "Sundowner," and the "Livestock Farmer"? This is what we want you to create with greater detail than before, capturing the full extent of core needs, attitudes, behaviors, and demographics.

Figure 7.9 is an example of applying this framework to HealthyWags. Mother Goose and Dog Mommy represent distinct female personas, one older, the other younger, with different attitudes and shopping behaviors. Mother Goose is the primary grocery shopper of the family and buys her pet food along with the rest of the family's food. That leads to supermarkets and mass merchandisers as preferred channels. And, she is looking for a nutritious snack from a brand-name manufacturer.

Dog Mommy is a distinctly different customer. This became the team's primary target. Dog Mommy could be married or single but views her pet as a child. She is highly receptive to all-natural health, seeks minimally processed food, tries new products, and pays for better quality. Importantly, this customer is willing to experiment with new brand names; in fact, she sometimes has a distrust of "big-name" manufacturers. Smaller is better. The all-natural goodness that she seeks for herself is what she wants for her special family member—her pet. Knowledgeable salespeople in a store are important to her.

The last "customer" is a male for whom the pet is a friend and "buddy." This customer seeks convenient, "fun" snacks and does not expect a pet snack to be particularly healthy—just as he views his own snacks! This attitude and set of behaviors pretty much applies to both younger and older males.

These are the types of insights we want you to have for your various potential target customer groups. The chart is a nice way of summarizing all these insights into a simple, readily accessible form. Not every target customer will fit perfectly into one of your specific groups, but there should be strong alignment by virtue of shared needs, attitudes, behaviors, and perhaps demographics.

For those of you venturing into the software and systems business, Health Monitoring Systems is a good illustration of different customer groups emerging from the combination of ethnography and validation in a reality check. That venture found two types of elderly: those chronically ill and needing constant supervision in a controlled medical environment such as an assisted-living center or nursing home and others who are still relatively healthy and live either in their own personal residence or a special elderly residence community. In its research, the team found that the typical cost of an emergency room readmission for an individual is over $12,000—and many of these are preventable by detecting problems before they become crises. The team decided to focus on elderly in assisted-living centers or still living at home—the

Target Customers	Core Needs	Attitudes (toward family or work or lifestyle)	Behaviors (include buying preferences)	"Hard" Demographics (including percentage of total market/survey)
Mother Goose	Perceived: Nutritional health Latent: Snacks matched as part of a nutrition system that includes main meal	• Caring to the pet, a member of the family • I feed my dogs just for love • Doesn't study ingredient list • Dog walking is another household to-do • Looks for brand name manufacturers	• Shops for pet food while shopping for the family • Looks at big bag as way to economize • Prefers grocery channel	• Married with children • Primary grocery shopper • Mature (over 35 years)
Dog Mommy	Perceived: Nutritional healthy snacks Latent: All-natural goodness, not over-processed, low fat	• Views pet as surrogate child • "I want my dog to be as healthy as I am" • Dog walking is major enjoyment event • Looks at ingredients • Seeks simple, all-natural goodness • Some want grains and vegetables only	• Shops for pet food separate from own food purchases • Prefers premium specialty channels, combination of PetSmart, PETCO, and independent retailers • Receptive to food innovations for self and pet • Likes to have a knowledgeable salesperson to speak with about product choices	• Single or married without children • "Professional" with disposable income
Pet Buddy	Perceived: between meal snacking Latent: A "fun" snack; an on-the-go convenient meal substitute	• Views pet as a friend, a buddy • "If he is happy, I am happy." • Looks for brand name manufacturers • Dog walking is personal fitness occasion	• Rarely shops for pet food • Likes big bag bulk purchases • Traditional cookies are good enough: "It's just a snack."	• Married or in steady relationship • Not primary grocery shopper; "impulse" buyer

Figure 7.9   HealthyWags' Customer Grouping

customer group where automated monitoring could make the biggest impact and where the sheer number of customers made the best business case. Lastly, for those of you venturing into services, Telestructures—the B2B telecommunications infrastructure firm—quickly found that the needs, attitudes, and behaviors of large corporations were clearly different than those of either medium-sized companies or small ones. Their target became the medium-sized segment.

Validating Your Product or Service Strategy and Its Positioning

The next step is to validate the attractiveness of your product or service idea of your venture with the target customers. There are several aspects to this: (a) the extent to which the customers are dissatisfied with their current solutions, and (b) the extent to which they find your solution distinctive (special and meaningful for their use case application) and (c) the extent to which customers value that differentiation with a willingness to pay more for it relative to existing solutions.

The stars align for your venture if target customers are highly dissatisfied with current solutions, your offerings are special, and customers appreciate that with a willingness to support premium pricing. The entrepreneur seeks a clearly differentiated position—one that stands out from the competition. And, this may not just be in terms of a dramatically lower price for customers. Since it is typically the established large-scale manufacturers or service providers that use economies of scale to drive prices down, often the most powerful points of differentiation for a new venture with limited volumes will come in an area other than price.

Conversely, customers might be very interested in your idea conceptually, but if they are already pleased with their current product or service, most customers will tend not to try your offerings due to switching costs and the uncertainty of working with a new firm. Or, they might perceive your concept as special but not special enough to support healthy pricing. To test these things, our field research guide has three questions:

Question 3: How satisfied are you with the current products/services you use now?
Very dissatisfied   Dissatisfied   Neither Dis./Sat.   Satisfied   Very satisfied

Question 4: Do you see the proposed offering as distinctive from the competitors?
Not different   Somewhat different   Highly distinctive

Question 5: How much would be willing to pay for this offering compared to the current products/services you use now?
Less   Same   More

Turning to the HealthyWags' consolidated data (Figure 7.8B), it is clear that certain target customers appreciate the premium, all-natural, health positioning. The reality check showed that premium features—all-natural nutrition—would command a price premium over current snacks. Some might say that a high price reinforces the premium perception in the hearts and minds of consumers. Let's take a look at the actual data:

Question 3: How satisfied are you with the current products/services you use now?
Very dissatisfied   Dissatisfied   Neither Dis./Sat.   Satisfied   Very satisfied

Mother Goose:	20% Dissatisfied or Very dissatisfied
Dog Mommy:	40% Dissatisfied or Very dissatisfied
Pet Buddy:	5% Dissatisfied or Very dissatisfied

Those "Dog Mommy" customers—younger females who view their pet as a child—show the highest level of dissatisfaction with current pet snacks. This makes them a primary target customer for the venture. That's what you need to find for your venture. Conversely, those "Pet Buddy" guys don't seem to really care about quality of snacks (including for themselves!). Those are the type of customers that you need to know about ahead of time so that you don't target waste your product development, distribution, and marketing money.

Question 4: Do you see the proposed offering as distinctive from the competitors?

Not different   *Somewhat different*   *Highly distinctive*

Mother Goose:	20% Highly distinctive
Dog Mommy:	30% Highly distinctive
Pet Buddy:	10% Highly distinctive

Question 5: How much would be willing to pay for this offering compared to the current products/services you use now?

Less   *Same*   *More*

Mother Goose:	10% would pay more
Dog Mommy:	20% would pay more
Pet Buddy:	100% won't pay more

Once again, the stars align for the team to target that younger female. She has the highest level of appreciation for the proposed product and will support it with her spending. Mother Gooses come in a strong second; Pet Buddy's a distant third.

The reality check should also provide support for your strategy regarding product line variety (often "good, better, best") and complementary products or services developed in Chapter 4. This is the purpose of the very last, open-ended question in the Field Research Discussion Guide, and it is presented as a way to increase the customers' perception of his or her likelihood of purchase by them if they would like to see additional features or offerings.

Question 11: What additional features would make you more likely to buy this (product or service)? (Open ended)

Mother Goose: Bulk packaging to buy it for less money per pound

Want smaller-portion treats for training purposes

Dog Mommy: A no-meat version because "I don't eat meat myself"

Pet Buddy: "Can you make it look like a bone?"

The Mother Goose primary grocery shoppers are always thinking about the family budget and, therefore, bulk packaging would make sense. Also, being experienced in training (children as well as pets), it makes sense that these customers might want a new type of healthier training snack in a "bite-size" portion. The Dog Mommy customer—that younger female typically not yet with children and who views her pet as her child—is very much focused on her own eating needs when she thinks about the pet. Eating less meat is a growing trend in such consumers and, therefore, that preference is passed onto the pet (even though dogs clearly love to eat meat!). Lastly, the male Pet Buddy is thinking about play and enjoyment with his pet. "Since dogs love bones, why not make it look like a bone?" Any of these ideas might be introduced at startup or later on once the business picks up steam.

The same type of reality check validation process for new product or service strategy applies equally well to our systems and services cases. The Health Monitoring Systems team found its offering of a noninvasive, 24/7 monitoring system to be distinctive and well valued over existing alternatives—which for many elderly was Philips Lifeline, a push-the-button alert system to a call center that the individual wears around his or her neck.[1] The team found that a significant percentage of its primary target customer—elderly with health problems and already receiving health services within an assisted-living center or from a home health agency—would pay more for an automated service compared to the traditional push-button alert system, especially when informed that the system would continue to monitor individuals at night while sleeping. The cost of push-button systems currently on the market was about a dollar a day. The product line strategy was flexed to serve different types of customers. Loved ones wanted visibility in their parent's medical monitoring and health history through the Web. So did the nurses providing care. And, assisted living center and home health agency managers wanted the "transactions" on the system to be fed into a database to track incidents and response times. With a growing elderly population, anything that could help manage patient health quality and nursing staff productivity would be "worth its weight in gold."

Telestructures, our telecom design services example, received similar support from its reality check. When the venture team talked to prospective customers, it found that "vendor independence" was a powerful differentiator. The other dimension that really "popped" from their field research was the concept of a full service provider. The target customers, medium sized companies, perceived being full service and vendor independent as a powerful proposition. Telestructures positioned itself as a one-stop shop for upgrading telecommunications infrastructure with the most cost effective, newest technologies and advanced software to remotely diagnose and fix any operational problems.

Validating Your Go-to-Market Strategy

Entrepreneurs in technology-intensive businesses often focus so hard on their products or services that they short-change the go-to-market aspects of the business. This can be a fatal flaw. Go-to-market is the hidden genie of any successful new product or service development. A bad salesperson or low-quality retailer can make the best of products appear inferior. Or, as we have

---

[1] Lifeline itself was a fascinating startup that grew to $100 million in annual sales before being acquired by Philips. It was started in 1974 in Watertown, Massachusetts, by Andrew Dibner, a geriatric physician at Boston University, who at first could not convince any manufacturers to produce his invention. He started his own company to manufacture and market the system. He ran a successful trial with the Veterans' Administration, and grew from that point onward. He was quoted as saying, "We nearly went broke. Almost lost our house. We had young children. It was awful! My wife and I were both academics, and we despised business at the time. But, we believed it was so important that we were determined to make it happen." The key to success was to switch its marketing strategy to sell to hospitals and nursing homes for their patients, as opposed to directly to consumers. Finding that "trusted source" for new technology and making it your distribution partner has worked for entrepreneurs across many industries. Source: http://www .fundinguniverse.com/company-histories/Lifeline-Systems-Inc-Company-History.html

seen so often in Web and software ventures, developing communities around a new product or service can create the buzz needed to create critical momentum in a marketplace that would ordinarily be out of the reach of an entrepreneur if he or she had to buy such market awareness through traditional media.

The reality check for your go-to-market strategy includes getting customer feedback on four key elements guiding a go-to-market strategy:

- Frequency of purchase
- Typically "spend" for each purchase
- Preferred place of purchase
- Preferred information channel for product or service information

In the next section of this book, we will also learn how to go back to customers to test the branding for a new product or service. For now, however, all we need to do is to validate and gain further insight into the four issues above.

Perhaps the most important aspect for entrepreneurs is to determine if target customers agree with the channel strategy. For example, do customers want to buy direct from you? Or, would they prefer to purchase from an already established channel member, such as a retailer for B2C ventures or an original equipment manufacturers (OEM; a larger firm) or systems integrator for B2B ventures. Remember, a successful channel strategy will accelerate your time to market and break even, increasing the return on investment for your startup company. However, this channel strategy must balance the ideal design for market coverage and meeting customer preferences with the costs of implementing that channel—particularly for a startup. For example, many successful entrepreneurs started first with a regional or "top ten accounts" penetration strategy before expanding to national and then global reach.

We want to emphasize that it is important to get feedback on all of these issues early and make any necessary adjustments now before going to market since making after-launch changes can be very expensive. The way we do that is by asking customers four simple questions in the Field Research Discussion Guide.

Question 6: How often do you buy similar products or services? (Open ended)

Question 7: How much do you spend each time you make a purchase? (Open ended but look for a dollar amount)

Question 8: Where is the best place to buy products/services such as this? (Open ended but look for a specific preferred channel and ways in which they test or try products/services)

Question 9: Where do you get your information about products/services such as this? (Open ended; look for preferred information sources)

To illustrate how consolidated data can validate or change a venture concept, let's turn to HealthyWags once again. Take a look at the data below.

Question 6: How often do you buy similar products or services? (Open ended)

Mother Goose:	Once a month
Dog Mommy:	Once a month
Pet Buddy:	Once every 2 months

These data support the team's focus on the female buyers as a startup strategy because they are more diligent, frequent shoppers.

Question 7: How much do you spend each time you make a purchase? (Open ended but look for a dollar amount)

Mother Goose:	$5
Dog Mommy:	$7
Pet Buddy:	$3

These data provide strong directional guidance that the younger female shoppers—those who view their pets as surrogate children—are less price sensitive than the older, primary grocery shopping Moms trying to manage a family budget. And those guys—well, the reality check reveals that they are simply "cheap" when it comes to pet snacks (and, we bet, their own snacks!).

Question 8: Where is the best place to buy products/services such as this? (Open ended but look for a specific preferred channel and ways in which they test or try products/services)

Mother Goose:	Supermarket (34%), pet specialty store (33%), Walmart (33%)
Dog Mommy:	Supermarket (20%), pet specialty store (50%) including independents, mass merchant (10%), club store (20%)
Pet Buddy:	Supermarket (60%), pet specialty store (10%), mass merchant (30%)

One of the team members was skeptical about the strength of the specialty channel for younger women—the primary demographic source for Dog Mommy. He went to a pet specialty store and discretely observed who was purchasing off the snack aisle over the course of an hour at the end of the working day. Sure enough, women were doing the vast amount of the purchasing, more younger than older and hardly any men other than himself! Both the data and the in-store observation supported the team's focus on the female buyers as a startup strategy because they prefer the pet specialty channel, such as PETCO, PetSmart, or independent retailers. From a practical matter, given the costs of getting shelf space in a supermarket, and the difficulty of breaking into mass merchants such as Walmart, the venture team found the pet specialty channel attractive for a venture—particularly the independent pet retailers who serve as a good test bed for new products. Then, the team reasoned, it would have the credibility to do national agreements with the large specialty chains. Dog Mommy continued to find support as a primary target customer.

Question 9: Where do you get your information about products/services such as this? (Open ended but look for preferred information sources)

Mother Goose:	Print, television, friends
Dog Mommy:	Internet, friends
Pet Buddy:	In-store

These data show that Dog Mommy—as a younger consumer—prefers social networking channels of information for new products (as well as services, we find). The traditional Madison

Avenue advertising approach (expensive print and broadcast/cable advertisements) for marketing to an older consumer is sometimes distrusted by this young consumer. The primary grocery shopping Mom, on the other hand, prefers these traditional information sources—costly for a fledgling company. And Pet Buddy—well, it seems that male pet owners in this reality check like to be sold right in the store through pamphlets, displays, or in-store samples. Taken together, the reality checks showed a clear alignment toward the Dog Mommy consumer for the premium, all-natural and healthy pet snacks that HealthyWags aspired to bring to market.

The go-to-market field research for Health Monitoring Systems supported a different set of go-to-market strategies. For example, the preferred channel was assisted-living centers and home health agencies versus selling direct to the elderly themselves, simply because technology scares many of the elderly. It was also a lot less costly in terms of advertising to build awareness. The elderly wanted to learn about new services from trusted sources, for example, their doctors and care providers. The field work also helped validate the revenue model. The elderly made the most direct connection to home security systems to prevent burglary—such as ADT. Such services carry an installation fee in the range of $300 and a monthly monitoring fee of $50. Those numbers became important for the financial modeling that the team had to perform to prepare its business plan to raise venture capital.

The Telestructures service business also received validation and further direction from its reality check. Small companies did not want to spend much if anything on systems design services and were reluctant to pay ongoing systems monitoring fees. Large corporations, on the other hand, most often had their own staff to do networking and telecommunications systems design and support. Telestructures would just be another vendor in their eyes. And the sweet spot in the market, fast-growing midsized companies showed both the need for vendor-independent and full-service consultancy as well as the cash to pay for such services.

Getting a Handle on Revenue for a Scaled-Up Business

You might have a great product or service idea, *but can it be the basis of a good business?* That, readers, is the $64 question (and for some of you, the $1 million to $3 million investment decision) that you and your potential investors must try to answer.

The reality check can begin to answer that question by providing a picture of the revenue potential for a scaled-up venture. By scaled-up venture, we mean a company that has started successfully, has its sea legs, and has expanded its customer base and product or service offerings. This is typically a firm that is two to three years old. In the next section of this book, we turn to an even more granular project of revenue and then projected expenses and profitability. However, for now, our focus is on *revenue—which for a venture is the source of all things good.* The failure to produce a consistent stream of growing revenue is difficult if not fatal.

The reality check goes a long way to making sure you are not walking down a dead-end alley. You need to determine the extent to which your target customers want and will demand your offering. *No demand means no venture.* Weak demand means a venture that will struggle along until such demand evolves and grows within your marketplace—and then, an established firm might enter your market and steal that demand.

We want you to use our "voice of the customer" reality check to create a *customer-driven projection of scaled-up revenue.* All too often we see revenue projections for new ventures that are based on assumptions such as obtaining at first 5% then 10% then 20% share of a given total market. Many business planning guides reinforce this top-down aggregate market share approach or have revenues result from projections based on costs and break-even numbers relative to investments. These revenue projections rarely stand up to time.

It is important to understand that there can be a significant difference between target customers' receptivity to buying your products or services and, moreover, a difference in interest in the concept and actually purchasing. In some cases, the idea sounds or looks better than the reality. This might be due to the inability to reasonably demonstrate the idea by virtue of not having a good sketch or physical prototype. Or, a concept tests well then fails in the marketplace. Or, it might perform better than in prelaunch tests. In consumer products, good packaging and in-store displays can truly make new products shine. Or, in software and services, an excellent sales force can make an unclearly differentiated product sell better than others.

With this caveat in mind, we still need to get a read from target customers on their likelihood of purchasing your product or service offerings—assuming that it is placed in a channel that they prefer and priced to match their perceived value. For this, we have two questions in the field research guide:

Question 10: How likely is it that you would be willing to buy this offering?
Very unlikely   *Unlikely*   *Neither likely or unlikely*   *Likely*   *Very likely*

Question 3: How satisfied are you with the current products/services you use now?
Very dissatisfied   *Dissatisfied*   *Neither Dis./Sat.*   *Satisfied*   *Very satisfied*

Question 3 moderates Question 10. Trial is often induced by dissatisfaction with current products. The reasoning is that while customers can express a high level of purchase intent (i.e., really like a new product or service), unless they are unhappy with their current solutions, most are not likely to try something new unless "novelty" is an intrinsic part of their nature. The answers to this question are therefore used to put some hard-nosed reality into expressed purchase intent.

For both questions, customers within distinct customer groups are asked to respond along that five-point scale ranging from *Very unlikely* to *Very likely*. We are interested in the percentage of the prospective customers in your reality check that select either *Likely* or *Very likely*. This is classically called a *two-box score*.

We then combine the answers to these two questions with three more questions from the field research guide that assess the frequency of purchase and the typical "spend" for each purchase for different customer groups:

Question 6: How often do you buy similar products or services? (Open ended)

Question 7: How much do you spend each time you make a purchase? (Open ended but look for a dollar amount)

Question 8: Where is the best place to buy products/services such as this? (Open ended but look for a specific, preferred channel and ways in which they test or try products/services)

When combined with some key external data on market size, we can then estimate revenue based on the following equation:

Revenue projection = Sum (1 to N = Customer Groups):

   Customer Group % of Total Market x

   Purchase intent % x

   Dissatisfaction % (with current products/services) x

   Channel penetration x

   "Spend" on each purchase $ x

   Purchase frequency (times per year)

Let's first focus on getting a reasonable sizing of the target market, and then the percentage of each customer group within that total market. For these elements of the equation, a simple question on the field research guide won't suffice. Instead, you have to go to the Web and dig into government reports or industry statistics. In Chapter 1, we reviewed methods for mining public data sources for market size and growth rates. It is that same type of work that you must do once again to get a handle on *market size* in the terms of the number of potential customers, be they consumers, companies, or government organizations. If you cannot find hard data on the total market size of the percentage of the market for your target customer groups, you are going to have to make a reasonable estimate—and then be able to back it up with some good old common sense and supporting information. In addition, many new ventures have a channel strategy which itself is restricted to a specific part of the broader target market. That channel strategy also needs to be factored into the revenue projection.

Next, in the second element of the equation—purchase intent—we need the percentage of the top "two-box" score for each customer group. You must add the *Likely* and *Very likely* respondents to get that top two-box percentage.

The channel penetration is also an important consideration. If a particular channel can ultimately reach 100% of the total market—no problem. However, if it only reaches a part of a market, then that percentage needs to be factored into the revenue projection. For example, in the pet snack case, pet specialty only reaches 30% of the total market, on average, and in the field research, the team gathered specific channel percentages for each customer to help guide its projections.

Next, if we know how much customers in the group, on average, spend on such types of purchases, we have another key part of the revenue projection equation. That would be Question 7. Here, you are looking for an approximate dollar amount for each purchase occasion—be it a visit to the store, a purchase on a Website, buying a new software license, and so forth.

Subsequently, we need to understand the purchase frequency—the number of times per year that individuals in each customer group purchase, license, or subscribe to your product or service.

Now, let's see how all of this works out for the HealthyWags case. Let's break down the equation into HealthyWags speak:

Our scaled-up revenue projection = Sum (1 to N for Mother Goose, Dog Mommy, and Pet Buddy groups)

* Mother Goose, Dog Mommy, and Pet Buddy size (% of the Total Market)
* Purchase intent % (Question 10)
* Dissatisfaction % (Question 3)
* Channel penetration % (Question 8)
* Spend on each purchase $ (Question 7)
* Purchase frequency (times per year) (Question 6)

Now, let's look at the data, remembering that the N was 30 dog owners for this particular reality check.

Total Market Size:

- A simple Web search shows that the 2009/2010 National Pet Owners Survey found 62% of all U.S. households own a pet, which equates to 71.4 million homes! This has increased from 56% in 1988. (We wonder what this trends means for the pet industry in developing economies coming into new found wealth!)
- Of those pet owners, 45% own at least one dog.
- The company wants to start as a regional player, focusing on New England. The breakdown of households, reflecting approximate numbers gathered from public data sources, for the six New England states is as follows:

State	Households
Massachusetts	2,000,000
Connecticut	1,400,000
New Hampshire	500,000
Maine	475,000
Rhode Island	400,000
Vermont	240,000

Customer Group Size: Industry data shows that about 75% of all pet food buyers are female. That percentage is even higher for pet snacks. The HealthyWags teams ethnography and reality check research supported those general observations: the Mother Goose represents 50% of all target customers, Dog Mommy 40%, and Pet Buddy (i.e., males) only 10%. Furthermore, the field research shows that while 100% of women interviewed considered themselves customers of a healthy pet snack product, only 50% of the males interviewed did the same, reducing the male participation in revenue generation by a further half.

Channel Penetration: From Question 8 above, we have the following:

Question 8: Where is the best place to buy products/services such as this? (Open ended but look for a specific preferred channel and ways in which they test or try products/services)

Mother Goose:	Supermarket (34%), pet specialty store (33%), Walmart (33%)
Dog Mommy:	Supermarket (20%), pet specialty store (50%) including independents, mass merchant (10%), club store (20%)
Pet Buddy:	Supermarket (60%), pet specialty (10%), mass merchant (30%)

Purchase Intent: From Question 10, we have:

Question 10: How likely is it that you would be willing to buy this offering?
Very unlikely   Unlikely   Neither likely or unlikely   Likely   Very likely

Mother Goose:	25% Likely/Very likely
Dog Mommy:	50% Likely/Very likely
Pet Buddy:	10% Likely/Very likely

Dissatisfaction With Current Products/Services: From Question 3, we have:

Question 3: How satisfied are you with the current products/services you use now?
Very dissatisfied   Dissatisfied   Neither Dis./Sat.   Satisfied   Very satisfied

Mother Goose:	20% Dissatisfied or Very dissatisfied
Dog Mommy:	30% Dissatisfied or Very dissatisfied
Pet Buddy:	5% Dissatisfied or Very dissatisfied

Spend on Each Purchase: And from Question 7 we have:

Question 7: How much do you spend each time you make a purchase? (Open ended but look for a dollar amount)

Mother Goose:	$5
Dog Mommy:	$7
Pet Buddy:	$3

Purchase Frequency: And from Question 6:

Question 6: How often do you buy similar products or services? (Open ended)

Mother Goose:	Once a month
Dog Mommy:	Once a month
Pet Buddy:	Once every 2 months

With these elements in hand, we can construct the revenue projections. Let's start first with one state and then expand to the rest. In fact, it would be reasonable for this venture to launch first just in Massachusetts, their "home turf" and the largest of the New England states in terms of dog owners and potential revenue. For just Massachusetts alone, the revenue projection equation would be:

Total market for Massachusetts = 45% of 2,000,000 households = 900,000 households.

Mother Goose (mature female, kids or empty nester, primary grocery shopper)

　　　　50% of dog households (900,000) = **450,000** customers x (Question 1)

　　　　25% purchase intent (likely/very likely) = **112,500** customers x (Question 10)

　　　　30% dissatisfaction = **33,750** customers x (Question 3)

　　　　33% channel penetration (pet specialty stores) = **11,137** customers x (Question 8)

　　　　$5 spend per month * 12 months = **$668,250 per year**

Dog Mommy (younger female, no kids, primary grocery shopper, pet is the kid)

　　　　40% of dog households (900,000) = 360,000 customers x

　　　　50% purchase intent (likely/very likely) = 180,000 customers x

　　　　40% dissatisfaction (dissatisfied) = 72,000 customers x

　　　　50% channel penetration = 36,000 customers x

　　　　$7 spend per month x 12 months = **$3,024,000 per year**

Pet Buddy = (male, not a primary grocery shopper, pet is friend/pal, not focused on healthy snacks)

　　　　10% of dog households (900,000) = 90,000 customers x

　　　　10% purchase intent (likely/very likely) = 9,000 customers x

　　　　5% dissatisfaction = 450 customers x

　　　　10% channel penetration = 45 customers x

　　　　$3 spend per month x 6 (every other month) = **$810 per year!**

Indeed, it doesn't make any sense focusing on those male shoppers unless the team can figure out a clever way to *bring more males into market!* But that takes a lot of time and a lot of advertising money—not the stuff for a new venture.

The total revenue projection for Massachusetts alone is therefore **$3,693,060.** This also assumes that those consumers who make an initial purchase continue to be "repeat" purchasers—which is not always the case. In fact, in many cases, entrepreneurs make estimates for initial and repeat purchase, with repeat purchasing being a percentage of initial purchase or trial. But, given that such a high percentage of the Mother Goose and Dog Mommy groups saw the product as distinctive, were dissatisfied with their current snacks, and showed a high purchase intent, in this case repeat purchase can be assumed as strong. Of course, once HealthyWags is in the market—and if its products fail to "perform"—all bets are off with respect to repeat purchases. Execution is so very important for any good idea.

Now, we can extend this framework to all of the states to get a picture of the scaled-up revenue for all New England—a reasonable sales target for this venture over the course of its second year of business. Take a look at Figure 7.10. You can see the projections marching through Connecticut, New Hampshire, Maine, Rhode Island, and Vermont. The business comes out to about $9 million in revenue per year business, just in New England alone.

We are not quite yet done, however. The price points stated by the three customers in the field research were retail shelf prices. As the manufacturer, HealthyWags is only going to enjoy 65% of that number. Therefore, the actual revenue projection is more in the range of $6 million a year.

If the business were to scale nationally, the revenue number is very attractive since the 5 million households in New England pale in comparison to more than 100 million households (Well, really it is not 100 million as not all households have a dog—only 45%). Now, that's a business! And in the next chapter, we will learn how to project expenses and then operating profit from such a business.

Most important, in Figure 7.10, you can see the direct connection between the 50% top two-box score for Dog Mommy—those young females still without kids for whom their pet is the child, our target market—and the resulting revenue projections. That young female is the HealthyWags sweet spot, for sure. The Mother Goose is No. 2; and any business from guys for all-natural health pet snacks is going to be incidental to the success of the business. And, most important, potential investors who know the pet industry are going to look at the bases for your revenue projections, couple these with the product concept, and see the sense in the numbers. *That is what you want for people reviewing your venture concept, your business model, and the revenue projections for a scaled-up business. The bottom line is that you have done your homework on the revenue projections. Investors will respect that.*

The reality check for Health Monitoring Systems and Telestructures also showed attractive revenue potential. However, the bases for those projections were obviously different. In fact, in some ways, HealthyWags was a more complex calculation because of the complexities of trial and repeat that one finds in consumer products.

Health Monitoring Systems simply had to identify large assisted-living and home health agencies, find out the numbers of elderly managed by those target accounts, and use the "student project" excuse to get interviews with managers in those target accounts. From these interviews, the team determined an installation and ongoing monthly fee amount that was much like what ADT charges for installation and maintaining home security systems. (Go to http://www.adt.com to see this benchmark pricing for installation and ongoing monitoring.) All the terms used in our Field Research Discussion Guide questions—such as purchase intent, dissatisfaction, purchase frequency, channel penetration, and so forth— applied to the monitoring business but with different meanings. The team made what it felt was a reasonable assumption that one new major account was practical each year—because each account represents tens of thousands of elderly customers. It also had to make an

State	Households	Dog Households	Customer Group	% of Dog Households	% Purchase Intent	% Dissatisfied	% Channel Penetration	$ Spend	Purchase Frequency	Amount
Massachusetts	2,000,000	900,000	Mother Goose	50%	25%	30%	33%	$5	12	$668,250
			Dog Mommy	40%	50%	40%	50%	$7	12	$3,024,00
			Pet Buddy	10%	10%	5%	10%	$3	6	$810
										$3,693,060
Connecticut	1,400,000	630,000	Mother Goose	50%	25%	30%	33%	$5	12	$467,775
			Dog Mommy	40%	50%	40%	50%	$7	12	$2,116,800
			Pet Buddy	10%	10%	5%	10%	$3	6	$567
										$2,585,142
New Hampshire	475,000	213,750	Mother Goose	50%	25%	30%	33%	$5	12	$158,709
			Dog Mommy	40%	50%	40%	50%	$7	12	$718,200
			Pet Buddy	10%	10%	5%	10%	$3	6	$192
										$877,102
Marine	500,000	225,000	Mother Goose	50%	25%	30%	33%	$5	12	$167,063
			Dog Mommy	40%	50%	40%	50%	$7	12	$756,000
			Pet Buddy	10%	10%	5%	10%	$3	6	$203
										$923,265
Rhode Island	400,000	180,000	Mother Goose	50%	25%	30%	33%	$5	12	$133,650
			Dog Mommy	40%	50%	40%	50%	$7	12	$604,800
			Pet Buddy	10%	10%	5%	10%	$3	6	$162
										$738,612
Vermont	240,000	108,000	Mother Goose	50%	25%	30%	33%	$5	12	$80,190
			Dog Mommy	40%	50%	40%	50%	$7	12	$362,880
			Pet Buddy	10%	10%	5%	10%	$3	6	$97
										$443,167
									Total	$9,260,348
									65%	$6,019,226

Figure 7.10   HealthyWags' Scaled-Up Revenue Projection

assumption about the penetration rate within each account year by year—the equivalent of "channel penetration." The reasoning was that a home health agency would not convert all 100,000 customers at once into a system such as this. Even 10,000 new customers a year would be ambitious. Nonetheless, from its calculations, the team quickly found that the venture represented a revenue opportunity of tens of millions of dollars over the course of four to five years. We will show you the detailed financial projections for this venture later on in Part II. Just know that these financials were so attractive that the real venture team behind the venture "disguised for this book" raised over $7 million in first-round (called Series A) venture capital largely as a result of its projections and experience and quality of the founding team. And just six months later, the team landed its first multimillion-dollar contract to install monitoring devices in the facilities of a large assisted-living provider.

Telestructures revenue projections came out to under $10 million as a scaled-up business—but at the same time, it was a self-funded business and that sort of revenue would be wonderful for the founders, both in terms of operating profit and what the business would be worth should they ever wish to sell it. This team's reality check process was to interview commercial property owners and tenants that represented large, medium, and small businesses. Everyone had some type of computer networking and telecommunications system already, unless these were new tenants going into an existing property or a new commercial campus development. Levels of dissatisfaction with current services were therefore important. However, the reality of the revenue projection was that it was limited more by the number of skilled staff to draft the designs and perform system implementations that the team could bring on board each given year.

Also note that in all three cases, as well as your own venture, an important part of this reality check is not just what customers will pay, but how they prefer to pay it. In other words, we are trying to validate the "structure" of revenues within the business model. HealthyWags and Telestructures are fairly straightforward: buy this, pay that. But software is increasingly tricky. The traditional model of software licensing is transforming in subscriptions—monthly or annual rentals—based on the number of customers. For an entrepreneur, learning the structure in which customers prefer to pay you is just as important as how much they pay. As you might recall in Chapter 3, we wrote of a new firm that had tried for an entire year to sell an expert system for finding "lost charges" in health care providers—with little success. A $250,000 piece of software is expensive, regardless if it saves or makes a client ten times as much money. However, the day that the founders decided to charge nothing up front, but rather take 20% of the new revenue found for their clients, the business literally took flight. That team would have had preferably learned that lesson in a two-week prelaunch reality check rather than beating its head against the wall for a year before getting the "Aha!" on its business model. So should you!

Reader Exercises

As in all our other chapters, we have exercises for you to perform. This set is perhaps the most important of the lot because it is a field-based validation of everything you have done so far—the venture concept, the business model, the product/service strategy, and the positioning strategy.

Step 1: Create the Venture Concept Statement

Prepare your textual, one-paragraph statement of your venture concept. It should be two to three sentences. Use the examples in the chapter as a guide. You should be able to communicate the essence of your venture to potential customers in about 30 seconds. This will be important because most customers won't give you much more time than that in this type of field experiment! Practice on yourselves first and then on friends outside of your team. Did those friends understand the concept in 30 seconds? If not, keep reworking the text statement until it is clearly understood by outsiders.

Step 2: Create the Discussion Guide

Using Figure 7.6 as a reference, prepare your own Field Research Discussion Guide. You should cover all the various bases that are shown in that figure. Once again, practice with teammates and friends outside your team.

Step 3: Conduct the Field Research

Talk with at least ten potential customers. If you have distinctive customer groups be sure to talk to people in each group (e.g., 3 customer groups, 10 each = 30). If you feel that you still have unanswered questions or a lack of clear insight on product/service requirements, positioning, channel, and price, find more prospective customers.

Step 4: Analyze the Data

Now, begin to analyze what you have discovered. Use Figure 7.8 (A–D) as a reference for organizing the data and interpreting the results. What does this data tell you? For example, are customers interested in the concept? Are they likely to buy? How much are they likely to spend on each purchase? Importantly, through which channel do they prefer to buy your product or service? If you gather a sufficient number of respondents, the data should really tell the strength of customers' preferences for these and other important areas.

Overall, does the venture concept you created in Chapter 3, the business model you designed in Chapter 4, the product/strategy you developed in Chapter 5, and the positioning approach in Chapter 6 collectively make sense given this direct feedback from prospective customers?

Step 5: Create a Rich Profile of the Target Customer

Now, armed with this information from your customer groups, describe them in rich and thick detail. Which group, if any, is likely to be the core customers of your venture? Harkening back to Chapter 3, what are their core needs, their attitudes, their behaviors, and any hard demographics such as age or gender or industry affiliation? Figure 7.11 is a good template for this purpose. Fill it out with your customer insights.

Under behaviors, also include any special purchase cycle factors, such as the budget cycle for a B2B venture selling to large corporations or occasion-specific timing for B2C ventures selling gifts of one type or another. An extreme case might be a technology company whose customers only design new generations of their systems once every five years or so, which means a "design-in" for the venture's technology occurs only rarely. At the other extreme is a

Target Customers	Core Needs	Attitudes (toward family or work or lifestyle)	Behaviors (include buying preferences)	"Hard" Demographics (including percentage of total market/survey)
Group A	Perceived: Latent:	• • •	• • •	• • •
Group B	Perceived: Latent:	• • •	• • •	• • •
Group C	Perceived: Latent:	• • •	• • •	• • •

Figure 7.11 Know Your Customer Template

Web-based information service (such as in the "Generate" case in the back of this book) where customers want the venture's outputs fresh on a daily basis. Knowing your customer also includes knowing when they want to buy your products, systems, or services.

Step 6: Take a First Crack at Revenue Projections for a Scaled-Up Business

Now, using Figure 7.10 from our pet snack example as a guide, construct revenue projections based on your reality check. Remember, you are multiplying the percentage of customers who are "likely" and "very likely" to buy your products or services times their actual "spend" on those purchases. To this, you must also factor frequency of purchase and overall penetration into the target market for the channels that you are going to use. Also remember that these projections are for a scaled-up business of some reasonable size—and not the revenues that are likely to be achieved in the first year or two of the business. The structure of your spreadsheet will differ in terms of the labels for the headers for the columns and the levels for the various rows. Make this spreadsheet reflect *your* business, not the pet snack venture used as a teaching example.

Do those revenue projections look attractive to you? Is this the type of business in which you want to dedicate your time and effort over the coming five years? If a business shows the promise of strong revenue, you can usually figure out "all the rest" in terms of people, expenses, and capital. Without strong revenue potential, everything else is so *very, very hard.*

Step 7: Summarize Your Reality Check

Take a good 30 minutes to complete the chart in Figure 7.12. The chart has fundamental questions you must answer. Answer them as succinctly and clearly as possible.

Use short, bullet-point answers, as if you were going to present this to an interested investor. Then, underneath each set of answers, indicate your confidence level for that answer (Low, Moderate, or High). For many students, this is the "money chart." Good answers with high levels of confidence are your ticket to the leg of this journey to entrepreneurial success. And then ask yourself, does all of this add up? Is it worth a go? Or, what else do we still need to learn before writing our formal business plan?

As in our other chapters, the completion of this work presents a fine opportunity for a checkpoint before proceeding forward. Accordingly, we encourage you to show your results to your trusted advisors, your professors,

	Your Answer and Confidence Rank (Low, Moderate, High)
1. What is the business? (product, system, service)	
2. Who is the target end-user? Who is the target buyer?	
3. What problems does it solve for the customer?	
4. How is it different from competitors in terms of what "it" does?	
5. Would the customer pay more, the same, or less than what they use now if your product was available today?	
6. Where does the customer want to buy offerings like yours?	
7. How much and how often will the customer buy your offerings? Are there occasion-specific or budget cycle drivers?	
8. Where do customers normally learn about offerings such as yours?	
9. What else do they want to buy with offerings such as yours?	
10. Can we produce a strong stream of revenue in this venture?	
11. What additional features do you think are important in a (product or service) such as this?	
Do the answers to these questions add up to a cohesive, powerful venture concept and an attractive revenue model?	

Figure 7.12   The "Go, No-Go" Reality Check Template

and your classmates. Have some fun with it! Nobody comes back from the field without a few surprises. This is what makes entrepreneurship not only challenging but fun. Think of yourself as a highly adaptive, fleet-footed individual who can respond faster to new insights than any established competitor in the target market.

*** *** ***

Well done! A market-tested venture concept and business model are a lot more than most first-time entrepreneurs have in their arsenal before writing a business plan and making a pitch to investors. We hope you now realize the power of your industry and customer insights and how this sets you apart from those many other would-be entrepreneurs who just "wing it" in writing a business plan.

The results of all this hard work are going to pay off "big time" in Part II—which comes next. So, take a deep breath. Give yourself a huge pat on the back. Go celebrate for a bit with your teammates and your advisors. And then, get ready.

In Part II, we will learn how to translate your work to date into a set of realistic financial projections, a well-written business plan, and a compelling pitch for investors.

part 2

Writing the Business Plan and Making the Pitch

Developing Financial Projections, Writing the Business Plan, and Making the Pitch

Part II of this book is focused on translating the venture concept and business model into a professional, pragmatic set of financial projections, a business plan, and a winning pitch. Whereas Part I was about industry insight, customer insight, competitors, and creative solutions, Part II is focused on execution. Now is the time to drive to the goal of getting startup funding.

Before starting down this path, it is essential to first understand the types of investors who finance ventures, their preferences, and behaviors. Chapter 8 walks through the different types of investors, how they think, and how they act. The entrepreneur needs to decide which type of investment source is most appropriate for his or her venture. This increases the likelihood of success; it also helps spare you a lot of wasted time and energy. If you have a classic niche-focused software company which—if all goes according to plan—can reach $20 million in sales over five years, it makes no sense going after venture capital firms that only touch companies where at least $50 million if not $100 million is the target for portfolio companies. Creating a $20 million a year, profitable business is a huge accomplishment; there are many other sources of startup and growth financing that will be interested in such ventures. Of, if you are not willing to give control over key management decisions to outside investors, then this too narrows down the field of suitable investors. The trick is to know who you are as an entrepreneur and as a venture, and then seek investors that fit you and your venture in terms of industry interest, the amount of money available to invest, and the degree of hands-on involvement required by the investor. Raising money is a sales process. Like any sales process, raising money requires that you know your customer (the investor) and what you have to sell (your company).

With these insights, we then have you march forward to create three deliverables:

1. A comprehensive set of financial projections for the revenues, expenses, cash flow, and assets of the proposed venture. This is the focus of Chapter 9. We take financial projections seriously and so should you. There is a lot of thinking that needs to go into modeling revenue and expenses for a venture. If you simply make up a bunch of numbers and use the power of spreadsheets to thoughtlessly replicate those numbers out into the future, investors will spot it in two seconds. Chapter 9 teaches the discipline of creating robust, pragmatic financial projections for new ventures. Fortunately, none of you are starting from scratch. Your work in Chapter 4 (Business Models) and Chapter 7 (The Reality Check) serves as the platform for creating a great set of financials.

2. An equally comprehensive business plan integrates market, customer, solution, sales, team, and finance all in a single, concise, and powerful document. However, before writing the plan, you also need to consider the skills and balance of your venture team—not only for what needs to go into the team section of the business plan *but to write the plan itself!* Chapter 10 addresses the organizational aspects of writing the business plan and launching a venture.

3. Chapter 11 focuses on actually writing the business plan. Here, too, all of your work in Part I of the book is the platform for writing a powerful plan. That plan needs to be a rifle-shot plan to hit your target market, creative yet pragmatic in its contents and appealing to investors. Throughout the chapter, we will provide the questions that are at the top of investors' minds as they read each particular part of the business plan.

4. Chapter 12 teaches you how to develop a short, compelling pitch for investors. There is definitely an art to making a successful pitch. Part of it is to know who you are pitching to. But the other part is to tell the story of your target customer and your business in a way that is clear, convincing, and engaging. How do you take all the information you have gathered and learned about your industry sector, your customer, your competitors, your products or services, and your business model and present this in ten slides or less? How can you stand out among dozens of entrepreneurs that professional investors see each and every month? These are the challenges tackled in this chapter, the last in our book.

So, while you have worked hard in the chapters leading up to this point, now it is time to work hard in a different way. You now have intimate knowledge of your industry, your customers, and your competitors. You talked with prospective customers and have direct feedback on your solutions for them as well as the key dimensions of your business model. Now is the time to shape all this knowledge into "the numbers, the team, the plan, and the pitch."

Part II is the launch pad for your venture.

chapter 8

Sources of Finance for Startups and Corporate Ventures

8

The Purpose of the Chapter

Family and friends, "angel" investors, and venture capital (VC) firms—these are the major sources of financiers for new ventures. Their investments tend to differ by the amount of the money provided, ranging from tens of thousands of dollars for family and friends, to hundreds of thousands for angel investors, to millions of dollars for venture capital firms and direct investments by existing corporations. And the structure of these investments—while primarily cash for equity in the venture—can vary by a range of specific criteria and financial instruments. This ranges from a startup loan from family members, to equity with warrants to buy more equity at a specified price, to debt with interest convertible to stock (under certain conditions) with full voting rights as if the debt amount were stock. But beyond these facts, there is a lot to learn about the style as well as the substance of venture finance. That is the purpose of this chapter.

It is also important that you keep venture finance in its proper context. Sure, most startup or corporate ventures need some startup capital to get up and running—and then to grow. However, don't let the importance of finding money distract you from the even greater importance of creating products and services that target customers want to buy and then, to convert that interest into revenue, and then the revenue into cash. As a friend who is a venture capitalist said, "Entrepreneurs should worry more about their customers than me or my colleagues with the money. Find an initial set of customers, serve them well, and you will find that the venture money will come to you."

Learning Objectives

In this chapter, we will learn about:

- The stages of company growth and the common uses of funds for each stage of growth
- How professional investors expect to make money by investing in your company
- The types and inclinations of different types of investors
- How investors will value your business for the purposes of investment
- Ways you can increase the premoney valuation of the your venture
- Some tricks of the trade for raising startup capital

The Stages of Venture Development and the Relevant Funding Types

Whenever successful entrepreneurs raise a current round of investment capital, their thoughts are always on the need and timing for the next round of financing to support the next stage of growth.

It is useful to think of a new venture evolving through distinct stages of growth where the company raises investment capital to achieve milestones in a current or next stage of growth. Here are four relevant stages of growth for startup ventures:

Seed/Startup Stage

At this stage, the founding team already has its venture concept and is trying to build a prototype of its product, system, or service. The entrepreneur's innovation is under development—which includes doing the user research as well as any sort of initial technology implementation—but the venture is not fully operational. This is where you are now having successfully completed the first section of this book. The goal is to make your product or service function, package it correctly for marketing, and get it to market through appropriate channels.

Such "ventures" have usually been in the "concept" stage for a year or less and the founders are seeking money to get to first commercial launch. Most technology-focused firms try to get to an initial "alpha" test of their product or service in three to four months, to a more full-scale "beta" test in another two months, and then to complete all the technology and marketing collateral development in another three months. This makes it a full nine months to a year to bring an idea to market and start generating revenue.

Over the years, this early stage financing has been called "zero-stage," "seed," or "startup." The most common term is "seed" financing.

This initial round of funding is usually limited to under $250,000 and is more typically under $100,000. When funds are less than $100,000, bootstrapping—using funds from the venture team itself, or from family or friends—is typical. When it is over $250,000, entrepreneurs tend to search for angel investors operating either individually or in "groups" in their local area (unless you have a rich uncle or aunt!).

In fact, over the years, venture capital and other forms of institutional money have drifted even further from the seed stage. Venture capital firms—which are formalized investments pools with general (or investing) partners and limited partners (institutional money)—have comprised only 5% of seed investments in the United States! If you had a perception that it is venture capital firms that fund startups *at the beginning,* the data do not support that perception. Only a handful of companies get their first-round financing from venture capital firms. In the teaching cases for this book, we include two cases of friends who were part of that handful—and we encourage you to read that in both cases, each talked to dozens of venture capital firms before securing an investment. All the other cases are startups that either were self-financed or were internal corporate ventures funded as part of the annual corporate budgeting process.

Development and Initial Launch Stage

Funding at this point in time is generally called "Series A" financing. At this stage, the product, system, or service has been tested with users and is in some form of pilot production. And in a significant percentage of cases, the product or service might be commercially available in some limited way. Usually, the venture has been in business for less than several years and, more typically, fewer than 12 months. These have been long, hard months where the founders have received minimal salaries, fought for an initial set of customers, and worked day and night to create a functional prototype. The venture may or may not be generating revenue. However, if you want to raise money from professional investors, even a little bit of revenue suggests that your venture concept is worth a customer's cash—always a good indicator to an outsider.

Today, the vast majority of Series A financing comes from angel investors—successful businesspeople who working alone or in groups pony up between $250,000 and $1 million to turn teams and working prototypes into money-making machines. For example, one of your authors is a cofounder and advisor to a medical billing services company that first spent 18 months with founder seed money, developing specific software and started generating revenue with several large hospitals. In early 2010, this company then raised approximately $1 million from a group of six angel investors for about 10% of the equity. The fundraising process, all told, took three months.

Typically, angel investors not only want to make money but to build a self-sustaining business as well. They have a certain amount of patience for trying things, learning, and adjusting strategies for growth.

For that handful of ventures that receive Series A financing from venture capital firms or other institutional investors, the financing amount tends to be higher. Only about 15% to 20% of Series A financings in the United States come from venture capital firms. One of the cases in this book—Sentillion, making medical software—received $2.7 million in Series A financing from venture capital firms. One of your authors had a hand in this venture as well. It took the better part of six months to secure the Series A financing. Moreover, this company was a corporate spin-off in which Hewlett-Packard had already funded the initial software development. As in the case of Sentillion, Series A financing from venture capital firms tends to be in the $2 million to $4 million range, and often the funding comes from multiple sources. Rather, the lead VC firm brings other firms into the round. This is called a "syndicated" investment. That means that you, as the entrepreneur, will have not just one partner of a VC firm on your Board of Directors but two or three! Be prepared because these are "active" investors and the clock is always ticking. Building a category-leading company is the clear motivation; but achieving "exit"—one way or another—is clearly another.

In addition to allocating invested capital in R&D and market launch, Series A investors—be they angels or venture capital firm partners—focus on building out the management team of a fledgling company. It is typically assumed that the venture has the technology smarts needed to be an excellent company—that is one of the foundations for the investment. However, it just as typically assumed that the founding team does not have the marketing or operations expertise needed to scale up a business in a competitive marketplace. Be prepared for "suggestions" to augment the capabilities of your management team with some experienced managers.

Expansion (Growth) Stage

This is generally called "Series B" investment. Sometimes, a follow-on Series C investment is made as well—all by the same core group of institutional investors plus new investors.

By this point in time, the company is two to four years old, has had a successful launch of its products or services, has an excellent management team, and is ready to scale. By *scale,* we mean that the company is set to increase production, engage in serious branding activities, expand market reach both regionally and globally, and substantially beef up its customer services and support. Next-generation R&D for new products and services is also on the table for investment consideration—as might be a select acquisition or two to buy new technology. Moreover, not only has the company expanded its revenue, but it has also achieved its first operating profit.

Each one of these activities takes a million dollars or more to accomplish. Put them altogether and one can see why this Series B financing is typically a multimillion dollar affair. While early angel investors may participate in this next round by matter of having clauses in their investment agreements that guarantee the right to purchase additional shares at an attractive price, the bulk of the Series B financings comes from venture capital firms. Sentillion, to continue the example from above, received $9 million in its Series B financing within three years of startup. The company channeled this money into all key parts of the business: It expanded the product portfolio through R&D, built a strong North American sales program, and beefed up its field integration services for customers.

Recent data show that 40% of all venture capital firm investment is made at this stage of growth.

Later (Maturity) Stage

This is generally referred to as "Series C" financing. In past years, entrepreneurs often referred to this as "mezzanine" financing, the step that gets the company to an initial public offering. Forty percent of all venture capital firm investment is channeled to this stage as well.

These later-stage investments are by venture capital firms with large funds to invest (sometimes in excess of a billion dollars to put to work!) or private equity investment firms such as Bain Capital. These later-stage investments tend to start at $20 million and can reach far higher. The goal here is to become the market leader in a specific category. Sentillion, for example, received close to $20 million in a Series C investment about four years after startup. All told, the company raised approximately $30 million in investment capital before Microsoft acquired the company for many times that amount.

If these numbers seem large to the reader, know that they are large for anyone, including most investors! And know further that the founder of Sentillion started off as a senior-level programmer in Hewlett-Packard with a vision and the common sense to ask trusted advisors the hows and whys of writing a business plan and pitching to early investors. (The Sentillion case is in the back of this book.)

Series C investments can also come in the form of direct investment from major corporations. For example, one of your authors cofounded a real-time operating systems company that received close to many millions of dollars in direct "strategic" investment from Microsoft in 2000, after having received its initial Series A financing from a local venture capital firm.[1]

Exit

Very few ventures achieve an initial public offering of company stock—the ultimate exit hoped for by investors because of the enormous (we have seen 100 times) returns often enjoyed with such events. Far more frequent is that "exit" is achieved by being acquired by a larger corporation. These acquisitions are called "mergers and acquisitions" because often the acquisition is structured as a merger to use stock for the transaction and take advantage of certain tax regulations.

Courtesy of Thomson Reuters and the National Venture Capital Association, Figure 8.1 shows the brutal reality for those seeking an initial public offering (IPO) for a startup. The number of IPOs in the United States dropped from a high of 84 in 2004 to a mere half dozen in 2008, and 12 in 2009. In contrast, exits achieved through the big company buying a small company route have remained fairly constant at about 350 deals. Even in the difficult 2009 timeframe, 271 such deals occurred. While 2010 was shaping up to be a more productive year for IPOs, mergers and acquisitions still dominated the exit landscape for ventures.

Figure 8.1 also shows why investors would prefer an IPO if that type of exit could be achieved in a reasonable period of time. Even though the average deal size for acquisitions and IPOs was roughly the same, the deal size for the acquisition is for the entire value of the company, while the deal size for an IPO is only for that percentage (say 10% to 20%) of the total company stock that is placed into the public offering.

		Mergers and Acquisitions Exits				IPO Exits	
Year	Total M&A Deals	M&A Deals With Disclosed Values	*Total Disclosed M&A Value ($ in millions)	*Average M&A Deal Size ($ in millions)	**Number of IPOs	Total Offer Amount ($ in millions)	Average IPO Offer Amount ($ in millions)
2004	349	188	16,043.8	85.3	94	10,481.6	111.5
2005	350	163	17,324.7	106.3	57	4,482.4	78.6
2006	377	164	19,034.8	116.1	57	5,117.1	89.8
2007	379	168	29,460.0	175.4	86	10,326.3	120.1
2008	351	119	13,775.4	115.8	6	470.2	78.4
2009	271	91	13,531.1	148.7	12	1,642.1	136.8

Figure 8.1 The Market for Acquisitions and IPOs in the United States (2004–2009)

Source: Thomson Reuters & National Venture Capital Association.

*Only accounts for deals with disclosed values

**Includes all companies with at least one U.S. VC investor that trades on U.S. exchanges, regardless of domicile

---

[1] Look up *Ardence* in Wikipedia. Ardence started off as VenturCom and received investment from Microsoft in July 2000, which also licensed the software—a real-time module for embedded applications software development. Ardence was later acquired by Citrix and then spun out again as IntervalZero.

While IPOs are relatively infrequent, they do occur. Take a look at Figure 8.2, which shows the value of the equity held by management and investors in A123 Systems the day after the IPO. This manufacturer of innovative high-energy-producing lithium-ion batteries went public in 2009, raising more than $350 million in capital from public markets, with a stock price that doubled in the first day of trading. This capital was coupled with a nonequity dilutive $249 million grant from the federal government for building manufacturing capacity in the United States for the green economy. The stock of the founders of A123 Systems was suddenly worth tens of millions of dollars and that of the venture capital investors hundreds of millions of dollars. An alumnus of our university, a partner with Northbridge Venture Partners, was one of those lead investors in A123 and remains a member of the Board. The equity of his firm alone in the A123 IPO was $180 million. Still, Thomson Reuters estimated that on average, A123's venture capital investors made about four times their money on this particular deal—good, but not the ten times that many VCs state as their investment objective.

Shareholder	Number of Shares	Percentage	Value as of Day After Trading
All Directors and Officers as a group (15 persons)	25,769,226	25.8%	$522,857,596
North Bridge Venture Partners	8,859,619	9%	$179,761,670
General Electric Company	8,280,622	8.4%	$168,013,820
Gururaj Deshpande (Chairman of the Board)	7,017,629	7.1%	$142,387,692
Qualcomm	5,351,864	5.5%	$108,589,321
Motorola	4,844,914	4.9%	$98,303,305
Morgan Stanley Emerging Markets	3,107,899	3.2%	$63,059,068
Sequoia Capital	2,886,506	2.9%	$58,567,207
AllianceBernstein Venture Fund	2,713,314	2.8%	$55,053,141
Anchorage Capital Master Offshore	2,497,919	2.5%	$50,682,777

Figure 8.2 A123 System's IPO: A Big Score for Management and Investors

Source: Thomson Reuters and the CleanTech Group, as posted in How A123 System's Investors Fared in the IPO, by Katie Fehrenbacher, http://earth2tech.com, Oct. 1, 2009.

While IPOs such as A123 are rare, in contrast one frequently reads about IBM, Oracle, Microsoft, Google, or some other large technology company buying yet another small company to add spice and breadth to their respective portfolios. Sometimes these acquisitions are just to gain access to a technology; but more often, it is to reach a new target customer group or serve a use within current customers.

Now turn to Figure 8.3. It shows the financial performance of a venture that is often attractive to the corporate buyer. The figure comes from yet another one of our teaching cases in the back of the book: Generate, Inc. Here, the entrepreneur started an information services company. It targeted professional sales forces by gaining access to thousands of real-time news feeds and filtering these to present information and business contacts simply and effectively, customized for individual preferences.

The founders had invested $200,000 of their own money as "seed" capital and for the Series A, $3 million as a direct strategic investment from one of their news suppliers with a highly

	Beta - 2005	2006	2007	2008
New Customers	2	30	49	147
Recurring Customers		2	34	83
Total Customers	**2**	**32**	**83**	**230**
Average Revenue per Customer	$17,000	$50,000	$50,000	$50,000
Recurring Bookings		28,900	1,066,831	3,020,568
New Bookings	34,000	1,571,000	3,034,043	8,458,897
Total Bookings	**34,000**	**1,599,900**	**4,100,874**	**11,479,465**
Revenue	$4,250	$1,001,844	$3,401,870	$10,102,559
COS	$59,250	$978,417	$1,185,000	$4,649,710
GM	(55,000)	23,427	2,216,870	5,452,849
%	−1294%	2%	65%	54%
OpEx	613,093	1,552,233	3,100,438	4,903,550
Op Inc +/−	(668,093)	(1,528,806)	(883,568)	549,299
Adjustments for Working Capital		(30,055)	(102,056)	(303,077)
Ending Cash	$3,774,144	$2,215,283	$1,229,659	$1,475,881
Headcount	11	33	73	91
FTE	5	27	55	81

Figure 8.3   Generate, Inc.: Financial Performance on the Road to Exit—A B2B Information Services Venture

Source: Generate, Inc., by Marc H. Meyer and Richard Luecke, Northeastern University, Boston, MA. 2010.

favorable valuation, leaving the founders with majority ownership of their company. After tremendous execution of the business plan, Dow Jones acquired this company three years later for an amount in excess of $50 million. From Figure 8.3, you can see that the company had reached $10 million in annual sales with attractive gross margins. And it had achieved a small operating profit even with sizable investments in information technology and marketing to grow sales.

The case of Generate is certainly a model for success for any entrepreneur to consider before going to institutional sources:

a. Seed a distinctive venture concept with your own savings,

b. Build the prototype and get your first customers,

c. Raise a Series A at highly attractive valuation from angels, VCs, or strategic investors,

d. Build a profit-generating company with strong sales growth over the course of three or four years, and then

e. Achieve an exit for you and your investors.

The A123 Systems IPO is once again an uncommon event. It went public, generating hundreds of millions of dollars in return for management and investors, and yet, according to plan, operating profit would come three years after the IPO! Moreover, all of this occurred in the middle of a huge economic downturn. It takes a very special company with very special technology aimed at a tremendous growth market to achieve a similar result.

The Sources and Types of Venture Funding

Equity Versus Debt

There are many sources of capital available for your new venture. At the highest level, there are two types of financing: equity financing and debt financing.

Of course, there is also a third type of investment—your own "sweat equity." This means working for no money during the startup period. Nearly all ventures have their share of that!

Equity capital is the investment made by an individual, partnership, or corporation in return for some form of ownership, typically through the purchase of stock at a predetermined price per share based on the premoney valuation of the company. When a company is formed, a certain numbers of shares, say a million, are created; some are issued to founders and investors, and other shares are held in abeyance for employee stock option plans or for future rounds of financing. The Board of Directors of a company can also decide to issue more shares for future rounds of financing, in which case current shareholders are diluted by the percentage that the new shares represent of the new total number of shares.

There are two classes of stock which concern investors: common and preferred. Preferred has special rights over common stock. When a company goes bankrupt and all assets are liquidated, debt holders get paid first, preferred shareholders next, and only then do common shareholders receive money—by which time is little or nothing. Or, if the company is going great guns and decides to issue dividends by choice or by the terms of the earlier funding deals, the preferred shareholders get paid before common shareholders. Most often, dividends for preferred shares are also structured as regular payments, whereas dividends for common stock are decided by the Board during its meetings. The preferred shares sit somewhere in between common stock and debt instruments in terms of rights in liquidation and dividend payments. And that is why most professional investors insist on preferred shares in early-stage companies.

It is also common in early-stage financings to have warrants issued to buy even more stock at a future date. The price of the stock for those warrants is set to be advantageous relative to what the stock should be worth if the business met its goals and were to raise another round of money. For example, a startup gets valued at $3 million with a stock price of $5 a share for a group of angel investors putting in $500,000. The team gets its product to market, generates $2 million in sales, and wishes to raise another $3 million to build R&D and a sales force. The valuation is set at $12 million, and the price per share for this next round increases to $20 a share. A venture capital firm is very interested in doing the deal. But factored into the valuation are warrants that allow the original angel investors to the equivalent of 10% more of the company at $10 a share, or an effective valuation of $10 million. The VCs push back for a lower valuation for themselves as well—and the negotiation begins!

Debt capital is money that an entrepreneur tries to borrow for working capital to pay for salaries and other operating expenses or to purchase equipment needed for operations. The startup must repay the principal with interest over a specific period of time. As a general rule, debt capital does not include any ownership interest in the venture unless you are dealing with particularly avaricious investors who try to structure your deal as debt with principle and interest payments that is also convertible to equity upon certain conditions—such as an exit event.

There are also many types of debt instruments used by entrepreneurs to fund startups: personal credit card debt, a second mortgage, or in some rare instances, a working capital line of credit from a commercial bank. However, without collateral in a startup, or receivables, it is hard to secure a line of credit for a new company. Revenue and assets need to be accumulated to secure such a loan—*particularly these days when credit for small business is tight*. Doing a seed financing on a personal credit card or a second mortgage on personal property is very common—and obviously, carries considerable personal risk!

The advantage of debt financing, however, is that the entrepreneur keeps his or her precious stock. Remember that at the end of the day, your fortune will be made on the value of the company in the form of equity—not your salary. The value of this equity will be in the stock or cash received from an acquisition, in the residual value of your holdings in an IPO, or in the pro-rata share of profits (without corporate taxation) that you are entitled to receive from a Subchapter S Corporation or a Limited Liability Company. Your venture's equity should be near and dear to your heart. You want to keep as much as possible for the founding team, knowing in advance that you will not be able to keep all of it if you need to finance growth. The disadvantage of debt, however, is that startups are always short of cash. With debt, you have to meet your payments whether or not the business is making money. Interest and principle payments are a cash drain on the business. Whether it is equity or debt financing, raising significant amounts of money is difficult to do. As the saying goes, there are only two ways to raise money: the hard way and the very hard way.

Sources of Venture Financing

While there are many different sources of financing for startups, the ones that are most common are:

- Your own savings for seed financing
- Family and friends for seed financing
- Angel investors, who invest their own money primarily for both seed and Series A financing
- Venture capital firms, who invest other institutions' money primarily into Series A, B, and C rounds. Increasingly, VC firms are focused on Series B and C rounds—putting more money to work at lesser risk relative to a brand-new startup. We think of VC firms as "institutional" investors because they draw their funds from institutional sources: pension funds, large corporations, and other investment companies.
- Direct strategic investment from large corporations. These may be suppliers for your venture, channel owners, large customers, or technology leaders who see synergy and leverage in your venture. This is an often overlooked source of Series A or later-stage financing. Experience suggests that valuations tend to be higher and covenants in the term sheets less restrictive in direct strategic investment than in traditional venture capital deals.

There are a number of other sources of financing for ventures as well. These include commercial banks, government programs that either provide direct research grants to technology companies or back commercial loans for any type of company, leasing companies, and direct investments by pension funds. Microcredit is also increasingly popular in emerging markets with loans of $500 or less. There are groups such as ACCION USA (http://www.accionusa.org/) that offer loans of up to $50,000 to entrepreneurs who have not historically had access to bank lending.[2] And, many universities have a business plan competition where winners get anywhere from $5,000 to $100,000. This is perfect seed money—but again, rare. The public markets are of course another source of business financing. However, none of these are common sources for the bulk of new ventures. So, let us focus on those that are.

---

[2] ACCION USA (http://www.accionusa.org/)

Founder Self-Financing

The most significant source of seed or early-stage financing for all new ventures, regardless of category, is the founders' personal savings. Seventy percent of entrepreneurs had used personal savings as a main source of funding for their first businesses, more than four times the number for any other form of startup financing. Friends and family and bank loans were a source of funding for around 13% to 16% of startups. While very popular in the entrepreneurial press as a source of startup capital, the fact remains that angel investments played a small role in the seed stage funding—just 9% of startups received early capital from angel sources. The same holds for venture capital firms: Just 11% of startups received venture capital.[3] For the entrepreneur, raising money from angels or institutional sources for a startup can only be viewed as "long odds."

As you might expect, the picture is a little different for serial entrepreneurs and their subsequent startups. More than half of the entrepreneurs still relied on their personal savings. But the proportion of entrepreneurs who obtain angel and venture funding increases with each subsequent business launch by the entrepreneur. A study of serial entrepreneurs found that 22% received private/angel financing and 26% received venture capital for their latest startup. Friends and family provided funding for 16%, and banks provided funding for 16% of the respondents' most recent startups. Direct strategic corporate investments comprised 7% of early-stage financing. Keep these statistics in mind as we discuss the various sources and types of venture funding.

When self-financing, the entrepreneur may draw upon any number of potential sources of personal funds, including the following:

Personal cash. Entrepreneurs who have some personal net worth may draw upon their personal assets to support a new venture. These funds may be invested directly into the business in the form of equity. Personal cash assets might come from cash in bank accounts or investments that can be liquidated. Common uses of personal cash invested in the business include buying equipment, inventory, and other startup expenses. Personal cash may also be used as a backup source of cash for personal needs for those times when a business is not able to pay the entrepreneur a salary. A common rule of thumb is to have enough cash saved to cover at least six months of basic personal living expenses before starting a business. It takes time for any business to reach breakeven and then to be able to provide consistent cash flow to pay the founding entrepreneurs. Many entrepreneurs are forced to give up a new business simply because they cannot afford to give business enough time to reach this point.

Other personal assets. Often a business grows out of a part-time endeavor, personal interest, or hobby. In such cases, the entrepreneur already will have purchased tools and equipment that they had purchased to support this interest or hobby. This equipment became an asset of the business and was treated as part of their equity contribution as shareholders of the business. Other common assets that are brought into a business include computers, cell phones, and office furniture.

Unsecured personal credit. A new venture is not likely to be able to secure credit financing. Many entrepreneurs will use personal credit cards or unsecured personal lines of credit to help finance a business startup. When personal credit is used for the business, it is essential to track personal versus business transactions very carefully to ensure clean recordkeeping. If an entrepreneur plans to use a personal credit card for the startup, it is preferable to get a separate credit card for the business transactions. Some credit card companies explicitly prohibit the use of personal credit cards for business purposes.

---

[3] Wadhwa, V., Aggarwal, R., Holly, K., & Salkever, A. (2009, November). The anatomy of an entrepreneur. Kansas City, MO: Ewing Marion Kauffman Foundation.

Entrepreneurs should read carefully the terms of use in the credit card contract for any personal credit card being considered for use in the business.

Second mortgage on property. For entrepreneurs who have built up equity in real estate, securing a second mortgage on a home or other property may be a way to fund a business startup through a bank loan. It is important to understand that this will be treated as a personal loan by the bank. The entrepreneur will be personally liable for the repayment of the loan independent of the success or failure of the business.

Pledging other personal assets. The entrepreneur also may be able to obtain a loan for the business by pledging personal assets that are easily liquidated and have verifiable market value, such as publicly traded stock or government bonds. Again, this loan will likely be considered a personal loan by the bank and not a direct loan to the business.

Working a second job. During the startup of a new business, many entrepreneurs continue to work their "day job" to support their personal expenses. If the new venture requires the entrepreneur to work during the daytime hours, the entrepreneur may pick up an evening job. If the business hours of the new venture are flexible, the entrepreneur may be able to keep a daytime job to make ends meet. A significant challenge is deciding when to phase out of the second job and rely fully on the proceeds of the transition. However, in reality the entrepreneur often faces a difficult, potentially risky decision of when to leap into a full-time, exclusive commitment to the new business.[4]

There are also some other novel ways that you can employ to self-fund your new venture. For those of you who are older (quite a bit older!), one source of capital can include your 401(k) retirement plan. Typically, early withdrawals of 401(k) funds face tax penalties. However, there are two ways an entrepreneur can use a 401(k) from a prior employer to fund their startup. First, the entrepreneur can convert those funds to stock in their company. This type of conversion requires a specialist to help establish what is called a Rollover as Business Startup or ROBS by the IRS. Alternatively, entrepreneurs can take their 401(k) from their existing employer, move the funds to a 401(k) in their new firm, and then take out a traditional loan against that new plan. Such loans are limited to $50,000 and must be repaid within five years. Either approach can be risky, because failure means the loss of retirement money. However, in tough times, the access to these funds to start a business can be critical. And you would be surprised at how many individuals become entrepreneurs as a second career upon retiring from a major corporation.

Some forms of self-financing can be problematic. Another form of sweat equity in startups goes under the label of "deferred compensation." Without cash from customers, entrepreneurs can choose to pay themselves little or nothing but enter what they consider a fair salary as a deferred liability on the balance sheet. They then expect to get that deferred salary redeemed upon successful financing. Unfortunately, most angels and venture capitalists will insist on writing that liability off the books as a precondition for funding. They simply do not want to see their money invested in yesterday's decisions.

Friends and Family

Another classic, important source of startup capital is friends and family. These are often gathered from the entrepreneur's individual and professional support network. It is useful to remember that friends and family have consistently been the most important source of startup capital for most types of entrepreneurial ventures, even technology-intensive ones. Walt Disney got started with funds from

---

[4] Cornwall, J. R., Vang, D. O., & Hartman, J. M. (2009). *Entrepreneurial Financial Management: An Applied Approach* (2nd edition, pp. 165–167). Upper Saddle River, NJ: Prentice Hall.

friends and family. This funding is secured most often at the seed funding stage. You are known to the funding source, a trusted entity, and they wish you well. On the upside, it is unlikely that there will be any sort of battle over the premoney valuation. Set a fair value. Again, for a well-reasoned idea—complemented by some type of reality check as described in Chapter 7—together with a well-executed business plan and perhaps a prototype, that valuation will typically be in the range of $1 million to $2 million. If you raise $100,000, these private investors get between 5% to 10% of your company. That is fair, particularly if your venture is grounded without the money.

There are downsides to taking money from friends and family—or more specifically, family! Let's say that your parents are physicians and clueless about the software company that you are starting. You have two other partners. One of partner's parents is a farmer and the other is involved in the newspaper business. You each borrow $25,000 from these family units. The parent-child relationship, while great for weekend visits, can prove difficult when real money in a real venture is involved. You cannot take calls every day in the middle of the day, even if the purpose of those calls is to wish you well. In addition, a board position for family members is awkward, at best. This venture is your time to stand up, be your own boss, and show leadership to people you bring into the business. The baggage of historical family relationships can easily distort the objective reasoning that you must have to grow your business. Therefore, if you take family money to start your venture—and yes, it is often the only source and therefore the best source—you need to set clear ground rules. Give your family members the stock they deserve at a fair valuation. As soon as you start generating profit, pay them back their seed investment in full and let them keep every share of stock as a warm thank you.

Angel Investors

Angels are an increasingly important component of entrepreneurship because they are professional investors who have a taste for seed and Series A financing. An angel investor is a wealthy individual that invests in startups—whether alone or in groups of like-minded individuals. Truly, these angel investors have become the financial engines for startups in our economy.

If you are going to raise money from an angel investor, you must understand their thinking and motivations. The majority of angel investors made their money by starting and/or building successful companies. The typical angel has already made the mistakes in his or her business career that you are about to make in the year or two ahead. Their desire is not only to put their money to work but to also put their experience to work to help make the investments worthwhile. While angels tend to have a lot of free time on their hands, they do not want to waste it. They want to find a younger entrepreneur who is serious about building a great company, one that is a good business as well as having or using good technology, and who will listen to and appreciate the angel's advice as much as his or her money. If you enter into conversations with prospective angel investors with this attitude—and a great business plan and PowerPoint presentation—you have a reasonable chance of success. If you appear arrogant, immature, or are a poor listener, you have no chance. An angel investor does not need to invest in you to feel fulfilled or become successful as a businessperson. He or she already *is*.

Therefore, angel investing is an individual decision on the part of private investors. In other words, they are investing a portion of their net worth. Even when angel groups put money into a company, shares are issued to the members of the investment group individually. Usually angels or angel groups invest less than $1 million per startup, and the more typical investment is in the range of $250,000 to $500,000. Of course, there are "super angels" that invest $1 million to $2 million in a new firm—but these are rare.

As an entrepreneur, there are certain rules or restrictions for angel-type investment. Figure 8.4 shows the U.S. Security and Exchange Commission's current definition of an "accredited investor" for the purpose of private equity investing. The idea is that you only want those individuals or organizations that can afford to lose all the money they are investing in you. Ventures are inherently risky.

Under the Securities Act of 1933, a company that offers or sells its securities must register the securities with the SEC or find an exemption from the registration requirements. The Act provides companies with a number of exemptions. For some of the exemptions, such as rules 505 and 506 of Regulation D, a company may sell its securities to what are known as "accredited investors."

The federal securities laws define the term accredited investor in Rule 501 of Regulation D as:

- a bank, insurance company, registered investment company, business development company, or small business investment company;
- an employee benefit plan, within the meaning of the Employee Retirement Income Security Act, if a bank, insurance company, or registered investment adviser makes the investment decisions, or if the plan has total assets in excess of $5 million;
- a charitable organization, corporation, or partnership with assets exceeding $5 million;
- a director, executive officer, or general partner of the company selling the securities;
- a business in which all the equity owners are accredited investors;
- a natural person who has individual net worth, or joint net worth with the person's spouse, that exceeds $1 million at the time of the purchase;
- a natural person with income exceeding $200,000 in each of the two most recent years or joint income with a spouse exceeding $300,000 for those years and a reasonable expectation of the same income level in the current year; or
- a trust with assets in excess of $5 million, not formed to acquire the securities offered, whose purchases a sophisticated person makes.

Figure 8.4 | Accredited Investors According to the Securities and Exchange Commission

Source: Securities and Exchange Commission.

Traditionally, the process of working with angel investors is that you will typically try to convince a single angel investor on the merits of your plan, and then he or she will contact a group of friends who each throw in the $25,000 or more each as a group to get you where you need to be. Ventures often put together a "private placement memorandum" that contains key elements of the business plan and the specific terms and conditions, including the number of shares offered and the offering price of those shares, as well as governance mechanisms (such as the Board of Directors) and other controls. Angels may want *preferred* stock rather than common stock because of preferential treatment on exit. They also tend to get issued "warrants" in the company at an attractive price per share relative to what the next round might be for new investors. Warrants are the sweetener in the deal.

Increasingly, individual angels work through angel groups. For example, the eCoast Angel Network (http://www.ecoastangels.com) is a highly regarded collection of angels working out of New Hampshire and Northern Massachusetts that has placed more than $20 million into a number of startups and supported these investments with deep operating experience among the members. And we have several others operating in the authors' Boston region such as CommonAngels or Launchpad Venture Group. The West Coast has dozens of its own angel groups, such as Tech Coast Angels, a large angel group that operates a number of "chapters" in Southern California or O'Reilly AlphaTech Ventures for Web 2.0 entrepreneurs in Northern California. The typical process is that the entrepreneur is invited to make a "pitch" at an angel group meeting. Expect to get grilled—often by individuals who are not particularly expert in your specific area of business or technology. If there is sufficient interest by angels in attendance, one of the members of the group will take the lead on investigating you, your team, and your business plan. This is called "due diligence." If you are fortunate to get a seasoned professional at this stage, visiting prospective customers or suppliers with them will be valuable for them and incredibly educational for you. The lead angel will also structure and negotiate a term sheet for a possible investment in your company. This term sheet with his or her recommendations will then be presented back to the other angel group members for investment. Your job is to make the lead angel your champion to his peers.

Angel investors play an increasingly important role in the funding of new ventures. Jeff Sohl, a professor at the University of New Hampshire's Center for Venture Research, has done a

Spotlight on Innovation: Tech Coast Angels

Tech Coast Angels (TCA; see http://www.techcoastangels.com) is known as the largest angel investor group in the United States. It has nearly 300 members, including a number of venture capital firms participating to get a lead on early-stage companies for later round investment. TCA has five chapters for angel investors operating in various counties in Southern California.

This is a very active angel group. In 2009 (which was a terrible economic climate for ventures in general), TCA still completed seven rounds of new investment deals and 17 follow-on deals. To do this, it raised $4.7 million directly from individual members (the typical member investment size ranges from $25,000 to $100,000) and $57 million follow-on financing through other sources, primarily venture capital firm affiliates investing larger amounts in later rounds. Since 1997, TCA has invested over $100 million in excess of 160 companies. These companies attracted over $1 billion of follow-on financing beyond TCA. TCA also segments its investments into seed and Series A projects. For a seed-stage venture, TCA's members will typically invest between $50,000 and $200,000, with a premoney valuation between $1 million and $2 million. For Series A situations—ventures with some traction and a good team—TCA's investment may range upwards of $750,000 or more, with premoney valuations in the range of $3 million to $5 million based on concept, team, closeness to commercial launch, or existing traction.

The typical scenario is that entrepreneurs will be prescreened by members with expertise in the industry. The entrepreneurs get feedback and some coaching at these meetings. Those proposals that advance to a formal screening will make a pitch to local chapters of TCA, where typically 15 to 20 members attend. If there is sufficient interest, which means 10 or more members expressing interest, a due diligence lead is assigned. Over the course of a month or two, the due diligence team does both the market, competitive, and solution investigation, and also negotiates the term sheet—including the premoney and postmoney valuation. There is a monthly meeting where the final presentation and term sheets are presented for individual member sign-up. Individual members can then decide whether they wish to participate in a specific deal. Those members that invest receive shares individually in the venture based on their contributions to the financing. This is different than a venture capital firm where the "pooled fund" receives shares and the proceeds from portfolio exits are then partitioned back out to institutional investors and the VC partners themselves. While term sheets are individually negotiated, TCA's investments tend to be structured as preferred shares with some warrants at attractive valuation in the future as a sweetener for the investors.

According to Richard Sudek, TCA chairman,

> "We take our responsibility very seriously as the key investment source for entrepreneurs in Southern California. TCA members are committed to assisting entrepreneurs reach the next level of success through funding and support."

Like other angel groups, TCA strongly believes that entrepreneurs get a lot more than just capital with an investment. As Richard remarked: (how he has helped a particular firm)

> "We see our role as more than just providing capital. We provide value to entrepreneurs by leveraging our expertise, experience, and personal networks. Approximately 70% of our members have started a company and provide expertise and assistance at many stages. Often our members will help our portfolio companies connect with strategic vendors, partners, clients, and VCs. Most TCA members join TCA not only to invest but to assist entrepreneurs in building successful fast-growth enterprises."

remarkable job over the years tracking the growth of the angel investment sector.[5] Jeff's research found that the total value of angel investment in 2008 was $19.2 billion, funding a total of 55,480

---

[5] Sohl, J. (2009, March 26). *The Angel Investor Market in 2008: A Down Year in Investment Dollars But Not in Deals.* Durham, NH: Center for Venture Research.

entrepreneurial ventures in the United States alone. During that same time period of 2008, the number of active investors was approximated to be 260,500 individuals.[6] Overall, Jeff found that like the venture investment in general, the total amount of money invested by angel investors declined from prior years, but the total number of deals actually increased. In other words, angel investors remain incredibly active—and with a rebound in stock portfolios, one can expect dollar amounts to increase as well.

It is no wonder that for many entrepreneurs, their local angel community remains the most feasible avenue for raising startup capital—with the caveat that the amount of those funds stays under $1 million for any given company. In other words, angels are a source of seed and Series A financing. In Jeff's most recent survey, 63% of all angel investments were for first-round investments, that is, seed financing. Angels also actively participated in later rounds of financing with 40% of their angel investments in the Series A stage. However, beyond that (Series B, etc.), angel investing drops precipitously. This is where venture capital firms and other forms of institutional investing take over, given the sheer amount of capital typically needed. In certain regions, angel groups are viewed as the "farm system" for the "big leagues" of venture capital.

There are also "specialty" angel groups with particular interests. For example, we have an old college classmate who has a small angel fund that focuses exclusively on "green" startups. There are also an increasing number of women's angel groups (Golden Seeds). In 2008, women angels represented 16.5% of the angel market. Women-owned ventures accounted for 15.7% of the entrepreneurs that are seeking angel capital, and 9.5% of these women entrepreneurs received angel investment in 2008. Minority angels accounted for 3.6% of the angel population, and minority-owned firms represented 3.7% of the entrepreneurs that presented their business concept to angels. The yield rate for these minority-owned firms was 11.3%.

There are many attractive aspects to angel investors generally. First, the angel investors we know have had management positions in operating companies. As noted earlier, they tend to have a lot of time on their hands, so they want to roll up their sleeves and help you succeed. They know what it takes to start a company and to build it. In addition, when things get tough with customer payments or suppliers, many angels help add some of that toughness back into your own thinking. This type of "mentor" capital is just as important as the actual money they provide.

Angel investors as a group tend to have reasonable performance objectives for a venture. Having been operating executives, they understand how hard it is to crack that first $1 million of revenue, the next $5 million, the next $10 million, and so forth. Our experience is that an angel investor will want to make three to five times his or her money over five years, have far fewer investments, and focus more on each one—compared to the typical venture firm that is driven hard, for a number of reasons that we will address momentary—to make at least twice that return.

Not all angels or angel groups are the same. It is essential that you try to find other entrepreneurs who have worked with a particular investor or an angel group to understand the dynamics of getting funding and working together to build a company. One useful site is thefunded.com (http://www.thefunded.com). It contains the opinions of entrepreneurs who have worked with VC firms across the country. Use the various filters to narrow the search down to your location, type of investor (angel or VC), and size of investment desired.

---

[6] The Center for Venture Research (CVR), at the Whittemore School of Business and Economics, University of New Hampshire, Durham, NH.

Spotlight on Innovation: Angels Are More Than Money: The Captain to the Rescue!

In your author's second company—another software firm started when our founding group was in our early 30s—we had one of the largest systems integrators in North America as the first key "reference" account. That company owed us several million dollars for some special software that powered the integrator's own next-generation solutions for major government and private-sector organizations. When we won the project, we saw that money as sparing us the need to raise outside capital to scale up our R&D efforts and marketing. Moreover, up until that time, we have been self-funding our venture to the tune of about $100,000. Well, that receivable stretched from 30 days to 60 days to 90 days, and there was no certainty that it would not 180 days. Meanwhile, the customers' programming staff was using our software and expecting bug fixes as well as new features—right away. We were in a true pickle: stuck with one large account that was eating up our resources, with someone in the treasurer's office of that company treating us like all other small companies (e.g., like dirt).

Enter "The Captain." One of the author's mentors was a serial entrepreneur who had launched half a dozen companies. In his youth, Mel—known amongst his friends as The Captain—had piloted planes in the Pacific during the Second World War. (Now approaching 90, The Captain still goes to work every day in a "new" company that he helped start in his 70s.) It occurred to us that perhaps if anyone could get us our money, it might be The Captain. And, as a mentor and Board Member in our first company, he would at least advise us. Mel drove over for lunch, we told him our problem, and the next thing we knew, he was on a plane down to the client. The Captain had two conditions: We had to pick up his plane ticket and we couldn't go with him. "You would only get in the way," he said. "And if I get you the money, you're going to have to give me some of it for my trouble; not that I need your money, but how else are you guys ever going to learn?"

Through other contacts, The Captain got 20 minutes with the general manager of the division that was our customer. And as the story is told, The Captain pulled out "the nuclear option"—unless the general manager personally called up accounts receivable and authorized a wire transfer that very day, no one in "Mel's" company would answer calls from the client's R&D group, starting as of 9 a.m. the next morning. The Captain explained how the software was mission critical to the client's future sales. He also assured the general manager that as a former pilot, he could easily enforce the no-call rule with any of those "young fellas" working up in Cambridge.

Of course, we had thought about doing this earlier but had feared losing our No. 1 key reference customer. The Captain had no such trepidations. "Not going to happen," he said later. "They need your software too much, whatever the heck it does." In fact, he said later that the discussion with the general manager of the division lasted 15 minutes and was not particularly unpleasant. He had offered the manager a discount on the invoice if payment was executed the next day. The general manager responded back, "three days." Sure enough, the customer wired the money owed less the discount to our bank account in three days. That money saved our company. In fact, we still think of that money not as the client's money or even our money—but rather as "The Captain's money." Seasoned angel investors—those with true operating experience—do such things for their investees and mentees. In fact, *they relish every second of it.*

Venture Capitalists

Venture capital is a fundamentally important segment of the private equity industry. In fact, many would contend that it has been the primary engine of technology-intensive entrepreneurship in the U.S. economy over the past 40 years. That success has brought a tremendous amount of money into the hands of venture capitalists—money that must be put to work in ventures that need and deserve that money. In 2008, for example, venture capital under management in the United States was estimated at $28 billion spread across over 3,800 deals. Those, we contend, are very big numbers fueling the next generation of our economy. Over the long term, the National Venture Capital Association reports that venture capital funds have paid out a net 15% to 20% internal rate of return (IRR) to their investors.[7] At one point, before the tech bubble in 2001, those returns were considerably higher—in the 30% to 40% range for the most successful firms.

Not only do venture capitalists have a *lot more money* to invest than angel investors, but in some ways, they also face greater challenges than a private investor. Venture capital firms are professional, institutional managers of risk capital that enable and support the most innovative and promising companies. When an investment is made in a company, it is an equity investment in a company whose stock is essentially illiquid and worthless until a company matures five to eight years down the road. Unless a company is acquired or goes public, there is little actual value.[8]

The venture capital firm itself has partners. There may be upwards of a half-dozen partners in a typical VC firm. The firm then creates "funds" (typically with ten-year terms over which proceeds are distributed to fund investors) and raises hundreds of millions of dollars for those funds. A venture capital firm will create a Limited Partnership with the investors as limited partners and the firm itself as the General Partner. Each fund or portfolio is a separate partnership. A new fund is established when the venture capital firm obtains necessary commitments from its investors, say $400 million. The money is taken from investors as successive investments are made. Typically, an initial funding of a new venture will cause the venture fund to reserve three or four times that first investment for follow-on financing. Over the next three to eight years or so, the venture firm works with the founding entrepreneur to grow the venture. The payoff comes after the venture is acquired or goes public. While there is a management fee ranging often in the range of 3% for invested capital, the VCs make their money on "the override" or "carry" on the invested capital.

This is how it works: Typically, most of the invested capital in the fund is committed over the first two or three years. That means just not the "A" rounds but the expected follow-on investments in a venture over successive rounds on the journey to exit. If a venture fund has $400 million in invested capital and four individuals in the VC firm as the managing partners, the typical scenario is that since a single person can only manage at best four to five ventures (as an investor and Board member), that means that the portfolio of ventures in the fund will be about 20 companies. Divide $400 million by 20 and one gets about $20 million that a single VC firm will invest over successive periods of financing in any given portfolio company.

Over that time period, the fund returns the invested capital back to its institutional investors, and then divides the gains above that amount in the form of 80% for the institutional investors and 20% for the VC firm partners. In "the good old days" of the technology bubble, we knew of several $200 million funds that grew to over $700 million. In those instances, the investors first received their original $200 million and then another $400 million. The four or five partners in the VC firm had the right to split up $100 million. That is serious money by any standards. And there are a number of funds where the venture capitalists did twice as well with even larger pools of money.

These days, the VC business seems to be a different and much more difficult animal. The declining market for initial public offerings has made achieving high returns a very hard thing to do. As noted earlier, in 2009, there were only 12 IPOs in the United States. Getting portfolio companies acquired remains as strong as ever. Here the numbers of acquisitions consistently number in the hundreds. (See Figure 8.1.) But the purchase price in an acquisition tends to be far less than the market caps of a successful IPO. The pressures of investing someone else's money and getting paid primarily on the 20% carry of the gains in those investments when the best way to make gains is largely absent—IPOs—makes the job of a venture capitalist anything but easy.

---

[7] Thomson Reuters (2009). *National Venture Capital Association 2009 yearbook.*

[8] Thomson Reuters (2009). *National Venture Capital Association 2009 yearbook.*

This means that whereas an angel might be satisfied getting three or four times his or her money from a venture investment, today VCs seek a ten-times return. Sure, there is the love of new ventures and new technology, but the payoff only comes from big successes on exits. In a portfolio of 20 startups within a venture capital fund or pool of $300 million to $500 million, six or more will be complete failures, and ten or more perfectly viable business that nonetheless cannot provide even a five-times return on an exit. That means that within any given portfolio, there needs to be those two or three stars that truly hit pay-dirt. Without those few "big hits" in a portfolio saddled by moderately valued ventures as well as good number of abject failures, a venture capitalist is going to gain a large personal benefit from the carry on the performance of the total fund. That is why the successful venture capitalist is so driven, so demanding, and so particular about his or her investments. Finding the jewel among the hundreds or more ventures that come across the table is so very hard—and yet, *it must be done*. And achieving strong returns is the only way the venture capitalist can go back to institutional sources to raise the hundreds of millions of dollars or risk capital to initiate another fund. While there are early-stage VC funds in the sub $100 million range, most today are in the $500 million plus territory. VC firms tend to raise new funds of this magnitude every three to four years, just enough time to put a current fund to work and free up time to put new money to work. It is an incredibly tough, demanding business—and this past recession has whittled down the ranks of those who call themselves venture capitalists.

Therefore, the fundamental insight for any entrepreneur visiting a top-level VC is that the person on the other side of table is under a tremendous amount of *pressure*. He or she has to put a lot of money to work in a very short period of time. Because ventures are so risky on so many fronts, there has to be two or three really big hits to make the math work. And you never know which one of the 20 portfolio companies will become that hit. Hits, in the form of IPOs or high-priced acquisitions, are exceedingly rare.

For all these reasons, it is also exceedingly difficult to raise money from a venture capitalist as a startup. And since VCs manage their own risk by syndicating with their associates in other VC firms, you typically have to sell two or three VC firms for an initial investment. It can be done, however. A case provided in the back of this book, SilverRail, describes an entrepreneur who raised $6 million from VCs to start his company. You will see that his target market is enormous, that he had a very specific niche within that industry as his business focus, and that his own experience in the industry was already substantial. Plus, his startup had a quick plan to acquire and then build upon proprietary technology. All this provided the potential of a big hit as well as some degree of risk mitigation for the VCs.

Therefore, if you have a company that over the first three rounds of financing needs to take in $20 million or more to generate a $100 million revenue per year enterprise, that upon exit can bring in hundreds of millions or reach a billion dollar market cap in a public stock offering— then venture capital is your ticket. It is nice to dream, but most startups don't fit that mold, nor do they need that much money!

For every 100 business plans that come to a venture capital firm for funding, usually only ten or so get a serious look, and only one ends up being funded. The venture capital firm looks at the management team, the size and growth potential of the target market, the distinctive compelling nature of the product or service concept, and sales and profit potential in the business model. The venture concept work we did in the first part of the book is essential homework for VCs. A new product or service concept that promises a 10% or 20% improvement on something that already exists is not likely to get a close look.[9] Just as important, the VC is going to analyze the projected financials to see just how much money is really needed over five years to build a scalable, category-leading enterprise. If you ask for $2 million and are expected give up 30% of your stock in a Series A financing, but the VC, based on past experience, believes that you

---

[9] Thomson Reuters (2009). *National Venture Capital Association 2009 yearbook.*

really need $4 million, the choice may be $4 million and 66% of your stock—or *no deal*. You thought you might keep controlling interest, at least until the second round. That is why entrepreneurs try to shop their ventures for the best-possible deal both in terms of dilution and terms. Unfortunately, however, VCs tend to share the same valuation insights and benchmarking services and structure their deals in similar ways: preferred stock, seats on the Board of Directors, participation rights in future offerings, preferential rights on exits, and various restrictive covenants that provide control and oversight on management decisions. While these terms and conditions are negotiable, the "Golden Rule" is in effect: "It is my money, so I rule!"

The VCs are also focused on certain key industries. They have to have expertise in the industry sector targeted by the venture team to provide value beyond money. If you want to call on a VC firm, visit that firm's Website. Look at its portfolio; read the backgrounds of the general partners. Do further research through the Web on the partner who invests in companies such as the one you wish to start or grow. And then try to find out a referral to that partner through a friend, a fellow entrepreneur, or an alumnus of your university. The least preferred method for reaching out to a venture capitalist is a blind mailing. It is the last item on their queue—and that queue is indeed already very long.

Many VCs also want the firm to be in the local geographical region simply because the lead partner on the deal is going to be an active board member. That means visiting the company every week or two in the beginning, calling on the telephone every day or two. Some VC deals are structured so that any significant financial expenditure must first be approved by the VC assigned to the Board. The VC is therefore a "hands-on" investor. Few inexperienced entrepreneurs approaching venture capital firms realize that that they are essentially asking for one-sixth of a person! And the VC is asking, "Can I actually work with this person? Will they listen to me?" Ask any venture capitalist who has had successful investments and he or she will tell you that ventures that break through the gravity of the early-stage growth evolved from the original business plan concept with the careful input of experienced board members and advisors.

Figure 8.5 shows the top industry targets for recent VC investments in 2008 and the geographical spread of these investments. For example, the top four industry sectors receiving venture capital investment represent over 60% of total venture capital investment (software, biotech, industrial/energy, and medical devices and equipment). Also, note that a single state—California—accounts for 47% of total companies receiving venture capital and over 55% of total venture capital investment.[10] For current data by industry, regions, and stage of investment, go to PricewaterhouseCoopers *MoneyTree* (http://www.pwcmoneytree.com).

The pressures driving VCs to make handsome returns on their portfolio companies have led to the nickname of "vulture capitalists." In their capacity as Board members, venture capitalists have driven out founding teams deemed inept or incapable of managing a business.

As a general rule, the objective of the entrepreneur is to raise as much capital as needed to achieve an exit or become self-reliant from operational cash flows—*without giving up majority control of the company to outside investors*. Once majority control of equity is relinquished, the founding team is truly subject to the Board of Directors' decisions because the founders can no longer control Board membership. As such, the Board can choose to remove the founding team from senior management. No entrepreneur wants to see that happen. So the objective for the entrepreneur is to try to keep majority control, and if not, preserve a Board that is friendly to the founders' wishes.

Boards of Directors are designed to hold senior management accountable for growth and profitability. For VC-funded companies, this gets ratcheted up a notch or two given the race against the clock to produce sales and operating profit. Even when an entrepreneur provides a minority stake in the company to a VC, they will insist on covenants as a condition of the financing that give the VC control over crucial decisions. These include any changes to senior

---

[10] Thomson Reuters (2009). *National Venture Capital Association 2009 yearbook.*

By Industry Category	% of Total VC Investments
Software	17%
Biotechnology	16%
Industrial/Energy	16%
Medical devices and Equipment	12%
Media/Entertainment	7%
IT services	7%
Semiconductors	6%

By State	No. of Companies	% of Total	Investment (millions)	% of Total
CA	695	47%	$5,917.30	55.20%
MA	138	9%	898.2	8.40%
NY	125	8%	768	7.20%
TX	56	4%	510.2	4.80%
WA	69	5%	405.2	3.80%
VA	37	3%	291.3	2.70%
IL	23	2%	229.5	2.10%
MD	32	2%	220.6	2.00%
NJ	33	2%	182	1.70%
PA	51	3%	168	1.60%
All Other States	223	15%	$1,123.70	10.50%

Figure 8.5   Venture Capital Investments in the United States (2008)

Source: National Venture Capital Association 2009 Yearbook, Thomson Reuters, 2009.

management, raising additional amounts of capital, and exits for the company, be it a sale or an IPO. The VC will want to know everything that you are doing—and if they disagree, you will not only know it but might find yourself under extreme pressure to either comply or make room for new senior management. You need a good lawyer on your side of the bargaining table. Insist on a full Board of Directors' vote for any change in management and require directors other than just the VCs themselves to sit on the Board. You will also need to resist having your founders' shares converted to options that vest over time, say in three years, as a condition of the financing. When times get tough—as they invariably do over the span of years—you don't want to see yourself out on the street with half your options unvested and returned back to the company. Hopefully, when you get ready to take VC financing for your new venture, you will come and read these pages one more time as you negotiate the term sheet with an experienced attorney at your side!

VCs are also notorious for playing hardball on valuations, including "down round" valuations that are less than prior rounds, which serve to further dilute early shareholders. But there are always two sides to any story: Many technical founders do not have the capability to manage and integrate all the functions of a business, and poor performance can well deserve a lower valuation in a subsequent round. But the most important thing to remember is that the entrepreneur's success is the VC's success. Most venture capitalists have done this enough times to know what it takes to grow successful businesses. This doesn't make the medicine any easier to swallow for the entrepreneur.

Receiving financing from a venture capital firm is a second form of marriage. You cannot expect to receive $2 million or more of someone else's money and not have them actively involved, particularly when their own investors want to see that money worth $20 million six or seven years down the road. Their entire, unswerving focus is to make your venture successful to the point that it achieves an exit that benefits all involved. And we have found that the connections that a good VC can provide throughout the industry for next-stage investments, channel partners, and technology add-ins are unparalleled.

As with angel investors, you want to search out entrepreneurs who have worked with a particular VC firm before you get too deeply involved. Again, you can check out http://www.thefunded.com, a Website that contains the opinions of entrepreneurs who have worked with VC firms across the country. Use the various filters to narrow the search down to your location and the size of investment desired.

TIP: SOCIAL VENTURE CAPITAL

There is also venture capital for social entrepreneurship, ventures that focus on social good, the environment, or tackling mature industries with new sustainable business models. For example, the Acumen Fund is a well-funded organization that makes investments (as opposed to grants) in health care, water, environmental, agriculture, and other types of social ventures in emerging economies. Its portfolio of projects is impressive. We encourage you to look at its Website (http://www.acumenfund.org) and consider for a moment about how this type of work might fit at some point in your own career. Groups such as the Good Fund (San Francisco), the Underdog Ventures (Vermont), or the Massachusetts Green Energy Fund work in various segments of social entrepreneurship in the United States. Many social enterprise groups make "grants" for community projects as opposed to equity investments in new types of companies. Seek those with highly experienced individuals with a business acumen managing activities and serving on the Board of Directors.

Corporate Financing

Working with large, mature corporations is an often under-looked source of venture finance. Clearly not appropriate for all situations, corporate money can still be the perfect complement to follow your own early-stage seed funding for a Series A or B, particularly given the long odds of raising money from venture capitalists. There are a number of forms of this type of investment. The three that we will describe here are direct strategic investment, corporate venture capital funds, and special innovation programs.

Direct corporate investment—often called strategic investment by entrepreneurs—takes personal contacts to get air-time with senior executives in a large corporation. If the entrepreneur can use these connections to raise capital, the money is only part of the benefit if the corporation is also a large reference customer. For example, the founder of Apropos, a call center software solution that identifies preferred customers and routes their calls to the front of the queue, was able to convince Allstate Insurance Company to participate in Apropos' $2 million early-stage financing. Since Allstate had one of the largest call center operations in the United States and became the venture's largest and best early reference site, the benefits were substantial. The founder, Kevin Kerns, made the poignant observation: "If some venture-capital firm uses our product, we can't say, 'They use our product at X venture-capital firm.' That means nothing. But Allstate is a name people recognize."[11]

Sometimes corporate investments are made directly from the C-Suite. More typically, the corporation forms its own venture capital fund to invest in early-stage companies. This "corporate venture capital" (CVC) is running between 6% and 8% of total venture capital investment or $1.2 billion to $2.0 billion in the United States.[12] Corporate money is known to be more patient than traditional venture capital, and some entrepreneurs have found that higher valuations are possible from corporate sources. There are significant investment programs in large corporations such as Intel, GE, Motorola, or IBM that make investments in entrepreneurial companies. If your venture is in the technology field, Intel Capital's Website is worth examining (http://www.intel.com/capital). Similarly, Google's commitment to invest $100 million a year in startups through Google Ventures (http://www.google.com/ventures) is another Website to investigate to get a feel about the foci and processes of corporate venture capital.

CVC programs in established corporations aim to learn about technology and business directions of strategic interest and then make investments that create new strategic opportunities for the corporation. By interacting with the firm's R&D and business operating units, CVC programs identify the operating unit's interests and priorities. CVCs support the corporation's existing businesses by introducing new technologies and partnerships to its operating groups. At the same time, CVCs help identify technologies and opportunities that fall between or beyond the corporation's existing businesses, which could then form the basis for new business directions.

GE shows the synergies sought in corporate venture capital. For example, in 2008, GE started a $250 million fund to invest in new health care technology companies. Typically, a CVC makes a financial investment—just as an independent venture capitalist does—and receives a minority equity stake in the entrepreneurial company. CVCs will also frequently syndicate with or work through traditional venture capital firms. Perhaps more important, large corporations look for synergies between their own parent company and the new venture. In the case of GE, for example, its medical divisions are already market leaders in diagnostic and imaging segments. The focus of the new fund is to advance solutions for disease prevention—that is, to move earlier in the health care continuum. GE has made a number of significant investments in the new energy sector as well.

Most if not all CVCs work hand in hand with traditional VCs, either syndicating with VCs on specific deals or making investments as limited partners in VC funds. By doing so, a CVC develops experience in venture investing, builds relationships in the venture capital community, and gains a view on the "deal flow" of technologies and companies seeking venture capital funding.

There are two important differences between most CVCs and traditional VCs. First, a CVC may make investments largely for strategic benefits and not just financial returns. A corporation may be interested in gaining a foothold on early-stage breakthrough technology that it knows will take ten years or more to ripen for wide-scale commercialization. A VC just doesn't have the luxury of waiting that long.[13] Second, in many corporate venture capital groups, the partners are paid differently.

---

[11] Popper, M. (1999, October 4). Hunting for venture capital? Don't ignore the corporate crowd. *BusinessWeek*. Apropos was later acquired by Syntellect.

[12] MacMillan, I., Roberts, E., Livada, V., & Wang, A. (2008, June). *Corporate Venture Capital (CVC): Seeking Innovation and Strategic Growth*. Gaithersburg, MD: National Institute of Standards and Technology.

[13] MacMillan, I., Roberts, E., Livada, V., & Wang, A. (2008, June). *Corporate Venture Capital (CVC): Seeking Innovation and Strategic Growth*. Gaithersburg, MD: National Institute of Standards and Technology.

Yes, there are bonus incentives for strong performance. However, typically these individuals do not participate directly in the override or carry on capital gains of investments. Remember, this is a powerful driver for the partners in a traditional venture capital firm, and it leads to certain tough-fisted behaviors. CVCs, on the other hand, do not have that same financial incentive. Many entrepreneurs feel that leads to higher valuations for their ventures and an involvement that is more patient than that of the typical VC. With that said, professionals working in a CVC are working to find good deals in great new companies, just like everyone else.

Corporate Innovation Programs

Some large corporations have established innovation programs to reach out to and partner with new ventures in specific areas of technology and application. These can be a great way for the young entrepreneur to gain the expertise and credibility of a market leader—in addition to money for R&D in the form of licensing revenue or a small, early-stage equity investment.

Procter & Gamble (P&G) is a great example of this approach. It has an open innovation program called Connect + Develop. It is a program where P&G collaborates with independent inventors and startups. The company seeks active proposals for game-changing products, technology, business models, trademarks, packaging, and design (inbound and outbound) to improve lives of global consumers. To date, Connect + Develop has more than 1,000 active agreements in place, and many of these are licensing or distribution agreements (as opposed to equity investments). We encourage you to visit the Connect + Develop Website (https://secure3.verticali.net/pg-connection-portal/ctx/noauth/PortalHome.do). The level of activity is impressive.

P&G also has another program that focuses specifically on equity investments for entrepreneurial new business ventures. This is called P&G FutureWorks. FutureWorks is funded by an "Innovation Board" made up of top P&G executives. It focuses on locating business opportunities outside the core business. "Personalization" of health and wellness products and services is a current thrust. In many cases, P&G will form a strategic partnership with entrepreneurs or independent inventors that will include capital investment to help mature the technology that will serve as the origin of a new $100 million business. FutureWorks is staffed by P&G personnel from R&D, manufacturing, sales, finance, and market research—all the diverse capabilities that entrepreneurs and inventors need to grow value. In sum, if you are an entrepreneur venturing in personalized solutions and services in health and wellness, FutureWorks would be a good entity to engage.

How Investors Make Money From Ventures

Angels, VCs, and Other Private Equity Investors

Now let's look at how equity investors (as opposed to debt holders) make money from their investments into startups.

Before you take a single penny of investor money, it is important that you understand the mechanics of how an investment in your venture appreciates in value through stages of growth. In very general terms, the basic formula is simple: If you need to raise $5 million and an investor believes the venture is worth $15 million, you will have to give that investor 33% of your venture in return for the investment, and all prior shareholders will see their holdings diluted by 33%.

Working through a specific example will help you understand how investors expect to make money from your venture. Take a look at Figure 8.6, which shows three rounds of investment, "Seed," "Series A," and "Series B," followed up with an acquisition.

	Seed	Series A	Series B	Exit	Times Return
Postmoney Valuation	$1,000,000	$5,000,000	$15,000,000	$75,000,000	
			6,000,000*		
Founders					
Investment	Sweat				
%	90%	72%	40%	40%	
Value	900,000	3,600,000	5,950,000	28,000,000**	
Family and Friends					
Investment	100,000				
% Equity	10%	8%	5%	5%	
Value	100,000	400,000	733,333	3,500,000 **	35
Angels					
Investment		1,000,000	500,000		
% Equity		20%	22%	22%	
Value		1,000,000	3,260,000	15,400,000 ***	10
VCs					
Investment			5,000,000		
% Equity			33%	33%	
Value			5,000,000	28,100,000***	6

* The right to purchase a fixed number of shares at a $6 million valuation was an incentive for the Series A invest-ment by the angel investors. The % equity holdings for angels shown in Series B (22%) is therefore a 33% dilution applied to their 20% holdings (yielding 13%), *plus* an additional 8% based on the equity value of their new Series B $500,000 investment at the $6 million valuation. Conversely, the founders come down to 39% because their Series A 72% equity holding is first diluted by 8% for the angel warrants, and then again by 33% for the VC investment.

** Founders and Family and Friends equity upon exit is based on their % holdings times the exit price minus repayment of all invested capital by the VCs.

*** The VC's equity at exit is the sum of getting their invested capital returned first, and then their % holdings multiplied by the balance of the proceeds.

Figure 8.6   Making Money on Equity in a Venture: A General Scenario

Let's say that you have a team of three partners (one technologist, one salesperson, and one operations person) who has developed the prototype of a system to help homeowners monitor and optimize their energy consumption from household appliances, lighting, computers, and so forth through a combination of sensors, metering software, a user portal, and a database to maintain historical information and show trends.

To build the prototype, you get $100,000 from family and friends in return for 10% of the company stock. Your team works nights and weekends to build a prototype and gains the interest of a local utility company in the result. They want to be a channel to reach their utility customers. You write a business plan. From the description above, we know that we are focused on a hot area in a growing industry. We also narrow down the market to a clear customer: individual homeowners living in moderate to upper-income neighborhoods. In VC terms, you have a well-defined and attractive addressable market. You also have a few people on your team who know the industry. And you have a working prototype. Companies raising money in the "new energy" industry sector are getting a "startup" valuation of $5 million postmoney.

After soliciting ten venture capital firms, all you get is "no." So instead you turn to the angel community. You find an alumnus of your university who is a highly successful entrepreneur and is known for doing startup deals. You have lunch and find him both incredibly knowledgeable and a good listener. You could see him as a valued mentor as well as an investor. Your financial projections show the need for about $1 million to get the venture to commercial launch. While that amount is beyond the alumnus' own personal limit, he knows of three or four other friends who he might convince to pony up $200,000 each, and he will cover the remainder. The milestones are focused on turning your prototype into a fully functional system and getting it into a "beta" test site with a group of ten households in your city. The *premoney* valuation for this Series A financing is $4 million; the *postmoney* valuation is $5 million. The simple math is that for their $1 million investment, the angel investors receive one-fifth or 20% of the equity. The $4 million premoney valuation is based on the Series A benchmark valuations for other companies funded over the past year in the same industry sector—and the sources to which investors subscribe that provide up-to-date investment and valuation information for different types of companies at different stages of growth. (VentureSource, part of Dow Jones, is one of the popular private equity information portals [http://www.dowjones.com/privatemarkets/venturesource.asp], as is Thomson Reuters' SDC VenturXpert data service. BIZCOMPS is another interesting, paid data service with all sorts of granular detail about private company transactions [http://www.bizcomps.com/].)

With this Series A investment, the founding team and their family members are diluted by 20%. Collectively, you now own 80% of the venture. Note from Figure 8.6, however, that your founding team's equity is suddenly worth $3.6 million on paper, and your family and friends have received a four-times return on their investment! At least, *so far.*

Nine months down the road, your team has successfully finished building the prototype and tested it in an even greater number of households. You have also reached a distribution agreement with your regional utility company to provide the system as a service for $2.50 a month plus a 50% markup on the cost of some simple, low-cost sensors. You beta test has shown that the average user will save at least five times that amount on a monthly basis through your system. Plus, you agree to provide community-wide information back to the utility company for its own purposes, at the cost of $50,000 a quarter.

You now go back to your investors. You need another $3.5 million in growth capital, half of which is to build a full marketing campaign to reach households in your region, to expand to other geographies, and to scale up computer operations. This is where things get interesting. You already have some initial revenue locked up and a channel for wide-scale marketing in your region. You meet with your current angel investors and agree that for the next round (Series B), the premoney valuation, based on your success to date, should be $12 million. With $5 million in additional invested capital, the postmoney valuation is set at $15 million. That $5 million will grab another 33% of the venture. This also means that all current investors will be diluted by 33%.

With the help of your angel group, you approach a number of VCs and hit pay dirt after the tenth visit. A local VC firm agrees to put in $3 million and brings along two other VC firms with whom it invests regularly at $1 million each. That gets your company the $5 million, with each VC receiving a Board seat on a five-seat Board. Some observers might say that this gives them effective control of your company even though they own only 33% of the stock! But you need the money for growth and to achieve your own successful exit, and all VCs want Board seats when they invest.

Further, as these things usually go, your first investors—the angels—have the right to participate in this new round of financing. One of the stipulations in their initial investment, however, was to purchase stock at a discount from the next round's price. The effective postmoney valuation for exercising these warrants is $6 million (only a million more than their Series B postmoney valuation.) The VCs agree to this but insist that the dilution must first come out of the founders' equity. You need the money and have little choice given the cash demands of your business. The angel group kicks in another $500,000.

Figure 8.6 shows how this works out in terms of equity holdings. Look at the Series B column:

- The new VC investors receive 33% of the equity for their $5 million investment.
- The angels' holding is more complex. The right to purchase a fixed number of shares at a $6 million valuation (structured as warrants) was a sweetener for their Series A investment. The percentage equity holdings for angels shown for Series B is 22%. This represents a 33% dilution of their original 20% holdings (or an 8% decrease in absolute numbers to 13%), *plus* an additional 8% based on the equity value of their new Series B $500,000 investment at the $6 million valuation.
- For the founders, their equity holdings decrease to 39% because their Series A 72% equity share is first diluted by 8% for the angel warrants, and then again by 33% for the VC investment.
- For the family investors, they are more simply diluted by 33% for the B round, leaving them with 6% equity.

With this additional capital of $5 million, your team executes flawlessly to plan over the next two years. You expand to new regions, develop new utility company partners, and get millions of consumers to use the energy monitoring and saving service. Revenue soars to $15 million in the 24 months to follow, and operating profits are achieved after 18 months. These are running about $2.5 million on that $15 million of revenue.

Microsoft hears about your company. They have long been fascinated with home automation and admire the way your team has executed on its plan with a cash-generating business model. Due to the recurring nature of revenues, the profitability, and the sheer amount of data you are gathering on household appliance electrical consumption, Microsoft wants to make an acquisition and pour more resources in to make you a new division in the business, go national, and then global.

After considerable negotiation, your Board of Directors agrees to a purchase price of $75 million, or six times revenue. The Board comprises two of the cofounders and three representatives of the VC firms. There is much to celebrate. In less than five years as a business, you and your investors have achieved an exit.

Before you and your cofounders can begin the party, however, you must calculate the numbers. There was a "restrictive covenant" that was imposed by the venture capitalists as part of their $5 million investment that said that before any proceeds from a sale are distributed, the VCs *first* get their original investment returned in whole. Then, the remainder of the proceeds is divided pro-rata to shareholders. While you might think that this is "double dipping" on the part of investors, it has become standard practice among venture and many angel investors. With this in mind, you calculate the numbers as follows:

- The VCs get their $5 million. And to this, they add their equity holdings at 33% of the remaining $70 million proceeds from the sale. The result is $28.1 million, a six-times return on their original investment. Not bad in this era of venture investing.

- The angel investors come next. Their equity holdings remain at 22%. Multiply this by the sale price minus the repayment of the VC's original investment. This yields $15.4 million, a ten-times return on their accumulated $1.5 million investment. Those warrants at a favorable price really improved the return.

- The family investors had a remarkable return. Their $100,000 seed financing, even with successive rounds of dilution, still left them with 5% of the company, worth $3.5 million even after the VC's original investment was returned first. That represents a 35-times return on the seed investment. Not only great, but rare!

- And the founding team, starting with 100% of the company and diluted down to 40% after three shots of investment—seed, Series A, and Series B—get to split $28 million, or more than $9 million each.

However, there are some strings attached. Microsoft writes some further provisions that the acquisition is contingent on the founders spending 18 months working within the new division. Salary and further stock incentives are structured based on achieving certain objectives. Nonetheless, your outlook on life has certainly changed. One of the first things you do is consider setting up a charitable foundation to provide ongoing grants to your university to seed new, young entrepreneurs!

We have described a rather ideal scenario. It is a win-win for all involved. In most cases, the owners of technology-intensive companies actually get far greater amounts of investment—not $4 million but $10 million or more. This means that the founders end up with far less stock. It also means that the investors are driven to a higher acquisition price. Getting to a $30 million revenue level might produce a $150 million plus valuation in an acquisition. If a group of VCs owned 75% of the stock, this would give them their desired ten-times return.

How Corporations Make Money From Internal Corporate Ventures

Since we are equally concerned in this book with internal corporate ventures, the "investor" in this case is the sponsoring executive. These projects are new products, systems, or services that either extend existing brands and/or product lines, or create new ones.

The executive team in the corporation will have well-developed measures for return that are based on the cash flows generated by the venture and the return on invested capital—either for operating expenses or in new plant and equipment. You must structure your financial statements to produce those measures from projected or pro-forma financial statements. There are two common metrics that we see used regularly within large corporations assessing the business plans for new internal ventures:

- Net present value (NPV). This is the value of cash flows from the venture discounted into current dollars, where the cash flows include ongoing investments into growing the business. The discount rate is typically the corporation's own weighted cost of capital. NPV's should represent a substantial contribution to the business, in the millions of dollars if not tens of millions. The reason why NPV "works" better for internal corporate ventures is that the projected stream of revenues and cash flows from the venture are far more certain if the venture is working within an existing market and product or service category that is already familiar to the corporation. The uncertainty is further reduced if the new internal venture can employ the corporation's existing sales channels—which is often the case. For all these and other reasons, including the fact that team leaders are often well-known and proven entities, the size and ramp-up of revenues for a new product or service can be matched to the corporation's prior experience.

• The return on assets (ROA). In large corporations, the numerator is net income divided by total assets. For a new venture, teams often use EBITDA (earnings before interest, taxes, depreciation, and amortization) since so many "games" are played on the way to net income. This is divided then by the ongoing accumulated investment in fixed assets for the venture itself—such as newly installed manufacturing machines. Again, for most mature industries, the ROA sought by executives will be between 5% and 15% depending on the specific industry.

You might also see your company using an Internal Rate of Return measure (calculated as the internal rate of return represented by the cash flows projected for a certain number of years), and with a certain minimum level of return deemed necessary for any new investment. This is often called the "hurdle rate." Again, whatever measures your company uses to prioritize investments and evaluate financial performance, learn the measures and include them in your financial projections and presentations.

How Investors Value Your Business _____

The real estate market is a good analogy for thinking about how to value new companies.

When you decide to sell a house, there is a fairly straightforward way of determining a fair market value. You find "comps." Comps are slang for comparable sales. This method involves finding homes sold within a recent period of time that compare in size, type of construction, age, amenities, and neighborhood. The values are reduced to price per square foot in order to compare apples to apples.

A "comp" approach is often used by investors to determine the value of a startup business, for either seed or Series A financing. The venture has little if any revenue, and no profits. As indicated earlier, the investors subscribe to data services to get current comparables by stage of financing for your target industry sector.

Mentioned earlier, SDC/VenturXpert (Thomson Reuters) VentureSource (Dow Jones), and BIZCOMPZ are all popular services in this regard. If 20 biotech startups received first-round funding for new drug research in the United States in the past quarter, an investor might take the average of the valuations for these deals as a benchmark for the new investment. The data sources that venture investors use to establish valuations for companies at different stages of growth are updated regularly and maintained data by (a) industry sector or type, (b) geographic region, and (c) stage of growth, for example, early stage, growth, expansion, and exit.

In this day and age, where it is so difficult to get startup money from institutional sources (e.g., VC firms), entrepreneurs tend to have to settle for less than they think their business is worth. As one passionate entrepreneur complained the other day, "I asked for $500,000 seed and they only gave me a $1.5 million premoney valuation. That's 25% of my company for not a lot of money!" If you don't have any other alternatives, no customer revenue, and no finished product, you may have no other choice!

Once a business is actually producing revenue, however, valuations are a different matter. You have a real business with real products or services that customers want to buy. Professional investors will subscribe to large-scale data sources mentioned earlier to find comparables by industry sector and stage of growth. In addition to these data sources, the primary driver of valuation is your own company's performance. There are fairly consistent multiples of the actual revenue and profit achieved by a venture in a specific industry sector. For mature industries, that might be two to three times revenues. For "hot" high-growth industries, the multiple might be as high as five or six times revenue. And the entrepreneur can often argue for *next year's projected revenues* based on the current year's performance. Achieve some type of operating profit on current revenues and your valuation at any given stage increases substantially.

Now, take a quick look at http://www.pwcmoneytree.com. It provides lots of information—but in aggregate. To get the specific information you need, which is the typical valuation by stage of growth for ventures in your specific industry sector, do what other entrepreneurs seeking external financing have done: Go to venture networking events. Talk to investors, professionals, and other entrepreneurs at the event. Arrange a private lunch with those that are not trying to sell you their services, but rather are actually in the field either starting a company, growing a company, or investing in companies at different stages. Also, see if the professors in the Finance Department in your business school have a subscription to Thomson Reuters SDC (Securities Data Company) VenturXpert for their own research. This will provide you with the comparables you require for your industry and stage of growth.

If you do a quick search on the Web for "venture valuation methods," we are certain that you will find valuation methods other than adjusted comparables for startups, and multiples of revenue and profits for later-stage ventures. These include calculating the net present value of projected cash flows over a five- to seven-year time period as a basis for determining what a company might be worth at exit years down the road. This is sometimes referred to as "the terminal value" of a venture. In the next chapter, we will teach you how to project revenues and expenses and make adjustments to cash flow for your planning purposes. And you can use the Web to find multiples on sales and profit for your industry sector to determine what the business *might be worth* in the future. However, these projections are not used by angels or VCs for a seed round or Series A valuation. The reason why is simple: Any projections beyond two or three years are usually complete speculation on the part of the entrepreneur, so working back from later points in time to the present doesn't add a whole lot of value. No, investors are going to look at "comps" and adjust from there based on your team, your venture concept, and your business model.

Now, for internal corporate ventures, NPV calculations are often far more reliable as a basis for making a "go/no go" decision. The reason why NPV "works" better for assessing internal corporate ventures is that the projected revenues and operating profit from such ventures are more predictable than in a startup. Most often, the markets are known, the routes to market are known, and much of the technology is leveraged from other parts of the company and its suppliers. The challenge is to figure out the new application and satisfy the user need. If the new internal venture can employ the corporation's existing sales channels, corporations are skilled at assessing levels of sales for launch and then, steady state. Team leaders are often well-known and proven entities. For all these reasons, NPV calculations tend to be much more reliable. Executives are looking for a nice positive number—hopefully, in the tens of millions of dollars. Depending on the industry, the time window for those NPV calculations can go well beyond the standard five-year planning horizon of startups. Ten years or more is not uncommon.

Some corporations—particularly manufacturers—will also focus on projected return on assets on an annual basis. ROA is simply the net income from the internal corporate venture divided by the total assets used by the venture. In our experience helping corporate teams, EBITDA is the number to use since large corporations have all sorts of tricks of the trade for charging a venture's corporate overhead or charging off shared manufacturing assets. This is then divided by the ongoing accumulated investment in fixed assets for the venture itself. Executives seek a 5% to 15% ROA depending on the specific industry.

Ways You Can Improve the Valuation of the Venture

First, let's assume that you have gone to one set of investors—say angels or VCs—and received a proposed premoney valuation of $2 million for your brilliant venture idea. This is Series A financing. You need $500,000 to improve your prototypes, engineered with your own savings, into finished products and into the market. The investor has derived that value by doing "comparables" in your industry sector and lowered the valuation based on the fact that your team is young and inexperienced in doing a startup. By agreeing to this valuation, you will be giving 20% of your stock to the investor. You know that to build a sales force you will need to raise another $2 million in 18 months. By then, you hope the company will have doubled in value, achieving a $5 million premoney valuation or a $7 million postmoney valuation. By taking in the $2.5 million, the new investors get about 35% of your stock. Doing the math, you realize that within several years, you will barely own majority control (about 51% if you work the numbers)—and you still expect to have to raise additional capital in order to scale up the business and achieve profitability.

Wouldn't it be great to increase these valuations at each stage of growth? What if you could get a premoney valuation of $5 million for the first round as you have heard other successful entrepreneurs achieve, $12 million for the next, and $20 million for the next? If you were able to do this, you would own a lot more of the equity as the company grows. How might you improve your valuations at each stage of growth?

For Series A financing, there are steps that you can take to increase the valuation. These steps include:

- If you are young (which means under 30), find yourself an experienced business person who understands the venturing process and knows your industry, and convince that individual to work with you—contingent upon financing. Their role might be VP of Sales, VP of Finance, or who knows, maybe CEO of the company! If it is the right person, he or she will also know investors from prior ventures. That network of friendly investors may generate millions of dollars in added valuation at the startup stage. Of course, you will also have to provide that individual with stock based on performance. Just make sure that they are willing to work as hard as you in terms of building a company. Adding "brand-name," credible individuals to your advisory board can also have a beneficial impact on valuation for new companies.

- Hustle on finishing your prototype to get a first beta customer or channel partner who will testify that your product or service is indeed a worthy offering. Putting a few dollars of customer revenue on the table will do wonders for your valuation. It removes a great deal of risk from the venture: You have made a product, someone wants to actually buy it, and they will testify to the innovation's benefits relative to competitors' offerings.

- While not directly addressing the valuation level, you can also seek to reduce operating expense so that you don't need as much capital, and therefore, do not have to sacrifice as much cash. In the example above, instead of $500,000, let's say that you find a way to get the work done for $200,000. You get that amount from investors—granted at the low valuation—but once completed and successfully tested with customers, and with some actual customer revenue, your *next* round can jump to that $12 million Series B level for high-performing ventures in your category. In other words, you can "parse" your financing and raise only the $200,000 necessary to commercialize an initial product, give up less equity, and then jump to a higher valuation and raise greater amounts of capital at a far more attractive price.

- And perhaps most important, try to bring in that first dollar of real customer revenue as soon as humanly possible.

We want to emphasize that the best way to win the valuation battle is to get paying customers signed up with your venture. Remember our opening statement in the beginning of the chapter: "You should worry more about customers with money . . . rather than venture capitalists with money. If you are able to gain some customers with money, then the venture funding will take care of itself." If you land a real paying customer, you instantly add value to your venture. In fact, some suggest that the value of a venture with revenue is at least twice as great as one without any revenue.

In successive stages of financing, revenues and profits drive valuations above or below the comparable valuations in your industry sector. A multiplier of five times revenues is often used for successive rounds of valuation. Achieve $3 million in revenue from a Series A financing, and your Series B might reach $15 million. Achieve $10 million in revenues from the Series B financing—with operating profit—and your Series C might reach $50 million. It has for many other entrepreneurs. Remember, *drive to revenue, then drive to operating profit.* This proves the merit of your products and services, and then proves the merit your business model. With each step, your business rises exponentially in value. And neither happens by accident. Once beyond startup, you require outstanding people who think smart and act brave.

The Dos and Don'ts of Raising Capital

Through our own experience and that of our students and friends who played the startup capital game, there are some clear dos and several don'ts for raising capital. Here are the top ones to keep top of mind:

Dos

Sharpen Your Focus

Sharpening your focus has two dimensions: making sure your venture is clearly focused and focusing your attention on the right investor. If you followed the guidance provided in this book, you have that focus. Investors want to know *what you are making and selling, who is buying it,* and *why they are buying it.* Then, they need to see how you plan *to monetize* the opportunity. You need to present a laser focus on these issues.

Know Who You Are Pitching To

It is essential that you do your homework on the angel, VC, or strategic corporate investor you plan to pitch. This is not so that you can flatter them on their past successes but rather, understand their industry interests and focus points. It makes no sense trying to raise money from a VC firm that has never done a deal in your industry sector. They are unlikely to invest, and if they do, the chances of them adding real value to the business in addition to money are small. Also, if your financial projections (next chapter) don't show the opportunity to create a $100 million plus business, forget pitching to top-tier venture capital firms. Instead, look toward angels, strategic investors, or niche-type VC firms. These investors are perfectly happy with a $15 million plus business that generates healthy amounts of cash and which can be sold at exit for $50 million or more depending on the size of their investment.

Try to Get a Referral Into the Investor or VC Firm

A trusted referral is worth its weight in gold for the investor, removing a significant element of risk. It might not get you the money, but it will certainly get you the meeting. Raising funds for a venture depends as much on personal relationships as it does the soundness of the business plan and business deal. The referral can be another entrepreneur, an investee of the investor, a lawyer, or an executive with a major corporation—or, another investor. Or, it can be an alumnus of your university or a professor connected into the investment community. Once you identify a list of potential investors, you want to do some groundwork trying to find someone who can make a personal introduction for you. *Do not* contact the potential investor before trying to secure this introduction. This is where picking the right advisory board and other professionals (e.g., accountant, attorney, etc.) proves invaluable.

Have a Good Advisory Board

The right advisory board carries with it many, many benefits. A good strategy is to have a board that has some "brand-name" experts from the particular industry in which you will compete. Also, make sure your advisory board is participatory—that is, the board members provide wise counsel and guidance. Moreover, do not be afraid to ask them for help in raising funds for the venture including having them make referrals and introductions. If you want a helpful and active board, offer them an incentive (a fee) for attending board meetings.

Have Good Legal Counsel

You should hire a good attorney from the onset, and you should look for one that has good connections and a network within the investor segment. You should also meet with several attorneys before making your selection. Find out if any will forgo their fees until the venture is cash positive or until investment funds are raised. Securities law can be very complicated, and you will need a seasoned attorney who can and will protect your interests. Plus, for any sort of institutional investment (e.g., a VC investment) you are going to be paying them $20,000 or more in legal fees—so you might as well get a top-flight firm for the money.

Make Sure You Have a Handle on Your Secret Sauce

This is usually technology embedded in your product, system, or service, but for some companies, the secret sauce can also exist in a channel strategy, a product positioning, or some combination thereof. Investors can be brutal with their questions, and one of the toughest is when they ask why your venture is different. Make sure you describe this secret sauce in a clear, easy-to-understand way that will resonate with the investor.

Have a Great Business Plan With a Great Executive Summary

We will teach you how to do this in Chapter 11. The executive summary of the plan is the entrance card for getting the chance to pitch to a professional investor. A great executive summary is the "bait," and your clear value proposition—how you plan to monetize the opportunity—is the "hook." In many cases, an investor might simply request an executive summary of your business plan. If he or she likes what they see, you may get a request for the whole plan. A poor executive summary will ensure you will not get a follow-up request from the investor. And, remember, an investor is looking for a reason to say *no,* not to say *yes.* If your business plan is flawed and/ or if you lack a great executive summary, you are going to get a *no.*

Line Up Your References, Particularly Early Customer References

Make sure the references you use are relevant to your industry sector and to the potential investor, and let them know that you are using them in your pitch. Also, make certain these references will really support you and advocate for you. The best thing you can do is to get an investor to make a customer visit. It builds a shared interest in the solution and will get the investor thinking on your behalf.

Be Specific About Your Funding Requirements

Any investor is going to ask how much you want and how you are going to spend the money. Therefore, you must be clear and specific about "the ask." This includes at least a year-by-year expenditure detail, and in some cases, the investor may request a month-to-month detail to assess your burn rate. You must also be sure to align your financial needs with timing objectives and valuation expectations. Investors who know your business sector will often have experience with what it really costs in terms of business execution and if your funding requirements are off (e.g., asking for too little or asking for too much), the investor will call you on it.[14]

Don'ts

There are also some major "don'ts" in raising capital. These can be deal killers, so be mindful of each one.

Financial Projections With Unrealistic, Unfounded Assumptions

We often see business plans with financial projections that are flawed because of poor assumptions, are unrealistically optimistic, or woefully lack validation. There are three potential problem spots:

a. **Crazy, wildly optimistic revenue numbers.** "I am calling on a VC that is expected to see a $100 million revenue number in Year 7, so by gum, that is what I am going to show." The VC will pick you apart in two seconds. Another common flaw is that first-time entrepreneurs think that they will close every customer that is visited and that all customers will become repeat customers. Think again. Entrepreneurs also often have fantasies about ramp-up. "I have $1 million in revenue for the first year, $10 million the next, $40 million the next, and $70 million the next. We are another Google." Prove it.

b. **Unrealistic expenses.** You are calling on an experienced angel investor with a plan to build a national direct sales force for enterprise selling at $150,000 per person. The "ask" needs to be for considerably more, yet you know that doubling the sales expense will kill the profitability of the venture for two more years. Guess what? Put in the correct numbers and figure out more products and more revenue for each salesperson to sell!

c. **Underestimating the total size of investment to achieve scale.** This means that over the course of three or four years and two or three rounds of capital, the total cost for the investor to build a viable, profit-generating enterprise is substantially underestimated by the entrepreneur. To build a powerhouse you might need, for example, to build a national customer service of systems integration capability. Or, you might need to spend as much money launching a brand in Europe as you did the United States, and then that same amount again penetrating Asia. Or, you have a manufacturing business and a $20 million capital outlay needs to occur in Year 3 and it is unlikely that any bank is going to pony up debt for a company of your size and maturity.

Investors tend to have a lot of money because they are smart business people. They can rarely be fooled. As we discussed in Chapter 7, one way to developed realistic numbers for revenue is to gain user input directly for your venture concept: the reality check. If you do not have this validation, any investor will immediately discount your numbers. At the same time,

---

[14] Evanson, D., & Beroff, A. (1999, August). Ready or not? *Entrepreneur*, pp. 56–69; Link, W. (2006). Pursuing venture capital. *Entrepreneurship* (5th ed.). New York: McGraw-Hill, pp. 90–92; Worrell, D. (2004, May). All in the delivery. *Entrepreneur*; and Jorgensen, B. (2001, May). The do's and don'ts of fund raising. *Electronic Business*, 29.

experienced investors can help you think through the activities and cost needed to build a great company. We will build on these themes in the next chapter on developing realistic financial projections.

Talking About Large, Generic Markets Instead of a Specific Addressable Market

All too often entrepreneurs focus their argument about the validity of the venture opportunity by talking about large, generic markets that amount to "billions of dollars." Remember, you need to focus on a specific market segment and then, specific customer groups within that segment. This is what we refer to as the "addressable market." It needs to be clearly defined and on its own, sufficient to support the revenue you plan to generate.

Focusing Only on Proprietary Technology at the Expense of Solutions for Users

Great technology companies are also great at finding, selling, and supporting users. While today's investors very much want to hear about your secret sauce, they know that successful companies are also strong on the market side of the business. And, never start with the technology first. That is a *big mistake*. Start off with target customers, your solutions, and why these are compelling for the users. Then, you can get into the weeds.

Asking for NDAs

Too many entrepreneurs believe what they are doing is so ground-breaking that they want to keep it a secret for fear someone else will steal their concept. They then make the mistake of asking potential investors to sign nondisclosure agreements (NDAs). This request puts off or insults the potential investor. The relationship between the entrepreneur and investor is based on trust and mutual benefit. Asking a potential investor to sign an NDA negates this possibility.

Focusing Too Much on the Future at the Expense of the Next 12-Month Milestones

Another fatal mistake the entrepreneur makes is focusing too much on what "will happen" to the venture in the far-off future. First, projecting future performance is very difficult. Doing so beyond one to two years is difficult at best. And yet, for most angels and all VCs, you must show the upside revenue potential of the business, say in five or six years. Do so with caution, and try to find benchmark analogous companies against which to compare your own upside potential. Second, investors want to know what steps are needed to get to your first commercial launch. That typically means some type of "alpha" and "beta" test milestones, followed by a series of steps to successfully launch your new product or service. Get tangible, and let investors know what specifically is going to occur over the coming months.

Avoiding a Discussion of Your Competition or Actually Claiming Your Venture "Has No Competition"

Please, never pretend that there are no competitors. There is always some form of competition, even if it is competition for the customers' total budget or "spend" in your area. Moreover, a larger competitor can easily decide to get into your target application through an acquisition or commercializing its own R&D. Pretending that your venture is "the only one" will seriously undermine your credibility with seasoned investors who have heard this all too often. Besides, a market with successful competitors may be positive from an investor's perspective since it indicates that customers are already spending money for current, albeit inferior, solutions. We find that the weakest part of many business plans and presentations is the competitive analysis section.[15]

Closing Thoughts: Getting Funded Is Not for the Faint of Heart

Ultimately, you must keep in mind that getting venture funding is very difficult. For example, the entrepreneur described in the SilverRail Technologies case visited 36 venture capitalists before he found the 37th who gave him a whopping $6 million in Series A financing. Another entrepreneur, whose venture is also the focus of another case in this book (Sentillion), visited two dozen VCs in his search for first-round financing of approximately $3 million. Their experience is the norm in this day and age of tight venture funding for startups.

If your business plan is going to call for greater than $250,000 in initial financing—which tends to take you beyond family and friends and angels—be prepared to work just as hard selling investors as you are trying to sell first customers. The odds are longer than you probably ever imaged. Some experts suggest, for example, that for every 1,000 plans that a VC sees on his or her desk, only two or three will get financing. So, do your homework and focus your efforts on investors who are interested in your industry sector and who have a history of investing in your type of business; be sure to get a personal introduction, have solid references, and of course, a great business plan.

Remember that if you are not passionate about your idea then no one else will be passionate. You are the messenger, the venture's chief salesperson. If you fail to be a passionate seller, you won't raise a penny. Investors not only want to see you put "skin in the game" (your own finances), but they also want you to be emotionally involved and passionate about the venture. Speaking from our experience on both sides of the table, an entrepreneur is going to have to live a 24/7 existence for at least the first three years of the business, making incredible sacrifices for marginal salary, at best. Be it late nights working with engineers in the office, endless road trips to customers, or countless lunches courting new employees and investors. You will never work so hard. And for most of you, it will be the most fun you will ever have—despite the challenges. Only passion and conviction will carry you through along the path to profitability. Seasoned investors know all this. If you appear unconvinced, uncommitted, or in any way, shape, or form passive about the venture, the game is over. "Committed" is different than "wild-eyed," however. Be professional as well as passionate about your venture concept and the business model you have created for it.

With that said, you need a thick skin on the hunt for investment capital. Do not take anything personally, because professional investors will be merciless with their questions! In fact, our experience in presenting to VCs is that they can have a feeding frenzy on who can ask the most difficult question. All the work we have had you do in the first section of this book should arm you well in the onslaught. Nonetheless, don thick skin! You are likely to talk to dozens of investors before finding the right one for your business.

---

[15] Jorgensen, B. (2001, May). The do's and don'ts of fund raising. *Electronic Business, 29.*

Reader Exercises

Raising capital has a lot to do with networking, getting the referral into an investor, or leveraging university connections. These reader exercises are designed to help you discover these connections:

Step 1: Find Angel Investors

Find out—any way you can—two or three angel investors who are alumni of your university. Determine further if you know anyone else who you know who knows these investors on a personal basis. It might well be your professor. See if there is a way to meet them for breakfast or lunch. Extra credit: Have that meeting with them!

Step 2: Get a Feel for Deals in Your Industry Sector

Go to http://www.pwcmoneytree.com. This is PricewaterhouseCoopers' *MoneyTree* site where you will find comprehensive reports on VC investment activities by industry, region, and stage of development. Navigate the site and study what activities are happening that are relevant to your venture concept. What kinds of conclusions can you draw as a result of your search?

Step 3: Learn About the Venture Capital Industry

Go to http://www.nvca.org. This is the National Venture Capital Association Website. Under "Research" study the latest statistics on venture capital industry statistics. Also, under the "About NVCA" tab, look at the Members page and the hundreds of members of the association. Clicking on the member firm's name takes you directly to their Website. There you can study their portfolios.

Step 4: Learn About Local VC Firms

Next, select three VC firms who have companies in their portfolios that are in the same industry sector as your idea. Learn what you can from the Websites of those portfolio companies. Do they seem to be successful? Identify the partners of the VC firms who are the lead investors in those companies. Look at their educational and work backgrounds. See if there is some type of personal connection for you. Do the same with the backgrounds of their investees in your industry sector. The goal here is to determine if there is an individual who can make a call on your behalf to a partner in that VC firm.

Step 5: Learn About Local Angels

Go to http://www.angelcapitaleducation.org. This is the Angel Capital Education Foundation, and it provides education, information, and research about angel investing. Under "Resources" you can find a listing of angel groups by region. Check out angels in your region and try to learn about who they are, what they do, and their investment strategies. Also, under "Research," check out the latest statistics on angel investment in the United States.

Step 6: Learn About Potential Corporate Investors in Your Region

Find a large corporation in your industry sector that has its own internal venture fund or direct investing activities. Once again, research the backgrounds of the executives—see if there is a connection for you, as alumni of your university or in some other way. Many executives in large corporations look for opportunities to help students or recent graduates of their alma maters.

Step 7: Develop a Strategy to Raise Funds

Develop a draft strategy for raising capital for your venture, including who you might visit, the rough amount of funds you think you need for Series A financing, and how much of the stock you would be willing to provide for that capital.

This is another opportunity for a check point with your trusted advisors, your professor, and your fellow classmates! You might be surprised at just how many angels, VCs, and corporate executives are networking into your university.

chapter 9

Projecting the Financial Performance and Requirements for the Venture

9

The Purpose of the Chapter

Planning how your business will make money is as fascinating and important as designing the new product, system, or service that the venture will sell to customers. The work you did in Chapter 4 on defining your business model is the essential foundation for this business planning. Think of this chapter as the execution and refinement of that business model into a crisp set of financial projections that are necessary both for you and your prospective investors. Teaching you how to do this is the purpose of this chapter.

In the process of translating your business model into actual numbers, you need to focus on projecting revenues, expenses, operating profit, the difference between "income" and "expenses" and actual cash flows, capital investments, and startup costs. And all the while, you need to make sure that these projections integrate with your R&D, production, and go-to-market strategies.

For that reason, we recommend that you develop the financial projections for your venture first before writing the full business plan. Besides, from Part I of this book, you already have your strategies for R&D, production, and go-to-market developed and tested with actual customers. These provide the insight required for effective financial planning. Then, with a first set of financial projections in hand, you can revisit various aspects of the business model and improve them to enhance revenue, increase profitability, or reduce startup costs.

For example, let's consider the implications of all three major financial statements, the P&L, the Cash Flow Statement, and the Balance Sheet for the business strategies of startups and internal corporate ventures.

- If you present a stream of revenues without recurring revenue, it may be best to rethink the product section of your business plan to include add-on products or services to create that recurring revenue. This directly affects your product and service strategies as well as your business model.

- Similarly, if your cash flow projections show huge lags between when sales are booked and when revenue is collected, you might reconsider the nature and structure of how you price your products and services (as in some up-front payments for services provided).

- Or, if you are developing an internal corporate venture—say in a manufacturing firm—your balance sheet projections might show large fixed assets relative to sales and profits generated from those investments—that is, a poor return on assets (ROA). This would cause you to use external subcontract manufacturers to shift your fixed costs into variable costs. Once again, this directly affects your production and supply strategy as well as your business model.

All of these are examples of how financial planning for a venture can reshape the strategies of the venture, and therefore, make anything you write in the business plan obsolete. Put otherwise, a venture is in the business to make money.

Learning Objectives

- Developing meaningful financial projections for a startup or corporate venture, and within this, different approaches for thinking about revenues and expenses
- Seeing how these approaches work for a product startup, a systems venture, a services venture, and an internal corporate venture

The Whiteboard Approach

Remember when we suggested in Chapters 2, 3, and 4 that the best way to design your venture concept and the business model was with team members working together on a whiteboard, and even perhaps with a beer or two in hand? Well, the same applies for designing the financial statements for your business. Except for this one, forget the beer. Creativity and the free spirit need to be replaced with pragmatism and discipline.

Using the whiteboard or pen and pencil may seem unusual in this day of the ubiquitous spreadsheet. However, we find that turning to the computer too quickly often leads to mindless financials. It is simply too easy to put some numbers into a worksheet, develop some standard percentage growth equations, and replicate everything into a rosy future scenario—that simply will never be real. Beautiful financials, perfectly formatted . . . that mean absolutely *nothing*.

So instead, use the spreadsheets *after* you have figured out the assumptions and reasoning behind your revenues, expenses, operating profit, and capital infusions. Do your financial prototyping on the whiteboard—at least for the first year or two of the P&L, and particularly for the revenue part of the P&L. *Revenue drives everything in a venture.* Then, once you feel comfortable with the number of customers and the streams of revenue they are likely to produce, you can turn on the spreadsheet to keep track of various expenses and how that leads to operating profit.

The Financial Projections Necessary for a Business Plan _____

If you are uncomfortable with the structure and integration of any of the financial statements described below, get someone to join you who possesses that knowledge. And don't be sloppy with your spreadsheets. Investors will eventually find and dismiss numbers that do not add up or fail to integrate across financial statements. There are 4 key deliverables in the financial planning for most ventures.

- A five-year, detailed **projection of revenues,** often based on the number of new customers, repeat customers, price per unit for products or services, and to produce "top-line revenue." The default format for startups seeking angel and venture capital financing is to show monthly projections and the growth rate of or changes to these components for the first two years and annually for outlying years. The reason for the monthlies is that it shows specifically when you plan to realize your first revenue and then, how that revenue ramps up over the coming 12 or 18 months. Your professor may require a different format, such as just annual projections for all five years. Or, a quarterly revenue projection may be requested for the first two years by your professor. However, to get to quarterly estimates, you typically have to do monthly projections anyways and then sum them up in an appropriate manner. Startup investors are most likely going to want to see the details of the first two years of revenue, with the number of customers or units sold scaling up month by month upon product or service launch. We suggest that you use a separate worksheet for this purpose, complete with the assumptions driving the numbers.

If you find that a particular investor or professor only wants to see annual projections, then the "hide" feature in spreadsheets is a simple way of covering up the monthly detail and showing just the summed annual amounts for the first two years. Moreover, PowerPoint presentations of business plans tend to show only annual amounts, and even those are in summary form. No one wants to look at figures in 8 or 10 font size on the projection screen!

Interestingly, for internal corporate ventures, most successful proposals that we have seen—such as the My M&M'S teaching case included with this book—only use annual projections for the first years or more, depending on the nature of the business. Perhaps that is because most internal ventures go through existing channels so that there is far less uncertainty about sales volumes during the startup period. "Make a great product and we are pretty sure we can sell it through our channels at reasonably predictable volumes," is the school of thought. This may also be the case if you are constructing a venture proposal for within your present company.

- A five-year **projected P&L** (the Proforma Profit & Loss Statement or otherwise known as the Income Statement) for the venture, structured in monthly periods for the first two years, and annually for third, fourth, and fifth years. The revenue line(s) for the P&L are fed by the revenue projections above.

Once again, formats can vary based on the demands of your professor or the nature of your venture. As we will see in the next chapter on writing the business plan, we recommend that you include a summary of number of customers, revenue, and operating profit (EBITDA—earnings before income taxes, depreciation, and amortization) in a simple table showing annual amounts over five years. Then, for some investors (or professors) you will need a more detailed P&L showing various expense items that is still based on annual amounts. Lastly, for those investors and professors who want to dig into the details, you need a P&L projecting revenues, specific operating expenses, and operating profit both before and after tax that is monthly for the first two years of the business, and then annually for Years 3, 4, and 5. It is therefore our strong recommendation that you first generate this more detailed monthly P&L and then summarize as needed for the particular audience and use.

Do not underestimate the importance of showing monthly figures for the first two years of the business for proving to investors that you have considered the specific needs and goals of the business. Monthly projections show investors the level of cash burn in the business before sales commence, and then, the timing when operating profit is achieved. The monthly numbers also show when key managers, R&D staff, or sales staff are brought on board as the business ramps up during the first several years.

More generally, most investors know that any numbers beyond the first two to three years in a projected P&L are largely speculation. However, the fifth-year estimation remains important because it gives some sense of potential exit value as a multiple of revenue and profit.

• A five-year **projection of cash flow** (the Proforma Cash Flow Statement), which varies from the P&L based on delays in collecting on sales, paying creditors, "capital" expenditures (such as equipment or computers), and infusions of money in the form of venture or debt financing. These projections should follow the monthly and annual format of your revenue and P&L projections.

Revenue recognition and cash conversion are critical issues for most startups. Startup investors tend to want to see a monthly cash flow analysis—to gauge the amount of invested capital needed by the business to at least reach operating profit. Corporate ventures tend to stick to annual projections throughout. In addition, executives funding internal corporate ventures will probably want to see the Net Present Value of discounted cash flow produced by the venture.

• A five-year **projected Balance Sheet** (only for startups—but not for internal corporate ventures.) Unlike the P&L and cash flow statements, the Balance Sheet can be kept to year-end annual figures. Internal corporate ventures do not require any balance sheet—but rather, a capital plan for projects requiring an investment in new plant and equipment. Executives will probably want to see annual projections of Sales to Invested Assets and then, Return on Invested Assets, where the return is the annual operating profits.

TIP: BIOTECH VENTURES REWRITE THE RULES! _____

Biotech financial plans rewrite the rules of the game because the average cycle time for starting R&D to getting a product to market is ten years or more. If your venture is to commercialize a scientific discovery of the biotech sort, your financial planning spans at least the 17 years that represents the protection period of a U.S. patent. For the biotech entrepreneur, there tends to be plenty of comparables in terms of revenues per year for certain classes of drugs, as well as benchmarks for the costs of R&D and clinical trial in the years running up to commercialization. Biotech entrepreneurs need to present and justify these long-tailed projections for investors to make an assessment of the considerable financial risk and reward.

Increasingly, investors are turning to "orphan drugs," which target disease populations of 100,000 persons or fewer, for example, rare diseases. The Orphan Drug Act (ODA) was passed by Congress in 1983 to provide incentives to spend the time and money needed to address small-population rare diseases. One of these incentives is seven years of market exclusivity once a drug-in-the-making is awarded orphan drug status by the Food and Drug Administration (FDA). In 2009, there were 150 drugs given this special status. The FDA also tends to give an expedited review to orphan drug applications, helping to shorten the development process. As a result, more ventures are pursuing these niche diseases. During the 2000s, orphan products comprised 22% of all new molecular entities (NMEs) and 31% of all significant biologics (SBs) receiving marketing approval by the FDA.

From these financial statements, you will also be able to produce what we think of as the financial "goalposts" for the venture. These goalposts include:

- **Startup costs**—these come directly from your cash flow statement, specifically from the month-by-month breakdown of operating expenses and capital investments in plant and equipment. We like to focus on the cash requirements until you launch your first products or services to market, or the first year of the business if you are in a heavy, long-tailed R&D situation. Remember that if you have included seed- or Series A–type infusions of cash as part of the cash flow projections, subtract these first before summing up your various cash needs for the first year of the business.

- **The time to first dollar**—when the business becomes "real." This information comes directly from monthly projections of revenue.

- **The time to first profit**—when the business achieves true investor value. This, too, can be found in the projected P&L.

- **First-round and anticipated second-round financing** amount (e.g., seed funding and Series A, or Series A and Series B, depending on the point at which you request capital). This is typically shown in the Proforma Cash Flow Statement.

- **Potential valuation for exit**—for example, the value of the company as an acquisition by a larger concern, and then, the money the investors might make based on their equity holdings and exit preferences. VCs are shooting for a ten-times return (often called a "10X" return) on their invested capital, and that is after all the money that they have invested into your company is *first* paid off. Angels hope for a 10X return, but our experience is angels will be perfectly happy with a three-times (3X) to five-times (5X) return over a five-year period. In one of the financial statement examples that we will show you in a moment, there is a specific row placed at the bottom of a projected P&L that shows possible exit valuations at Year 5 at an industry standard multiple of sales and EBITDA.

Do not minimize the importance of understanding the time to first dollar and the time to first profit. These will be primary questions of any professional investor—even after they have read an outstanding business plan: "How long do I have to wait before seeing proof that it is a viable, money-making business?" It should be your question, too.

Creating Realistic, Granular Projections _____

You are going to have to spend quality time developing your financial projections—and it all starts with projecting revenues.

The *very first two years of revenue* projections matter most for professional investors and corporate executives. We have attended investment meetings where prospective investors and executives have dug into those first two top-line numbers in a way analogous to a root canal for the entrepreneurs! Whatever numbers you present, you need to back them up with as much detail as possible. Think of this as a separate worksheet that feeds into the top revenue rows of your projected P&L.

Let's look at a few examples of how to develop granular—or what we like to think of as "bottoms-up"—revenue projections that can withstand investor challenges.

The most important aspect of projecting revenues is the assumptions behind the numbers. This will vary for every different type of business. You also took a first stab at this in Chapter 7 (the "Reality Check") where you developed a rough estimate of the annual revenue potential for your venture. Grab those assumptions now and use them as a starting point.

A few examples are helpful. In Chapter 4 on business models, we used an example of a more traditional manufactured product (healthy dog snacks), a systems example (health care monitoring for the elderly using sensors and software), and a technology-intensive services example (an engineering services venture to design and install telecommunications infrastructure for businesses). Each one is indicative of the types of assumptions that come into play for different types of companies.

In the **pet snack business,** there are a number of critical assumptions, each one of which requires that you do the type of homework we described in the first section of this book:

- The number of **stock keeping units** (SKUs)—the items on the shelf—and how that number of SKUs expands over time
- The on-shelf or **list price** of each SKU
- The **margins provided to retailers** (35% for the pet specialty channel), margins for distributors (10%).
- The **number of stores** for its major channels to market, in this case PetSmart (about 1,000 in 2009), PetCo (about 900), Pet Supplies Plus (about 200), and the independent pet specialty stores (about 15,000). Remember, the focus of this venture was premium products and pricing; it therefore avoided the grocery and mass merchandiser channels.
- The **launch strategy** of hitting local New England pet specialty stores for the first two years, expanding nationally, and also securing PetSmart in Year 2, PetCo in Year 3, and also Pet Supplies Plus (in Year 4).
- The team also learned that the independent pet retailers did not want their products also sold in PetSmart or PetCo. Therefore, four new SKUs with somewhat different ingredients and very different packaging and branding would be introduced in Year 3 to hit the major retail chains.

If you turn to Figure 9.1, you can see how these assumptions translate into a simple projection of revenue, and from that, an estimation of gross profit. The estimates from raw materials, conversion, packaging, and shipping were all developed with the owners of the Pet Bakery with whom the MBA student team partnered on this venture. Also note when the venture gets to "first dollar."

In the **health monitoring business,** there are a number of equally important assumptions driving revenue. You might recall that this venture sought to provide automated alerting for serious medical conditions for elderly persons by combining new body sensors with elegant workflow software. The two channels selected by the team were assisted-living centers and home health agencies. Each channel partner was in many ways its own market segment, because each organization controlled a fixed amount of patients who were target customers for this new technology. Take a look at Figure 9.2 to see how this vision translates into a granular projection of revenue. If you have a venture where this level of detail can be achieved, we certainly recommend that you do it because the detail helps relieve one of the major questions of investors: "What's really in that revenue number?!"[1]

There are a number of assumptions behind the revenue model for the medical monitoring venture:

- **The "service" offerings.** This is a system offered as a service case. Based on its customer research, the team identified three services: monitoring the elderly, providing a portal for medical staff caring for the elderly, and a portal for family members to get up-to-date information on their loved ones in skilled care or still living at home.

- **The pricing for these services.** The team had benchmarks for other nascent health monitoring ventures—plus the benchmark of ADT in home security. $79 per month per patient seemed very reasonable for 24/7 health monitoring and alerting—even if this would limit the market to middle-class individuals and above, up until the time that private and public insurers saw the wisdom of proactive alerting and initiated reimbursement. A fee of $12 per patient per month was set for access to informatics on emergency response and patient health for care providers (including the heads of nursing for assisted-living businesses and home health agencies). And then, to help families keep apprised of their elderly loved ones, and to relieve a little guilt for not visiting more, the team set a price of $24 per patient per month for a loved one's portal.

- **Charging for installation.** This could be a contentious issue for similar service-type businesses where the idea might be to install at no cost, and make up the money throughout recurring service revenue. However, the team decided to charge $249 for installation because the elderly residents being monitored might not be around long enough to make the no-charge install feasible. One visit to an assisted-living center revealed an average length of stay of about three years!

- **Licensing server software to assisted-living centers.** After discussions with several assisted-living center companies, the team decided to license its server software—the software that aggregated all the wireless communication, signal processing, alerting, metrics, and user identification—at a fee of $1,000 per month per facility. Certain portions of the software would reside locally on a computer residing in the facility itself that would be linked to the venture's own centralized servers for partner-wide reporting, medical record access, software downloads, and backups.

- **Penetration rates in each channel.** You can see from the detailed numbers in the figure that one needs to be brutally realistic about the penetration rate of new technology. In just about any market, there are lead adopters who are very small percentage of the market (say 5%), and the later-stage adopters. The team hoped to get that 5% in each channel partner over the first six months, and then expand to 12% to 15% or more of elderly residents in the coming years.

- **Staging.** The team targeted sales and deployment into assisted-living centers because of the more controlled environment with the residences themselves. These multidwelling units tended to be "cookie-cutter" in spatial design: one bedroom, one bathroom, one toilet, one kitchen/dining area, and one living room. This made placement and test of the various sensors much easier to accomplish in a specific building. These sensors were fitted onto beds and reading chairs (for pulse, breathing, and activity monitoring), hallways and bathroom floor (for fall detection). It also made

---

[1] These and other spreadsheets with examples of financial projections for startups and corporate ventures are available from the authors and on the Website associated with this book. Using these templates can give you a jump start on your own financial projections. At the same time, never use anyone else's numbers blindly. Each and every number must be your own!

Four SKUs	On-Shelf Price	Retailer Margin	Wholesale	Trade Allowance (Samples, etc.)	Net Sale Price	Spin rate per Month per Store (All grain half spin of meat)
1 Meat and Oats (300 gram - small)	$7.00	35%	$4.55	8%	$4.19	24
2 Meat and Oats (1 kilogram - bulk)	$24.00	35%	$15.60	8%	$14.35	8
3 Oats only (300 gram)	$7.00	35%	$4.55	8%	$4.19	16
4 Oats only (1 kilogram)	$24.00	35%	$15.60	8%	$14.35	4

	Development	Test		Launch			Expand Independent Pet Specialty						
	Jan	Feb	Mar	Apr	May	Jun	Jul	Aug	Sep	Oct	Nov	Dec	Yea
Revenue Projections													
Independent Pet Specialty Stores (15,000)	0	1	15	25	35	45	70	95	120	145	170	195	19
PetSmart (1000) (new versions of 4 SKUs)	0	0	0	0	0	0	0	0	0	0	0	0	0
PETCO (900) (new versions of 4 SKUs)	0	0	0	0	0	0	0	0	0	0	0	0	0
PetSupplies (200) (new versions of 4 SKUs)	0	0	0	0	0	0	0	0	0	0	0	0	0
Total stores selling products	0	1	15	25	35	45	70	95	120	145	170	195	19
SKU 1 revenue		100	1,507	2,512	3,516	4,521	7,032	9,544	12,056	14,567	17,079	19,590	92,0
SKU 2 revenue		115	1,722	2,870	4,019	5,167	8,037	10,908	13,778	16,648	19,519	22,389	105.
SKU 3 revenue		67	1,005	1,674	2,344	3,014	4,688	6,363	8,037	9,712	11,386	13,060	61,3
SKU 4 revenue		57	861	1,435	2,009	2,583	4,019	5,454	6,889	8,324	9,759	11,195	52,5
Total revenue		340	5,095	8,492	11,888	15,285	23,776	32,268	40,760	49,251	57,743	66,234	311,
Total units sold		52	780	1,300	1,820	2,340	3,640	4,940	6,240	7,540	8,840	10,140	10,1
P&L Projections													
Gross Sales		340	5,095	8,492	11,888	15,285	23,776	32,268	40,760	49,251	57,743	66,234	311
35% Raw materials (35% 1st year, declining next years)		119	1,783	2,972	4,161	5,350	8,322	11,294	14,266	17,238	20,210	23,182	108
10% Conversion to finished product (10%)		34	509	849	1,189	1,528	2,378	3,227	4,076	4,925	5,774	6,623	31,
5% Packaging (5%)		17	255	425	594	764	1,189	1,613	2,038	2,463	2,887	3,312	15,
3% Shipping/logistics (3%)		10	153	255	357	459	713	968	1,223	1,478	1,732	1,987	9,3
Gross profit		160	2,395	3,991	5,587	7,184	11,175	15,166	19,157	23,148	27,139	31,130	146
Gross margin		47%	47%	47%	47%	47%	47%	47%	47%	47%	47%	47%	47
Sales and marketing		1,000	5,000	5,000	5,000	5,000	7,500	7,500	7,500	7,500	7,500	7,500	66,
R&D (not full time in 1st year)	2,500	2,500	2,500	1,000	1,000	1,000	1,000	1,000	1,000	1,000	1,000	1,000	14,
Manufacturing engineering/extra materials	5,000	5,000	1,000	1,000	1,000	1,000	1,000	1,000	1,000	1,000	1,000	1,000	15,
Other G&A		5,000	5,000	5,000	5,000	5,000	5,000	5,000	5,000	5,000	5,000	5,000	55,
Operating profit/loss to LLC Members	(7,500)	(13,340)	(11,105)	(8,009)	(6,413)	(4,816)	(3,325)	666	4,657	8,648	12,639	16,630	(3,7
Net profit margin before tax													−1

Figure 9.1   Projected Revenue and P&L for the Healthy Pet Snack Venture

						Add PetSmart and expand Independent Pet Specialty								Add PETCO	Add PetSupplies
Jan	Feb	Mar	Apr	May	Jun	Jul	Aug	Sep	Oct	Nov	Dec	Year 2	Year 3	Year 4	Year 5
245	245	295	295	345	345	395	395	445	445	495	495	495	600	800	1,000
200	200	200	200	200	200	1,000	1,000	1,000	1,000	1,000	1,000	1,000	1,200	1,400	1,600
0	0	0	0	0	0	0	0	0	0	0	0	0	500	900	1,100
0	0	0	0	0	0	0	0	0	0	0	0	0	0	200	250
445	445	495	495	545	545	1,395	1,395	1,445	1,445	1,495	1,495	1,495	2,300	3,300	3,950
44,706	44,706	49,730	49,730	54,753	54,753	140,147	140,147	145,170	145,170	150,194	150,194	1,169,401	2,772,806	3,978,374	4,761,994
51,093	51,093	56,834	56,834	62,575	62,575	160,168	160,168	165,909	165,909	171,650	171,650	1,336,458	3,168,922	4,546,714	5,442,278
29,804	29,804	33,153	33,153	36,502	36,502	93,432	93,432	96,780	96,780	100,129	100,129	779,601	1,848,538	2,652,250	3,174,662
25,547	25,547	28,417	28,417	31,287	31,287	80,084	80,084	82,955	82,955	85,825	85,825	668,229	1,584,461	2,273,357	2,721,139
151,150	151,150	168,134	168,134	185,117	185,117	473,831	473,831	490,814	490,814	507,798	507,798	3,953,689	9,374,726	13,450,694	
12,740	12,740	15,340	15,340	17,940	17,940	20,540	20,540	23,140	23,140	25,740	25,740	25,740	31,200	41,600	52,000
151,150	151,150	168,134	168,134	185,117	185,117	473,831	473,831	490,814	490,814	507,798	507,798	3,953,689	9,374,726	13,450,694	
52,903	52,903	58,847	58,847	64,791	64,791	165,841	165,841	171,785	171,785	177,729	177,729	1,383,791	2,812,418	3,900,701	4,508,021
15,115	15,115	16,813	16,813	18,512	18,512	47,383	47,383	49,081	49,081	50,780	50,780	395,369	937,473	1,345,069	1,610,007
7,558	7,558	8,407	8,407	9,256	9,256	23,692	23,692	24,541	24,541	25,390	25,390	197,684	468,736	672,535	805,004
4,535	4,535	5,044	5,044	5,554	5,554	14,215	14,215	14,724	14,724	15,234	15,234	118,611	281,242	403,521	483,002
71,041	71,041	79,023	79,023	87,005	87,005	222,701	222,701	230,683	230,683	238,665	238,665	1,858,234	4,874,858	7,128,868	8,694,040
47%	47%	47%	47%	47%	47%	47%	47%	47%	47%	47%	47%	47%	52%	53%	54%
15,000	15,000	15,000	20,000	20,000	20,000	25,000	25,000	25,000	30,000	30,000	30,000	270,000	843,725	1,210,562	1,449,007
6,000	6,000	6,000	6,000	6,000	6,000	6,000	6,000	6,000	6,000	6,000	6,000	72,000	468,736	515,610	567,171
2,000	2,000	2,000	2,000	2,000	2,000	2,000	2,000	2,000	2,000	2,000	2,000	24,000	46,874	67,253	80,500
15,000	15,000	15,000	20,000	20,000	20,000	25,000	25,000	25,000	30,000	30,000	30,000	270,000	656,231	941,549	1,127,005
33,041	33,041	41,023	31,023	39,005	39,005	164,701	164,701	172,683	162,683	170,665	170,665	1,222,234	2,859,292	4,393,894	5,470,357
												31%	31%	33%	34%

Monthly Service Fees For the Health Monitoring Venture

Wellness monitoring	99	99	99	99	99	99	99	99	99	99	99	99	99
Wellness portal for providers	12	12	12	12	12	12	12	12	12	12	12	12	12
Wellness portal for loved ones	24	24	24	24	24	24	24	24	24	24	24	24	24
Installation fee per residence	249	249	249	249	249	249	249	249	249	249	249	249	249
Installation fee per facility	12,000	12,000	12,000	12,000	12,000	12,000	12,000	12,000	12,000	12,000	12,000	12,000	12,00

	Mar	Apr	May	Jun	July	Aug	Sep	Oct	Nov	Dec	Year 1	Jan	Feb
Primary Markets/Channels			*Test/Trial with Partner #1*										
Assisted-Living Companies													
Partner #1													
# of residents								50,000	50,000	50,000	**50,000**	50,000	50,00
Incremental penetration rate								0.5%	0.5%	0.5%	**1.5%**	1.0%	1.0%
# of new residents to be automated								250	250	250	**750**	500	500
Total # of residents automated								250	500	750	**750**	1,250	1,75C
# of facilities (rounded up)								3	5	8	**8**	13	18
Wellness monitor and report								24,750	49,500	74,250	**148,500**	123,750	173,25
Wellness portal for providers								3,000	6,000	9,000	**18,000**	15,000	21,00
Wellness portal for loved ones								6,000	12,000	18,000	**36,000**	30,000	42,00
Installation fee for new residents								62,250	62,250	62,250	**186,750**	124,500	124,5
Installation fee for new facilities								30,000	30,000	30,000	**90,000**	60,000	60,00
Subtotal #1								**126,000**	**159,750**	**193,500**	**479,250**	**353,250**	**420,7**
Partner #2													
# of residents													
Penetration rate													
# of new residents to be automated													
Total # of residents automated													
# of facilities													
Wellness monitor and report													
Wellness portal for providers													
Wellness portal for loved ones													
Installation fee for new residents													
Installation fee for new facilities													
Subtotal #2													
Partner #3													
# of residents													
Penetration rate													
# of new residents to be automated													
Total # of residents automated													
# of facilities													
Wellness monitor and report													
Wellness portal for providers													
Wellness portal for loved ones													
Installation fee for new residents													
Installation fee for new facilities													
Subtotal #3													
Partner #4													
# of residents													
Penetration rate													
# of new residents to be automated													
Total # of residents automated													
# of facilities													
Wellness monitor and report													
Wellness portal for providers													
Wellness portal for loved ones													
Installation fee for new residents													
Installation fee for new facilities													
Subtotal #4													
Subtotals for Assisted Living											Year 1		
Residents Monitored								250	500	750	**750**	1,250	1,75
Facilities								3	5	8	**8**	13	18
Revenue								126,000	159,750	193,500	**479,250**	353,250	420,7

Figure 9.2   Revenue Projections for the Health Monitoring Systems Venture

Please view the remainder of this spreadsheet at the textbook's companion Website: www.sagepub.com/meyer

99	99	99	99	99	99	99	99	99	99	99	99	99	99
12	12	12	12	12	12	12	12	12	12	12	12	12	12
24	24	24	24	24	24	24	24	24	24	24	24	24	24
249	249	249	249	249	249	249	249	249	249	249	249	249	249
12,000	12,000	12,000	12,000	12,000	12,000	12,000	12,000	12,000	12,000	12,000	12,000	12,000	12,000

Mar	Apr	May	Jun	Jul	Aug	Sep	Oct	Nov	Dec	Year 2	Year 3	Year 4	Year 5
			Launch 4th Qtr.										
50,000	50,000	50,000	50,000	50,000	50,000	50,000	50,000	50,000	50,000	**50,000**	53,000	56,000	59,000
1.0%	1.0%	1.0%	1.0%	1.0%	1.0%	1.0%	1.0%	1.0%	1.0%	**12%**	15%	15%	15%
500	500	500	500	500	500	500	500	500	500	**6,000**	7,950	8,400	8,850
2,250	2,750	3,250	3,750	4,250	4,750	5,250	5,750	6,250	6,750	**6,750**	14,700	23,100	31,950
23	28	33	38	43	48	53	58	63	68	**68**	147	231	320
222,750	272,250	321,750	371,250	420,750	470,250	519,750	569,250	618,750	668,250	**4,752,000**	17,463,600	27,442,800	37,956,600
27,000	33,000	39,000	45,000	51,000	57,000	63,000	69,000	75,000	81,000	**576,000**	2,116,800	3,326,400	4,600,800
54,000	66,000	78,000	90,000	102,000	114,000	126,000	138,000	150,000	162,000	**1,152,000**	4,233,600	6,652,800	9,201,600
124,500	124,500	124,500	124,500	124,500	124,500	124,500	124,500	124,500	124,500	**1,494,000**	1,979,550	2,091,600	2,203,650
60,000	60,000	60,000	60,000	60,000	60,000	60,000	60,000	60,000	60,000	**720,000**	954,000	1,008,000	1,062,000
488,250	**555,750**	**623,250**	**690,750**	**758,250**	**825,750**	**893,250**	**960,750**	**1,028,250**	**1,095,750**	**8,694,000**	**26,747,550**	**40,521,600**	**55,024,650**
											15,000	20,000	25,000
											12%	15%	15%
											1,800	3,000	3,750
											1,800	4,800	8,550
											18	48	86
											2,138,400	5,702,400	10,157,400
											21,600	57,600	102,600
											43,200	115,200	205,200
											448,200	747,000	933,750
											216,000	360,000	450,000
											2,203,200	**5,875,200**	**10,465,200**
												50,000	53,000
												12%	15%
												6,000	7,950
												6,000	13,950
												60	140
												7,128,000	16,572,600
												864,000	2,008,800
												1,728,000	4,017,600
												1,494,000	1,979,550
												720,000	954,000
												11,934,000	**25,532,550**
													35,000
													12%
													4,200
													4,200
													42
													4,989,600
													604,800
													1,209,600
													1,045,800
													504,000
													8,353,800
										Year 2	Year 3	Year 4	Year 5
2,250	2,750	3,250	3,750	4,250	4,750	5,250	5,750	6,250	6,750	**6,750**	16,500	38,100	54,450
23	28	33	38	43	48	53	58	63	68	**68**	165	381	545
488,250	**555,750**	**623,250**	**690,750**	**758,250**	**825,750**	**893,250**	**960,750**	**1,028,250**	**1,095,750**	**8,694,000**	**28,950,750**	**66,684,600**	**91,022,400**

response by skilled nurses faster and more reliable because skilled nurses were usually already on site. Penetrating the home health agencies come in the third year of the revenue model. This was an important assumption. (Several home health agencies approached the team for a partnership during the startup period!)

*** *** ***

Next, **for a service,** we can turn to Telestructures, the engineering services businesses proposed by one of our students. The services were to design, install, and maintain telecommunications infrastructures for office building owners and leaseholders. The basis of revenues is the number of proposals generated for prospective customers and the close rate on those prospective customers.

Turn to Figure 9.3 to see how this translates into a simple financial model that summarizes the revenue into just annual projections for the first five years (to show you an example of how internal corporate ventures seem to skip the monthly projections for the first two years and go straight to annual figures). You can see that some of the key assumptions shown in that figure are the percentage of customers who buy "design" versus "installation" versus ongoing "maintenance" for their telecommunications systems. Pricing for these services is another crucial assumption for the revenue projection of this venture. In this case, the partners were already providing

Startup Capital investment	Year 0
Applications software development (2 persons, 6 months, $15K/month)	180,000
Middleware tools (server/dbms)	25,000
Server upgrade	25,000
Field hardware for testing	25,000
Data analyzers	15,000
Additional laptops	10,000
Other equipment	10,000
Total Startup Capital Investment	**290,000**

	Year 1	Year 2	Year 3	Year 4	Year 5
Sales					
Number of Sales Staff	1	2	3	4	5
Number of proposals per month	5	10	15	20	25
Number of proposals per year	60	120	180	240	300
Planning and Design Services					
Purchase Rate	20%	25%	33%	35%	40%
Number of Projects	12	30	59	84	120
Average Revenue per Project	$15,000	$15,000	$15,000	$15,000	$15,000
Total Revenue	$180,000	$450,000	$891,000	$1,260,000	$1,800,000

Figure 9.3   (Continued)

Implementation		12		30		59		84		120
Purchase Rate		13%		17%		22%		23%		26%
Average Revenue per Project		$50,000		$50,000		$50,000		$50,000		$50,000
Total Revenue		$396,000		$990,000		$1,960,200		$2,772,000		$3,960,000
Maintenance										
Purchase Rate		13%		17%		22%		23%		26%
Average Revenue per Project		$2,400		$2,400		$2,400		$2,400		$2,400
Total Revenue		$19,008		$66,528		$160,618		$293,674		$483,754
Gross Revenue		**$595,008**		**$1,506,528**		**$3,011,818**		**$4,325,674**		**$6,243,754**

Field Service Staff

Service Teams (each team has 3 people)			1		5		10		15		20
	Salaries	**Qty**	**Total**	**Qty**	**Total**	**Qty**	**Total**	**Qty**	**Total**	**Qty**	
Project / Account Manager	130,000	1	130,000	2	273,000	3	409,500	4	546,000	5	682,500
Design Engineer	90,000	1	90,000	2	189,000	3	283,500	4	378,000	5	472,500
Installation / IT Engineer	75,000	1	75,000	5	393,750	10	787,500	15	1,181,250	20	1,575,000
Total Salary cost per year			**295,000**		**855,750**		**1,480,500**		**2,105,250**		**2,730,000**
Total Marketing and Technical Staff			10		18		26			34	
Sales & Marketing Expense (20% of sales)			59,501		150,653		301,182		432,567		624,375
R&D Software/Test Expense (software rev in Year 3)			125,000		137,500		250,000		275,000		302,500
Customer Support Staff (20 accounts per staff person)			50,000		99,500		197,510		336,110		534,110
G&A Overhead Charge (10% of revenue)			59,501		150,653		301,182		432,567		624,375
Operating Profit Before Tax			**$56,006**		**$211,972**		**$678,954**		**$1,080,289**		**$1,962,503**
					14%		23%		25%		31%

Potential Adjustments to Cashflow Before Tax

Adjustments for A/R (30 days)		(49,584)	(75,960)	(175,025)	(185,448)	(334,865)
Working capital: startup & ongoing	(290,000)	(50,000)	(45,000)	(80,000)	(115,000)	(150,000)
Cashflow	**(290,000)**	**(43,578)**	**91,012**	**423,929**	**779,841**	**1,477,638**
NPV (15% cost of capital plus risk factor)	**1,043,643**					
ROI			70%	204%	350%	547%

Figure 9.3 Revenue Projections and a Proforma P&L for a Telecommunications and Network Infrastructure Consultancy

Please view the remainder of this spreadsheet at the textbook's companion Website: www.sagepub.com/meyer

these services for a small number of clients and wanted to scale up the business. They had already had direct conversations with a number of IT and facilities managers in office parks in the region. From their current work, the team came up with pricing goals of $15,000 for network design, $50,000 for implementation, and $2,400 for ongoing off-site help/support for systems administrators. Again, if your plan is to start a similar type of engineering services firm, go to your customers and determine your own pricing. These numbers are for you to learn by, not use.

Figure 9.3 shows the team's:

- Projected startup expenses,
- A granular projection of revenues for design, implementation, and maintenance services,
- How projected revenues then drive down into a P&L based on body counts for different types of employees and various operating expenses (sales and marketing, R&D, customer support, and a general overhead charge for office expenses and so forth),
- An adjustment to cash flow for accounts receivables and capital equipment purchases,
- And then an NPV and ROI on cash flows derived from the venture.

All on one worksheet! This simple, inclusive approach worked for our student . . . and it might work well for you, too!

The Top-Down, Share of Market Approach

While we are advocates of the "bottoms-up" approach to projecting revenue, in some cases that is simply not possible.

One case might be the sale of a service through a Web channel to reach a broad target market. In fact, SilverRail Technologies—one of the teaching cases in this book—is precisely such a case. The founder, an alumnus of our university, raised a $6 million Series A right in the middle of the recession in 2009.

Aaron based his revenue projections on capturing 10% of the market over five years for booking passenger rail travel, first in Europe, and then in other target markets. His venture concept was to become an aggregator of all open seats on railcars from railroad companies across Europe, make that inventory accessible to online travel sites as well as traditional travel agents, and then manage the financial transaction for the booking. In Aaron's case, there was no other company aggregating the inventory of open rail seats even though demand for high-speed rail travel in Europe was blowing by air travel between major cities. If a ticket sells for 50 Euros, Aaron's company receives a 5% commission, or 2.50 Euros.

While we will leave it to you to read the case and prepare revenue projections using the facts provided, this top-down share of the market was the best way for Aaron to build his P&L. And still, Aaron had a number of critical assumptions to make. While all travel sites and agents of any size would want to use his service, not all travelers were likely buyers. He focused on high-speed rail travel between major European cities. This narrowed the total market (to about 60% of the total rail market). Then, there was the critical assumption of how the business would start and scale: 1% of the target market in the first year, 2% in the next, and so forth. And as for the 10% share as a five-year goal, Aaron told us it was based on the VC's heuristic view that anything less than 10% of a target market was not viewed as sufficiently aggressive, and anything more as naively optimistic. Again, while we prefer a granular, bottoms-up approach for any venture, you must do what works best for those individuals from whom you wish to raise your investment capital. If it's 10% for VCs investing in your space, so be it—have your numbers scale to 10%—but be able to back them up with specific market data, customer needs, and the compelling nature of the products or services you wish to provide.

Biotechnology ventures also tend to use top-down revenue projections. Each venture focuses on a specific disease (or set of related diseases). The entrepreneur finds the number of individuals both in the United States and abroad who suffer from that disease. A benchmark pricing is established with analogous therapies and multiplied against the patient population to get an annual revenue number. These products are so very long in the making (ten or more years!) that any sort of granular revenue projection that far ahead in the future make little sense. If the drug cures a disease, it is a safe assumption that those patients who can afford it or with the insurance that covers the therapy will receive the drug. These revenue projections also tend to show how new therapies move across international borders to build revenue.

Being Specific About the Assumptions Driving the Revenue Model

Let's assume that most of you can do a bottoms-up revenue model. Whether your business is selling products, systems, or services, you will have to provide your reasoning for the assumptions that affect your revenue projections. For many businesses, there is a common thread of:

- **What are the elements within your product line or services?** Think of these as specific rows, each with its own specific revenue stream. Product manufacturers think of these as SKUs; systems developers think of these as base-level licensing or subscription, then add-ons for more features and services; and services companies tend to "productize" their offerings into different capabilities at different fee structures—just as we saw above in the engineering services firm. Your new product/service strategy from Chapter 5 is the input needed for this key assumption.

- **How many points of exposure do you plan to have over time to prospective customers?** This could be the number of stores, inquiries from or visits to a Website or "infomercial," customer calls by a direct sales force, or any other lead generation and customer contact mechanism that suits your business.

- **What is your "close" rate for first time use**—what some might call "trial" or initial adoption? How is the closing rate different for the various products or services that you plan to offer?

- **What is the "sales cycle"** to close each customer? A sales cycle is the period between the first exposure of a product to customers and receipt of orders. During that period, the product's features and benefits must be communicated and customers must make decisions. For impulse consumer products, the customer decision process may be very brief. For expensive goods, specialty goods, and industrial goods, the decision process may be many months; buyer committees are often involved. Technology products, for example, are very complex and their sales cycle can extend over many months. The sales cycle is only one of the good reasons to have a person with sales experience on the team—if only on a part-time basis.

- **What is the "repeat" or continued usage rate** by customers who have started using your offerings?

- **What is the "list" or other form of end-user pricing** for your offerings (including those for "good, better, best" items)? The reality check in Chapter 7 is critically important here. In many instances, the current market will suggest a suitable pricing structure. A team starts with a product strategy that leads to a certain positioning for its new products or services along a continuum of "good, better, best"—and this drives pricing. In other instances, price is not often so easily determined. That is where the reality check steps in. McKinsey, the prominent consulting firm, provides insight into the pricing issue: "Companies consistently undercharge for products despite spending millions or even billions of dollars to develop or acquire them. The incremental approach often underestimates the value of new products for customers."[2] We can't tell you how many times we have seen business plans where entrepreneurs are essentially giving away fantastic new products just to achieve "market share." The problem with this approach is that low prices or free-price tarnishes any appearance of a premium product or service—and it kills any hope of achieving an operating profit.

- **What is the growth rate year to year for many of these key assumptions?** Most ventures start off slow in the first year of selling and then ramp up over subsequent years. What are reasonable initial penetration rates for contact, close, and repeat customers? How will these improve over time?

- **What is the timing to achieve first revenue?** For "products," there tends to be a lag for full product and packaging development, and then another lag for manufacturing or outsourcing the supply of finished products to go into channel. That entire lag may be just three months for you, but for most product ventures it is six months to a year. For a startup, don't start showing revenue before it is realistically feasible.

Use these bullets as a checklist to guide your own revenue projections. And, don't forget the whiteboard approach. Think through your assumptions and quickly rough out a set of revenue projections. Then, turn to the spreadsheet. Put in a set of rows stretching out month by month for the first two years, and annual for Years 3, 4, and 5 that contain your key assumptions behind the revenue streams for your venture. Try to be as realistic as possible about your revenue goals in the first couple of years—including when you can actually start selling a commercial product, system, or service.

Revenue Recognition

Revenue recognition is one of those difficult and sometimes nasty issues that can ensnarl the inexperienced entrepreneur. And not all accounting classes spend sufficient time helping students appreciate the important subtleties of revenue recognition.

If you are selling a consumer product—such as the healthy pet snacks venture described earlier in this chapter—then it is relatively straightforward. Let's say that the pet entrepreneurs sign a contract with PetSmart to supply stores with what is expected to be $3 million worth of product (at the price that PetSmart pays) in a given year. Those sales cannot be placed onto the P&L all at once. Rather, you book or "recognize" the revenue when product is shipped to PetSmart's distribution centers or directly to its stores. Invoices are generated for shipped product, which then convert to cash typically in 30 to 45 days when PetSmart pays its invoices.

If you sell to wholesalers—in the pet venture this means selling to distributors who are selling to independent specialty pet store retailers in a geographical region—that cash conversion can often occur within two weeks upon invoicing. And if you are selling through a Web store, it is a matter of your credit card merchant agreement—typically sales convert to cash within several days to a week.

Let's say that you have a software venture. You sell a site license to use the software to a major corporation with 50,000 users. The contract is for $250,000 that begins on March 1. The corporation plans to make the software instantly available to all of its employees. And, its

---

[2] McKinsey & Co. (2004, June 15). Pricing new products. *The McKinsey Quarterly.*

payment period to small firms such as yours is 60 days—that tends to stretch to 90 days—no matter how much you beg, scream, or holler. That would be a two- to three-month delay in that $250,000 or booked revenue hitting the all important cash flow statement.

But, it can become much more complicated. Let's say that you are providing your software as a service. That means a monthly service fee for those 50,000 employees, which might come to $250,000 a year, but which cannot be recognized all on March 1. Rather, the revenue can only be recognized month by month and the structure of the revenue is typically the number of users "provisioned" or given access to the software times the subscription fee per user negotiated with the corporation. Bottom line: The revenue recognition is stretched out over time.

Similarly, let's say that your venture makes a new breed of environmental sensors. You sell a major contract with IBM for one it's "Smarter Planet" governmental customers, valued at $10 million for the calendar year. Unfortunately, IBM only wants to take shipment of these sensors when it needs them for each new Smarter Planet initiative. Your accountants will not let you book the revenue until actual sensors are shipped to IBM at the price per unit as agreed to by IBM.

When you prepare your financial statements, you must walk through these scenarios and generate numbers that reflect the reality of your proposed business model in terms of recognizing the revenue.

Shortening the Sales Cycle

This is what every entrepreneur would like to achieve, of course. But for complex products, systems, and services, this is easier said than done. Here are some tricks of the trade that might prove useful for your planning:

- **Mitigate the risk by starting small.** Many business-to-business (B2B) ventures create systems and other related technology that can be used across the entire organization. But the same positioning as a new, innovative company also scares decision-making executives in mature corporations. They want innovation but are also concerned with risk. The answer often is to create a test-site within the client organization where the system can prove its worth before widespread adoption. And, it is not necessary to give the test away for free. Rather, hold firm on your prices, but simply restrict the scope of the application. However, it is a good idea to provide no-cost technical resources to help the customer integrate and install the software—just so the trial can start quickly. Also, these first-phase uses need to be constrained to specific periods of time. Two to three months is a reasonable number for both parties.

- **Allow easy entry with a "good, better, best" upgrade strategy.** This is another version of risk mitigation. Depending on your product or service, consider offering a no-frills version at a moderate relative price—and then allow easy upgrade options for customers once they have become comfortable with your solution. Of course, a certain percentage of your target customer market will want "the best" right from the start. Just make sure you have them pay adequately for that privilege!

- **Create a "win-win" for the customer.** One of your author's current ventures is a software company selling error detection systems to hospitals. This company has some pretty fancy data-mining software that identifies missing medical charges by physicians and other care providers. The company adopted a strategy *to sell its capabilities as a service, as opposed to selling complex enterprise software.* By selling a revenue-finding service, the company could sell to the CFOs of client physician groups and hospitals, individuals known for quick, objective decision making. The venture asks for 20% of the missing medical charges once the client collects its money from the health insurers, making this a risk-free proposition for the CFO. This new selling approach has reduced the sales cycle from the typical nine months for selling enterprise software to committees comprising IT professionals and doctors to, on average, 60 days. In its first year of business, the company signed up several dozen major accounts—due primarily to this "win-win" selling proposition for customers.

- **Sell up the organization.** Information technology companies selling enterprise software find that the higher up the organization they go in terms of selling, the more rapid the decision-making process. An example is a storage management software company that was experiencing a very long sales cycle selling software that reported on all the files stored over enterprise storage networks. Part of the delay was because the team was selling to information technology managers with constrained budgets and who labored over price/performance analyses for each procurement. The team decided to build an add-on module that produced all the data needed for "chargeback" to end-user departments for space used on central storage machines. This allowed a sale directly to the CIO of target companies. Allowing client executives to "make money" with the system dramatically shortened the sales cycle. Many software companies creating "cloud computing" applications are finding that building in a "chargeback" capability is a strong purchasing incentive for senior managers in enterprise customers.

- **Manage stakeholders in any enterprise procurement decision.** What might seem to be a 60-day sales cycle can turn into many more months because other individuals inside a corporate customer in a B2B play are part of the sign-off process for a significant purchase. The entrepreneur must know who these individuals are and take specific steps to inform them about the products or services to be sold. You are going to have to do it sooner or later—so best sooner to avoid any nasty surprises in trying to close a corporate sale. Make a list of all the key stakeholders in your customer's decision-making process. Establish a "call list" for having a conversation with these individuals and note any follow-on steps required. These individual meetings before "the big meeting" go a long way toward ensuring your success with a large client. B2B ventures need internal champions in enterprise customers. Getting access to senior-level managers in an enterprise customer takes networking and diligence.

You should know the nature of the sales cycle facing your venture from your Reality Check (Chapter 7). If you feel that this is going to be a problem, don't hide it in your revenue projections. Rather, adjust your product/service and pricing strategy to shorten the cycle, and reflect these approaches in your revenue projections. Rest assured that your investors are going to be asking detailed questions about the sales cycle!

Last, but Not Least: Identify and Show the Recurring Revenue

Achieving recurring revenue seems to be one of those "truisms" for successful ventures. Want to please a prospective investor? Show recurring revenue in your projections, and then have the customer input to back it up.

Experienced entrepreneurs will tell you that it is a lot of harder to win each new customer than originally expected. Rarely does a new venture enter into a clean market space. There are existing competitors, each with their own sales pitch and incentives to keep current customers. For software types of ventures, enterprise customers have often developed so many customer interfaces between all their various computer systems that switching to a newer, better alternative represents a huge leap of faith and substantial cost. Or, consumer products entrepreneurs underestimate the difficulty of stealing shelf space from existing competitors or the cost needed to establish a brand presence in the market. That is why once you get a customer, investors want to see an aggressive plan for extracting additional revenue from each customer. That means add-on products or value-added services.

For many types of ventures, recurring revenue is a natural part of the business. For example, most services companies have recurring revenue; try it once, and use the services forever. A software company providing energy analytics probably won't have to work too hard convincing clients to buy a subscription model for information flows that are continuous and never ending. Or, a third-party logistics venture can well expect to receive a continuing stream of business from corporate customers—if it proves that it does an effective job arranging the shipment of goods and materials around the world. Health sciences entrepreneurs naturally get recurring revenue by creating diagnostic kits, therapies for disease treatment, and various regimens for ongoing disease management. Prove it once and well for customers and you win a continuous stream of business—at least until the point where the quality of your service deteriorates or a competitor re-enters the market with a major price disruption. (Think "open-source" software or generic drugs.)

However, most ventures have to work hard to think through the meaning and nature of add-on products and services. You can be like Microsoft or Intuit and try to convince your installed base to upgrade to a new version of the software once every two to three years or so. Or, you can mirror Symantec with annual renewal subscriptions (for its daily anti-virus updates.) We like this model! Or, your recurring revenue might be professional consulting or integration services on top of a piece of software or third-party plug-ins; or, a line of accessories for a consumer electronics product. Harley-Davidson, for example, realizes about 8% of its revenue from selling Harley-Davidson–branded general merchandize made by third-party suppliers. Or, Apple achieved about $4 billion of its $43 billion of revenue in 2009 from the sale of music and other digital content through the iTunes store, iPod services, and Apple-branded and third-party iPod accessories. That is a remarkable number for a business that was launched just six years before!

Your investors will want to see a similar eye for the potential of recurring revenue in your business. This should appear as a separate line item or two in your revenue model.

Generating the P&L

Now we move on to generating the complete P&L projection. Since by now you have the revenue portion of the P&L well in hand (or at least all set to try!), we will focus on the various expense items that come underneath revenue to get to operating profit.

Figure 9.4 is an example of a proforma P&L, using our health monitoring case as the learning example. While we have constructed this case for the teaching of this book, we modeled it directly on an actual startup. You can see that for this case, we have chosen for the purposes of this presentation to show monthly projections for the first two years of the business, and then annual projections for Years 3, 4, and 5. Please view the entirety of this spreadsheet at the textbook's companion Website: www.sagepub.com/meyer. The on-line spreadsheet has very detailed financial projections for the health monitoring venture: a) the P&L, b) the departmental budgets for this venture incorporated into to the P&L, and c) the staffing and headcount forecasts that are a major component of the departmental budgets. Scan through these worksheets and have them at your finger tips as we read on. And yes, we know that these are highly detailed—but it is with such detail that most ventures are successfully planned and funded.

For those readers interested in getting an actual copy of these and other financial projections for new ventures, go to our book Website. We have templates that you can freely modify for a number of different types of businesses! Go to www.sagepub.com/meyer.

The projected P&L in Figure 9.4 has all the standard line items that one expects to find for a startup. In this particular venture, revenues do not start until the ninth month after startup. The monthly breakdown of expenses is useful to show the cash burn and the ramp up of expenses in successive months. Moreover, the most powerful driver for spending in this type of

Revenue	Mar	Apr	May	Jun	Jul	Aug	Sep	Oct	Nov	Dec	Year 1
Recurring Service Revenue											
Assisted-Living Monitoring	0	0	0	0	0	0	0	126,000	159,750	193,500	479,250
Home Health Agencies Monitoring											
Total Revenue	0	0	0	0	0	0	0	126,000	159,750	193,500	**479,250**
Less 5% commission to channel partners	0	0	0	0	0	0	0	6,300	7,988	9,675	23,963
Net Sales	0	0	0	0	0	0	0	119,700	151,763	183,825	**455,288**
Cost of Goods											
75 Installation in residencies ($100)	0	0	0	0	0	0	0	18,750	18,750	18,750	56,250
600 Sensors, PC, wireless modems ($500)	0	0	0	0	0	0	0	150,000	150,000	150,000	450,000
5% Application hosting (5% of revenue)	0	0	0	0	0	0	0	6,300	7,988	9,675	23,963
Total Cost of Goods	**0**	**0**	**0**	**0**	**0**	**0**	**0**	175,050	176,738	178,425	**530,213**
COGS as % of Revenue											1
GS&A											
Executives and support staff	23,933	22,333	34,933	33,333	33,333	33,333	33,333	33,333	33,333	33,333	314,533
Sales	0	0	0	0	0	0	0	32,333	41,033	55,533	128,900
R&D	62,617	64,917	63,500	63,500	76,067	76,067	76,067	80,900	80,900	80,900	725,433
Technical support	0	0	0	0	21,167	20,367	35,017	33,417	33,417	33,417	176,800
50 Subcontract field support for residences											
System field test for new channel partners	200,000										200,000
Accounting service fees	350	350	350	350	350	350	350	350	350	350	3,500
Legal fees (including patent)	24,000	12,000	2,000	2,000	2,000	2,000	10,000	2,000	2,000	2,000	60,000
Insurance (product/commercial)	0	0	0	0	0	0	0	10,000	10,000	10,000	30,000
25,000 Public relations/media ($25K/yr.)	0	0	0	0	0	0	0	0	0	0	0
50,000 Direct marketing ($50K per partner/yr.)	0	0	0	0	0	0	0	4,167	4,167	4,167	12,500
20 Rent and utilities ($20K foot)	5,833	6,667	8,333	8,333	10,833	10,833	12,500	14,167	15,000	15,833	108,333
Postage	100	100	100	100	100	100	100	100	100	100	1,000
Tradeshows ($60K per show)	0	0	0	0	0	0	60,000	0	0	0	60,000
24,000 Misc. office expenses (supplies, Etc.)	2,000	2,000	2,000	2,000	2,000	2,000	2,000	2,000	2,000	2,000	20,000
Total Operating Expense	318,833	108,367	111,217	109,617	145,850	145,050	229,367	212,767	222,300	237,633	**1,841,000**
Operating Income	(318,833)	(108,367)	(111,217)	(109,617)	(145,850)	(145,050)	(229,367)	(268,117)	(247,275)	(232,233)	**(1,915,925**
Operating Margin											
Depreciation (see Cap Budget)	5,103	5,103	5,103	5,103	5,103	5,103	5,103	5,103	5,103	5,103	51,033
Interest Income											19,616
Provision for Taxes (33%)											0
Net Income	(323,937)	(113,470)	(116,320)	(114,720)	(150,953)	(150,153)	(234,470)	(273,220)	(252,378)	(237,337)	**(1,947,342**
Profitability on Sales											

Figure 9.4   Proforma P&L for a Health Monitoring Venture

Please view the remainder of this spreadsheet at the textbook's companion Website: www.sagepub.com/meyer

Jan	Feb	Mar	Apr	May	Jun	Jul	Aug	Sep	Oct	Nov	Dec	Year 2	Year 3	Year 4	Year 5
53,250	420,750	488,250	555,750	623,250	690,750	758,250	825,750	893,250	960,750	1,028,250	1,095,750	8,694,000	28,950,750	66,684,600	91,022,400
													5,607,000	19,812,000	45,855,000
53,250	420,750	488,250	555,750	623,250	690,750	758,250	825,750	893,250	960,750	1,028,250	1,095,750	**8,694,000**	**34,557,750**	**86,496,600**	**136,877,400**
17,663	21,038	24,413	27,788	31,163	34,538	37,913	41,288	44,663	48,038	51,413	54,788	**434,700**	**1,727,888**	**4,324,830**	**6,843,870**
35,588	399,713	463,838	527,963	592,088	656,213	720,338	784,463	848,588	912,713	976,838	1,040,963	**8,259,300**	**32,829,863**	**82,171,770**	**130,033,530**
37,500	37,500	37,500	37,500	37,500	37,500	37,500	37,500	37,500	37,500	37,500	37,500	450,000	0	0	0
00,000	300,000	300,000	300,000	300,000	300,000	300,000	300,000	300,000	300,000	300,000	300,000	3,600,000	7,650,000	15,240,000	23,850,000
17,663	21,038	24,413	27,788	31,163	34,538	37,913	41,288	44,663	48,038	51,413	54,788	434,700	1,727,888	4,324,830	6,843,870
55,163	358,538	361,913	365,288	368,663	372,038	375,413	378,788	382,163	385,538	388,913	392,288	**4,484,700**	**9,377,888**	**19,564,830**	**30,693,870**
												1	0	0	0
5,235	44,435	44,435	44,435	44,435	44,435	57,985	57,185	61,069	60,269	60,269	60,269	624,455	845,481	885,346	915,717
2,633	61,833	61,833	61,833	61,833	61,833	69,616	68,816	84,333	83,533	83,533	83,533	845,159	990,820	1,359,473	1,412,795
3,349	83,349	83,349	83,349	83,349	83,349	93,190	91,690	91,732	101,532	109,832	108,332	1,096,401	1,352,871	1,433,039	1,486,541
4,398	43,598	43,598	50,198	49,398	49,398	51,590	51,590	60,381	59,581	66,181	65,381	635,291	1,104,698	1,434,918	1,851,518
													150,000	550,000	1,300,000
												100,000	100,000	100,000	100,000
350	350	350	350	350	350	350	350	350	350	350	350	4,200	4,620	5,082	5,590
3,000	3,000	3,000	3,000	3,000	3,000	3,000	3,000	3,000	3,000	3,000	3,000	36,000	39,600	43,560	47,916
0,000	10,000	10,000	10,000	10,000	10,000	10,000	10,000	10,000	10,000	10,000	10,000	120,000	132,000	145,200	159,720
2,083	2,083	2,083	2,083	2,083	2,083	2,083	2,083	2,083	2,083	2,083	2,083	25,000	26,250	27,563	28,941
4,167	4,167	4,167	4,167	4,167	4,167	4,167	4,167	4,167	4,167	4,167	4,167	50,000	150,000	250,000	350,000
8,333	18,333	18,333	19,167	19,167	19,167	21,667	21,667	24,167	25,000	26,667	26,667	258,333	30,000	30,000	30,000
100	100	100	100	100	100	100	100	100	100	100	100	1,200	1,320	1,452	1,597
0	0	0	0	60,000	0	0	0	0	60,000	0	0	120,000	120,000	120,000	120,000
2,000	2,000	2,000	2,000	2,000	2,000	2,000	2,000	2,000	2,000	2,000	2,000	24,000	60,000	70,000	80,000
5,648	273,248	273,248	280,681	339,881	279,881	315,748	312,648	343,381	411,614	368,181	365,881	**3,840,039**	**5,107,659**	**6,455,633**	**7,890,336**
5,223)	(232,073)	(171,323)	(118,006)	(116,456)	**4,294**	29,177	93,027	123,044	115,561	219,744	282,794	**(65,439)**	**18,344,316**	**56,151,307**	**91,449,324**
												(0)	1	1	1
6,938	6,938	6,938	6,938	6,938	6,938	6,938	6,938	6,938	6,938	6,938	6,938	83,250	117,267	91,433	87,750
508	508	508	508	508	508	508	508	508	508	508	508	6,096	11,102	218,721	1,071,087
													0	6,057,288	18,602,109	30,531,736
1,652)	(238,502)	(177,752)	(124,436)	(122,886)	(2,136)	**22,748**	86,598	116,615	109,131	213,315	276,365	**(142,593)**	**12,180,864**	**37,676,486**	**61,900,925**
												−2%	35%	44%	45%

technology startup is the spending on various types of employees—not just management, but salespeople, programming and quality assurance staff, and customer support personnel.

Also, note from the staffing and headcount projections contained in the spreadsheet for this health monitoring venture on the textbook's companion Website (www.sagepub.com/meyer), that the venture is judicious on when to hire certain types of people. For example, it doesn't make sense to bring on an expensive VP of Sales until the development of the software and sensors that the company needs is nearing completion. Conversely, the venture needs to hire technical managers and staff in the very first month. Similarly, hiring technical support staff for installing systems and training channel partners only begins in earnest in Year 2.

All these headcounts in the spreadsheet then feed the departmental budgeting, which is also included under a separate tab in the spreadsheet on the textbook's companion Website (www .sagepub.com/meyer). This is where computers, telecommunications, and other types of expenses are added to the labor cost on a person-by-person basis. Yes, these figures are detailed—that is what most investors expect when real money is at stake. Once you are running an actual business, you will be even more focused on each hire and the costs associated with that hire. Think of it this way: Each employee consumes your hard-earned sales dollars (or hard-won investments)—and therefore, each person must produce at a high level according to their role and responsibilities.

It is not our purpose here to teach you the structure of a proforma P&L or any of the other financial statements that we will use in this chapter. We trust that you have already taken at least one accounting course and have learned the fundamentals of the income statement, the cash flow statement, and the balance sheet. For example, at the very top of the P&L for the health monitoring venture is a 5% sales commission to incentivize assisted-living center companies and home health agencies for helping to market the service. This 5% is deducted from Sales to obtain Net Sales. Selling through channels or strategic partners requires that you adjust your revenue projections accordingly. Similarly, some businesses need to account for "Returns"—hopefully a small percentage of Sales!

Perhaps most important, we hope that you have had some practice showing how certain elements of these financial statements flow from one statement to the other. This might be how Net Income from the P&L flows into the cash flow statement and as earnings for the balance sheet. Alternatively, it might be how sales in the income statement drive accounts receivables in the balance sheet as adjustments to working capital in the cash flow statement. Inventory is the same way, being the materials used to produce sales, the cost of which hits the balance sheet and your timeliness of paying suppliers affecting working capital on the cash flow statement. If this is all unfamiliar to you, we can recommend as supplemental reading, *Financial Intelligence for Entrepreneurs: What You Really Need to Know About the Numbers*, by Karen Berman and Joe Knight.[3]

What most accounting books don't teach, however, are the basic considerations for the entrepreneur behind the various expense items in the P&L. Just as we dug into the details of modeling revenue, we need to do the same for projecting expenses. Whether you call it "Op Ex" or "cash burn," managing these expenses carefully is an essential part of getting a company to operating profit. Entrepreneurs need to be very careful about conserving the cash raised in a seed or Series A financing because one never really knows just how long that cash will need to last before revenues start to roll in from your first products or services.

The bottom line is that the entrepreneur must be tight-fisted on operating expenses—both in the planning of the venture and in the actual execution of the plan. Investors will try to gauge your maturity and frugality. Here are some of the key areas that will be front and center:

Management Salaries (Including Your Own Paycheck!)

The staffing and headcount projections that we described above feed into the departmental budgets, and then, those department budgets feed into the expense line items in the P&L (Figure 9.4). Now, let's talk about your salary and those of fellow team members.

---

[3] Berman, K., & and Knight, J. (2008). *Financial Intelligence for Entrepreneurs: What You Really Need To Know About the Numbers*. Boston: Harvard Business School Press.

If you are an MBA student developing a plan to start a new company with $100,000 to $250,000 of angel money, you should be able to live with a salary in the $50,000 to $75,000 range for the first year or two until the venture becomes cash positive. This is probably a pay cut for many of you. However, remember that you are working for the value of your equity and few if any will own as much of that equity as you in your new venture. Later on, once the business becomes cash positive, you bring your salary up to market par.

The salaries of CEO and VPs of Sales and Engineering of ventures raising $1 million to $3 million or more for Series A financing have salaries that are generally in the $120,000 to $150,000 range. It is easy to see, however, that with those three or four senior managers, half a million dollars of that precious cash is consumed before any of the R&D salaries, manufacturing expense, or sales commissions are paid to people doing the more detailed work of the company. Once sales begin to accrue, these salaries tend to bump up by $30,000 to $50,000 in outlying years. Ventures backed with $3 million or more in Series A financing tend to have senior management salaries in the $150,000 to $175,000 range.

If you have gone to our textbook companion Website (www.sagepub.com/meyer) and looked carefully at the staffing and headcount projections, you can see how the various management salaries quickly add up. In addition, you can see why a monthly breakdown of expenses is useful because it allows you to more accurately reflect the hiring of personnel to when you truly need them. This, in turn, has a direct impact on cash flow. Most entrepreneurs have highly detailed breakdowns of how positions are filled over the first two years of the business, position by position, as shown in the department budgets in the online spreadsheet for this health monitoring example. It is a good idea to create a separate worksheet on the timing and amount of personnel costs if these are one of the major expense components of your business. The textbook's companion Website has projected P&Ls for different types of businesses, so be sure to look at these and see which one might help you as a starting point for your own financial projections.

Spending Money on Office Space and Furniture

The moment you move out of a home office, rents tend to be the second biggest expense for new ventures after salaries. Most nonretail startups will have two or three cofounders, and over the course of the first year, perhaps ten other employees. That's three offices, a dozen cubicles, a conference room for meetings and selling, storage area for supplies, and a small kitchen area. Add all of these up and it is no surprise that many startups look for between 2,500 and 5,000 square feet of space to lease in the first year of operations, hopefully with some adjacent options to expand. The simple table below shows the tremendous impact on operating expense on the price per square foot.

Cost per Square Foot ($)	Space Needed	Lease per Year	Cost per Month
8	5,000	40,000	3,333
13	5,000	62,500	5,208
22	5,000	110,000	9,167

$8 per square foot might represent some converted warehouse space ideal for software development; $15, a well-accommodated space in an office building with certain amenities, located outside a major city; and $25, the same within the city. Look at the immense differences in cash outlays on a yearly basis. This is of course a balance. You have to be where young, hardworking employees want to come to work; and, for the "adults" helping to manage the business, you might have to spend more for parking spaces near your office. The bottom line is that you have to hunt for a good deal for your office space—and if you can—work out of your home offices until you begin to hire employees.

Incubators are another option for entrepreneurs. An incubator is shared office space where angel groups or venture capital firms essentially subsidize rent for startups. Once you need to hire additional employees beyond the founders, then it's time to move out and find your own office space. If you use an incubator, however, be careful about giving up your equity in return just for office space, basic services, and supplies. There has to be a lot more value added to the business to warrant dilution for such commodities.

Talk to your friends in a similar position starting ventures. For example, in one of your author's first companies, our group of cofounders checked around our university community regarding office space. We heard about an alumnus who was leasing office in the attic of his commercial building to students wishing to start new companies at the whopping price of $2 a square foot! There were certain conditions: no walls, a willingness to share computers, and not minding when the chemists from downstairs came running up to the attic asking us to quickly open all of our windows (chemistry experiments were running on the lower floors). All of this sounded just fine to us. This alumnus had his hand in dozens of startups during his informal yet highly effective incubator.

Every office needs desks, couches, kitchen appliances, and other accessories to make the office a fun place to work. That does not mean that the furniture has to be purchased new. Read the classified advertisements in your local paper, find the bankruptcy auctions of office equipment, or visit your local low-cost office furniture and suppliers discounter to get bargain-basement prices for used items. The only place where you need to impress visitors is in the reception area and the conference room—and even there, you can typically buy used items that are still very attractive. Another option is to look at leasing plans for new equipment. However, you can't really beat used office furniture at a "fire sale." Countless entrepreneurs have done this and so can you.

Hiring Engineers

Entrepreneurs sometimes turn to "search firms"—otherwise known as recruiters—to fill marketing and technical positions. Since these firms are paid 20% to 30% of the first year's salary for successful placements, that can be a hugely expensive way to find new employees. Instead, use your network, your investors, your classmates, and your professors to spread the word that you have certain positions to fill. Moreover, rather than just putting jobs up on the Web, you want to get some sort of reference for each person you hire. Even one *B* player in a 15-person company can cause terrible harm, be it with customers, the suppliers, or in the technology itself.

You can also be creative in your search for new employees. Throw a few office parties, invite everyone in your network, and spread the word among your local university community. Let other people do the drinking while you talk to everyone attending, learning their interests and seeing if they are good listeners and collaborative in nature. If so, you can float the idea of working with your company—first on a trial basis to get to know one another and then, ongoing. Your authors have hired dozens of new technical employees in their various startups in years past, all without paying a single recruiter fee.

In terms of financial projections for technical salaries, there are standard levels of pay for certain disciplines that you can determine by networking with other entrepreneurs or referring to the various templates on our own textbook Website. And be sure to include a small bonus pool at the end of each year for your technical people. Five percent goes a long way at Christmas time as a gesture of appreciation and will help retain your best engineers. Be assured that if they are talented and achieve success in your company, these same individuals will be receiving calls from other companies for employment. There is no doubt that the human dimension of a business also drives financial projections.

Many entrepreneurs feel that what you need to find and hire is a strong project manager who can organize a combination of engineering employees and external subcontractors found to augment the team in certain important areas. These include the exterior design of the product, packaging, or user interface. See the accompanying shaded text region to learn how to work lean in the area of product development.

Spotlight on Innovation: Agile Development: Resources for the New Venture

"Agile development" is a significant trend in the startups now. We asked one of our colleagues, Tucker Marion, a professor at Northeastern University, to share a few of his thoughts. Tucker is an expert in agile development in small firms and an industrial designer of new products himself. This is what Tucker said:

Over the last ten years a perfect storm has developed that enables new ventures to design, develop, prototype, and test new concepts more efficiently and effectively than ever before. The combination of Web-based services, low-cost rapid prototyping, and the freelance economy has fostered this storm. Capabilities that were once only available to the largest of companies are now accessible to the garage inventor—seeding the ground for an explosion of innovative products and services in the coming years.

There are now a wide range of services that allow a startup team to design, source, manufacture, and test new product concepts. These services can help turn the fledgling startup into a fast-acting virtual company. For example, if a company needs to find a microcontroller for a new device, it can go to DigiKey—a leading supplier of electronic components (http://www.digikey.com). Do you need to find a manufacturer to build your product and provide detailed quotes for cost engineering? Uploading your product designs on MFG.com can net dozens of potential manufacturers in several days (http://www.mfg.com). Other entrepreneurs have found Guru.com a useful source for finding just about any type of type of engineer, from software to mechanical engineering (http://www.guru.com).

Services such as these for prototyping and limited production runs are relatively inexpensive and fast compared to taking the time to hire, train, and organize your own extensive engineering and manufacturing staff. This also helps maintain low overhead—maximizing funds for R&D and marketing.

Tucker continued with his passion for agile development for entrepreneurs:

In the 1980s, technology was developed that allowed virtual computer-aided-designs (CAD) of products to be built quickly using new technologies such as stereolithography (SLA). These prototyping machines were expensive—and available only to the largest of firms such as automobile manufacturers. However, over the last ten years, new technologies combined with refinements in existing machines have lowered the cost exponentially. There are now desktop machines that can create parts for several thousand dollars, approaching the point of being affordable for small companies. Additionally, these fast prototyping machines—combined with Web services such as Quickparts (http://www.quickparts.com)—can turn around look and feel prototypes in a matter of days, sometimes faster. These parts can be used for rapid feedback on design efficacy and from target customers—allowing firms to move quickly to market. Rapid prototyping has also entered other more complex spaces such as electronic circuit board turnaround, and production tooling (http://www.protomold.com).

For new ventures, this ability to quickly design, prototype, and iterate has many ramifications. Entrepreneurs can pitch their business plan with a prototype in hand. Or, they can initial sales without investing too heavily into fixed assets by subcontracting manufacturing for initial production runs. Or, startups can gain access to world-class design talent for their first new product without having to bear the cost of hiring half a dozen full-time employees. Control the architecture of your product or system in-house, but then consider subcontract engineers to build certain components. Freelance experts are used to working in this manner and most often will hit the ground running.

To find industrial designers to help you improve the look and feel of a new product, packaging, or system, Tucker suggested Coroflot (http://www.coroflot.com) or iFreelance (http://www.iFreelance.com).

Thank you, Tucker!

Hiring and Compensating Salespeople

Hiring salespeople is an entirely different matter. It cannot be so easily subcontracted out to independent sales representatives or other companies. Revenue is the lifeblood of any venture, and sales are something that you must not only control but excel at. Therefore, a few select sales or business development people are essential for the success of nearly all new ventures. A small firm needs *A* players especially in this area. And, if they make more take-home pay than the founders based on sales commissions, well that's a good thing because their success is making your equity worth millions. However, it is hard to know if any given sales candidate will prove successful selling your products or services *until they are actually doing it*. Some salespeople are very good at selling entrepreneurs on large, rich pipelines of customers *that never materialize into actual sales*. And, by the time you know it in six months, it may be too late for your fledgling company. Your author speaks from painful experience on this matter in one of his other startup companies.

> *There was once a guy named Dan,*
>
> *who every day sold us a big pipeline, "man to man,"*
>
> *but good old Dan never put a penny of real revenue into our can.*

The Dan in this rhyme was all too real. Relying on him to generate sales led to a tough startup year and almost proved fatal to the fledgling business! Unfortunately, most entrepreneurs make this mistake at one time or another in their ventures. The only way to be sure about avoiding a similar type of mistake is to do your due diligence on every salesperson you hire. Find out their performance to sales quota over the past three years. If someone doesn't work out, you have lost three months between firing that individual, finding someone new, training them, and turning them loose onto customers. Ventures can ill afford three months of lost time.

In terms of how these ideas hit the financial statements, if you have the choice between a $100,000 base and a 3% commission, versus a $50,000 base and a 5% commission, choose the latter. In fact, tier the commission level higher for more sales. For example, if it's software, 5% for the first $500,000, 6% for the next $250,000, 7% for the next $250,000, and 8% for anything beyond. The message is the more business you close, the more money you make on each sale. A good salesperson will jump all over this and work tirelessly to succeed.

Spending Money on Lawyers

Retaining good legal counsel is money well spent in a new venture.

Unfortunately, it is going to cost you a lot of money. In the health monitoring venture's projected P&L, you can see that we have budgeted $60,000 in the first year, which for that case, included incorporation, an employee stock option plan, a patent, and helping to structure the legal agreement with the first assisted-living company. In writing this book, we asked former students and friends who have had ventures funded by angels, VCs, and corporate investors to share with us their startup financial projections. We observed attorneys' fees ranged from $20,000 at the low end to $100,000 at the high end for high-roller, technology-intensive ventures. Expect some significant upfront fees for incorporation, shareholder or partners agreements, and employee stock options plans. You will also incur further upfront fees for "private placement memorandums" (which include the guts of your business plan) for angel-type investments. Or, if you are doing substantial venture capital fundraising—be prepared for attorneys fees that are in excess of $30,000! Insist that the legal fees for venture capital fundraising are taken out of the post-raise piggybank, that is, to be shared with the investors, and not borne by you alone.

However, after these initial expenses, with careful management, your attorneys fees can come back down to earth. In our health monitoring venture, for example, the second-year fees come to $3,000 a month, or $36,000 for the year. For most technology ventures that is not an unreasonable number, although we have seen many with expenditures twice that amount—and much more if patent work is involved.

At the same time, a good attorney is worth his or her weight in gold. As in so many other areas of entrepreneurship, the best way to find a good attorney is to network with other entrepreneurs in the area. See who your *successful* peers recommend. While the brand name on the firm is important, remember that you are hiring an individual. You want to try to get the name of an attorney who is highly experienced doing work in your specific industry sector.

In addition to keeping you out of trouble in matters of standard business practice, attorneys from well-established firms will introduce you to investors, angels as well as venture capitalists. Those from the largest firms may also have colleagues who represent other organizations that just might be your first set of hard-to-win customers. The types of advice that you will receive include how to best distribute founders' shares, to establish employee stock incentive programs, and where and how to incorporate or structure the business to serve the interests of both investor types and liability protection. For example, angel investors will have no problem with a Limited Liability Company because the losses of the startup are passed on through to the unit holders on a pro-rata basis. Venture capitalists, on the other hand, want preferred stock, which takes you into the C Corporation status. If your attorney cannot show insight into these fundamental matters, they are not the correct attorney for you. The attorneys you want will also have access to seasoned intellectual property (IP) staff that can help protect the "secret sauce" of your company.

You want to try to get a "special deal" on first-year attorneys fees—or at least until you are well funded. Good attorneys have a nose for high-potential ventures and will cut you a very good deal on fees up until the point you are generating solid revenue as a business. Their time with you is an investment on their part into helping grow a long-term client.

Also, be forewarned that using a good attorney can be addictive. The meter is always running. To reduce legal expenses, your attorneys should be able to provide you with standard boilerplate-type contracts for customer and employee agreements. It should then be okay for you to fill in the blanks or modestly amend them without final review for each agreement. Entrepreneurs who send everything to their attorneys will find themselves with twice the bill for which they had planned.

For patents, you need to work with the very best IP attorneys in your city or area because the implications of a successful patent application can be enormous for the ultimate value of a venture. First, entrepreneurs who think they have developed some type of "secret sauce" should first file a provisional patent through their attorneys—and this typically costs less than $5,000. Then, there is the formal patent application for a technological process or method. This work can run the entrepreneur upwards of $50,000. No two patents are the same, and each one takes thoughtful preparation.

We have also observed ways to reduce this expense. We are advisors to a recent startup presently that spent "only" $12,000 for a first-rate patent application (at least they hope!). By the lawyer's own estimates, this patent would have ordinarily cost the venture about $40,000 to prepare. The reason for the difference was the document that the team handed to the attorneys was also so highly detailed and well prepared. The founding team had already done its homework with friends and associates, several of whom had an extensive legal background.

Spending Money on Accountants

We strongly recommend that you find a reasonably priced, well-regarded accounting firm. This is not just to do your company tax returns but to provide advice and assistance on your bookkeeping system and your own personal tax situation. If you spend $2,500 a year for various filings prepared by professionals, it is money well spent. You will also find yourself asking your accountant about how to handle difficult issues about revenue recognition, tax issues in doing business abroad, and to participate in bank negotiations for working capital loans and the like. And, while QuickBooks might be the best tool for small business ever invented, you as the entrepreneur do not want to spend your time entering data and producing the reports. Either hire a co-op student from your local university, or ask your accounting firm if it can provide some "in-sourced" talent during the startup months of your business. Later on, you can bring in a controller to manage the books—but until then, you and your founding team want to spend every waking second either selling customers, developing products, or raising the next round of capital from investors.

Spending Money on PR Firms

Many an entrepreneur will tell you that being the focus of an article in a local newspaper or trade publication led to critical sales in the early years. This type of publicity makes a small firm look larger and better established. The focus of these articles tends to be an exciting new product announcement or a major customer "win." Or, sometimes articles are written on a new emerging market or technology trend and the entrepreneur is interviewed as a subject matter expert.

We have worked with some entrepreneurs who are natural PR machines, fearless about reaching out to business reporters or trade journal editors. But most simply do not know how to do this and are shy about engaging with the press. That is where a good PR firm comes into play. Their job is to get your firm visibility. PR firms often work on a monthly fee for a pre-specified set of activities with tangible milestones. As with any supplier, you should create a trial period in which the PR firm can prove its capabilities before entering into a longer-term contract. Here, too, network with fellow entrepreneurs to find out the local PR firm that delivers best for firms like yours. PR firms tend to have contacts with media types in specific sectors.

Closing Comments on the P&L

Amongst all your various projections, investors will turn to your projected P&L first—and then come back to it repeatedly as they read a section of your business plan and then see how it translates back into a particular area of revenue, expenses, or profitability. They will then most likely turn to your revenue model to dig further into the top revenue line(s) in the P&L, and then, to the cash flow statement to gauge the need for the amount and timing of investment

	Mar	Apr	May	Jun	Jul	Aug	Sep	Oct	Nov	Dec	Year 1
Beginning Cash	0	1,915,857	1,795,373	1,671,839	1,549,698	1,391,121	1,233,080	990,458	757,732	464,348	
Net income	(323,937)	(113,470)	(116,320)	(114,720)	(150,953)	(150,153)	(234,470)	(273,220)	(252,378)	(237,337)	(1,966,95
Less Adjustment for A/R (30 days)	0	0	0	0	0	0	0	(126,000)	(33,750)	(33,750)	(193,50
Add Adjustment for A/P (30 days)	0	0	0	0	0	0	0	175,050	1,688	1,688	178,4
Add: Interest Income 2%	0	3,193	2,992	2,786	2,583	2,319	2,055	1,651	1,263	774	19,6
Subtract: Interest payment 12%	0	0	0	0	0	0	0	0	0	0	
Add: Depreciation	5,103	5,103	5,103	5,103	5,103	5,103	5,103	5,103	5,103	5,103	51,0
Less: Capital Expense	(15,310)	(15,310)	(15,310)	(15,310)	(15,310)	(15,310)	(15,310)	(15,310)	(15,310)	(15,310)	(153,10
Free Cash Flow	(334,143)	(120,484)	(123,534)	(122,140)	(158,577)	(158,041)	(242,622)	(232,726)	(293,385)	(278,832)	(2,064,48
Net Change in Cash	(334,143)	1,795,373	1,671,839	1,549,698	1,391,121	1,233,080	990,458	757,732	464,348	185,516	(2,064,48
Equity Financing	2,250,000	0	0	0	0	0	0	0	0	0	2,250,0
Debt Financing	0	0	0	0	0	0	0	0	0	0	
Ending Cash	1,915,857	1,795,373	1,671,839	1,549,698	1,391,121	1,233,080	990,458	757,732	464,348	185,516	185,5

Figure 9.5 Proforma Cash Flow Statement for the Health Monitoring Systems Venture

capital. And, for most startups, it is not the balance sheet that is used to assess company value over time (e.g., a book value of the business), but rather some combination of a multiple of sales and operating profit in the outlying years—where the multiple itself is based on current deals in your target industry sector. Either way, the P&L becomes a central communication and selling tool in your business plan. It needs to be done carefully and well. This includes a complete set of reasonable assumptions that guide the numbers.

In most cases, you will need a summary version (say just annual numbers) for an initial discussion, and then a detailed version (monthlies for the first two years) for deeper discussions. Once again, if you do take the more granular approach to projecting revenues and expenses, you can always do a "hide" columns command in your spreadsheet to produce the summary versions as needed.

Digging Into the Cash Flow of the Venture

Figure 9.5 shows a detailed projection of cash flows for the health monitoring venture, following the monthly format for the first two years, and annual for Years 3, 4, 5. Figure 9.6 shows the balance sheet. Here, as do most investors when examining the projections for new ventures, we will focus on the cash flow statement, looking for any challenges in or long delays between converting finished products or services into hard cash in the bank account!

Note the line items that affect cash (or often referred to as adjustments to working capital).

- First, there is a line item for accounts receivables (which reduce cash on hand and that will grow as your sales increase for most types of businesses)

- Another line item for accounts payables (which increase your cash on hand and also increase as your production or unit volumes increase over time)

- And another line item for interest income (which is the interest paid by banks on the cash balances or CDs in your commercial accounts), and/or conversely, a line item that you must pay (say to commercial banks) for any sort of debt that you have in the business

an	Feb	Mar	Apr	May	Jun	Jul	Aug	Sep	Oct	Nov	Dec	Year 2	Year 3	Year 4	Year 5
5,516	1,150,044	848,217	542,511	353,738	102,076	133,869	26,473	46,873	33,199	76,144	159,219	185,516	369,607	10,566,467	42,987,861
1,652)	(238,502)	(177,752)	(124,436)	(122,886)	(2,136)	22,748	86,598	116,615	109,131	213,315	276,365	(142,593)	12,180,864	37,676,486	61,900,925
9,750)	(67,500)	(135,000)	(67,500)	(135,000)	(67,500)	(135,000)	(67,500)	(135,000)	(67,500)	(135,000)	(67,500)	(1,239,750)	(2,879,813)	(7,208,050)	(11,406,450)
6,738	3,375	6,750	3,375	6,750	3,375	6,750	3,375	6,750	3,375	6,750	3,375	230,738	781,491	1,630,403	2,557,823
309	1,917	1,414	904	590	170	223	44	78	55	127	265	6,096	11,102	218,721	1,071,087
0	0	0	0	0	(1,000)	(1,000)	(1,000)	(1,000)	(1,000)	(1,000)	(1,000)	(7,000)	(12,000)	(12,000)	(12,000)
6,938	6,938	6,938	6,938	6,938	6,938	6,938	6,938	6,938	6,938	6,938	6,938	83,250	117,267	91,433	87,750
3,054)	(8,054)	(8,054)	(8,054)	(8,054)	(8,054)	(8,054)	(8,054)	(8,054)	(8,054)	(8,054)	(8,054)	(96,650)	(102,050)	(75,600)	(85,600)
5,472)	(301,827)	(305,705)	(188,773)	(251,663)	(68,207)	(107,396)	20,400	(13,674)	42,945	83,075	210,388	(1,165,909)	10,096,861	32,321,393	54,113,534
9,956)	848,217	542,511	353,738	102,076	33,869	26,473	46,873	33,199	76,144	159,219	369,607	(980,393)	10,466,467	42,887,861	97,101,395
0,000	0	0	0	0	0	0	0	0	0	0	0	1,250,000	0	0	0
0	0	0	0	0	100,000							100,000	100,000	100,000	100,000
0,044	848,217	542,511	353,738	102,076	133,869	26,473	46,873	33,199	76,144	159,219	369,607	369,607	10,566,467	42,987,861	97,201,395

- Another item for depreciation expense (which adds to your cash flow because it is deducted directly from operating profit before taxes are paid)
- Another line item for "capital" investments such as purchasing computers, vehicles, industrial equipment, buildings, and other physical assets
- And lastly, line items for infusions of cash coming from either new equity or debt investments

All of these line items represent adjustments to the working capital (i.e., the cash) available at any given time for your business.

As with the projected P&L, it is a good idea to have someone on your team who is fluent in accounting so that this cash flow projection can be correctly structured. However, it is the meaning behind the numbers that you, as the entrepreneur, need to master. Cash flow numbers reflect how you plan to operate the business from a day-to-day money perspective. Investors need to see that you have a keen interest not only in generating sales but also cash.

The cash flow statement also provides insight into the amount of startup money needed by the business. We think of startup costs in three parts:

a. How much money is needed to get the product or service to the point of an "alpha" or proof of concept test with a live, kicking customer? (If you can do this right away— which is often the case for a service—all the more power to you!) To use the terms from the prior chapter, this can be considered "seed financing."

b. How much money is needed to complete the product or service, and if necessary to manufacture an initial amount, to sell to the first wave of customers? This can be seen as Series A financing.

c. How much money is needed to scale up the business to achieve first operating profit? We think of this as the next round or Series B financing.

	Year 1	Year 2	Year 3	Year 4	Year 5
Assets					
Cash	$185,516	$369,607	$10,566,467	$42,987,861	$97,201,395
Accounts Receivable	193,500	1,095,750	2,879,813	7,208,050	11,406,450
Equipment (Net of Depreciation)	102,067	115,467	100,250	84,417	82,267
Total Assets	**$481,083**	**$1,580,823**	**$13,546,530**	**$50,280,327**	**$108,690,112**
Liabilities					
Accounts Payable	178,425	392,288	781,491	1,630,403	2,557,823
Debt					
Short-Term Debt	0	100,000	100,000	100,000	100,000
Long-Term Debt					
Total Liabilities	**$178,425**	**$492,288**	**$881,491**	**$1,730,403**	**$2,657,823**
Equity					
Invested Capital	302,658	1,088,536	3,500,000	3,500,000	3,500,000
Retained Earnings			9,165,039	45,049,925	102,532,289
Total Equity	**$302,658**	**$1,088,536**	**$12,665,039**	**$48,549,925**	**$106,032,289**

Figure 9.6 Proforma Balance Sheet for the Health Monitoring Systems Venture.

Different types of businesses represent different amounts of time and money for these three milestones. And we have worked with ventures where operating profits were achieved so quickly after first revenue that only a small amount of working capital or "bridge" financing was needed to fill the cash gap. On the other hand, most ventures are not so fortunate. Either way, the cash flow statement should show these points in time.

The simplest way to estimate financing requirements is to look at the accumulated cash deficit in the business until the business becomes cash positive, without any equity, debt, or other cash infusions during that time period. This is the gap you will need to cover with some type of financing. Your investors will then piece up that total amount into stages of financing that are appropriate for your type of venture (e.g., the seed, Series A, and Series B financing).

Revenue Rich, Cash Broke

"Cash is king" has been the long-standing mantra of entrepreneurs. There are many reasons for this. Perhaps foremost is the proverbial "cash crunch" that most entrepreneurs confront at one time or another. And this goes well beyond being short on cash for startup.

There are times in the ramp-up period for ventures when sales grow beyond expectations and at *the same time,* it becomes difficult to meet the biweekly payroll. When this happens once, you can live with it. When it happens month after month it means that while you have focused on managing the revenue dimension of the P&L, you have failed to adequately plan for cash needs. There tends to be two causes to the problem:

- To meet increased levels of sales, you have to pay contract manufacturers and materials suppliers (for product companies), or application hosting suppliers (for software firms), or contract labor (for services firms) in advance of when revenue can be collected from customers, particularly large ones. In other words, your COGS (cost of goods sold) are eating up the cash in the business that you need to pay yourself and your full-time employees.

- With the increased level of sales, it becomes increasingly hard to actually collect that money, either because you have simply that many more customers to chase down for the money, or your customers are becoming increasingly large and laggard in payment. Sales are great but because of the accounts receivable collection problem, the cash situation is poor. You, as an entrepreneur, find yourself spending morning after morning calling up corporate customers for payment!

Entrepreneurs then go to their commercial bank seeking a working capital loan—typically structured as a line of credit secured on collateral in the company—against which the company can borrow funds for short-term needs. Before the economic worries of 2009, most entrepreneurs could walk into their bank with proof of a strong and growing P&L and a strong balance sheet (where Total Assets exceeded Total Liabilities by a factor of 2:1) and walk out with that line of credit. However, these days, that visit to the bank has become far more difficult. Many entrepreneurs have been forced to turn to other measures to both conserve and raise short-term cash—second mortgages on their personal property, reduced credit terms to their own customers, squeezing suppliers, and yes, reducing headcount. *The hardest time to raise additional money—short term from banks or longer term from investors—is when you really need it.*

Showing an Understanding of the Cash Conversion Cycle

Investors and serial entrepreneurs have lived through this type of problem a number of times in their careers. This makes the proforma statement of cash flow for a new venture all the more important for prospective investors. They want to see that you fully understand the cash conversion cycle in your business.

- For a product type of venture, that means the time period between (a) when you have to pay for materials and the conversion of those materials into finished products in inventory, then (b) when the products are sold into channels to generate sales from customers, and then, (c) when these sales from customers convert into cash as checks or electronic funds transfers deposited and cleared in your company's bank account.
- For a software or services venture, the cash conversion cycle typically boils down to how to get customers to pay you in a timely manner. Either way, that cash conversion cycle is crucial to how investors will think of you and your venture!

Needless to say, the shorter the cash cycle, the better. The question is, what can you do as the entrepreneur to shorten it? For example, a homebuilder will ask customers for a down payment before construction begins. Should consulting ventures try to do the same? Otherwise, the consultant will do the work, invoice for time and expenses at the end of the month, and then wait 30 to 60 days for payment. Meanwhile, the consultant has had to pay his or her credit card company for expenses incurred. Better to estimate the project fee and immediately invoice for 25% of that amount with a two-week "rush" on payment so that the work can commence right away.

Similarly, most contracts have interest penalties for late payment beyond 30 days from receipt of invoice. Moreover, in some businesses, one finds incentives for early payment—such as a 2% discount for payment within 15 days.

On the other side of the equation, you need to manage your own suppliers carefully. You need to find suppliers that will give you terms of credit as well—and then treat those suppliers with respect and timely payment. The last thing an entrepreneur needs is to be the last in line to receive essential materials or components for a finished product or service that a large customer is expecting to receive at the end of the month!

A Capital Plan for Investing in New Machines for a Corporate Venture _____

Some ventures will require investment in plant and equipment. The word of caution to you is to try your best to find reliable contract manufacturers in the first two years of your business before tying up precious capital in developing such assets. In other words, you want to try to shift all fixed costs into variable costs—until the point in time where you are generating strong revenues and might then be able to benefit from the depreciation thrown off from such assets.

Across nearly all industries, there is a broad range of suppliers available to the entrepreneur. Unfortunately, there are risks incurred in any subcontract manufacturing. First, you will not be able to directly control the quality. Second, you are making another company smart about your products and embedded technology—creating the potential that the partner could migrate forward and become a direct competitor. Outsourcing carries with it substantial risks that can only be mitigated with well-designed contracts and timely face-to-face interaction with contract manufacturers. If, for example, you have a product that can be made for a far lower price in Asia, you are going to have to approach that relationship carefully and cautiously, investing your own time to find trusted suppliers, observing their operations, and thinking about how best to still control certain proprietary technology. Without this attention, the reputation of your company could suffer once products are in the hands of customers.

For internal corporate ventures where a capital limitation is not as significant a problem, teams need to produce financials that show the efficient utilization of manufacturing assets. That means you must show how sales and operating profit provide a return on invested capital. That return must meet the corporation's hurdle rates for Return on Assets and Sales to Fixed Assets (sometimes call the Fixed Asset Turnover Ratio).

Figure 9.7, which is also on the textbook's companion Website, shows the financial planning of an internal corporate venture inside a large consumer products manufacturer. The sales volumes are shown at the top as a function of unit orders by customers. This was an initiative to modify standard mass market products and sell them directly to consumers through a Website. The figure ties everything together on an annual basis over five years:

- Unit and revenue projections.

- Manufacturing, logistics, and other cost of goods sold—leading to a gross margin.

- Variable operating expenses that include marketing, R&D, IT (Web and production systems), and other General and Administrative costs—leading to net operating margin.

- The capital plan for installing new manufacturing machines. This plan is driven by the capacity of each machine, the projected unit volumes, and the cost of procuring and installing each new machine (shown as $500,000 in the top box in the figure).

- The cash flow from operations, adjusted downward by a rounded estimate of 5% of annual sales for various delays in customer payments, as well as for the capital invested in new machines. The line labeled "production machines" shows that more than 30 machines for this specific product are needed to handle the volumes projected for Year 5.

- And lastly, the metrics at the bottom. One of these is the Net Present Value of the discounted cash flows. The two others are asset utilization measures. One is the FATR (Fixed Asset Turnover Ratio), which is current annual sales divided by accumulated fixed assets. In the corporation described here, any measure over 4.00 was seen as a strong result—such as deriving $100 million in sales from $25 million in accumulated assets. The other is the ongoing Return on Assets, which divides the operating profit by the invested capital in the average amount of fixed assets for the time period. The numbers shown here are highly attractive because of the high margins within the product itself.

Internal corporate ventures tend not to have to deal with depreciation, income taxes, and the like within investment proposals—since these elements are handled in consolidated financial statements for the entire corporation.

How These Financial Projections Impact Investor Valuations of New Firms _____

If we step back for a moment, the larger purpose of these financial projections is to show investors that your good product, system, or service concept can be turned into *a good business*. That means a business that produces a growing revenue stream, and from that stream, cash. Just as you might think of an "architecture" for a product or service, your financial statements are really the "architecture" for how you plan to make money for all concerned.

These are just projections. For most of you, *there is no business yet*. As we described in the prior chapter, seed or Series A financing will be based largely on two things: (a) comparables for similar types of ventures at given stages of growth in the same target industry and market space, and (b) the experience of your management team. Investors have a number of online sources they can turn to for private equity deals—Dow Jones VentureSource being perhaps the leading service. If ventures in your "space" with prototyped technology or services and little if any actual customer revenue are getting valued at $5 million postmoney for Series A financing, then that is going to be

	Price/unit	$30.00	Units/shift			350	
			Shifts/year			480	
			Units per machine per year			168,000	
			Cost per machine			500,000	
	Development	Year 1	Year 2	Year 3	Year 4	Year 5	
Volume Projections							
Total orders/day		150	300	700	1,500	2,500	
Average units per order		4.00	4.00	4.00	4.00	4.00	
Units per year		216,000	432,000	1,008,000	2,160,000	3,600,000	
P&L Projections							
Gross sales		6,480,000	12,960,000	30,240,000	64,800,000	108,000,000	
Manufacturing cost per unit		6.00	5.70	5.42	5.14	4.89	
Total conversion		1,296,000	2,462,400	5,458,320	11,111,580	17,593,335	
Shipping (per unit)		4.50	4.28	4.06	3.86	3.67	
Shipping		972,000	1,846,800	4,093,740	8,333,685	13,195,001	
Gross Margin		65%	67%	68%	70%	71%	
	Startup costs						
Advertising (traditional & Web)	250,000	648,000	1,296,000	3,024,000	6,480,000	10,800,000	
E-commerce site Outsourced	250,000	275,000	302,500	332,750	366,025	402,628	
IT Ordering/Fulfillment	250,000	125,000	137,500	151,250	166,375	183,013	
Product R&D	1,500,000	750,000	750,000	750,000	750,000	750,000	
Other G&A (5% of sales)	200,000	324,000	648,000	1,512,000	3,240,000	5,400,000	
Operating Profit	(1,950,000)	2,490,000	5,956,800	15,401,940	34,884,735	60,261,664	
% Gross Sales		38%	46%	51%	54%	56%	
Capital Infusions for Operating Assets							
New production machines	1	1	3	6	13	21	
New capital invested	500,000	642,857	1,285,714	3,000,000	6,428,571	10,714,286	
Fixed Asset Total	**500,000**	**1,142,857**	**2,428,571**	**5,428,571**	**11,857,143**	**22,571,429**	
Business Metrics							
EBITDA	**(1,950,000)**	**2,490,000**	**5,956,800**	**15,401,940**	**34,884,735**	**60,261,664**	
Working Capital Adjustment (5% of EBITDA)		(124,500)	(297,840)	(770,097)	(1,744,237)	(3,013,083)	
Cash flow	**(1,950,000)**	**2,365,500**	**5,658,960**	**14,631,843**	**33,140,498**	**57,248,581**	
NPV of cash flows (15%)	53,406,493						
Fixed Asset Turnover Ratio		7.89	7.26	7.70	7.50	6.27	
Return on Assets		303%	334%	392%	404%	350%	

Figure 9.7 The Business Case for a New Product Line in a Food Manufacturing Company

Discount rate: 15%, 10% WACC plus high risk factor of 5%
Annual Sales/Accumulated Capital Investment

the starting point for you as well, even if your financial projections show $100 million in annual revenue down the road. The quality of your management team should get you a bump on that valuation. In some cases, we have seen younger entrepreneurs who have recruited a serial, successful entrepreneur as the CEO and seen their financing valuations *double*. Plus, that CEO brings in his or her prior VCs into the deal. However, this is not a viable option for most entrepreneurs, simply because experienced entrepreneurs will only join you after you have productized your technology or service idea and actually sold products to live customers. And for most you, that will take some seed funding to get to the point of proving your venture concept in the marketplace.

Once your business starts generating revenue, however, your financial statements do become a foundation for company valuation, either to raise the next round of financing or for acquisition valuation by a larger firm. Again, as noted in the prior chapter, investors will turn to sources such as VentureSource and look for multiples of sales and multiples of earnings for companies similar to yours. Obviously, you need to update your monthly financials with company results—both for revenues and expenses—and revisit the outlying annual numbers with each passing month. And, there is no single way that investors or acquiring corporations set a value on a business. Some simply do an industry-segment multiple on the mix of current year and next year's projected sales. Others do a mix of an industry segment multiple of EBITDA—of operating profit before the "funny business" of advanced accounting. And others will do a blend of a multiple of sales and earnings. But for most small firms, profits are scarce, and the driving force for valuation is the current revenue and the growth of that revenue.

Let's take a quick example. One of your authors helped an entrepreneur craft a business plan that focused on a specific aspect of enterprise-wide software used in large hospitals. The entrepreneur built a great company that became the leader in the specific *use case* or application in his specific market niche. After a decade or so, revenues grew to $30 million plus a year with clear prospects of hitting $40 million the year after. Operating profit had been steady at about 20% of revenue—not uncommon for successful "traditional" (i.e., B2B) software startups but impressive during the travails of the 2008–2009 economy. Soon after, his company was acquired for in excess of $150 million. That represented a multiple of about five times revenue and about 20 times EBITDA. A similar type of company was acquired for 4.7 times revenue just the year before. And P/E ratios for publically traded healthcare IT companies at that time were 20 and higher. The financial projections that we had made in the early days turned out to be "real" in terms of dollar amounts, but like most entrepreneurs, it took far longer—about four years longer—to actually hit those numbers than originally hoped. Still, the venture was a great success for all involved.

A Closing Thought: Realistic Revenue, Please!

Perhaps most important, try not to be so enamored with your own venture concept that your revenue projections become wildly optimistic. Listen to your own reality check (Chapter 7)! Remember, a team will have to defend its numbers "six ways from Sunday" in front of investors. Putting silly numbers on a spreadsheet isn't going to fool anyone.

Several years ago, one of your authors was invited to observe a team's presentation to senior management for a new, exciting corporate venture. The team had prepared a detailed set of financial statements and was prepared to make its business case by explaining them page-by-page. That didn't happen. Instead, one executive grilled team members for over an hour on the set of revenue numbers of just Year 1 and Year 2. When I asked him later why the intense focus, the executive said, "Marc, revenue drives everything. Get it right, and we have a fairly good handle on cash flow and capital asset requirements. Get it wrong, however, and everything else is wrong. We've lost a lot of money in the past on revenue projections that were completely off base."

This executive wanted to know the sources of those revenues, their lower and upper ranges, and which sources were greatest. Who would be their best customers? This executive showed little interest in market share expectations in outlying years. Instead, he drilled down on the details of the early years: "How many units do you expect to sell through each channel month by month?" he asked. "How does that compare to competitors' sales in the same category? How can we establish a beachhead with the best customers in your target market, make them reference accounts, and leverage out from there?" He understood that not all customers are equal. He also wanted to know about the team's proposed channel partners. "How will these partners give us more unit sales than those of current market leaders?" The executive was also curious about the impact of a higher price on sales projections. "A higher price might improve the profit margin, but it's bound to reduce unit sales," he told them. "So, how many unit sales will a 10% price rise cost us, and how does that net out?"

His approach was "bottoms-up" and fine-grained. Will you encounter investors or corporate executives with the same level of detailed curiosity? The only safe way to proceed is to be prepared to answer questions that go to the heart of a team's projections—the assumptions, key customers, the most important drivers of both revenues and costs, and how the projections will change if those assumptions and drivers are altered.

A team preparing to defend its financial projections must be realistic. Most investors have had their fill of unreasonable, unachievable sales projections. Figure 9.8 shows one example taken from studying the corporate ventures initiated by a particular corporation over the past decade. The figure shows two-year projected revenues and those actually realized for nine new product lines, where the revenue is disguised (but think in tens of millions of dollars) into a scale of 1 to 10. In most cases, the gap between projected and actual was substantial. Don't become part of this "liar's club!" Only two proposals—shown at the far right of the bar chart—met their projections, and it is not a surprise that they were two internal ventures launched by the same team!

Remember, all startups and most new corporate ventures start small. It is okay for you to do the same. The investors and executives doing the grilling have been around long enough to recall the modest beginnings of today's 10X exits or corporate cash cows. Investors and executives expect and appreciate realistic numbers.

Besides, should you get your funding, you will be held accountable *to those same numbers!* So don't oversell. Don't create unachievable expectations that will get everyone in hot water a year or two down the road.

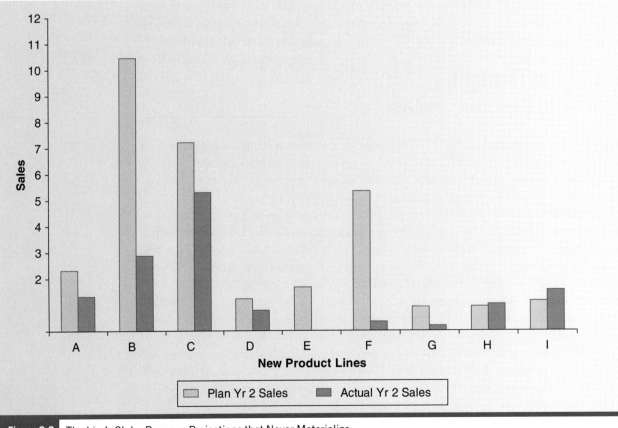

Figure 9.8   The Liar's Club: Revenue Projections that Never Materialize

Source: Adapted from Marc H. Meyer (2007), *The Fast Path to Corporate Growth*, The Free Press, N.Y.

Reader Exercises

Now it is your turn to develop your own financial projections. To guide you through this process, you can find financial templates for various types of companies on our Website.

Step 1: Develop a Granular Projection of Revenue

- Determine the format desired by your professor. We recommend monthlies for the first two years, or until you become cash flow positive. Then, annual projections are fine. Your professor may just want annual projections for all five years. Ask.

- Run through various scenarios on the number of customers, the products and services you are selling, and the unit prices for those commercial offerings. Don't forget to start on a whiteboard first before becoming too heavily engaged on a spreadsheet. Spreadsheets sometimes lead individuals into blind replication of numbers. Investors will challenge you on all your numbers; they do not appreciate thoughtless financial projections. Be realistic about customer ramp-up. Think hard about concrete objectives that lead up to the "scaled-up" revenue potential that you determined in the reality check. (We think of that as a revenue target for the fifth year of operations.)

- Also think about recurring revenue from existing customers, as well as new revenue from new customers. Build these into your projections as well.

- If you are a products company, think about any services that you might offer with your products (if that is the case), the pricing for those services, and how these ramp up over time. Show these as separate line items.

Step 2: Develop a Proforma P&L (i.e., a Projected Income Statement)

Summarize your revenue projections into the top portion of the projected P&L. Then think through your cost of goods. Try to do a "bottoms up" estimate of the materials and conversion or assembly cost on those materials. For benchmarks, the COGS of manufactured products often come in at 30% to 40% of revenue; for software-based businesses, COGS are far less, from 2% to 15% of revenue; and for labor-intensive services, often 35% of revenue. Then, apply the guidance in this chapter to consider carefully your various operating expenses.

More generally, most investors know that any numbers beyond the first two or three years in a projected P&L are largely speculation. However, the fifth-year estimation remains important because it gives some sense of potential exit value as a multiple of revenue and profit. Once again, internal corporate ventures can satisfy with annual P&L projections. Take your best shot, remembering the "scaled-up" revenue projection you determined in the reality check.

Step 3: Develop a Cash Flow Projection

Cash flow is so important to entrepreneurs—where every dollar often means the difference between paying yourself a modest salary, or not, during the startup period. This is where you take your learning from accounting classes and apply it to your venture. These are the key questions to consider:

- What are the adjustments to working capital? The big items here are to adjust working capital for accounts receivable (increase working capital), inventory (increase working capital), accounts payable (decrease working capital), taxes (decrease working capital), and any prepaid expenses (decrease working capital).

- Are there adjustments due to fixed capital expenditures, such as spending money on machines of some sort?

- Are the increases to cash due to any short-term borrowing, such as amounts taken from a line of credit with a commercial bank or longer-term commercial notes?

- And last, are there any infusions of capital from investors?

The last point might lead some to question the extent to which to include seed, Series A, and successive rounds of financing in the cash flow projections. Figure out how much you need to cover cash shortfalls and to meet required investments in people, plant, and equipment. We suggest that you include those rounds of financing needed to (a) get your product to market, and (b) get your company to a cash flow positive footing. That might be $200,000 right in the beginning to complete development, $2 million in six months to build a sales force, and $4 million in two years to scale nationally. Often, services can be cash flow positive from the start, so the amount of money required is to hire the people and buy or lease the computers and office space needed to start delivering those services. Once again, your business model should be driving these projections.

Step 4: Develop a Balance Sheet

Balance sheets are a snapshot of performance, year by year. Venture investors expect to see a balance sheet as part of a complete set of financial statements. However, unless you are planning on debt financing during the first year or two of operations, it is unusual to see an equity investor focus on the balance sheet. Startup valuations are based on the comparables we mentioned in Chapter 8, and exit valuation speculation using sector-specific multiples of revenues and EBITDA. However, make sure the numbers add up in the balance sheet.

Step 5: Establish Financial Goalposts

- **Startup costs**—these come directly from your cash flow statement, specifically from the month-by-month breakdown of operating expenses and capital investments in plant and equipment. An investor will dig into the cash flow projections to ask a million questions, one of which will be to pinpoint "startup costs" over the first six months to get to "alpha" or "beta test" and the "launch" costs of successfully introducing a new product, system, or service to market. Remember, if you have included seed- or Series A–type infusions of cash as part of the cash flow projects, you should subtract these first before summing up your various cash needs to achieve specific milestones. Obviously, the purpose of those funding rounds is to cover the cash shortfalls on the path to profitability.
- **The time to first dollar**—when the business becomes "real." This information comes right from monthly projections of revenue.
- **The time to first profit**—when the business achieves true investor value and this, too, can be found in the projected P&L.
- **First-round and anticipated second-round financing** amount, that is, seed funding or Series A, or Series A and Series B, depending on the point at which you are requesting capital. As mentioned earlier, these rounds of financing are typically shown in the projected cash flow statement and carried on to the balance sheet.
- **Potential valuation for exit**—for example, the value of the company as an acquisition by a larger concern, and then, the money the investors might make based on their equity holdings and exit preferences. VCs are shooting for a 10X return on their invested capital, and that is after all the money that they have invested into your company is *first* paid off. Angels may hope for a 10X return, but our experience is angels will be perfectly happy with a 3X to 5X return over a five- to seven-year period.

*** *** ***

It is hard to develop a comprehensive set of financial projections alone. And rarely can they be done quickly. Set aside two or three solid working days to accomplish the steps outlined above. And take the opportunity to share your results with your advisors—including your professors. You need to be challenged on the numbers by trusted, friendly parties before running the gauntlet with professional investors.

For when it comes to the numbers associated with a business plan, the phrase "root canal" is a fair description of the nature of probing that VCs and others will perform on your projections. The three questions that will run continuously through their minds will be:

1. Are the sales projected for the business both sufficient and based on a realistic revenue model?

2. How much will it really cost to get this business to scale? Is it really a million dollars, for example—as the entrepreneur suggests—or is it really two or three million?

3. And if this business works as planned, what is the possible exit valuation based on performance in Year 5? More specifically, a million invested today will be worth how many millions down the road?

Your financial projections must answer these questions. While many investors get excited about new venture concepts, business model innovations, and the passions and experience of a venture team, *all investors* drop their smiles and become all too serious when it comes to the numbers. Prepare to defend your numbers, again, again, and again.

## chapter 10

Organizing the Venture Team

10

The Purpose of the Chapter

Venture capitalist Arthur Rock once said, "Good ideas and good products are a dime a dozen. Good execution and good management—in a word, good people—are rare."

The purpose of this chapter is to introduce you to the importance of organizing the right venture team. This includes first thinking about the legal organization of your venture, assessing yourself as founder of the venture (both in terms of personal characteristics and business skills), understanding the two types of venture teams—the one responsible for writing the venture business plan and the one who will execute the venture business plan, your Advisory Board, official Board of Directors members, and other stakeholders such as a customer Advisory Board. Organizing the right team is critically important for venture success.

Learning Objectives

In this chapter, we will have a number of important objectives. We will learn about:

- The characteristics and business skills of successful venture founders
- The differences between the team that writes the business plan and the team that implements the plan to build a venture
- How to make the venture team work effectively
- The importance of constructing a solid external Advisory Board

(Continued)

> (Continued)
> - The roles, talents, and responsibilities for official Board members
> - The role other stakeholders can play in the venture, including a customer Advisory Board
> - The legal organizational options for the venture and the implications for liability protection and taxes
> - Rewards and incentives for the venture team

The Characteristics and Skills of Venture Founders

Entrepreneurial Characteristics

By engaging in this book, you have already started your entrepreneurial journey. Gaining industry, customer, and competitive insight, and then forming distinctive solutions and solid business models, is how most successful companies get started. And, as you know by now, it is a lot of work.

There are some fundamental personal characteristics that separate a successful entrepreneur from unsuccessful ones. Do you have what it takes to succeed in the toughest field in the business world? Just as important a question is do your teammates have the "right stuff" for venturing?

Your initial questions to ask yourself are: Do I have commitment, motivation, skills, and talents to start and build a venture? And, can I locate individuals to join my management team who have the skills and talents to help me succeed? Then, you need to ask the same questions of your founding team. Do they have the commitment, motivation, and skills needed to build a dynamic company—and do they know people who they might bring into the business with funding and the need to build capabilities as well as more capacity for work within the venture?

We suggest that you start your personal assessment by honestly comparing yourself to successful entrepreneurs. Perhaps the most important personal skill comes under that elusive heading called "leadership." Even young entrepreneurs have a good sense if they have the makings of a strong team leader. This means having the ability to make a decision with imperfect information. It also means being able to motivate and inspire others through thick and thin. Successful ventures invariably have a strong leader.

Beyond leadership characteristics, successful entrepreneurs possess the following personal characteristics:[1]

- **Drive and energy:** Successful entrepreneurs have the ability to work long hours for extended periods of time and can still function at a high level.

- **Self-confidence:** Successful entrepreneurs believe in themselves and their ability to achieve success.

- **Set challenging and realistic objectives:** Successful entrepreneurs have the ability to set challenging and realistic objectives.

- **Long-term involvement:** Successful entrepreneurs make a commitment to the business and fully dedicate themselves to the business for the long haul.

---

[1] This section is based on A. Dingee, B. Haslett, and L. Smollen's, "Characteristics of a Successful Entrepreneurial Management Team," in *Pratt's Guide to Venture Capital Sources,* 1997, pp. 23–28; and F. Crane and E. Crane's, "Dispositional Optimism and Entrepreneurial Success," in *The Psychologist-Manager Journal,* 2007, *10*(1), pp. 1–13.

- **Use money as a scorecard:** Successful entrepreneurs use money as a scorecard or measure for how well the venture is doing as opposed to an end in itself.

- **Persistent problem solving:** Successful entrepreneurs have an innate desire to solve problems and persist until they achieve positive outcomes.

- **Ability to tolerate uncertainty:** Entrepreneurs must feel comfortable making tough decisions without perfect information. This ability to thrive under conditions of high uncertainty differentiates the entrepreneur from, say, a scientist who needs to resolve ambiguity before proceeding forward.

- **Learn from failure:** Successful entrepreneurs learn from failure and use those lessons to avoid future failures. They accept failure as part of the entrepreneurial journey, but they are not discouraged by it.

- **Use constructive criticism:** Successful entrepreneurs seek out constructive criticism from informed experts, and they act on it.

- **Take initiative:** Successful entrepreneurs take initiative when they see opportunities. They also seek out situations where personal initiative can pay off.

- **Make good use of resources:** Successful entrepreneurs readily identify and use appropriate expertise and assistance to achieve their objectives.

- **Compete against self-imposed standards:** Successful entrepreneurs establish their own benchmarks of performance and focus on competing with themselves to improve personal performance. They don't need someone else to set goals for them. Successful entrepreneurs drive themselves hard.

While this list may seem long, every point is worthwhile and important. Equally important is that entrepreneurs generally have a positive outlook on life and a belief that good things will be abundant and bad things scarce. In essence, they are "glass half-full" individuals even when times are tough! We call this "dispositional optimism."

Additionally, entrepreneurs want to work in small companies! Don't forget that when you encounter a highly experienced individual who comes from a large corporate environment, looking to be a VP in a venture capital–backed startup with a hunk of stock. Has that person ever scheduled his or her own appointments, made the pot of coffee for others first thing in the morning, cleaned up the conference area for visitors, worked on a steel desk purchased from a lead on Craig's List or a discount furniture store, flown regular class, or more generally, understand that the company's money is their money? These are tough questions to ask—but they need asking!

You should rate yourself on each of these characteristics (strong, average, or weak). To give these ratings a dose of reality, compare yourself to other individuals you know who rate strongly on these characteristics. If you rate yourself average or weak on most of these characteristics, it's a warning sign that a career in a larger, more mature organization might be the best ticket for you—at least for the time being. We have found that business skills are simply not enough to succeed. The psychology of an entrepreneur is essential for success. Granted, no single entrepreneur possesses all these attributes, yet many are attributes that you can begin to practice on a daily basis such as setting clear and challenging objectives for yourself or using constructive criticism to the best-possible result.

We also want to emphasize that if you don't view yourself as a gambler—a wild risk-taker—that's okay, in fact, more than okay. Most successful entrepreneurs are calculated risk-takers and constantly think about how to manage and mitigate apparent risks with specific strategies across the entire spectrum of the business. For example, if you are only average in organizing work and making optimum use of scarce resources, bringing on board a more experienced manager with proven operational skills might be just the ticket.

The Team That Writes the Business Plan: Guard Your Founder's Stock Carefully _____

There is often a difference between those individuals who help write a business plan—say in an entrepreneurship class—and the actual founding team for a funded venture. Usually one or two people from the class march forward and do all the work it takes to raise money and build a business. Everyone who helps work on a plan gets bragging rights years down the road when the venture is successful; but realistically, only those few who lay their careers on the line deserve founder's stock. It is a hard lesson for student teams but an essential one when term projects transform into startup enterprises.

Do not promise stock to anyone other than a rock-solid core team member. Contributors during the startup phase come and go. You will find that most people don't have the stomach for the risk, anxiety, and beyond-normal commitment required for new ventures. Giving stock away early on to people who may or not stay with the venture—or on student teams who may not even be part of the venture can take millions of dollars out of your own retirement.

For example, let's say that you are one of those rare entrepreneurs who sell their company for $100 million and realize a 100-times return on the value of founder's stock at that price. At the very beginning, you sold a certain number of shares of stock for $10,000 to a classmate who helped write the business plan. Other than giving you a little bit of money, the classmate didn't do much else thereafter. Ten years down the road, after the acquisition, that passive participant's $10,000 is worth $1 million. And you, having raised many millions in venture capital, have been taken down to about 9% of the company stock—typical in cases of successive rounds of financing. You walk away with $9 million. But, it could have been $10 million. That hurts, particularly after paying taxes. In hindsight, it would have been far better to offer individuals such as this classmate some "friends and family shares" for say, $100. At exit, that would be a $10,000 thank you, not a $1 million one. Remember, every share of stock you give to people outside the core team dilutes your own shares; investors will insist on this with their Series A and follow-on financing. Guard your stock carefully; it is the primary asset that you will be working for over the next several years—not salary, bonuses, or paid vacations.

Moreover, every mature person that you encounter in the process of a startup knows that working hard for a new venture and contributing in a meaningful way leads to stock. Professional investors have clear expectations for the percentage allocation of stock to key managers in a venture. If an individual becomes part of your management team funded by professionals, stock will come because investors know that stock ownership (or options to own stock) is a major part of incentivizing employees to work 24/7.

Now, let's consider the skill sets required for writing a business plan. Writing a business plan helps teams think through their strategy and then integrate all the different functions in a business toward a cohesive whole. In business school, we learn a lot about how to do an industry or market analysis. We also learn a lot about the basic mechanics of putting together a set of proforma financial statements.

However, when it comes to an R&D and product strategy, and a sales or channel strategy, there is no substitute for experience. If your plan includes developing a technology-intensive product or service, it is best to have someone who has done that before. That person needs to understand that products are different than services and that both require underlying platforms, be they homegrown or created with third-party toolkits.

Experience in the target industry sector is another great asset for a business plan writing team. If you are mapping out a channel strategy, it would be good to have someone on your team who has actually sold products or services before in a similar market space. It's easy enough to say, "We are going to sell through Whole Foods to reach premium consumers" or "IBM is going to be our channel partner into the health care space," but the complexities of actually getting into these or any other powerful channel require as careful a staging as any R&D effort.

Therefore, before you start working on the business plan, ask yourself who are the "right" types of people to have on your team and what it will take to get them to participate.

Some might be direct team members, others advisors to the team. Particularly helpful advisors might include someone already working in your channel—such as a store or regional manager for a consumer product, an industry sales executive in a large computer company for a software venture, or a manager of business development in a pharmaceutical company for a life sciences venture. Similarly, for your financial statements, you or one of your team members should be able to put together a set of coherent projections. We find, however, that the assumptions behind those projections always require bullet-proofing before the show-and-tell with investors. Find any tough, experienced business person who has had to "carry a bag" (i.e., sell) and collect cash from customers—and ask them to play the devil's advocate for your projections.

Every team needs to find a devil's advocate who tries to poke holes into an emerging business plan. Like anything else, if you are too close to a project it is hard to be sufficiently critical of the project. As professors, we take the greatest pleasure from teams that approach us every several weeks for selective advice and counsel. This is far better than receiving a plan, sight unseen, the last day of the semester. This allows your professor to also play the devil's advocate—as well as cheerleader.

Many universities have established mentor networks of individuals like these who want to help new entrepreneurs like you. Even before you start writing your plan, find out if such a network exists and plug into it. You want to try to schedule meetings with your assigned mentor as soon as possible. Obviously, try to get a mentor who has worked in the industry that you wish to pursue. This will bring the benefit of decades of experience into your business planning.

For the corporate entrepreneur, all these ideas apply as well. You need to bring people with a diverse set of skills onto your venture planning team. It would be foolhardy to fall so much in love with your own idea that you fail to see the landmines both in the market and within the corporation. A strong devil's advocate helps avoid these traps by asking the tough questions and being somewhat skeptical *for your own good.*

Building the Team That Builds the Venture _____

Strive for a Balanced Management Team

Clearly, the success of a new venture is partly based on you, the founder. The irony is that while you want to hire people who are equally entrepreneurial, you do not want to hire people just like yourself in terms of competencies. The venture's performance relies far beyond the skills of any single founder and the founder's skill set. Scholarly research shows that the management team, working together, explains much in terms of what we know about venture success. Successful ventures have strong, diversely skilled teams at the core.[2] This typically means someone who excels at sales and marketing, another person who excels at technology (depending

---

[2] Roberts, E. B. (1991). *Entrepreneurs in High Technology: Lessons from MIT and Beyond.* New York: Oxford University Press; Hambrick, D. C. (1998). Corporate coherence and the top management team. In D. C. Hambrick, D. A. Nadler, & M. L. Tushman (Eds.), *Senior Leadership and Corporate Transformation: CEOs, Boards, and Top Management Teams in Turbulent Times* (pp. 24–30). Boston: Harvard Business School Press.

on the nature of your business), and another person who is highly competent in finance and/or operations. "One-person" shows rarely succeed because no single founder is good at everything, and the founder's skill limitations will soon limit the growth of the venture. This has actually been called "founder's disease."[3] Ventures constrained by the limited skill sets of their founders typically suffer the fate of "the living dead," little companies that reach a million dollars in sales and never a penny more.

Accordingly, investors look very carefully at the venture team before determining whether or not to invest. This is not the plan-writing team, per se, but the company building team. Once again, the "bullet points on two sides of the page" method works well. There are two dimensions to this: personality (which we reviewed above, such as self-driven, highly motivated) and business skills. Let's talk about the necessary business skills required on a startup or corporate venture team.

- **Sales and marketing.** Someone on the team must have solid skills in the marketing and sales area, including marketing research, strategic sales, sales management and merchandising, direct sales, customer service, distribution management, marketing communications, branding, product management, and pricing. For Sales Directors, it is essential that they walk in the door with direct customer leads that can quickly translate into revenue. To do this, they have to know the industry, key customers, and how to sell. It is the ultimate litmus test for hiring a VP of sales for both startups and corporate ventures.

- **R&D,** with a big emphasis on the *D*. Someone on the team must have specialized skills and expertise in R&D, including leading and managing the R&D process and management of engineering. The person you hire needs to have brought a product or service such as yours to market as a successful commercial offering. Anything less and you are playing a game of Russian roulette.

- **Running a business or operation.** Sometimes called "general management," this is a key skill that must be on the venture team. Some might think of this as an individual with a few gray hairs in spirit (if not in the hair) that has helped build an organization of a significant size. This person must take charge of personnel, project management, planning, and overall administrative matters. In some cases, for young entrepreneurs, you might think of this person as a co-CEO of the company.

Depending on the business, you might also need a team member who knows how to run a manufacturing operation and how to manage suppliers. Similarly, usually after the first round of financing (Series A), ventures bring on a professional CFO type who is experienced in finance and accounting processes. This individual helps structure subsequent financings; manages cash flow, credit and collections; and puts in the systems needed to maintain and produce financial information.

Ultimately, your job as founder is to put together a management team that is skilled, highly motivated, and cohesive. In fact, management team cohesion has been found to be positively related to new venture growth.[4] So, choose your team wisely. If you fail to build the right team—a team that will stick together in good times and bad—the future of your new venture is likely to be truncated. And every single person you bring on board in the startup phase needs to be

---

[3] Roberts, Edward B. 1997. *Entrepreneurs in High Technology: Lessons from MIT and Beyond.* Oxford University Press, NY, 1991.

[4] Ensley, M., Pearson, A., & Amason, A. (2002). Understanding the dynamics of new venture top management teams: Cohesion, conflict and new venture performance. *Journal of Business Venturing, 17*(4), 365–385.

highly competent in their own particular area. Competition is generally so fierce across an industry that you can ill afford to do otherwise.

This means that you must also assess your business skills. This is a simple personal audit of your strengths and weakness with regard to the basic functional areas of business that are necessary to start and grow a business. Consider the key areas of sales and marketing, R&D, general or operations management, finance and accounting, customer service, and supplier/manufacturing management. Rate yourself as strong (high skills and abilities), average (limited skills and abilities), and weak (low level of skills and abilities).

No professional investor expects a single individual to be strong in all of these areas. In Microsoft, for example, even the great Bill Gates (the product person and technologist of the business) had Steve Balmer to run sales and operations. Therefore, discern your business strengths and weaknesses. Let this be the driver of composing the startup team, *not just people who you like or who are your friends or acquaintances*. Ventures that are just another type of social club amongst friends rarely become dynamic businesses. A venture requires disciplined activity across the major functions of the business, where key managers are held directly accountable for their respective activities and outcomes. If a founding team has two or three key members, count on the fact that one of these will not survive the first two or three years of the business due to skill and performance issues. Your goal is to find the necessary skills and abilities in others that complement your own to serve the needs of the business.

Spotlight on Innovation: A Mentor Provides a Life-Long Lesson

One of your author's mentors shared an approach to team formation that has served well across dozens of startups and corporate ventures. I was all of 23 years old and my partners were not much older. Mel, our mentor, didn't beat around the bush.

"You guys, for all those brains between those ears, don't know how to hire people, do you? And what's with these fancy headhunters, anyways? They cost *way* too much for a little outfit like yours."

So, we listened.

"Take a blank piece of paper and write all the things that you and your partners are good at on the left side of the page. Then write down all the things on the right side of the page where you have no proven abilities—dreams perhaps, but nothing real. By the way, you have four cofounders and that is way too many chiefs to run the show, but we will deal with that later."

So we wrote down the skills in which we excelled: Technology and face-to-face direct selling appeared on the left side of the page. We had no one who had ever run a significant business operation, knew how to put together a real budget and manage to it, or managed a nationwide sales force. These gaps were on the right side of the page. Meanwhile, the sales of our product were starting to escalate. Our weakness as a team stood out like a sore thumb. The needs were fairly obvious. Yet, in our interviewing, all of us were still fixated on hiring brilliant software architects and programmers, and the few of us who could sell were spending more and more time on the road pulling in enterprise sales.

Our mentor stated the obvious. "All you guys want to do is meet other techies, go out and have a great lunch, talk code, and write it off on the business. That is because you feel comfortable meeting other programmers, and meeting people who aren't like you—the people you really need for the business—isn't so much fun. Well, it's time to grow up. Tear that piece of paper in half. Throw out the left side (the things you are good at) and keep the right side (the things you stink at), and only have lunch with people who can fill those gaps. Got it? Can I make it any simpler for you?"

Let his powerful method serve you as well as it has served us over dozens of startups and corporate ventures.

The Importance of Building a
High-Performance Culture of *A* Players

The list of personal entrepreneurial characteristics provided earlier in the chapter (and later on as a template in the Reader Exercises) is a good place to start. Consider scoring team candidates on that same list of attributes. This is the beginning of creating a certain performance-oriented culture for your company that will produce results.

Perhaps most important, an entrepreneur needs *A* players on the team. Any weak team member hurts a small firm more than in a larger corporation. There is simply no margin for error in a startup. That means that you cannot give up looking for an *A* player just because you are tired and have someone willing to take the job who is a *B* player. Experience dictates that the suboptimal choice never works. Rather, keep on looking for that *A* player and convince them to take the job even though the salary is less than corporate positions. They will do that with a reasonable and appropriate amount of stock and for the sheer excitement of working on a dynamic venture team *with other* A *players.* That's the secret. A *players sell themselves on joining ventures.* Introduce an *A* player to weak members on your team or unimpressive Board of Directors or Advisory Board members, and the party is over.

To assess an individual's motivation and capabilities, look to their past behavior. Past behavior is a reliable predictor of future behavior. Try to discover the individual's record of achievement and self-motivation. As you interview a candidate, not only ask for key decisions that he or she had to make in the past, but the "why" behind those decisions. You might also want to ask individuals about concrete examples of situations they have been in and how they dealt with those situations. For example, you might ask, "Have you had a setback and, if so, how did you deal with it?" You could also follow up with a follow-up question, "Why did you choose that course of action?" The answer to this question further reveals insight about the individual's motivation.[5]

As noted elsewhere in this book, when it comes to hiring sales and marketing professionals, a track record of success in your own specific industry sector is essential. Every entrepreneur has made the mistake of doing otherwise at some point in time, with deep regret. The sales and marketing hire has to be not just an *A* player but an *A* player within your industry. For R&D, software skills are wonderfully portable. The same reasoning applies to finance and accounting skills. Same with general and operations management. But sales and marketing is a different animal. You just don't have enough time for someone to learn who the customers are and how to sell to them in your target market. On the very first day they have to be running hard and producing results.

Every hire is critical. The customer support staff needs to wear smiles on their faces and at least not show the frustration they might feel for defective product or bad code; the financial controller must be tight-fisted on operating expenses and contract terms with suppliers, and be a great presenter to your investors and Board of Directors. Even the receptionist is a critical hire. This person will be the face of the company, literally or on the phone, day in and day out. In other words, in their own way, receptionists can be *A* players, too.

The goal of all this is to have a high-performance culture driven by a team of *A* players. Surround yourself with people better than you in certain key areas. Let them know what you expect and reward them for being overachievers. At the end of your first year in business, you want to sit back and say "I have the best darn team around. They work hard, they are great people, and they are totally dedicated to the company. They are family to me. And I will do anything and everything to help them be successful." That success is your gain.

---

[5] Slaughter, M. (2004). *Seven Keys to Shaping the Entrepreneurial Organization*. Kansas City, MO: Kauffman Center for Entrepreneurial Leadership.

Creating a Shared Vision and Culture of Teamwork and Success

Your job as a founder is to communicate your vision and values to everyone who joins your team. There are two sides for a startup. The first is your vision and values for the customer. Ventures that are highly customer focused seem to excel time and time again. The second side is your vision and values for your employees. The words "teamwork," "personal growth," and "financial gain" are often used without substance. In your company, make these words have real meaning by the actions you take with how you approach problem solving, career advancement, and financial incentives. It is all about finding the best people to work in your company and doings things that deserve their respect and loyalty.

You must communicate a binding, forceful vision for your venture to all involved. A vision is all about the purpose of the venture and its long-term destiny. You, as leader, must get each team member to buy into this vision. Ultimately, you are trying to create a unity of purpose that energizes everyone in the venture to work together to achieve this vision. The vision must be clear, consistent, purposeful, and unique to the venture. For example, McDonald's vision is to be the best at providing good-tasting, low-priced, quality fast-food in clean restaurants for people pressed for time. The vision can be written as a statement and shared with everyone, and it can also be vividly expressed verbally as a compelling story. It sets the tone and culture within your company. Set a target to be the very best in your target industry at *something,* and then articulate to your team what it takes to be *the best.* This helps everyone understand the importance of each and every function inside the company. You want your team to rally around this vision, be it the engineers who are working to make the most-easy-to-use software that is still powerful and bug-free, the salesperson who represents your company with pride and purpose, or the front office receptionist who greets visitors as a committed representative of your company. If all members of your company understand and believe in your vision, you will have a high-functioning team that shares a common purpose and goals. And when these goals are accomplished, do not forget to celebrate them! Special meetings of the entire company, a weekend get-together, or a simple walk down to the local pub where very choice words are said—these all provide the opportunity to step back, appreciate a win, and build collective energy to charge forward. These are simple yet fundamentally important concepts that have served entrepreneurs well time and time again.

It is equally important to provide clarity with regard to the roles, responsibilities, and accountabilities of every team member. This is often hard to do in a startup where everyone enthusiastically wants to do everything: a little bit of R&D, a little bit of selling, a little bit of customer service. But this simply doesn't work. Each team member needs to have a clear focus that aligns with his or her skills. The entrepreneur as manager has to provide clarity with regard to such questions as, "Who's going to do what?"; "What part of the job is mine and what is yours?"; "Whose responsibility is it?"; and "How are we going to be held accountable?"[6]

It is also important that you understand the basic principles of retaining good, loyal venture team members:

1. Preach what you practice: Communicate the values, vision, and objectives of the venture. Practicing what you preach is also imperative.

2. Be selective in hiring: Hire people with values consistent with the venture.

3. Make use of small, talented teams for most tasks and give them the authority to act. Assign new marketing, product, or sales challenges to small teams of people empowered to give you a straight answer.

---

[6] Slaughter, M. (2004). *Seven Keys to Shaping the Entrepreneurial Organization.* Kansas City, MO: Kauffman Center for Entrepreneurial Leadership.

4. Supply excellent rewards for excellent performance. This means setting aside a portion of the operating budget—say 5%—to selectively reward excellent work.

5. Listen hard, talk straight. Honest, two-way communication is required to build trust.[7]

Finally, it is extremely important for team morale to celebrate your victories. Everyone wants to be associated with a winner. So, it is imperative that each victory (e.g., attracting a new client) be celebrated. This provides needed motivational fuel to keep the venture team working at optimal levels.

Boards in a Venture

Create an Advisory Board From the Get-Go

We believe that building an Advisory Board should precede the formation of a formal Board of Directors. Your Advisory Board is a group of individuals that you will invite to provide you with advice, counsel, and guidance as you attempt to build and grow your venture. But, unlike your official Board of Directors, your Advisory Board has no legal status and is not subject to the same regulations as the Board of Directors, including possible legal liability. The entrepreneur can begin building an Advisory Board from Day 1 of the venture.

An Advisory Board should consist of experienced individuals across the spectrum of functions: sales, technology, venture finance, and so forth. They are there to help you on a phone call, to help the entrepreneur make tough decisions. And the Advisory Board gives quasi-officialdom to their contribution, coupled selectively with financial rewards. This might be a small amount of stock (options) for participating on the Advisory Board, additional stock for making the introduction to major accounts that result in revenue, an annual retainer to provide monthly reviews of technology plans and choices, and reimbursement for travel to the meetings you wish to conduct. For the most part, however, Advisory Board members are engaged individually by the entrepreneur and his or her key team members.

Our experience is that entrepreneurs form such Boards but, in the heat of battle, fail to use them as regularly and effectively as originally intended. Don't make the same mistake. These individuals can really help you with that outside, independent opinion. The types of calls that might be made by the entrepreneur to Advisory Board members include:

- "I need to hire a new VP of Sales. Our current guy is good at managing current accounts but not busting into new ones. And, he isn't a closer. I would like you to meet him and get your opinion. If you can't have lunch, can you take a phone call?"

- "We are trying to crack into Company X. Do you know anyone who is an executive with that company? We need a referral into the account."

- "We need to start raising our next round of capital. It would be great if we could get the next round from angel investors. What do you think about that approach versus VCs? Would you be interested in participating? Do you have others in your network that we can talk to?"

- "My technology lead wants to shift to open-source tools. I am concerned that we might be sacrificing power or support of some sort. What do you think? Do you know someone I can talk to about this?"

- "This new product we have been talking about is ready to go live. I need help finding a beta test site. Where do you think we should go? Can you go in there with me to talk with the customer?"

---

[7] Reichheld, F. (2001, July). Lead for loyalty. *Harvard Business Review*, 76–84.

Advisory Board members are valuable for their personal networks. Most entrepreneurs look at initial Advisory Board members as individuals who can help produce revenue for the venture through their personal contacts. But beyond this, the entrepreneur should look for people with a range of expertise to expand his or her knowledge base. Some companies, particularly in the biotech space, have both a business Advisory Board and a technical Advisory Board (with distinguished scientists). Importantly, you should seek out people who will be candid and honest with you and willing to bounce ideas around. The typical Advisory Board will consist of highly experienced individuals from sales and marketing, investment, and technical backgrounds. You might even find a few professors sitting on those Boards!

On the other hand, not every person working with your company deserves an Advisory Board position. For example, it is not uncommon to find entrepreneurs who place their professional services providers on the Advisory Board with some stock included. But be careful here. You are paying these professional services providers for their services anyways. For a technology-intensive venture, figure at least $25,000 for a major financing and an ongoing amount of at least $5,000 a month. You are getting their advice anyways and paying handsomely for it! On the other hand, if you are fortunate enough to have an attorney who can network you into your region's angel investment and venture capital community, then they truly deserve a taste of stock in your company that comes with Advisory Board membership. In other words, the value-add has to be beyond the specific professional service contracted.

The same reasoning applies to the accounting firm you retain for the business. These days you will be paying market rate for their services. (In a difficult economy, professional service providers have little desire to take equity in lieu of cash.) With that payment, you have the right to ask for additional advice. If, on the other hand, you feel that your accountant has operating experience and can spend time in your company helping to set up control systems and coach people hired to run operations, then an Advisory Board position makes very good sense.

The Board of Directors: Proceed With Care (If You Are Given a Choice)

The notion of having an official Board of Directors is largely driven by the form of organization you select to develop. (We will explore this issue in greater detail later in this chapter.)

If the entrepreneur decides to formally incorporate the business, a formal Board of Directors is required by law. The Board of Directors serves to protect the interest of the shareholders in a way that is independent of the managers of the business. It provides oversight and governance on key decisions and the managers making those decisions. But beyond this, you will find startups recruiting prominent members of the business community to serve on the Board of Directors to lend credibility to the venture. In addition, members of the Board play an active hand in raising subsequent rounds of funding.

The Board of Directors is typically composed of several key officers of the company (such as the CEO and the CFO) and then three or more outside members responsible for the oversight of the affairs of the venture. Boards that are greater than seven individuals prove unwieldy and incapable of making fast decisions. The more typical number is five individuals, keeping to an odd number to avoid deadlock in certain critical issues such as basic strategy, senior management changes, financings, and exits.

The Board of Directors is elected by shareholders based on a slate of Directors put forth by the management team. In reality, if your venture is financed by angels or venture capitalists, you can expect them to request a seat on the Board so they can closely watch how their money is being spent. Since most investments are "syndicated," that means that the Board will consist of you, perhaps one other cofounder, and two or three professional investors. They will outnumber you and, if you are not the right person to build the company, your days at the helm are numbered. That's the price of taking outside money from professional investors. In ventures just getting going, one will often find even smaller Boards of Directors, say two founders and one key angel investor. This is often more comfortable for the entrepreneur, although not necessarily better. It is a business and everyone, even the founder, needs to be held accountable for his or her decisions and actions.

Taking professional money is analogous to getting married. The Board of Directors' role is ultimately the investor's "stick" to demand a divorce, to keep the house, and proceed forward without you. That is why when you convince an investor that they should invest in your company, have a serious heart-to-heart with your partners to determine whether you can see having that particular angel, VC, or corporate strategic investor sitting on your Board holding the sword of Damocles over your head. And yes, you need to try to talk to a few other entrepreneurs who have lived under the sword of that same individual. In many if not most cases, it is a wonderful, productive relationship where the investor adds incalculable value to the business—value well beyond the money itself. But in other cases, the relationship becomes "a pain in the neck" and distracts the entrepreneur from building the business he or she wants to build. You obviously want to try to avoid this latter situation, and it all comes down to a matter of individual personalities. Do your homework on investors because they will most often be sitting on your Board.

The Board is expected to meet on a regular basis (typically monthly for startups). It will take a major role in setting strategic direction, appointing the officers of the firm, declaring dividends, approving major purchases, and reviewing the performance of management. The Board will also be involved in reviewing operating and capital budgets, assisting with your business plan and its execution, providing support for daily operations, overseeing proper use of resources, and resolving conflicts among owners and/or shareholders. That means that you, as the entrepreneur, must allocate several days (hopefully over the weekend before Board meetings) working with your management team to prepare the presentation to the Board as well as necessary financial statements. These need to be short, focused presentations and an accurate set of current month, past month, and quarterly financial statements. The details matter on revenue creation, cash on hand, and monthly burn.

Revenue Creation

Revenue is the cure for many sins in a venture, and your Board members will want to dig into the revenue situation of the company. Expect Board members to want to see a breakdown of customers in the pipeline, customers closed, and the revenue expected or realized from each type of customer. They will want to help you build the pipeline but also hold your feet to the fire on closing sales.

As noted above, if you take outside professional money, it is your investors who will hold the "outside" Board seats—and they will most often outnumber the "inside" Board seats of you and your founders. In fact, the composition of the Board will be a specific condition of the financing itself. The investor will already have his or her stock by virtue of the investment, and while the company remains privately held, there are no additional director's fees or payments expected or required. These investors/Directors are working to achieve an exit—just like you.

It is also possible to not have just investors sitting on your Board of Directors. These can be executives working in major corporations or the CEOs of other successful startups. In some cases, there might even be a professor with business experience sitting on the Board! The advantage of this type of noninvestor, outside Board member is that they can provide the external perspective on strategy and tactics that is not totally driven by "exit." For example, some venture capitalists have little or no true operating experience building and running a company. They are strictly "financial" types. If that is the case in your company, you can argue for finding an outside Board member who has already created the $100 million company that you wish to create. Prudent investors will want this as well.

For outside Board Members who are not direct investors in your company, it is customary to provide between 1% and 2% of the stock in the business. This is compared to the .1% to .2% stock provided to Advisory Board members. That is ten times as much stock for at least ten times as much work. When giving this amount of stock, there is no need to pay Board members a monthly retainer—even though many entrepreneurs have found themselves agreeing to a retainer of some sort just to get the experienced, senior business person to attend meetings. Moreover, in some cases, we find outside noninvestors getting upwards of 5% of the stock—but this is indeed rare. That Board member has to do a lot for the venture beyond the Board meeting themselves to deserve that amount of stock—help write the business plan, raise the seed or Series A financing, or help recruit and hire the management team. Of course, for the young entrepreneur, 5% does not seem like a big number. Trust us, it is. You can easily make the mistake of giving up a lot of stock to a senior individual who promises to do a lot and doesn't contribute much of anything over the course of time. Get an attorney experienced in startup deals to structure Board of Directors and Advisory Board shares as options that vest over time based on continued participation.

It is also extremely important that you set expectations and requirements for each Board member who is of the outside, noninvestor variety. For example, Board members must be able to devote 12 days a year to attend monthly meetings. In reality, that is closer to 20 days because Board members will meet with key managers outside of Board meetings. Their advice is both needed and important. Board members often communicate with management on regular if not daily basis by phone or e-mail. Getting this involvement won't be a problem if an individual has money at stake in your business. Otherwise, it needs to be part of the deal for Board participation.

Of course, if you do not go the incorporation route, and instead elect for a sole proprietorship, partnership, or limited liability corporation, a formal Board of Directors is not required by law. Deep, experienced counsel can be rewarded through the Advisory Board described earlier. However, if you have outside investors with "member interests" (sometimes called "units" or "shares") in a limited liability corporation, they will insist on some form of oversight and governance. This includes periodic meetings. It is also achieved by preparing quarterly written "member consents" where investors approve certain major business decisions and actions undertaken over that time period, including additional financings, financial performance, and changes in corporate structure. But there is no structure through which you can be "fired" as the CEO. Poor performance simply means that you will not get additional investment simply because any future investor will want to talk and rely on the experience of current investors. Handcuffs of a different sort than steel.

Form a Customer Advisory Board

Another important stakeholder group that entrepreneurs tend to overlook in terms of seeking counsel and advice is the venture's own customers. An important emerging trend that we are seeing and recommending to new ventures is the establishment of a Customer Advisory Board. This is also known as a Customer Advisory Council. It is a representative group of existing customers who meet with your team on a regular basis (two to four times per year) to offer advice to your venture and its future direction. A Customer Board offers feedback on customer satisfaction with the venture and its products and services; provides early warnings on shifts in customer needs and emerging opportunities; offers input on new product development; makes referrals to other customers; and provides intelligence on competitors' tactics and strategies. You may also be able to use a Customer Advisory Board to discover how customers are actually using your product and learn about future technologies your customers are currently evaluating.

Entrepreneurs who build deep relationships with their best customers create a great advantage over larger, stodgier competitors. It's well known that your top 20% of clients typically generate 80% of a typical firm's revenue. Therefore, engaging key customers on a Customer Advisory Board is essential for the entrepreneur (once products are launched to market).

Membership typically consists of ten to 20 customers (again, representative of that 20% of customers that generate 80% of your revenue). Participation is voluntary. Customers love the feeling of influencing product or service direction. Advanced training on product features, for example, is a nice "throw-in" to these meetings.

Ideally, meetings should be held either at your company facility or at a nearby hotel so that as many employees can attend as is appropriate. Some groups meet in field offices for maximum regional participation. We believe it is important that you, as founder of the venture, make an appearance at these meetings. The entrepreneur must be willing to act on customer advice; otherwise, customers will soon quickly learn that attendance is a waste of time.

Invitations should go out well in advance, a couple months if possible, to allow customers to schedule the meeting appropriately. In most cases, a good member of a Customer Advisory Board will pay their own expenses to come to your office. Supply the meals, however. This is money well spent given the insights you will gather.

Once at the meetings, be sure everyone is introduced, company and customer participants. Take the time to discuss the challenges faced by your customers when dealing with your company and its products or services. Then, discuss strategic initiatives and/or new products/services to get customer reactions and input. Leave lots of time for open discussion. You might also consider breakout sessions to get feedback from small groups that represent different customer types. Finally, find the time to do a recap of the meeting so participants receive confirmation that their voices have been heard.

A more recent trend with Customer Advisory Boards is to run them entirely online. Going online allows for scalability and global reach at reduced cost. We know of one firm that went from ten Customer Advisory Board members attending an in-person meeting to over 40 members participating from multiple sites around the globe. Another advantage of an online Customer Advisory Board is you can increase the frequency of contact and obtain more insight and feedback.[8]

The Legal Organization of the Venture _____

Standing apart but related to team issues is the legal form of business, or "entity type," that a founding team should adopt to begin operations and raise capital. There are a number of options open to the entrepreneur—and each has important considerations for liability protection, taxes, and the classes of stock that certain types of investors prefer.

While there are many options, we will concentrate on the five major types used by entrepreneurs for different reasons:

- A sole proprietorship
- A partnership
- A Limited Liability Company (LLC)
- An S Corporation
- A C Corporation

Let's learn the differences.

With a **sole proprietorship,** you are the single owner and have full responsibility for the venture's operations. You retain total control. A significant benefit of a sole proprietorship is

[8] Carter, T. (2003). *Customer Advisory Boards: A Strategic Tool for Customer Relationship Building.* New York: Routledge. If you wish to learn more, visit http://www.customeradvisoryboard.org/.

that there is only one level of income tax on the business income, which is paid directly by the owner on his or her personal income tax return. The income is only taxed once, unlike a corporation where there are business income taxes and then personal taxes on profits paid out to shareholders in the form of dividends. In the sole proprietorship, all revenue, expenses, and depreciated assets are reported directly on the Schedule C as part of your personal tax return. Losses (under certain conditions) are also passed through onto your personal income tax returns. The downside to a sole proprietorship is that your personal assets—your bank accounts, personal investments, and personal property—are exposed to liability claims from customers, employees, or anyone else for that matter who interacts with your business. Thus, creditors could seize any assets you own outside the business to satisfy any outstanding debt the business has incurred. You are also legally liable in the case of any lawsuit made against the business. To help mitigate this risk, you can purchase insurance against commercial damages (typically up to a million dollars) on a sole proprietorship that can be attached to your personal homeowner's policy. The cost of such policies typically runs less than $1,000 a year. However, if you have full-time employees or a large number of customers, a sole proprietorship makes no sense whatsoever given the liability risks involved. Anything can happen at any time. It is just not worth the risk.

With a **partnership,** two or more individuals pool their resources to start the venture. And, there can be some general partners and some limited partnership owners. As with a sole proprietorship, the partners share personal liability. The only legal protection for partners is to purchase insurance against liability suits and placing partner assets in someone else's name. There are rather complex "partnership agreements" that must be executed that stipulate the various rules of engagement in such entities, including the distribution of profits, decision-making rights, and ownership rights upon the exit or death of a particular partner. The partners in a partnership also enjoy the benefit of "single taxation" as well as participating in operating losses under certain conditions. Profits or losses are reported on the Schedule K-1 of the tax return. At the same time, however, partnerships operate "naked" in terms of potential liability. Traditionally, law firms were formed as partnership because no one had the courage to sue a law firm! That's changed, however, and entrepreneurs and professional service firms alike have shifted to our next major form of company structure.

We believe one of the great business innovations for entrepreneurs is the **Limited Liability Company** (LLC) almost complete liability protection to the business owners ("members" in the LLC form and "partners" in the LLP form). At the same time, the taxation is similar to that of a partnership or sole proprietorship. Profits and losses flow through to the "members" of the LLC based on the allocations set forth in the LLC agreement. Members own "units" of the pool of total outstanding "units" ("units" being the LLC equivalent of corporate "stock" or "shares"). Investors may purchase these units in successive rounds of financing, just as in a stock equity corporation. LLCs also file federal income tax returns, but only to report the business income and to which members that income is allocated. Members receive Federal Schedules K-1 showing their flow-through income from the LLC that must be included on the member's personal income tax return. As an added plus for angel investors, the early start-up losses may be eligible for tax deductions against the angel's other investment gains. While LLC's have the full flexibility of determining income allocations, agreements are often written to be like a traditional corporate structure in terms of voting rights, board members, meetings, and so forth.

The next form of corporate structure for the entrepreneur is an **S Corporation.** This is what many entrepreneurs preferred as a corporate structure before the emergence of the LLC as an alternative. The S Corporation is a special type of corporation where profits and losses are distributed to stockholders and taxed as personal income. A formal Board of Directors must be established for an S Corporation—not a small matter for the entrepreneur. Like the LLC, an S Corporation also combines the tax advantages of a partnership and the liability protection of a traditional corporation. And like the LCC, the S Corporation has only one class of stock, in this case common stock. Unlike the LLC, tax returns for the business must be filed quarterly as well as annually. Shareholders report their income or losses on the Schedule K in the personal income tax return. In addition, the limit on the number of shareholders is set at 100 persons—and they must all be U.S. citizens. (These restrictions do not exist for an LLC.) That means that an entrepreneur cannot take an S Corporation public. Nor can a strategic corporate investor put money into an S Corporation entity. But the entrepreneur can also convert later from an S Corporation to a traditional C Corporation described next.

The **C Corporation** is the gold standard of liability protection and flexibility in the number of shareholders, their citizenship, and the classes of stock. Venture capitalists tend to insist on this form of incorporation because it offers multiple classes of stock, in this case preferred shares (which is what the VCs will insist on owning) and common shares (for the entrepreneurs and employees). Should bankruptcy occur, or an exit in the way of acquisition, the preferred shareholders move to the head of the line before the common shareholders. A C Corporation has other benefits for investors: Shareholders can include individuals, other corporations, trusts, partnerships, and LLCs. The downside is that the C Corporation carries double taxation for shareholders—first corporate and then personal. Moreover, the losses incurred in the early years cannot be passed onto investors—a major detriment to certain types of early stage investors, namely the angels. Tax filings are also more complex and quarterly as well as annual. In short, entrepreneurs tend to save the C Corporation for a much later point in time.

In general, it is advantageous for most entrepreneurs to start out with a simple flow-through (in terms of business income) entity type. This is due primarily to the tax benefits for early stage angel investors. If partners or investors are not needed, and legal liability is limited, a sole proprietorship may work fine and you can purchase liability insurance if you have any concerns. When partners or early stage investors are important, an LLC may be the right choice. The LLC provides solid liability protection for the entrepreneur's and investor's personal assets. Others might find that an S Corporation may be best when a more corporate legal structure is desired while still retaining the benefits of flow-through of business income and losses. However, the S corporation has been overtaken in popularity by LLC's as a startup entity form. This is due to the wide flexibility of LLCs in terms of forming rules and governance structures while still preferring the flow-through tax benefit of the sole proprietorship, partnerships, or S Corporations.

Bottom-line: You'd best do your homework first and then talk to a business accountant who advises startups. And if the accountant doesn't mention (unsolicited) an LLC or S Corporation in the first two minutes of serious discussion, say "thanks" and run the other way!

Providing Rewards and Incentives for the Venture Team

A common question from entrepreneurs is the best way to reward and incentivize a team. This invariably leads to a discussion on "how to slice up the pie." Our two over-riding principles are to share the wealth equitably with those who helped you start and grow the venture, and grow the pie as big as possible.

This is a tough question to answer. On one hand, you want to be stingy with your stock for advisors or employees who talk a lot but don't do a lot and disappear over the hill within six months or so. That happens frequently in new ventures. The faces seem to come and go. On the other hand, you want to recruit *A* players onto the team, and that takes stock. Those faces seem to stick and become the bedrock of your company. Therefore, guard your equity well. But do not forget that 51% of nothing is still nothing. Thus, you have to be prepared to share the pie and focus on the growth of the pie.

It is important to first test people before giving stock. Find the *A* players, set certain rules by convention or personal design for granting stock options based on performance, and then stick to the plan. For example, in a venture capital–funded startup, after several rounds of financing, the management team and employees might own as much (or as little depending on your perspective!) as 30%. That might mean 10% for the CEO; 3% to 5% for the VPs of Sales, R&D, and Finance, respectively; and about 10% for the rest of the various employees. Directors and advisors other than investors might account for another several percentage points of the total. Stock is not unlimited. Other rules of thumb are:

- Grant stock as options based on level or position that vest over time. (This applies to everyone except the founding team: *Do not* let the investors force you to convert all of your shares to options, then take control of your Board, and throw you out on your ear without any stock!) Your Advisory Board and attorney should be able to provide guidelines for ventures in your industry sector. If not, find an additional advisor and/or a new attorney!

- Reserve additional stock option incentives for stellar performance, be it in sales, delivering a new product out of R&D, or installing a complex system in a large, corporate customer.

- Make sure that every employee, even that front-office receptionist, gets a taste or more of stock. You want to create a "rugby team" atmosphere in the venture—and stock is an important element to achieving this.

- Review the stock option plan every year. Create (which may mean having the Board of Directors approve) additional stock incentive pools to provide to top performers across the company every year in addition to their current holdings. The goal is to have all employees be winners. Seasoned professional investors will require a future stock option pool (often 10% of the fully diluted company) set aside for attracting future talent and rewarding current employees.

There are a variety of compensation and reward plans available to stakeholders of a new venture. These include director stock option plans, cash bonus plans, future performance plans, stock option plans, stock purchase plans, and 401(k) retirement plans. Your Advisory Board and attorney are there to help you navigate through these waters. Proper plans take considerable forethought and reflection.

*** *** ***

Always remember the type of contribution made by core team members, advisors, employees, and yes, classmates. It is our sincere advice to not let "stock" get in the way of life-long friendships that are created in entrepreneurship classes. In a team of three or four persons working on a group project, chances are that only one or two has the taste for the risk and incredibly hard work required to actually raise money and launch a venture. Setting expectations ahead of time in terms of stock ownership is begging for disaster.

Our recommendation: Agree to not talk about stock until the team is formed to raise capital. To do this, you will have to assign roles and responsibilities—positions—in the company. One of you will have to be the CEO; another, run sales; another, R&D; and so forth. If you all get along famously and have the desire to "do a company" then the stock will take care of itself once investment money is in the offing. But some team members are likely to move onto other careers. Or others simply will not have the experience to take a certain position in a competitive market context. They need to work for such a person first, even if it is in a venture that they helped create!

Setting expectations up front—making commitments—will only lead to hard feelings down the road when a silent partner owns as much stock as several hardworking entrepreneurs. Leave the equity decision until after the class is over and you have made your first investor pitch, been thoroughly and completely grilled, and then see *who has the stomach for more*. Those team members who politely drop out of the venture can be fairly and warmly rewarded as the first and well-deserving members of the Advisory Board.

Sound good? Stay friends, first and foremost, and use fairness as the guide for dishing out the founder's equity in your venture.

Reader Exercises

Step 1: Conduct a Personal Characteristics Audit

Use Figure 10.1 to rate yourself as strong, average, or weak on the personal characteristics known to be important to successful entrepreneurship. The goal is to determine what personal strengths you bring to the venture and to identify your weaknesses. Use the results when you are constructing your team.

Personal Characteristics	Strong	Average	Weak
Have drive and energy			
Possess self-confidence			
Can set challenging and realistic objectives			
Can provide long-term involvement			
Can use money as a scorecard			
Am a persistent problem solver			
Can tolerate ambiguity and uncertainty			
Can learn from failure			
Can use constructive criticism			
Can take initiative			
Can make good use of resources			
Can compete against self-imposed standards			
Have an optimistic outlook on life ond overcoming challenges			

Figure 10.1 Personal Characteristics Template

Step 2: Business Skills Audit

Now do the same audit on your own personal business skills. Rate yourself as strong, average, or weak on the business skills discussed in the chapter (marketing and sales, operations/production, R&D, finance and accounting, general management, legal, and IT).

Skills	Strong	Average	Weak
Sales and marketing			
R&D management			
Finance and accounting			
General and operations management			

Figure 10.2 Business Skills Template

Step 3: An Aggregated Business Skills Audit for the Team

Have each of your team members apply the Business Skills Audit Template to themselves. Aggregate the entire lot and see where the gaps remain. Be sure to play the *devil's advocate* for one another. Five to seven years of work experience with a proven record of accomplishment in an industry sector aligned with the venture might qualify as "strong." Remember, the focus of this is not just for writing the business plan but for implementing the plan, that is, to start and grow the company.

From this discussion, try to complete the template shown in Figure 10.3. If there are gaps, simply put in "TBD" (to be determined).

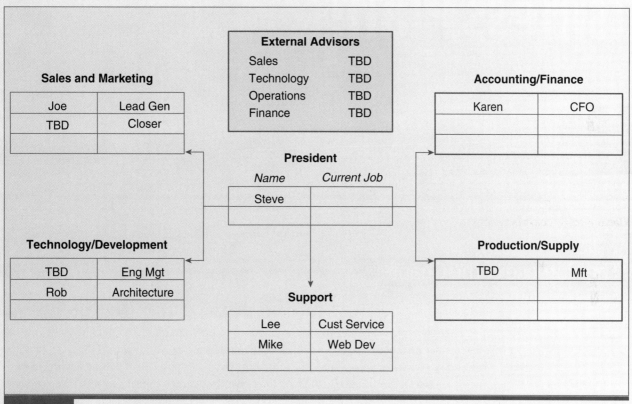

Figure 10.3 Build Your Team Template

Step 4: Begin Building an Advisory Board

Start thinking about who might be available to you to serve on your Advisory Board. Consider the trusted advisors you might have already gathered in the process of doing the work for this book. Think about mentors who might be available to you through your university's network, or the different types of investors you might have encountered in your research on the types and sources of venture finance in Chapter 8. Begin to write down a few names. You can place these directly on the template in Figure 10.3 as well.

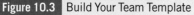

One name you should probably *not write down* is that of the professor teaching this class! Save that for when the class is over. Otherwise, your dear professor will have to think of you as a student to be mentored and graded on one hand, and a ticket to early retirement on the other! That's hard to do. Neither one of you needs the complication. Soon, school will be over and you can both decide the best relationship moving forward.

chapter 11
Writing the Business Plan!

11

We will take the perspective in this chapter that a business plan is a sales document. Sure, writing a business plan can help you organize your business, sharpen your thinking, and consolidate all the market research, solutions design, go-to-market, and financial planning that you must do to start a venture—but at the end of the day, your purpose in putting together a business plan is to get someone else to invest their own hard-earned capital into your company.

In prior chapters, we have described how your venture might be valued for the purposes of providing investors with a certain percentage of the company equity for their investment. We have also considered the different types of investors that invest in new companies as equity participants. And, we have worked through the details of projecting financial requirements for growth, as well as the financial outcomes of successful execution of a venture strategy. Now, we are going to take all these pieces of the puzzle and put them together into an actionable, sellable plan for investors—leveraging all the insights you developed in Part I of this book.

To do this, we will work through the particulars of writing a business plan, step by step, providing instruction in terms of the information needed for each section of the plan—and perhaps most important, the most essential questions that will be top of mind for investors as they read each section. These questions come from our own experience working with teams to raise funds from various types of investors. We have also helped corporate venture teams apply this to their own projects. Following this chapter will help you produce a concise document no more than 20 to 25 pages in length, with three or four pages of financial statements added at the end. With all the research and thinking you have done up to this point, writing a great business plan should be the icing on the cake!

Unlike prior chapters, there are no specific exercises at the end of the chapter. Just go write your plan, mindful of all the templates you have completed in prepartion for this moment. These, and your reality check, are powerful ammunition on your journey to raising capital. Be sparse with your words. Keep your wrting short, powerful, and full of the facts you have gathered from your industry, customer, and competitor research.

Learning Objectives

Write a plan to raise startup or growth capital. This chapter provides an outline for a business plan and practical advice on what investors are generally looking for in each section. It will also highlight where you might integrate templates from the first part of this book—either to help write the text or as outright exhibits. The deliverable is the first draft of a comprehensive business plan to which you will attach the financial projections created in Chapter 9.

The Outline of the Business Plan and Where Your Prior Work Fits In _____

The major sections of the business plan are:

1. Executive Summary

2. The Business Model and Financial Goals

3. Market Analysis: Demand, Customers Profile, and Competitive Analysis

4. Solutions: Technology/Intellectual Property, Products, and Services

5. Go-to-Market: Channels, Pricing, Promotion, and Sales Plan

6. Operations, Production, and Supply

7. Organization

8. Major Milestones With Funding

9. Financial Projections

In addition to key questions to answer for each section, we will provide a task organizer for each section so that you and your team can take responsibility for doing the research and writing of the text.

A quick note: For those of you who have seen other business planning structures, note that we do not include a special section stating the key risks and strategies to contend with these risks. While such a section is traditionally found in other business planning guides, we have reasons for excluding it. First, as stated earlier, a business plan is primarily a sales tool for raising capital for a startup, pure and simple. The risks will come up in the Q&A with your prospective investors. No need making them gun-shy right from the start. You want investors to fall in love with your venture idea, and then let the various strategies and projected financial outcomes win their minds. And if you are honest about it, there are so many risks in any new venture that a thorough review of how to mitigate these risks could easily consume two or three pages in your business plan—precious pages that you do not have to spare. Professional investors know the risks—and if you get the right ones—they will know how to better manage those risks than you. That is why investment capital is called mentor capital.

Figure 11.1 shows where your prior template work fits into the businesss plan outline. These templates are guides for what you should write in each particular section. In some cases, elements of these templates might be useful as actual illustrations in the text. If you look at the figure closely, you will also see that we have a few more concepts to learn in this chapter as well. These include frameworks for thinking about underlying product or service platforms, for structuring channels to market, for defining a coherent brand strategy, and creating a set of major milestones that will drive everyone's efforts once you get your financing.

Business Plan Section	Reference templates from earlier parts of the book	
Executive Summary	• Venture concept summary, • Venture concept template,	Chapter 7, beginning of the chapter Chapter 3, Figures 3.7 and 3.8
Business Model and Financial Goals	• Business model template,	Chapter 4, Figure 4.12
Market Analysis	• Industry attractiveness • Market segmentation template • Customer group template • Competitive positioning template	Chapter 1, Figure 1.9 Chapter 2, Figure 2.6 Chapter 2, Figure 2.3; Chapter 3, Figures 3.2, 3.3, 3.7, 3.8 Chapter 3, Figure 3.4; Chapter 6, Figure 6.3
Solutions (Products and Services)	• Product strategy template • "Good, better, best" template • Platforming concepts	Chapter 5, Figure 5.5 Chapter 5, Figure 5.3 To be provided in this chapter
Go-to-Market	• Business model template • Channel and branding	Chapter 4, Figure 4.12 To be provided in this chapter
Operations, Production, and Supply	• Startup and scale-up operations	To be provided in this chapter
Organization	• Organization template	Chapter 10, Figure 10.1
Major Milestones	• Milestone template	To be provided in this chapter
Financial Projections	• Revenue projections • Projected P&L • Projected cash flow • Projected Balance Sheet	Chapter 9 financial templates

Figure 11.1   Mapping Templates to Sections of the Business Plan

At this point, we would like you to create nine temporary folders on your computer or shared drive labeled for each of the sections shown in Figure 11.1. Begin to place copies of all your template work in the appropriate folders. If you have downloaded important articles from industry trade journals or other market studies as part of defining your venture scope and your target market, place these in the Market Analysis folder. The Organization section will require paragraphs on venture team members and key advisors. You can start gathering brief biographies and resumes right away. Place them in the Organization folder. In all of this assembling of materials, keep your eye open for graphs, illustrations, or digital photographs that will liven up your written document.

Appreciating Your Reader: The Professional Venture Investor

Venture investors put their time and money into good people with good ideas focused on clearly targeted and growing markets. You must be prepared to prove and defend your ideas and your team time and time again—until you launch your products or services and get checks. Then, the market begins to do the talking.

So your business plan must speak to the prudent investor with confidence: "We have a great idea for a growth market, a solid strategy for executing on that idea, and a great team."

The business plan is a product in its own right. In the development of any product, you need to put yourself into the shoes of the customer—in this case, the investor. It is part of your responsibility to do some homework on the investors you approach: Where have they succeeded? Where have they failed? What do other entrepreneurs think about these individuals as investors? Are they antagonistic and disruptive or truly helpful and work to open doors into major customer accounts and raise additional capital? If you try to approach investors who have no interest or experience in your industry segment, or prefers second- or third-stage company investments as opposed to startups, you are wasting both their and your time.

Beyond this, there are certain facts "on the ground" that you need to consider that should influence the style and the content of your written plan.

Fact 1: You will be one of many teams trying to get that investor's money. Raising capital for new ventures is a highly competitive situation. Friends of ours who are venture capitalists in the Boston and Silicon Valley areas throw around formidable percentages: For every 1,000 business plans that come across their desk, they will be seriously interested in ten and will invest in one or two of those ten. Those are not very good odds. That means that you have to have a very thick skin. You will be told "no" time and time again; but if you believe in your venture, and it needs investment capital beyond the $50,000 or $100,000 that you might be able to get from your family and friends, there is no choice but to suck it up and keep tackling investors.

TIP: STANFORD'S ENTREPRENEURSHIP CORNER

We recommend that you go to the Stanford University Entrepreneurship Corner (http://ecorner.stanford.edu/). Search for the entrepreneurship video called "Attrition Rates for Potential Investors," where two seasoned angel investors talk about the factors that lead them to actually listen to pitches from just a very few of the plans coming before them. The investors (very active "angels") talk about receiving five new plans a day, coming to about 150 a month, of which just one will receive investment. And the deals they receive are initially triaged based on the source or reference of the deal.

Fact 2: Your business plan is your bona-fide instrument for getting a face-to-face meeting—or most often, a return telephone call before the meeting—with an investor. So obviously, it must be very well written. That means concise, clean, and error-free. If you don't take the time to clean up the language, and write carefully and meaningfully, the investor is probably going to discard your plan. If you are not a particularly good writer, get someone on your team who is! The business plan must also be engaging in certain ways. We find a few choice graphs and charts helpful.

Fact 3: It is a fairly safe assumption that a professional investor will not read your plan from the first page to the last in the very first sitting. Rather, they will read your Executive Summary, then your Business Model section, fast forward to your Team/Organization section, and hit your projected P&L. If they don't like what they see in these first four sections of your plan, they won't read the rest and you will certainly not get the meeting.

Jeff McCarthy, an alumnus of our university and partner in a very successful venture capital firm, shared his thoughts on what he looks for first before reading the entire business plan:

> "Before I read a single page, I first look for a trusted referral. If we know the person who referred the entrepreneur, it makes a huge difference. Then, I go straight to the Executive Summary. If I understand what they are going to make, who they are going to sell it to, and why those customers are going to buy this product over any other product in the market, then I'm interested in reading more.
>
> I next go to the Team section. Has anyone on the team done a successful startup before? Do they have an established track record of success? Is there operating experience present? Do they have a good understanding of the market they will be attacking? The team is always the most important ingredient to us. If the team looks solid, then I read on.
>
> I next need to see how they plan to make money—not just get customers interested in the company's products or services, but to get them to actually buy and deploy the product. And then as I read the Financial section, what I am really looking for is two things: What is going to be the true capital required to finance the company and get it to scale? Second, is the revenue opportunity sufficient to make it worthwhile? For my firm, if it doesn't represent a $100 million plus revenue opportunity, we are not really interested.

Of course, there are other types of investors—ones who do not have hundreds of millions of dollars to put to work as do Jeff and other high-end venture capitalists—who will be interested in that $20 million, $30 million, or $50 million revenue opportunity. But for all the other elements, professional investors are *just like* Jeff McCarthy. Here is what they need to see:

- The Executive Summary has to shine—to give the vision and promise of the market, the compelling solution, the technology within the solution, and team—all in a page or so.
- The Team section must show that even if you don't have all the key players, you are taking steps to find them. Professional investors want to see a member of the founding team who has successfully started and grown companies before. That experience also brings with it a network of other key team members that need to be recruited to supplement the founders in the first critical years of the business.
- The Business Model section also has to shine—to show that your approach to monetizing on the vision and opportunity is pragmatic and reasonable. As we emphasized in the Business Model chapter, investors want to see a structure of revenues that clearly features some type of recurring revenue. Even if you are selling an airplane, there should be line items for replacement parts, add-on systems, and ongoing services in your financials.
- The Financial section must show projections that are both exciting yet reasonable. Investors will also want to see a path to profitability (a positive operating profit) occurring over 18 to 24 months, unless of course you are proposing a biotechnology or similar type of deep, R&D-intensive venture. Investors will look at the assumptions behind the revenue projections carefully as well as those behind the operating margins once revenue is generated. If the assumptions behind the financials seem unreasonable or random, you won't get the meeting.

Fact 4: Most people with a lot of money and who wish to invest it in new venture are of a certain age and tenure. Their tolerance for examining financial statements that go on page after page in font size 8 is nonexistent. (One of our particular beefs with the popular "question and answer" business planning software packages is that you answer a bunch of questions and it produces a dozen pages of incredibly detailed financial statements—minutiae.) Think of it this way—you must be prepared to defend any and every number that you put in the back of your business plan. So like the plan itself, remember to keep your financials concise, powerful, and integrated. Spend just as much time on stating the assumptions behind your revenue, expense, and cash flow projections as on the numbers themselves. These assumptions tell an investor how you think about your venture *as a business*—and it is that thinking that he or she wants to understand, assess, and hopefully, improve.

Fact 5: Investors live by the "golden rule." He or she who has the money rules! Professional investors—serious angels, VCs, and strategic investors—believe that they know best how to build a profitable, money-making enterprise (whether this is true or not) and expect you to show a willingness to listen to what they have to say. So even if you have put together the greatest business plan of the last decade, unless you are Steve Jobs or Bill Gates, if your investor likes your idea, he or she is still going to want to make inputs and changes to certain elements of it. And it is unlikely to come in the areas of target market or product strategy—rather, it will be in the finer aspects of the business model—how to convert your idea into money. *Be prepared to listen and adjust.* The ability to try something, learn from it, and quickly integrate that learning into a scalable business is how the best investors view new ventures. The same goes for executives sponsoring internal corporate ventures. It is exceedingly rare that a venture hits a home run right in the first inning; rather, it's in the second or third where the pitching becomes familiar and the team begins to pick up its full stride. Harry Keegan, a successful entrepreneur and alumnus (or use alum across these three pages) of our university (who started and runs his own pharmaceutical company) is also an active angel investor. Harry views managing the trials and tribulations of new ventures this way:

> Setting up a communication avenue with investors and using it both to inform and to solicit guidance is not a sign of weakness. Rather, it is utilizing resources who want to help and expect to contribute more than money. The vast majority of angel investors earned their wealth in the school of blood, sweat, and tears. Not to tap that wellspring in favor of learning the hard way by yourself is surely folly. Everyone makes mistakes. More can be learned from those that are honestly shared than from the war stories of victories long past. Nothing warms the heart of a mentor better than a pixel of contribution where the student avoids calamity or expands the scope of a success.

Fact 6: Investors hate being caught unawares. They invest in a plan and ordinarily expect you to stick to it. However, any business needs to adjust to conditions on the field. Just don't veer from the plan without first talking to your investors. That might be a competitive announcement that you should have known about and they learned before you. Or, it might be a serious delay in a sale to an initial important customer that you promised would occur by a certain date. Bad news doesn't necessary get an entrepreneur in trouble with his or her investors; surprises will. As noted once again by our friend Harry Keegan:

> Entrepreneurs have an obligation to adhere to the business plan upon which the investment is solicited and not to run naked into the woods as soon as the checks clear. If course corrections are needed based on real-time feedback, angels need to know as surprises are not welcome.

Fact 7: Every investor has been badly burned by what they had once felt was a highly promising venture at some point in time. There are many reasons why a venture can go sour—the biggest ones tend to be market related (the market wasn't ready yet or competition was not fully understood) or team related (individuals who were poor managers, inexperienced in the industry, or difficult personalities). As the investor reads your plan and gets to know you, he or she is going to be on guard for those subtle and not so subtle warning signs that you might be one of those horrible disasters that had cost the investor endless time, aggravation, and considerable money. If you set off a risk trigger—which can happen in the most unexpected ways because you have no way of really knowing how that investor got so badly burned in the past unless he or she tells you—then it is likely that *there is nothing you can do to turn things around.* You've got to be prepared to to pack your bags and move on. Most entrepreneurs literally talk to dozens of potential investors before they find that particular individual who is willing to commit and bring other investors along.

Fact 8: Even if an investor loves your idea, he or she is still going to worry about how to best mitigate all the attending risks associated with any new venture. One way to mitigate these risks is to seek funds and go-to-market partnerships with major, well-established corporations. These partnerships may represent a technology or R&D "shortcut," a go-to-market channel, or a way to provide high levels of customer service from the get-go. A partnership with a major corporation can help speed time to market and establish your credibility as a player in the industry. The word of caution on this is that even if you have channel partners, it is most often advisable that you own the customer—at least in the beginning. This allows you to directly learn from the customer. Second, it allows you to directly introduce new products and services to the customer over time rather than have a channel partner control that decision. So, sell with and through established players, but be part of the marketing and selling process. Tom Aley, an alumnus of our university and the focus of one of our teaching cases in the back of the book, put it this way:

> Institutional investors, such as VC firms, are always looking for ways to reduce the risk in a new venture. One of the best ways for a startup to reduce risk for investors is to convince a large, industry player to be one of the investors. This gives immediate industry credibility for the VC. Someone with domain experience has agreed to invest. The VC will talk with the industry partner to learn as much as he or she can, as quickly as possible, to convince other VCs to invest.

The bottom line for writing a business plan comes to this: Above all else, clear writing is essential. Brevity is a must. Investors (and sponsoring executives for a corporate venture) want to see evidence of:

- A well-defined, robust MARKET,

- A distinct product or service SOLUTION that target customers need and want to buy,

- A balanced, experienced TEAM,

- A sensible BUSINESS MODEL, featuring recurring revenue and that generates cash with each sale and operating profit within a reasonable period of time.

Perhaps most important, investors want to see a clear, driving **FOCUS** in everything that you propose and do.

Lastly, if you get told "not interested" by the first 15 investors that you send your plan to read, *welcome to the club of entrepreneurs trying to raise money!* Only the most successful entrepreneurs, with a track record of making money for investors in the past—often multiple times through a series of successful ventures—can pick up the phone, call a former investor, and get commitments for a new venture over the course of several weeks.

For those of you who are starting corporate ventures, all of these "facts on the ground" apply for potential executive sponsors. There are many people vying for their attention, and in the vast majority of cases, the executives who can fund your venture are also busy operating executives responsible for core businesses or functions in major corporations. Their time is short; their patience for poorly conceived or written business plans is even shorter.

There are a few additional "got to haves" when appealing to the strategic or corporate investor, or the executive helping to run a major corporation. One is that the plan must clearly show how (a) the venture will leverage existing corporate technology, or (b) will significantly add to the corporation's portfolio of technologies and products, and (c) can leverage the corporation's brand and channels to accelerate the creation of value.

Now, for the team seeking to create a new business within a business, and appealing to the executive team of the parent corporation for seed funds, you may find that your executive suite prefers to see just a PowerPoint with all the details of a venture rather than a full written plan itself. However, we believe that a short written plan must still accompany the PowerPoint presentation—as will all the same sort of detailed financial statements that startups developed for angels, venture capitalists, or externally focused corporate venture groups. Moreover, unlike going to most VCs, our experience is that corporate executives will want an informal meeting before the meeting to provide their input into your plan and your milestones.

In addition, while the startup entrepreneur needs to typically manage one or several investors for the Series A financing, the corporate entrepreneur needs to manage a broader number of stakeholders within the corporation. These might include the CEO and his or her executive committee. These might comprise the general managers of adjacent lines of business, the CFO, the chief legal counsel, and the senior vice president of marketing and R&D. Again, this means a lot of meetings before the official meeting if you want to have any realistic chance of getting sponsorship and financial support from within a major corporation. And all of these stakeholders will be thinking about the risks inherent in "rocking the boat" with a new corporate venture. "Risk mitigation" strategies and customer or sales force migration plans will be even more important to corporate executives. While most will seek venturing that leverages core technology as a good path for growth, taking venture-type risks will not appear in any of their job definitions!

Before Writing, "Storyboard the Plan"

You can save yourself a lot of time and have a much more effective result if you first bullet-point the major elements of each section of the business plan before writing anything. We call this storyboarding the business plan. It means walking through the plan from front to back and outline the major ideas in each section and see how they align and integrate to your core strategy, that is, the Venture Concept and Business Model.

Figure 11.2 shows a storyboarding template. Each section of the business plan is shown in that figure, with the major bullet points that you should think about with each section. The one section that isn't shown is the Executive Summary. The other sections feed into it. We have put a graphic icon to illustrate the seminal framework for most of the sections, followed by the major bullet points for which you should have clarity and a strategy as you write your plan:

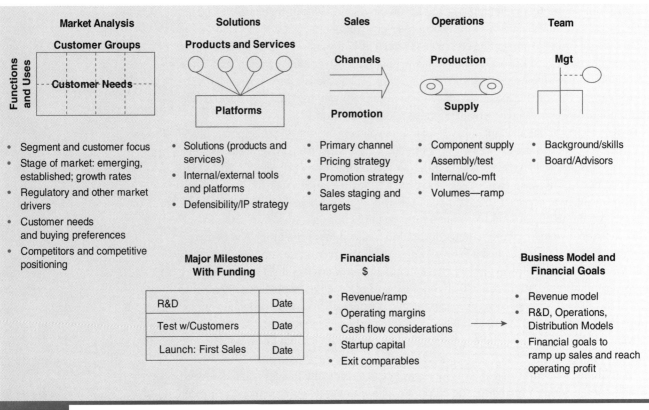

Figure 11.2   Storyboard Your Business Plan

- **The Market Analysis** section shows a segmentation grid—the framework used to identify different types of customers, different types of uses cases by customers, and customer needs within those use cases. By working through the first part of this book, you should be able to easily storyboard the major points about your target market, market size and growth rates, customer focus and customer needs, competitive positioning, and any sort of regulatory events or trends that make your target market particularly advantageous—or less so. Without a clear focus for this section, nothing else in the plan will really work as needed.

- **The Solutions** section shows a graphic representation of an underlying platform and the products or services that utilize the platform. The idea here is that successful companies provide a range of products and services over time. Platforms are underlying parts, systems, or processes shared across multiple products or services that allow a company to achieve greater levels of profitability by virtue of increasing volumes of shared parts and systems. This section also contains your intellectual property (IP) strategy (patents, etc.) if your venture is based on a new core technology.

- **The Go-to-Market** section is represented graphically by a straight arrow—reflecting the channel by which your products or services reach the customer. Entrepreneurs often underestimate the importance and cost of creating effective channels. Put another way, the greatest products or technology in the world will *not* meet their commercial promise without an equally powerful channel strategy. This section also contains a bullet point for your pricing strategy, which is a combination of your competitive positioning defined in the first section and your decisions regarding the structure and nature of revenues in the business model chapter (Chapter 4). Promotion and branding is another essential part of a sales plan. The last bullet point is the sales staging and rollout. This simply means whether you plan to do some type of regional or limited rollout in the first year and then expand nationally or have one initial original equipment manufacturer (OEM) channel partner and expand to others over time.

- **The Operations, Production, and Supply** section is represented by a supply chain icon. Here, your business model decisions can be so important. Will you be doing R&D in-house as most firms, or subcontract design and development? Will there be key technology or component suppliers? Also, will you do manufacturing in-house or as many new firms producing physical products, use subcontract manufacturers? If you are running a Web services business, will you host your own services or use a secure third party (as do most startups)? If you have storefronts, this part of the business plan deals with location and store operations for the first several years of the venture. Or, if you are shipping products to customers, a logistics vendor needs to be identified. It is this part of the business plan that may take considerable research in addition to all that you have done in earlier chapters—for you will need to investigate certain approaches and understand the fixed and variable costs of these approaches. For storyboarding, set forth your preferred strategies for each of these areas. This will help identify the calls you have to make. For ventures with manufactured products, we prefer to have a section in this part of the business plan that defines production goals in terms of volume for products.

- **The Organization** section is represented by an organization chart icon. New venture teams are notoriously nonhierarchical. The CEO is chief executive and bottle washer. Nonetheless, professional investors will want to know who is the top decision maker and his or her key staff for R&D, sales and marketing, production/operations, and finance. A number of these may be cofounders. Others may be people with whom you have already spoken and who have the skills you require to balance the team but will not leave their current jobs until you secure funding. Others may be people you do not know yet but know you need to hire. Storyboarding a winning team is one of the most important things you can do up front. Getting the right people involved will help you write a much better plan. Thinking about good external advisors at this point is also important for the same reason: They can help make your plan better.

- **The Major Milestones With Funding** section is represented by a task list. For the written plan, your investors will want to know what you plan to do with their money across all major functions within the business. For storyboarding, we prefer that you consider pragmatic objectives for getting your product or service in test mode with a customer(s), often called the "beta version"; bringing your first product to market for commercial sale; bringing in your first dollars of revenue; and, the time period when you achieve first operating profit. These four key milestones, plus a few select hires to fill major gaps in your management team, are the stakes in the ground that you need to set if you are going to have a real business.

- **The Financials** section draws from your fine work in the prior chapter! Just bullet point the highlights: the revenue ramp, the operating margins, any unusual considerations for converting revenues into cash, and the money you need to get the business started. Also, to add some fire to the discussion, do a quick search on the Web to find out the exit valuations for similar types of companies over the past several years. Most of these exits will be acquisitions by a larger corporation. Try to find the multiple on revenues for those deals—then look at your own thoughts about revenue ramp and think to the future!

- **The Business Model and Financial Goals** section is a simple bulleted list. Even though this section is presented in the written plan right after the Executive Summary, for storyboarding we like to have it come last—as an ending scorecard for all the prior sections. The structure and nature of revenues is the key bullet. So are your approaches to R&D, products, and sales. Lastly, investors want to know "the time to first dollar" and "the time to first profit." These goals should be clear from your financial modeling in the prior chapter. State them in months from startup for your storyboard.

Now, for work process. We suggest that you try to develop your own war room for storyboarding the plan. That might be your kitchen or a conference room. This is also a full-day work session—so you'd better plan on doing it over the weekend. Find a big whiteboard, buy some new dry-erase markers, grab some pizzas and beer (only after lunch!), and start mapping out your storyboard for your business plan. Have fun with it—it is your future.

As you fill in each section, step back, take a look, and see how the pieces fit together. Again, writing a good business plan is akin to writing a good story that will be sold to investors—tight, customer focused, pragmatic, and pointing to attractive financial outcomes. It takes a lot more thinking and elbow grease to write a powerful short business plan than to write one that is long and rambling.

When you are done completing the storyboard, take a moment to show it to your advisors and friends. It is the prototype of your business plan. You want your advisors to candidly tell you any elements that seem unclear or that don't make sense.

The Business Plan Sections _____

Now we transition from getting prepared to write the plan to the plan itself. In the pages to follow, we go through each section and tell you what investors expect and their top-of-mind concerns as they read each section.

The Title Page

The title page must have the name of your business or corporate venture and your contact information. We also prefer to see the amount of funds requested for startup or the corporate venture. **Do not forget to include your personal contact information!** One of our VC friends who runs a firm that receives several thousand plans a year (and invests in only a half dozen or so) once told us that he regularly discards new business plans because personal contact information was not on the front page.

Executive Summary

The Executive Summary must grab the reader. It might be the only page or two that they read! As indicated earlier, most investors and executives will only read the Executive Summary, then go straight to the resumes, and then to the financials. If they like what they read, only then will they read the rest of the plan.

Remember, professional investors want to see (a) a solid, growing market, (b) well-defined customers who need what you have to sell, (c) an attractive business model that produces cash, and (d) a team suited to the task. The Executive Summary hits (a), (b), and (d) all in a page or two; and the next section of the plan, hits (c)—the business model.

Therefore, the Executive Summary is a concise statement of the purpose of the proposed venture—its vision of greatness in the form of a distinctive market position that you hope to achieve.

The first thing you need to write is two or three sentences which present the vision of what you wish to create and the market position you wish to achieve. This is often referred to as "The Company" section. It is imperative that these first few sentences show the clear focus of your venture. This opening paragraph is so very important—it sets the stage for everything to follow. For starters, you can take a look at your venture concept statement for the Reality Check in Chapter 7. Our guidelines for that were:

ABC is our business that (solves *what problem*) for (*who—which target customers*). It is different from the current competitors because of (*why customers buy*). The benefits that we expect to provide (name the major benefits) will make ABC stand out from all competitors.

Now, we recommend that you front load it with key words that include "to be a market leader" in the well-defined "target market."

ABC is a (startup, spinoff, internal corporate venture) seeking to be a market leader in the target segment of (name your target segment.) The Company is focused on (solves *what problem*) for (*who—which target customers*) in that target segment. The (products or services) of the Company will provide (name the major benefits) that will make it unique in the marketplace.

Here are a few examples from business plans that received funding in years past, with company and product names disguised. The first contains the initial paragraph for a private placement memorandum for a financial services company that selected medical billing as its target. It raised $1 million from angel investors at a postmoney valuation in excess of $12 million!

Company X is a Web-based health care software services company that provides health care providers solutions to efficiently recapture lost revenue due to missed charges without requiring either investments in new enterprise software or significant changes to the way providers conduct business. The Healthcare Financial Management Association estimates that health care providers fail to bill approximately 3% to 5% of all reimbursable charges. Our company brings immediate financial and administrative benefit to its health care provider clients, generating sales primarily from a revenue sharing arrangement with its clients based upon reimbursed missed charges. Our lead-users have already proven that this win-win business model leads to a quick sale and rapid business growth.

Here's another one for a "green" engine company that received a combination of equity and debt financing to produce a new type of engine with extremely low emissions needed to comply with the new federal law:

XYZ Engine Technologies' goal is to become a market leader in the OEM segment for small vehicle or craft production. The company is commercializing proprietary technologies for lightweight high-performance 4-stroke engines that dramatically reduce pollution emissions as will be mandated by future federal and state law. These clean engines are ideal for motorcycles, snowmobiles, watercraft, all-terrain vehicles, and microcars. The first engines are in the tooling stage and should be ready for production by the end of 2XXX, with several other engine designs soon to follow. With commitments for significant orders on hand, XYZ Company now needs capital to complete manufacturing engineering and tooling for production.

Then, following "The Company" section, write one short (very short) paragraph for each of the four topics:

- The **market opportunity** in terms of target market segment, target customer, and the customer problems to be solved. Summarize the size and growth characteristics of the target market in a way that demonstrates a robust, attractive target (or addressable) market.

- The **distinctive products, services, or distribution assets** you seek to provide and the extent to which it either creates intellectual property (IP) or leverages current IP. The IP statement can be critically important for certain types of biotech, materials science, or information technology ventures.

- The startup/management team, hopefully with a combination of **industry experience** and a **balance of skills.** If you don't have a management team—that is, it is just yourself—use a few sentences to identify key management that you seek to recruit in the first few months of the venture. An investor is going to want to see that you have the right people involved from the start or at least know what types of persons you require so that the investor can help you build a powerful team.

- **The funds** requested for the venture at this stage of growth and **the uses of those funds in terms of achieving major milestones.**

The entire Executive Summary can be single spaced within the paragraphs, but double or tripled spaced between paragraphs, making for a concise, one- or two-page presentation. Some professors might advise to save writing the Executive Summary for last—but from our own experience, we know that this is virtually impossible to resist. So give into the urge. Write a first draft of your Executive Summary and let it serve as a follow-on to storyboarding to help guide all the more detailed business plan sections to follow. When the plan is completed, set aside a couple of quiet hours to revise and improve the Executive Summary. It needs to be concise and powerful.

The Business Model and Financial Goals

In this day and age, investors (and sponsoring executives for corporate ventures) are getting back to basics. They want to know that the products and services are *real,* and that there is a solid business model generated from these products and services. They want to know that customers have the cash to pay for what you wish to sell. And, they want to see that the business itself generates cash. Jeff McCarthy, the venture capitalist quoted earlier, noted further that:

> "In this era, we see a lot of plans that promise to bring millions of users to a Website, without ever really answering what all those users are going to do and buy once they arrive. We need to see plans that show how to monetize on any given opportunity. Without a clear plan on how to make money, it is a nonstarter."

This requires not only a robust target market and compelling product or service solutions but also some prudent decisions on how to best stucture the revenue model as well as how to structure operations in terms of R&D, production, and distribution.

The framework we learned earlier provides an excellent tool to guide you through writing this important section of the business plan. If you did the exercises in Chapter 4, all of the hard work is already done. We reproduce that framework in Figure 11.3. Each of the sections below is a short, concise paragraph that explains each of the rows in that figure.

Business Model Dimensions	The Approach for Your Venture	Rationale for That Approach
1 **Revenue Model** Products and services The structure and nature of revenue? The number of distinct revenue streams? Pricing relative to competition? Recurring revenue?		
2 **R&D Model** Build technology or buy? Focus of "value-add" in product/service R&D?		
Production Model Manufacturing—internal or outsourced? Gross margin targets on products and services.		
Go-To-Market Model Channel? Strategy for building awareness Startup approach versus ramp-up approach?		
3 **How Do these All Fit Together as a Business?** Logically, and then goals for revenue, gross margins, and operating margins.	**4** **Taken as a Whole, Is this Business Model Distinctive Relative to Competitors in the Marketplace?**	

Figure 11.3 Defining Your Business Model

Revenue Model

Briefly describe the types of products or the types of services provided by the company. Then, within this "mix," is the percentage of the projected revenues that are derived from each and the margins from each. You might also want to indicate how these percentages will change as the business grows. Also, indicate how your pricing for products and services compares to direct competitors. This should reflect your competitive positioning: premium performance/pricing strategy or low-cost player. And very importantly, put in a sentence on what creates recurring revenue. This is a hot button for any investor. Figure out what it means for your venture and put that into this paragraph.

R&D Strategy

This is the make-or-buy approach. In most complex ventures, there is a combination of internal R&D that is complemented by some external infusions of technology for various components or add-on features. For example, are you building a software application on top of open-source tools or the Microsoft Development Studio? Explain what this means for your company. If you have or need to have trusted partners or suppliers for parts of your products or services, say who they are and what stage of development that relationship exists. (IP was covered already in the Executive Summary, so no need to cover it here.) Most professional investors are suspicious if you decide to outsource every bit of R&D to a third party because that introduces a new type of risk to the venture (e.g., no control over the technology and hence, no barrier to entry on the technology front should the venture become wildly successful). Moreover, if you get into a contractual or personal disagreement with that third party, your business is at risk. We recommend that you try to determine a particular crown jewel of knowledge or technology in your business, create that in-house, and then build around it with logical partners. And if you are a software company, a robust third-party developer program is a must!

Production/Manufacturing Strategy

This is the in-house versus supplier strategy. For startups, it is essential to stretch out your invested capital—and that means doing whatever you can to keep it from getting tied up in hard, physical assets. Later on, once you have proven your business and it is scaling in terms of customers and revenue, you can consider how to bring these capabilities in-house to improve operating margins. But for a startup, your focus needs to be on surviving to the point where the business is generating unencumbered cash. For software and Web services firms, if you need to accommodate large amounts of traffic or data, there are numerous hosting services available for both computational needs and storage or backup. If you need high-performance computing, look at Amazon's cloud solutions—they are inexpensive.

Distribution Strategy

This means channels. While we will have more to say about channel strategies later on in this chapter, for now, this paragraph is a summary of the best route to (a) sell your products and services and (b) to provide support customers. One of our mentors, Al Lehnerd (the fellow who invented the Dustbuster) used to say, "Think of being the product yourself. How would you want to go to market, to get into the hands of the customer?" You then need to put in one or two sentences that state "we will build a direct sales force," or "we will sell through independent distributors," or "we will sell through mass merchandizers," or "the Web is our preferred channel." Or, your best channel may be other manufacturers or systems integrators. This is often called selling through OEMs or VARs (original equipment manufacturers or value-added resellers). Then, provide a statement that indicates the cost of a sale given your channel strategy—a 5% sales commission to your own salesperson, a 30% margin to a retailer, or a 40% margin to a VAR, or a large volume discount to an OEM.

Financial Goals

No business model is complete without providing goals derived primarily from the projected profit and loss (P&L). For many entrepreneurs, this means (a) the number of customers, (b) the revenue or bookings per customer, (c) the total revenue, and (d) the operating profit (EBITDA—earnings before income taxes, depreciation, and amortization—is easiest) from the business. In this part of the plan, you want to show this in summary form: annual projections over the first five years of the business. This should be a simple table. Investors will think of multiples of revenue and EBITDA in Years 4 and 5 to get a sense of the value you can create. In fact, it might not be a bad idea to include a single sentence here stating the current multiples used for exits within your specific industry sector.

Questions on the Investor's Mind

a. Is there solid, recurring revenue in this business?

b. Does the team have the "chops" needed to execute on its R&D strategy internally? If they use R&D partners, are these credible outfits or small, fly-by-night operations?

c. Is the team taking advantage of agile supply chains for production and logistics?

d. Does the financial performance table look over the top? Are the entrepreneurs naïve? On the other hand, do those same revenue projections after the business scales produce the type of exit that I, as an investor, need to achieve? It may be a good business but not the business for me.

Market Analysis

This section has three parts: The Target Market, Customer Profile, and Competitive Analysis.

The Addressable Market: The Industry, Target Segment, Size, and Growth

This section provides information on the total size of the market, its major segments, the growth rate of those segments, and the specific segments or niches that your business will target. The size of your target niche in the larger market becomes the "addressable market" for your venture. It is part of the lexicon of VCs and other professional investors.

This information needed to define and size your addressable market typically comes from Web or library sources, your own company studies, published government statistics, trade association data, business magazine articles, and so forth. Footnote key sources as part of the credibility game. **You must have data!** You need to be able to prove your choice of target industry segment.

Also in this section, we include a description of major trends that affect buyers and buying behaviors in the target segment. These trends might be regulatory in nature, political threats or concerns, disruptive technologies, new science, or the emergence of new channels to market. This is *environmental scanning*. Entrepreneurs are wise to look for signs of turbulence or chaos in an established market—this presents opportunities for creative problem solving.

Now refer to the templates listed earlier in Figure 11.1 that apply to this particular part of the business plan. We recommend that you use your prior work in Chapter 1, Figure 1.9 and Chapter 2, Figure 2.6 as the supporting data for this section.

Professional investors pride themselves on asking a whole bunch of smart questions. Since our goal in the book is to help you succeed, part of that is making sure you do not get caught unaware. For each of these sections, we have listed the major types of questions that will be on the investor's mind when they read each particular part of the plan. For the Market Analysis section, this is what is likely to be on the investor's mind:

Questions on the Investor's Mind:

a. Is the venture placed in a robust, growing market? Does the entrepreneur have hard, current data to back up his/her assertions that this is a robust market?

b. Has the entrepreneur defined an "addressable" or target niche within a broader market in a manner that is clear, pragmatic, and actionable? For example, are specific customers with specific needs identified?

c. Can the entrepreneur capture 5% to 10% of the defined addressable market over five or six years, and does that represent a large enough company to sell or IPO (to make a ten-times return if the investor is a VC, or five times for an angel or corporate investor)?

d. Are there compelling societal, governmental, technology, or industrial trends that are causing turbulence in a market, creating a compelling need among customers for new solutions? Is the venture riding a "wave" of consumer or industry demand and need?

The Customer Profile and the Compelling Applications/Solutions That They Need

Every entrepreneur needs a clearly defined customer. This section provides specific information about customers' needs and preferences relative to your product and service. You should provide an in-depth profile of the target customer's relative size in terms of the overall market, needs and frustations, current solutions and limitations of those solutions, buying preferences, and needs for related products and services in addition to your own. If there is a difference between the end-user and the buyer, then state that clearly in this section, and list their respective needs and requirements. State how these fundamental insights drive your proposed product or service offerings.

The most effective way to gather this information about customers is to observe and talk to them in their own environment. Go to their place of use, and go to their place of purchase. If you use a questionnaire, summarized responses should be enclosed in an appendix.

If you are a representative customer (which is how many new companies begin), you must still go out into the field to understand the needs of other end-users and buyers. Your own insights will be shaped by what they have to say. A shortcut is to find other organizations or companies that have recently completed a customer requirements market research study. If you can find this, all the power to you. It becomes part of your arsenal.

You should have a wealth of "ammo" for writing this part of the plan from Chapters 2 and 3 of this book. Chapter 3 really digs into these topics and the Reality Check in Chapter 7 should have validated your customer insights. Incorporate the use case scenarios that are the focus of Figure 3.8 and the customer insights in Figure 7.11 into this part of the plan.

Questions on the Investor's Mind:

a. Does the entrepreneur have a crisp picture of the target customer, and the target buyer in terms of what they need and how they buy? Is that based on reading what others have written or firsthand, intimate experience with customers? Has the entrepreneur invested time with customers? Does the entrepreneur have data, or is it just conjecture?

b. How is the entrepreneur's appreciation of the customers' needs special or different than current competitors? Is the entreprenuer addressing problems that no one else is addressing that are or will be a priority within the target market segment?

c. How does that understanding of the target customer translate into a compelling product or service offering? Does the business model proposed by the entrepreneur align with these customer insights?

d. What customers can I visit myself to validate what I am being told? Professional investors will do due diligence by talking to a number of customers on their own as part of their recommendation to their fellow investors. (Your Reality Check in Chapter 7 is the right stuff here. Customer prepayment for a new product or service is even better.)

Competitive Assessment

Competitive assessment identifies either the flaws in your direct competitors or gaps in the market that are not addressed by them. Go down the list of commercial offerings, functions, and features for your competitors. This is far more than a simple Web search, however. If appropriate, go to both the place of sale as well as the place of use for your competitors' products.

One of the primary reasons why investors often shun business plans is that entrepreneurs think that they are the only show in town and simply have not spent the time to understand the strategies and activities of companies already in the market—large as well as small.

Summarize your competitors' marketing concepts and strategies—and their vulnerability. Where are the gaps? How will your venture differentiate? Is it in the area of product or service, in pricing, or in channel? Once again, **you must have data** from competitors or more generally, about existing solutions to the problem you are trying to solve.

Competition doesn't always have to be direct. The real competition for a business-to-business (B2B) venture might be the customer's own internal R&D or IT development teams. If your new product or system is too expensive, they just might say, "Let's build it ourselves." This needs to be factored into the competitive assessment as well.

You've also already done a lot of homework in this area and should bring these data to this section. Specifically, look at what you did in Chapter 6, and in particular Figure 6.3.

Questions on the Investor's Mind:

a. Who are the primary competitors? What are the "big boys" in the mainstream market doing in this area? If they aren't working on it, why not?

b. Is the customer itself a form of competition? How does the venture handle "we can build it ourselves" for corporate customers?

c. What other funded startups are working in this space? Who are the investors, and do I know them? Whom can I call to find out the action that is happening in this space?

d. What are the clear points of competitive differentiation that the entrepreneur is proposing? How is that achieved? By feature, by cost, or by sales capability?

e. How do actual target customers perceive the proposed products or services? What do they think about current competitors? Are customers so loyal to current competition that it will be extremely hard to unseat current suppliers? Once again, what live customer can I check this out with?

f. If this team is successful, are any of the large, established players in the market potential buyers for an exit strategy?

Final Checklist for the Market Analysis Section

The bottom line for the Market Analysis section of the business plan is that anyone listening to you and who reads this section must see:

- That the target market is healthy and growing;

- That you are focused on a specific part or segment of the larger market that is well defined, sizable, and in need of what you have to sell;

- That you deeply know customers' needs; and

- That you can beat "the guys next door."

This section is incredibly important for both a startup and corporate venture. **In many ways, this entire project hinges on the quality of your insight into customers and competitors.** Part Web research and part field research in the place of use and the place of sale, your work here is the foundation of everything to follow. If you do not have a team member with experience in the industry that you wish to start the company, forget it. Look somewhere else!

We typically like to see a few charts or graphs showing size and trend of demand and an exhibit showing competitive offerings.

Writing a business plan that will help raise you money requires that you be highly organized in the research and writing of the plan. To that end, edit the table below to fit your venture and assign team members to the work.

Team Activities for Writing the Market Research Section

Activity Description	Team Lead	Status/Date
Market size, trends, growth rates		
Environmental scanning		
Customer research		
Buyer research (if different than end-users)		
Competitive analysis		

Solutions: Technology, Products, and Services

The purpose of this section is to describe the product and service portfolio, the staging of that portfolio, and the development effort and time needed to get the first product or service in the market. If your venture is to strictly be a reseller, then use this section to define those products and services you hope to distribute to the target market.

This is one of those sections we need to get into some detail not covered in prior chapters. This section should only be several pages with a figure or two. But to write those pages well, you need to learn a lot.

Product Strategy

Here you need to describe your product/systems/service portfolio. Terms such as "good, better, best" often work well here. Also, showing how your portfolio maps out against target market segments or niches can also be a powerful addition to the plan. *Professional investors do not invest in "onesies."* They need to see a product line, or a base-level service that can be customized to particular customer group needs. This is also a good opportunity to describe your "follow-on" or "add-in" strategy for driving recurring revenue.

Don't propose a strategy to conquer the entire world. Start off highly focused. Hand-waving doesn't work here. Understand what you know and what you don't know. Don't make stuff up. If you don't the answer, be honest about that and get back with an answer later.

Another important part of a product strategy is evolution of the portfolio over the first three years of the business. Who is your first target customer in the first year, and what are you selling to that customer? Once you have established this "beachhead," what additional products or services do you wish to bring to market in the second year? What do you propose to add in the third year? Also, are you going to expand from your initial customer group to an adjacent set of customers after several years in business? All these are important in driving a product strategy that has "legs"—that fuels the growth of a dynamic enterprise.

Here again, the work you did earlier in the book should be all that you need to write this section of the plan. Chapter 5 focused on this. Specifically, look at your completed version of Figure 5.5 (the product strategy template). Think about the various examples we discussed in that chapter for "good, better, best," such as the health monitoring systems or the enterprise software company. Then, take a quick look at Figure 5.7 that showed the fishing boots example with all the different applications based off a common boot and sole connection interface. Certainly one of these examples should strike home for your venture. Build that insight into this part of the plan. And at the same time, stage things out. Do not try to create a richly diverse product line or service suite all in the first year. It's best to get an initial set of commercial offerings out as soon as possible, learn as much as you can from the in-market experience, and grow your offerings from there with an even better understanding of customer needs and other market opportunities.

Questions on the Investor's Mind:

a. Is this entrepreneur trying to do too much in the first two years? Is he or she sufficiently focused? (You would be surprised how the well-intentioned enthusiasm of "youth" can produce anxiety in an investor who relishes innovation but also wants to mitigate and manage risk. Yes, go conquer the world, but let's first start by creating a highly focused business providing X to customers Y. Then, we can expand.)

b. After the beachhead is secured, does the entrepreneur truly have a dynamic product or service strategy that can create a niche or segment leader that can provide the investor with a home run?

Product or Service Design

This section is the translation of customer needs and requirements from the Market Analysis section into a new product and service design. What is the minimum level of functonality? What are the added levels? How does the "good, better, best" strategy get added to your offerings? Think of this as the *product or service charter.* It provides a clarity of purpose. A graph or diagram of the product, system, or service design is an important illustration in this part of the plan.

The principles of good product and service design are best learned by example. The one we would like to quickly share with you is of one of Honda's SUVs. Whether the SUV is your cup of tea or not doesn't really matter—it is the approach to translating customer needs into specific designs in various parts of a product or service that does matter.

Figures 11.4 and 11.5 tell the story. Figure 11.4 is an encapsulation of the needs and behaviors of the target customer for this case—the young male driver: socially active, likes to have fun, and uses his vehicle for all sorts of various activities . . . moving in and out of apartments, sports, and partying. These "use cases" are shown in the middle of the figure. Then, on the right side are the major design drivers for Honda's engineers. Figure 11.5 then shows how these engineers implemented concepts to meet these needs into specific parts of the vehicle: a funky exterior styling, B-pillarless clamshell doors for maximum entry/exit allowance, totally flexible seating to create maximum cargo carrying space, and a floor without a stitch of carpeting. Honda even designed a moonroof that is in the back of the vehicle and pops off entirely to move large bookcases.[1] Our friend who was one of the lead engineering managers on the Element told us how his team systematically translated these customer needs into specific subsystems designs, step by step. And then, the management team would look at the integrated whole to make sure that the result was balanced and fit within the product's tight cost constraints—another end-user need!

---

[1] Meyer, M. H. (2008, May). Perspectives: How Honda innovates. *The Journal of Product Innovation Management, 25*(3), 261–271.

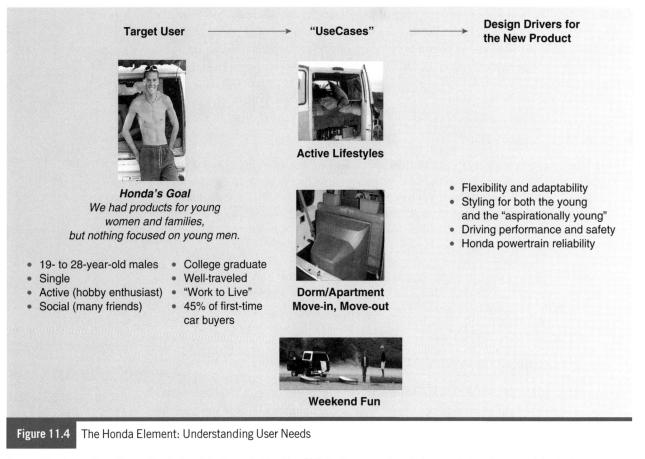

Figure 11.4   The Honda Element: Understanding User Needs

Source: Honda case from Meyer, *The Fast Path to Corporate Growth*, 2007; Portions reproduced with permissions from Honda Motor Company.

The same approach works for software and services. One of the teaching cases in this book (Sentillion) is of a software engineer who tackled the problem of doctors having to log in with different IDs and passwords to a dozen or more computer systems used in a hospital for patient care over the course of a day. Rob Seliger and his team invented a "single sign-on" software product, front-ended with a biometric thumbprint reader, that the physician used just once and then the software did all the rest for all the information systems the doctor had to access. Rob's venture became the market leader in secure sign-on for the health care industry—and Rob's company was acquired ten years down the road for close to five times its annual revenue!

Now, you should think about Honda or Rob and try to do the same thing for your venture. Design a solution that speaks to the needs of the customer in a direct, compelling way. Be the product yourself, and then think about how you can best bring a smile to the customer's face. Then, draw some sketches to capture your thinking. Frame these into an interesting, meaningful exhibit as an appendix in the business plan.

Questions on the Investor's Mind:

a. Are the insights discovered and presented in the Market Analysis section driven into a compelling base-level product, system, or service design? Does that design "sing?" Or, do we need to get some professional product designers on the case? That's okay, but it will cost me more money.

B-pillarless for maximum entry/egress
Clamshell wide aperture tailgate

Flexible seating

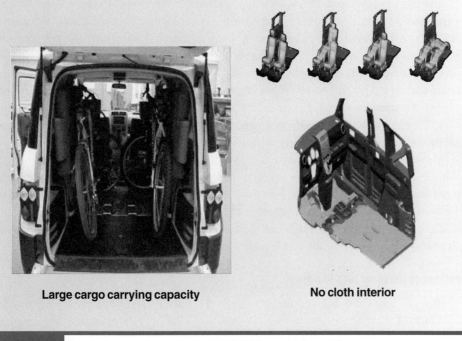

Large cargo carrying capacity

No cloth interior

Figure 11.5 Translating Needs Into Designs: Flexibility and Adaptability

Source: Honda case from Meyer, *The Fast Path to Corporate Growth*, 2007; Portions reproduced with permissions from Honda Motor Company.

b. Is this entrepreneur trying to do too much in terms of product or service development the first two years? Can we get an initial offering out to market faster and see if it actually appeals to customers?

Proprietary Technology, Intellectual Property

For biotech, medical device, materials, and energy ventures, and to some extent even software ventures, you would be surprised how the IP issue can be a show-stopper for professional investors. This is often an essential component in technology-focused businesses because *IP can create an "unfair" winning advantage.* If you haven't figured out an IP strategy, the investor may walk away.

When entrepreneurs think about intellectual property, they think about patents. Patents, which are applied for through the United States Patent and Trademark Office (http://www .uspto.gov), are typically prepared by an attorney—and hopefully—one with lots of experience working through this process. The manner and method in which patent applications are filed takes time, experience, and to varying degrees, familiarity with the area of science or technology involved in the patent. The classic patent is a "design patent"—which is the design or architecture of a new invention. Once a patent is received—a process that now typically takes several years—it is still up to the entrepreneur to enforce the patent against copycats. Your legal "monopoly" lasts for 17 years from the date that the patent is issued.

There are also patents which can be granted for the creation of a new business method in the most general sense. New workflows or methods for accomplishing a given task count here. Entrepreneurs often try to patent new business methods and models. For example, there are patents surrounding various aspects of online auctioning, or risk management in life insurance, or even the delivery of rich media content over mobile networks.

Bottom line, if you are starting a technology-intensive venture, you need to find yourself an experienced IP attorney and get a read on whether your idea is patentable. But first, ask the attorney about the patent application process. If the attorney is vague, they may not be a specialist. If, however, the attorney goes into lots of specifics and speaks to examples of inventions in your field of work, then you might have the right person. Also, get a read on the cost of filing a patent, starting at $7,000 to $10,000 for a simple technology or method and running upwards of $50,000 for complex filings. However, this is one of those cases where you get what you pay for. Go with an inexperienced, cheap attorney, and you can waste a year and get turned down by the Patent Office for the very same idea that an expensive attorney would have filed successfully.

Most entrepreneurs working technology spaces work with an attorney to take the initial step of filing a "provisional patent application." This is a relatively short summary description of the design or method patent that serves as a placeholder for 12 months from the filing date, in which time the entrepreneur can spend the time and money to develop a full-fledged patent application—and you can use the words "patent pending."

Questions on the Investor's Mind:

a. Is there any IP in this venture, and does the entrepreneur appreciate the importance of it for the value of the company?

b. Is the entrepreneur's proposal to create a true barrier to entry with IP believable? The investor then asks him or herself, "Who do I know who can punch holes in this theory?"

c. Is the entrepreneur working with a law firm that is good in this area? Or, do I have to find a better one for them?

Underlying Platforms

Platforms are shared subsystems that are used across multiple products or services. They can also be a common production process used for multiple products or services. A product platform might be the same engine used across different types of vehicles. Honda, for example, shares powertrains across its passenger cars and SUVs. A software platform might be a common database management system that stores and provides access to the data used by multiple applications. Oracle Financials, for example, uses the Oracle database as an underlying platform. A service platform might be an insurance company's rules and procedures for risk management that are then adapted to specific indiviuals or groups applying for life, health, or property insurance. A production platform might be common manufacturing or information technology assets used in all three cases above. Platforms create *points of leverage to reduce cost of goods sold (COGS) for individual products or services and speed time to market* for new ones.[2]

Platforms fit within a broader product line or service *architecture*. That architecture shows all the major subsystems or building blocks used within the product or service. A platform is simply one of those building blocks that is used time and time again across multiple specific offerings. Today, everything has become so modular that it is common to see that certain platforms used internally within a product or service are actually licensed from a third party. For example, if you are making a new software application—say to help a hospital collect all its money—you would be foolish to spend the time and money needed to build your own database management system. MySQL or Postgres are perfectly fine and extremely powerful database management systems that, for starters, are free! The same would apply for Google's Android operating system for developing mobile applications. Or, you might decide to license (and pay for) one of Microsoft's own powerful toolkits because your business is focused on the Windows marketplace. Either way, you need a paragraph that explicitly describes what portions of the product or service are licensed from the outside versus developed in-house. Here, once again, a single diagram accompanied by a brief technology description serves the purpose.

As an entrepreneur, you need to be prepared to articulate the underlying design or architecture of your product or service, its major components, and those that over time will prove to be your own powerful platforms.

Questions on the Investor's Mind:

a. Is there the possibility of creating a product or service platform that becomes an industry-wide standard for the next generation of technology in their industry?

b. Are these folks being smart about R&D? Are they trying to recreate the entire solution stack?

Development Plan and Key Milestones

This should also be a brief written section, accompanied by a short milestone table for developing your product or service. For most technology-intensive ventures, the typical flightplan is:

• Complete the "alpha" version and show it to key prospective customers.

• Complete the "beta" version and provide it to a few select customers for actual use. If you have done your work well, there shouldn't be much difference between the beta and the final commercial release.

• Complete and release Version 1.0.

• Develop and release follow-on features and improvements for the next version.

In a software company, typical time periods are three months to alpha, and an additional three to six months to get to beta and commercial release respectively. The terms also apply to a new retail concept, where there is a design of the store layout and merchandizing (alpha/beta depending on your point of view), and the opening of the first store (the "beta" or Version 1.0, again depending on if your plan is from the start to open a multistore operation). Designing and opening a new store, with all the various commercial contracts required in the process, tends to be a six-month journey. For a consumer packaged goods venture, a year's effort from concept to commercial release is also not unrealistic, particularly if you use outside subcontracted manufacturers for production. And the "alpha" is used for customer research, the "beta" for a local or

---

[2] Meyer, M. H., & Lehnerd, A. P. (1997). *The Power of Product Platforms: Building Value Cost Leadership*. New York: Free Press.

regional test market with select retailers, and "commercial release" the beginning of national distribution. However, if you are working in the biotech space, there is an entirely different set of terms and time cycle calculus—FDA-mandated milestones take years for each major step!

Beyond your strategy for getting the work done, investors also want to see someone on the team who has had the experience of successfully bringing a new product or service from the idea stage to commercialization, someone with judgment, maturity, and strong organizational skills to run new product or systems development—even if the original "insight" comes from younger, brilliant engineers or scientists!

There are also many other things that a venture must do to launch a product—such as developing marketing collateral, tradeshow attendance, and promotion. Incorporate these, however, in the Sales section of the business plan.

Questions on the Investor's Mind:

a. Do they have a sense of urgency? Do they understand "agile development"—develop, test, and develop some more?

b. Can they get the work done? Do I need to make the founding technologist a CTO and bring on an experienced product development or IT manager?

c. Do they know who their beta customers are going to be? (Note: For a consumer packaged product, it's the first retailer; for a B2B software or service, the first large account; for a medical device/product, the test or clinical trial partner.)

Development Costs

We like to see a short section on the costs associated with R&D for your major milestones included in this section of the business plan. These costs then tie into the Financial Projections section of your business plan, first as part of the Assumptions and next, a part of the Proforma P&L (e.g., the projected income statement for the venture). You need to think about in-house engineers or programmers, testers, fees to partner developers, and any sort of licensing costs incurred in developing the product, system, or service. It is easy to scare investors away without a good manager of projects on a team. It is also easy to scare investors by being totally unrealistic about how much it will really cost to get a functional product to market. Investors want realism, good R&D management, and a bunch of doers who are hungry to create new products.

Questions on the Investor's Mind:

a. Do they have an engineer who knows what is at stake? Can they make a deadline? Do they know that "the Perfect gets in the way of the Good"? My money is at risk here, and I need a product in the market as soon as possible.

b. Do they have a solid core team driving development (be it for a product or a system or to design a new store)? Do they already know who they want to bring on board for key positions if I give them the money? Are they doers or managers of process? (If not, that could be a **problem**).

c. Is this venture going to cost twice as much as they think it is going to cost to get product ready for market?

Final Checklist

The reader needs to walk away with the impression of:

- A robust product and service strategy that will offer choice as well as value to the target customer.

- An understanding of what it takes to develop commercially viable products or services. If you don't have a member of your team with engineering (for products) or domain expertise (for services), you had better find someone with that experience to be a part of your team or at least advise you.

- If your venture is a technology venture, the reader wants to see an IP strategy and understand why your IP is potentially valuable to other companies in the industry.

In this section of the business plan, it is also customary to see diagrams or higher-level schematics of the product or systems architecture. If you are solving a workflow problem, a diagram of the "before" and "after" workflow would make for an excellent exhibit. You can also include a diagram that shows how your product family or services roll out over the first three or so years of the business. Also, if you have prototypes, include product prototype pictures in an appendix. Definitely bring these prototypes to your investor presentations.

A word for technologists here: Even though you could easily write 30 pages in this section, **don't.** You do not want to tell the reader specific technical details in this document—just technology strategies.

Team Activities for Writing the Solutions and Technology Section

Activity Description	Team Member (s)	Status/Date
Product strategy		
Product, system, or service design		
Intellectual property		
Underlying architecture and platforms		
Development plan and key milestones		
R&D cost plan		

Sales Plan: Customer Targets, Distribution, Branding, and Pricing

Executives and investors are going to want to see three basic things in the Sales Plan:

- That you understand the importance of selling—and will not short-change investment in building sales capability in the first years of the business.

- That your go-to-market strategy is spot-on with the target buyer for your venture. This requires a tight "fit" between your **channels,** where and how the customer prefers to buy, and a compatabililty between the features and price of the product and the channels selected.

- That your **promotional strategy** is similarly compelling and forceful.

- That you have a compelling **brand** that will resonate with the customer.

- That you have a good strategy for scaling distribution once a successful launch is achieved.

There are a few basics on developing go-to-market strategies that are well worthwhile reviewing here before getting into elements of specific sections of this part of the business plan.

Simply put, think of the distribution channel as the pipeline through which your product/ service flows. The key to success to selecting the appropriate channel is to be the product, system, and service yourself, and then see how you would prefer most to be brought into the hands of the customer. Sounds simple, but it is a technique that tells you a lot! This, combined with your customer research from Chapter 3 and the business model strategy you developed in Chapter 4 (Figure 4.12), should be all that you need to know the proper path to market for your commercial offerings.

There are a number of direct channels. The most obvious is a direct sales force—salespeople who are employed by your company to sell its products, systems, or services to the customer. Ventures are well served having a good salesperson on the team from early on to help sell the first one or two customers. Nothing proves the merit of a venture concept like real customer money, and it typically takes great skill and persistance to achieve this for a company that is new and doesn't have any other customers! You also have to be very careful bringing on salespeople. They need to have a track record of success in your target industry—not just a good style but also customers who you can call to find out what it was like to be sold to by this particular individual. Entrepreneurs in B2B ventures probably make more mistakes hiring their first one or two salespeople than in any other area. The entrepreneur gets sold a "pipeline" by the salesperson that simply never materializes. Month after month, the only thing that gets done is that your precious cash disappears on travel expenses and base salary. And we have found that the only way to hire correctly is to have one experienced salesperson hire other salespeople. That means having such a person as a team member and, just as well, as a trusted advisor. You can never be too careful about who you hire to represent your company in the field, and you will depend on these people to produce the lifeblood of your company—customer revenue.

There are of course other direct channels. Your venture might have its own retail stores or its own e-commerce Website. Or, you might find it best to propose a multichannel option in your business plan—combining a retail channel, for example, with a direct Web or mail order channel. For example, your authors sometimes purchase fishing gear from a company called Cabela's. Cabela's started off as a catalogue mail order business for outdoor sportsmen. It then opened its own retail stores, first in the Midwest, and is now expanding across the country. And, it now has a robust Web order business. Since it owns all three channels, these are all "direct to consumer." L.L.Bean does the same.

Then, there many different types of indirect channels or selling intermediaries. These include:

- **Retailers** obviously sell directly to the end-users or consumers of products. Increasingly, they are selling services as well. For example, in the pet food industry, PetSmart now houses the Banfield veterinarian clinics as well, becoming a one-stop shop for the consumer. **Dealers** are typically synonymous with retailers, and your automotive dealer will be trying to sell you XM satellite radio and extended warranty services in addition to the vehicle itself. In the boating industry, for example, boat manufacturers reach the public through a network of boat dealers—who themselves, tend to carry three or four different brands of boats. Retailers or dealers expect to make a 30% to 50% margin on the end-user price of a product, and generally, less margin for add-on services.

- **Distributors** are intermediaries who perform a variety of distribution functions, including holding inventory and marketing to and supplying retailers. Typically, a distributor buys your products at a price that provides it with 5% to 10% margin on the final customer price of the product. Distributors tend to cover an entire region or country for a certain class of product or service. **Wholesalers** are typically synonymous with distributors.

- **Agents** are intermediaries who market a product/service for a fee. These are often referred to as a manufacturer's agent or selling agent. You might retain an agent, for example, to find distributors or retailers in a foreign market or to get you into the front door of a large national retailer. Be sure to ask for evidence of the agent's effectiveness before signing an agreement! Many entrepreneurs have been promised "the moon," paid hefty monthly retainer fees for six months, and not seen a single penny in additional revenue. Do not be one of them!

• **Brokers** are intermediaries who bring buyers and sellers together to negotiate purchases. They do not take title to anything but tend to work on some type of commission basis. You will find numerous brokers across the various financial services industries, for example.

• **OEMs** are manufacturers through whom you sell products or systems where these are included as part of their own manufactured products. The term "OEM" stands for "original equipment manufacturer" and one tends to find the term used in the computer and automobile industries. For example, one of your author's first companies sold its real-time operating system software on an OEM basis to the old Digital Equipment Corporation (DEC). DEC bundled that software onto its mini and desktop computers. (One of our favorite applications was process control for brewing beer!) OEMs offer the promise of high volumes and in return expect to buy your product at a huge discount (sometimes up to 70%) of whatever "list price" you might establish. OEMs also take a lot of upfront work because your component or software has to be designed into their own systems.

• **VARs** are "value-added resellers" who buy your products (typically computer hardware and software or devices of some sort) and then add their own software and services as part of the sale to the customer. VARs tend to also expect a significant discount off your list price, in the range of 30% to 40%. The great thing about VARs in certain high-tech industries is that they are focused on a specific vertical market or niche and have highly specialized direct sales forces that work directly with accounts in that niche. At the same time, VARs need support. You will have to assign an engineer to work with the VAR's own engineering staff to learn how to make your products or systems sing and integrate them with other technologies in their solution stack.

With indirect channels, you can also have a multichannel strategy—but here you must proceed with utmost caution. Many software companies sell both through retailers and directly to consumers through the Web. Just think of Intuit or Symantec for examples of well-managed, multichannel strategies in software. Microsoft adds to this with a robust OEM strategy—with its software bundled by manufacturers onto their own computers.

This does not mean that the independent retailers are happy. Further, this type of channel conflict—offering two ways to buy the same product—can confuse the buyer. It can also lead various channel partners to begin to discount your products in order to get the sale. As soon as that happens, even the best product can be blemished. Salespeople tend to say the best things about the products with which they make the highest commissions. Salespeople rarely present discounted products as the best choice to customers, because the salesperson doesn't make as much money selling those products as others that are not discounted. Moreover, a channel partner is making an important commitment to your company by carrying your product. This involves training its own sales force and comarketing your product or service. They will be maddened if your own sales force or Website steals customers away from their own sales staff. If you are going to use channel partners, your commitment must be to support *their sales* as best you can.

Becoming a channel for other companies that disintermediates current suppliers and channel members has become a valid venture concept in its own right. **Disintermediation** means the removal or bypassing of established channel players to reach customers directly. In many ways, the Web has disintermediated many industries, allowing producers of products and services to develop direct relationships with customers. Apple bypassed the music stores with its iTunes, becoming the dominant new channel for content owners (e.g., the major record labels). Now, iTunes offers a lot more than just music to its loyal followers. Zappos is another example. This powerful online fashion merchandiser specializes in contemporary shoes and apparel backed up with best-in-class delivery and customer service. It disintermediated traditional shoe retailers. Started only in 1999 outside of Las Vegas as an online retailer, Zappos was approaching a billion dollars in sales before it was acquired by Amazon in 2010!

Beyond such dramatic venture successes, there is a long established history of successful software companies adding incremental streams of revenue to their P&Ls by becoming a channel for third-party software developers. The software company externalizes its own software libraries as an SDK (software development kit) and markets its ability to provide access to customers to other independent software firms. These firms build applications on top of the venture's own software environment and are then marketed on the venture's Website as add-on applications. Not only does the venture receive a small sales commission, but it also presents a broader solutions portfolio to current and prospective customers. This is not disintermediation, per se, but it is becoming a channel in your own right—a "Pied Piper" for a community of like-minded software developers.

Think about how this concept has any application to your own venture.

Source: Illustration by Kate Greenaway (1846–1901). Copyright expired and in the public domain.

**** **** ****

We also need to go through a few principles of "branding," because branding will be an important aspect of this part of the business plan. The first thing that every reader sees when they get your business plan is the name of your company—on the cover page in a very large font. That name is a cornerstone of your branding strategy! Then, they will try to go to your Website. What will they see? What will they feel? Will it be powerful, meaningful, and speaking to customer value? Or, the opposite—just another Website, confused or vacant in terms of its messaging, and nerdy instead of speaking to customer value.

To the basics: A **brand** is a name, sign, symbol, design, or combination of these elements intended to identify the offerings of one company and to differentiate them from those of the competition. The brand embodies your offer of value—your promise—to the customer. It can and should be a powerful asset, developed and managed.[3] There is both the name and the visual aspect and logo surrounding the name. Both are incredibly important in the eyes of the customer.

We think that the best way to approach all of this is to establish a "brand architecture" for your company. It starts with the name of your company and the messaging behind that name. For example, we all know Apple, and the messaging behind Apple is "easy to use." Then, there is IBM—(which originally stood for International Business Machines)—with a dual messaging on complex systems and services for a "Smarter Planet" and being a trusted partner for client organizations. Then, comes the naming and messages of specific product lines or services. Apple's "Mac" brand includes a number of computer and peripheral products, just as its "i" brand covers a range of products and services. Then comes the naming and branding of individual elements within its product line or service: MacBook, MacBook Pro, and MacBook Air; or iPod, iPhone, iPad, and of course, iTunes. Apple has a created a robust brand architecture and spends heavily to promote both broad and individual product/service messages within it. Apple's overall branding, as well as its individual product and service branding, is wonderfully clear, upbeat, and meaningful to target customers.

Brand name and the visual icon and imagery around the name need to follow certain rules. You want the branding to be directly relevant to the customer—to speak to the distinctive value you wish to offer them. The word and images need to "resonate." It would also be great if all the specific elements within the brand architecture were mutually reinforcing, consistent, and unifying. Moreover, from our chapter on business models, it would be great if your branding work could support some type of premium pricing for great new products and services. In other words, do not use messaging such as "good and cheap." If cheap is anywhere around your company, the established Walmarts of the world are always going to win the attention of the target consumer who wants low prices. Rather, emphasize the value you provide to customers. You can see this type of thinking in many of the cases provided with this book: My M&M'S (personalized M&M's); Catch a Piece of Maine (a gifting service that supports the lobster fishery of Maine); Generate (a company that helps B2B sales forces generate and learn about leads into companies); and SilverRail Technologies (a portal for providing open seats for intercity rail travel in different countries). These are direct, meaningful company names that begin the branding process. Then, each is supported by specific product or service names—and the entire lot by Websites, advertising, and other forms of promotion.

In addition, when it comes to product names, we suggest the following simple but important checklist:

- The name should suggest key product benefits. For example, "Bug-Be-Gone" clearly describes the benefits of purchasing this product.

- The name should be distinctive and convey a positive meaning.

- The name should fit the company or product image.

---

[3] Good resources to learn about the basics of branding are: K. Keller's, *Strategic Brand Management* (Mahwah, NJ: Prentice Hall, 1998); Leslie de Chernatory and Malcolm McDonald's, *Creating Powerful Brands* (London: Butterworth Heinemann, 1992); and Philip Kotler and Gary Armstrong's, *Principles of Marketing*, 10th ed. (Upper Saddle River, NJ: Pearson, 2004).

- The name should have no legal or regulatory restrictions. (Increasingly, brand names need a corresponding address on the Internet. This further complicates name selection because millions of domain names are already registered.)

- The name should be easy to pronounce and remember.

- The name should have an emotional appeal.

- The name should translate easily into foreign languages.

We must emphasize that branding is not something that the entrepreneur can leave to three or four years down the road. Jump on it right away! Your own venture's branding is important for competitive differentiation. If you brand well, this also helps ease the perceived risk or fear that a prospective customer might have in purchasing goods or services from a new company. It allows them to recognize you and to understand the core value that you wish to bring to them. And, good branding does not always require a lot of money. In fact, you can start right away by implementing a carefully considered brand, imagery, and messaging right on your company's new Website.

With this information as the foundation, now we can turn to writing this part of the business plan.

**** **** ****

Customer Targets

In many businesses, the primary user is not the primary buyer; the grocer versus the consumer; the pet owner versus the pet; the IT department versus the office worker; the logistics department manager versus the truck driver. In this section of the business plan, you need to be specific about this difference if it exists for your product, system, or service. Then, if there is a difference, you need to get very specific about the needs and wants of these buyers. Approaches used in the Market Analysis section for customers should apply here to buyers: industry description, size, growth rate, buyer needs and concerns, and the best way to reach these buyers.

B2B enterprise selling is complex. One of the first things an investor is going to want to know are the key stakeholders in a company who are part of the purchase decision—and how long that extends the sales cycle. In tough economic climates, the sales cycle extends even longer.

Questions on the Investor's Mind:

a. If the buyer is not the end-user, does the team have a deep and clear of an understanding of the buyer as they do about the end-user? Is there any sort of seasonal or calendar type of buying cycle? How and where do these buyers become informed about new products?

b. Is "the sale" a lot more complex than the team is presenting in its plan? If this is a B2B venture, who are other key stakeholders in a business customer that need to be influenced in favor of the venture's products or services?

c. Is this something that has to be sold face to face, or can they use telemarketing? Face to face is going to be very expensive—but if it necessary, so be it.

d. Does the team also know about the buyer's preferred buying amounts/volumes and financing methods for purchases?

Trade/Channel Strategy

In this part of the plan, you need to describe the channel structure, that is, if it is direct to the customer or through intermediaries. If you will use middlemen, describe who they are, their location, and importantly, their standard margins. If you are going to pursue multiple channels, how will they be synchronized and how will you avoid channel conflict?

As many an entrepreneur has learned (the hard way), the biggest channel partner is not necessarily the best, because they may be carrying a thousand other products in addition to yours. For example, you will find new food products appearing in Whole Foods Market as opposed to a traditional, large grocer such as Kroger's or Walmart. Same might go for targeting the True Value hardware stores as opposed to The Home Depot. The larger outfits have a tendency to not want to work with small firms who have limited resources to promote their new brands and a limited number of SKUs (stock-keeping units) to create on-shelf brand awareness—in other words, a lot of bother for not a lot of money. If working with a Home Depot or Walmart is part of your launch strategy, you had better show that you understand what it takes to reach an agreement with a large channel partner and demonstrate some type of access to that partner. When working with any large, established retailer, the details of developing marketing collateral, a sampling program, and a cooperative marketing program can be overwhelming for the inexperienced. Here, too, there is no substitute for experience. If you plan to sell products through a major retailer, get either a direct team member or a gray-haired advisor who has successfully launched products "to trade" in a prior job. This will make your work proceed much faster.

Perhaps more important, an initial set of conversations with buying decision-makers in large channel partners of any sort, or store owners in small independent chains, is an essential part of doing your homework prior to pitching investors. How else is an investor going to know that you can deliver the channel in your plan as well as the revenue associated with that channel?

Another important element in this section of the business plan is to describe your activities regarding supporting the channel, be it for your own direct sales force or a channel partner, and to determine what it takes to make the seller successful. This might include training and product samples.

It goes almost without saying that for whatever channel strategy you choose, you must understand the margins and incentives needed to motivate your sales force and channel partners.

For those of you selling through your own direct sales force, do not be cheap with commissions. Consider *increasing* the sales commission percentages for superstar salespeople. That might mean 5% plus base for the first $1 million, 7% for the next $500,000, 9% for the next $500,000, and so forth. If these superstars end up making more salary than you (as the CEO), you should be delighted. Every extra dollar they bring into the company increases the value of your company and your owner's equity. In fact, show a good salesperson how they can make more cash salary than you and challenge them to do it! Also, any good B2B or channel salesperson is going to want you to go on the road with them to meet customers and help drive revenue. Do it!

An understanding of the sales pipeline is critical. For many technology industries, the typical ratio is to have 3:1, three times the number revenue opportunities in the pipeline compared to monthly revenue goal. The VC is going to ask you this—and you need to know the answer for your industry sector. And salespeople have got to be closers—that means seeing their performance against quota for the past three years. Then, you must do your own due diligence to make sure that candidate hit his or her numbers.

Questions on the Investor's Mind:

a. Is there anyone on board who has "carried a bag" for a living? (That means sold products or services for a living.) If there isn't, would the founders ever listen to what a saleperson might tell them about what it takes to sell effectively? This is where many small companies fail.

b. Success in a venture is all about revenue—at least in the first couple of years. Do these folks understand how to "engineer" revenue as much as they understand how to engineer their product or service?

c. Do they understand what it takes to prime a channel—to get the sellers in that channel competent in demonstrating and selling the venture's wares?

Branding, Advertising, and Promotion

Describe your company's brand architecture: the company name, the name of its product or service lines, and then, the specific product names. Also describe the messaging around this branding. Then, in just a few sentences, explain why this branding is relevant and truly meaningful to your target customers. Do you have any data—such as data from your reality check—that proves this? And, how does your branding differentiate your venture from current competitors?

Then, you need to briefly describe the venture's promotional efforts in terms of **the message** and **the media** or other form of promotional outlet, such as tradeshows. Investors will also want you to have done your homework on the cost of these different venues and work that into your projected P&L. Moreover, if you select a particular promotional channel, it must be one that is respected and used by the target customer. These are expensive and important investments.

Questions on the Investor's Mind:

a. How much work are these folks going to need to make a first-rate impression in their target market?

b. Do they have an attractive Website right now? If not, is that because they are working in stealth mode or don't really care about marketing? And if they have a Website, what is the messaging conveyed? Solutions? Reliability? Customer value? Or, just a tech or services shop?

c. Do I like what they are going to call their product or service? Does it make any sense to the target customer?

d. Are their approaches for generating awareness and demand appropriate for a startup venture? Are they being clever about how they want to spend my money? Have they thought about how to get free publicity?

Pricing Strategy

This is where you bring to bear your research on competitors and the positioning of your products or services. Using the words "premium" or "parity" or "discount" are important signals for investors. Even though we are fans of the low initial volume, premium pricing revenue model, it is okay to have predatory pricing to gain share. Just look at Twitter or the early years of Google. However, you are going to have to prove to the reader in the Financials section of the business plan that you have a strategy for making money, typically within a one- or two-year period from startup.

This is also where you should add the concept of recurring revenue. Think about the following types of questions for your venture:

- If you are providing a physical product of one form or another, what will you charge and what accessories and services might be provided with the core product?

- If it is software, will you be selling plug-ins and/or charging maintenance fees? If it is a service, will you be providing a "good, better, best" suite of value-added services?

- Does bundling mean anything for your business—such as combining different products together at a price break for customers?

- If you are going to be a reseller for other firms' products or services, what do you expect to be your commission off list price?

Your reality check in Chapter 7 should have tested the concepts of additional products and services, bundling, and overall pricing relative to competitors. If you have the data, this is the place to use it!

Questions on the Investor's Mind:

a. Does the entrepreneur's price support the positioning of the venture relative to competitors?

b. Are they giving stuff away just to get customers, and what type of precedent will that set in the company? A reference account or two based on a "freebie" is okay, but how does that translate into hard revenue soon afterwards?

c. Has he or she thought cleverly about how to make additional money from hard-won customers? Is that thinking also part of the R&D plan?

Layout and Merchandizing (for Retail Ventures or Retailed Product Ventures Only)

A diagram of your proposed store layout or on-shelf/in-store display would be a very useful exhibit here. The investor wants to see that you appreciate key principles of merchandizing—where to place things in a store and how to place them for your target customer. If you are providing products to sit on retailers' shelves, how will you draw attention to SKUs in a crowded retail environment? Will it be with in-store sampling and displays or posters? Will it be through a point of sale "shipper" or rack? Here, too, an experienced hand on the team or a trusted advisor can make all the difference for a successful launch. You can also learn a lot by calling local vendors who are in the business of creating these materials.

The Question on the Investor's Mind:

a. Do the entrepreneurs really know what they are talking about? Let's go to a store together and see. It will also be a great opportunity to do a quick competitive check.

Final Checklist

Should you receive funding for your venture, a lot of money and effort over the next five years is going to be allocated to building a powerful go-to-market capability. More than any other section in the business plan, these four (and if your venture is a retail product, five) elements must fit together in a cohesive, pragmatic, and affordable fashion. This is a great opportunity to apply everything that you should have learned in your marketing classes—and even better—work experience into creating a dynamic market strategy for your own business. Perhaps more important, the investor must come away convinced that you have sales experience on your team and that you have truly listened to those team members. If you don't have a person with selling and channel experience, find that person and include him or her on your team or as a trusted advisor.

Team Activities for Writing the Sales Section:

Activity Description	Team Member (s)	Status/Date
Understanding the target buyer		
Channel strategy		
Branding and promotion		
Pricing strategy		
Layout and merchandising		

Operations, Production, and Supply

This section typically describes the "back end" of your company—all the important activities that happen outside of R&D and sales or distribution. For most businesses, this section is critical because the management of production and manufacturing, and of the suppliers that come before manufacturing, is the key to achieving operating profit. The buzzwords are easy to say—low-cost, high-quality suppliers or low-cost, high-quality manufacturing—but hard to achieve. At this point in your business planning, what you need to do most is to show readers that you understand the importance of these matters and have developed some excellent if not world-class options for your venture.

Figure 11.6 shows the key elements that you need to consider in writing this section. All you really need for the purposes of a business plan are *strategies* for each of these elements—suppliers, production, logistics/fulfillment, and customer service—that fit together in a cohesive and coherent manner and are then carried forward as base-level assumptions in your financial projections to drive cost of goods, operating expenses, and investments in "plant and equipment." Keep it simple, and keep it real.

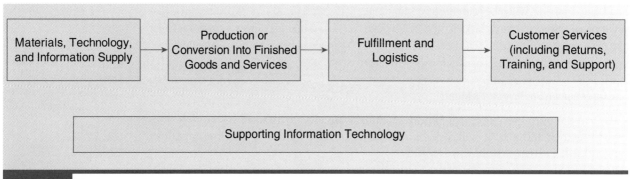

Figure 11.6   Key Elements in Operations, Production, and Supply

The thinking behind each of these is to make smart decisions about *what you do in-house, what you do external to the company,* and for those areas that are external, being very careful about the external partners with whom you are going to entrust a major chunk of your operations. For example, if you are going to be shipping physical products directly to consumers or businesses, use UPS or FedEx, not some other fly-by-night operation that might cost a little less. This holds true for all other expects of the supply chain. What you put into your product, how it is put together, how it is delivered, and how it is serviced *all matter.* And a poor choice of partner in any one of these areas can lead to a tarnished image in the eyes of the customer—just like an ineffective salesperson or channel partner.

Managing Suppliers

The world is your oyster here. A simple Web search will quickly reveal all the major suppliers of components that might go into your product. That might be food ingredients, electronic components, entire computers, or chemicals. Select one or two well-known suppliers that match your venture's needs and then call their sales offices to find unit prices based on volumes. Use the most sensible of these choices in your financial projections. Or, if your company is making a software product, what are the toolkits that you or your engineers want to use, and what is the cost of these toolkits? (This might be somewhat redundant to text in the R&D section of your business plan—but that is okay.) Here, you need to talk about ongoing licensing or "run-time" costs for deploying these tools in volume. Most entrepreneurs are looking to Red Hat, MySQL (now owned by Oracle), or Microsoft for low-cost tools solutions—that are nonetheless, extremely powerful. If your venture focuses on technology-intensive services, these days that means getting your hands on streams of data, crunching those data, and incorporating the results into services for target customers. A great example is the "Generate" teaching case in this book. That business created a specialized search engine that crunched through thousands of real-time news feeds from around the world. Even better, the entrepreneurs got one of the providers of those news feeds to provide growth capital. The supplier became the equity investor!

Managing Production

In the "old days," entrepreneurs would carefully design and install their own production equipment and processes and then gradually ramp up production to meet growing demand. However, today, just as products have become modular, companies have as well. Many entrepreneurs now find larger, well-established manufacturers who will cut, shape, extrude, and otherwise assemble finished products on a subcontract per unit basis. The good ones have extensive quality control systems that would take years and considerable sums for an entrepreneur to develop on his or her own.

At the same time, there is also risk in externalizing production. You need to invest considerable time and effort specifying materials to be used for both the product and packaging and do systematic sampling of outputs to make sure that finished products meet your quality standards. If you can get a patent on some aspect of design, this provides you with some measure of protection against deceitful contract manufacturers. But vendors need to be carefully investigated and contracts written carefully to provide penalties for late delivery and poor quality. And of course, the availability of subcontract manufacturers is industry specific. The bottom line, however, is that this is an option that every entrepreneur should explore before writing a business plan that requires millions of dollars to buy, install, test, and operate dedicated machines. This transforms "fixed costs" into variable costs—a good working principle for entrepreneurs.

If you work for a large corporation and are planning an internal corporate venture, there will be considerable pressure for you to use existing plant and equipment. Executives reading your plan might say, "Let's give them a shift on one of our lines." Be careful, however. The overheads on those manufacturing lines might be totally acceptable per unit when there are thousands of units being produced each and every shift. However, for your small initial volumes, the overheads can be crushing—so much so, that the resulting COGS may kill your business altogether. Run the numbers, talk to people, and if you need to use a less expensive subcontractor to get started, be sure to support your strategy with numbers. You will need them.

Even businesses that do not make physical products can benefit from the same approach. For example, companies making complex software can "rent" machines from Amazon's cloud computing business unit at a truly fractional cost for extra computing power. Or, a service business that needs to crunch huge amounts of data in the delivery of its service can contract with any one of thousands of infrastructure service providers who will host your key applications. And most entrepreneurs go to a service provider to build and host their Websites—particularly those requiring e-commerce capabilities.

This is another area where getting that gray-haired advisor who has manufacturing and supply management experience in your target industry can be of tremendous help. When it comes to manufacturing, or using subcontract manufacturers, there is no replacement for field experience. There are just too many details and too many potholes where an inexperienced entrepreneur can make a critical error without knowing it. This is particularly true for entrepreneurs seeking low-cost manufacturing partners abroad. Knowing the lay of the land in an offshore business environment is essential for successfully negotiating business agreements and nurturing a productive working relationship with offshore partners.

Managing Logistics/Fulfillment

This one is getting easier and easier. For small packages, there is UPS and FedEx. For larger shipments, there are dozens of well-established third-party logistics firms that will organize the shipment of your containers around the world, handling customs and other regulatory affairs that would take the typical entrepreneur years to learn. For ventures providing software, the Web is the logistics channel. Simply go to Symantec or salesforce.com (http://www.salesforce.com) to see how online subscription management and software/services delivery should be done.

Stepping back, the message here is *do not* buy your own trucks, or do not print manuals or CDs unless your business or customers absolutely demand it. It is better to invest your capital into R&D to create new innovations and into sales programs to generate revenue from those innovations.

Managing Customer Service

Making sure that your customers feel well treated—particularly when they have problems or concerns, is the key to establishing long-term repeat customers. In this part of the business plan, you need to present a simple, effective process for providing customer service—whatever that means for your type of business. For some companies, that might mean training customers; for others, fixing bugs or problems with software; and for others, handling billing and account management questions. You cannot underestimate the importance of establishing good customer service for a fledging business. It is not the small problem here or there that will lose you a potentially lifelong customer; rather, it is the failure to respond to such problems with clarity and speed. You need to think of your customers as an extension of your sales force—and that means eating the cost of whatever it takes to "make things right."

Designing customer service can't be left to chance. We remember as young software entrepreneurs ourselves how customer support calls would be channeled through our little company. First, a call would go to our front desk receptionist. Then, the call would be sent back amongst the programming staff, many of whom took great delight in speaking to live customers. However, after a few months, it became all too apparent that the programmers were enjoying their new friendships a little too much. The mornings were increasingly consumed responding to issues that came in the day before. Not only did we have to hire a customer support person, soon followed by others, but also a manager. We also had to implement a "bug reporting" system to keep track of issues, resolutions, and serve as a valuable input to R&D.

Increasingly, computer systems can help you manage these different functions—and some of these are being provided on a Web services basis—which means rather than an expensive up-front license, a pay-as-you-go option in terms of usage. Investigate these and work subscribing to such services into your financials when your company begins to scale in Years 2 and 3.

At a more mundane level, you can use this part of the business plan to also specify the office space and location of your "headquarter" facilities to take you through the first several years of the business.

Questions on the Investor's Mind:

a. Do their operations plans show an analytical approach to assessing suppliers, subcontractors, and shippers? Has anyone worked the numbers?

b. Are they wasting money on a fancy office and furnishings?

c. Is there anyone on the team that has managed a business operation before? If not, can I find them one? And how much time do I have to do that? How far away are they from needing to scale up their operations?

Team Activities for Writing the Operations Section

Activity Description	Team Member(s)	Status/Date
Suppliers		
Production/internal and outsourcing options		
Logistics		
Customer service		
The company headquarters office		

Organization Plan

This section first provides a description of the management team and your key advisors. It draws upon your thinking in Chapter 10 on how to best build winning teams for putting the business plan into motion.

No need to beat around the bush here. You require experience, a balance of skills, and individuals who have a track record of success in prior jobs. Even better, a successful serial entrepreneur on your team or advisory board adds tremendous assurance to investors that *someone on the team has gone through the process before and made investors money*. The part of the plan has three sections: the management team, a staffing plan for ramp-up, and the Board of Advisors (or Directors if you are seeking growth capital).

The Management Team

The simple yet powerful method is to take the business model template you complete for your venture (Chapter 4, Figure 4.12) and look at the human skills required for your R&D, production, and customer-facing strategies and/or activities. First, look at your management team. This will include not only the founding team but other types of experienced individuals that will complement your own skills and capabilities. Look at the skills that you and your present team possess. Then look at what is missing. Add those missing parts to your management team as part of your organization plan. It might not be right away, but by the end of the first year for most businesses, the key management personnel need to be on board. For example, we have seen quite a few successful software companies in which for the first six months the founders themselves did all of the direct selling to enterprise customers. Then with a few customers and some cash flow, these firms were then able to bring in an additional professional sales manager to build the channel. This would be shown as a new key hire six months from startup. Similarly, a highly experienced CFO might only come a year or more down the road, well after a far less expensive controller. (Unless, of course, you have raised $5 million in venture capital and your investors want a CFO to help watch the money, right away!)

Now, let's talk about you. These days, startups that raise venture capital (from an institutional source such as a VC firm or a corporate venture fund) always seem to have an experienced hand at the tiller. It is a fact of life. If you don't have experience and have proposed a business that needs more than $1 million for startup, you are going to have to find yourself a partner with that type of track record.

However, as we learned earlier, only a small fraction of startups are actually funded by institutional sources. Most are funded by angel investors or by the founders' family or friends—where a little bit of money is used to quickly begin to produce cash from customers to fund further growth. Angel investors actually enjoy the enthusiasm of youth, and the energy and excitement of young entrepreneurs, as long as there is a solid, pragmatic plan behind them. Most angel investors are themselves prior business executives and entrepreneurs with extensive operating experience. Of all the angel investors we have met, the vast majority are just the type of people who you want as advisors as well as investors.

The Staffing Plan

The entrepreneur needs to be so very careful in hiring each and every person, particularly during the first two years of the business. Even one weak person in a new company can sink the ship by losing a key customer through poor service or sloppily implementing a flaw in the product. In our experience as entrepreneurs, even positions that you might not think all that important can make or break the business. For example, the front office receptionist can be critical for a new company. Professional, communicative, warm—this is the type of personality that you need to have at the front desk to meet and greet key customers or suppliers as they sit in the waiting area to meet you and your team. That receptionist sets the tone for the visit.

For young entrepreneurial teams, we cannot underestimate the importance of having an experienced office manager who can take care of all the little details of running an office operation that are wasteful time-sinks for the entrepreneur. Once your company grows to be over 20 or so employees, spending on an office manager is short money. Same thing goes with a controller to manage the books. As an entrepreneur, you want to be spending the bulk of your time working with customers, investors, or for some, the technology itself.

Staffing plans take direct form in the financial projections for most types of startups. Figure 11.7 shows a cutout from the staffing plan of software startup that fed into a higher-level P&L. That figure was not submitted to investors as part of the formal plan—but served as the planning for the P&L. You can see that it is very specific about job titles, salaries, and when these expenses are brought on board to match development requirements and sales revenue. As a company grows, entrepreneurs must add staff across key functions to augment the amount of R&D, production, and selling that the business can accomplish.

Even if you are outsourcing key functions, you still require qualified personnel to manage these external relationships. In the financial projections, it is not uncommon to see fairly detailed breakdowns of human resources requirements and the salaries and overhead for particular types of individuals that are then summed up and carried forward into the appropriate areas of an aggregated P&L.

Board of Advisors/Directors

There are highly experienced individuals who can provide your team with the mentor capital it needs to deal at both the strategic and tactical levels of startup and growth. You should have someone who is an expert at sales in your industry; another in technology (if appropriate for your type of business); and another who is an expert across a broad spectrum of finance, be it raising money or establishing banking relationships for working capital. This would translate into a current or former VP of Sales, a CTO, and a CFO, respectively. It is also strongly advisable to consider your attorney a close advisor as well as the person who will prepare your business taxes. *Both* serve the role of keeping you out of trouble, *so listen to them!*

The difference between a Board of Advisors and a Board of Directors is that the former has no fiduciary responsibility to shareholders, including investors. The norm is to provide advisors some stock options in a startup. A Board of Directors is typically comprised of just one or two founders and two or three investors. The fact is that if you take investment capital from venture capitalists, you are not going to have any real choice in terms of who sits on your official Board. If is their money, and if you mess up they will be in the position to remove you as part of the original financing agreement.

Even if you have an official Board of Directors (which you must have for certain types of corporate organizations such as a C-Corporation or Subchapter S-Corporation), we still advise you to form a Board of Advisors and use them frequently as well.

**** **** ****

Department/Position	No of FTEs	Annual Salary	2007 (Jun–Dec)	2008	2009	2010	2011
General Administrative							
CEO and President	1	150,000	75,000	175,000	200,000	210,000	220,500
COO	1	140,000		105,000	160,000	147,000	154,350
CFO	1	110,000		55,000	115,500	121,275	127,339
Controller	1	75,000	37,500	75,000	78,750	82,688	86,822
Assistant Controller	1	55,000				55,000	57,750
IT Manager	1	85,000			85,000	89,250	93,713
Network Manager	1	70,000	35,000	73,500	73,500	77,175	81,034
Network Engineer	1	65,000				65,000	68,250
Application Support	1	60,000			60,000	63,000	66,150
Application Support	1	65,000				65,000	68,250
Communication Specialist	1	65,000		65,000	68,250	71,663	75,246
Communication Specialist	1	55,000			55,000	57,750	60,638
Operation Manager	1	52,000	26,000	54,600	54,600	57,330	60,197
Office Admin	1	30,000	15,000	30,000	31,500	33,075	34,729
Office Admin	1	30,000			30,000	31,500	33,075
Office Admin	1	30,000				31,500	31,500
Office Admin	1	30,000				30,000	30,000
Office Admin	1	32,000					32,000
Total General Salaries			188,500	633,100	1,012,100	1,256,705	1,381,540
Bonuses					100,000	200,000	250,000
Total General Compensation			188,500	633,100	1,112,100	1,456,705	1,631,540
General Headcount			5	8	12	16	18

Figure 11.7 (Continued)

Department/Position	No of FTEs	Annual Salary	2007 (Jun - Dec)	2008	2009	2010	2011
R&D							
VP Engineering	1	125,000	62,500	125,000	131,250	137,813	144,703
Application Development Mgr	1	60,000	30,000	63,000	72,450	81,144	85,201
Product Manager	1	95,000	31,667	95,000	99,750	104,738	109,974
Product Manager	1	70,000			70,000	73,500	77,175
Product Engineering							
System Architect	1	85,000		85,000	89,250	93,713	98,398
Web Engineer	1	85,000	28,333	85,000	89,250	93,713	98,398
Web Engineer	1	85,000			85,000	89,250	93,713
Software Engineer	1	52,500	26,250	55,125	57,881	60,775	63,814
Software Engineer	1	75,000	37,500	75,000	78,750	82,688	86,822
Software Engineer	1	75,000	37,500	75,000	78,750	82,688	86,822
Software Engineer	1	80,000		80,000	84,000	88,200	92,610
Software Engineer	1	80,000			80,000	84,000	88,200
Software Engineer	1	80,000			80,000	84,000	88,200
Software Engineer	1	85,000				85,000	89,250
Software Engineer	1	85,000				85,000	89,250
DB Developer	1	90,000	37,500	90,000	94,500	99,225	104,186
DB Developer	1	90,000		90,000	94,500	99,225	104,186
DBA	1	75,000		75,000	78,750	82,688	86,822
Total Engineering			291,250	993,125	1,364,081	1,607,357	1,687,725

Figure 11.7 A Partial Staffing Plan for a Technology Venture

Final Checklist

The bottom line of this section is that you must not give short shrift to thinking about both your immediate and extended team. It may be the deciding factor for investors or executives in your corporation (if you are planning an internal corporate venture). Include brief resumes of key management in an appendix. If you are doing a biotech venture, forget the word "brief." If you have a scientist on the team with with page after page of journal publications, put them all in.

Questions on the Investor's Mind:

a. Can I see myself working with this team?

b. Does the team have substantial experience and talent? If not, do they realize that? How hard will it be to convince them to "beef up?" If they don't have anyone who has been a CEO before, are they ready to take one that I supply?

c. Does their advisory board have some serious "chops"—namely, deep experience and talent in sales, technology, and financial matters?

d. Do they have a good law firm and accounting firm to keep them, and me, out of trouble?

Team Activities for Writing the Organization Section

Activity Description	Team Member (s)	Status/Date
Management team		
Staffing plan		
Board of advisors/directors		

Major Milestones With Funding

This section of the business plan is critically important in your selling effort to prospective investors. It presents the major milestones that your business is committed to achieving with the specific round of financing. This needs only be a page featuring a task list with key dates. We also like to see a sentence or two on how to mitigate the risk of these key milestones at the bottom of the page. And even though it is only a page in length, you can be asssured that if you have truly interested investors, you will spend hours working with them to sharpen these milestones and determine the people, partners, and resources needed to meet, if not accelerate, achieving them.

As noted earlier, there tends to be specific types of "development" milestones for startups:

• **Alpha.** This is the "alpha" version or prototype of your product, system, or service. In reality, most investors want to see that prototype with the business plan. However, in some cases, developing that "alpha" will be your first order of business. If it's more than two or three months in time, most investors will shy away. "Come back when you have a prototype, and then we will talk about investing," they will say.

• **Beta.** This is the "beta" version, a much more complete and working version of an alpha that is actually placed into the hands of lead users for test, feedback, and improvement. The time duration for achieving a beta varies widely on the type of venture; a consulting service can start providing services to clients right away, a software company might get to beta in three to six months, or a new pet food company such as that described in the first part of this book can get product for test marketing within several months with the use of contract manufacturers.

• **First commercial release.** This is the "Version 1.0" of your product, system, or service, together with a full marketing plan for launch and initial customer support. Sometimes this is referred to as the "first dollar" milestone. This is also another way of saying early customer milestones, including key accounts, distribution relationships, or an e-commerce Website going live, depending on the type of business. In most types of start-ups, investors expect to see a fairly quick follow-up to the beta test for full-scale commercial release. Unless you are working in the biotech or medical device space, try your best to get a first product or service to market within six to nine months from startup.

- **First operating profit.** This fourth milestone is derived from your projected P&L. Wouldn't it be great to achieve an operating profitability with the release of the first product or service? Unfortunately, there is often a lag. Investors want to see a path to profitability that falls within 18 to 24 months. Any longer will scare away most.

Of course, these time frames may well change for a particular type of venture. A retail concept will have its first test store that is both beta and first commerical release in the same shot. At the other extreme is a drug discovery venture. Your authors have invested in such a firm and don't expect to see a penny of return for eight years after startup, unless a large pharmaceutical firm buys the startup for its technology before it enters into full human clinical trials. However, a far shorter time horizon is expected for discovering new science and the filing of patents. Compared to all the other examples used in the book, *biotech is such a long haul.* But we know that even a single successful drug will generate hundreds of millions of dollars or potentially much more on an annual basis once brought to market.

Other types of milestones can also often be found in the planning of new ventures. The two most prominent are:

- **Key hires.** Certain investors will also see the hiring of managers in your firm as important milestones. Often, this is a VP of Sales.

- **The next round of financing.** The next round is best planned well in advance and should match the needs of the growing business to achieve the next set of major milestones. That might be $1 million to build the next-generation product or service, $2 million to build a professional direct sales force, $3 million to expand manufacturing to support major channel partners, or some combination of these and other company milestones.

Questions on the Investor's Mind:

a. Are the venture's milestones well considered and appropriately staged?

b. Are these milestones sufficiently aggressive? What can we do to speed things up?

c. How long will the money last before we have to raise the next round? Does the current money give the venture enough time and evidence to prove that this is a viable market and good business opportunity? In other words, it is enough for me to get an uptick on my valuation?

Team Roles for Writing the Activities Section of the Plan

Activity Description	Team Member (s)	Status/Date
Development milestones		
Key hire milestones		
Financing milestones		

Financial Projections

This section contains your financial projections for

- A granular, "bottoms-up" projection of revenues that gets bundled into the P&L (which means number of customers, unit prices, and other volume factors—as opposed to broad assumptions of getting a certain "market share,"

- The Profit and Loss Statement,
- The Cash Flow Statement, and
- The Balance Sheet.

For planning purposes, you might also want to create a detailed breakdown of startup expenses and then scale-up expenses. Professional investors really want to know how much the business is going to cost—not only to start, but also to scale into a significant company. Is it a $3 million investment over three years to reach $20 million in revenue, or a $30 million investment to reach $100 million plus in revenue? Is the company destined to be a small, niche player—albeit highly profitable—that can be sold to a larger corporation five or six years down the road? Or, does it represent an opportunity to build a global powerhouse, one that can employ thousands of people around the world, reach markets around the world, and achieve an IPO? A large venture capital firm is unlikely to be interested in the former. A small firm or angel investors will.

The standard format that we observe in most funded business plans is to have a monthly breakdown of revenues and expenses for the first two years of operations and then annual projections for Years 3, 4, and 5. As noted in the prior chapter, your professor may ask for a different time period breakdown for financial information, such as quarterly projections instead of monthly ones. And we have rarely seen financial projections for internal corporate ventures that are anything but annual projections, even for the first year or two of the venture. However, we feel that the monthly projections reveal a much more precise analysis of cash burn before initial sales, and then, the path to achieving operating profit once sales commence. If someone only wants to see quarterlies or annuals, you can simply roll up your more detailed projections as needed. You will have to do so regardless because in the first section of the business plan, we ask you to show the number of customers or units, annual revenue, and operating profit over the course of five years as a summary of the financial performance of the venture.

Even though the annual projections for Years 3, 4, and 5 are totally speculative, they do paint a picture of the size of the business and the value it can achieve in an ideal scenario. Plus, investors tend to look at industry sector multiples of sales and profits in those outlying years to get a notion of what your business *might be worth* if successfully implemented.

As important as any of the specific projections in this part of the business plan are *the assumptions* behind the numbers. We covered this material in the prior chapter. Your assumptions should include:

- Unit prices for products, systems, and services and any discounting of those prices for volume procurements
- The number of customers by time period, and if need be, broken down by channel
- Any materials, direct labor, and subcontracting costs that drive COGS for the business, also on a per unit basis
- Officer salaries are often a major factor in GS&A expenses. Only pay the management team what the business can afford. Unpaid salaries placed on the balance sheet as debt are the first things wiped out in subsequent stage financing. The founding team in a startup typically receives salaries of about $100,000. If it is a venture capital–backed business, they will hold between 10% and 20% equity after the first two rounds of financing. Angel-backed firms tend to leave the founders with substantially greater equity.
- Any specific difference between "sales," revenue recognition, and cash. Investors will want to understand these differences with an eye on appropriate revenue recognition and incentives that can be provided to customers to shorten the cash conversion cycle. Bottom line: Investors will want to know if there is a significant lag between sales and cash.

In general, any set of factors that have a major impact on your projected P&L should be noted in the financial assumptions. Same for cash flow and investments into fixed assets of any sort. **Do not** short-change these assumptions. One way or another, these will come up as questions from discerning investors. We also have financial templates available on both our academic and book Websites that you should freely download and adapt to your own specific venture. Some of these are for ventures making physical products, others software or systems, and yet others for pure services plays. You might find that they save you lots of time!

What we don't want you to do is use any of these templates blindly. Even worse is to buy one of the popular commerical business planning packages that ask you to answer 50 questions and then generate a dozen pages of detailed, small-font financial statements. You need to think through your financial projections as carefully as anything else in your business. Unfortunately, the human tendency is to let computers do the thinking for us. For venture finance, that simply doesn't work. It is far better for you to take the first pass at your P&L by hand—preferably on a large whiteboard surrounded by teammates to bat around the assumptions and the numbers. Start with a granular "bottoms-up" projection of revenues. Then, when it is time to start adding expenses, turn on the computer and use a spreadsheet.

For those of your doing intrapreneurial ventures, you need to understand the financial metrics used by your company to evaluate new proposals. Measures such as ROA (return on assets) or FATR (fixed asset turnover ratio) are common amongst large manufacturers. And nearly all major corporations now use the net present value of discounted cash flows to evaluate new business proposals. Bottom line, take the time to learn how executives in your company measure business success and plan accordingly.

We need to reiterate: It is easy to print out 20 pages of spreadsheet projections that have little value and that are virtually impossible to defend. Your financial statements must be concise and realistic. Don't make your investors work too hard to understand your numbers. And be prepared to defend your numbers again and again—particularly your projections of revenue over the first three years of the business.

Questions and Expectations on the Investor's Mind

Investors also want to see that your financial projections reflect an understanding of certain key principles:

- **Produce a robust stream of revenue:** a clear structure and nature of revenue, the time to first dollar, and how revenues scale.

- **Turn that revenue into cash:** incentives for customer payments and how you manage your accounts receivables.

- **Produce strong operating profits:** Unless you are doing a biotech startup, the bottom line is that operating three years in the red while revenue ramps up is no longer feasible. You need to show a clear path to profitability in 12 to 24 months—and the sooner the better. This is known as the path to profitability. Anything that you can do to reduce cash outflows should be strongly considered. Deferring paying up front for supplies, software, or services is essential. Office overhead, including computers, should be considered with extreme care. You might be able to sublet space at attractive rates, and avoid longer-term leases, from a larger corporation in the process of cost cutting.

- **Return on investment:** Most venture investors are looking for a ten-times return on their invested capital upon exit, preferably within five to seven years, even with dilution based on later rounds of financing. The way that investors tend to calculate this type of return is not on the book value of your balance sheet but rather as a multiple on the sales and profitability in your P&L in the out-years. Multiples on sales and profitability for recent "exits" are simply applied to your own projected revenues in Year 5 on your Proforma P&L to get a feel for the potential exit valuation of your venture.

Each one of these expectations can be turned into specific questions:

a. Is there a solid revenue stream with recurring revenue from existing customers as well as new revenue from new customers?

b. What is the product–service mix? Am I comfortable with that mix?

c. Is there a structural cash conversion problem in the business? What can be done to shorten that cycle?

d. When does the company achieve operating profitability? Have they really asked for sufficient investment capital to reach that point?

e. Taken all together, do the business plan and the financials lead to a world-class global company that can achieve an IPO, or is it really a niche company that would be the candidate for an acquisition by a large corporation down the road? And, is that acquisition likely to be a $30 million, $50 million, or $100 million plus type deal? How does that scenario fit with my own investment objectives and priorities?

Team Activities for Financial Modeling

Activity Description	Team member(s)	Status/Date
Granular revenue projections		
P&L, Cash Flow, and Balance Sheet statements		
Startup expenses (for later)		
Equity of "cap" table (for yourself)		

Closing Thoughts

A potential investor will do their own due diligence on your business plan. If your information is inaccurate or you leave out a critical fact or detail, good investors will find the error or gap and hold you accountable. Every element of the plan needs to be considered carefully.

The most important questions your business plan must answer to the satisfaction of the investor are:

1. Is the venture situated in a robust, growing market?

2. Is there something clearly different and distinctive in what the venture proposes to make and sell that differentiates it from competitors?

3. Is there a well-defined addressable market that has a clear motivation to buy what the venture intends to sell?

4. Is there a strong, balanced team, some of whom have successfully developed new companies before and others with strong operating experience? For some investors, this is often the very first question.

5. Does the business plan clearly show how the opportunity can be monetized—how the business can make money? Within this, are the revenue and expenses realistic and is a longer-term profit picture attractive? And are those revenues and profits sufficiently large to warrant the type of return on investment required by the type of investor to whom you are pitching?

It is also important to remember that investors are ideally looking for 20- to 25-page business plans, cleanly written, nicely formatted, with a few selected diagrams or illustrations at key sections, and equally clear, reasonable financials. Many professional investors take new plans on a business trip or to their home office. Guess what tends to happen to a 100-page "heavy" binder? It gets left behind!

Reader Exercises

Step 1: Storyboard Your Plan

Creating a compelling, seemless story about the focus and promise of a new venture is your objective here. Planning the different parts of that story and how they connect is the purpose of storyboarding. Use Figure 11.2 as a template. Convene at a large whiteboard if possible and fill out with just a few bullet points each part of that chart. Sit back and assess. Do the parts fit? Does the story flow? Can you give a two-minute elevator pitch that captures the essence of the storyboard for each section?

Step 2: Fill in the Activities/Roles/ Status Table for Each Section

At the end of each section, we have provided a simple table that you can use as a template for defining plan writing activities and responsibilities for team members. Edit these tables to fit your venture. Then, take a pass through each section and assign the work. Also, leave time someplace for editing, consolidation, and "beautification" with a few choice charts and illustrations.

Step 3: Write the First Draft of the Sections and Assemble

Assemble all of your materials from the prior chapters and write the first draft according to team roles and responsibilities. Each section should be no more than two to four pages, single-spaced, with several lines as paragraph breaks. The financial statements are attached at the end of the plan.

Step 4: Review and Critique

We have provided typical questions that investors will raise at the end of most of the sections of the business plan. Organize a team meeting and work through these questions, section by section. Role play if that is helpful. Having a "devil's advocate" is a tried and true method for improving projects. Remember that it often takes more work to make a section of text shorter and more powerful. Leave sufficient time for such editing.

Step 5: Get Even More Specific on the Assumptions for the Financial Section

For the financial section, pay particular attention to the list of key assumptions for revenue, expenses, cashflow adjustments, and capital expenditures. Assume that the investor or an analyst working for the investor will pore over your financial statements back at the office. This part of the business plan must be self-explanatory.

Step 6: Review "Milestones With Funding" Section as a Team

Assess with team members and trusted advisors the strategies for reducing the time to achieve major milestones and the amount of money needed to accomplish these goals. The quicker you get to market, the quicker you not only produce revenue but also begin the essential process of market learning from customers and sellers on how to make a better product or service. Also, the less money you need to raise, the more equity you get to keep.

Step 7: Polish—Formatting and Graphics

We recommend single-spacing, with several blank lines between paragraphs. Font size should be either 12 or 11, depending on the font selected. We also recommend that you start each major section on a new page, for example, the Business Model, Market Analysis, and so on should each start on a new page.

Financial statements should probably be no smaller than font size 10 because anything smaller becomes hard to read. Landscape printing for the projections is totally acceptable. Please make sure that the numbers add up, and that the different financials integrate correctly for items such as operating profit, working capital adjustments, and longer-term investments. These come at the end of the plan.

Traditionally, documents of this sort have a Table of Contents. However, if your plan is short and focused, we don't think that a Table of Contents lends anything to the plan. In fact, for some investors, it might make the document feel "academic." Most investors know what to expect in each part of the plan and where those parts fit within the overall plan.

You might wish to include resumes of key team members in the back of the plan in an appendix. For biotech or other scientific ventures, this is mandatory because investors will want to see the backgrounds and research publications of technical leaders. Your authors vividly recall reviewing a business plan where the "plan" itself—calling for the development of a new generation of antibiotics by two brilliant professors at our university—was about 20 pages. However, the resumes in the back of the plan went on for over a hundred pages! There were two key principles and each had hundreds of publications and dozens of research grants. A patent was also included as was the reprint of a seminal article in a leading journal.

We also strongly recommend that you incorporate a few choice graphs or charts into the business plan. Break up the text with some eye-candy. The Market Analysis section could use some type of industry analysis or competitive positioning chart, just as the Solutions section might benefit from a product/service architecture illustration or a development milestones chart.

Last, don't forget to put your name and contact information on the front page! Also, put in a very small font, a correctly formatted copyright notice on the bottom of the pages in the text.

**** **** ****

After this chapter and all the work you have done leading up to it, there should be no question about what to write. *Go for it!*

The next chapter—our last—turns to the PowerPoint presentation needed for investor pitches and that accompanies the business plan. As in this chapter, we will also share our thoughts on what to expect from investors in such presentations.

chapter 12
Making the Pitch

The Purpose of the Chapter

You've come a long way to the point of launching your enterprise. You have defined and tested both a venture concept and the business model for that concept. You have created a powerful, focused business plan with financial projections that show attractive and growing streams of revenue and operating profit. Your cash flow statement should also give a good approximation of the funding tranches that you require to achieve alpha-beta-launch, and then, to scale the business to achieve operating profit. For most of you, that capital can be clearly segmented into "seed," "Series A," and perhaps even "Series B" financing. Given the nature of the venture, the amount of money needed to fund startup and growth, and the Reader Exercises you did to hunt for angels, venture capitalists, and strategic investors in Chapter 8, you should also know *who* you wish to target for the capital raise.

Now, it's "show time." In the parlance of American football, you are now within ten yards of the goal line—within scoring distance. Everything you've done to this point has fortified your understanding of the opportunity, the market niche and users you aim to serve, and how the venture will make money. Your confidence has grown apace with that understanding and with your mastery of the venture concept.

Just one more push—one more task for most of you—and you will be across the goal line.

That last task is to pitch your venture to investors with the money you need first for startup and then for growth. As we noted in Chapter 8, that capital may come from friends and family, business "angels," or in rare cases, from venture capitalists or strategic corporate investors. If yours is an internal corporate venture, your "ask" will be to one or several executives who control the purse strings for new product, service, and business development.

No matter the source of capital, you will be obliged to make a *presentation.* The quality and persuasiveness of that presentation must be first rate. Helping you achieve that end—to get your money—is the purpose of this chapter.

Learning Objectives

- The structure and content of the investor presentation
- Questions to expect during the presentation
- Getting the meeting with investors for the presentation

There Are Presentations, and Then, There Are Investor Presentations

Contrary to your inclination after all the hard work in this book, and the numerous templates you have completed—the shorter the presentation, the better. All the other detail will come into play in the questions and answers during and after your presentations, including the extensive *due diligence* that professional investors will undertake in the weeks to follow.

Guy Kawasaki, the noted observer of technology industries and a successful venture investor in his own right, stated this so very well in a blog post that he titled "The 10/20/30 Rule of PowerPoint":[1]

> "Most of these pitches are crap: sixty slides about a "patent pending," "first mover advantage," "all we have to do is get 1% of the people in China to buy our product." These pitches are so lousy that I'm losing my hearing, there's a constant ringing in my ear, and every once in a while the world starts spinning."
>
> I am evangelizing the 10/20/30 Rule of PowerPoint. It's quite simple: a PowerPoint presentation should have ten slides, last no more than 20 minutes, and contain no font smaller than 30 points. While I'm in the venture capital business, this rule is applicable for any presentation to reach agreement: for example, raising capital, making a sale, forming a partnership, etc.
>
> - **Ten slides.** Ten is the optimal number of slides in a PowerPoint presentation because a normal human being cannot comprehend more than ten concepts in a meeting—and venture capitalists are very normal. (The only difference between you and venture capitalist is that he is getting paid to gamble with someone else's money.) If you must use more than ten slides to explain your business, you probably don't have a business.
>
> - **Twenty minutes.** You should give your ten slides in 20 minutes. Sure, you have an hour time slot, but you're using a Windows laptop, so it will take 40 minutes to make it work with the projector. Even if setup goes perfectly, people will arrive late and have to leave early. In a perfect world, you give your pitch in 20 minutes, and you have 40 minutes left for discussion.

---

[1] Read Guy Kawasaki's blog at http://blog.guykawasaki.com/2005/12/the_102030_rule.html#axzz0ui VGgxtj)?.

- **Thirty-point font.** The majority of the presentations that I see have text in a ten-point font. As much text as possible is jammed into the slide, and then the presenter reads it. However, as soon as the audience figures out that you're reading the text, it reads ahead of you because it can read faster than you can speak. The result is that you and the audience are out of sync. The reason people use a small font is twofold: First, they don't know their material well enough; second, they think that more text is more convincing. Total bozosity."

Guy goes on to suggest that the entrepreneur takes the oldest person in the investor meeting, divides that age by two, and uses that as the average font size for text in the presentation. Most professional investors will be between 50 and 60, and for angel investors, older by a decade or more. In our experience, anything less than a font size of 20 is probably not a good idea. As for the ten slides, we might extend that to a dozen—but no more! And if you have been able to create a prototype of your product, system, or service, at the end of your presentation definitely ask the investor if he or she would like to take a look!

You must also realize that most professional investors are, by nature, skeptical. They listen to so many venture proposals, often several or more a week. The sheer volume of these presentations, the repetitive nature of the pitch-criticize-decide process, puts a hard shell on the active investor and makes the entrepreneur's task all the more difficult. Interesting ideas can become "so-so" in comparison to so many others.

With so many interesting ideas circulating in the entrepreneurial milieu—it is that presentation which translates an interesting idea into a dynamic venture concept that shows a clear path to generating profit that stands apart and gets the investment capital. Often, it is the passion and conviction that the entrepreneur shows for his or her venture that makes the difference above and beyond anything else, particularly for angel investors.

The Foundations for a Great Investor Presentation

Throughout this book, we have explored the most important features of any new venture, the same sought by prudent investors. These boil down to:

a. A well-defined, attractive addressable or target market—with the size of demand and growth over the next five years that can support a well-conceived venture

b. Solutions—be they products, systems, services or some combination of them—for which target customers have a compelling need, and sufficient evidence that your solutions can actually solve the identified problem or need

c. That the business around these solutions is based on a pragmatic cash-generating business model—a model that can be well tested as a startup, improved, and scaled into a major force in the target market niche

d. And perhaps most important, that there is a strong, committed team behind the venture, with the knowledge and experience needed to make the idea a working reality

Put these points on the wall next to your desk, front and center as you work on each slide and assemble the presentation.

Spotlight on Innovation: Cheryl Says . . .

Cheryl Mitteness, a colleague at our university, studies the decision-making process of angel investors by actually sitting in on literally hundreds of individual presentations. She and her research partners find the reasoning behind the "yes" and "no" angel votes. We thought it a good idea to ask Cheryl to share her insights into what works within this increasingly important source of seed and Series A financing.

Cheryl's research has shown that:

- When pitching to angels, an entrepreneur should focus on convincing them that the business opportunity is strong. Then focus on why the entrepreneur is the best person to pursue the opportunity.

- Angel investors are hardly a homogenous group. To increase the likelihood of receiving angel capital, entrepreneurs need to be aware of the characteristics of the audience evaluating the pitch. Angels with direct startup experience are more forgiving of younger, less experienced entrepreneurs—perhaps because they see an opportunity to teach the entrepreneur the keys to success. Those angels who are primarily financial or corporate types without startup experience are much harder on the young entrepreneur. *Look for angels with successful startup, operating experience.*

- Above all else, an entrepreneur needs to be authentic in all interactions with angels. Angels are looking for trustworthiness, coachability, and passion. Don't try to be someone you are not. *And bring passion to the presentation.* If you don't believe in your idea, nor will anyone else. Passion and conviction are essential criteria in angel decision making.

We believe that Cheryl's research applies to VCs and strategic corporate investors as well.[2]

An Outline for the Presentation

The goal here is to create a short, powerful pitch for investors. We recommend the following format as a guideline for the investor presentation:

1. **The Team:** The background, experience, and motivations of the founders (No need for a slide here—address this in your opening statement. Investors want to know who they are talking to.)

2. **The Customer and the Problem:** The target customer, the customer's problem to be solved, and the cost or importance of that problem for the customer

3. **The Market Opportunity:** The size and characteristics of the addressable market that this target customer and the problem to be solved for the customer represent

4. **The Solution:** The new product, system, or service that solves the customer's problem, and how this translates into a product or suite of services. Also, include "the secret sauce" (if any) lying at the heart of the solution.

5. **The Competitive Positioning:** Not only the competitors, but the venture's positioning of the venture against them in classic price/performance terms, and then, the open opportunity space from the customer's perspective

---

[2] Sudek, R., Mitteness, C., & Cardon, M. (2010). The impact of perceived entrepreneurial passion on angel investing. *Frontiers of Entrepreneurship Research*.

6. **The Business Model:** This includes the structure and nature of revenue (sale, license, subscription, service, etc.), and your approach to R&D, production, and sales that leads to gross and operating margins and profit. The goal is to show a cash-generating business model within a reasonable time period from startup.

7. **Summary Financial Projections:** This is a high-level P&L for five years, plus key revenue drivers such as number of customers and unit prices.

8. **The Go-to-Market Strategy:** The route to market, key channel partners, and promotional and branding factors that will power growth in sales. Strategies to reduce the sales cycle or secure major channel agreements are described.

9. **Major Milestones With Funding:** The timeline and allocation of resources to achieve major milestones. Terms such as "alpha," "beta," first dollar sale, and first operating profit used as appropriate. The funding requested should be staged and with a clear purpose.

Adapt this outline for your own venture. In addition to covering these essential elements of information, you must be comfortable with the flow of the presentation. If you wish to shift elements to a different order, try it! Chances are that you will have multiple opportunities to give your pitch and will soon come to the order which works best for you.

Create a Compelling Story

There is much more to the presentation than simply covering these elements, however.

Audiences of just about any kind, including investors, don't care to listen to a rote presentation of facts, detached from the excitement you wish to create in the marketplace. Instead, you want to capture the investor's interest—and to do this, you want to craft a story that is both interesting and compelling, first from the point of view of the target customer, and then, from the perspective of creating a money-making business.

There are excellent books on preventing "Death by PowerPoint." We prefer those that recommend a story-telling approach, using pictures as much as text, and creating simplicity in layout and design. *Presentation Zen,* written by Garr Reynolds, is a worthwhile read.[3] The goal is to deliver a short, powerful story that leaves a crisp image in the listener's mind.

For the entrepreneur, there are three stories to be told within a dozen slides in the investment presentation:

a. **Story A: The story of *you* and your team**, the backgrounds, experience, and motivations for starting the venture. As noted above, this doesn't necessarily even have to be a separate slide. It could best be a 30-second introduction where you are making direct eye contact with the investors sitting at the table. Show your passion and conviction for the venture concept.

b. **Story B: The story of the target customer.** Focus on the target customers and the problem that you wish to solve for them. Then, the clear value of solving that problem in terms of saving the customer time or money or bringing unparalleled levels of convenience or pleasure in a leisure activity.

c. **Story C: The story of your business**, which means how your business can become a leader in its target market, and how your business model will generate the type of revenue flow and cash needed for hungry investors.

Tell Story A first, B next, and then get to Story C.

---

[3] Reynolds, G. (2008). *Presentation Zen: Simple Ideas On Presentation Design and Delivery.* Berkeley, CA: New Riders.

The Story of Serving the Customer

The approach we recommend here is to create a "tension" in the form of an important problem or unexploited opportunity on the part of the target customer. This requires intimacy with that customer. If you've worked through the first part of this book, you are now the master of customer knowledge. Now is the time to show it.

There is no doubt that investors enjoy a crisp identification of the target customer, the target buyer (if different), and the needs not yet filled by competitors currently in the marketplace. Show these insights and you are off to a good start.

Define the Customer, the Customer's Problem

First, clearly define the customer, their role, position, stage of life, or economic level depending on the nature of your business. Then, explain the customer problems and frustrations associated with the current situation. In the case of our three running examples in this part of the book, this would be the lack of healthy pet snacks for pet owners, the fear of the elderly falling and dying unattended in their own homes, or the difficulty of keeping up with the latest in cost-effective networking and telecommunications equipment for building owners. In earlier chapters, we dug deeper into these customer situations in the form of developing "use case scenarios," and these were featured in your venture concept diagrams. Showing your insight into the "world" and needs of the target customer should take, at most, a slide or two. Remember, prudent investors will want to see for themselves through customer visits before making an investment. At this point, your goal is to prove customer insight. Figure 12.1 provides the essence of a "springboard story" that creates a tension around the problems of the customer that your venture exists to solve.

- Captures attention of the investor
- A specific user scenario that is compelling
- The customer's current "negative" outcome creates tension
- Your solution to the customer problem relieves the "tension"

Figure 12.1 The Springboard "Problem" Story From the Perspective of the Target Customer

The next part of the story of your customer is to dimensionalize the customer problem into an economic or opportunity cost. In other words, for the specific use case scenario, what is the cost or penalty of doing business or performing an activity under the current situation? How significant or large is this cost for the user? Is this a little problem, or one that is truly compelling? This might be included as just a bullet point on one of your first two charts.

Define the Addressable Market

The next essential step in the presentation is to describe how your target customer represents a substantial market opportunity. That opportunity represents the "spend" or economic activity for your target application or problem area. You have the data from the first part of the book—and in the business plan—so use it. For example, "the market for pet snacks in the United States is . . . ," or the "money spent on emergency admissions for the elderly is . . . ," or the "design and implementation services niche within the telecommunication network infrastructure market in North America is. . . ." This is where you create a single slide that shows the size, growth rate, and competitive dynamics of the target market. A graph here that shows the current size and growth rate of that target market is a good addition, with a bullet point or two describing additional salient trends.

That addressable market should be substantial if you are seeking investment from an angel, a VC, or a strategic corporate investor. In their minds, these investors will be thinking, "if those folks can capture 5% of that defined market, it translates into a $50 million a year business, or 10%, a $100 million a year business." Many will then quickly work the multiples for acquisitions in your industry sector on revenues, and start thinking about the potential value of owning 20% of the equity five years down the road as part of a larger syndicated investment group. This sizing up not only of your customer knowledge but of the business opportunity it represents happens surprisingly quickly. In five minutes, you want to get the investor thinking about his or her own possible financial returns in large, unsolved problem spaces.

The Solution to the Customer's Need, the "Secret Sauce," and the Competitive Positioning

This is where your creativity, customer insight, and nose for the competition have to really shine.

First, use a slide to present your new product, system, or service—its key features, functions, and performance. If it is a consumer product, a good photograph is useful here. If it is a piece of software, best leave the imagery for a demonstration of your prototype—reprints of computer screens never look as good as what appears on a live screen. On the other hand, graphics showing the context of use can help bring a new technology to life. If you are enabling a new business process, a very simple process diagram that shows the improved process is good, again highlighting the benefits for the customer.

As you are talking to this slide, it is also very important that you address the following four points:

- First, describe the compelling, distinctive aspects to the product, system, or service in the eyes of the customer. Not what you think is "cool" but what the customer perceives as a compelling benefit based on the results of your Reality Check. (Those data are a good set of additional slides to have in your back pocket.) Place a few large bullet points next to your images on this slide that convey these customer benefits. Remember, often the benefit of an innovation is cost savings or productivity gains for the customer. Try to be specific here and dimensionalize the scope of these benefits.

- Second, describe the product line or suite of services that emerges from your product, system, or service idea. Remember to use the words "good, better, best" here if appropriate. They mean a lot to certain types of investors who have pragmatic operational experience; these investors know that customers want choice.

- Third, describe the proprietary technology or process lying with your offerings. If you have such secret sauce, this too deserves a separate slide with high-level bullet points presenting the points of unique intellectual property. If your "secret sauce" is in a nonpatentable process, such as a method for integrating different systems in a customer's facility or for interpreting the results of particular types of data or analytics, then you should address these as well. All investors are looking for some type of special "know-how" to give a venture competitive advantage.

- Fourth, share your insights regarding the competitive positioning of your solution. This also deserves a separate slide focused on the competition—but much more than just a list. The perceptual map is an interesting and powerful idea that professional investors will appreciate. They are searching for solutions that occupy some sort of "white space" relative to competitors.

Figure 12.2 shows examples of visual aids for a product and system solution that come from two of the teaching cases in the book: Catch a Piece of Maine's seafood gifting service and Sentillion's single sign-on security and provisioning software for health care. Illustrations such as these bring the venture concept to life.

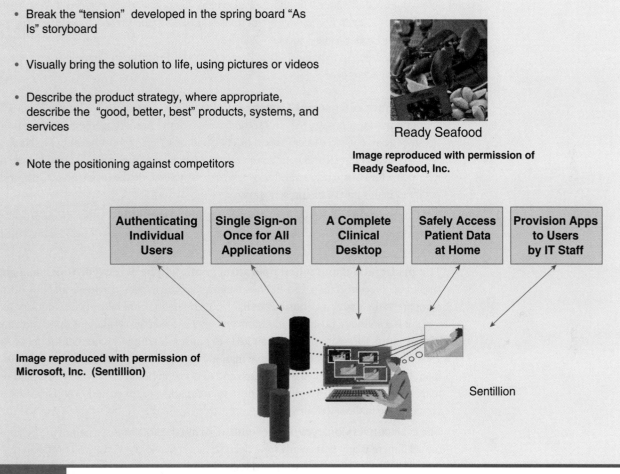

- Break the "tension" developed in the spring board "As Is" storyboard

- Visually bring the solution to life, using pictures or videos

- Describe the product strategy, where appropriate, describe the "good, better, best" products, systems, and services

- Note the positioning against competitors

Ready Seafood

Image reproduced with permission of Ready Seafood, Inc.

| Authenticating Individual Users | Single Sign-on Once for All Applications | A Complete Clinical Desktop | Safely Access Patient Data at Home | Provision Apps to Users by IT Staff |

Image reproduced with permission of Microsoft, Inc. (Sentillion)

Sentillion

Figure 12.2 Your Compelling Solution for the Customer

**** **** ****

Put all of these together and you have a rich, compelling story about how your venture will serve the needs of the customer—the foundation for becoming a leader in the market that the customer represents.

Students have asked, "The venture concept templates summarize the target market, the customer need, the solution, and positioning all in one page. Why not show it to investors?" Good point. But it is a lot of information on a single page and investors might get lost in that detail. It is best to partition the information into two or three slides focused on the key themes of that template.

The Story of Your Business

Describe the Business Model

This story—the "story of the business"—focuses on creating a business that not only produces revenue but one that generates operating profit once the business achieves reasonable scale. In this part of your investor pitch, you need to provide the impression of a clean, powerful business model.

In Chapter 4, we had you develop the business model for your venture, and in Chapter 7 you tested it. Then, we had you develop a set of financial projections based on that model in Chapter 9. This work is the platform for this part of your investor pitch.

You can simply describe the business model to the investor. Then again, a simple bullet-point slide wouldn't hurt either. The slide will also help you organize your story and keep to the straight and narrow—even if you decide not to use the slide in the presentation. Investors will want to understand your business model.

Using your planning in Figure 4.12 (the Business Model Template in Chapter 4), create a set of bullet points that focus on:

- **The structure and nature of revenues,** for example, a retail price, a license fee, a subscription model, a project fee, and so on for each of the primary elements in your product strategy articulated earlier (as part of The Solution). Pricing must be addressed here as well. The reality check and your competitive research should give you a good handle on the pricing for your products and services. Also, try to include the magic words "recurring revenue" in this part of the presentation.

- **Your approaches to R&D, manufacturing, and distribution** when the approaches have a significant effect on either gross margins (cost of goods sold) or net margins before tax (such as an outsourced model for any of the areas described above).

- **The profit model and when operating profit will be achieved.** Your comments should be directed at the gross and net margins that you expect to achieve and how these compare to the margins of businesses like yours operating generally in your industry sector. If it is a software business, investors will expect to see gross margins approximating 90% or more, for example, but high R&D expenses, leading to a net before tax of say 25%. Check the Web for comparative margin benchmarks in your industry sector. In a manufacturing business, gross margins tend to come in between 40% and 50%, and net margins before tax at 15% to 20%. These benchmarks are for scaled-up businesses, as yours will be in three to four years.

- **The cash conversion cycle for revenue** must also be addressed as part of the business model if there is any particularly long delay, beyond say 45 days. You will find that experienced investors view this as a critical issue.

- **The upside after five years.** This is the potential business value based on the revenues and profits you think are reasonable after five years, using industry benchmarks on multiples of sales and profits.

We want to emphasize to use the Business Model Template to help you think—but not necessarily to show in an investor presentation. Simple, large-font bullet points work best! We also want to reiterate that reasonable sales projections are essential here.

Summary Financial Projections

Provide a very high level P&L for five years. You should also include other key data, such as revenue drivers (the number of new customers and repeat customers, and/or the unit volumes and price per unit), which come as rows above the revenues. The challenge here is to create a summary in a reasonably large font from the detail you developed in the financial projections in Chapter 9. This summary can be the same basic figure used in the Business Model section of the business plan. In other words, you should already have something close to what is required here. The numbers have to be shown on a projected screen—so keep the font rather large—say size 16 or greater. Figure 12.3 provides an example—and even that figure verges on the "too small" for an investor presentation. The figure is part of the Generate, Inc. teaching case in this book.

	Year 1	Year 2	Year 3	Year 4	Year 5
New customers	2	30	49	147	303
Recurring customers		2	34	83	147
Total customers	2	32	83	230	450
Average revenue per customer	$17,000	$50,000	$50,000	$50,000	$50,000
Recurring bookings		28,900	1,066,831	3,020,568	7,350,000
New bookings	34,000	1,571,000	3,034,043	8,458,897	15,150,000
Total bookings	34,000	1,599,900	4,100,874	11,479,465	22,500,000
Revenue	4,250	1,001,844	3,401,870	10,102,559	20,925,000
COS	59,250	978,417	1,700,935	4,649,710	8,997,750
Gross margin	(55,000)	23,427	1,700,935	5,452,849	11,927,250
%		2%	50%	54%	57%
Operating expense	613,093	1,552,233	3,100,438	4,903,550	10,156,514
Operating income	(668,093)	(1,528,806)	(883,568)	549,299	1,770,736
%				5%	8%
FTE	5	27	55	81	105

Figure 12.3 Readable Financials: Large Font!

Bring printouts of your more detailed financial projections to the meeting. Should the investors start asking specific questions, reach for your bag and bring out the heavy ammunition!

Remember, no wild projections! In particular, the sales projections should be reasonable. However, there is a fine balance between being conservative and underselling the potential of your venture. If you undersell, no one will invest. If you oversell, investors will run the other way. It is a balance that you will have to learn to achieve.

Describe the Go-to-Market Strategy

There are so many entrepreneurs with clever ideas, technology intensive or not. But few make the transition to an equally clever, aggressive sales strategy for their wonderful inventions. And it is those few that are far more likely to get funded.

The Go-to-Market Strategy deserves a separate slide. The bullet points on the slide need to include:

- The primary route to market (a direct sales force, a channel partner such as a major OEM or retailer, the Web, or one of the other alternatives described in the prior chapter). As part of your work in this book, you should know the best channel partners for your venture. If you are serious about starting a business, you should take the initiative to find out what it takes to do business with these partners and have begun that process. This will show investors that you are truly serious about this side of the business.
- The branding activities you plan to pursue. As IBM has shown, branding is not something left to consumer products companies alone. All companies need to design and implement a branding strategy. This includes the name of your company, the name of your products and/or services, and the messaging for these offerings that is consistent with how you have positioned them relative to competitors.

Perhaps above all else, you need to show investors that *you like to sell* as opposed to selling being a necessary evil that every new company must undertake. Going into the market and busting it wide open is a challenge that you and your team relish. Remember this as you speak to this slide. Selling produces revenue, and revenue—for new ventures—makes the rest of the business tick with energy and excitement.

Describe the Major Milestones and the Funding

Feasibility and timeliness should be the questions on investors' minds now that you have sold them on the stories of your customer and your business. Have a simple, clear slide showing your milestones to achieve the "alpha," "beta," first dollar sale, and first operating profit as these apply to your business. A horizontal timeline works well here. Then, show the dollar amounts of funding that your financial projections show you require to achieve each stage of growth. See Figure 12.4 for a general example.

| Figure 12.4 | Milestone Chart and Financing to Achieve Goals |

A milestone chart sounds simple to create, but it takes a lot of careful planning to establish sufficient, reasonable levels of funding—as well as a conviction in your voice that you truly believe in the milestone dates with the funding proposed. Once again, keep it simple and direct. We prefer to see the milestones and funding shown together in a single slide, to show that the money requested has a specific purpose and that the entrepreneur fully understands the successive stages of funding needed to achieve scale.

Use Graphics and Illustrations, but Avoid Sensationalism

Good stories are complemented by interesting graphics and illustrations. For example, investors will expect to see a graph of the market demand, a picture of the target customer, and illustrations of the product concept.

By some estimates, people remember only 25% to 45% of what they hear, but a much greater percentage of what they *see*. Bring your slides to life. At the same time, a standard clip or word art in PowerPoint will come off as amateurish and silly. Animations also come off as "cute." Skip these. Same with garish colors.

Simplicity in the slides is essential. Keep the slides straightforward and unencumbered. Remember Guy Kawasaki's dictum on font sizes. Offering a slide that is so complex that its creator must read or interpret it to the audience is a no-no in the world of presentation arts. Slides should *highlight* your presentation; they shouldn't *be* your presentation. Whatever time and attention your audience devotes to viewing slides is time and attention diverted from you. And you should be the center of attention.

Presentation Style

Don't read the slides! Speak to your audience. Let them read the slides. Point to trend lines on graphs if you have them, or to design points in a picture of your new product or the architecture diagram of your system, but otherwise, your eyes must be front and center whenever possible.

Once again, please ***do not read*** the slides! This is a classic mistake made by entrepreneurs somewhat nervous in the occasion. It is a fatal mistake for an investor presentation. It is also a good rule of thumb for any presentation.

Naturally, repeated rehearsals before an audience of colleagues will help you uncover and repair the holes and the weak spots. Rehearsal will also increase your self-confidence—and you need to be the very image of self-confidence.

As you rehearse, experiment with the various techniques that speakers use to engage and maintain audience attention and involvement:

- If you've been given a lectern or podium, escape from its confines every so often. Even step in front of it occasionally, as if to remove a barrier between you and your listeners.

- If you feel disconnected from the investors listening to you, you can ask a question. For example, "Has anyone here had an elderly friend or family member who had to be taken into the hospital every week or so for monitoring that might have been done at home?" Getting responses from investors can help lighten up what is typically a tense atmosphere.

- Build hand-offs into the presentation. For example, if the technology whiz of the team is not the main presenter, shift the presenter role over to that person at appropriate times. These shifts and the variety they bring will give a little jolt to the crowd.

- For certain forums, you might have the opportunity to demonstrate a prototype. The prototype makes the venture all the more "real" for potential investors.

These proven tactics will help you convert part of your presentation from "talking *at*" to "talking *with*" the audience. Remember, preparation is so important. Go through the slides in a final edit to eliminate any words that are not really necessary. Remove the silly stuff, remove the "fat," and strive toward a lean and powerful presentation.

**** **** ****

If you have captured the investors' attention and sincere interest in the slides leading up to this point, now is the time for "the close." The close in this case is a commitment to a rapid due diligence process to getting the check. If the investors are truly interested in your venture, they will begin a rapid fire of questions—and it is for these questions that you must be prepared.

Prepare for a Grilling (Where You Are the Meat)

During investor presentations, most (if not all) entrepreneurs feel as if they are a tasty slice of rare, roast beef sitting warming in front of hungry diners (the investors) who relish the opportunity to feast on any real or perceived weakness in the market insight, the solution, the business model, or the team. It's just the nature of the game.

Wear that thick skin—and even though it is difficult, try not to take criticisms personally. In fact, an investor may be deliberately trying to get under your skin just to see how you handle pressure. The pressures in the startup world are intense; those thinking about giving you their money are trying to make an assessment of your ability to think on your feet, to work under pressure, and to stick to your convictions. The same applies to internal corporate ventures—plus the heat of internal corporate politics!

Take confidence however, in all the work you have done in this book! You have the data needed to make a robust defense. Bring these data the table. Take your time. Patiently show that you know as much about the market, the customers, and the competitors as anyone else. Reveal how you did deep dives with customers, ran your reality check, and obtained direct and specific feedback on the design of your product, system, and service, as well as guidance on the percentage uptake in the target market for the commercial offerings you wish to sell. The customer insight work and the reality check in the first part of the book comprised powerful stuff. Don't leave these at home. Take confidence in the insight you have gained! If a particular investor doesn't "get it," pack up your show and find an investor who does. All but the most successful serial entrepreneurs get dozens of *no's* before they get to a *yes*. And in the current economic climate, it is a rough ride for everyone seeking to raise startup capital.

Perhaps most important, be prepared to defend your numbers during investor presentations! As Aaron Gowell, an alumnus of our university on whom we wrote a teaching case for this book, said, "Be prepared to defend you numbers six ways from Sunday." This means having the numbers to back up your numbers: market size and growth, the size of the specific target niche or addressable market, the revenue model, the sales cycle and cash conversion cycle, and the margins in production and other operating expenses.

Our recommendation is to keep your PowerPoint presentation to 20 to 30 minutes in duration. If it hits the mark, the discussion afterwards will probably continue for another 90 minutes or so—just in that first meeting. The really hard work—the money time—comes in the dialogue after the presentation.

In the prior chapter, we ended each major section of the business plan with the common questions and concerns of an investor reading the plan. You must prepare yourself to answer these same questions in an investor presentation. We constructed those questions based on our experiences as entrepreneurs and investors. We also reviewed those questions with friends who do angel investing or are venture capitalists. For better or worse, those questions are real and you will encounter them in your search for startup or growth capital. Take confidence in the fact that you enter these meetings armed with all the work you have done in this book. Without being arrogant, wear that confidence on your sleeve.

So with the questions from the prior chapter in mind, assume that the following types of responses and questions are raised either during or after your presentation:

1. *"Let's run through those market numbers again."* Here, the investor is going to try their best to poke holes into how you have defined and sized your target market, for example, that specific addressable market from which you plan to get revenue.

2. *"How does it really work and tell me again why the target customers really need it."* Expect a question of this sort. Walk the investor through the most common use case scenario for the customer. Explain what they use now and why they are still having problems. This is also the point where you can bring out the data from your reality check and work through indicators showing favorable response. Also remember that the best investors will want to go talk to some of those customers. You might jump ahead of this by saying, "Would you like to see this for yourself? Why don't we go visit some customers together next week?" In other words, you may be able to facilitate this part of the due diligence process.

3. *"Why isn't Company X already doing this?"* Experienced investors often find that young entrepreneurs "don't know what they don't know." This becomes particularly relevant when it comes to competition. Proposing a new product that is already in the portfolio or on the immediate radar screen of a current industry leader is not a recipe for success. Being in the pack with a bunch of startups all focused on the same general target is not a bad thing—if you know who else is in the race. Show the investor that you are not naïve here. Show knowledge of the industry by responding with the activities of major corporations as well as other relatively new companies.

4. *"Walk me through the sales cycle and then tell me how long you think it takes until revenue gets converted into cash."* The investor wants to make sure that you fully understand the cash cycle in your business. Use a specific number of days here as opposed to general types of answers. The more specific, the better.

5. *"Who are you working with on IP? What do they think about your chances of getting a patent?"* For those readers with technological ventures that have the promise of proprietary intellectual property, the way to answer this question is with the name of an attorney in a reputable law firm. The investor will have his or her own personal network to get further insight into any claims made—but it is unlikely that you will have to go into significant details in the first meeting.

6. *"What's to keep a market leader such as Company X from learning about your idea and doing it themselves and then having a much larger sales force to capture the market?"* This is a tough but important question. There are three answers to it. First, owning some type of intellectual property is a barrier to entry by a large corporation. Second, developing a loyal customer following—"owning" your customer—is another powerful barrier to entry. And third, large companies seem to be slow going after new technologies and new market opportunities. Using all three points in your answer with specific reference to the current market leaders in your industry sector should suffice. Of course, everyone knows that if a global leader wants to compete with you, they can do so. But generally, there are other large competitors who might then be even more motivated to acquire your venture to get to market first with a well-oiled, robust product or service.

7. *"You say that your primary channel is through Company Y. How real is that? What's to prevent them from owning the customer and shopping around for a substitute at a lower price in 18 months?"* Another important question. The first order of business here is to have actually had conversations with that channel partner and being able to

honestly say that they are highly interested in helping to sell your products or services. Second, you should then describe your approach to make that channel partner successful in terms of training, samples, marketing collateral, and selling support in the field. Third, you should indicate that you, too, think it is important for startups not to rely 100% on a single channel partner and that you are already looking for other partners—be it an OEM or retailer, and so forth. Lastly, you should then describe your strategy for reaching directly to customers even though they are buying the product through someone else. This might be a Website for end-users to purchase additional products or services. Or, it might be conference attendance where you interact directly with customers. These responses might not eliminate the risk of overreliance on a channel partner, but at least it shows that you are thinking about motivating and managing channel partners. Successful entrepreneurs know their customers; being totally shielded from customers by a large, controlling large channel partner puts the venture in the backseat in terms of understanding what customers need and how to best serve them.

8. *"How much money are you looking for? Let's go through those key milestones again and see what you plan to spend it on."* Come through hard and clear in your response. Walk through the specific steps within your key milestones. Talk about the number and types of people needed to achieve alpha, beta, and commercial launch. Then, share your insights on the number of people and financing needed to achieve substantial scale as a business and—with that—healthy operating profit. Stage the timing and cash needed to achieve these steps, digging a little deeper into the milestone chart you have in the presentation. Show that you know what needs to be done and can organize the work. While there are numerous stories about investors finding their own managers to run a new company, they would vastly prefer to have the entrepreneurial team be fully capable of getting a business through its first stage of growth.

9. *"How much equity are you prepared to provide for my investment?"* Some investors will actually ask you for your thoughts on company valuation to see if you are in the same ballpark as they. So, you had better be ready to provide a simple, direct answer. Beating around the bush serves no purpose here. Learn the comparable valuations for seed or Series A financings in your industry sector. Perhaps suggest something higher (this is a negotiation!) and justify it! And conclude with the impression that you understand fully that this is a matter for further thought and consideration.

Then there are the advanced class questions that will invariably come during one of your follow-on meetings. They will come in the form of: *"What is your vision for exit? What are comparables?"*

A venture capitalist who is intrigued by your presentation will want to see your thinking on exit. Whether it is in the first meeting or the second, this question is going to come up. If you have an answer prepared, it shows the VC that you are already aligned with his or her own priorities on creating value and providing a return for shareholders. Figure 12.5 shows a spreadsheet that one of our former students used to answer this question for several venture capitalists. Note that the figure was developed for a deal executed in 2005. The numbers are not relevant for anything that you might be doing today! However, the thinking and format fit the purpose of answering this type of question.

On the top part of the spreadsheet are publically available stock prices, number of shares, market caps, and an adjusted "enterprise value" upon which multiples are created. Comparables are typically based on enterprise value rather than market capitalization. The reason is that in the event of an acquisition, the buyer would (a) have to take on the company's debt and (b) pocket its cash. Enterprise value is simply the market cap adjusted by the amount of "net" cash in the

Company X (Information Services)   (Created for an investment valuation in February, 2005)

Public Comps		Stock price Feb 2	Equity market cap $m	Cash $m	Enterprise value $m	Revenue estimates $m		Enterprise value/ revenue		Gross Margin
						CY05	CY06	CY05	CY06	
Salesforce.com	CRM	13.30	1,370	110	1,260	174	283	7.2x	4.5x	80.00%
InfoUSA	IUSA	11.32	605	6	599	395	415	1.5x	1.4x	68.89%
ChoicePoint	CPS	47.22	4,190	23	4,167	1,000	1,150	4.2x	3.6x	45.00%
Equifax	EFX	28.80	3,750	39	3,711	1,270	1,330	2.9x	2.8x	58.12%
Dunn & Bradstreet	DNB	57.85	4,002	275	3,727	1,440	1,530	2.6x	2.4x	68.76%
Thomson	TOC	34.97	23,130	483	22,647	8,000	8,640	2.8x	2.6x	
Monster	MNST	29.11	3,470	142	3,328	853	1,000	3.9x	3.3x	52.43%
Factset	FDS	52.27	1670	67	1,603	309	332	5.2x	4.8x	70.27%
CoStar	CSGP	41.64	761	113	648	112	135	5.8x	4.8x	67.37%
McGraw Hill	MHP	93.58	17,770	423	17,347	5,650	6,000	3.1x	2.9x	59.92%
United Business Media	UNEWY	10.34	3,540	1000	2,540	1,000	1,001	2.5x	2.5x	38.93%
SAP	SAP	38.61	47,970	2640	45,330	10,480	11,590	4.3x	3.9x	51.17%
ProQuest	PQE	33.44	955	8	947	462	494	2.0x	1.9x	60.08%
							Max	7.2x	4.8x	
							Min	1.5x	1.4x	
							Median	3.1x	2.9x	
							Mean	3.7x	3.2x	
							Mean (Ex. Max/Min)	3.6x	3.2x	

Private Comps: Precedent Acquisitions

Date	Target	Acquirer	Revenues (million)	Transaction Value (million)	Multiple
Jan-05	SRD	IBM	$8	$40	4.7x
Jul-04	Seisint	Reed Elsevier	$119	$775	6.5x
Dec-04	BitPipe	TechTarget	$10	$40	4x
Dec-04	Prime Assoc	Metavante	$5.2	$28	5.4x
Oct-04	Pinacor	MarketWatch	$7.0	$18	2.5x
Jun-05	IHI	Thomson	$88	$441	5.1x
Sep-04	CCBN	Thomson	$50	$188	3.8x

Figure 12.5 Developing Comparables for Setting an Exit Goal

Source: From personal contacts and published sources.

business, that is, subtracting the debt and adding the cash on hand. It can differ significantly from the market capitalization and that is why it is often used in exit valuation analysis.

On the bottom of the spreadsheet are acquisitions of private venture funded companies that our former students were able to dig up through their friends and published sources. Those ventures that are acquired five to seven or eight years down the road are typically valued as a multiple of revenue, and some, on next year's projected revenue. Operating profit sweetens the deal, but unlike the price/earnings ratios of publically traded companies, it is not typically the foundation for the acquisition valuation. But pay attention to those gross margins! When your business scales, it needs to achieve similar gross margins because these ultimately drive the bottom-line profitability of the business.

You can see in the figure that the multiples on revenue and earnings for private company deals are lower than the comp's on publicly traded (and arguably more commercially successful) public companies. It is then a matter of arguing for a middle ground between these two averages. You will also find yourself arguing about the companies included in the comparables basket. Nonetheless, doing the work needed to complete this template for your own venture will impress the investor with the fact that you are thinking about making both of you a lot of money!

**** **** ****

If you "get past go," the investor is going to want to check your references. Give him a list of names that will testify to your character and hard work. If possible, include the name(s) of an individual who is a prospective customer or channel partner. The investor will surely call his or her own network of professionals for an outside opinion.

The "experience factor" is obviously problematic for young entrepreneurs (say below 27 years old). One of your own authors went into his first startup at the age of 21—and we did well. But that was with money from friends and family, incredibly tight-fisted operating expenses (we didn't pay ourselves much and rented the cheapest office space in town), and a hunger for good, old-fashioned customer revenue as soon as humanly possible. This is the best approach for young entrepreneurs. There are other ways as well. Getting a "salt and pepper" haired experienced entrepreneur to join your team or serve as an active venture advisor can prove invaluable. That individual will help ease investors' concerns about a young entrepreneurial team, and he or she should know angel investors and venture capitalists on his or her own. Just be careful with your stock and have good legal counsel to help you set up performance-based grants of stock (e.g., stock options). You just don't know if an individual who you have not worked with earlier is going to be a good fit for you and your company.

And there are other ways to surmount the experience factor. Rather than take just any job before, during, or after your MBA, look for those that are either in a large, well-established player in your general market or who are representative of the target customer for a B2B venture. All the while you can be thinking about how to best improve your venture concept and the business model. You will also run into new potential team members. If you are young, working within the target market in an interesting position is probably the best thing you can do in preparation for a successful startup. Either way, view each and every investor presentation as a learning experience.

Thorough preparation—just as you would for the most rigorous examination in your college or graduate career—is so important for a successful outcome. That preparation quickly becomes clear to investors. It really impresses them. Even if a particular investor finds that your particular venture is outside his or her preferred investment focus, a strong showing will often motivate that investor to call friends who are interested in your field of work.

The bottom line is that investors need to walk away from the meeting with an impression of your passion, knowledge, and conviction for the venture. They know that you and your key team members will require all of these to get through the tough times ahead.

Understand That No Matter How Good the Pitch, It Just Might Be the Wrong Investor for Your Venture

Most professional investors have other parameters that serve as a lens through which they see any new proposal. An angel investor is often going to want to have some type of operating experience in the industry in which he or she is investing. That is the value-add that they can bring. It is a good idea to do your homework beforehand. When you speak to an angel who is meeting you privately or who is introducing you to an angel investing group, ask that person about his or her background in a way that is interested, not pushy. In other words, try to find out how they made their money. That should tell you whether the meeting is worthwhile for you or not. You have to decide whether you want to restrict your meetings to individuals who are likely investors. Often, however, even if an angel investor is not interested in your type of venture, chances are that if they like you over breakfast or lunch, they will make the introduction to a peer who is experienced in your industry sector. The Web remains a powerful tool for doing a little research on angel investors and their present or prior companies.

Venture capitalists have areas of portfolio specialization. These focus points are provided directly on the VC firm's Website. They are highly unlikely to invest outside of those industry sectors. So do your homework once again. Find out the VC firms in your region. Visit their Websites. Look at their portfolio companies. Determine if there are companies in the same area as your venture. If not, keep looking for VC firms that do specialize in your field. The most common investment areas for VC firms are software; networking equipment; biotech; Web-enabled health, financial, or entertainment services; social networking ventures; or clean technologies. But there are also boutique VC firms that specialize in consumer products or industrial products. The National Venture Capital Association's Website (http://www.nvca.org/) is a good place to begin.

Once you create a list of VC firms that work in your industry sector, find out the partner(s) in the VC firm who specialize in your area and the names of the companies on which they sit on Boards of Directors. Do a quick Web search on that individual(s). Learn their background—see if there is an educational connection for you or members of your team. Look at the companies where hopefully those VCs had operating experience before becoming VCs—for those are the VCs that we find are by far and away the most valuable in working with to help staff, structure, and scale a venture. Then, find out the companies in which that partner has led the VC firm's investments. Do a quick Web search on those companies. Even better, see if you know anyone working in one of those companies, and if so, inquire about the interaction with the investor and see if your acquaintances know the partner in the VC firm who is working with their company. In other words, arm yourself with knowledge about the background, experience, and current activities of the individual you are going to meet. And, don't forget to check out social networking Websites such as http://www.thefunded.com to gain insight into the level of knowledge and speed in specific investment firms.

Strategic investors—corporations making direct investments into smaller firms—obviously need to have that company provide synergy to the larger company's business. So, here, once again, you need to do your homework on the Web to try to find a match between the corporation's interests and yours. As we described in Chapter 8 on sources of financing, there are a number of major corporations with dedicated innovation programs geared to outside innovation. These programs will each have their own form of paperwork to complete, but we strongly advise you to first make a call. Sell yourself and your idea to someone working within the innovation program and seek their advice on suitability and the best way to approach the corporation for support. The person on the other end of the phone may become your internal champion for navigating the different business units and R&D groups within the corporation.

If you get a chance to meet the R&D group of a major corporation, some caution is required. You will probably be asked to sign a nondisclosure agreement (NDA). Rather than being forced to sign that in the corporation's conference room, it is best to have the NDA e-mailed to you beforehand. Read it carefully and make sure you can live by its terms and conditions. If not, propose a few select changes (typically to the term or length of the agreement and the process by which a party can terminate the agreement). Some of the larger innovative companies have NDAs that are far too lopsided to the benefit of the large company and against the interests of the entrepreneur. For example, here is an actual clause from a corporate NDA that entrepreneurs (friends of the authors) received from a Fortune 100 company that would be the perfect go-to-market partner and strategic investor for the venture:

> Except for the obligations of the parties with respect to Confidential Information disclosed prior to expiration or termination, this Agreement shall (unless extended by mutual agreement) expire or terminate at the earliest of the following events:
>
> a. One (1) year after the Effective Date of this Agreement, or
> b. Thirty (30) days after written notice of termination provided by either party to the other.

Obviously, the Fortune 100 company could simply write a letter voiding the NDA, and even if they did not, a year's protection is nothing for a new firm that needs at least two to three years to enter the market and achieve some scale. An NDA with these types of clauses is analogous to throwing a drowning person an anchor!

The lesson is clear: Find legal counsel experienced in your domain of work. A good NDA and a provisional patent will provide a good degree of protection for the entrepreneur—and neither should cost you very much money. The last thing you want to do is to give your idea away to an R&D department in a major corporation that has trouble thinking for itself.

But remember, you won't have this problem with angel investors or VCs. They are not going to give you an NDA, nor should you force one upon them.

The Last Important Step: Go Get That Meeting!

Sending a business plan or presentation blindly through the mail or e-mail to an investor—any type of investor—is a fool's errand. No matter how good the idea or how well written the plan, the chances of getting a meeting through this approach are virtually zero. For example, VC firms receive numerous business plans "over the transom," that is, blindly sent through the mail. These end up on the desks of "associates" or analysts working for these firms who will review the plans and forward them to the general partners. Our experience is that adds at least two to three months to your fundraising process, and for some reason, plans forwarded by an associate to a general partner never seem to take priority.

As we noted earlier in the last chapter, professional investors such as VCs want a trusted referral first. And with that trusted referral, a solid venture concept, and a well-written business plan, the chances increase substantially for getting that meeting.

So, the question becomes, what is the best way for you to get that trusted referral into an angel group, VC firm, or strategic investor? Here are some methods that our own students use to find that trusted source.

Getting a Meeting With Angels

Use your university's alumni network. Do not discount the utility of successful alumni wanting to help "the next generation" at their respective colleges and universities. Many have formal mentor networks where an administrator will connect you with an experienced business person who matches your particular interests. Forums and panel sessions geared toward entrepreneurship in different fields are also common in education institutions. University business plan competitions are another common venue for meeting successful businesspeople looking to fund new ventures. All of these are great networking opportunities for the young entrepreneur. Attend, dress smart, have a firm handshake, look people in the eye, and have a set of business cards printed beforehand with your contact information. Again, suggest a phone call or coffee/breakfast/lunch and show the courtesy of picking up the tab if the location is of your own choosing. You are asking your guest to do you a very big favor. If your guest is an experienced businessperson friendly to your university, there is a strong probability that they are either private investors or know other angel investors.

Getting a Meeting With VCs

There are four effective methods for getting a meeting with a top-flight venture capitalist.

a. Be a serial entrepreneur who has made money for VCs in a prior company. Unfortunately, this is a rare situation. You goal perhaps is to work yourself into that position over time!

b. Retain a first-rate law firm as the corporate counsel for your venture. Remember our earlier remarks about such firms offering a discounted billing rate as a startup in the hope of more, full-priced work in the future. With that in mind, prominent business attorneys are well connected into both the angel and "institutional" money (which means VCs and private equity funds). If you have the right attorney, you will probably get a meeting with the appropriate VC. Be prepared, however, to have to sell that attorney on the qualities of your venture.

c. Develop a relationship with another entrepreneur who has successfully raised money from a VC firm that invests in your area of interest. The basis of that relationship can be one of seeking advice or mentorship, appreciative of the fact that VC-funded entrepreneurs have barely a second during the work week to focus on anything but their own company. Nonetheless, a breakfast or lunch might just produce an e-mail or telephone call to the general partner of the VC firm that sits on that entrepreneur's board. That's what you need.

d. Meet with alumni of your university, as described above, for coffee/breakfast/lunch. If these alumni are successful in businesses, chances are that they know a few partners at local VC firms as well as angel investors.

Another way to get access to a VC for the meeting is to retain a special boutique investment firm in your city or region. These firms are often run by former VCs. Their job is to help ventures find money, and they work on a sales commission on the money raised—typically 5% to 8%. Unfortunately, many if not most are small-time operations that can consume a lot of your time. Further, most VCs do not take kindly to seeing 5% of their money going to pay a sales commission to an intermediary.

Getting a Meeting With Corporate Strategic Investors

The very best way to get investment meetings with strategic investors—large corporations—is to first develop a relationship with them as a customer or channel partner. In other words, do business with a manager in that corporation. Here, too, you will invariably share a meal at some point—and it is typically at such occasions that the manager will say, "And how are you folks doing for money? Maybe we should get involved." Again, a call to the investment arm from a senior business manager in the corporation is the best type of referral for this type of investor.

There is also another source of contacts into major corporations: your college or university. If your institution is well established, it will have many alumni that are executives in important companies. We have found that the "development" (fundraising) officers in universities are the best source for this type of information. They manage events where successful alums come on campus to participate in advisory boards and related events. Ask for the opportunity to get a cup of coffee or tea with a visiting alumnus but remember, at this point you are only seeking advice—not money—from that alum on your venture idea. In fact, be sure not to bring up the word "money" to your development officer because this will surely make them feel threatened for obvious reasons.

Additionally, if your school has an executive MBA program, ask your professor to network for you into the students enrolled in that program. These will tend to be seasoned professionals—middle- to high-level operating managers already. Ask to see a class roster and identify those who work in the industry sector where you wish to venture. These are also very busy individuals—working and going to school at the same time. Perhaps you can meet for 30 minutes before their class. Or better yet, go out for a beer or two. See if there is synergy with that executive MBA student's company as a potential customer or channel partner. Again, the goal is to develop a business relationship with that company as a lead user or early adopter. From there, strategic investment can follow.

The Bottom-Line for Making Investor Presentations

Your job is to infect the audience with your own enthusiasm for the opportunity. Remember that. This is definitely a sales process. And if the investor tells you that he or she is not interested, try not to get mad or frustrated. Ask "why?" and dig a little deeper into those whys. Incorporate their thinking into your plans and presentations for the next group of investors. After each pitch, grab a cup of coffee or a beer and think about what you have learned.

If you have to speak to 15, or 20, or 30 investors before reaching the right one, simply know that *countless entrepreneurs have walked this road before you and have achieved success.* You are the next generation carrying the entrepreneurial torch. The opportunity is yours for the taking.

Be bold, be smart, and above all else, remain true to your vision.

Venture Cases

SilverRail Technologies, Inc.

November 2009

Aaron Gowell sat at the desk in his home office. The laptop monitor illuminated the dimly lit room and the pile of papers in front of it. Peering into the screen, Aaron contemplated the rough outlines of a five-year financial forecast for the new venture he would be pitching to venture capitalists in less than two weeks' time. That venture, dubbed SilverRail, would be the first-ever aggregator of rail passenger seats for corporate and online travel agencies, with a focus on the booming market for high speed train travel across Europe. With the glaring exception of rail, every mode of business and vacation travel booking—air, car rental, hotels, and cruises—had moved to the Web. This represented a huge hole that Aaron aimed to fill.

In Europe, train travel was the dominant form of intercity transportation and by 2009, an $80 billion industry—50 times the size of its U.S. counterpart. Aaron aimed to develop B2B e-commerce software that travel agencies could use to view schedules, prices, and availability, and make reservations—just as they currently did for other modes of travel. Aaron's company would aggregate the inventory from all the different European national railroad systems and make the combined result available to corporate travel agencies like Amex and online travel agencies like Expedia. His new company would receive a commission on all bookings through the system. Even with very conservative assumptions, net revenues and EBITDA could be huge within five years.

Aaron was no newcomer to the online travel business. He had worked the numbers and made successful investor pitches in prior ventures. Now he had to do it again. The question was, would the VCs share his confidence in the future of rail travel, and the opportunity for SilverRail as an inventory aggregator? What would they have to hear and see before they'd open their wallets? And, beyond the pitch, what deals would he have to strike along the way with European rail systems and on-line travel sites to validate the plan?

These thoughts were on his mind as he planned his fund-raising presentation. That presentation would include a pro forma P&L and a set of PowerPoint slides. To spark the interest of venture capitalists in the gloomy economic environment of late 2009, that presentation would have to be *very* powerful.

Aaron Gowell

Launching a new business was the furthest thing from Aaron Gowell's mind in the 1980s.

As a member of the U.S. Army's 82nd Airborne Division, Aaron was more concerned with launching himself with a parachute from the belly of a C-130 airplane. But after combat tours in Panama and Gulf War I, he returned to civilian life. Under the GI Bill, he completed college at

Written by Marc H. Meyer and Richard Luecke. Copyright © 2011, Marc H. Meyer.

Northeastern University with an MS in Finance. Graduating summa cum laude in 1996, he was one of the rare few "coops" who was hired by Bain & Company, a prestigious management consulting firm headquartered in Boston, where Gowell helped found Bain's highly successful private equity consulting practice that consulted to companies during acquisitions, such as when AOL acquired Compuserve.

Two years later Aaron was on the move, this time to General Catalyst Partners. General Catalyst was a private equity firm with major investments in the travel industry. One of the firms General Catalyst had acquired was a cruise business—National Leisure Group with the idea of turning it into the travel industry's first online cruise agency. The managing partners of General Catalyst dispatched Aaron to help build the business. He quickly became the chief operating executive. (See Appendix A for an article describing Aaron's work at NLG). Aaron described his venture capital firm's activity:

> GC decided to buy a small traditional travel company that understood cruises and built an Internet travel company around it. We called it National Leisure Group (NLG), and I was appointed as CEO. I wrote the business plan, raised money, and built a team and the technology—the whole thing.

NLG built the cruise industry's first online booking system, which aggregated all of the cruise suppliers into one e-commerce platform—and then provided white label Websites to online travel agencies like Expedia, Orbitz, Priceline, and Yahoo! Travel.

Under Aaron's leadership, NLG grew its business and made a series of strategic investments, increasing employees from 80 to 1,800. It eventually owned or operated 20 private-label vacation brands. The NLG cruise platform was similar to the airline industry's SABRE system. NLG's system made it possible for travel agents and on-line Web services to see all available cruise inventory and prices in real time, and then, book customers. As Aaron noted:

> NLG specialized in complex travel and grew to be one of the largest travel agencies in the country. Expedia and Travelocity were focused on airlines, cars, and hotels, but they entirely ignored cruise vacations—a $16B market!

Over the course of six years, Gowell grew the business from $110M in sales to over $1B and successfully sold the business in 2006.

Mission accomplished, Aaron returned to General Catalyst as an "Entrepreneur In Residence." From this perch, he was exposed to all important developments in the travel and vacation space.

One opportunity that caught his eye was a small firm whose R&D unit had developed a beta version of online booking technology for rail travel. "That company had lots of problems," he recalls, "and General Catalyst withdrew its interest."

Aaron, however, was intrigued by the possibility of doing for rail travel what NLG had done for cruise vacations, and what Expedia and others had done for air, car and hotel rentals. The little company might have problems as a money-making business in its present form, but Aaron thought the new technology within the company was outstanding.

Aaron started hitting the Web and making telephone calls. A little research made it clear that rail in auto-centric America was limited to the perennially money-losing Amtrak with no immediate prospects for significant growth. For the rest of the developed world, however, passenger rail travel was huge and growing, driven by new 250 mph trains, often at expense of air travel. Aaron sized the broader opportunity in rail travel this way:

> "Whenever rail connects two cities that are less than three hours apart, new high speed trains take most of the market away from air travel between them." Once the Chunnel was built between London and Paris, 80 percent of travel between those cities shifted from airplanes to trains—and that was the heaviest traveled air route in the world!"

With more and more high-speed rail projects on the drawing boards in Europe and Asia, it was clear that rail's share of the travel market—already substantial—would grow even larger. Fueling the entrepreneurial opportunity was the European Union's push to increase train travel across the continent—because rail had a much lower carbon emissions footprint compared to both air and car travel. Aaron got his hands on the high speed rail installation plan published by the European Union over the coming decade. It was clear that the Chunnel-type projects for intercity travel was a major investment priority for Union members. Other factors, such as the growth of European equivalent on-line travel sites similar to Expedia, Travelocity, and Orbitz, further wetted his appetite.

Aaron thought it was time to approach the owners of the troubled software company with an offer to buy their technology in return for cash and an ownership interest in his new venture. They agreed in principle to the transaction, realizing that their technology would only see the light of day with a person like Aaron behind the wheel. Now it was time to put together a business plan and a presentation to raise the capital to complete the software and create the operations needed to support the global rail marketplace.

Rail Industry Research _____

Numbers to substantiate the market opportunity and prove the addressable market were going to be crucial. Thanks to his Bain training in industry analysis, Aaron had a good idea about how to proceed:

> I learned at Bain to get as much information about an industry or company as I possibly could and then develop a story from it.
>
> At Bain we used to say that we could win every argument if we had enough data. If you're going to approach VCs, you'll have much more success if you're in command of all the facts and done all your homework. They have a hard time saying no to a fact-based case.

A self-described "research hound," Aaron worked hard to gather data on the market size, the forces that were driving more consumers to rail travel, and opportunity to make rail travel information and booking more accessible. Some of the information he needed was available online. He also relied on PhoCusWright, the leading source of data for the online travel industry.

Current Market Sizes _____

These industry data[1] revealed a large and growing market. In 2007, the worldwide market for rail travel was roughly $300 billion and projected to increase at a compound annual growth rate of 8 percent.

Aaron found great variations in the dollar size of national markets, with small geographic entities have disproportionately large rail travel expenditure in many cases. For example, the tiny Benelux countries accounted for $7.2 billion in annual passenger rail receipts in 2007, the UK stood at $12 billion, and Germany led the Euro league at $23 billion. In total, European spending on trail travel was $80 billion. In contrast, U.S. travelers spent a mere $1.6 billion (Exhibit 1).

---

[1] "International Railway Statistics" International Union of Railways (UIC), Paris, 2007, and a "Ten Year Growth Report" made available by the Association of Train Operating Companies in June 2007.

USA	$ 1.6
Canada	$0.3
Australia	$ 6.7
Japan	$ 7.9
Korea	$12.0
China	$18.0
Russia	$16.0
Europe	$80.9
India	$20.0

Exhibit 1 2007 Spending on Passenger Rail Travel (rounded, billions $)

Source: "International Railway Statistics," International Union of Railways (UIC), Paris, 2007.

Rail Versus Air Competition

With all the security in air terminals plus increased passenger volumes in the post-9/11 world, frequent travelers like Aaron were keenly aware of the pain and frustration associated with air travel. They had to arrive an hour before take-off, run a gauntlet of metal detectors and X-ray devices. Passenger volumes in Europe had increased substantially as well with the growth of budget carriers such as Ryan Air, and security had become increasingly tight.

The Europeans were also much further along in rail travel compared to the United States. Major cities were amply linked with rail service. Many of these were high speed and offered passenger amenities that airplanes lacked, such as Wi-Fi access, unrestricted usage of cell phones, laptop power sources, and so forth. And unlike airplanes, these trains traveled between city centers, making long, expensive taxi rides from outlying airports unnecessary. Except for Amtrak's operations in the Northeast Corridor, U.S. travelers had few alternatives to the annoyances of air travel for distance travel.

Given the expanding high speed rail infrastructures of their respective countries, Europeans, Koreans, Japanese, and others were turning to rail travel in high numbers as the preferred alternative to intercity plane flight. Aaron's research revealed that rail's share of the travel market (versus air) was especially high along rail routes greater than 1 hour and less than four hours in duration. This became the sweet spot in his target market. His data sources showed the relationship between rail travel time and rail's market share (versus air) in the EU countries (Exhibit 2). Of the total European market for rail travel of $80 billion, the one to four hour travel focus still left him with a well-defined addressable market of approximately $48 billion a year.

Travel Time (hour)	Rail's Share
1.5	90%
2.0	80%
3.0	58%
4.0	40%
5.0	23%

Exhibit 2 Rail's Market Share Relative to Rail Travel Time

Sources: Thalys NBTA, May 2009; Travel Weekly, 4 December 2009.

Short-haul high speed rail between major European cities would clearly disrupt the trend of low cost air carriers that had emerged over the past decade. Europe had 3,700 kilometers of high-speed rail in 2009, but was projected to have 9,000 kilometers by 2020.[2] Aaron recalls:

> Based on these data, I estimated that high-speed rail would effectively eliminate air travel as a competitor between routes of 600 kilometers or less. All of that business would be captured by trains.

Supporting Factors Behind the Business Opportunity

A number of political and environmental factors pointed to a rosy future for passenger rail. Many governments were pushing their citizens toward rail travel as a solution to climate change, highway congestion, and to reduce their dependence on foreign oil.

As a centralizing decision-making authority, the European Union was moving strongly towards rail. It had made the bold decision to begin to deregulate the European rail industry in 2010, making it possible for carriers to compete across borders. The plan would allow a German carrier, for example, to take passengers all the way from Munich to London, competing directly with French or Dutch or Belgian or English carriers along the way.

This would be an enormous change from the two centuries of history where strong national governments established dominant national governmental organizations to build and operate rail travel for passengers and freight. Rail gauges were often deliberately built in different sizes to disrupt resupply by rail from invading forces. Booking systems were different, currencies were different, and in more recent decades, computer systems were different. Now, all of this was going to change.

The EU had stepped up and committed $250 billion to develop new high-speed rail infrastructure across the continent! That is compared to the meager $18 billion plan presented for high speed rail in the United States. Globally, Aaron's research showed an expected 4x increase in high speed track over the next 15 years.

Using mostly freely available Web sources, Aaron found evidence of other factors that favored train travel:

- Rising fuel costs—rail was more fuel efficient per passenger miles than air or autos. Some researchers had found that rail moved people at *700 miles per gallon of fuel*—far better than all other modes of transport.
- Climate issues—*rail produced 89 percent less CO_2 than air travel* and 70 percent less than automobiles on a per passenger mile basis
- Shorter travel times for consumers versus air on most routes of 300 miles or less due to no early security checks, and city center-to-city center routes.
- Greater passenger comfort and more on-board amenities provided in trains compared to no-frills budget air carriers that had emerged across Europe.
- New 250 mph trains, allow travel times to compete with air travel.

These finding pointed to the simple, powerful conclusion that rail travel in Europe and Asia was already huge and growing. One study forecasted a growth rate of 8 percent per year over

---

[2] International Union of Railways data.

the next 15 years.[3] This signaled a healthy and buoyant environment in which to launch a passenger rail-related venture.

Booking Rail Travel: Industry Research

Aaron's vision was to create a Global Distribution System (GDS) for booking rail travel. Here, thanks to his past experience as CEO of National Leisure Group, he had substantial working knowledge of the industry and well as existing relationships with many of the key players in the channel.

For the U.S. and Europe, Aaron's research showed that the travel booking market was estimated to be $600 billion per year. It included air travel, car rentals, hotels, cruises as well as rail. Over 50% of that travel was booked through two competing channels: corporate travel agencies and online travel agencies.

Corporate Agencies

Corporate travel agencies are companies that sell travel products and services to business travelers on behalf of suppliers: airlines, car rentals, cruise lines, hotels, etc. Notable agency examples include American Express, Hogg Robinson, and Carlson Travel.

All of these travel agencies source the product info through the GDSs that included SABRE, Amadeus, and Galileo. These GDSs aggregate the inventory from suppliers and make it easily available for search and booking by the travel agents. The GDSs' business model is to charge booking fees to the supplier equivalent to roughly 5% of sales on anything booked through their systems.

There were GDSs for air, hotels, rental cars, and so forth, *but none yet for rail travel.* While agencies could book rail by communicating directly with the individual rail supplier, there was no single source to see open seats from all rail carriers. Each customer inquiry required a separate phone call or online check with a particular rail service. If a customer needed to travel between different countries, that meant a number of phone calls or Web checks to different systems—and then, the skill and knowledge on how best to put forward an integrated itinerary for the customer. This was highly inefficient. The result is that in spite of the fact that travel agencies sold >50% of all travel, they sold less than 1 percent of rail travel! These agencies knew that they were missing out on a large and growing segment of the travel industry.

Online Booking

By 2009, online travel agencies (OTAs) such as Travelocity, Orbitz, Expedia, and PriceLine had taken a huge chunk of commission business from traditional travel agencies. Increasingly, the consuming public was Internet savvy. In 2009, 60 percent of all U.S. travel was booked online; in Europe the percentage was 50 percent. And for the U.S., 71 percent of non-commuter trips were booked online through Amtrak's Website. All of these various percentages were climbing year-over-year.

Like their corporate agency rivals, online travel agencies relied on the same GDSs, and gave customers information and booking access to the same range of travel products and services. And, like their corporate rivals, the on-line travel portals lacked access to a rail travel GDS aggregator and booking broker.

---

[3] Association of Train Operating Companies; Amadeus Rail Market Whitepaper.

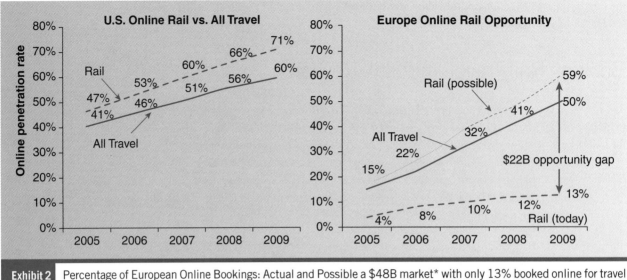

Exhibit 2 Percentage of European Online Bookings: Actual and Possible a $48B market* with only 13% booked online for travel between 1 to 4 hours

* Long distance leisure + business, excludes commuter and regional

Sources: PhoCusWright 2007 Travel Report, PhoCusWright 2007 EU OTA Travel Report.

In Europe specifically, only 13 percent of rail travel was booked online. The more Aaron thought about Europe as an initial target market, he saw a huge gap between actual rail travel and the percentage of that travel booked online, particularly in his sweet spot of travel between 1 to 4 hours in duration. (Exhibit 2)

The only way to bring online rail books in line with other travel—and with its potential—was through a GDS such as the one Aaron wanted to create. Without it, rail bookings would remain complex and frustrating for agents and consumers doing it on their own.

To prove his point, Aaron developed a range of use case scenarios for booking travel between cities within and between different European countries, counting the number of steps required to book each trip using various national rail and travel agency Websites. He found that to travel from London to Brussels, for example, required seven steps, and from Brussels to Cologne, nine steps! Even going from Manchester, England to London required seven specific steps. So, if a passenger wanted to travel from Manchester, England to Cologne, Germany, 23 separate steps were needed. That included three separate rail bookings, using three different Websites, and two currencies. Aaron noted:

> That includes three credit card transactions. You have to buy UK tickets in pounds and other tickets in Euros.

One of Aaron's industry sources indicated that two-thirds of attempted rail books in Europe *failed* due to a combination of booking and financial transaction complexity. He remarked:

> "That's as clear a customer need as you will ever find. The rail supplier sites present information on travel in ways that are not uniform or easy to understand. There's no Expedia to clean it up and make it easy. The result is a terrible consumer shopping experience."

This situation reminded Aaron of one of entrepreneurship's Golden Rules: Opportunity lurks wherever you can save a customer time or money, eliminate pain, and remove frustration.

Going after the $48 billion addressable market in Europe, Aaron figured that if his venture could capture, and apply the 5 percent fees charged by other GDSs, he could realize a whopping $3.5 billion in annual revenues! Even if he could only get a third of the booking, his business could still become another NLG.

The SilverRail Solution _____

With the U.S.-based technology he knew he could purchase as the software GDS engine, Aaron set out to build an "aggregator" that would contain all seats on all routes offered by European rail lines—a rail version of the SABRE GDS that every travel agency and every online ticket service used to serve their air travel customers.

Though train companies in the UK, Germany, France, and other nations maintained separate databases, Aaron knew that his software had the flexibility and power to bring all these data together, store them in a standard, accessible format, and present easy-to-use screens for users. With this integrated system, a customer taking Aaron's hypothetical trip from Manchester to London to Brussels to Cologne could book the trip with one search and four

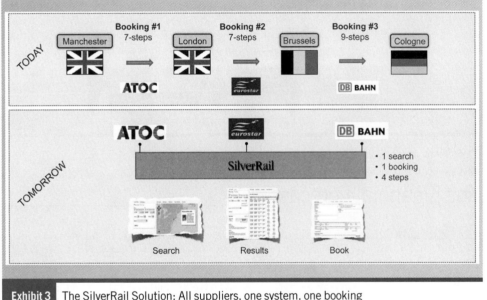

Exhibit 3 The SilverRail Solution: All suppliers, one system, one booking

ATOC, Eurostar, and Bahn are current national rail travel booking Websites, each with different formats, and representing two different currencies.

steps—not three searches and 23 steps required previously! (Exhibit 3) Customers would see a booking page very similar to those used by Expedia and other online systems (Exhibit 4).

Would the travel agencies and online ticketing services be interested? His inquires through old NLG contacts returned nothing but enthusiasm. The travel agents knew they were not participating in Europe's hottest travel segment. The online travel portals were seeking to simplify complexity, reduce cost, and increase their business in cross-national rail travel. Aaron's venture would put money on each of their respective tables.[4]

_____

[4] While Aaron's focus was to be a B2B GDS travel services provider, he learned that if he wanted to be licensed as a GDS doing business in Britain, he would also have to create a B2C direct consumer site. This raised the potential of competing with his channel partners and he had to make sure that they knew that his consumer site was a regulatory requirement. This B2C rail travel site, Quno, was launched in the first year of business.

Booking Page With a SilverRail Channel Partner

The Financial Forecast

Aaron now had to create a compelling story around the data he had assembled. He could image how his VC audience would respond even to such compelling market data: 'That's interesting Aaron, but how will you make money from all this—and how much?'

To answer that question convincingly, he would have to build and refine a financial forecast that was reasonably conservative, *yet* contained the expectation of a very high return.

The Revenue Model

Aaron had the data to show that the worldwide market for rail travel was about $300 billion. As a startup, he was also in no position to address the world market right away. As he saw it, the best initial opportunity was Europe. This represented $80 billion in annual rail bookings. The one to four hour sweet spot gave him 60% of that number, or $48 billion. Next, the "opportunity gap" he had discovered between possible and current online rail bookings was about $22 billion (47% of the $48 billion, as shown in Exhibit 2). That $22 billion was what he would use for his initial addressable market. Then, he would expand to other regions of the world. Aaron noted,

> "When pitching VCs, it's very important not to talk about tackling the whole market, but to segment the market down into something more believable and achievable—it builds credibility with the VCs who are tired of companies pitching them on how they're going to "capture just 2% of the total market," which is simply not a believable approach. If you talk about tackling the whole market, you're going to get kicked out of the room. The more detailed you are in your segmentation, the more credibility you gain."

Industry practice in air, rail, and cruises awarded GDS operators 5 percent of booking, and Aaron had assure himself through contacts with rail companies that they would pay him the same percentage if he could create a system that would make online bookings easier for travelers and agencies.

With the 5% standard industry commission for GDS providers in other travel segments, Aaron had his annual revenue target: $1.1 billion in annual revenue for his new venture.[5]

Next, Aaron knew that VCs tend to think in 5 year windows for exit valuations. Based on this, Aaron figured that:

> If I estimate capturing more than 10 percent of the $1.1 billion by the end of Year 5, they won't believe me. If I estimate less than 10 percent, they'll think I'm not sufficiently aggressive. $110 million in revenue seems a very achievable target. If we knock it out of the park, we might even get to $300 million.

Aaron then ran detailed projections on the revenues possible from selling rail through the major European corporate and online travel agencies. This more granular revenue projection also got him into the hundreds of millions of dollars by the end of Year 5.

He also knew that his percentage of market capture would have to ramp up to that 10 percent by Year 5. It wouldn't happen overnight. Starting at 1% in Year 1 seemed reasonable. Assumptions would have to be made for Years 2 through 4. He further assumed that software development would take yet another six months from the point of Series A financing to create a better user interface as well as greater scalability in the database design. When revenues did begin, the ramp would be slow for the next three months as the first customers went live with a few kinks to be resolved. Aggressive ramp up of sales would then start in the last three months of the first year and continue forward.

Looking at the end of the five year planning horizon, Aaron figured that 10 percent of the $22 billion market in year 5 would give SilverRail *gross* bookings of $2.2 billion. And if suppliers would pay him 5 percent of that amount, the new venture would be looking at *net* revenues of $110 million. This calculation, however, did not account for the anticipate 8 percent annual growth in rail bookings indicated by his research. Aaron went back and recalculated his total and addressable market figures to reflect that growth.

Aaron also found out that wholesalers/brokers in the travel business could expect a 40 day average receivables period from agents. Not ideal, but still, manageable in terms of preserving working capital in the business with appropriate funding.

The Path to Profitability

Aaron continued with his five-year financial forecast, estimating anticipated costs for scaling up SilverRail's technology systems and the venture's general and administrative expenses. He developed detailed monthly forecasts for systems operating costs (which were integrating data from the various national railroad systems and hosting the GDS with trusted third parties), programming and customer support staff, as well as other types of GS&A expenses. The results of this planning are provided in Exhibit 5.

Within the GS&A were extraordinary year-one costs for setting up business in Europe. This included:

- $200K in legal expenses
- $80K in travel costs
- $120K in recruiting costs
- $200K in computer hardware
- $100K to set up a UK office

[5] One would think that over a billion dollars of annual, recurring revenue would be enough to whet any VCs appetite, but Aaron had to make 36 different presentations to VCs before he got his Series A financing—from presentation #37! "Raising $6 million for a startup during the economic downturn since the Depression was incredibly hard," he noted. "My combat experience came in handy."

	Year 1	Year 2	Year 3	Year 4	Year 5
Systems operating costs	$283,000	$7,053,000	$22,323,000	30,913,000	$40,374,00
GS&A expenses	$2,148,000	$5,184,000	$5,836,000	$5,848,000	$5,941,000

Exhibit 5 Estimated Costs and Expenses

Subtracting these expenses from projected net revenues would give him annual EBITDA figures, from which a valuation could be estimated, using a travel industry multiple. Based on his research of comparable ventures, Aaron determined that multiple to be eight times EBITDA.

The Series A Capital Structure

Aaron needed to raise money to complete the purchase of the booking software, create an R&D team to scale and otherwise improve it, and build a marketing and operations capability in Europe. Looking at his cashflow projections, he thought that $5 million should be sufficient for the first round, which should last him 18 months before a second round was needed— hopefully at a much higher valuation than the first round. Being an experienced entrepreneur, Aaron also wanted to leave himself a cash cushion for unexpected expenses during those first 18 months. He thought that an additional $1 million would be sufficient for that purpose. He knew that in the present economy, raising a $6 million Series A would be no small feat, even for an individual with a track record such as his own. He was prepared to visit dozens of venture capital firms over the next two months.

As part of this financing, Aaron had agreed to give the former owners of the technology a 10% equity position in the business, post Series A financing. In addition, Aaron researched the market average for employee ownership in new ventures such as the one he wished to start, and found that 30% ownership for the team was reasonable. The result was that he was prepared to provide 60% of the business to investors for $6M, giving him a post-money Series A valuation of $10 million.

It was time to get to work preparing the investor pitch. Now that he had thought through the various elements of his presentation, Aaron was ready and eager to put everything together in a compelling and convincing package. "If I have enough data," he reminded himself, "I can win any argument."

Student Assignment _____

Put yourself in Aaron's shoes. Using the information provided in the case, do the following:

1. Develop an outline of Aaron's verbal presentation to venture capitalists (less than one page). What should be his major points?
2. Create a set of presentation slides for his pitch.
3. Prepare a five-year financial forecast in the form of a P&L. Be sure to account for the 8 percent CAGR estimated for passenger rail travel over the planning period.
4. Determine the year in which the venture will be cash positive.
5. Calculate the SilverRail's value at the end of year five, using a multiple of 8 times EBITDA. Assume two rounds of investment: a Series A from one VC at the start for $6 million and 60% of the stock, and a Series B in Year 2 for $15 million for another 25% of the stock ($5 million from the first VC, and two $5 million tranches from two additional VCs for expansion of services beyond Europe.) What would the founders' and investor's stock be worth if your Year 5 company valuation became an actual exit point?

Appendix 1

6 Boston Business Journal boston.bizjournals.com February 6-12, 2004

NLG ready to top $1B, eyes larger share of the market

BY JILL LERNER
JOURNAL STAFF

WOBURN — After making waves with a $110 million acquisition late last year, officials of Woburn-based cruise and vacation company National Leisure Group Inc. say they are poised to sail near the $1 billion sales mark this year.

In November, privately held NLG acquired the U.S. cruise division of Del Ray Beach, Fla.-based MyTravel Group, rendering the Woburn company — which owns or licenses approximately 20 private-label vacation brands, including Filene's Basement Vacation Outlet and 1-800-CRUISES, one of the largest providers of cruise vacations in North America.

The acquisition increased NLG's total employment rolls to 1,800 nationwide, including 400 in Massachusetts.

But despite its size, NLG still only commands about 1 percent to 2 percent of the $150 billion U.S. leisure-travel market, and its young co-CEOs say there is opportunity to grab a bigger share by taking advantage of dramatics shifts in the way consumers buy travel, and the resilience of the cruise industry amid a generally sluggish travel market.

About 60 percent of NLG's revenue comes from sales of cruises, with the balance coming from other vacation services.

"The room for growth is tremendous," said Brad Gerstner, 32, who along with Aaron Gowell, 35, helms the company.

Venture capitalists Joel Cutler and David Fialkow started NLG in 1986 as a means to resell excess travel inventory in bulk at reduced rates. Later that year, they joined with Filene's Basement to open a second brand, Vacation Outlet, in the downtown Boston store.

In 1995, they sold the company, and in 2000, they began their Cambridge venture firm, General Catalyst Partners. Throughout the 1990s, NLG added brands, such as BJ's Vacations and the Vacation Store, to its portfolio, and in 2000, in conjunction with Newton-based private equity firm Softbank Capital Partners, Cutler and Fialkow's firm bought it back for $125 million.

Following the untimely death of company president Greg Davis, the investors installed Gerstner and Gowell as co-CEOs in 2002.

"It was very clear to David Fialkow and me ... the migration from off-line to online travel was very real," said Cutler.

"Buying back the company seemed to make more sense than doing a raw start-up," he added.

In recent years the company has invested heavily in technology, growing its staff of technologists from 10 to 120, in order to capitalize on market shifts in the way consumers buy travel, said its CEOs.

"As of the late 1990s, you still had a local travel agency on basically every street corner in America. ... We realized the desire to buy travel online would drive massive consolidation," said Gerstner.

In fact, traditional travel agencies nationally continued to fold last year, with the number of agencies dropping to 25,620 from 29,522, according to the Airlines Reporting Corp.

A big factor in the decline is consumers' shift to e-commerce travel sites like those operated by NLG, which can provide vacations at lower prices because technology

Aaron Gowell and Brad Gerstner, co-CEOs of Woburn-based cruise and vacation company NLG, say they are on track to generate $1 billion in sales this year.

lowers their costs for distribution.

Additionally, whereas traditional agents often re-sell vacation packages, NLG negotiates its own wholesale agreements with its lodging and transportation suppliers, further reducing the prices it can offer.

NLG charges fees for its services and says its margins are about 20 percent.

Another key factor in the company's success is the resilience of the cruise industry.

"The cruise industry ... remains the fastest-growing segment of the travel industry," said Brian Major, a spokesman for the New York City-based Cruise Lines International Association, who noted cruise vacation retailers continue to consolidate.

Last year saw the launch of 14 new ships, and in 2003, the industry increased its passenger load by 11 percent, according to the American Society of Travel Agents.

Fifty-six percent of people who have ever cruised have done so in the past five years, according to CLIA.

Cutler, who says the business is "nicely profitable," says Gerstner and Gowell's performance has "far exceeded anyone's expectations," and the co-CEOs themselves are bullish on NLG's market opportunity.

The company is going after JetBlue Airways Corp.'s vacation service, and executives say they plan to increase their marketing budget by 25 percent this year to promote existing brands.

Appendix 2

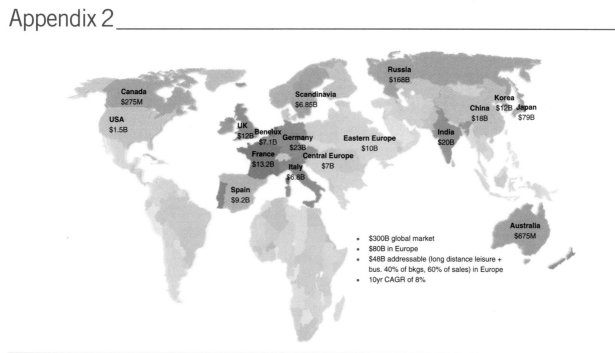

Rail travel in major national markets (2007)

Sources: UIC "International Railway Statistics" (2007); TOC "Ten Year Growth Report" (6/07).

Appendix 3

High Speed Rail is transforming the travel landscape. In 10 years,
European air travel on routes <600km will be virtually eliminated.>

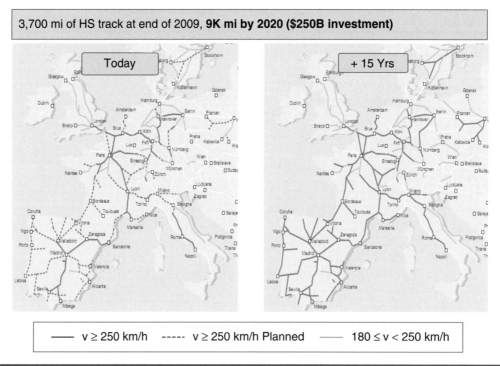

The Growth in European High Speed Rail

Sources: UIC "International Railway Statistics" (2007); TOC "Ten Year Growth Report" (6/07).

Ready Seafood

Business Model Innovation and Venturing in a Mature Industry

Marc H. Meyer, Matthew Allen, and Fredrick G. Crane
Northeastern University
Boston, MA

Corresponding Author: mhm@neu.edu

Introduction

It's a perfect September day in Portland, Maine. Crisp and clear. And the harbor side location of Ready Seafood is already busy. A lobster boat has pulled up alongside the wharf and is unloading its morning's catch. The boat's skipper, who has been on the water since before sunup, relaxes on the pier, regaining his land legs as a Ready employee examines and weighs the lobsters, then puts them into a holding tank with dozens of their crustacean kin. Within a few minutes the lobsterman has been issued a check and is casting off , heading seaward to check his other traps.

A lobster boat at the Ready Seafood dock.

Source: Catch a Piece of Maine, with permission.

Forthcoming in The International Review of Entrepreneurship.

Meanwhile, inside a 5,000 square feet leased building, several young men are busily pulling lobsters out of super-cooled holding tanks and packing them into specially designed cartons for a journey that will speed them by truck to Logan airport, then on by air express to distributors in Europe and Japan. Others lobsters will be taken to the loading dock for local and regional distribution. The holding tanks in the backrooms could contain 45,.000 pounds of lobster at any given time.

The Ready operation just described is quality-oriented and highly efficient. With the exception of its overseas sales, however, its business model differs little from the model followed by other lobster and seafood distributors on the same wharf and up and down the Atlantic coast. That model is simple and straightforward: take in freshly caught product from boats on one side of the wharf and sell it at a modest markup out the other side to local restaurants, supermarket chains, and other buyers. If a distributor can manage its cost, he or she can earn a 3–5 percent operating margin.

While Ready has the appearance of a standard seafood distributor, a small, cramped office with two employees on the building's second floor is creating something new and different— and immensely more profitable: catchapieceofmaine.com. This small but growing operation has established a direct supply link between ruggedly independent Maine lobstermen and the far flung individuals who purchase and consume their harvest. That link is tight and personal: the customer owns an interest in a lobster trap, and knows the fisherman who regularly baits and checks it. And she'll hear from him often. "Hello," says a voice on the phone as a customer is preparing a special meal for her guests. "This is Captain John from the Port of Cape Elizabeth, Maine. I'm on the boat and just calling to see if your lobsters arrived today in good condition. I caught them yesterday."

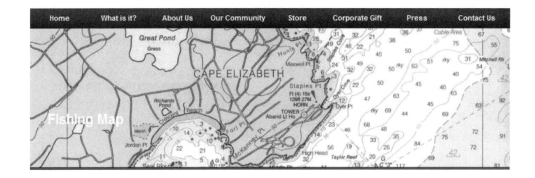

John and Brendan Ready grew up in Cape Elizabeth, just south of Portland, Maine. Their uncle Ted, like many other local men, was a commercial lobsterman, and through him they learned the trade. The business is dangerous and physically demanding to the point of breaking strong men before their time. But the two young men couldn't get their fill of being out on the water, baiting and hauling traps. Before either was ten they owned their own boat and gear and were earning modest incomes. "Lobstering was our passion," says John Ready, "and the older lobstermen were our heroes."

Off the Water and Onto the Dock _____

The brothers continued lobstering through elementary and high school. Then Brendan went off to Stonehill College, where he majored in marketing. John enrolled in Northeastern University's "coop" business program, a five-year undergraduate curriculum characterized by alternating periods of work internships and classroom study. While there, John took a "venturing" course which, among other things, required him to develop a plan for a new business. His choice of business, with Brendan's participation, was a lobster distributorship. "We realized that the working lifestyle we so admired could not be sustained as we got older," says John. "We could see that in the older men we had looked up to as kids. Being out in rough weather day and night, lifting traps and heavy equipment, and so forth, takes a huge toll on your back, your knees, your whole body."

There was also a clear economic reason for moving a step up the supply chain from harvester to distributor. Lobstermen are stuck selling a commodity product at a price dictated by supply/demand forces over which they have no control. They also feel the full force of bad harvest seasons and rising fuel costs. One or two years of low prices or bad harvests can force even the hardest working lobsterman to sell his boat and quit the business. And because a license holder can work no more than 800 traps, a lobsterman's potential income has a ceiling. Says, John:

> There are some five thousand full-time licensed lobstermen in Maine. Because of the trap limit, and other dynamics such as the amount of fierce competion amoung harvesters, it is difficult for a lobsterman to catch more than 50,000 pounds each year. At the current $2.50 per pound dock price, that means $125,000 in revenue—tops! After boat payments, insurance, fuel, equipment, and so forth, it's hard to net more than $50,000 in a year of very hard work.

A distributor, in contrast, works "out of the weather." He can ride the spread between harvester and retailer and may squeeze out a bit more profit margin through operational innovations and efficiencies. And if he has good marketing sense, he can scale up volume by generating more or larger accounts.

When they finished college in 2004, the Ready brothers began implementing John's business plan which, coincidentally, won Northeastern's undergrad business plan competition that year. With the financial support of friends and family and an SBA-guarantee bank loan, they leased a building on Hobson's Wharf just off Portland's bustling Commercial Street, purchased holding tanks and other necessary equipment, and used their contacts to generate initial customers. "It was a grind," John confesses.

> During the first 18 months I spent most nights here in the building, sleeping on a cot. You never knew when a lobster boat would pull up wanting to sell its catch. Someone had to be here at night, but we didn't have the cash to hire anyone.

To preserve cash, the brothers took turns running the shop while the other was out catching lobsters. That catch was distributed without payment to the business.

Distribution is a simple and straightforward business. As described by the brothers, "We buy lobsters from one side of the building [dockside] and sell them out the other side [the loading dock where vans and trucks make pickups]. For the many lobster distributors in Portland and elsewhere along the New England coast, this business model produces low margins: about 5 percent. "It's an easy business to enter," according to John. "All you need is a building with boat access, a winch and scale, and a tank system."

The Ready's built their small distributorship buying lobsters from their local Maine lobstermen and selling their lobsters to restaurants and fish markets in Maine and its surrounding states. Although finances were extremely tight, they reached $2 million in sales within two years, and the profits from that allowed both to "get off the water."

From Local to Global Distribution _____

Once they had their feet on the ground, the Readys turned their attention to optimizing the three key factors that affect margins in their industry: buying, holding, and selling lobsters.

- *Buying*. Eager to assure a reliable supply of product, the Readys adopted a strategy of buying both direct from lobstermen as well as indirect from dealers. Dealers who would work as middlemen to accumulate lobsters from the lobstermen and then sell to the Ready brothers. They located and signed deals with different buying stations/middlemen up and down the Maine Coast to secure supply. The Readys also adopted a COD, "fast pay" buying plan. This practice aimed to make them a *preferred* buyer among local lobstermen. By their estimate, 90 percent of rival distributors make both harvesters and middlemen wait weeks for payment.

- *Holding*. The Ready Seafood has a number of seawater holding tanks where live lobsters are held until they are packed for shipment. The brothers invested in cooling apparatus that keeps water temperature in two of these tanks at a very low 38° F, a technique that reduced mortality among lobsters shipped long distances from an industry average of 5 percent to 1 percent. The brothers also developed low cost packing materials that further enhances survivability over long shipping routes. By their calculation, that one improvement has reduced costs by $40,000 per year.

- *Selling*. Most of the Maine distributors that cater to the eastern seaboard market fight intensely for sales to supermarket chains, fish retailers, restaurants, and individual customers. Their success depends on quality, reliablity, and price—but mostly price. Brendan and John managed to carve out a modest niche in this traditional market; but unhappy with low margins, they decided to seek out more profitable opportunities. By means of persistent phone calls and personal visits, they established a number of accounts with major seafood dealers in California and other distant states. Following a suggestion by the Maine International Trade Center, the Ready brothers traveled to Europe where they met with and forged relationships with distributors in Italy, France, and Spain. These customers put greater stock in product quality and less on price. France and Spain also represented volume markets that provide large bulk orders for fresh seafood, making them highly attractive to a growing company like Ready Seafood.

Within four years, Brendan and John were shipping almost 2 million pounds of Maine lobster each year from a facility that could hold 20,000 pounds of lobster at any given moment. They had their eyes on expanding on the same dock, renting additional warehouse space to double capacity. This was generating domestic and international sales of approximately $10 million. Margins were roughly 5 percent, somewhat better than those of their local competitors. As revenues grew, however, overhead costs also increased. It became more important than ever for the Readys to examine all aspects of their operations—from customer order processing, to transporting lobsters from harbors up and down the coast, to the backroom lobster holding tanks, to shipping product to customers—to make these as efficient as possible to preserve their margins. The operation had become a lot bigger and more complex than the typical Maine distributorship. It had leased two trucks, had banking relationships, was paying workers compensation and interstate licensing fees. "We were much much bigger, but not proportionally more profitable."

Left to right: John and Brendan Ready.

Source: Catch a Piece of Maine, with permission.

Connecting With End-Users

The brothers viewed entry to the distribution business as a means to more profitable end. Their intention was to use it as a financially reliable base from which to seek out higher-margin ventures within the lobster business. Once that base was secure, John and Brendan began thinking about those other ventures.

During his senior year at Northeastern University's business school, John Ready learned from an entrepreneur professor how Mars, the largest U.S. confectionary company, had successfully carved out a direct connection to the people who consumed its candies, generating higher profit margins in the process. Mars is a master at mass-producing M&M'S, Snickers, and many other candies and selling them by the truckload to mass market retailers, supermarkets, convenience store chains, and other intermediaries. Like Ready Seafood distribution, Mars is a high-volume, low-margin business. But thanks to a technical innovation that made it possible to print short personalized messages on individual M&M'S candies, a development team at Mars created a profitable and growing business selling small volumes of custom-printed candies to individual customers for weddings, retirement parties, birthdays, and other special occasions. They successfully bypassed layers of middlemen and sold direct at higher prices to end-users who appreciated—and were willing to pay for—the personalized aspect of the product. That professor, Marc Meyer, had helped the internal Mars venture team organize and launch "MyMMs" to market.

Two years after the brothers launched Ready Seafood, John recollected the M&M'S story. His old professor had challenged him to consider what the MyMMs business model might mean for Ready Seafood. John wondered if he and Brendan could do something similar to break out of their high-volume, low-margin business. Could they premiumize a commodity product and position it as a service for special occasions?

The Aha! Moment

One day in the fall of 2006, the Readys were visited by a New York banker for whom John had worked briefly as part of his Northeastern co-op program. The brothers thought it would be nice to give their visitor some live lobsters to take home for dinner. So when a boat pulled up to the dock, they took their guest onboard, introduced him to the skipper, and invited him to pick out the lobsters he wanted. "He thought this was so cool," John recollects. "Being on the boat and meeting the guy who had caught his dinner really made his day. That experience meant more to him than his lobster dinner."

Bingo! That episode on the dock got John and Brendan thinking that many customers, like their banker friend, would value and pay for a piece of the lobstering *experience*.

> Our gut feeling was that we had more to sell than a commodity seafood product. We tested that idea through focus groups of affluent summer visitors to Maine—people who loved Maine and loved lobsters but didn't see all the people and all the work that brought food to their tables. We also talked with friends and acquaintances in different parts of the country. What we learned was that most of them valued and would pay a premium for something that connected them to life here in Maine—call it the Maine mystic.

Despite lots of positive feedback, the brothers recognized that this would be a risky venture. "But we had a solid and profitable business [Ready Seafood] as a safety net if our idea failed."

Developing the Concept _____

Over the course of twelve months, the Ready brothers fleshed out their concept and processes for marketing and delivering it to customers throughout the United States. "It had to be more than simply selling lobsters online," says John. "Other people were already doing that. We wanted to sell a piece of the Maine experience."

As initially conceived and offered, the "product" was the annual catch of a single lobster trap, along with other dinner items. For $2,995, the customer would receive a *minimum* of 13 gourmet lobster dinners delivered anywhere in the country with free shipping: i.e., at least fifty-two 1–1/2 pound lobsters, clams, mussels, and Maine-made desserts. A "partner" customer would be assigned a lobsterman who would fish the partner's trap over the course of the season. Partners would capture some of the excitement of the lobstering experience by monitoring their traps online. They would also get to know their assigned lobstermen via online video clips and DVDs. And as an added personalized touch, they would receive a phone call from their lobsterman on the day of shipment.

Each customer would also receive literature about the Maine lobster culture, and how their participation helped support lobstering families, a sustainable fishery, and working waterfronts on the coast of Maine. For their part, participating lobstermen would receive a premium price for their catch. In this sense, the Ready's concept was analogous to the "community farm share" and "buy locally grown food" movements then sweeping the country. Both aimed to help the small family producers who were doing the hard but poorly rewarded work at the very beginning of the food supply chain. The Ready's tactic of connecting customers with their assigned harvesters via Internet and telephony put a human face on this concept.

The brothers had to engineer every piece of the process that made their offer possible and financially viable, from recruiting seven Portland area lobstermen, to creating and staffing an e-commerce site, and dozens of logistical arrangements. They also set up Catch a Piece of Maine as a limited liability company, with Brendan and John as shareholders.

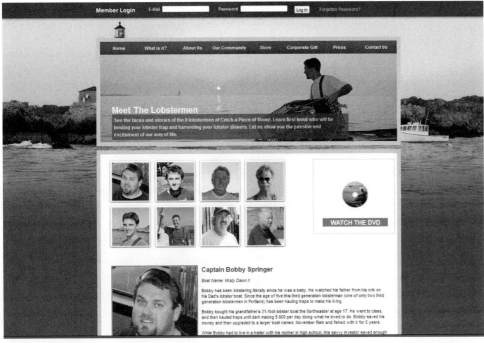

"Meet the Lobstermen." Catch a Piece of Maine, with permission.

Making a Wave

In November 2007, a year after conceptualizing the new business, the brothers launched Catch a Piece of Maine, with John as manager. For his part, Brendan would tend primarily to the ongoing distribution business.

Their launch immediately caught the attention of the Associated Press, thanks to a personal call from John. The uniqueness of the offer and its beneficial intentions for struggling lobstermen presented a good story opportunity. *USA Today,* a huge nationwide daily, ran a feature on Catch a Piece of Maine. The next day, 30 people purchased full-trap partnerships, producing roughly $90,000 in sales in the first few hours—until the Website crashed. "This was a great start," says John, "and we didn't spend a bundle on advertising and, unlike the distribution side of the business, we didn't have to wait thirty to sixty days for our money. With credit card purchases we were paid in a few days."

More Ready-generated publicity followed on Fox News and other media outlets with the result that November and December 2007 brought in $200,000 in revenues. John and Brendan were amazed. Media coverage continued into 2008, with some reporters traveling to Portland to film the company's lobstermen at work. When the *CBS Sunday Morning* television show ran a segment on Catch a Piece of Maine, the company's Website crashed under the weight of incoming orders—but not before booking $60,000 in ten minutes. Revenues for that year totaled $375,000 with profit margins five times higher than the core business. And despite a terrible economy, the company appeared on its way to $500,00 in sales for 2009.

While recognizing the beneficial impact of media news stories, John Ready attributes much of the company's revenue growth to "viral" marketing "an infectious message spread by happy users of a brand or product. . . ."

Many of our customers are businesses. They'll buy a full trap for $2,995 then gift each of its 13 shares to a key client or outstanding employee. Each of those 13 recipients receives a great meal for four people, gets a personal call from a lobsterman, and a piece of the Maine experience. The next thing you know, those gift recipients are calling us to order shares for *their* friends or *their* business associates. And so far they keep coming back. Eighty percent of share purchasers have renewed their shares for the coming year.

The benefits of viral marketing were not immediately apparent. As a result, the company spent several hundred thousand on traditional advertising before it realized that traditional ads were not cost effective.

Tweaking the Offer

Despite good initial results, market research by the company confirmed that the initial product offer at $2,995 left too many potential customers on the sidelines. So the company created an alternative. It subdivided every trap into thirteen "shares," each priced at $249. One share consists of four 1–1/2 pound hardshell lobsters, along with four servings of mussels and Maine-made desserts (e.g., whoopy pies), a map showing where the lobsters were caught, a DVD, and a personal phone call from a lobsterman timed to correspond with their package's delivery. "For many customers, this is the perfect gift for a friend, family member, or business client," says John Ready. "And the personal phone call makes a huge difference. It separates us from anyone selling lobsters online."

The "share a trap" program was launched for the holiday season in 2008. With economic times becoming even harder and luxury spending dropping, the "share program" began to exceed "total trap" purchases. Most customers were now looking for lower price points. Even very highly influential customers were stressing that they wanted a lower to entry price point making the "share a trap" an attractive option.

Sales hovered around the same level but the brothers decided to limit their spending for the time being on costly outward bound marketing programs. Their focus was to keep existing customers happy and using them to recommend new people.

The brothers launched promotions following certain gift-giving cycles such as the Christmas holidays, Valentine's Day, and other special occasions. They found that promotions created secondary spikes in demand following those holidays.

Managing Growth

Sales continued to increase into late 2009, and the fact that 80 percent of share and trap partners were renewing for a second year inspire much confidence in the future. Participating lobstermen were also doing well, receiving a year-end bonus equal to 40 cents per pound of the catch they sold to the new enterprise. This could potentially increase their annual revenue by 20 percent.

All of this good news, however, brought John face-to-face with an unanticipated problem: building an infrastructure capable of handling current and future business. He had his eyes on a 15,000 square foot facility on the other side of the harbor that would triple his holding tank capacity to 150,000 pounds of lobster and offer the potential of tripling his revenue if marketing efforts were successful. Finding employees was also a challenge. They needed to be personable and effective on the telephone and this was proving difficult. "We can't grab just anyone off the street for this type of work. I had to go through four people before I found the two effective employees I have today. Competent people are proving to be an important constraint."

And he did not consider his e-commerce site (www.catchapieceofmaine.com) capable of handling much more in the way of new business. "It simply isn't up to the demands of a much larger business," John complained out loud.

We'd like to be able to put Webcams in waterproof housings in the traps, so that our customers can tune in anytime to see what is going on. Can you imagine the excitement they and their friends will feel watching lobsters coming in for the bait? We'll need a better system for that.

Discussion Questions _____

1. Apply the Figure below to identify and discuss the four distinct business models that the Ready brothers have journeyed on their path to success. Are the Ready brothers selling just lobsters in their direct-to-consumer business?

Business Strategy

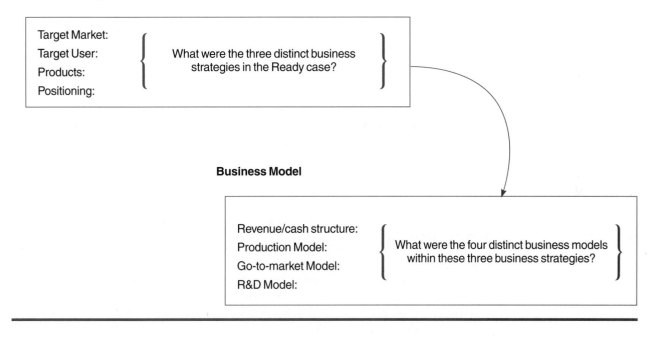

2. Why did the Ready brothers shift their entrepreneurial efforts from harvesting lobsters to distribution, and then, to expand from distribution to a direct-to-consumer business?

3. The company is presently operating under two different business models. Is managing two different business models too much to handle? What are the benefits and drawbacks of staying in both businesses?

4. What are some things the Readys will have to do to in terms of operations to double or triple the size of Catch a Piece of Maine? Please consider the marketing skills and capabilities that the Readys need to bring into the company. Also consider the limitation of its current facility (a 10,000 square foot facility on the docks, filled with holding tanks that could contain 50,000 pounds of lobster at any given time).

Evergreen Memories

A Truly Green Business

Introduction

Evergreen Memories is located in the heart of Northwest Ontario. Surrounded by crystal clear lakes and a beautiful forest, this eco-friendly (green) business is inspired to create and deliver earth-friendly favors and gifts to its customers. In doing so, this company has become a commercial success while also helping to preserve the planet. But there is a story behind this entrepreneurial journey.

Background

The original business was called Tamarac Nursery. The company had a single-minded focus: to grow tree seedlings for re-forestation purposes only. However, this market was basically a commodity-based market where price was often the key determinant for the customer. Moreover, demand for forestry seedlings was also declining. It doesn't take a genius to figure out that under these conditions this company's future was likely to be truncated. So, the company set out to determine how to sustain and grow the business. A review of other possible markets for its existing product resulted in some possible options. After much discussion, the idea of entering the "wedding favor" market emerged. However, the wedding favor market would be a chance for the company. It would be a business-to-consumer (B2C) play and not the current business-to-business (B2B) play which was the original focus of the business. But, the company decided to give it a try. With very little marketing and promotion of this new idea the company had three requests from "brides to be" for tree seedlings that could be given out at their weddings to their guests.

But, in addition to limited marketing and promotion, the company was also not well-prepared to execute in this new market. The presentation of the wedding favors, according to the company, was not well executed in the beginning. So, the company began to experiment with how to best prepare and present the wedding favors. The company began to further study the wedding favor market and began experimenting with different decorating techniques. One day the company experienced a "eureka" moment. It sent some personnel to attend a major wedding show in Toronto, Canada. There the company finally found some insight into its competitive set of offerings and how those offerings were being presented and merchandised. The company also made contact with personnel from several wedding magazines. These contacts provided some insightful assistance and encouraged the company to advertise their new wedding favor offerings in their magazines. Within a few months orders began pouring in. At the same time, the company made continual improvements in its product presentations. The company also began listening to customers' feedback in order to make further refinements.

The New Concept, the New Vision, the New Mission

Tamarac Nursery was evolving from a commodity-based business to a new value-added enterprise. Enter, new owner of Tamarac Nursery, Margot Woodworth. She would be the perfect fit for the company's new focus. Margot was always very conscious of the importance of preserving and protecting the natural environment. That love and respect for nature was something that was ingrained in her growing up in her native Germany. Germany has been a leader in promoting green behavior for many years. Yet, when Margot arrived in Canada 20 years ago, the emphasis on "green" was in its infant stage. In contrast to Germany, Canada appeared to be a "throw away culture" to the detriment of the natural environment. Margot believed that every product came from the Earth and would inevitably return to it in one form or another. Her hope was that Canadians would soon realize the importance of preserving the planet for future generations.

So, with her nursery background, Margot began the task of really building this green business. She knew, for example, that billions of dollars annually were being spent on weddings in North America. Margot believed some of those expenditures could be turned into ones that would support a green business—a business committed to the environment and to social responsibility. Margot believed that the company's new earth-friendly wedding favors (the tree seedlings) focus was a good one. But, she also believed the company needed a broader product portfolio. So, she began to design seed packages for an alternative favor to give during the winter months and also developed other green options suited for giving on every occasion. She also undertook the design of a professional Website that would enable the company to accept customer orders from all across North America. And, importantly, she also believed that the company needed a new brand name, one more consistent with its new focus. She renamed the company, Evergreen Memories.

Business Growth

Margot was extremely passionate and committed to her new business. Margot considered her green favors as "gifts of oxygen" since trees clean our air as well as fight global warming and prevent soil erosion. Margot believed that by the time her customers celebrated their silver wedding anniversaries, their wedding guests would have nurtured small forests that both beautified and protected the planet. In addition to her tree seedling product line, Margot added her packaged seed line for special occasions. Margot also discovered that many large eco-friendly companies were also interested in using "green favors" as part of their promotional efforts. So, she decided to embark on a marketing effort to gain some customers in this corporate space.

Margot also believed that entrepreneurs have an obligation to be good citizens and to give back to their communities. Therefore, Evergreen Memories became a sponsor of school projects, as well as other charity and fundraising events. Margot believes that starting and growing a successful business is very similar to growing a tree from seed. Both endeavors require much care and nurturing. She sees her business success as inextricably linked to her love and passion for nature and the planet. Ultimately, she has demonstrated in a very tangible way that a green business can be a success; a success both in terms of profitability and the preservation of the planet.

Under her stewardship, the company doubled its sales in its first year. Since then, sales have increased 30 percent per year. These results are impressive considering the business only operates six months a year (April-October).

Currently, 60 percent of total sales come from tree seedlings/seed favors sold as wedding favors. The other 40 percent of sales is derived from corporate sales to companies such as Xerox, Honda, Jamieson Vitamins, Bell Canada and TD Bank as well as sales to school districts.

The company sees major growth potential in the United States. Currently, about 30 percent of total sales are derived from US-based customers. She believes the wedding favor market in the US is 10 times bigger than in Canada. Currently, there are over 2 million weddings per year in the United States. The average cost of a wedding is close to $20,000 making the market size over $40 billion. The average wedding size is 100 guests. Margot roughly calculates that the average expenditure per wedding favor per wedding guest is $5. Thus, she believes the wedding favor market in the US is approximately, $1 billion. As part of her plan for US expansion, Margot is advertising online and in bridal magazines in the US. She is also attending wedding trade shows and corporate trade shows. She has also purchased the Web domain name evergreenmemories. com to complement her evergreenmemories.ca Website. She also discovered that some gift-giving occasions in the US are much different and much bigger than in Canada. For example, there is a major opportunity to market green gifts during American Thanksgiving.

Finally, Margot entered the Dragons' Den, a Canadian television show that has entrepreneurs meeting with potential investors in the hopes of securing venture financing. Margot won the competition and received angel financing for her US expansion plans. She also believes that her exposure on this nationally televised program will bring her new business, both wedding favor clients and corporate clients.

Questions

1. What does the evolution of Tamarac Nursery to Evergreen Memories tell you about the entrepreneurial journey?

2. What other opportunities do you see for Evergreen Memories in terms of sustaining the growth of its enterprise? Be specific. What market segments and product offerings do you recommend? Why?

3. What advice can you offer Margot as she makes her move to expand into the United States from her home-base in Ontario, Canada. For example, where should she build a beach head? What do you think of her way of calculating market size for wedding favors in the USA?

My M&M'S®

An Internal Corporate Venture

MY M&M'S® is a customizable version of the familiar M&M'S® product found at almost every supermarket checkout counter and convenience store. It emerged from innovations in process technology that enabled the printing of personalized images or expressions on every tiny candy piece. These customized candies are now a popular item at birthday parties, weddings, and other special occasions. The case underscores the challenges faced by managers innovating within companies whose success has been built on a very different business model.

Hackettstown, New Jersey. USA. June, 2003.

When Neil Willcocks moved from Britain to the United States to work as director of Mars, Inc.'s Advanced Development Group, he was fascinated by the success of the company's M&M'S® candies. "It had become part of Americana—like Coca Cola." He found it on store shelves and display racks wherever he went. And when the company experimented with selling individual orders of the tiny candy pieces in a customer's choice of color, the market response was enthusiastic. People ordered pounds of orange and black candies for Halloween, green ones for St. Patrick's Day parties, and red, white, and blue mixes for July 4, U.S. Independence Day.

Wondering about other possibilities, Willcocks engaged an artist to create images that might be printed on each candy piece. Mars had been printing the letter "m" on M&M'S® candies for years using a 1950s engraved rolling drum technology (offset rotogravure). Why not print something else and sell it as a special occasion, customizable product?

The process development group Willcocks directed was behind the idea and began thinking broadly about how more effective printing technology could be developed and applied. But when Willcocks shared the artist's images and the new business idea with other managers, the response was lukewarm. He was told, in effect, not to waste too much time on personalization.

Indeed, the idea of making and selling a customized product flew in the face of Mars' operating philosophy that had made it the world's largest candy and snack food company: high volume, low cost. "But my process engineering people," he recalls, "wouldn't take no for an answer. They wanted to keep working on the concept." Willcocks agreed to support them. Together, they would handle it as an underground project.

Though Willcocks's initial concept had encountered resistance, top management's concerns with market saturation and anemic growth would give him a second chance.

The Company and Its Culture[1] _____

Mars, Incorporated, is among America's ten largest privately held enterprises, and a consumer products powerhouse with more than fifty business units operating in 65 countries around the

---

Written by Marc H. Meyer and Richard Luecke. Copyright © 2011, Marc H. Meyer.

[1] To learn more about Mars and its culture, see Chapter 10 in The Fast Path to Corporate Growth, by Marc H. Meyer, Oxford University Press, 2007.

world. With some 64,000 employees (in 2009) and an estimated US$27 billion in annual revenues, the company owns some of the world's most popular snack food and confectionary brands, including M&M's®, Snickers®, Milky Way®, 3 Musketeers®, Dove® chocolate and ice cream bars, Kudos® snacks, and Skittles® candies. It is not only the world's largest confectionary maker; it is also the largest manufacturer of pet food, with brands such as Pedigree®, Whiskas®, and Royal Canin®.[2] Mars' experience in snack food retailing had also led it to develop the Klix® electronic vending equipment business and, in Europe, Flavia® packet-based coffee and teas. Its 2008 acquisition of Wrigley Company added that enterprise's brands to its list.

Frank Mars founded the company around the turn of the last century in Tacoma, Washington, where he produced a small line of locally marketed gift chocolates. In 1920, he moved to Minneapolis to grow the business. There, after visiting a local drugstore, Mars got the idea for a chocolate and malted milk snack that could be enjoyed anywhere. The result was the Milky Way bar—an immediate success. Snickers, a peanut-filled bar, followed, as did 3 Musketeers. All have been enduring successes. Frank's son, Forrest Mars, joined the family business in the 1930s and established the enterprise in Europe with a manufacturing plant outside of London. He also used an acquisition to enter the pet food business.

As Forrest Mars traveled through Europe in the 1930s, he observed a Spanish company producing panned candies, coated in chocolate, with sugar providing both a barrier and special taste. That encounter inspired his development of the now ubiquitous M&M'S®, which was introduced in 1941 as a chocolate candy that would not melt in a person's hands during hot weather.

Through the years, the company developed an egalitarian culture and relatively flat organizational structures. Those characteristics remain in place today. There are no private offices in any of the company's plants or offices. And despite Mars' size, people still know other people around the globe to a remarkable extent. Every employee, including the President, punches a time clock, and the company offers a "punctuality" bonus to people who show up on time. There are no executive parking spaces. Whoever arrives at work first is entitled to the best spaces.

Volume and Efficiency Rule

Efficiency is a key operating principle at Mars and has led to sophisticated process engineering and careful management of supply chains. Though product R&D has always been important, high volume, low prices, and distribution to grocery, mass merchants, and convenience channels are king. "Tons R Us" is an expression commonly bandied around by Mars people. Cost of goods and conversion costs, measured by the tonne, are important metrics for any business plan seeking senior management approval.

By the late 1990s Mars had begun feeling the effects of market saturation. As one Mars executive put it:

> We already owned a huge percentage of available retail shelf space, leaving little room for growth. A big sales effort would increase revenues somewhat, but not enough to move the needle in a major way. Marketing and R&D would periodically come up with extensions or different package sizes of our successful brands, but introducing them was costly, and many would experience sales slips once we let up on the initial promotional effort. In some cases these new products simply cannibalized sales of our other brands. It was like pushing water up hill.

---

[2] M&M's®, Snickers®, Milky Way®, 3 Musketeers®, Mars Bar®, Dove® Kudos®, Skittles®, Pedigree®, Whiskas®, and Royal Canin® are registered trademarks of Mars, Incorporated.

Experimentation

Given the maturity of its current market categories, senior management in Mars knew that it had to break out into new food occasions to achieve meaningful organic growth. Mars already had specialty M&M'S® shops located in four key cities and a high-end chocolate store (Ethel M's) in Las Vegas. These were not dramatically moving the sales "needle" but they were useful test beds for new business model approaches. For instance, the four M&M'S® shops allowed customers to create their own color blends, using stock M&M'S® colors—an offer that proved fairly popular.

The idea of customization caught John Helferich's attention. As Vice President of R&D, Helferich was Neil Willcocks' boss. "I was scanning the horizon, looking for some way for us to build confidence in our ability to work outside Mars' core model." He recalled Willcocks' idea and asked him to develop it further. Tapping his R&D budget, Helfrerich gave Willcocks' team $250,000 to work with. Their goal was to experiment with different ways to print—both words and pictures—on flat chocolate surfaces using inkjet technology and edible ink. And before long they had a working model.

Willcocks found himself in an uncomfortable position. He had an idea and a functional inkjet printer, but no real interest from marketing or top management, who viewed the idea of customization as interesting, but "not a big idea" capable of supporting a serious new business outside Mars' core. The only interested party was a manager in the UK, who wanted to use the new inkjet printer for a local product promotion. Feeling that he had come to a dead end, Willcocks agreed to ship the equipment straight away.

Hours before the printed equipment was scheduled for air shipment across the Atlantic, Willcocks received a call from, Paul Michaels, general manager of Mars USA. Michaels, who had guided the M&M'S® brand growth years earlier, had gotten wind of events and told Willcocks that *no way* would the equipment leave the building. "I wondered if I was in deep trouble," Willcocks recalls. Instead, his project was about to get a new lease on life. Michaels talked to him and Helferich about the concept of customized M&M'S® and their market possibilities, and he gave them the green light to pursue it aggressively.

The team pushed the customization concept forward using fellow employees as an initial test market. Using the old rotogravure technology, they began making up small batches of personalized candies for company events: employee birthdays, retirements, and weddings. These were a big hit with employees, and the team received more and more requests as word of personalized M&M's traveled around the Hackettstown facility. "Each event required us to engrave a special rotogravure printing drum at about $1,500 apiece. That wasn't a major expense," Helferich recalls, "but it certainly wasn't the path to cost-effective customization."

The team redoubled its efforts to master ink-jet printing on the curved surfaces of M&M'S®, and it soon had a working prototype. This opened new commercial possibilities. With ink-jet technology, order lead times for internal event candies dropped from five weeks to a matter of hours, and the $1,500 cost of each order set up disappeared. "We seemed to have the basis for a real business—one for which we could charge a lot of money."

Getting Serious

Within a few months, a landmark event appeared on the Mars calendar. Caught by a case of innovation fever, Mars' senior management asked product line and R&D managers to make a case for their latest and most promising new ideas. An off-site "Pioneer Week" was planned two month in the future as the setting for this show-and-tell event. John Helferich didn't have to think twice about his unit's best and brightest idea. But could they put together a plan for a real business in just 60 days? Neither he nor anyone else on the team had any business start-up experience. No one had given any thought to the operation elements of this potential new business: pricing the product, communicating with individual customers, taking and fulfilling orders, safeguarding peoples' credit card numbers, and so forth. Every team member was acculturated to a giant firm that produced 100 million M&M'S® candies every day, loaded them onto 18-wheel trucks, and sent them off to Wal-Marts and similar distributors. Could they model a profitable business that produced one or two thousand candy pieces for a small number of individual customers? Would the company's marketing, finance, and manufacturing people embrace their idea or try to kill it?

The venture team had just sixty days to answer those questions and to create a business model and a business plan for what they dubbed "My M&M's ." (See Figure 1)

Figure 1 Custom-printed candies: the earliest versions

Learning the Business_____

Since no one on the team had ever planned or operated a new venture, a consultant was brought in to help. With his coaching, they developed a segmentation strategy, a Web channel plan, and a business model that included estimates of capital and financial projections. The market segmentation strategy (Figure 2) shows a sharp contrast between the segment focus of standard M&M'S® (a commodity candy) and the many possible usage occasions for customized MY M&M'S®.

Launch and Learn _____

Everyone knew that their estimates and plans were unlikely to survive initial contact with real customers. Consequently, the team decided to develop and launch an internal version of the business to test out its concepts and systems. Mars employees in this experiment would represent the market. An *intra*net site would be used as an order taking link to "customers." And a small scale printing/packaging line would handle manufacturing. The reasoning behind this internal prototype was simple: use customer feedback to better calibrate pricing and minimum order sizes; improve and perfect all systems of the business prior to a public launch of the My M&M'S® enterprise; and do it all within 60 days.

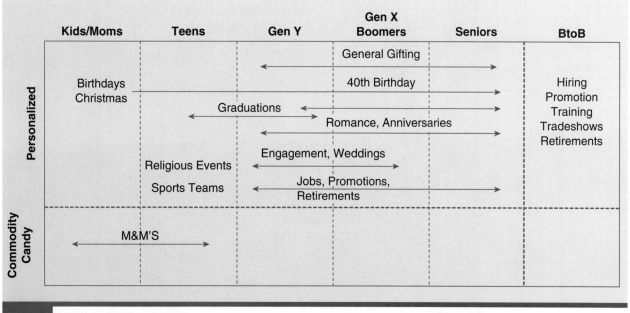

Figure 2 | Initial market segmentation

Source: Adapted from Marc H. Meyer (2007). *The Fast Path to Corporate Growth.* Oxford University Press, N.Y.

Pricing was an initial point of contention. The team felt strongly that personalized candies should command a substantial price premium over standard M&M'S®. Willcocks felt that a unique, one-of-its-kind product, supported with the tremendous branding of core M&M'S®, justified premium pricing, plus he knew that there would be substantial R&D expense to refine and improve the product in the years ahead. The company's marketing department was more cautious, however, and requested a low test price. The team bowed to their wishes and set the price at about twice the retail price of standard M&M'S®.

The Website launched with no advertizing or public relations other than word of mouth amongst M&M enthusiasts working with Mars itself who wanted customized candies for their own personal occasions. At the launch price per pound, these "customers" buried the Website with orders. After being "live" for just 4 hours, the My M&M'S® team had enough orders for the entire month, given its single production machine. The team decided on the spot to double the price hoping to keep orders in check. When the Website was turned on again the following week, just the opposite happened. The team had to turn off the Website after just two hours. *The more they raised the price, the more consumers wanted to buy!* Higher price conveyed the special nature of customizing the world's most popular candy brand.

Marketing staff in the company, however, remained cautious on pricing. They were fearful that this early high-demand experience might be an unsustainable aberration. Unable to reach a consensus, the parties initiated a consumer research study.[3] Respondents in the study were asked to make trade-offs between product features, packaging features, and price. One finding was that $20 per pound before shipping costs was about right. Another finding was that male respondents were substantially less price sensitive than women and professed that they would continue to buy even as the price continued to increase (See Figure 3). After further discussion and analysis, the team tried to choose a middle-ground price point between the female and male segments. And, shipping was made an additional charge. The team also reduced the minimum order size to two pounds. (Since launch, the MY M&M'S® team has supported its premium pricing relative to traditional M&M'S® with a range of new features, including the ability to print jpegs on the candies! See Figure 4.)

---

[3] The study was conducted by students in the High Technology MBA Program at Northeastern University.

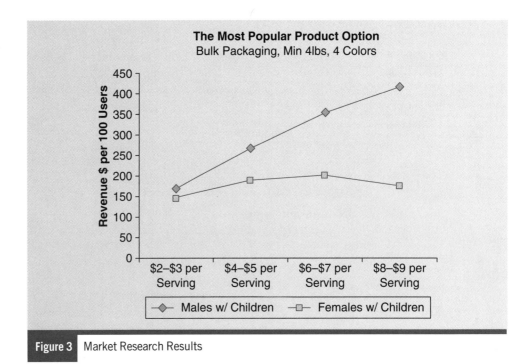

Figure 3 Market Research Results

Source: Adapted from Marc H. Meyer (2007). *The Fast Path to Corporate Growth.* Oxford University Press, N.Y.

Figure 4 The Next Generation of My M&M'S®

Source: Image used with permission of Mars, Inc.

Creating Financial Projections to Make the Business Case for Senior Management

Based on its experience with internal sales and pricing changes, the team put together financial projections for the business showing sales, cost of goods, shipping costs, and other expenses. It also estimated the cost of adding new printing machines and the number of new machines needed as volumes grew. The major assumptions that the team used for its financial planning were as follows:

- The price per pound: $25, which did not include shipping and handling.

- Shipping and handling: Since special insulated cardboard boxes were involved, delivered by UPS, an average price of $12 was added to shipping and handling. Large order amounts over 10 pounds would be charged twice as much for shipping and handling. Given the labor intensive process for packaging goods and the special box materials, the team did not expect to make any profit on these shipping and handling fees—at least not in the beginning.

- Minimum order size: 2 pounds. The majority of consumers would order between two and four pounds of candy. Business customers would order less frequently, but in much greater volumes, with an average order size of about 10 pounds of custom printed candies.

- Orders per day: The team thought that 300 orders per day in the first year was reasonable (based on the test launch of the MY M&M'S® Website internally). The team thought that this amount could easily double year over year over the course of the first five years. The team also segmented its buyers into consumers and businesses. In the beginning, it thought that only 5% of the orders would come from businesses—but that over time, the B2B part of the business would grow to 20% of the business by the fifth year of operations. Within these segments, the team also saw three quarters of the demand coming from first time users, and the other quarter coming from repeat purchases by existing customers for other family occasions. These percentages were just the opposite for business customers who would purchase the candy for hiring, promotion, retirement, product announcement, and educational events.

- Cost of goods: in the range of $3 per pound, including labor and the use of clear cellophane bags as the packaging for the product. The team expected that over time, it could add all sorts of value-added packaging that would be supplied by third parties. As noted above, the cost of the insulated shipping cartons was born by a "breakeven" shipping charge—separate from this cost of goods.

- Capital invested into printing machines. Willcocks' process engineers had done a marvelous job designing high speed printing equipment for the round M&M candies. Conveyor belts load within the candies (blank side up) would zip by and special purpose piezo electric printheads would add the customized messages. (Several years later, this technology would be enhanced to print high quality images on the same surface area!) The team performed calculations on the throughput rate for improved versions of its prototype machine and determined that each one could produce 200,000 pounds of printed candies a year. And it estimated that each machine, loaded up with multiple printheads, a conveyor system, and control technology would cost about $500,000 fully loaded with equipment, installation, and maintenance.

- Advertising to grow revenue. The team had been amazed by the explosive demand for the product just in its internal trials. Word of mouth had capped out production capacity on the prototype machine in under 4 hours! However, the team knew that it would have to advertise to generate the hundred plus million dollars in revenue that it wanted to achieve in the future. Speaking with the company's advertising agencies, the team determined that for this type of business planning, $1 in advertising could be expected to generate $10 in revenue.

Show and Tell

The proforma P&L developed from these estimates and assumptions prompted the first executive to see it to remark, "You are in the ballpark. That would be a very nice business." This was encouraging, and specific line items in the P&L were refined over the next month in consultation with experts from different parts of the company.

Getting approval from top management, however, would not be easy. Many aspects of the nascent venture were troublesome. Order taking, fulfillment, and logistics were going to be entirely different than those used to support conventional M&M'S® and Mars' other snack food products. My M&M'S® would involve small, discrete orders shipped directly to thousands of customers—the opposite of traditional M&M'S® transactions, which were characterized by large quantities shipped in bulk to a handful of retailers and distributors. Indeed, the company was totally geared for mass production, not small batches. "Ton R Us" was baked into the DNA of company decision makers. Could a small order business earn enough to make the venture worthy of attention?

As they prepared for "Pioneer Week," Helferich and Willcocks wondered how they should make their presentation. With all the excitement generated by the internal trials, this was still not going to be a walk in the park. Not even close. They knew that there would be challenges such as, "How do you know that personalization is just not some new fad?" Or, "What do we know about making print heads or developing specialized inks?" Or, "I like it, but it can't be a pet project in R&D anymore. It's time to place it under the core M&M'S® team." What could Helferich and Willcocks say to the executive committee to get behind My M&M's® as a new business?

Discussion Questions

1. Define a business model for this venture and explain how it would differ from the model followed by traditional M&M'S® candy. What parts of the core business does My M&M's® leverage?

2. Create a simple P&L using the estimates and assumptions provided in the case. Then, develop a capital plan for buying the machines that scales with your revenue projections. Calculate a return on these assets.

3. If you were the team leader, how would you sell the venture to senior executives schooled in "Tons R Us?"

In Search of a Viable Business Model

Marc H. Meyer
Northeastern University

Neil de Crescenzo
Oracle

Bruce Russell
Northeastern University

In Search of a Viable Business Model _____

David Perry, CEO of Ventro Corporation, describing to an eCompany magazine reporter how he had to change business models rapidly during 2000: "Think about how fast that is. You go public as Chemdex in July, by September you're two companies, and by December you realize this idea of independent marketplaces doesn't make sense and you've got to get bricks-and-mortar companies involved. Our entire business changed in a five-month period. Not externally, but our internal understanding."[1]

eCompany reporter to Michael Dell, CEO of Dell Corporation: "What has been the biggest waste of money [during the Internet age]?"

Michael Dell: "The biggest waste of money has been all the investment in companies with so-called new-economy business models. Business fundamentals haven't changed, and a lot of investors lost sight of that—and are paying for it."[2]

Professor Michael E. Porter of Harvard University, writing in the March 2001 issue of the Harvard Business Review: The misguided approach to competition that characterizes business on the Internet has even been embedded in the language used to discuss it. Instead of talking in terms of strategy and competitive advantage, dot-coms and other Internet players talk about "business models." This seemingly innocuous shift in terminology speaks volumes. The definition of a business model is murky at best. Most often, it seems to refer to a loose conception of how a company does business and generates revenue. Yet simply having a business model is an exceedingly low bar to set for building a company. Generating revenue is a far cry from creating economic value, and no business model can be evaluated independently of industry structure. The business model approach to management becomes an invitation for faulty thinking and self-delusion.[3]

*** *** ***

Adapted from Marc H. Meyer, Neil de Crescenso, and Bruce Russell (2004). "In Search of a Viable Business Model," *International Journal of Entrepreneurship Education, 2*(2), pp. 31–43. Used with permission.

[1] "Why is David Perry Smiling?," eCompany, Will Bourne, January 2001.

[2] "If I Knew Then What I Know Now," eCompany, March 2001.

[3] "Strategy and the Internet," Michael E. Porter, *Harvard Business Review,* March 2001, p. 73.

This case explores the rise and fall of one of the most praised and high flying start ups of the dot com B2B bubble. Chemdex started with a focused strategy and business model to create a B2B trading exchange in specialty chemicals that was attractive enough in the financial climate of 1999 to enable the company to raise $45M in venture funding and to float an IPO that quickly valued the company at over $1 billion. Soon, the valuation was driven in excess of $7 billion on the public markets. The case describes the changes in strategy and business models that management subsequently pursued to try to "earn" this extraordinary market valuation. Chemdex, which focused on providing a single industry vertical on-line exchange for trading specialty chemicals, became Ventro, which developed multiple trading exchanges. Ventro then changed its focus, closing down these industrial vertical on-line exchanges to become a vendor of the underlying technology and services, seeking to sell them as a tool kit to other companies wishing to set up their own on-line marketplaces. Then, Ventro transformed into Nexprise through an acquisition of a group-ware company, and has since focused on that strategy with a rather traditional software products company business model. The case offers a cautionary tale of the difficulties and challenges in changing strategies and business models, of overselling the promise as opposed to the reality of a business, and of the extraordinary speculation that occurred during the Internet bubble.

Since the late 1990s, the concept of a "business model" became a much discussed aspect in business venturing. The concept was nothing new to business: it only restated the fairly obvious point that a company had a clear description of how it would make money, how much money it would make, and how this translated into increased shareholder value. Business models take form in a firm's financial statements, primarily in its profit and loss statements (P&L) and how earnings from the P&L enhance the balance sheet and ultimately the company's valuation.

At a deeper level, a business model links a firm's business strategy—its target markets, products, and services—with its financial outcomes. A company must know how to differentiate itself in a target market and how to provide clear benefits in its products and services. These offerings must lead to sales, earnings on those sales, and improved shareholder value. The business model is therefore the dynamics of and behind the P&L. These dynamics have five important dimensions:

- The first dimension comprises the structure and nature of revenues, and how these change as the volume of product and services increase. To obtain funding and successive infusions of growth capital, an entrepreneurial firm must be able to substantiate the design and growth of its revenue stream.

- The second dimension of the business model is the firm's approach to R&D, the research and development needed to create its new products or services. This also includes the investment needed to do that R&D internally or to secure and fund external development partnerships and/or technology licensing arrangements.

- The third dimension is the approach to manufacturing, typically involving either the development of in-house production capacity (for either physical services or for delivering services) or the use of subcontractors or some other form of rented capacity. These business model decisions have telling impacts on both the investment requirementsfor new plant and equipment and the financial outcomes of the firm in terms of operating margins and working capital deployed to build and maintain inventories.

- The fourth dimension is the firm's go-to-market approach, which includes channel strategy, promotional strategy, and its branding strategy. These decisions within the business model will have profound impacts on the investment into things such as channel partners or media buys, as well as the operating margins realized in the business.

These four factors—the structure and nature of revenues, and the approaches to R&D, manufacturing, and go-to-market—are the essential ingredients of "the business model" that any new or growing firm needs to articulate for prospective investors. The business model is not so much the P&L, but what is behind the P&L that makes it not only believable but compelling.

A company's decisions on each of these four dimensions can lead to a different business model. The classic business model for manufacturers of physical products is to set a retail price double its cost of goods, to invest from 2% to 10% in R&D, to have substantial capital requirements, and to expect a sales to fixed asset ratio of 4 or more within several years of launching new product lines. A classic service business model for consulting firms is to charge out professionals at three times their cost to the company and have little if any internal R&D. A software products company, by contrast, will spend upwards of 25% of its revenues on R&D, and will generate gross margins in excess of 90% and operating margins above 50%. Each one of these business models is described by the four dimensions listed above.

Further, by the turn of the millennium, investors also appreciated the potential of creating and scaling a new business model. In the computer industry, Dell had transformed the PC business with direct order efficiency and Ebay was taking its commissions in the new world of on-line auctions. Popular search engines, such as Google and Yahoo! were charging fees to "advertisers" who wished to be profiled on the results pages of matching Web searches. (Search for "fly rod" on Google, for example, and Orvis might be featured on the results page, even though thousands of other "hits" are displayed for the user's perusal.)

Just as there were positive examples, the disaster cases provided perhaps the most lasting impression of the importance of business models. During the latter part of the 1990s, a new breed of Internet companies flourished apparently unconcerned with operating margins. It seemed as if many entrepreneurs and investors alike had disassociated the income statement from the balance sheet. In the words of one venture capitalist, "earnings didn't matter." Companies losing enormous sums of money so long as revenues were growing were still being valued for the purposes of next stage investment or acquisition on extraordinary multiples of sales. In some cases, firms with minimal revenues and large operating losses had billion dollar market capitalizations.

The press and Wall Street searched for reasons to justify these valuations. They found entrepreneurs and investors backing plans built on the hope that if a company spent enough on marketing, it would grab enough "eyeballs" to justify hefty advertisement revenue, and eventually, e-commerce transactions, be it from consumers or business-to-business trade. Perhaps an odd and incomplete business model, but a business model nonetheless. Moreover, for a while, these business models themselves seemed to justify extraordinary valuations.[4]

In March 2000, it became clear how much Wall Street had based their support for Internet company valuations on a business model that said "If you spend enough on marketing, and grab enough eyeballs, sooner or later, earnings will come." The Internet bubble burst and the NASDAQ Composite Index declined over 67% from its high in March 2000 over the next twelve months. The projected P&Ls of Web software and services companies that were so highly praised in 1998—2000, the ones showing earnings coming in 5 or 7 years down the road, were no longer found believable.[5] Indices that include primarily Internet or dot.com companies fell even more than the NASDAQ. The Interactive Week Internet Index declined over 80% between March 2000 and April 2001.

---

[4] Day, G.S., Fein, A. J. and Ruppersberger, G. (2003), "Shakeouts in Digital Markets: Lessons from B2B Exchanges," *California Management Review* 45(2): 131–150.

[5] See for example: "The B2B Internet Report: Collaborative Commerce," Morgan Stanley Dean Witter, Charles Phillips and Mary Meeker, April 2000 ("Many B2B business models look suspect and most will probably fail . . ." page 4).

What follows is a fascinating and painful story of one firm's extraordinary rise and equally dramatic fall, and its search for a feasible business model where an attractive business strategy could actually be turned into operating income. The company has been known by various names: first Chemdex, then Ventro, and finally, Nexprise. Each change of the company's name featured a different business model.

Chemdex: The Startup

Chemdex had many of the elements of a classic start-up story. David Perry and Jeff Leane founded the company in 1997. Perry had just received his MBA from Harvard Business School (HBS) and Leane was a former consultant for Andersen Consulting and a technology entrepreneur (Leane later left the company to pursue other interests). Perry had a B.S. in Chemical Engineering from the University of Tulsa and had been a supervisor at an Exxon Refinery before entering business school.

While attending business school, Perry had assisted two Harvard scientists in starting a biotechnology company. While involved in that start-up as Acting President, Perry discovered that the processes for purchasing lab supplies, and particularly complex specialty chemicals used in laboratory research, were based upon relatively inefficient paper, fax and telephone communications. He felt that by using the Internet this purchasing process and the market for these products could be made more efficient and benefit both the vendors and the purchasers. This was the "Aha!" driving the new venture.

Perry and several classmates wrote a business plan for such a business that would use the Web as the supply chain for the biotechnology and pharmaceutical industries. The team named their company Chemdex and submitted their business plan as part of the First Annual HBS Business Plan Contest.[6] They were named a runner up in the contest. Perry then hooked up with Jeff Leane, and the two further refined the business plan leveraging Leane's industry expertise. Perry and Leane founded the company in September 1997.

The Business Strategy and Its Business Model: A Life Sciences Online Marketplace, 1998–1999

Chemdex was one of the first business-to-business (B2B) exchanges. The specific application was a life sciences specialty chemicals marketplace. As pioneers, Perry and Leane initially had difficulty raising capital for their new company. It was a new type of business, and his financial statements represented a new type of business model. However in September 1997, Perry raised seed funding of $560,079 from CMGI@Ventures, a venture capital firm that specialized in funding Internet-based companies, and Bob Swanson, the co-founder and CEO of Genentech, Inc. Swanson was a pivotal figure in the company's early success because Swanson's company, Genentech, became Chemdex's first major customer. Swanson himself was a legendary businessman. Many felt that he had "started" the biotech industry when he founded Genentech with Herb Boyer in 1976. At that time, Swanson was a 29-year-old venture capitalist with Kleiner Perkins, which continues to be a leading venture capital firm. Kleiner Perkins became a major investor in Chemdex the following year in May, 1998.

It was not atypical for technological entrepreneurs to have a combination of large early customers as well as venture capitalists as first round investors. CMGI@Ventures was an

---

[6] Described in "Chemdex.com," Harvard Business School Case 9–898–076, June 22, 1999, prepared by Senior Research Fellow Laurence E. Katz under the supervision of Professor William A. Sahlman and Lecturer Michael J. Roberts.

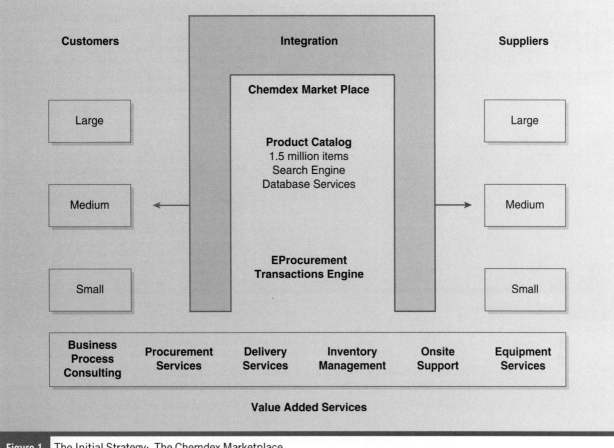

Figure 1   The Initial Strategy: The Chemdex Marketplace

aggressive early stage venture capital firm based in Massachusetts and an active participant in university business planning events and other related activities that enhanced its own "deal flow." CMGI continued to participate in subsequent financing rounds prior to the IPO. In fact, if it had not participated, new investors probably would not have participated in these rounds.

Swanson mentored Perry and created connections for Chemdex throughout the industry. Significant revenues also came from business directly with Genentech. By November 1998, Perry had a working Web-based system for specialty chemical ordering and fulfillment. Figure 1 shows a representation of Chemdex's basic business strategy. With this strategy, a business plan, and a working prototype, Perry was able to raise almost $13 million from a syndicate of top-tier venture capital firms. Figure 2 contains a history of Chemdex's venture funding before the company's IPO. By April 1999, the total investment capital into Chemdex had grown to $45,224,784.

As a B2B exchange, Chemdex listed suppliers' products in an on-line catalog and allowed scientists and/or administrative staff to search and order these products through a secure, browser-based interface. The end user accessed the catalog, which was hosted and maintained by Chemdex at a site that Chemdex itself leased. Chemdex charged listing fees for a product in its on-line catalog as well as a sales commission for completed transactions. The company did not charge users to access the marketplace because it did not want to discourage volume.

The business model accompanying this strategy was that of a niche B2B exchange. In terms of revenue dimensions, the model sought to get as many customers as possible within the life sciences market. From these customers, the company targeted four distinct revenue streams: a 5% transaction fee on supplies purchased through the marketplace, systems integration fees for directly connecting large users' inventory and purchasing systems to the Chemdex marketplace,

Date	Amount	Investors
September 1997	$560,079	Bob Swanson CMGI@Ventures
December 1997	$1,395,198	Bay City Capital Fund CMGI@Ventures
May 1998	$12,974,988	Kleiner Perkins Caufield & Byers Warburg, Pincus Ventures CMGI@Ventures Bay City Capital Fund
March & April 1999	$30,294,519	Galen Associates Kleiner Perkins Caufield & Byers Warburg, Pincus Ventures CMGI@Ventures Bay City Capital Fund
Total	$45,224,784	

Figure 2 Ventro/Chemdex's pre-IPO Funding

repackaging and reselling of customer data to chemicals manufacturers, and "placement fees" for chemical manufacturers who wanted to launch new products through Chemdex's Website.[7] In terms of cost of goods, the company was spending heavily to integrate its major customer's (Genentech) internal systems with the B2B marketplace. In a race to build share, Chemdex was also marketing heavily while R&D expense also accelerated forward.

By the summer of 1999, Chemdex's marketplace for life sciences products offered 240,000 stock keeping units (SKUs). The company had $191,000 in revenue through 3/31/99 (though 82% of the company's revenues were from its first customer, Genentech) and an accumulated deficit of approximately $15.7 million.[8] Nevertheless, with the excitement over Internet and dot com stocks reaching a fever pitch, Chemdex's board decided to go forward with a public offering.

Having major venture capital firms as investors—CMGI, Kleiner Perkins, Warburg Pincus—it was clear that Chemdex would seek a timely and successful "exit strategy" to provide a handsome return for these very investors. Of the two primary exit strategies, to be acquired or to go public, during 1999 IPOs provided the greater potential return for shareholders.

Chemdex completed its IPO on July 27, 1999, selling 7.5 million shares at $15 per share and raising $112.5 million in gross proceeds. In the first day of trading, the stock reached $34 a share, providing a market capitalization of $1.11 billion. CMGI an early and multiple round investor, that owned 16% of Chemdex at the time of the IPO, saw its holdings worth $177 million.[9] CMGI, being one of four professional firms that had invested a total of $45 million prior to the IPO, realized one of those legendary "15x pops" on an investment. To achieve this in just two years was extraordinary.

By March 2000, Chemdex had 95 enterprise (corporate) customers, with over 24,000 registered users, accessing almost a million stock keeping units (SKUs) in its electronic catalog.[10] The company would also issue corporate debt in March of 2000 of almost $250 million, even in a time when NASDAQ was tumbling in free-fall. Figure 3 contains the company's financial transactions post IPO.

---

[7] Chemdex.com, Harvard Business School Case 9–898–076, by William A. Sahlman; Michael J. Roberts; Laurence E. Katz, 1998.

[8] Chemdex Corporation S-1 registration statement filed with the SEC on 5/14/1999.

[9] William Barker, "Dueling Fools," the Motley Fool, August 4, 1999.

[10] Ventro Corporation preliminary common stock prospectus, issued March 14, 2000, p. 41.

07/27/99 Chemdex: Strategy: Build more branded marketplaces Strategy: Partner with other companies to create B2B marketplaces	IPO: $112,500,000 For 16% of company stock. Debt $250,000,000 $50,000,000 P&L loss.	Bought: Promedix: $325m SpecialtyMD: $108m Model: listing and transaction fees
03/01/00 New name: VENTRO Strategy: Leverage "platform" through partners		Model: franchise type sign up fee and revenue sharing
2/25/01 VENTRO Strategy: Sell technology & services to anyone who wanted to build an on-line marketplace	Market Capitalization: 7,900,000,000	Valuation based on <$1m revenue, $600 million operating loss, and a business plan transitioning to Web marketplace infrastructure (Ariba) Model: license server software and tools, Website development services
07/21/01 NexPrise Collaborative Software	$100 million cash on hand	Bought a Collaborative Software Company, NexPrise, $2.3 million in revenue, for $27 million. Model: License Server Software and Tools
01/01/04 New Strategy: Business process automation	Total assets: $20 million	Revenue: $4 million Model: License server software

Figure 3 Post IPO Financial History

Using proceeds from the IPO, Chemdex began to selectively acquire other companies. In September 1999, the company agreed to purchase another B2B marketplace that provided specialty medical products to hospitals (Promedix) for stock valued at $325.3 million at the time of the agreement. In December 1999, the company agreed to purchase SpecialtyMD, a provider of search and content functionality, for stock value at $107.7 million.

A New Strategy to Scale the Initial Business Model: 2000

On February 22, 2000, Chemdex sought to continue to scale its strategy of owning and operating specialty exchanges. The company announced that it was repositioning itself as a "leading builder and operator of B2B marketplace companies." The Board changed the company's name to Ventro Corporation to emphasize its new strategy and financial goals, e.g. its new business model. Figures 4 and 5 contain Ventro's income statement and balance sheet information for the years 1999 through 2002.

The new Ventro would now seek to provide services, technology and investment in multiple B2B marketplaces and estimated that it would have as many as 10 sites in place by year-end 2000. Aided by strategic partners, Ventro would expand beyond life sciences by creating a family of specialty on-line marketplaces. The business model would essentially be the same as that in the original life sciences chemicals marketplace, but scaled by creating addition marketplaces through a combination of internal developments, joint ventures, and acquisitions.[11] The

---

[11] Some readers might find the far higher investment level required to build new marketplaces itself justifies calling this expansion an entirely new business model. However, we think not. The structure for producing revenue and operating marketplaces remained the same. The analogy is to a successful retail operation that figures out its business in its first pioneer store, and then raises capital to replicate its recipe for success through multiple store openings, e.g. Staples or the Home Depot.

Period Ending	12/21/1999	12/31/2000	12/31/2001	12/21/2002
Total Revenue	**30,840**	**0**	**1,042**	**2,802**
Cost of Revenue	29,306	0	797	2,393
Gross Profit	**1,534**	**0**	**245**	**409**
Operating Expenses				
Research and Development	17,734	35,030	24,580	5,295
Sales, General and Admin.	33,376	30,855	25,117	10,556
Non-Recurring Items	0	4,891	18,843	12,051
Other Operating Items	1,992	532	0	0
Operating Income	**(51,568)**	**(71,308)**	**(68,295)**	**(27,493)**
Add'l income/expense items	3,163	(9,415)	(5,389)	(1,204)
EBIT	**(48,405)**	**(80,723)**	**(73,684)**	**(28,697)**
Interest Expense	168	12,813	5,646	749
Earnings Before Tax	(48,573)	(93,536)	(79,330)	(29,446)
Net Income-Cont. Operations	(48,573)	(93,536)	(79,330)	(29,446)
Discontinued Operations	0	(524,561)	0	0
Extraordinary Items	0	0	159,762	0
Net Income	**(48,573)**	**(618,097)**	**80,432**	**(29,446)**

Figure 4 NEXPRISE, INC. Income Statements

software that Chemdex applied to its first marketplace became the "platform" from which other marketplace offerings were generated.

Chemdex continued to be the name of the company's life sciences products B2B marketplace. As the company stated in its Annual Report later that year:

> As a leading builder and operator of B2B marketplace companies, Ventro was created in February 2000 to leverage the corporate assets originally developed in its Chemdex life sciences business. Fueled by its speed of execution, scalability, technology architecture and operational expertise, Ventro is poised to transform the supply chain in businesses around the world. Ventro provides its marketplace companies with the ability to unite enterprises, buyers and suppliers to streamline business processes, enhance productivity and reduce costs. Ventro marketplace companies offer complete e-commerce solutions consisting of extensive online marketplaces, electronic procurement, the systems integration needed to interface with third-party and back-office systems, and comprehensive services and support. [12]

Wall Street and the press appeared to endorse Ventro's new business model. Ventro's stock price rose from $90 on 2/1/00 to a high of $240 on 2/25/00, giving Ventro a market capitalization of $7.9 billion! A Morgan Stanley Dean Witter report later that year stated

> While the model is still evolving, we believe that Ventro's net market capabilities provide compelling value added, its management is top notch, it's got scalable, robust technology, and it has demonstrated that it can attract strong industry partners.[13]

---

[12] Ventro Corporation 1999 Annual Report, p. 1.

[13] Morgan Stanley Dean Witter, Ventro Corporation stock note, Mary Meeker and Marie Rossi, July 21, 2000.

Period Ending	12/31/1999	12/31/2000	12/31/2001	12/31/2002
Current Assets				
Cash and Cash Equivalents	21,934	91,348	13,565	3,225
Short Term Investments	81,161	94,987	8,150	7,050
Net Receivables	12,414	4,269	814	560
Other Current Assets	5,041	21,923	1,642	1,512
Total Current Assets	120,550	212,527	24,171	12,347
Long Term Assets				
Long Term Investments	5,000	8,103	3,832	0
Fixed Assets	10,264	21,797	2,675	339
Goodwill	0	0	11,652	0
Intangible Assets	13,107	0	8,829	9,150
Other Assets	512	7,943	1,266	1,168
Deferred Asset Charges	14,500	6,938	200	0
Total Assets	**163,933**	**257,308**	**52,625**	**23,004**
Current Liabilities				
Accounts Payable	38,051	26,053	7,740	3,180
Short Term Debt	369	0	0	0
Other Current Liabilities	0	28,122	639	1,047
Total Current Liabilities	38,420	54,175	8,379	4,227
Long Term Debt	494	250,000	8,803	11,843
Other Liabilities	0	206	0	0
Total Liabilities	38,914	304,381	17,182	16,070
Stock Holders Equity				
Common Stocks	7	9	10	10
Capital Surplus	189,842	630,140	631,082	631,764
Retained Earnings	(57,465)	(675,562)	(595,130)	(624,576)
Other Equity	(7,365)	(1,660)	(519)	(264)
Total Equity	125,019	(47,073)	35,443	6,934
Total Liability and Equity	**163,933**	**257,308**	**52,625**	**23,004**

Figure 5   NEXPRISE, INC. Balance Sheet (in '000's)

A high-tech industry publication, *The Red Herring,* also wrote in March 2000 that

Chemdex is a case in point [of vertical (industry-specific) marketplaces becoming horizontal (multiple industry) marketplaces]. Last week, while the NASDAQ traded in 100 point swings, the B2B chemicals exchange renamed itself Ventro and announced that it would change its strategy to operate a broad portfolio of B2B marketplaces. That's not only smart, it's brilliant. Ventro's goal is to evolve into four vertical markets, creating even more top-line opportunities in a business where, once scale is achieved, the operating margins within a B2B exchange become enormous.[14]

---

[14] *The Red Herring,* "When Verticals Go Horizontal," Peter Henig, 3/6/00.

A reporter wrote:

Chemdex/Ventro, having gone from vertical to horizontal, was valued at $7.8 billion, up more than $41 a share since Friday, February 25, alone. It represents the possibility for Internet investors of even higher valuations on these stocks. If any of the current or future B2B holding companies can truly execute and create the dominant exchanges in their verticals, $50 billion market caps might even seem like bargain-basement prices.[15]

Despite the turmoil in the stock market, Ventro continued to develop new B2B marketplaces, as its expanded business model required. A marketplace for general hospital and medical supplies (Broadlane) was created in December 1999 through a joint venture with Tenet Healthcare. A marketplace for fluid-processing plant supplies and equipment (Industria) was also formed in January 2000 with DuPont Corporation. A marketplace for the food services industry (Amphire) was also formed in April 2000 with a major food distribution company. In addition, Ventro announced the formation of Ventro Life Sciences Europe in April 2000 in order to expand its Chemdex life sciences marketplace into Europe. Finally, in August 2000, Ventro announced a joint venture with American Express Corporation (MarketMile LLC) to provide a marketplace offering general office supplies to small and medium-sized businesses.

While Chemdex, Promedix and Ventro Life Sciences Europe were wholly owned subsidiaries of Ventro Corporation, the company held only minority interests in its subsequent marketplaces. This was viewed internally and externally as a way to reduce Ventro's financial and operating risk in starting these new marketplaces. Ventro stated that each marketplace would only become profitable when it had 80% of the products end users wanted to buy in that niche, and the end users would only use the market when the products were there. Therefore, by partnering with industry participants, Ventro's new marketplaces began with a larger critical mass of buyers and/or suppliers than they would have been able to achieve on their own. These joint ventures also reduced Ventro's financial risk by having both industry partners and financial partners co-invest in these new marketplaces.

A New Business Strategy: A B2B Marketplace Infrastructure Provider, 2001

Despite the initial excitement this new business model initially generated on Wall Street, and the new joint venture marketplaces Ventro announced throughout the year, the business was still bleeding cash. Wall Street had fundamentally changed, where future promises were being cast aside for present realities. Even though Ventro's overall loss per share had been better than Wall Street expectations, it would be reporting more than $93 million in operating losses for the year of 2000.

Further, during the third quarter of 2000, transaction volume and gross margins for Ventro's two existing, wholly owned marketplaces (Chemdex and Promedix) had not met Wall Street's estimates. The bloom was coming off the rose.

While Ventro management felt that in the prior year it had articulated a business model that moved the company beyond just the life sciences marketplace, virtually all operating revenues and profits still came from that first marketplace. Perhaps Ventro had not found the right strategic partners, or perhaps it lacked the operating knowledge required by these different vertical markets. Whatever the reason, these new niche marketplaces were not gaining traction. Management felt compelled to develop a new strategy.

Another option, of course, would have been to use cash on-hand to first reimburse debt obligations, and then, provide the remaining funds back to equity holders. Management teams

---

[15] *The Red Herring*, "When Verticals Go Horizontal," Peter Henig, 3/6/00.

with failed business models never took this dramatic step, however, unless absolutely forced to do so. Rather, they sought to create viable businesses with funds raised from successful IPOs and debt issues rather than cease operations and admit failure.

The company announced a new business model along with its third quarter 2000 results on October 19, 2000.[16] Ventro stated that its new business model was to become a "Marketplace Service Provider," or MSP. As an MSP, Ventro would provide technology and services to marketplaces, including the marketplaces currently wholly or partially owned by Ventro or, in the future, marketplaces in which Ventro held no ownership interest and was purely a provider of services and technology. In this new business model, the company would license its technology, typically with annual maintenance and support fees, to other companies seeking to build their own on-line marketplaces. Ventro would become a tools provider. The advantage, just like any other software tools provider (such as Oracle) was the applications development productivity that this new set of customers could enjoy by deploying Ventro's tools for their own Website development. This advantage could be substantial given the complexity of the task.

Like other tools vendors, Ventro also planned to charge its new customers for professional services. In other words, Ventro would help its customers develop their own marketplace Websites, and integrate these with corporate and other types of databases.

This new strategy was a Web infrastructure play. Ventro would no longer own its own on-line marketplaces, but rather, help other organizations to build their own respective marketplaces. Ventro Chief Operating Officer Robin Abrams noted the change in approach, stating "Owning was fundamental to the way we viewed ourselves in the market, but that's not the case anymore."[17]

Management could take comfort that other companies appeared to be doing well as Marketplace Service Providers, i.e. selling tools for transactional Website development and helping customers use these tools. Companies considered as players in this space included software providers Ariba, Commerce One, and Purchase Pro. They also included established IT service providers like IBM Global Services, EDS, and CSC, as well as newer Internet-oriented IT service providers such as Scient, Viant, and Sapient. In July 2000, Scient, for example, had a market capitalization of $3.5 billion on annual revenues of approximately $300 million and an operating loss of over $20 million.[18] This was unprecedented for what was essentially a consulting firm with little intellectual property. In September 2000, Ariba had a market capitalization of $41 billion on annual revenues of less than $400 million.

There were obstacles however. A look at the backgrounds of executives who worked for Ventro at that time showed that the existing leadership team had little or no experience making general software tools.[19] Also, the company's Chemdex marketplace technology was the result of proprietary code and business processes linking over 20 third party software products. The end-result was not easily "modularized" or "packaged" into code that could be sold as a software license (as Ariba and other e-procurement software providers did with their software). Therefore, the R&D to transform a complex application (the Chemdex marketplace) into a robust and flexible toolkit (the new MSP strategy) would be both extensive and costly.

Also, while some managers felt that the company's original business model was fundamentally unsustainable, and therefore had both a sense of anxiety and urgency to establish a better strategy for the company, this conclusion was not a broad-based consensus. CEO Perry described his opinion in May 2001:

---

[16] Ventro Corporation press release, 10/19/00.

[17] *Upside,* "Inside Ventro: A costly lesson," Daryl Carr, 1/6/01.

[18] All market data and company financial data used in this paper is from Yahoo!Finance or Multex.com, unless noted otherwise.

[19] The CEO had a chemical engineering background and had worked for Exxon prior to business school, the CFO came from the biotech industry, the COO came from the computer hardware industry, and the Chief Technologist/CIO came from the internal IT department of a major brokerage firm.

"It's not that we thought we could never get Chemdex to be profitable," says Ventro's CEO, Dave Perry. "It had been growing at 20 percent to 30 percent per quarter. But it was burning a lot of money. We decided that, in an environment where raising capital is difficult, it wasn't where we wanted to spend the fixed amount of money we have."[20]

Six days after reporting its third quarter results, Ventro issued a press release about its MSP strategy and posted a presentation describing its MSP business model to its Website. The company stated that

> The opportunity for Marketplace Service Providers remains large, with over 1,500 current marketplaces. Currently, B2B marketplaces spend between $10–$25 [million] annually on technology, including software, hardware and consulting. Ventro sees an opportunity to target significant margins from the portion of these services addressed by its Marketplace Service provider offering. [21]

Ventro also announced that since it had decided to concentrate on revenues from providing technology and services, it intended to seek strategic partners for or sell its wholly owned marketplaces (Chemdex and Promedix).

The company stated that "changing to the Ventro Marketplace Service Provider model, whereby Ventro reduces its wholly-owned interest in Chemdex and Promedix, is expected to reduce Ventro's cash burn, accelerate the path to break-even, and improve gross margins. The timing of any financial improvements is not possible to predict given current uncertainties."[22] This was something of a shock to some observers, since Chemdex had been the company's only source of operating revenues and profits.

These announcements and press releases did not halt further declines in the company's stock price, which dropped from $8 at the beginning of October to $1 by the end of the year, giving Ventro a market capitalization of $46 million.

On December 6, 2000, Ventro announced a restructuring whereby it shut down its Chemdex and Promedix marketplaces. Management and its investment bankers had not been successful in finding a buyer or strategic partner for either marketplace. The company said it expected to record aggregate restructuring charges of approximately $380 to $410 million in its fiscal year-end results in connection with these activities, which would include an estimated reduction of approximately 235 personnel (out of total headcount of over 400).[23]

On February 20, 2001, Ventro announced its fourth quarter 2000 net loss was $451.6 million and that its total net loss for the twelve months ended 12/31/00 was $618.1 million. Ventro also announced that its Chief Operating Officer, Chief Financial Officer[24], and Vice President of Marketing had given the company notification of their intended departure by the end of the first quarter of 2001.

The Board also decided to use the company's cash to clean up its balance sheet. It announced that Ventro was tendering all its outstanding convertible notes at a price of $270 in cash per $1000 principal amount.[25] The notes had recently been selling at prices as low as $160 per $1000 principal amount due to Ventro's problems and the fact that the strike price ($90.78)

---

[20] *Upside*, "Who will survive?," Stan Draenos, 4/17/01.

[21] Ventro Corporation's "Marketplace Service Provider October 2000 Briefing" at http://www.ventro.com/ir/0010_briefing/index.html

[22] Ventro Corporation's "Marketplace Service Provider October 2000 Briefing" at http://www.ventro.com/ir/0010_briefing/index.html

[23] Ventro Corporation press release, 12/6/00.

[24] That Chief Financial Officer was one of the authors of this case.

[25] Ventro Corporation press release, 2/20/01.

at which the notes could be converted into Ventro common stock was far above the current stock price (approximately $1).[26] On March 28, 2001, Ventro announced that it had purchased approximately 74% of its outstanding convertible notes pursuant to its tender offer. [27]

On April 30, 2001, Ventro announced its first quarter results. Excluding the gain from its purchase of its convertible notes, the company lost $28.8 million. The company also announced that it would be reducing its workforce by two-thirds, to 85 employees, and taking a further charge of $10—$20 million in the second quarter of 2001 to reflect this and other restructuring activities. Perry's comments in the press release suggested that Ventro might adopt a new business model in the future:

> During the quarter we made progress towards defining our target market and thus, our future business model. We ended the quarter with approximately $96 million in cash and investments, which, together with the $11 million Broadlane note receivable [Ventro had settled various disputes with Broadlane and received this note as part of the settlement], provide adequate funding to execute on our business plan. Additionally, we are continuing to focus on streamlining our organization to fit the needs of our transitioning business model; we expect to reduce our ongoing operating cash expenses to less than $7 million per quarter, once our restructuring actions are completed.[28]

Uncertainty was pervasive within the company. The entire original senior management team had left the company as of April 1, 2001, except for the CEO. The company's headcount fell from over 400 at its peak to a stated objective of 85 by the end of the second quarter of 2001. These actions clearly were an enormous burden on the Ventro employees' professional and personal lives.

If it was of any comfort those who remained with the company, Ventro's major competitor as an MSP infrastructure provider, Ariba, was suffering extremely hard times, too. In the first week of April 2001, Ariba announced a loss of $0.20 per share for the second quarter vs. Wall Street expectations of earnings of $0.05 per share. Revenue for the quarter was approximately $90 million, half of what had been previously forecast and down 47% from the first quarter. Ariba also announced reductions of one third of its workforce (700 people), write downs for real estate investments and other items of $50—$75 million, and the collapse of its deal to buy collaborative software provider Agile Software. Keith Krach, Ariba's CEO, said "The [B2B] exchange business . . . has seen a dramatic falloff, and we don't think there'll be a recovery in marketplace revenue."[29] Ariba's market capitalization sank to $1.1 billion, compared to $41 billion on annual revenues of $400 million in just six months earlier.

Another Business Strategy:
Client Server Collaborative Software, mid-point 2001

Figure 6 shows the dramatic rise and fall of Ventro's stock price over the course of three years. With its stock price battered to less than a dollar per share by the summer of 2001, Ventro management changed the company's business model yet again.

Sitting on almost $100 million in cash, management decided to transform itself into a more traditional software company, seeking a more traditional stream of earnings.

On July 16, 2001, Ventro announced that it would acquire NexPrise, a software firm that developed product design and engineering, complex procurement and strategic sourcing tools.

---

[26] Per conversations the author had with a convertible debt trader at DLJ Securities during December 2000.

[27] Ventro Corporation press release, 3/28/01.

[28] Ventro Corporation press release, 4/30/02

[29] *Upside,* "Ariba Falls Hard, Fast," J. T. Farley, 4/3/01.

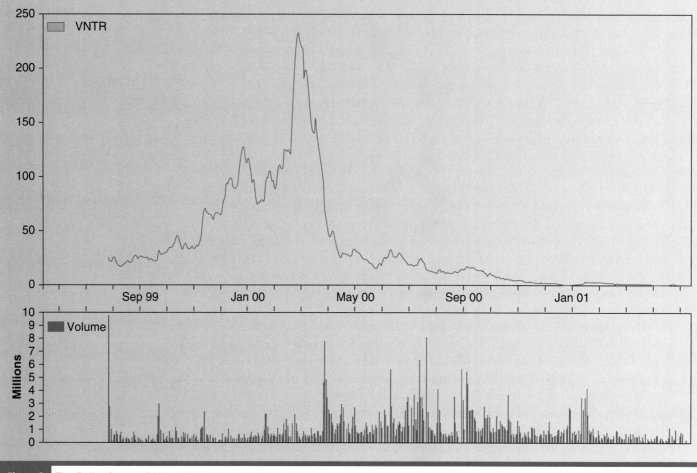

Figure 6 The Roller Coaster Ride—Ventro/Nexprise's Stock Price

Its business was collaborative computing within and between organizations with a focus on document management. Ventro paid $27 million for NexPrise, which had 110 employees and $2.3M in annual revenues. Ventro also formally changed its name to Nexprise.

Customers licensed this enterprise collaborative computing software, and in certain instances, paid Nexprise fees for systems integration and training. It is a highly complex field of technology, with major firms such as Documentum (now owned by EMC) and IBM (Lotus Teamroom) pursuing the same target user. This new strategy required continued and substantial investments in R&D, as well as a direct sales force to penetrate large corporate accounts. For the year ending December 2002 NexPrise reported revenues of $2.6 M and a loss of $29M, $11.6M of which was a write down of goodwill.

Looking Back at it All: circa 2004

A group of former Chemdex/Ventro employees were sitting at a bar in California, contemplating the roller coaster that they had experienced over the past several years. Few would disagree that Ventro Corporation's management, employees and shareholders required a new business model for the company as it navigated the turmoil in the B2B space in 1999–2001.

However, the question that kept bothering everyone was whether management, investors, and they themselves as options holders had all been collectively too greedy. Should the company have gone public, on revenues of less than $200,000 and significant losses? That IPO and the subsequent $250 million convertible debt put the company on a stage where it was not prepared to act.

Upon going public, especially after having been underwritten by some of Wall Street's most prestigious investment banks, Ventro underwent the typical scrutiny of analysts, investors and the press that public companies can expect.[30] Ventro received even more attention than most other Internet companies, since it had a photogenic and charismatic CEO and was in a space (B2B marketplaces) that was briefly valued at astronomical levels by investors. Since stock prices inherently reflect investors' future expectations for a company, there was substantial pressure for Ventro management to reflect continued progress and a detailed and realistic path to profitability when it communicated externally. However, Ventro was still very much in start-up mode. In fact, on Ventro's conference call with analysts on April 30, 2001, Perry stated that Ventro was essentially a start-up (again), and pointed out that its market capitalization was only about one-third of its cash balance.[31]

Clearly, being public creates additional challenges for a company seeking to change its business model. When AT&T started acquiring cable companies and wireless communications companies under its new CEO, Michael Armstrong, for tens of billions of dollars in 1997, some analysts pronounced the strategy as misguided, but overall Wall Street and the press supported Armstrong's initial acquisitions. Ultimately, the detractors were proven right.[32] If a large company had trouble changing business models, for a company like Ventro, with a limited and relatively unsuccessful operating history, the challenge was even greater.

These changes had been hard on the former employees sitting at the table. Ventro could ill afford extensively cataloging its problems and challenges in public. Ventro employees were unsure whether the public pronouncements of Ventro's new business model as being "evolutionary, not revolutionary," and the listing of corporate assets Ventro had in-house, were entirely accurate, or produced primarily to comfort Wall Street.[33]

All agreed that both Ventro and Ariba had suffered cruelly as Web infrastructure suppliers. Would Ventro have been better off sticking to its guns in 2000 and remaining as an owner/operator of specialized B2B marketplaces? Some former managers in the company even thought that the company should have stuck to its first life sciences market strategy of 1998–1999, finding new ways to create value-added services for that sector. Even though the IPO had originally achieved enormous high valuations, it had also raised expectations to an unrealistic level and hurt the company's ability to patiently pursue a focused growth strategy.

---

[30] Chemdex's IPO was underwritten by Morgan Stanley Dean Witter, BancBoston Robertson Stephens, and Volpe Brown Whelan & Company. The company's convertible debt offering in April 2000 was underwritten by Morgan Stanley Dean Witter, Robertson Stephens, Chase H&Q, and Deutsche Banc Alex Brown.

[31] The conference call is available at www.streetfusion.com.

[32] AT&T's stock price declined from a high of $96.125 during the initial years of Armstrong's tenure (January 1999) to $21.98 on 5/17/01.

[33] See for example Ventro Corporation's press release on 10/25/00 ("Ventro Provides Details About New Strategic Direction"), where CEO Perry stated, "Our move toward a MSP model is a natural evolution as we continue to leverage the core of our capabilities."

Generate, Inc.

Partnering With a Strategic Investor

Concord, Massachusetts

On a cold winter day, Tom and Darr Aley, twin brothers in their mid-forties, were busy working in a spacious office above Tom's attached garage. Shafts of midday sunlight warmed the room. Tom's dog, Billje, slept in the corner.

Having successfully sold their company, Generate, Inc., Tom and Darr now had the financial wherewithal and the leisure to choose their next opportunity. As serial entrepreneurs, the brothers would not be idle for long. "We're both ADD types," they liked to joke. In fact, Darr was at that moment creating a Webpage for their newest opportunity, a social venture project that aims to help single mothers re-enter the workforce.

As Darr was working, Tom thought back to their experience in starting, developing, and eventually selling Generate, Inc. "What a journey that was." And their relationship with a strategic corporate investor had helped bring the journey to a happy conclusion.

Tom worked for his father for two years following college, then went on to work for several technology ventures, including a speech recognition software developer. He would add an MBA from Northeastern University's High Tech MBA program to his résumé. While in that program, Tom took a product management job with ZDNet, the Web arm of the Ziff Davis computer publications empire, where he rose to found and lead its e-commerce business, creating a number of new services, including one of the first successful PC e-tailing sites: "ComputerShopper.com"

Tom, however, had the entrepreneurial bug and left ZDNet to help found OneZero Media, which created a CBS-backed nationally broadcast TV show called "The Wild Wild Web." The show featured the lifestyles and sports of the young and wild, and drove viewers to a Website where they could purchase products featured on the show. It was one of the first true "convergence plays," attempting to marry traditional media with an e-commerce back-end. After several years of national syndication, the company was acquired for over $20 million by GT Interactive Software, game software company most well known at the time for "Doom." GT Interactive Software had gone public the prior year with one of the largest public offerings of the time.

Moving on, and working with Darr, he helped to create Net Value Holdings, a multi-city business incubator that went public during the halcyon days of the Web bubble.

> Using about $5 million of investor capital, we began funding promising companies in many cities around the country. Shortly after going public, our market value approached $50 million. Analysts were telling us that we were the next CMGI [at one time, a hugely successful publically traded venture investment company.] However, most of that value evaporated when the market bubble burst in 2000.

Written by Marc H. Meyer and Richard Luecke. Copyright © 2011, Marc H. Meyer.

Tom knew it was time to move on and to try his hand at another side of the venture finance business.

Between 2000 and late 2004, Tom worked in the corporate venture capital wing of Reed Elsevier, the $8 billion leading global publisher and information provider with prowess in legal (LexisNexis) science and technology domains. In that position, he worked with an interval venture capital team, sniffing out investment opportunities for Reed Elsevier. During this time, Reed Elsevier made a number of successful investments in software and information products companies that in one way or another leveraged its own formidable information assets.

This was good preparation for Tom's next venture, Generate. He had learned how to evaluate the merits of different opportunities and, equally important, to understand the mix of market opportunity and management talent that made venture capitalists sit up and take notice. He had also learned the ins and outs of the different types of venture financing: angel investing, "institutional" venture capital (typically, VC firms), and corporate or "strategic" investing.

While Tom was building his finance and deal-making skills, brother Darr was also working in several successful startups. One of these was Lycos, one of the top search engines of the 1990s. Subsequently he co-founded an "e-procurement" company that was acquired by Accenture, and was recruited from there to run Amazon's entry into the procurement market. He later helped run corporate development and strategy, helping Amazon identify and make several acquisitions.

Experience in marketing and finance for information intensive industries, and their combined networks of software and computer infrastructure development, prepared the twin brothers for a new, bolder venture.

The Seed of an Idea called Generate, Inc._____

While at Reed Elsevier, Tom marveled at the success of one of that company's business units, a $2 billion legal data service called LexisNexis. Lexis offered subscribers searchable data bases from newspapers, periodicals, legal documents and other printed sources. This provided real value to users—the legal research community—allowing them to slice and dice a wealth of information with a few simple keystrokes. For Reed Elsevier, LexisNexis became a source of continually recurring revenues as subscribers came to rely on it in doing their work.

Lexis's combination of real value delivery and recurring subscription revenue got Tom to thinking about other information services for the corporate world. Several already existed in an industry estimated at $200 billion per year. These included Dun & Bradstreet, Bloomberg, ThompsonReuters, Hoovers, Experian, Equifax, MarketWatch and InfoUSA. Yahoo!Finance provided a wealth of free information, choosing to make its money off advertising. These information services provided mountains of financial, credit, and transactional data (e.g., on mergers and acquisitions), and also listed corporate executives.

Other ventures had tried to gather detailed information about public and private companies, such as product information and the names of executives in charge of different parts of a company. These included Individual, Inc. and Corptech, both started in the Boston area. While neither of the ventures was particularly successful, the idea of allowing individual users to set filters to screen real time events and announcements for specific companies was an important building block in Tom's thinking.

Something new entered the game in the early 2000s. By 2004, Web-based social networking had taken hold. Tom looked at LinkedIn and liked what he saw. That Website allowed users to develop personal networks of business contacts, and then, through the magic of database cross referencing, provided a modest ability to find out "who knew who," making it possible to bridge across personal networks.

By November 2004, Tom was eager to make a move. He had learned a great deal at Reed Elsevier but did not want a big company career. He wanted to do a startup instead—and with his brother. For his part, Darr had enjoyed great success as an Amazon executive, but he too wanted to get back into a startup. Together, they had enough money saved to provide seed funding for a new information products/services business. And the more they talked, the more they were convinced that combining social networking capabilities with the real-time news feeds and data aggregation represented solid opportunity. Their vision was to create an information service for the business-to-business space that would harness a world of information and put it at the finger tips of B2B sales people, wealth managers, investment bankers, and many others. "Our vision," said Darr, "was to provide people like us with all the *who, what, where* in real-time about executives and their companies, and then provide them with a path on how to reach an executive through a personal social network. There was nothing like it and people needed it." He continued:

> For example, if a computer systems salesperson were to open the *Wall Street Journal* and read that XYZ Inc. had just taken in $250 million through an IPO, he'd immediately think, 'XYZ is growing and probably needs to buy more computing power—and it has $250 million in the bank.' The sales person would now have a prospect company. The next step would then be to arrange a sales call. Everyone knows that cold calls are tough and will do whatever is possible to avoid making them. So, the salesperson would ask, who is the executive in charge of IT? Who do I know that might introduce me to that executive? When I get a chance to talk to that person, how can I break the ice and develop a relationship? What can I learn about the executive's background, his or her prior jobs, or whether he sits on company boards?

The Aley brothers played through this and a number of other use case scenarios—such as the sales triggers created from real estate transactions, new product announcements, and legal proceedings. And the more they did this the more they were convinced that such a service would deliver concrete value to corporate sales forces around the world.

A Company is Born

At the beginning of 2005 each of the brothers decided to put up $100,000 as seed capital for their new company, and would have to double this amount over the course of the year. "We were fortunate to be our own seed investors," said Tom, "because we didn't have to give up half our company just to get started." Having their own skin in the game would also mean a lot for the next round of investors.

The brothers left their respective corporate jobs "on good terms." And Darr, to the chagrin of his warm-weather loving wife, moved his family from the Seattle, Washington area to Concord, Massachusetts to work out of Tom's home office. Tom had just built a house near the banks of the Concord River, upstream from the Old North Bridge, scene of the celebrated battle that touched off the American Revolutionary War. After being there 4 years, however, Tom and his wife would sell that house and invest some of the capital in the new company. The family then moved into a smaller house on the other side of town. Tom had three young kids; Darr, two. Both families were putting a lot on the line to make this venture successful.

The number one job at this point was to capture company and executive information in real-time and make it accessible to the B2B sales community via a front-end portal on a subscription basis.

GENERATE'S BUSINESS MODEL

Most enterprise subscriptions to Generate's service were sold "per seat" (initially $3,000) with volume discounts. Generate also licensed it's content and functionality to News and information publishers (OEMs) who used it to provide more compelling services to their end-users, and in turn derived ad revenue and incremental subscription revenue.

OEM's such as Dow Jones and Dun & Bradstreet came onboard as customers in 2006, when the company was very needy of cash. Revenues in that year were $500,000, thanks largely to these information providers.

"Our plan was to license-in corporate data through one of the current services—data was a commodity" Tom recalls. "But that was only half of the puzzle. Information on executives was thin and there was nothing available to tie those people to the companies." Convergence had been an important element in Tom's career—be it at ZDNet, in the television show, or overseeing Reed Elsevier's venture investments. "We wanted to do a convergence play between information about executives and information about their companies, and then personalize it to the individual salesperson via our relationship mapping services." The brothers decided on a strategy of performing extensive Web searches on people's names and then building their own proprietary extraction and indexing scheme to not only link individual with corporate information, but do so within a social networking framework.

For the first piece of the puzzle—information supply, such as company news and events— Tom and Darr talked with a number of established information suppliers and, over the next six months, came to terms with several major players. One of these was Thomson Financial—which held a massive amount of financial data on companies around the world. (Thomson subsequently merged with Reuters to become an even larger, global powerhouse.) Another important information supplier was American City Business Journals (ACBJ)—publisher of 44 regional business journals across the United States. Within a year or so, Thomson was not only a supplier, but also a major OEM customer, private labeling Generate's service as part of its own offerings. ACBJ evolved from information supplier into a potential equity investor in the business.

For the second piece of the puzzle—gathering information about the lives and events surrounding business executives—Tom and Darr knew that they needed a specialized Web search crawler. From his Reed Elsevier days, Tom knew of a small private firm in Montreal called NetVention. NetVention had a Web-crawler that gathered and aggregated company information from designated Web pages; Tom and Darr, along with Howard Schneider, the CTO of Generate, felt the technology could be re-engineered to also crawl and extract data about individuals, a very compelling, non-commoditized market opportunity. Tom and Darr thought they could rent the same capability from companies like ZoomInfo, but figured that the cost would be prohibitive and that they would sacrifice control over a key part of their business. Acquiring NetVention's technology outright might be another possibility. Said Tom Aley:

Our vision was to capture and aggregate company and executive data from the Web and then map the relationships between the people and the organizations we found. Using LinkedIn-like software, we aimed to reveal connections between those executives and our users, up to three degrees of separation. In effect, we'd have LinkedIn meets Hoover meets Dun & Bradstreet on steroids—with the ability to filter out information that individual subscriber didn't need. They would also have a key ability to show subscribers corporate hierarchy and governance—something LinkedIn was not chasing.

Thus, if a Generate subscriber needed information on Jeff Bezos, Darr's old boss at Amazon, he would get whatever biographical information existed on the Web, along with data and news stories about Bezos and his company. The service would also reveal how the subscriber was related to Bezos through other people (relationship mapping). For salespeople and others looking for clients, this capability would save huge amounts of time, create new selling opportunities, and provide personal information on prospective clients that the sales person could use to initiate an interesting, meaningful conversation. The Aley brothers saw this as the essence of relationship-based selling.

The third piece of the puzzle was how to tie everything together within a scalable computer system. That meant building databases, connecting people with companies, creating user-defined filtering mechanisms on the raw data, and a portal for users to access everything. Infrastructure! Tom and Darr knew that they couldn't outsource this part of the business—it was the core engine. A large part of their invested capital would be used to hire the people needed to build that engine. The first of these was Howard Schneider, whom Tom had known at ZDNet. The information repository that Howard had built at ZDNet could slice and dice the information from thousands of articles across Ziff's various computer publications and make it available for individual search. The brothers made Howard an offer to join the company with a salary plus some stock, and he accepted in February 2005.

Going for the Money— The First Try

While Howard was designing an "alpha" version of the system, Tom and Darr further developed their concept, better defined the target market, and created what they believed to be a powerful business plan and presentation. Being a VC himself, Tom knew what VC investors were looking for. "I thought that getting funding would be a fairly easy. I knew these companies and their partners knew me." The plan was to show them a business plan and an alpha version of the software in three months, raise between $1 and $2 million in a Series A financing, and release a beta version four months later. They planned on having paying customers within 12 months.

Tom's first stop was Union Square Ventures, where he knew one of the partners. That acquaintance, Fred, seemed receptive. He liked the concept and had confidence in Tom and Darr because of their successful startup experience. Fred made a soft verbal offer of $3 million on a pre-money valuation of $4 million. That would leave Tom, Darr, and Howard with about 57% of the company. In the next round of financing, a Series B presumably to build a sales force, Tom knew that the outside investors would have majority control.

Fred wasn't the only interested party. "By the end of Q1 2005," says Tom, "I thought that I had three big New England VCs who were very interested." The brothers twice left meetings with one of these financiers thinking that the deal was a *fait accompli*.

But funding would not be completed that easily. "We love the team," said one VC, "but it's a little early." Others had questions about the market: Was it large enough to support a knock out venture? "How can you prove demand?" said another. Tom thought these questions were ironic since Generate would provide a first of its kind service, and VCs were supposed to relish first of its kind technologies.

There were also concerns about the product itself: "You're adding too many bells and whistles and I'm getting distracted," said another VC. Tom's plan to acquire two or three small tech companies (including NetVention) to power Howard's system architecture also raised a red flag for some VCs: agreement on the valuation of these companies was not obtainable. Nor did most funding prospects fully understand the technology: "It feels like you're doing too much sausage-making," one complained.

By this time, Howard had identified four programmers he wanted to hire immediately to begin building out the system. Tom and Darr gave the okay, and before long Howard and his crew were busily working in Howard's basement. Tom and Darr now had to buy some computers and begin paying five monthly salaries. Their initial $200,000 contribution was now gradually moving from their personal bank accounts into those of the new employees.

"We had a two-stage plan at this point," recalls Tom.

Stage 1 was to build an alpha version of the front end of the product, which we hoped to wrap up in three to four months. A beta version would occupy stage 2, with an end date of November 2005. In completing these, we'd have something to show potential customers and gain their commitment.

Tom and Darr were unconcerned about potential rivals stealing the march on them. In their view, the big B2B information providers (Dow Jones, Dun & Bradstreet, etc.) needed what Generate was building, but were not sufficiently tech-savvy or entrepreneurial to build it themselves.

Even as he kept up communication with interested VCs, Tom continued to make contact with other potential investors. "You have to turn over every rock. Placing all your bets on one VC is like putting a gun to your head. You have to talk to as many as possible while giving the impression that they are the only one you're courting."

Beyond Institutional VCs

The VCs approached by the brothers Aley were in the business of taking money from large institutions, such as pension funds, and investing it through limited partnerships in technology-focused companies. Most, however, had been badly burned during the crash of 2000–2001 and were gun-shy of new startups. At this point in time, their preference was for second or third stage equity investments. For these, "venture capital" and "venture startup" had become oxymoronic.

Frustrated by their reticence, Tom began turning over rocks elsewhere. During July and August of 2005, he began talking to "mega-angels," investors capable of putting a million dollars or more into a venture. Unfortunately, while Tom valued the operating experience of these private investors, and recognized how much they could help him grow the business, $1 million was simply insufficient. Consequently, he began courting potential strategic investors: large corporations that might wish to invest in a startup that would add to their own product or service portfolio. A corporate strategic investor might also increase the value of its equity holdings in the venture by being a sales channel for the start-up's product or service. A corporate investor might also want to acquire Generate outright at some point further down the road.

Knowing in his bones that Generate's product would have real value for any purveyor of business-related information, he cold-called American City Business Journals (ACBJ) the largest U.S. publisher of metropolitan business news weeklies, with 44 business journals across the country. ACBJ was owned by the $8 billion Advance Publications Inc., which also operated Conde Nast Magazines, Parade magazine, the Golf Digest companies, Newhouse Newspapers, and cable television interests.

Though its parent company focused on consumer products, Tom knew that ACBJ understood the market for B2B information and seemed a logical beneficiary of Generate's innovation—as either an outright owner or investor. Moreover, Generate would benefit greatly from access to the publisher's deep information sources. Perhaps a deal could be arranged.

Tom connected to an executive with ACBJ, Tim Bradbury, senior vice president of ACBJ's Interactive business. More than his colleagues on the print side of the business, Tim understood information technology and its value to the enterprise. Though his company didn't normally invest in new ventures, Tim was intrigued by Tom's idea and offered to visit him when the alpha version was available. In the meantime, curious as to how Generate might handle ACBJ's data, Bradberry offered Tom a free data "feed."

In the meantime, Tom kept knocking on the doors of VCs, all of whom remained non-committal:

"That's interesting. Come back and see us when you have customers."

Or, "Let's talk again when you have a CEO—preferably a guy who has delivered for us before. You lack operating experience."

Even the initial group of interested financiers, people who knew Tom well, were reluctant to move forward—at least on their own. Most proposed syndicating the deal as a way of hedging their bets.

"Where's the 'venture' in venture capital," Tom asked himself. His frustrations continued until September 2005, when Howard and his tech team unveiled the alpha version of the product. By that time, the venture was scraping the bottom of the cash barrel, forcing each brother to put another $100,000 of his own savings into the enterprise. This was the point at which Tom and his wife sold their big house and moved to more modest quarters across town.

Three Potential Series A Deals

In September 2005, Howard unveiled his alpha version of the system's front end. Tom and Darr had their business plan worked out. (See financial projections in Exhibit 1.)

True to his word, Tim Bradbury traveled to Boston to see the system in action, using his company's data feed as one key input. Tim was impressed. He invited the brothers to visit ACBJ's Charlotte, NC headquarters in the next month and meet with the CEO Ray Shaw, a former Dow Jones executive, was an old school newspaper man who, Bradbury warned, would be more interested in Generate's people and concept than in the details of its technology.

Meanwhile, two of the VCs Tom had been courting came through with term sheets. VC #1 (called Great Capital for this case), and VC#2 (Ocean Capital) both had their fears allayed when Howard finished the alpha version and felt comfortable that beta was only three to four months off with proper funding. Great Capital put a pre-money valuation on the deal of $4 million. Ocean Capital's pre-money valuation was a little bit better at $4.5 million. The term sheets from both VCs were remarkably similar—and equally painful for Tom and Darr. Tom remarked:

You have to be very careful about terms. A VC offer to buy 40% of the company typically leaves you with majority ownership but don't confuse ownership with control. There are always "protective provisions" in the term sheet—usually five to fifteen—that many uninitiated entrepreneurs fail to consider. Typically, these say that even though you own majority ownership, you can't sell the company, can't raise more capital, can't spend more than X dollars, and can't add a board member without their approval. Effectively, they can block any big decision the company faces. Additionally, the money that *you* put in vests over a number of years. So much for control. And if they don't like you, out you go!

He then shared another frustration: "participating preferred" shares. This was one of the provisions in the term sheets received from both Great Capital and Ocean Capital. Tom and Darr were aware that this type of structure was typical, especially in New England and in Series A-C term sheets.

Here's how those work. If the VC puts in $3 million for a 30% ownership stake, and the company eventually sells for $30 million, the VC will take back its $3 million, before anyone else gets a dime, and then have a right to 30% of the remaining $27 million. In the industry it's called 'double-dipping.' The VC is first in line for a payout and then enjoys its pro-rata ownership of what's leftover. This can be very painful the more money a company raises. The only place this is legal is in the world of venture capital!

Tom Aley's reflections on those term sheets continued:

They insisted that we create an incentive pool for future employees, which we wanted to do anyway. One firm proposed setting aside 10% of all equity, and the other, 20%. Fair enough. We want to incentivize our employees. But the problem was that the 10% or 20% option pool had to be taken out our own founders shares first, *before the VCs put in their money.* They want the entrepreneurs to take all the dilution. Again, Tom and Darr weren't strangers to these types of terms—they're the very ones that Tom had negotiated with entrepreneurs during his 6 years of being a VC himself. "That didn't mean it tasted good."

Darr reflected further on these VC deals:

Here's the worst of the provisions. One of the VCs, Great Capital as I recall, wanted us to reconstitute all of our founders' shares as options that would vest over three years. This is called reverse vesting—and it is a lousy deal, but it's pretty standard with VCs. This doesn't sit real well—I mean we invested the same hard cash as the VCs and they want us to vest into *our* shares?! We bought those shares just like the VCs are buying theirs. We're not asking *them* to vest into their ownership!

This meant that if the company needed another round of capital in 12 months—a certainty if the enterprise were to grow—the founders would face an impossible dilemma. First stage investors are expected to participate in later rounds. If they don't, that sends a bad message to other potential investors. Thus, a VC sitting on a startup board who doesn't think the entrepreneur is the right person for the job might then say, "Listen, you've done a pretty good job so far, but we don't think you are the right person to run the business moving forward. You need to go start another company and let us build this one. For all your work, you can keep the first year's vested stock, but you need to forgo the rest. We are going to need it to bring on a professional management team. If you don't agree, your company will probably be dead and all of your stock won't be worth a dime."

Tom and Darr had seen a number of VC deals from both sides of the table. Tom had a special caution for the legal profession:

You need a good lawyer to wade through all these provisions. And the rub of it is that your own lawyer—the person who you trust to represent you and tough it out in final negotiations—may not be entirely on your side. He wants the deal to get done so that he can get paid—usually $20,000 to $30,000, which comes out of the proceeds. The attorney has an incentive to urge you to sign. He'll say, 'These are standard terms,' which is true enough, but they're all in the VC's favor.

Also during October, Tom and Darr flew down to Charlotte to meet Ray Shaw. The meeting went well. Tom, who later described Shaw as one of the smartest, warmest, most genuine business people he'd ever met, was full of confidence.

With Tim Bradbury's endorsement, the CEO asked them, "What's the deal?" Generate had just signed three paying customers for its forthcoming beta version—one of them being ACBJ![1] Tom told him that he needed to raise $3 million. Shaw was agreeable and deferred to the Aley's request to eliminate most of the protective terms that Tom and Darr found so painful to swallow in the VC deals. Further, the investment would be structured without participating preferred shares. An incentive pool was set up, but with all owners contributing to it on a pro-rata basis.

As important as anything else was the valuation of Generate. Tom proposed a $9 million pre-money valuation on Generate, which for $3 million would leave the founders with 75% of the equity. Ray did not immediately say no, but as an experienced executive running a cash generating business, he said:

> "Tom, I like your team a lot. Tim says your system is going work just fine. But please explain to me now, why is a company with no revenue worth $12 million?"

Discussion Questions

1. What are the pros and cons of each deal? Which deal should Tom and Darr take?

2. How can the brothers justify their valuation to Ray?

Appendix A: Generate Proforma Financials

	Beta–2005	2006	2007	2008
New customers	2	30	49	147
Recurring customers		2	34	83
Total customers	2	32	83	230
Average revenue per customer	17,000	50,000	50,000	50,000
Recurring Bookings		28,900	1,066,831	3,020,568
New Bookings	34,000	1,571,000	3,034,043	8,458,897
Total Bookings	34,000	1,599,900	4,100,874	11,479,465
Revenue	4,250	1,001,844	3,401,870	10,102,559
COS	59,250	978,417	1,185,000	4,649,710
GM	(55,000)	23,427	2,216,870	5,452,849
%	−1294%	2%	65%	54%
OpEx	613,093	1,552,233	3,100,438	4,903,550
Op Inc +/−	(668,093)	(1,528,806)	(883,568)	549,299
Adjustments for Working Capital		(30,055)	(102,056)	(303,077)
Ending Cash	3,774,144	2,215,283	1,229,659	1,475,881
Headcount	11	33	73	91
FTE	5	27	55	81

[1] ACBJ signed a three-year subscriber agreement at $60,000 per year paid up front. The other two were T-Mobile, which has a large enterprise sales force, and Deloitte & Touche.

Appendix B:
Explaining the Term Sheet Provisions _____

The offers that Tom and Darr Aley received from VCs were loaded with restrictive covenants. We will take one of these offers and examine the key terms and provisions.

Pre-money valuation: $5 million. This is the valuation set by one of the VCs on Generate before investment. The VC offered to invest $3 million at this valuation. The post-money valuation would therefore be $8 million, and the VC would therefore receive 37.5% of the company stock in this Series A financing.

Participating Preferred Stock

Tom, Darr, and Howard all owned common shares, which represented ownership in the venture and carried full voting rights. These were founder's shares. The VC didn't want common stock. It demanded preferred stock. This type of security has numerous protections that a VC can use to limit its loss in the event of company failure or poor performance. The preferred stock had full voting rights in its pro-rata participation in all equity issued by the company (e.g. 37.5%). It also comes with liquidation preferences that are described next. It was also structured as "participating preferred stock," which means that upon any liquidation event, the preferred stock would convert immediately to common stock to participate pro-rata in the distribution of the company assets.

Liquidation Preferences

The participating preferred stock came with liquidation preferences. VCs usually have a broad definition of "liquidation," which includes an acquisition, bankruptcy, and the sale of company's assets. The purpose is that the VC wants to get its money *ahead* of the founders. This is usually structured as a 1X liquidation preference with terms attached. In the Generate case, Great Capital put a 1.5 times liquidation preference into the term sheet. Consider the following two scenarios:

1. If Generate was liquidated (acquired or went into bankruptcy) for only $4.5 million dollars, then even though Great Capital owned only 37.5% of the stock, it would still get all of its original $3 million dollars back plus another $1.5 million before the founders.

2. If Generate was acquired for $30 million, Great Capital would still get its $4.5 million right off the top before the common shareholders, and then 37.5% of the remaining $25.5 million, or $9.5 million, making for a total of $14 million or close to 5X its original investment.

Dividends

Great Capital also insisted on dividends on its preferred stock in the amount of 5% or $150,000 on its $3 million investment. If the company wasn't cash flow positive, then that amount would be paid in additional preferred shares.

Reverse Vesting. Great Capital insisted that Tom, Darr, and Howard put all their shares into the employee option pool, and then have their pro-rata amounts vest over a period of three years, losing effective control of the company even though the Series A investors owned only 37.5% of the venture! Even if Tom and Darr could negotiate the first third to vest immediately, that would still leave the founders with only 20% voting rights. In other words, Great Capital could decide as a Board Member to replace the founders and get a new management team at any time, in which case 40% of the founding stock would go back into the kitty for whatever purposes the VCs thought best.

Reserved Stock

Great Capital requested that an employee stock option pool of 10% of all outstanding shares be set aside pre-money. For Tom, Darr, and Howard, that meant that they would have to give up 10% of their collective stock—e.g. dilute themselves by 10%—before Great Capital put in its money. That meant that Great Capital would still own 37.5% of participating preferred stock with a 1.5 X liquidation preference, and that Tom, Darr, and Howard's collective 62.5% ownership would drop to 52.5% ownership.

Great Capital's term sheet contained other significant clauses. These included:

- A "take me along" clause. If the founders wished to sell some of their stock to another party, they had to also sell the same percentage of the VC's at the same time unless the VC approved otherwise. This would prevent Tom, Darr, and Howard from using their stock to bring in another investor to effectively run the company.
- Preemptive rights. Great Capital also put clauses into the term sheet stating a right of first refusal to preserve any portion of its 37.5% equity stake in subsequent rounds of financing.
- A rachet clause. If the price of the stock dropped below the Series A price per share in any subsequent round of financing, Great Capital would first be issued additional participatory preferred shares in the amount that would preserve its 37.5% ownership. This was effectively an anti-dilution clause. For example, if the Series A price was $10 a share, and the next round was only $5 a share, Great Capital would be issued the same amount of shares that it already held to preserve its ownership stake. New investors coming in at the lower $5 per share price would effectively be diluting the common shareholders, e.g. the founders.
- Regardless of Board Membership, Great Capital inserted approval rights on any expenditure of cash over $100,000.

Taken together, these provisions meant that even though Great Capital would be a minority shareholder after its Series A investment, it would still effectively control the company.

Sentillion, Inc.

The Anatomy of a Corporate Spin-off

"Do you think it's really possible to start a company to do this type of thing?"

—Robert Seliger, Co-Founder and CEO, asking a friend
about spinning off technology from HP into a
new company April, 1999, Winchester, Massachusetts

Rob Seliger was sitting across from John Douglass at his kitchen table. Rob Seliger had been an R&D manager in Hewlett Packard's Medical Products Group. John had been a marketing manager in the same division. Together, the two men were now partners in a new healthcare IT venture and had just raised $2.7 million in Series A financing. The process of spinning out their new company from HP had been a year-long journey. And with the funding, their work had just begun.

Origins in HP

The Medical Products Group was located in Andover, Massachusetts, an entire continent away from HP's Silicon Valley headquarters. The Group at that time accounted for roughly $1.5 billion of HP's $40 billion annual revenues. Seliger had arrived at HP 18 years earlier, at the very beginning of his career. An electrical engineering graduate from Cornell, he had added an MIT masters in computer science to his resume, thanks to a fellowship from his new employer.

Over the course of those 18 years, Seliger had risen to become the senior software technologist in the Medical Products Group. Being on the opposite side of the country from HP headquarters, and serving the specialized market of healthcare systems, had given the Group a fair amount of operating independence. It handled nearly all of its own business functions—ranging from R&D, to sales, manufacturing, finance, and customer service. This relative independence had made the Medical Products Group a training ground for up and coming HP executives. Lewis Platt, for example, a prominent CEO of HP during the 1990s had first been the General Manager of the Medical Products Group.

The 1990s had been a decade of transition for HP. Historically the company was a creator and manufacturer of high margin, sophisticated electronics, measuring instruments, and software for niche applications in industrial, scientific, and medical markets. With the advent of client server and home computing, however, management redirected the business to lower-margin, high-volume businesses such as servers, PCs, ink-jet and laser printers, scanners, and so forth. And management wanted more of the same.

The Medical Products Group was not "more of the same." It was the market leader in patient monitors for adults and infants, and in ultrasound machines for cardiology applications—all complex systems. The Andover facility also had its own automated surface mount manufacturing machines to fabricate the unique, multi-layered printed circuit boards for its various products. These products departed sharply from the new path that corporate HP was pursuing, and top management was finding it harder and harder to keep these different businesses under the same roof.

Hospital managers at this time were urging their vendors to integrate diverse data sets into electronic medical record systems. Care providers were convinced that such integration would improve the quality of care, reduce medical errors, and lower administrative costs by eliminating redundant processes and databases. As a gifted software architect, Seliger understood their need and believed that well designed software could bridge different types of systems with different specific purposes. His customer visits convinced him that this was what users wanted.

At the time, Seliger was an architect working on a highly advanced clinical information system that gathered data from a patient monitor and displayed computerized flowsheets and reports that in most hospitals were still documented manually by physicians and nursing staff. He wanted to connect the data in his system with other systems produced by the Group but he found no resources to develop such connections. In fact, he saw that different units within the Group were doing just the opposite of what customers wanted. Everything was decentralized. Each product line had its own R&D team building its own applications software to its own self-defined standards, using the tools of their own choice.

Seliger's R&D executive, Mark Halloran, also recognized the problem but was struggling for ways to get the division business managers to allocate resources to the development of common "software platforms." He knew that such platforms—common databases and application programming interfaces—would allow for seamless interconnectivity between the Group's different product lines. The same platform could also be opened to HP's partners. However, division managers were so focused on near term improvements to feature and functions in their own systems that common software for the common good was not an issue of interest. The impact on customers was predictable. Said Seliger:

> There was no connectivity. Cardiology had its computers and ran cardiology applications. Obstetrics had its computers, which ran applications for it alone. This did not bode well, for example, for treating pregnant women with mitro valve prolapse, a common heart condition among pregnant women. Customers would complain to us that they had bought a system for the intensive care unit, another for radiology, and another for the OR, but they didn't work together. And they were right. Different departments were using different operating systems, had different standards, and so forth. You couldn't have made these systems less integrated if you had tried.

Doctors and nurses who wanted to use these information systems to get a complete picture of their patients and patient care were frustrated at every turn.

> They would first have to find the application of interest—say radiology—then log on and enter their password. But if they were in the radiology application and wanted to check a lab report, they'd have to log into the lab's system, which required a different id and password. Want to order a medication for the patient? Then the doctor would have to log into yet another system. This was so frustrating and time consuming that most care providers stuck to their paper records and manual systems. Using the computer system was just too painful. At best, they would log into the single application most pertinent to their discipiline and ignore patient information available elsewhere.

"A company should organize the way it's wants it's products to operate," Halloran would say. He believed that the Group needed a small centralized R&D unit to build common components to be used across all divisions.

In 1996, Halloran hired a consultant to size up opportunities to create common parts and pieces across both hardware and software in the Group. Working with senior technologists such as Seliger, the consultant—known as "The Professor" because of his affiliation with a local university—found numerous opportunities for platforming. In software alone, there were different database management systems, programming languages, and even operating systems across the five different divisions. It was during this time that Seliger and Halloran kindled a friendship based on their shared interest in the power of product platforms. Halloran built support among Group executives for the creation of a new, central R&D team to create common software components to connect the five different product lines. He asked Seliger to lead the team.

At the time, being a formal leader at HP was not what most people would expect. HP culture was to give managers lots of responsibility but no real authority, as Seliger quickly discovered. He was charged with bringing the divisions together to build common software components. However, he was given few resources to get the job done. Nor did he have much leverage over the other R&D managers. They all had tight deadlines to meet in their other jobs and these had priority.

Forming an Industry Consortium to Create a New Standard

The opportunity to create common software existed at two primary levels. The first was at the database level, as common formats for identifying and storing information about patients, medications, or clinical procedures. By 1997, various industry standard groups had created fairly well defined database standards to address these needs, and most medical device and software developers had adopted them. Even HP's medical divisions had begun to incorporate these industry standards.[1]

The second opportunity to create common software was at the user interface level. Nothing existed within HP or any other medical systems vendor that standardized how physicians and nurses interacted with clinical software.

- Patient information resided in multiple clinical IT systems
- Doctors, nurses and other caregivers required access to many applications
- Navigating among those applications was cumbersome and time-consuming
- Even if a "single sign-on" for caregivers existed, it would not, by itself, get them into the specific applications they needed to see.
- There was no working technology to synchronize applications to present a single patient's data across the multiple applications used by caregivers.

As a result, each physician had to maintain a separate log in and password for each software application used over the course of the day—up to a dozen or more in many situations. There was also no way that a single patient's information could be populated across these myriad applications

---

[1] HL/7 (which stands for Health Level 7) is an important set of standards for the electronic interchange of clinical, financial, and administrative information among health care oriented computer systems. It specifies a number of flexible standards, guidelines, and methodologies by which various healthcare systems can communicate with each other. Within HL/7, document, data, and messaging formats have been proposed and adopted by the industry. DICOM was a major database standard. It stands for the Digital Imaging and Communications in Medicine (DICOM) standard for distributing and viewing any kind of medical image regardless of the origin.

once the doctor logged on. For each application, s/he would have to look up the patient's ID and wait for the system to access that information. When the doctor changed or added information (which is the whole point of providing care assisted by computers), s/he would have to update each clinical application separately. If the doctor had to race off to answer a page, for example, those systems might never have the correct information. Or, the results of a laboratory analysis shown in one system were not carried over into ordering drugs into another system. Incorrect or missing information could lead to suboptimal care, causing further illness, and sometimes, worse! For example, it was well known that in the United States alone, giving people the incorrect medications in the hospital was the cause of over 100,000 deaths each and every year!

These were the problems—for physicians, nurses, and other care providers—that Seliger wanted to try to solve. In his new position as the head of the Medical Product Group's central R&D team, that became his responsibility. But, as noted earlier, he had no authority to make any of the R&D managers in the five HP divisions help design and use common software infrastructure. None. Frustrated, he began asking for advice—of the political sort. Wes Rishel, a personal friend and industry consultant, offered a potential solution:

> Rob, why don't you create an industry standard? Focus on your ideas about patient and user context management. If you get people outside the company to embrace that standard, that might compel HP developers to fall into line with everyone else.

Going outside to encourage collaboration inside seemed a strange way to reach the goal, but at this point, Seliger was willing to try any good idea. He invited companies that worked in the healthcare IT space to come to Boston and form a consortium to create tools to identify care providers and synchronize patients across their respective systems. In March, 1997, twenty companies showed up for the first meeting of what became the Clinical Context Object Work Group, or CCOW. Of those, a number were HP's archrivals. Yet, everyone realized that these standards, if well designed and implemented as a new type of healthcare IT "middleware," would significantly improve the productivity of care providers using computers and eliminate a wide range of errors.

Seliger's middleware initiative had, until now, gathered little attention from top HP management. The fact that archrivals were participating in CCOW, however, gave his work greater visibility, and he was given a staff of programmers to get the job done.

Taking the lead within the consortium, the HP team developed an application programming interface (API) that any vendor could use to enable caregivers to sign on only once in order to use any application they are allowed to use. They also began work on a second set of software that would allow different systems to synchronize on a patient across different applications. By the end of 1997, Seliger's team had created the first version a software toolkit that offered the promise of being an industry-wide platform.

What to Do with the New Technology?

For Seliger, success bred both more success, and then new challenges.

The HP Medical Products Groups was always one of the major exhibitors at medical device and information systems tradeshows. As word spread about CCOW and HP's implementation of it emerging standards into a working toolkit, competitors quickly began to seek him out at trade shows, asking if they could license HP's new software to enable their own applications.

HP management took notice, and in early spring 1998 asked Seliger to continue his work in Andover *and* take over R&D responsibility for managing the software development of all of Medical Products Group, which had recently been combined into a single business unit. Now, with the top R&D job in the business unit, as well as increasing demand for his new software toolkit, things appeared to be looking up. Nevertheless, there were so many pressing priorities that transforming MPG's clinical information products into a suite of interoperable solutions continued to be elusive.

Seliger was getting increasingly concerned. He was the top R&D person in the Clinical Information Systems Business Unit and he had never been more on top of his game in terms of architecting software and leading people to build it. Still, he wondered if there was a different way to ignite the interoperability opportunity, especially in the form of clinical context management. During a quiet, reflective moment following a weekend of hiking with his family, he contemplated this challenge—and had an epiphany: maybe the new technology needed a new company to fully develop it and bring it to market. Perhaps he should start his own company! "Once that idea infected me," Seliger recalls, " I had trouble concentrating on anything else."

On Monday morning, he called The Professor. Seliger's friend had been a cofounder of a venture capital backed software company several years earlier and been involved in other startups. Seliger asked, "Do you think it's really possible to start a company to do this type of thing? Could we spin the technology out of HP and build it in a separate company?"

Over the next thirty minutes, The Professor fanned the flames, describing how other software entrepreneurs had created corporate spin-offs with the blessing of their former employers. He described what had to be done and ways of doing it. He talked to the software engineer about product strategy, writing a business plan, developing realistic projections of revenue and startup expenses, and the level of financing that might be necessary. He sent his friend various planning templates and financial boilerplates. "But one of the first things you have to do, Rob," the Professor said, "is have a heart to heart with your boss, Cynthia. You need to sell her on your vision for the technology."

Cynthia Danaher was the senior executive of the Medical Product Group. Cynthia had risen quickly to become the head of marketing for the company's industry leading ultrasound system division, and then, its General Manager. She had exceptional insight into HP as a company and the Medical Products Group's role within it. She had been a strong supporter of developing the CCOW standard, but knew the company well enough to know that HP corporate had a limited appetite for Seliger's type of project—at least at that time. In fact, corporate was probably in the process of spinning out its entire sensor and industrial systems businesses (which became Agilent), although this was certainly not known to Seliger at the time. The Medical Products Group would be packaged into that new business. Given that the Group's patient monitors, ultrasound machines, and clinical information systems were so different than industrial systems, it was only a matter of time before decision-makers in what would become Agilent would also seek a buyer for the Medical Products Group.[2]

When Seliger spoke to her about spinning out the CCOW technology into a new venture, Danaher quickly agreed. To her, the idea made sense because it would be good for HP, as the technology would help HP address the interoperability requirements that the market was increasingly demanding. And to Seliger's surprise, she offered to get HP Board approval for it and introduce Seliger to her friends in the venture capital industry. Seliger even wondered if seed funding for the venture might come in the form of licensing payments from HP to use the initial software products from the venture for its own "next generation" clinical information systems.

High Anxiety

Word of the possible spin-out quickly leaked out within the Medical Products Grooup. Some of Seliger's peers resented the idea of HP's technology working to his personal advantage and

---

[2] Phillips acquired the Group a few years later.

went out of their ways to create stumbling blocks. One individual even circulated misinformation about an outsider's interest in purchasing the technology from HP—which would have left Seliger high and dry! None of the rumors were true, but the turmoil they caused left Seliger anxious and somewhat disoriented. The idea of leaving HP was also disconcerting.

> I had only had one job interview in my entire career—with HP. I'd been with the company at that point for 18 years. It had been my whole world. I was well-known within the company and had access to people and resources. I knew nothing about the world outside of HP, and even less about starting a company or about venture financing. And here I was about to take this huge leap.

During the period when the spin out was being negotiated (May through November 1998), Seliger experienced a level of anxiety he'd never felt before. "I'd wake up in the morning with shortness of breath—hyperventilating. I'd tell my wife that I couldn't get out of bed and go to work." Seliger had climbed every rung on the technical career ladder within HP Medical and had a big, talented team working for him. He was earning a very good income and had a company car and stock options.

> "All that was about to go away because of my crazy idea. I'd ask my wife, 'What will I do if this doesn't work out?' and she'd tell me 'Don't worry—you can get another job.' But I didn't want another job. I liked working at HP. "

It wasn't until several months into this period that he realized that leaving HP wasn't the source of his anxiety—it was the fear of his spin-out plan falling through and *not* getting to create this company. "I was so excited about the idea and fixated on starting the company that every rumor and stumbling block triggered anxiety. Once I recognized that, my anxiety evaporated, and I never looked back."

Writing the Business Plan

Seliger called his friend The Professor, inquiring about the form and structure of a business plan. They reviewed some templates and Seliger went to work. With coaching from his friends and advisors, Seliger wrote the plan over the course of a month. A dozen improved iterations would follow over the next six months as the entrepreneur sharpened his strategy and secured funding

The first question that Seliger confronted was "What products am I going to sell?" The CCOW software he had developed in HP was a toolkit to implement the CCOW standard. As good as this new "platform" was technically, Seliger was skeptical that his new company could produce substantial revenue by selling a software toolkit to other medical software companies. "People don't buy platforms; they buy solutions. Good solutions, however, need to be built on strong platforms," he remarked. "We had the platform, but now we needed to create solutions that could be sold as products."

He focused on an initial product for end-users and on a software developer's kit (SDK) for software developers. The initial end-user product, *Vergence,* provided a single sign-on product that would allow care providers to sign-on just once, and be securely logged onto all the applications to which they were entitled. Vergence also provided patient context sharing, so that a user need only select the patient of interest once in order for every open application to "tune" to and display that patient's data. The software toolkit was comprised on a set of reusable components and an API that other medical software developers would use to simply if the process of "CCOW enabling" their applications for single sign-on and patient context management.

Armed with this basic product strategy, Seliger turned his attention to building a projection of revenue over the first three years that he could defend with confidence. Countless hours were spent in discussion with his advisors on the assumptions behind the revenue projections. These included:

- The number of hospitals buying these software products over the first five years
- The number of users in each hospital
- The price per user per year for the various software products
- The number or medical software companies buying the SDK a year, and what if anything, he should charge them for it

Given the pressing need among health care providers for this capability and strong interest by the dozens of companies who had attended the CCOW meetings, Seliger felt confident in the following assumptions:

- A dozen hospitals would adopt the single sign-on product during the first year of its release, with several dozen following in the year after.

- There were over 5,000 hospitals in the United States alone. The new venture's primary target market would be large health care providers which had, on average, approximately 1,000 physicians and 4,000 nursing and related support staff. Also, certain key accounts represented dozens and dozens of facilities in different geographic locations, the Veterans Administration and Kaiser Permente being two prime examples. Getting those accounts would anchor Seliger's position in the medical IT market.

- Seliger knew that pricing was a great challenge for new products. However, he had now spent several years talking to hospital administrators, doctors, and nursing staff. Hospitals were already buying identity management products from vendors such as RSA on a per user license model. And many were spending millions on enterprise software for electronic medical records and clinical information systems. Based on all this, Seliger felt that he could charge a per user fee for the single sign on, and an additional fee for the patient context management.

- To seed the market, Seliger also felt early on his new company was probably going to have to give the CCOW software development kit away for just a nominal fee. He also suspected that he would have to allocate his own programming staff to help other medical software companies enable their own applications. This came to be called the "immersion program" in which Seliger's team helped vendors perform "software surgery" on their applications.

Working Toward the Spin-out

Once he had a business plan, Seliger began pitching it to venture capitalists, some of whom were acquaintances of Danaher. In this process, he had a phone conversation with Bruce Bauer, a Silicon Valley financier with Newbury Ventures. Bauer had been tipped off by a key HP R&D executive that Seliger was working on something important. This piqued Bauer's interest, as he had wanted to do a deal with HP for a long time. The two agreed to meet at an industry tradeshow at which HP would profile CCOW to the medical technology community.

The two met and got into deep conversation. At the end of it, Bauer gave Seliger some advice: Rob had too many jobs to do. If he wanted to launch a company, he had to make it his only priority. Seliger reflected, "That was the best advice I could have received. Besides being an early investor, Bruce and I became and remain close personal friends."

Two days later he was in Cynthia's office, explaining what Bruce had told him. As he recalls. "She was in total agreement, and to my amazement, gave me the next four months to work on nothing but the spin off." Moreover, Danaher teamed Seliger up with one of her staff who was experienced in structuring agreements with VCs. Her one caveat was that if Seliger couldn't make the deal work—i.e., failed to gain external financing—he had to reassume his operating responsibilities as a full time head of R&D.

It took three months, but by November 1998, the HP Board or Directors approved the spin out and agreed to an intellectual property agreement with the venture.

Building a Team

Seliger knew that he had to quickly assemble a skilled and knowledgeable team, a task that proved easier than anticipated. As word of the spin-out leaked, he was approached by a senior product manager for one of the large medical device divisions, John Douglass. Douglass came up to Seliger in the cafeteria line and said a bit too loudly, "Tell me all about this!" Seliger quickly shuttled Douglass off to a vacant section of the cafeteria where he could talk about the project without being overheard. Douglass listened and liked what he heard. He joined as co-founder, and later took a lead role in defining and launching the company's first wave of products.[3]

Staff on the technical side of the business was also needed. Once the HP Board approved the spin-out in November, things could be out in the open. A standard exit agreement restricted Seliger from soliciting HP personnel for the new business. However, MPG was considering a downsizing due to challenging business conditions. To his surprise, the Group's HR manager presented Seliger with a list of people he could hire without violating the "non-solicit" agreement. "I couldn't believe the names I saw on that list—these were some of the very best," he said later. Several people were hired directly from that list, and others later joined on their own volition, including a brilliant software engineer from Germany—Ralf—who later became Seliger's head of R&D in the new company and led many of its most important projects. When the spin-out became a live company, in March 1999, Seliger had a total staff of 10 employees, 6 of whom were former HP colleagues.

Series A Funding, Key Milestones, and Important Decisions!

Bauer became the lead investor and brought along two other VC firms in a syndicated Series A financing. The $2.7 million round closed in March 1999, almost a year to the day after Seliger had returned from his fateful hiking trip. (Subsequent B and C rounds are also provided in Exhibit 1). His exit from HP was a *fait accompli*. In February, after considering many potential names, Seliger decided to call his new company Sentillion. The name satisfied Seliger's desire for a "cool" and unique name for which the Web domain name was also available.

With help from Bauer and other investors, he and John Douglass had to establish key milestones for:

- R&D, including the beta test and first commercial release for the Vergence, i.e. the single sign-on service.
- A program to get 3rd party software companies to incorporate Vergence into their own software according to the CCOW standard.

---

[3] Douglass left the company in 2003 to sail around the world with his wife and two children.

- First key hospital accounts.
- Intellectual property, including a patent and clarity on ownership of the IP relative to HP.
- Key hires for major functions inside the new company.

Driving all this planning for the question on the ongoing relationship to be formed with HP now that startup funding was secure. Should HP own Sentillion stock? What would that mean for Sentillion's position as the "Switzerland" in the industry? How else might HP gain from Sentillion's success? Seliger knew that this question was the elephant in the room.

The race was on. The team needed to achieve these goals in order to raise the next round of financing. Bauer and other advisors thought two to three times the Series A financing should get the company to operating profitability.

Questions _____

1. What is a corporate spin-out?

2. How should Seliger try to structure the deal with Hewlett Packard, including the handling of equity and intellectual property?

3. What is the market opportunity facing Seliger and his team?

4. What is Sentillion's core IP and what types of products do you see based on that IP?

5. What should be Seliger's key milestones with the Series A funding?

Series A:	March	1999	$2.7 million
Series B:	March	2000	$9 million
Series C:	August	2001	$18 million

Exhibit 1 Sentillion's Equity Financing

The Applications

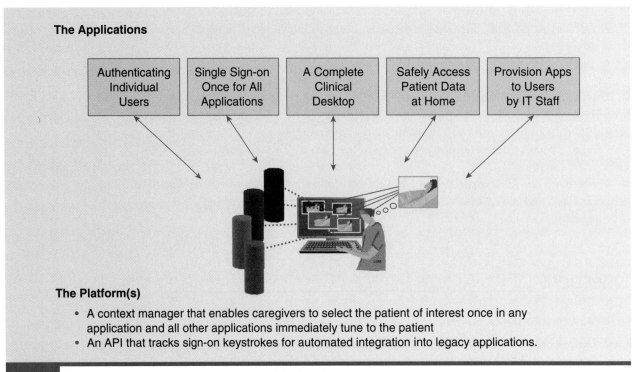

The Platform(s)

- A context manager that enables caregivers to select the patient of interest once in any application and all other applications immediately tune to the patient
- An API that tracks sign-on keystrokes for automated integration into legacy applications.

Exhibit 2   Developing a Product Strategy Focused on Major Use Cases

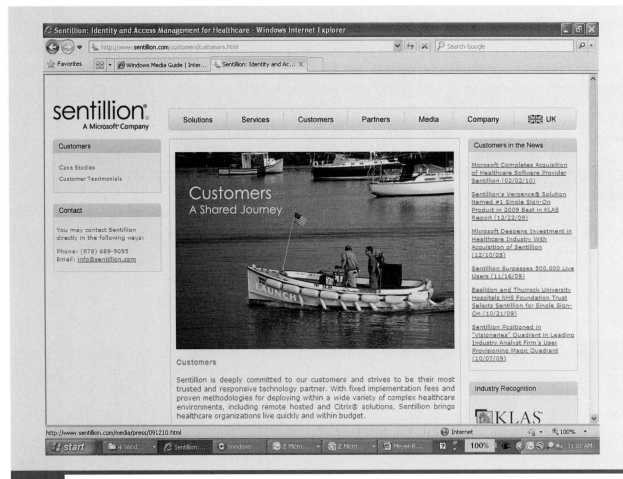

Exhibit 3   Sentillion's Website 12 Years After Startup

mInfo

SHANGHAI, CHINA. SEPTEMBER, 2010. CEO Alvin Huang Graylin and CTO Derrick had come a long way in a very short time. From the launch of their mobile Internet search company in early 2005 until now, they had built a company of 100 employees with a user base of tens of millions of mobile subscribers. And the company's performance had reached cash flow breakeven since Q4 of 2009. This had not been easy. Though born in China, Graylin had been raised and educated in the United States; thus, he had to learn the ins and outs of Chinese business culture, and was generally perceived as a foreigner by regulators and telecom company clients. Threading a course through government officialdom had also been a challenge. Entrepreneurs in the Peoples Republic of China—both foreign and domestic—had to master an opaque regulatory system and patiently build relationships with bureaucrats.

China was very different than the hi-tech entrepreneurial environment in which Graylin had forged his career. He had spent five years after graduate school helping Intel in its Shanghai Office, doing business development in the PC industry. Now, with five years of mInfo under his belt, with mInfo, and with the help of his Chinese co-founder, he had learned how to get things done.

The Company and its Service

mInfo was initially founded as an SMS mobile (text messaging) search service. Within six months, and after using their own savings, the two founders had developed a working prototype. With the backing of US and domestic investment capital[1], the company was soon able to address the search needs of the large and growing Chinese market of mobile Internet users, and had become that country's leading English and Chinese language mobile search service. mInfo was also China's only "natural language"[2] search provider. "We've only raised about $6 million in financing," says the CEO, "but here in China, where operating costs are much lower, that kind of money can take you a long way."

For Graylin and CTO Huang, mobile Internet computing represented the next big wave in an industry cycle that began with mainframe computing in the 1950s (Figure 1). Mobile Internet technology made it possible for people to use "smart phones" such as the iPhone and Droid

---

Written by Marc H. Meyer and Richard Luecke. Copyright (c) 2011, Marc H. Meyer.

[1] From its inception through mid-2010, mInfo raised $6 million in capital through a seed round and two A financing rounds. Roughly 70 percent of that capital had come from US investors, with balance put forward by Chinese financiers.

[2] Natural language processing refers to the interaction of computers and human, or natural,

to send and receive email, access the Web, and conduct online searches for news, weather, phone numbers and addresses, restaurant reviews, and other information. Because smart phone screens were small and their bandwidths are narrower than those of desktop and laptops machines, mobile online searches were limited in the volume of information they could deliver. These constraints represented challenges to search service companies such as mInfo. Since these companies cannot deliver page after page of search results, they must assure that the results they provide to subscribers are on target and the best available. "It has to be fast, and it has to be right," said founder Graylin.

mInfo's initial technology strategy was to provide mobile SMS. Over time, that strategy migrated to mobile search on the Internet, and then to a hybrid "automatic/operator" model. The latter delivered some 90 percent of search responses automatically; the remaining hard-to-find subscriber queries were addressed through a combination of search engines and human operators. This use of human operators raised the cost to mInfo, but it assured higher quality service to subscribers.

China's mobile telecom market was the world's largest. Dominated by China Mobile, China Unicom and China Telecom, it had grown from 400 million subscribers in 2004 to over 800 million in the U.S. 2010. In contrast, the number of mobile subscribers in 2010 was only about 270 million.[3] Subscribership in China was forecasted to continue at a rate of more than 7 million *per month* over the next several years. The rate of penetration of this technology (though less than half the penetration rate of the US) had far surpassed those of fixed-line telephone and PC-based Internet communication (see Figure 2).

Not all telecom subscribers, however, owned devices capable of mobile Internet search. Smart phones (3G +) were more costly in China than in the West, often running to $500–700— easily twice the monthly salary of a worker in China's urban commercial centers. Consequently,

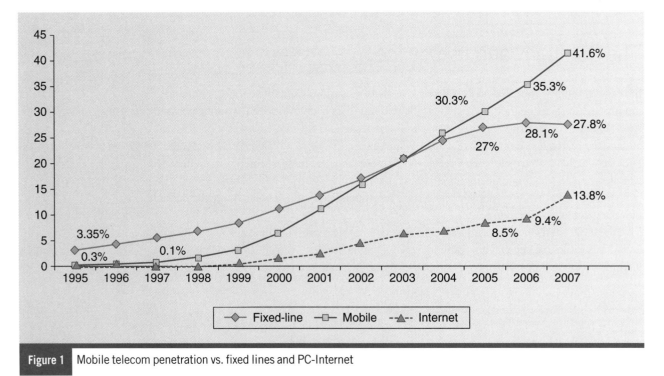

Figure 1 Mobile telecom penetration vs. fixed lines and PC-Internet

Source: Information from the Ministry of Information Industries, the People's Republic of China.

---

[3] World Bank, "World Development Indicators," updated 27 July 2010.

only 15–20 percent of mobile phone users subscribed in 2010 to Internet services. Rising incomes and the relative decline in smart phone costs, however, were likely to increase that percentage. With China's GDP growing at 8–10 percent per year, rising household incomes and buying power would increase demand for smart phones—a highly prized personal luxury item in China's modern cities and a symbol of personal success. And the number of mobile Internet searches would escalate in step. One industry analysis forecasted 52 percent compound annual growth in the number of those searches between 2007 and 2012.

WHAT ARE MOBILE INTERNET USERS SEARCHING FOR?

According to the company, in 2010, 65 percent of mobile subscribers searched for news; 59 percent use it to "chat"; 42 percent read novels on their mobile devices; and 39 percent searched community forums for information. Others searched for stock prices, directions, phone numbers, weather forecasts, and so forth.

Business Model

By 2010, mInfo had successfully negotiated service contracts with several telecom companies, including the country's two giants: China Telecom and China Mobile. During the Beijing Olympics, it won the contract to be the Games' official search provider.

Under the terms of its agreement with provider clients, mInfo received a fixed annual fee plus incremental revenues once the number of subscriber searches exceeded a particular annual level. The company also generated revenues by placing ads on its pages. It has agreements with many ad companies. As of 2010, Graylin believed that it has only scratched the surface of this potentially huge revenue source. Much more was anticipated as 3G mobile technology and broader bandwidth continued to gain a broader foothold in the Chinese market.

An Entrepreneurial Journey

Graylin was born in China in 1971. His Chinese father was a Western art professor of over 20 years at the Guangdong Art Academy; his mother—half Chinese and half American—was a dancer with the BJ ballet troop who had studied for a time in the United States. Eager to give Alvin and his siblings an opportunity to experience life in the West, the parents moved their family in 1980 to Seattle, Washington. They were among the first Chinese families to do so as their homeland emerged from decades of isolation.

The move to Seattle was economically difficult. "My parents came to the US with only $500 in their pockets," Graylin recalled. "My father couldn't find work in his field immediately and had to take two jobs painting ad signs and whatever else he could find. My brothers and I were expected to help the family by taking odd jobs after school."

After completing high school, Graylin attended the University of Washington, where he majored in electrical engineering. Midway through that program, he took a nine-month internship with IBM in Minnesota. Inspired by that first taste of real world technology development, he returned to Seattle and finished his degree, graduating at the top of his class.

During those final years at UW, Graylin and four classmates launched and ran an enterprise that provided systems integration and custom programming to local educational institutions and small businesses. At its peak, the venture generated about $500,000 per year, half of which was profit.

Intel

Upon graduation in 1993, Graylin took a chip design and system architecture job with Intel, which would employ him in many capacities over the next seven years. One of his early assignments (1994) took him to Shanghai, where he and two other US expats set up a new office and he led a team 25 employees focused on growing the Chinese consumer PC business. Its goal was to develop and bundle hardware and software, and find a business model that would break through the then-sluggish pace of Home PC adoption in China. This was a large order for a 23 year-old with limited experience, but Graylin rose to the challenge. As he recalled, "It gave me a chance to hone my management skills, and it kindled my interest in business." Within three years, his Shanghai unit was able to reduce the retail price of consumer PCs from roughly $2,000 to a more affordable $600. This greatly expanded the sales of PCs to consumers in China, many of which had "Intel Inside."

MIT and iCompass

His assignment completed in 1997, Graylin rotated back to the US, and to life in the corridors of Intel. The pay was good, and he enjoyed being back where he would spend more time with his relatives and friends. But missing the independence and responsibility he had enjoyed in Shanghai, be began looking for another situation. He found it at MIT in 1998, where, with Intel's support, he enrolled in a dual masters degree program in business management and computer science, in the University's renowned "Leaders in Manufacturing" program.[4]

While at MIT, Graylin entered two business plan competitions with a team of classmates. One of them was for an Internet marketing analytics company called iCompass. The company's proprietary technology was capable of discerning the search patterns and profitability potential of online shoppers—something that direct and online retailers were eager to know.

The iCompass concept and technology attracted attention from both investors and potential customers, enough so that Graylin and his colleague were able to raise $1 million in a first round of financing. Shortly thereafter, however, in March 2000, the "dot-com" bubble burst, share prices fell off a cliff, and investor interest in technology companies evaporated. Like many comparable startups, iCompass folded in 2001. But for Graylin, "Getting customers, raising money, and hiring a team had been a great learning experience,"which he would carry forward to subsequent ventures.

Back to China

Between 2001 and late 2004, Graylin worked for two security software companies, the first in Taiwan, the second in the United States. In each case he was given business unit responsibility and opportunities to deal with people in North America, Europe, and Asia.

Frustrated by the internal politics of the last of these firms ("We had three CEOs in one year"), Graylin was ready for self-employment. So, in late 2004, he quit his job and spent the next several months looking for a promising new opportunity. Among his first contacts was Derek Huang, a Chinese electrical engineer he had hired years earlier, during his days with Intel in Shanghai. Huang was familiar with the mobile messaging business in China and shared Graylin's entrepreneurial spirit. Huang had been the CTO of two VC funded startups after leaving Intel in 1999. After a lunch meeting discussing opportunities, the two identified a potential opportunity that was still unfilled in China. Mobile Search. Graylin had been working on search related projects with a VC firm since leaving his last job and Huang was an expert in mobile

---

[4] Later named the "MIT Leaders for Global Operations."

technologies and had access to a qualified technical team in Shanghai. The next day, they both wrote emails to each other, saying there could be a billion dollar market for this space long term. Working together, they planned and launched mInfo in mid-2005.

Graylin's initial investments came from wireless/tech industry angels in the Seattle area and they provided a lot of support and advice for getting the project off the ground. Graylin was also able to recruit former WA governor, Gary Locke, to serve on his board for over three years until he was picked by President Obama to be the US Commerce Secretary. Locke was viewed as a rock star in China being the highest ranking Chinese American in the US government At that time. He helped open many doors during his term with mInfo.

Graylin's earlier experience in mainland China had been useful, but much had changed in that country over the past decade. Besides the usual startup challenges of business development and connecting with customers, he and his partner had to overcome difficulties in several other important areas: special if not unique to the Chinese business and consumer environment.

Human Resources

By the mid-2000s, China's blistering GDP growth (typically 9–10 percent per year) had created wage inflation, particularly at mid- and upper-levels of the technology and managerial labor markets. Further, demand for individuals with proven skills had grown so strong that that recruiting and retention were very difficult. Many talented employees could pull up stakes one week and begin work with a competitor the next—often at a higher salary.[5]

Graylin and Huang had to cope with this situation as they began recruiting programmers in 2005–2007. As Graylin recounted later, "Hiring was and remains one of our most difficult issues." He discovered that only a minority of experienced technical people in China were attracted to small, unknown entities, and very few had entrepreneurial experience. In general, both seasoned and newly minted engineers and programmers preferred employment at large, stable, "brand name" firms. Many experienced people were working for state-owned companies; Graylin found most of these skilled workers unsuited by temperament and work ethic to the requirements of a startup entrepreneurial firm.

In the end, the two entrepreneurs found that the most productive approach to their human talent needs was to recruit directly from the best technical universities. New people were brought on as interns, giving the company an opportunity to assess their abilities and work ethics as a prelude for formal employment. Graylin explained his HR strategy further: "We provided a combination of industry average cash compensation, stocks and generous social/welfare benefits. Our cash comp wasn't the best, be we were generous with stock and had many fun activities for the team. Even still, finding and keeping staff was not easy. And most people didn't know the value or potential value of Stock Options.

Graylin continued: "In terms of salary, the cost of low-level employees is very inexpensive. The salaries of mid- and upper-level people are lower than their counterparts in the States, but not dramatically lower."

The mobility of technical workers was a large concern for Graylin and Huang because it jeopardized mInfo's emerging intellectual property. This was in a computing culture where, at the time, the majority of software used on desktops was unlicensed or pirated. mInfo decided to take specific steps to assure that no individual employee had access to the entire code base. Huang designed and controlled the architecture and then assigned specific teams to program certain pieces. Only a small and highly trusted team under Huang's direct supervision assembled these components for the final build and test.

---

[5] The Economist Intelligence Unit/Mercer HR Consulting, 2009.

Government Bureaucracy

Regulators presented another hurdle for the founders. mInfo needed a special telecommunications operations license. To obtain that license, Graylin had to have a specified level of capital in the bank. And as a company with foreign backers, mInfo needed a three-tier structure: it had to be under the umbrella of a foreign holding company; it had to register as a wholly-owned foreign entity; and it had to give evidence that it had contractual relationships with local Chinese partners. The company's US legal counsel handled these details, setting up the holding company in the Cayman Islands at a cost of roughly $50,000. The lawyers deferred payment of that bill until such time as the company had completed its first financing round.

To meet the capital requirements of the law, Graylin and Huang borrowed the requisite amount of money and put it in their company bank account.

Adherence to regulatory requirements was the easy part. Getting approvals from an inscrutable bureaucracy was another matter. In contrast to the US, where licenses and other approvals can often be obtained in straightforward ways, often online, Chinese regulators must be appealed to with personal visits and, in many cases, gifts.

As a westerner, Graylin found these requirements both frustrating and time consuming. "Sometimes an official would make us wait four hours or more for a five-minute meeting. In other cases, scheduled meetings would be canceled at the last minute for no apparent reason. They'd say, 'Sorry. Reschedule next month.'" Many officials did not return phone calls. Patience and persistence were the entrepreneur's only recourse in dealing with this system.

He also discovered the importance of gifts. Gift giving is part of Chinese culture and extends into the world of government. The tradition is to bring a gift when visiting an official. "And during holiday periods, the expectation is that gifts will be more valuable—for example, you might bring a $700 smart phone as a gift." Graylin also noted that officials where much more open to visits during holiday periods, when the expectation of a fine gift was highest.

Contracts

In the West, any contract that does not violate the law or public policy is enforceable in court. In China, contracts are less than "iron clad."

mInfo successfully negotiated contracts with several mobile telecom providers and advertisers—and it depended on those contracts for its success. In several cases, however, and mid-way through the life of their contracts, customers would ask to renegotiate contract terms. "They'd figure," says Graylin, "'Well, those guys [at mInfo] are making lots of money. Let's cut them back.'" mInfo had very little power to oppose these requests from valued customers. In the end, mutual self-interest, and not the language of contracts, ruled.

Interpersonal Protocols

Graylin also discovered the importance of properly matching hierarchical "levels" when conducting business with customers, suppliers, and regulators. In contrast to the informal and egalitarian culture of the US, Chinese culture expected that CEOs meet with CEOs, that mInfo sales representatives meet with mid-level customer officials, and so forth. Mismatching levels during sales calls and negotiations were deemed breaches of protocol.

RELATIONSHIPS COME FIRST

It's often said that "relationships" are an essential part of business life in China—and in Asia in general. Research by Edward Hall and Mildred Hall[6] has identified "low- and high-context" cultures. In the former (e.g., northern European countries and North American), business people like to get right to the point with little ceremony and a minimum of perfunctory small talk. In contrast, business in high-context cultures (which include Korea, Japan, China, and Arab countries) is preceded by more extensive formalities and relationship building. For example, a prospective Asian customer will ask to know about the visitor's company and about the visitor's personal background. A luncheon or dinner may be a necessary prelude to any substantive discussions. According to Hall, these preliminaries may take substantial time, but time is less important to people in high-context cultures. For low-context Westerns, who are eager to get down to business, the value of these formalities and relationship-building activities are not always appreciated.

[6] Edward T. Hall, *Silent Language* (Garden City, NY: Doubleday, 1959) and Edward T. Hall and Mildred R. Hall, *Hidden Differences: Doing Business with the Japanese* (Garden City, NY: Doubleday, 1987).

Discussion Questions _____

1. Alvin Wang Graylin is a highly skilled and energetic businessperson, with experience in many parts of the world. Why do you think he was so attracted to China?

2. Put yourself in Graylin's shoes as he began his venture in Shanghai. As you organize and develop your business, what would you describe as "different" from the US or other non-Chinese environment? What would be the same?

3. If you found an irresistible hi-tech venture prospect in China tomorrow, what preparations would you make for handling that country's unique labor market and its business and regulatory cultures?

4. What are the lessons learned by this entrepreneur operating in a foreign country?

BioBlood

M&A in the Biotech World

Marc H. Meyer[1], John H. Friar, Steven R. Kursh and Dennis Shaughnessy
Northeastern University, USA

Introduction

William O'Brien, Alewife Sciences' Vice President of Business Development, hung up the phone and took a deep breath. He had just been told by Dr. Jonathon Masters, founder and president of BioBlood, that the meeting with shareholders was not going well. In fact, Dr. Masters was about ready to throw in the towel. Before doing that, he wanted to know if William had any flexibility in his offer to acquire the company.

O'Brien's offer was based on his valuation of the company. Although O'Brien was aware that different valuation methodologies could be used he believed, based on his experience, that the best approach was the traditional discounted cash flow model. The DCF approach enabled him to consider the company's operating profit and the capital required to grow if Alewife Sciences decided to do the acquisition. For his own part, Dr. Masters wanted to get out from under his investors. Like many small businesses, Dr. Masters had taken startup capital from private investors who were not professional investors and expected Google-type returns from all of their high-tech investments. Now, these very investors were rejecting O'Brien's offer. Dr. Masters needed something more to get them to say yes.

O'Brien, 46 years old, had worked in the investment arena for many years. After earning his law and MBA degrees, he worked with a prestigious law firm handling technology deals in the New England (U.S.) region. In 1988, he went to work for Alewife Sciences, a U.S. company. He became Vice President, Corporate Development in 1994 and was responsible for overseeing their business development initiatives on a worldwide basis. He had concluded a successful string of acquisitions. He enjoyed the excitement of making acquisitions. His approach to buying and managing businesses was to place an emphasis on cashflow, the "Warren Buffet" model as applied to the pharmaceutical industry, rather than other valuation methods that he believed were not appropriate given the uncertainties in the business, changing industry dynamics, and the type of companies that Alewife Sciences targeted, *i.e.* companies in need of cash, management, and infrastructure to scale to grow

---

[1] Please contact Marc Meyer, (mhm@neu.edu) for the teaching note for this case. Additionally, we have prepared an Excel spreadsheet to help students work the details of the financial analysis and company valuation. © 2008, Senate Hall Academic Publishing. All Rights Reserved

significant value. O'Brien's goal was to find small operating companies that not only had successful technologies, but also, had proved a business model, *e.g.* they had figured out how to make attractive levels of profit on sales. Further, O'Brien wanted to find companies for whom capital infusions, and Alewife's own distribution channel were the key to scaling up. This approach was in stark contrast to the approach used by many of O'Brien's peers in the biotech venture world who focused purely on the market potential of new technologies.

But now on this cold February day in 2005, O'Brien might have hit a dead end with BioBlood. All the potential for synergy, growth, and operating profit was there, but he had to get Masters to get his investor group to agree to a package.

Alewife Labs

Alewife Labs (Alewife) was founded fifty years ago by a young veterinary school graduate to breed laboratory animals used for pharmaceutical research. By 2005, it operated more than thirty production facilities, some of which were overseas. From these facilities, the company produced animals used in biomedical research, consumer product safety testing, and animal health care. Alewife also produced biological raw materials for human therapeutic applications.

The company's focus was to expand across the full value-chain of drug discovery services, helping pharmaceutical companies to develop and test new drugs at all stages of development. Traditionally, the company's "core" business was the production of genetically defined and specific pathogen free (or "clean") rats and mice for laboratory research. Alewife grew rapidly in the 1960s and 1970s. During the 1980s, the company diversified into new product lines in the biotechnology and biomedical fields, including production of monoclonal antibodies for therapeutic purposes, animal organs for human transplantation, and embryo cryopreservation for human and animal fertility applications. Despite this incremental broadening of the product portfolio, the company still derived more than 80 percent of its revenues from the sale of laboratory animals.

Alewife's core business had been declining in unit volumes in the range of 1–2 percent per year for the last several years. The industry had undertaken systematic efforts to reduce unnecessary or duplicative animal tests. Mergers in the pharmaceutical industry had consolidated R&D labs - meaning fewer customers - and there was increased pressure on pharmaceutical companies to keep prices under control. Because pharmaceutical companies were being pressured to limit their drug price increases, they, in turn, pressured suppliers such as Alewife to limit their own price increases.

Alewife had been a financial success throughout its fifty-year history. (Its recent financials are shown in Exhibit 1.) Alewife had consistently maintained operating margins at or near 18 percent and had grown in both sales and earnings on an historical average basis of 15 percent to 20 percent per year. It achieved price to earnings ratios ranging from a low of 20 to a high of 60 during the 1980s. During the 1990s, however, Alewife found it harder to achieve the 15 to 20 percent growth in earnings in the laboratory animal business and now was focused on diversification into new but closely related areas. Alewife wanted to acquire companies with outstanding technology to which they could add management expertise, money, marketing know-how and sales-force infrastructure. As important as anything, Alewife wanted to find companies that were twice as profitable on an operating basis as its own core business - with 36 percent operating margins as opposed to 18 percent. Operating margins in the range of 36 percent would, O'Brien knew, provide sufficient cushion against some of the risks associated with acquisitions and further increase Alewife's average operating margins.

The LAS Assay

One method William O'Brien used for seeking out potential acquisition targets was to look for technologies that could have an impact on the use of animal tests. One such technology was an *in vitro* technique known as the LAS assay, a specialized reagent used to test for the presence of certain diseases. The LAS (Limulus Amebocyte Lysate) assay had already been recognized by US regulatory authorities as a fully acceptable *in vitro* alternative to the use of a whole animal.

LAS was based on endotoxin. Endotoxin was a component of the cell wall of gram-negative bacteria.[2] It was found almost everywhere in nature, especially in water. Also known as a "pyrogen" for its fever producing effect, endotoxin was generally harmless to humans except when it entered the blood stream. At levels as small as a few hundred nanograms, endotoxins could cause fever, shock, hemorrhage, and ultimately death. For this reason, medicines, fluids, and medical equipment, which were used in intravenous therapy, needed to be free of endotoxin contamination.

The rabbit fever test, developed in the 1940s, was the standard test for endotoxins until the approval of the LAS test by the FDA in the 1980s. In the rabbit test, healthy rabbits were injected intravenously with a sample of drugs or with a wash from a medical device. Then the temperature of the rabbits was monitored for three hours. If a one-degree or greater rise in temperature was observed, the product was considered pyrogenic. As many as one million rabbit tests were performed annually prior to US regulatory acceptance of the LAS alternative.

In the 1960s, a university-based pathologist observed a large number of horseshoe crabs dying on a beach on the northeast coast of the US. He found that their blood was clotted and that they were infected by gram-negative bacteria. A hematologist colleague of the pathologist also studied the crabs' disease because it mimicked the course of human infection. The hematologist's research showed that the blood cells of the horseshoe crab were responsible for the clotting, and that endotoxin from the gram-negative bacteria was the cause. From these blood cells, the hematologist developed a test reagent and began research on testing for endotoxins in patients with serious infections. He named this reagent LAS.

As the merits of the LAS test were identified and expanded, the FDA and the pharmaceutical industry began to develop standards and regulations to allow widespread use. The drug companies began providing multi-million dollar orders to suppliers in the early 1980s. In December 1987, the FDA issued guidelines outlining the steps necessary to obtain approval for LAS use in lieu of the rabbit fever test for release testing of drugs and medical devices.[3]

---

[2] Gram-negative bacteria are those that do not retain crystal violet dye in the Gram staining protocol, which is a common diagnostic method in the life sciences. Gram-positive bacteria, on one hand, will retain the dark blue dye after an alcohol wash. In a Gram stain test, a counterstain is added after the crystal violet, coloring all Gram-negative bacteria a pinkish color. The test itself is useful in classifying two distinctly different types of bacteria based on structural differences in their cell walls. The reason why this classification is important is that many types of Gram-negative bacteria are pathogenic, causing disease, and endotoxins are one of the more common, and harmful, components of Gram-negative cell walls. Endotoxin triggers a response in the immune system which begins the inflammation in tissues and blood vessels.

[3] Under these federal guidelines, the FDA's Center for Biologics Evaluation and Review (CBER) must first test and release each lot of commercial LAS prior to sale by the original manufacturer.

The Market

William recognized the potential threat of the LAS assay, but he also wanted to investigate its potential opportunity. He found that the estimated market for the LAS reagent and related test materials to detect endotoxins was approximately $200 million in 2005 and was expected to double over the next five years.

The end-users of LAS tests were comprised principally of drug manufacturers, biotech companies and medical device manufacturers. In excess of 90 percent of all LAS applications were for "fever" or pyrogenecity testing of FDA-approved, injectable human drugs. The US market was estimated to comprise 60 percent of the total market for LAS products. The European and Japanese markets were estimated to be 40 percent of the total, with the highest rate of growth expected in the near-term in Western Europe. Emerging pharmaceutical research in regions such as India, China, and Russia were also expected to contribute to market growth for LAS in the years ahead. In fact, industry observers expected the LAS business to grow at 15 percent a year, the rate realized since the FDA approval of the LAS test in December 1987.

The industry was highly profitable, with the three leading LAS manufacturers maintaining estimated operating margins of approximately 30 percent. The market was sensitive to quality, service and price, in descending order of importance.

The biotech industry was expected to use more LAS testing, as nearly all-existing and anticipated biotech products were administered by injection. The veterinary LAS testing industry was also expected to experience substantial growth, as veterinary pharmaceutical companies increased their LAS testing activity in response to new regulations. In addition, regulatory changes impacting manufacturing process quality testing were expected to increase the level of raw materials testing. The opportunity in new markets and for new applications equaled or exceeded the current market for existing applications. When O'Brien looked at these numbers, he knew that LAS was an area in which participation by his own company should be seriously considered.

LAS Suppliers

William considered the market to be interesting and started to sort out which company might be the best acquisition target. There were four major companies in the LAS industry, one of which was BioBlood. The other three were:

- *MarineBio:* a privately held firm U.S. founded in 1977. This company was the historical market leader with 2005 sales estimated at $67 million. This represented a 45 percent share of the commercially-supplied market (*i.e.,* excluding in-house production by biotech and pharmaceutical companies). The company had lost market share to its competition in the last few years due to product quality problems and service deficiencies. It nevertheless continued to enjoy a high level of brand recognition throughout the world. The firm had not significantly increased the price of its products over the past five years in an attempt to avoid further market share deterioration.
- *Endotox:* a division of a publicly held company, also headquartered in the U.S. The company's LAS operation had grown rapidly in recent years, principally at the expense of MarineBio with LAS revenues standing at about $60 million in annual

sales, a 40 percent market share. The company had used extensive marketing and a large direct sales force to grow. Its products were known for good overall quality in the high-end segment and held a significant price premium.

- *BioDetect:* a privately held firm with less than $6 million in sales despite a long operating history, this U.S. company competed primarily on price and provided only limited technical service.

About twenty companies had tried to enter the LAS industry since 1980 without success. The technical "know-how", the specificity of customer needs, and the rigors of the FDA approval process had proven strong barriers to entry.

BioBlood

William O'Brien began scouting out MarineBio and BioDetect as potential acquisitions to enter the business. His standard practice was to find customers of his own company that were also using the products of a potential acquiree, and to find out the strengths and weakness of those products and the companies behind them from the eyes of the customer. As he was doing this for endotoxin testing products, several Alewife customers mentioned that there was this other player in the market, BioBlood, a small privately held company in the Southeastern U.S. that had great technology.

O'Brien's initial inquiries found that in contrast to the other three companies BioBlood was growing, had proprietary technology, and seemed to be generating operating profits even at its small size. He learned that Dr. Masters had worked with LAS reagents since 1974 as a university professor but did not start BioBlood until 1993. The innovation in LAS technology he had developed was a proprietary method of chemically formulating the gel clot reagent to a variety of sensitivities as determined by customers' specific requirements. This allowed the reagent to achieve compatibility across a broad range of tested products, along with a consistent and unequivocal low end point at all levels of sensitivity. Dr. Masters held several patents on his chemical formulation process. His approach minimized interference with test results from the product being tested. This resistance to interference was a key competitive advantage. The BioBlood reagent had also gained recognition for its performance in terms of reliability, ease of use, extended bench stability, clot firmness (leading to easier, more objective interpretation), and conformance to label claims for shelf life.

BioBlood's mission was to offer the most interference resistant, reliable, and stable pyrogen test for pharmaceutical LAS testing. The FDA first approved BioBlood's production facility and gel clot product at the beginning of the 1990s.

BioBlood had slowly increased its sales in the years following FDA approval. By the end of 2004, more than two-thirds of its existing business was the result of conversions of customers from one of the two market leaders, and sales had reached almost $3.6 million. BioBlood made its first profit in 2002. Dr. Masters had hired an operating manager into the company several years early, and with that hire, came greater financial discipline to build a profitable, albeit small business. (See Exhibit 2 for BioBlood's recent financial statements.) For O'Brien, the company warranted the next level of investigation.

Due Diligence

O'Brien phoned Dr. Masters in June 2004 and floated the idea of Alewife purchasing BioBlood. He told Dr. Masters that he had done some checking on the company and that he found that Dr. Masters had a very good reputation. He told Dr. Masters that he would like to get to know him and his team further by visiting the company. He also warned Masters that he intended to perform due diligence by visiting the company's competitors to validate BioBlood's proclaimed advantages, by having a technical expert assess the quality of BioBlood's technology, by speaking to BioBlood's customers in an extensive manner. Eventually, he would also have to examine BioBlood's financial statements.

Before starting these efforts, however, he wanted to find out whether Masters was willing to stay with the company if acquired and to work hard to make it grow as a business unit within Alewife. O'Brien explained the concept of an earn-out deal:

> We like senior management of newly acquired companies to have an incentive to really grow the top and bottom lines. We want them to be investing all of their time and energy into taking their company to the next level. We think they should be rewarded for a real breakthrough level of growth. For this reason, we can incorporate earn-outs in any deal.

Dr. Master's had never heard of an earn out before, so he asked O'Brien for an example. O'Brien responded:

> The structure of an earn out might be, for example, that we project forward for five years the sales based on your current annual sales growth rate. If the business achieves beyond those projections, say over the next five years, we will provide a percentage of the up-side directly to you as a bonus. In one of our acquired companies, the annual growth rate was 25 percent year by year, and we decided to give the founder 5 percent of sales above those projections as a bonus. He did very well. In fact, he had so many shareholders by the time he sold the business to us that he really didn't own that much stock. That earn out is where he is going to make most of his money. Plus, he is getting the satisfaction of watching his company become a world-class business.

Dr. Masters said he was interested and they arranged a visit by O'Brien in several weeks. What O'Brien found was that BioBlood was indeed a profitable company. It had both a working product and a viable business model. The company had net margins close to 37 percent on $3.6 million in sales, for a net profit before tax of $1.19 million dollars.

O'Brien also learned that Masters had made some classic mistakes in raising money, mistakes that would limit the growth of BioBlood. Simply put, Masters had lost control of the stock by giving it out too freely. Further, Masters might be generating over a million dollars of profit now, but he had lost use of half that cash because he had promised the investors to pay the half of operating profit back out to investors as either interest or dividends.

To start the company, Masters first used nearly all of his family's savings, $60,000. He later turned to neighbors and professional acquaintances for additional money. Masters raised another $500,000 by word of mouth in his hometown through a network of lawyers and bankers. Because LAS was regulated by the FDA as a "drug", BioBlood had required nearly three years of start-up time to acquire the necessary FDA licenses and permits. During this period, the company had no incoming cash and was unable to obtain a bank loan. There had been no interest on the part of the venture capital community, as the market opportunity then seemed rather limited. Besides, Masters had never run a business before, nor did he work with lawyers and accountants with experience and sophistication in venture investing.

Masters had been careful to keep his payroll and expenses as low as possible during the start-up phase. By the close of 2004, the company had only 15 full-time employees. He had periodically enlisted the help of consultants and other professionals to solve operational problems. Having no cash, he had offered them instead a "piece of the company". BioBlood's investor group eventually grew to sixteen. Combining the shares paid in lieu of cash and the investors' shares, Masters ended up owning only 28 percent of the stock and the other investors 72 percent.

Not only had Masters lost control of the company, he had also boxed himself in with cash payouts. The total amount of capital raised from the investors was $500,000 in loans and equity. The typical shareholder of BioBlood invested $50,000 in the company with 90 percent of that amount structured as a loan with a higher than bank interest rate. The remaining 10 percent was structured as equity, at a low startup valuation level. Masters' deal with the investors was that once profits were achieved and retained earnings were positive, he would provide half of after-tax earnings to them and keep half of the earnings to reinvest in the business. He also had to pay back interest on the loan amounts to investors. All told, these consumed more than half of his operating profit in 2004. He had paid $670,000 to investors that year! He desperately needed that money to grow the business, but the investors were not willing to change the deal. More than several were lawyers and threatened legal action if Masters changed the deal.

BioBlood might continue to grow without raising outside money, but it would at a much slower rate than would be possible with a million-plus dollars invested every year into sales, manufacturing, and service.

O'Brien's overtures seemed a way out of this dilemma. While Masters was BioBlood's largest shareholder, he had no effective control. His hands would be forever tied. Plus, it was clear that Alewife called on many of the same customers that BioBlood wanted to reach. A deal with Alewife would clearly accelerate his own sales efforts.

Valuing the Company

O'Brien began to work on a valuation for BioBlood so that he could put together an offer. He understood that the three primary methods for valuing closely-held companies were the market approach, the income approach (DCF), and the asset approach. He quickly reviewed some notes that he had regarding these approaches (Exhibit 5).

Most of O'Brien's peers used the market approach or the asset approach, valuation methods based on some combination of multiples of sales and multiples of earnings, and benchmarked these against comparable acquisitions in recent months. O'Brien knew that the market approach using multiples on sales and earnings was a simpler and more common valuation technique. Small technology firms in life sciences (defined by analysts as having sales under $50 million, 15 percent sales growth, and at least 10 percent operating margins) were being acquired for 7 to 10 times trailing EBITDA (earnings before income taxes, depreciation, and amortization). This would put BioBlood's valuation at about $13.5 million. Other companies were being acquired on the basis of a multiple of sales, about 4-times sales. For BioBlood, this would yield a $14 million price. Alewife also had internal "comps" as benchmarks. The year before it had completed two acquisitions of privately held companies, one at 6.5 times EBITDA (a vaccine materials company) and the second at 7 times EBITDA (a medical instruments company).

O'Brien, however, preferred to use the income approach, *i.e.* to calculate the net present value of discounted cash flows because he wanted to see the cash generated by sales growth as well as factor in the capital investments needed to expand the business. This also meant that he had to determine the terminal value of the business - the value of the cash-flow generated by the business in perpetuity.

O'Brien created a discounted cash flow (DCF) model as a baseline to run scenarios. He developed a DCF computer spreadsheet model using BioBlood's historical unaudited financial statements. (Exhibit 3 shows a back of the envelop template that O'Brien used. That exhibit also provides a step-by-step process for working through the template.)

BioBlood had sales of $3.6 million in 2004 and operating margins of about 37 percent. He agreed with Masters that BioBlood could grow to $10-15 million a year over the next 4-5 years, or at about an annual rate of about 30 percent. He felt that its profitability should continue in the 37 percent pre-tax net income range. Now that the company had turned profitable, however, it would need to begin paying taxes. O'Brien assumed a 40 percent tax rate for BioBlood - the same rate that Alewife had been paying. He also felt that BioBlood would need a substantial infusion of cash, $250,000 a year over the next five years for new plant and equipment.

In addition to operating income derived from the future growth of the business, O'Brien also wanted to factor in changes to cash position based on increases in three specific items: accounts receivable, accounts payable, and inventory. (Exhibit 4 lists O'Brien's assumptions in these areas.)

To compute net present value, O'Brien decided to use Alewife's own weighted average cost of capital, which at that time was running at 10.9 percent.

It was important to O'Brien to keep the projections of revenue conservative for several reasons. First, he did want to overpay for BioBlood. Second, and equally important, was that those same spreadsheet projections used for valuation would serve as the going forward business plan for the new division. Further, if Alewife included an earn out, Masters' bonuses would be based on the projected numbers. Too high, and Masters might not receive any bonus. In fact, part of O'Brien's own compensation package was based not only on buying companies, but on their trailing financial performance for three years. His own management thought that this approach would ensure that O'Brien created realistic growth plans for acquired companies. As he said to Masters:

> We need to be careful here, since our valuation in the acquisition will surely end up as our business plan for the following year once we run the business. That's the Board's way of ensuring that we believe in the valuation, tying our bonuses to achieving the assumptions in the valuation.

O'Brien also visited some of BioBlood's lead investors. He felt that they had to know that Masters was himself frustrated and that Masters' energy and enthusiasm for the business was bound to decline over time. Yet, they seemed content to milk the profits from the business and didn't really understand that this was limiting the company's growth. O'Brien sensed that Masters would have to play hardball with his own investors. He had to tell them if they didn't take a reasonable deal he would leave the business and let them figure out what to do with it. Getting the kind and earnest Dr. Masters to do this would be no easy matter.

The Decision

O'Brien had decided to offer a total package of $7.5 million for BioBlood. The package consisted of a $500,000 in cash and $7,000,000 worth of Alewife stock. Alewife would also pay off some $200,000 of BioBlood's debt. This would remove a lien on Masters' house that he had taken to obtain working capital from a bank a few years earlier.

O'Brien thought that the $7,500,000 represented a handsome return for the early investors. Already, 2005 was looking to be a tough year for small biotech firms that had taken venture capital and had trouble getting more.

Masters' phone call indicated the opposite. Some of his shareholders held the fantasy of the next Google. Those that were more realistic were still looking at a multiple of sales and wanted a valuation twice the size of the Alewife offer.

O'Brien had also structured the deal to be the cash and stock for the assets of BioBlood, as opposed to a merger of the companies. This meant that the shareholders would still be held liable for lawsuits from prior business operations. Since some of BioBlood's shareholders were lawyers, this was proving to be a heated point of contention, even though the firm had never been sued.

What should O'Brien do? Should he increase the valuation of BioBlood? Large pharmaceutical companies were beginning to suffer from blockbuster drugs coming off patent, shedding their own research staffs, and turning to small biotech firms to rebuild the pipeline of new drug applications.

Should O'Brien change the stock for assets nature of the deal? Should he try an earn out for Masters? If he did, did he have to tell the other shareholders about the earn out? And perhaps most important, should he set a date for the investors to either fish or cut bait? O'Brien himself had other fish to fry -he was looking at about a half dozen other companies in other categories equally important to Alewife Sciences.

Income Statements (in thousands)

	2003	2004
Revenue	$ 99,300,000	$ 102,800,000
Cost of Sales	69,300,000	72,000,000
Gross Margin	**$ 30,000,000**	**$ 30,800,000**
SG&A	$ 12,400,000	$ 12,700,000
Operating (Loss)/Income	$ 17,600,000	$ 18,100,000

Exhibit 1 Alewife's Income Statement 2003, 2004

Income Statement

	2003	2004
Revenue	$ 1,710,88	$ 3,598,516
Cost of Sales	4, 671,108	1,470,990
Gross Margin	$ 1,039,776	$ 2,127,526
SG&A	$ 345,092	$ 780,000
Operating (Loss)/Income	$ 694,684	$ 1,347,526
Interest Expense	113,446	105,450
Depreciation Expense	50,000	55,000
(Loss)/Earnings Before Income Taxes		
Income Taxes ($0 due to tax loss carried forward)	$ 531,238	$ 1,187,076
Net (Loss)/Earnings	**$ 531,238**	**$ 1,187,076**

Exhibit 2 (Continued)

Assets	2004
Current Assets	
Cash	$ 66,352
Accounts Receivables	591,537
Inventory	735,495
Total Current Assets	$ 1,393,383
Fixed Assets	
Plant and Equipment	$ 2,500,000
Depreciation	(570,000)
Net Fixed Assets	$ 1,930,000
Total Assets	**$ 3,323,383**

Liabilities and Stockholders Equity	2004
Current Liabilities	
Accounts Payable	$ 362,710
Income Taxes Payable	-
Total Current Liabilities	$ 362,710
Notes Payable	703,000
Total Liabilities	**$ 1,065,710**
Common Stock ($1 par value) Masters	$ 280,000
Common Stock ($1 par value) Investors	720,000
Additional Paid in Capital	-
Retained Earnings	1,257,674
Total Equity	**$ 2,257,674**
Total Liabilities and Stockholders Equity	**$ 3,323,383**

Exhibit 2 BioBlood's Unaudited Financial Statements, 2003 and 2004

Notes: No taxes were paid in either year due to tax loss carry forwards.

10 Simple Steps

1. Establish Base Point (from current P&L) for Sales, Gross Margins, Net Margins—so as to get Operating Income and Net Income before tax.

2. Determine market growth rate; establish projections for 5 years on Sales.

3. Project operating income on reasonable margins and net income.

4. Look at both Receivables and Materials/Payables to see if cash is being consumed to the extent that net income needs to be adjusted. (Once you buy the business, you can generate more cash by improving the collection of receivables or the reduction of inventories.) The balance sheet might also have to be cleaned up in terms of retiring undesirable debt.

5. Look to Business Plan and determine reasonable capital investments into the business for plant and equipment, and other types of expansion.

Exhibit 3 (Continued)

6. Determine tax rate.

7. Determine Discount Rate—The companies estimated weighted cost of capital, adjusted for extraordinary risk on particular deals, is a commonly used discount rate.

8. Layout Cashflow over five years, then discount back into today's dollars.

9. Establish terminal value. There are many different methods for doing this. A simple, useful way is to take net income for year five, and divide it by your discount rate, adjusted for the terminal growth rate. Then, discount that back to today's dollars.

10. Add 8 and 9 to get your valuation.

Details of Steps

The first step is to build a summary five year projected P&L for the target business. Start by analyzing the historic financial trends in the business, and then project out into the future. The key assumptions are sales growth rate, gross and then operating margin, and net operating assets. Growth in sales and operating profit is obviously a source of cash. Changes in net operating assets, such as investment in manufacturing capacity, are either a source or use of cash. Assumptions about these primary sources and uses of cash can only be developed by thoroughly analyzing the existing dynamics of the business and the future opportunities that can be exploited according to a plan for growth.

- sales growth,
- profitability,
- capital requirements, for things such as manufacturing capacity,
- the discount rate for the cost of capital
- and terminal growth rate, which is the growth rate applied to sales after the initial five year valuation period for asset valuation

Once profits derived from operations are calculated, one must consider other elements affecting cash flow:

- **Cash tied up in Accounts Receivables:** An average accounts receivables collection period of 60 days is typical in the pharmaceutical supply industry. Therefore, 60 days sales outstanding (DSO) is useful for the calculation (divide the projected yearly sales by 365 and multiply that by 60. Do this year for year, and look at the difference for an increase or decrease in A/R as a use of cash).
- **Cash tied up in Inventory (materials used in production):** It is not atypical to find that about half of the Cost of Goods Sold (COGS) is comprised of materials. Accordingly, students can apply the gross margin (to sales) to determine the cost of goods sold, divide that by half, and compare to find increases in materials inventory as the business is projected to grow. Such increases are also a use of cash.
- **Cash used for new plant and equipment:** As for net operating assets, Masters considered how best to grow the business in terms of adding new plant and equipment. He believed that an investment of about $1 million in additional manufacturing capacity (to make Endolab's MLA gel clot reagent) would be needed over the course of five years.

With five years of cash flow, we need to start the processes of determining a terminal value. With the discount rate in hand, the terminal value is generated for the deal by simply dividing the net income after tax of the fifth year by the discount rate. This provides a simple but precise short-cut to the nominal, or undiscounted, terminal value of the business. Terminal value represents the value of the continuing cash flow, in perpetuity. If only the discount rate is used as the denominator, the assumption is that growth in cash flow will be equal to the assumed rate of inflation. If one believes that the business will continue to grow at a rate greater than inflation, then a terminal growth rate needs to be added to the cash flows. This is done by simply subtracting the terminal growth rate (let's say 2 percent) from the discount rate (10.9 percent

Exhibit 3 (Continued)

minus 2 percent, resulting in 8.9 percent). The fifth year net income after taxes is divided by that number (8.9 percent) to produce the nominal value of future cash flows. A significant terminal value growth rate (say 5 percent) will obviously have a major impact on the terminal value, and thus, on the valuation itself.

Terminal Value = (Year 5 Net Income) / (Project Discount Rate – Terminal Growth Rate)

Now that you have a nominal terminal value, it too needs to be discounted back to present value dollars using the discount rate. The same discount rate should also be used to obtain the present value of cash flows from Years 1 through 5. The result is the total operating value of the business, expressed in current dollars and reflecting the buyer's investment cost.

| Exhibit 3 | A Valuation Template Based on Net Present Value of Projected Cashflow |

Once profits derived from operations are calculated, he considered other elements affecting cash flow:

- **Cash tied up in Accounts Receivables:** An average accounts receivables collection period of 60 days is typical in the pharmaceutical supply industry. Therefore, 60 days sales outstanding (DSO) is useful for the calculation (divide the projected yearly sales by 365 and multiply that by 60. Do this year for year, and look at the difference for an increase or decrease in A/R as a use of cash).
- **Cash tied up in Inventory (materials used in production):** It is not atypical to find that about half of the Cost of Goods Sold (COGS) is comprised of materials. Accordingly, apply the gross margin (to sales) to determine the cost of goods sold, divide that by half, and compare to find increases in materials inventory as the business is projected to grow. Such increases are also a use of cash.
- **Cash used for new plant and equipment:** As for net operating assets, Masters considered how best to grow the business in terms of adding new plant and equipment. He told O'Brien that an investment of about $250,000 a year into plant and equipment (to make BioBlood's LAS gel clot reagent) would be needed over the course of five years.

| Exhibit 4 | O'Brien's Assumptions |

Unfortunately, there is no one single method for valuing high technology companies. Instead, we need to use a combination of approaches and methods. These approaches and methods enable us to establish a range of value for what we call the subject company. The three most prevalent approaches are the market approach, the income approach, and the asset approach.[4]

The Market Approach

The market approach is based on the assumption that the best way to determine the value of a subject company is to study closely the values of other companies that have been involved in transactions that provide an indication of value. These transactions normally involve sales

---

[4] Our discussion assumes that we are valuing the subject company for the purpose of a sale, but, as noted above, the processes that an analyst would follow are essentially the same with the other valuation purposes. Note, however, that the analyst would need to account for additional factors such as a minority discount or a controlling interest when doing valuations for some of these other purposes.

| Exhibit 5 | (Continued) |

of an equity interest in the public markets (i.e. an IPO) or to another company. Other types of transactions may also be useful; for example, the sale of a division or a product line may provide useful data.

The key concern with the market approach is that the comparison companies should be as similar as possible with the subject company. Obviously, it is impossible to have identical companies or exact historic transactions. The analyst, thus, needs to proceed through an iterative process of developing and applying common metrics and then adjusting the results to reflect differences between the comparison transactions and the subject company.

One of the primary challenges facing the analyst who uses the market approach is finding suitable comparable transactions and related data. Some sources to consider are general business publications including *The Wall Street Journal, The New York Times, Fortune, Forbes,* and *Business Week.* The technology industry also has several publications; investment bankers and industry trade associations are also good sources.[5] Finally, documents filed with the SEC and other federal agencies provide a wealth of useful data.

The analyst also needs to consider the "currency" used in the comparable transactions. There is obviously a difference between a transaction where the buyer pays cash versus stock that has significantly appreciated over the past few months in combination with a requirement that the seller hold the stock for a period of time. As compared with cash that the seller can use immediately, the stock is subject to market fluctuations. Similarly, transactions prior to 2001 that involved a pooling of interests often provided significant tax advantages that could have impacted the sales price.[6]

The Market Approach

Several metrics may be used when applying the market approach with technology companies. Three of the most common are:

Earnings Multiples—As with publicly-traded companies, one method of valuing companies is to apply a multiple to either present earnings or projected earnings, what is commonly known as the P/E ratio. This metric is generally more applicable for companies that have already established a market position and are profitable. Newer companies cannot typically be valued using this metric since management is more likely focused on growing revenue than in showing profits.

The analyst needs to be careful not to apply indiscriminately earnings multiples from publicly-traded companies when valuing most technology companies. The publicly-traded companies are usually larger, better capitalized, and have proven business models and, accordingly, better growth prospects. As an alternative in selected situations, the P/E ratios of publicly-traded companies may be possibly be used if adjusted by at least a factor of between 25 percent to as high as 75 percent depending on the similarities between the comparison companies and the subject company.

Normalization of the Income Statement

Typically, use of the earnings multiple metric with closely-held technology companies requires normalization of the income statement. Normalization refers to reviewing the income statements and tax returns and adjusting for discretionary spending and other factors that effectively reduce net operating income.[7] It is particularly important that the metrics used are

---

[5] Several state and regional technology associations work with local accounting firms and consulting firms to gather and summarize financial data from their members.

[6] The FASB eliminated the "pooling" method of acquisition accounting as of June 30, 2001. The changes and new purchase accounting requirements are codified in Statement No. 141, Business Combinations, which replaced APB No. 16.

[7] Recognizing that accounting income and taxable income are different, whenever possible the analyst should review both the financial statements and tax returns.

Exhibit 5 (Continued)

consistent. For example, as discussed below, one metric often used is the ratio of sales price to earnings. While seemingly a simple ratio, in fact, the analyst needs to make sure that "earnings" are defined the same among the set of companies. Is it earnings from operations? Was/were there one-time events, even in normal operations, that impacted earnings? Or, is it earnings after-tax? The ratio could also be based on earnings before-tax.

Revenue Multiples—One of the more popular metrics used to value technology companies is multiples of revenue. Typically, this metric is useful when the subject company is experiencing rapid growth and has the strong likelihood of continuing to grow at or near the same rate in the intermediate future. It is also among the most easiest to apply to comparison transactions involving closely-held companies, since revenue is shown on income statements in a more consistent manner than earnings.[8]

Another advantage of revenue multiples is that analysts can make general assumptions about total market size and market share for the subject company and then apply a revenue multiple to obtain one data point for the valuation.

One factor to keep in mind when doing a valuation of a closely-held technology company based on forecasts is that the prospective buyer and the seller are likely to disagree on what numbers to use in the forecast. The buyer will want forecasted numbers based on the past, while the seller will obviously prefer to use numbers in the forecast that reflect future opportunities. Indeed, one of the statements one often hears in negotiations is that the buyer wants to pay based on last year's numbers and the seller wants to be paid based on next year's numbers!

Cash Flow Multiples—The traditional metric used to value most closely-held companies is cash flow, or, more specifically, free cash flow that the purchaser can use to finance debt or draw from the subject company. Since this metric is typically determined in the context of the amount of debt that can be supported, the analyst should be aware of interest rates at the time of the transactions used to develop the multiple. A company generally should have a higher value under this metric when interest rates are trending down, since the cash flow will be able to support more debt financing.

Adjustments

Unfortunately, applying any valuation tool using a multiple or some variation requires the development and "cleaning" of information about the "comparables". Each transaction is, by definition, unique, and the analyst needs to make adjustments in order to use the data to develop and apply one or more of the multiples. Obviously, the factors to consider when making adjustments to the data will vary with each subject company, but some of the most important to consider are:

1. Company size—Does the transaction involve companies of similar size and scope? Obviously, a transaction involving a company with $200 million in revenues is not likely to be a good comparable with a subject company that has revenues of less than ten million.

On a related note, using data from companies that have gone public as comparables with companies that are closely-held and much smaller is often not effective; companies that have gone public, with the exception of the dot-com boom, have proven business models, management, and scalability as compared with closely-held firms.

2. The other company in the transaction (*i.e.* typically the buyer)—How does the other party in the transaction compare with the list of prospective buyers of the subject property or one specific purchaser? A purchase by a company that has historically paid for acquisitions with stock and often has paid a premium based on the market

---

[8] This does not, however, eliminate the need to confirm the reality of the revenue numbers.

Exhibit 5 (Continued)

potential of the company being acquired is clearly different than a purchase by a company that is buying for more traditional, finance-based reasons. This different in approaches is defined by some observers as "strategic" or "investment" versus "financial-proven" purchases.

3. Market potential—What is the market size for the subject company's products and services as compared with those in the comparison group?

Products and services focused on a specific vertical market are likely to have less potential market size than those focused on the general public or companies. (Again, one of the reasons why using data from companies that have going public is often not a good idea.) Market potential is, however, an important factor when the acquiring company can easily assimilate the assets of the business being bought and scale the new business quickly.

4. Company business model—A major consideration when reviewing transactions is to assess the business models of the other companies. Even if the comparison companies are in the same markets, their business models may be quite different.

5. Company market position—What is the market position (pricing, reputation, etc.) between the comparison companies and the subject company? As with the business model, the analyst needs to make adjustments if the subject company is competing on a different basis than those used in comparison group.

6. Company tangible assets—Although often not a significant factor, the analyst may need to account for tangible assets when making comparisons with the subject company. Some of the comparable transactions may have included, for example, prime real estate, research facilities, or distribution facilities. An analyst needs to recognize that other tangibles, including cash, inventory, and accounts receivable are often not part of asset acquisition transactions, a primary form of purchases of smaller technology companies. Instead, purchasers seek to acquire technology and other intellectual property, *i.e.* copyrights, patents, and trade secrets, and often permit the sellers to keep the cash and working capital assets.

7. Company intangible assets—Obviously one of the most important considerations when making comparisons is the intangible assets. Indeed, the very basis of most transactions involving technology companies is intellectual property.

8. Company management—Often one of the major differences between companies is the quality and reputation of management. Did the comparison company transactions involve on-going management contracts? Or, was the transaction based solely on the company's tangible and intangible assets? How does this compare with the subject company transaction?

9. Financial structure—All comparisons need to be adjusted for the respective company financial structures and tax factors. For example, the analyst needs to determine if the price included assumption of debt or hybrid securities. One particularly difficult aspect of the financial structure is payments made for non-compete agreements with the selling company's key personnel. These agreements are rarely publicly disclosed. Also, the type of transaction. As noted above, a transaction a purchase with cash often needs to be valued differently than one involving stock, since the seller may be subject to holding periods with the stock and the tax treatment may be different depending on how the transaction is structured.

The analyst also needs to consider other factors that had a material impact on the price. Some examples of these material factors are litigation risks, *(i.e.* was the company acquired in litigation or under the threat of litigation of a material magnitude), accounting policies, and foreign business implications.

Exhibit 5 (Continued)

Income Approach

The income approach is essentially the development and application of a discounted cash flow analysis for the subject company. The key tasks for the analyst are to develop projections of revenue, develop a discount rate, and use the discount rate with the revenue projections to estimate the value of the subject company.

Developing the revenue projections requires more than simply taking the prior period numbers and applying an estimated growth rate. Specifically, the analyst needs to confirm that the subject company's business model is sufficiently scalable for the projected growth. Will, for example, new capital investments in fixed assets be necessary as the company grows? Each item on the income statement and balance sheet needs to be examined thoroughly, as well as staffing levels, market size/share, and distribution channels. Fundamentally, the projections need to be defensible with industry data and trends. As with the market approach, the income statement should be normalized to remove discretionary spending that reflects management's desire to reduce tax liabilities or is specific to the existing management team and not needed going forward. For example, the owners of a technology company may choose to have extraordinarily high spending for office space and first-class travel for senior management; these expenses would be minimized by new owners and professional managers.

Recognizing the volatility of the technology industry, it is usually best to limit the projections to no more than five years. Even going beyond two years for many technology companies may be difficult. Similarly, if a terminal value is used to account for a perpetual stream of cash flows, the analyst typically should be conservative. Indeed, recognizing the inherent risks and volatility of the technology industry, the analyst needs to confirm that the future terminal value does not account for a major portion of the estimated value of the subject company.

It is also important to limit the impact of assumptions pertaining to growth and market share when doing the projections. These assumptions are obviously important in estimating the potential of a company, but not in developing a valuation based on existing information and data.

Estimating the Cost of Capital

Obviously, a key factor in estimating value using the income approach is the discount rate. This rate represents the subject company's cost of capital, but estimating the cost of capital, particularly when risk factors are considered, is a difficult task. Unlike with publicly traded companies, the cost of equity capital cannot be easily estimated, and, accordingly, the use of the traditional financial tools of weighted average cost of capital (WACC) and the capital asset pricing model (CAPM) to estimate the cost of capital is almost impossible without making several assumptions that essentially define the outcome.

One of the most popular ways to estimate the discount rate is to use what business appraisers call the "build-up method". The build-up method is relatively simple to apply. First, the analyst establishes the risk-free rate of return at the time of the valuation. Typically, the rate on 20-year or 10-year Treasury bills is used as for the risk-free rate of return.

The next step in using the build-up method is to add factors or "risk premiums" for company size, loss of key personnel, liquidity, industry, business, and other company-specific risks. Here it is important not to "pile on" with every possible risk factor and, instead, to focus on which risk factors are most important. For example, the size risk premium usually encompasses other risk factors like liquidity. Another advantage of the size risk premium is that the analyst can draw from several published studies that estimate the relationship between size effect and equity returns. While these studies focus on publicly-traded companies, they are very helpful in establishing the magnitude of the size effect on equity returns and the costs of capital for technology companies.

The risk premiums used in the discount rate should also reflect a company's business model and earnings streams. Companies with recurring revenue streams supported by executed contracts from customers are clearly less risky than companies with earnings streams based

Exhibit 5 (Continued)

on transaction revenue. Put slightly differently, companies with customers and prospects with inelastic demand are likely to have a much smaller business risk premium and, in fact, perhaps, even a *positive* risk premium (i.e. the discount rate should be lowered), as compared with companies with customers and prospects with elastic demand.

There is some difference of opinion among some analysts as to how best account for the risk in the subject company's income returns. The traditional approach, as discussed above with the build-up method is to increase the discount rate, thus, reducing the net present value of the future cash flows. More recently, some analysts have suggested that the risk should remain in the cash flows with the discount rate representing solely the effective cost of capital for the subject company. Under this approach, the analyst uses several different cash flows with the same set of discount rates for the projections.[9]

The analyst should also be aware that the costs of capital will usually significantly vary between the subject company and the prospective buyer, particularly if the buyer is a publicly-traded company. More specifically, publicly-traded companies typically have a much lower cost of capital than closely-held companies, and using the buyer's lower cost of capital rate may have a dramatic impact on the valuation of the subject company.

Asset Approach

The asset approach is based on the assumption that the subject company has tangible or intangible assets that have value to the purchaser. In effect, the purchaser is valuing the subject company from the perspective of a "make versus buy" decision for the subject company's technology, client base, technical staff, or some other assets.

The analyst can often apply the asset approach using methods similar to the market approach. For example, the value of a technology company may be based on a dollar figure multiplied by the number of users (or customers). Other possible metrics for technology companies include multiples based on one or more intangibles including, for example, the number and quality of distributors, the quality and number of technical staff, and the size and quality of prospects in the subject company's product pipeline, patents, copyrights, trade secrets, and even name or market reputation.

Analysts need to be particularly careful when applying an asset approach (as well as indirectly the other approaches) to valuing specific technology programs and intellectual property, including copyrights, trade secrets, and patents, that enable technology functionality. More specifically, some analysts may mistakenly equate functionality related to intellectual property with the investment and process of creating the respective technology programs when doing comparisons.

Finally, although not a frequent situation, the analyst may find that a particular company or technology product has a greater value in liquidation than as a going concern. This typically occurs when a company is not growing or even experiencing declining revenue and has tangible and intangible assets that may be of greater value to other companies. Similarly, there may be transactions, particularly acquisitions, where the buying company effectively liquidates the selling company in all but name. The liquidation might include, for example, stopping research and development investments on products licensed by the selling company, eliminating support for the products licensed by the selling company after a specific period of time, and using the intellectual property of the selling company in products and business practices.

---

[9] For a discussion of this alternative approach see, Dixit, Avinash, K., and Robert S. Pindyck, *Investment Under Uncertainty.* (Princeton, N.J.: Princeton University Press, 1994) and Luenberger, David, G., *Investment Science.* (New York: Oxford University Press, 1998).

Exhibit 5 Valuation Approaches and Methods

Index

About the Authors

Marc H. Meyer is the Robert J. Shillman Professor of Entrepreneurship at Northeastern University as well as a Matthews Distinguished University Professor. Northeastern is ranked as the No. 1 Cooperative Education academic institution in the United States, where student work experience is closely integrated with academic programs. Dr. Meyer is the founder of Northeastern's Entrepreneurship and Innovation Group in the College of Business Administration, where he has helped numerous students and alumni start their own companies. He is also Director of the High Tech MBA, a program focused on innovation within established corporations. In addition, Dr. Meyer currently leads Northeastern's executive education programs in innovation and corporate venturing, including IBM's program for designing and selling Smarter Planet solutions. The focus of all this work is innovation, entrepreneurship, and enterprise growth.

In research, Dr. Meyer is an internationally recognized scholar in the field of innovation. *The Power of Product Platforms* (written with Alvin P. Lehnerd, The Free Press, NY, 1997) continues to be a leading work in the management of architecture for products, systems, and services. *The Fast Path to Corporate Growth: Leveraging Knowledge and Technologies to New Market Applications* (Oxford University Press, NY, 2007) provides methods to link innovation with enterprise growth, the focus of Dr. Meyer's work throughout the industry over the past several decades. He is the recipient of the Maurice Holland Award from the Industrial Research Institute for this work.

In this new book, *Entrepreneurship: An Innovator's Guide to Startups and Corporate Ventures,* Dr. Meyer returns to his roots as a technology entrepreneur. He has been part of the startup teams of companies that include VenturCom (acquired by Citrix), Intervista Software (acquired by Platinum Technology - Computer Associates), Sentillion (acquired by Microsoft), and AcuStream (Great Falls, VA). He has helped entrepreneurs and corporate innovators design next-generation products and launch new businesses across a broad range of industries, including consumer products, industrial equipment, health care systems and new financial products. It is the richness of these diverse work experiences that Dr. Meyer brings to his teaching and research.

Dr. Meyer is a graduate of Harvard College and holds masters and doctoral degrees from MIT. While a PhD student in his mid-20s, he left MIT for five years to build his first software company before returning to complete his PhD. He remains a Visiting Scientist in the MIT Engineering Systems Division. Throughout, Dr. Meyer has relished working with the next generation of technology entrepreneurs.

Frederick G. Crane is an Executive Professor of Entrepreneurship & Innovation at the College of Business at Northwestern University, editor of the Journal of the Academy of Business Education, and a Research Fellow at the Institute for Enterprise Growth. He was formerly a professor of marketing and entrepreneurship at the University of New Hampshire and a chair and full professor at Dalhousie University. He currently teaches courses in entrepreneurship, innovation, and entrepreneurial marketing.

Dr. Cane grew up in a family business and also founded and operated several of his own businesses. In addition to being a serial entrepreneur, he has also been an investor in several startups, served on the advisory boards of entrepreneurial firms, and worked as a consultant for angel investors, venture capitalists, and government agencies on venture funding projects. In addition, he has developed and delivered numerous training programs and workshops for entrepreneurs and small-business owners.

His academic research activities have resulted in more than 100 publications, including eleven books, and he currently sits on the editorial boards of several academic journals. His current research stream intersects the domains of marketing, entrepreneurship, corporate venturing, and innovation, and he is conducting ongoing research on the psychology of entrepreneurship, entrepreneurial education, entrepreneurial branding, and innovation readiness. Dr. Crane is also an award-wining educator who has received numerous honors for teaching excellence over the past twenty years.

SAGE Research Methods Online
The essential tool for researchers

Sign up now at www.sagepub.com/srmo for more information.

An expert research tool

- An **expertly designed taxonomy** with more than 1,400 unique terms for social and behavioral science research methods

- **Visual and hierarchical search tools** to help you discover material and link to related methods

- Easy-to-use navigation tools
- Content organized by complexity
- Tools for citing, printing, and downloading content with ease
- Regularly updated content and features

A wealth of essential content

- The most comprehensive picture of quantitative, qualitative, and mixed methods available today

- More than **100,000 pages of SAGE book and reference material** on research methods as well as editorially selected material from SAGE journals

- More than **600 books** available in their entirety online

Launching 2011!

⑤SAGE research methods online

X